# KNOWLEDGE FOR JUSTICE

## AN ETHNIC STUDIES READER

# KNOWLEDGE FOR JUSTICE

## AN ETHNIC STUDIES READER

EDITORS

DAVID K. YOO

PAMELA GRIEMAN

CHARLENE VILLASEÑOR BLACK

DANIELLE DUPUY

ARNOLD LING-CHUANG PAN

Cover artwork: Darryl Mar and Critical Asian Pacific Islander Studies for Action, details of *Education through Struggle* mural, 1995. Mixed media on steel, 16 × 8 feet.

Cover and interior layout: William Morosi

*The AISC at UCLA acknowledges the Gabrielino/Tongva peoples as the traditional land caretakers of Tovaangar (Los Angeles basin, So. Channel Islands) and are grateful to have the opportunity to work for the* taraaxatom *(indigenous peoples) in this place. As a land grant institution, we pay our respects to* Honuukvetam *(Ancestors),* 'Ahiihirom *(Elders), and* 'eyoohiinkem *(our relatives/relations) past, present and emerging.*

Library of Congress Cataloging-in-Publication Data

Names: Yoo, David, editor. | Grieman, Pamela, editor. | Dupuy, Danielle, editor. | Pan, Arnold Ling-Chuang, editor. | Black, Charlene Villaseñor, 1962- editor. | University of California, Los Angeles. American Indian Studies Center. | University of California, Los Angeles. Asian American Studies Center. | University of California, Los Angeles. Chicano Studies Research Center. | Ralph J. Bunche Center for African American Studies at UCLA.
Title: Knowledge for justice : an Ethnic Studies reader / editors, David K. Yoo, Pamela Grieman, Danielle Dupuy, Arnold Ling-Chuang Pan, Charlene Villaseñor Black.
Description: Los Angeles, California : UCLA American Indian Studies Center Publications, Asian American Studies Center Press, Chicano Studies Research Center Press, and the Ralph J. Bunche Center for African American Studies, 2020. | Includes bibliographical references and index. | Summary: "Knowledge for Justice: An Ethnic Studies Reader is a joint publication of UCLA's four ethnic studies research centers (American Indian Studies, Asian American Studies, Chicana/o Studies, and African American Studies) and their administrative organization, the Institute of American Cultures. This book is premised on the assumption articulated by Johnnella Butler that ethnic studies is an essential and valuable course of study and follows an intersectional approach in organizing the articles. The book is divided into five sections-Legacies at Fifty, Formations and Ways of Being, Gender and Sexuality, Arts and Cultural Production, and Social Movements, Justice, and Politics-with each center contributing one or more articles or book chapters to each. In focusing on the intersectional intellectual, social, and political struggles that confront all of the groups represented in this anthology, the selections nonetheless articulate the specificity of each racial ethnic group's struggle, while simultaneously interrogating the ways in which such labels or categories are inadequate. The editors selected articles that not only address intersectional issues confronting various ethnic constituencies, but that also complicate the categories of representation undergirding such a project itself"-- Provided by publisher.
Identifiers: LCCN 2019025449 | ISBN 978-0-935626-70-4 (Paperback : alk. paper)
Subjects: LCSH: Ethnology--Study and teaching.
Classification: LCC GN307.8 .K56 2020 | DDC 305.80071--dc23
LC record available at https://lccn.loc.gov/2019025449

Printed in the United States of America
Printed on recycled paper by McNaughton & Gunn, Inc. ♾

Published by the UCLA American Indian Studies Center Publications, Asian American Studies Center Press, Chicano Studies Research Center Press, and the Ralph J. Bunche Center for African American Studies

Distributed by University of Washington Press
www.washington.edu/uwpress

# DEDICATION

To Dr. Claudia Mitchell-Kernan

Vice Chancellor Emerita, UCLA Graduate Studies
Dean Emerita, UCLA Graduate Division
Professor Emerita, Department of Anthropology and Department of Psychiatry and Biobehavioral Sciences
Director Emerita, Center for Afro-American Studies (now Ralph J. Bunche Center for African American Studies)

With sincere gratitude for her exemplary and visionary leadership, as well as outstanding scholarly contributions, during her oversight of the ethnic studies research centers.

# ACKNOWLEDGMENTS

We, the editors, are deeply grateful for and pay tribute to those who have come before us—literally thousands of people—ancestors, elders, community folks, students, staff and faculty members who together have breathed life into and sustained our centers over the decades. Similarly, we thank the current caretakers of our centers and the IAC for their labors. And we look forward to the next fifty years, hopeful that the struggles and sacrifices borne thus far will yield a future characterized by greater justice and an enduring peace.

# CONTENTS

## II. FORMATIONS AND WAYS OF BEING



## III. GENDER AND SEXUALITY

## IV. ARTS AND CULTURAL PRODUCTION



## V. SOCIAL MOVEMENTS, JUSTICE, AND POLITICS

# ABOUT THE EDITORS

Charlene Villaseñor Black is professor of art history and Chicana/o studies at UCLA, where she also serves as associate director of the Chicano Studies Research Center and editor of *Aztlán: A Journal of Chicano Studies*. Black is the author of the prize-winning *Creating the Cult of St. Joseph* (2006) and the editor of *Chicana/o Art: Tradition and Transformation* (2015). She has held grants from a number of institutions, including the Getty, the National Endowment for the Humanities, and the Fulbright, Mellon, and Woodrow Wilson Foundations, and in 2016 she was awarded UCLA's Gold Shield Faculty Prize.

Danielle Dupuy is the executive director of the Million Dollar Hoods project and director of Research and Programs at the UCLA Ralph J. Bunche Center for African American Studies. Her career has focused on reducing racial health inequities by addressing structural racism. Prior to moving to Los Angeles, Dupuy worked for Metropolitan Chicago Breast Cancer Task Force, Sinai Urban Health Institute, and Washington Park Consortium.

Pamela Grieman is the acting editor of the *American Indian Culture and Research Journal* and the assistant director of UCLA's American Indian Studies Center. She received her doctorate in English literature from the University of Southern California. Her work focuses on the representation of leftist political violence in fiction and nonfiction literature and media.

Arnold Pan is associate editor of *Amerasia Journal* and a staff member at the UCLA Asian American Studies Center. Prior to joining the staff of the Asian American Studies Center, Pan earned a PhD in English at the University of California, Irvine; his dissertation research is on representations of race and space in early twentieth century literature. In addition to his academic background, Pan has worked as a freelance writer on music and culture.

David K. Yoo is vice provost of the Institute of American Cultures and professor of Asian American studies and history at the University of California, Los Angeles. His publications include the *Oxford Handbook of Asian American History* (lead editor). He is also the former senior editor and a continuing board member of UCLA's *Amerasia Journal*.

# INTRODUCTION

PAMELA GRIEMAN
DAVID K. YOO

*Knowledge for Justice: An Ethnic Studies Reader* is a joint publication of UCLA's four ethnic studies research centers and their administrative organization, the Institute of American Cultures (IAC). The reader is a marker and celebration of their collective fiftieth anniversary during the 2019–20 academic year. Indeed, since 1969, a critical part of the legacies of the American Indian Studies Center (AISC), the Asian American Studies Center (AASC), the Ralph J. Bunche Center for African American Studies (CAAS), and the Chicano Studies Research Center (CSRC) has been the research produced and the many publications in print and online. Moreover, the centers and the IAC engage in a wide range of research projects, organize events and symposia, curate exhibitions, collaborate with many community partners, and advocate for faculty, staff, and students of color, grounded in the greater Los Angeles area, but extending outward across the state, the nation, and beyond.

While fifty years is a relatively brief period of time, anyone familiar with the beginnings of university-based ethnic studies knows well the tenuous nature of the origins and the challenges of sustaining such spaces in the midst of indifference and outright hostility. Those struggles are hardly an artifact of the past, and so, given such realities, there is much to be proud of in terms of what the IAC and the centers have accomplished and continue to do as part of larger social movements rooted in liberation and justice: increasing the numbers of underrepresented students, staff, and faculty in the academy; working with generations of students and community organizers; producing accurate and compelling scholarship about the histories and current practices that continue to marginalize people of color; and striving to change racist and inaccurate representations in the entertainment industry, media, government, business, education, and policy and health-related fields. Moreover, as recent events have shown, racially motivated harassment and hate crimes continue today and reveal how much work remains to be done.[1]

This book is premised on the assumption articulated by Johnnella Butler that ethnic studies is an essential and valuable course of study, not only as a means by which to complete the study of humanities and social sciences, but on its own interdisciplinary grounds.[2] According to historian Philip Deloria, ethnic studies scholars and graduate students often conceive of American studies as the "area study" of "United States white people" and he states that the relations between American studies and ethnic studies during the past thirty years has only exacerbated that tendency.[3] He argues, "If American studies has encouraged a kind of idiosyncratic approach to interdisciplinarity and practice, ethnic studies has always been a center—perhaps *the* center during the last four decades—for aggressive challenges to disciplinary imaginaries, institutional structures, ethical assumptions, and political consequences."[4] The contributors to this collection, representing work produced across the decades, take up the mantle of challenging scholarly orthodoxy and perceived norms.

In organizing the articles and book chapters reprinted herein, the editors are following the intersectional approach first articulated by Kimberlé Crenshaw, which emphasizes the interconnected nature of social categorizations such as race, class, and gender that link the centers' respective struggles and intellectual and educational endeavors.[5] Accordingly, the book is divided into five sections—Legacies at Fifty, Formations and Ways of Being, Gender and Sexuality, Arts and Cultural Production, and Social Movements, Justice, and Politics—with each center contributing one or more articles or book chapters to each. In focusing on the intersectional intellectual, social, and political struggles that confront all of the groups represented in this anthology, the selections nonetheless articulate the specificity of each racial ethnic group's struggle, while simultaneously interrogating the ways in which such labels or categories are inadequate. Pacific Islander Studies is sometimes linked to Asian American Studies, for instance, though Pacific Islanders are often Indigenous peoples. Some people of Chicanx/Latinx descent also claim Indigeneity. Many African Americans, such as the Cherokee Freedmen, former African slaves who until 2007 had been granted the full rights of Native Cherokees, identify as Indigenous. American Indians belong to hundreds of discrete tribes, each with its own history; furthermore, they identify as a political entity rather than a racial "minority," as federally recognized tribal members have political rights enshrined in treaties that have not been granted to any other peoples in the United States. Finally, many mixed-race peoples claim multiple identities. This book addresses such intricacies, but does not attempt to resolve them.

The editors of *Knowledge for Justice*, therefore, selected articles that not only address intersectional issues confronting various ethnic constituencies, but that also complicate the categories of representation undergirding such a project itself. It opens with descriptions of the origins of the individual centers in the "Legacies at Fifty" section—delving into the formative strategies, aims, and concerns that animated the drive to create the four ethnic studies centers in the late 1960s. It is noteworthy that UCLA is the only campus within the University of California system with four ethnic studies organized research units (ORU). The authors also discuss the shared struggles, at a time of major cultural upheaval in the United States, when oppressed and marginalized minorities found new openings in the longstanding struggles for self-determination and for equality. UCLA students of color, as part of a larger coalition of individuals and organizations, marched, protested, and argued for their own educational programs and needs, to study and learn about their diverse histories and cultures. In ideological solidarity with late 1960s and early 1970s resistance to the mainstream politics of imperial war, patriarchy, and conservative societal and cultural norms, those advocating for the centers focused more specifically on fighting against the racist representations of people of color, their mis- and underrepresentation in all aspects of American society and work, and the erasure of their specific histories and contemporary lives from the public record.

These forms of resistance occurred in universities and many other spaces in the United States and in other parts of the world. In March 1968, for example, roughly 5,000 students from five Los Angeles high schools took to the streets to demand a fairer education for Chicana/os; for culturally relevant curricula, books, and materials; and for culturally informed educators. Don Nakanishi, the founding publisher of *Amerasia Journal*, cited the problematic internalization of racist stereotypes as one underlying reason to publish a journal dedicated to the study of Asian American history and culture. He elucidated three goals for the journal: to attempt to accurately assess the past, to attain a clear knowledge of the present situation, and to pose plausible, well-defined visions of the future.[6] Black students' struggles intensified when two Black Panthers were shot and killed at UCLA during the formation of leadership initiatives. American Indian students demanded that UCLA—a land-grant institution—provide an education for the students upon whose land the university is built, and they joined UC Berkeley Natives in the occupation of Alcatraz and the Bureau of Indian Affairs building. As this volume demonstrates, many of the protesters joined forces with other underrepresented groups: Prominent activists urged African Americans to refuse to participate in a war against their "Asian brothers" in Korea (63), and comparisons have been made between the internment of Japanese refugees and the USA Patriot Act (42ff). As the "Hollywood Diversity Report" and the discussion of the Los Angeles uprising/riots of 1992 indicate, the shared struggles did not end in the 1970s but continue into the present day. The diversity report reveals how little progress has been made in the twenty-first century and a 2012 roundtable discussion of the ramifications of the 1992 uprising shows the dangers of ethnic communities pitted against each other as the mainstream media and other entities elide the structural roots of the socio-economic and political conditions those communities faced (112ff). The roundtable, in particular, speaks to the intersectional spirit of this project, as members of the Critical Race Studies faculty at the UCLA School of Law discussed the 1992 uprisings to detail the varied, complementary, yet sometimes conflicting perspectives of Los Angeles's minority communities.

Section II takes readers beyond the formative histories into the intellectual debates that animate the remainder of this edited volume. "Formations and Ways of Being" interrogates the ways in which structural and institutional racism undergird the specific historical experience of the various racial ethnic groups represented in this anthology. Several chapters in this section consider the meaning and status of immigrant as opposed to "native" American (lower-case to signify people born in the United States, not Indigenous peoples). St. Clair Drake traces the evolution of intellectual conceptualizations of Black Power and the "Black Experience" as an introduction to his effort to analyze blackness before white racism overdetermined representations of African peoples. The extract from his book, *Black Folk Here and There*, conceptualizes "slavery, skin-color prejudice, and racism as three distinct phenomena, each of which had existed separately from the other prior to the period of the great European overseas explorations but which became intertwined and mutually interdependent in the African diaspora of the Western Hemisphere" (139).

Haunani-Kay Trask argues that, in Hawai'i, Asian settlers have substituted the term "immigrant" for "local," claiming to be Native to the land and thereby erasing the history of the Indigenous peoples who preceded them (189). Theresa Delgadillo further complicates the meaning and history of the term. She claims that the mythos surrounding the "ideal immigrant"—who is conceptualized as "a hardworking, heterosexual, white ethnic male [who] lifts himself and his family up by virtue of his own efforts"—evinces preference for ethnicities who arrived in the nineteenth and early twentieth centuries, such as the Irish, Italians, and Poles. She further argues that this trope "muddles the difference between native, settler, slave, refugee, and exile . . . [and] displaces African Americans, Native Americans, and Mexican Americans from the status of 'true' citizen, since they are not originally immigrants" (206).

Rafael Pérez-Torres redefines immigration as a retaking of a lost land by analyzing the multiple significations of Aztlán in Chicana/o intellectual thought. Aztlán represents "a nationalist homeland, the name of that place that will at some future point be the national home of a Chicano people reclaiming their territorial rights," in part by the migration and immigration of Latinos to the United States through both legal and extralegal means. It signifies resistance to the US taking of land in the nineteenth century. Pérez-Torres argues that the meaning of Aztlán has shifted from "homeland" to "borderland," thereby signifying not an origin, but a contested place of identity construction, in other words, as a "site of numerous resistances and affirmations" (229).

Sharon Milholland's contribution does not address immigration, as American Indian peoples existed on what is now US land prior to the arrival of settlers, slaves, and immigrants. Her piece examines the ways in which sovereign Native peoples are forced to work within values, concepts, and languages of the dominant Western society that do not consider traditional Native knowledge systems and values she calls "necessary for meaningful protection and access to sacred lands" (247). However, its juxtaposition against Pérez-Torres' piece ascribing indigeneity to Chicana/os begs the question of claims to Indigenous identity. Federally recognized American Indian tribes have land bases enshrined in legal treaties, and although they too dream of retaking lost land bases, to consider Chicana/o claims to land might be considered part of the "Western" value system. Although Milholland alludes to several sacred sites across the United States, she focuses on Navajo sacred sites to explicate precisely how Navajo values serve to protect the land and demonstrates how federal laws actually work to "erode tribal identity and sovereignty" (250).

Section III interrogates the intersection of gender and sexuality with race, bringing to light cultural specificities with respect to LGBTQ issues. Daniel Enrique Pérez articulates a theoretical framework he calls mariposa theory, in which he combines elements of postcolonial theory, queer theory, an examination of butterfly imagery in ancient and contemporary cultural texts, and "the reappropriation and resignification of the term mariposa" (269). He traces the racism and homophobia that has tried to render LGBTQ Latinos ashamed of their identities and deploys mariposa theory as a decolonial method of empowering people who identify as queer by associating queerness with ancestors who are deities and warriors (290).

Glenn Magpantay examines census data to support his contention that the increase in the population of Asian Americans and Pacific Islanders will lead to greater acceptance of LGBTQ people in the future. He supports this assertion by pointing out that current education efforts are leading to a greater understanding and acceptance of nonheteronormative preferences and that future voters are currently supporters of LGBTQ rights. He states, "I believe that multiculturalism within existing legislation, programs, and agencies will normalize, and civil rights protections will more sufficiently address discrimination in a more dynamic and diverse American society" (304).

Valerie Lambert notes that American Indians are largely missing from debates about LGBTQ rights, in particular same-sex marriage, an absence she attributes to the fact that such debates typically take place in legislatures, the national government, and the Supreme Court, where Native peoples are barely represented. In her article, she documents Native peoples' participation and involvement in such debates from 2005–2015 in Indian country, that is, around tribal homelands, tribal legislatures, tribal legal and public institutions, and other Indigenous spaces. Even though the arguments for and against same-sex marriage are similar in Indian country, the debates take place within the context of Indigenous, rather than national, governance (321).

Although Section IV's emphasis on arts and cultural production canvasses the vast scope of ethnic artistic production, it also reveals interconnections in artists' responses to political and historical events. Russell Leong closely examines the work of several Japanese, Chinese, Filipino, Vietnamese, and Korean American poets between 1968 and 1978. He calls them a "tribe of storytellers," defining tribe as an "affiliation based upon blood and generational lines, upon folk and cultural ties. Tribal bespeaks of the consciousness of the third world—of attempts to rescue memory and culture from total colonization, or to reclaim and transform that which is left from annihilation. 'Tribal' is based upon shared experience—even the shared experience of subjugation—and on an integration of self with community" (332). During the decade under study, Leong points out that several themes regularly emerge—the Vietnam War, identity and cultural issues, historical lineages—but his close reading also focuses on poetics: the poets' frames of reference, the unity of the speaker, the elements of the oral tradition, the reversal of stereotypes, and the "compilative, archival approaches to language and speech" (333).

Like poets, visual artists also design their work as a commentary on current and historical experiences. In his chapter, Paul Von Blum profiles four African American painters, contextualizing their work within the political and social events that took place during their lifetimes. He argues that their work "must be viewed in the context of slavery, racism, and their more subtle sequelae, the changing dynamics of race relations in contemporary America" (356). He characterizes their work—as reflected in the book title from which these profiles are taken—as resistance, dignity, and pride.

In her chapter, Nancy Marie Mithlo identifies the key themes underlying an Indigenous artistic aesthetic. She argues that the defining quality of Indigenous life and identities is "a continued engagement with the colonial experience" and that "defining sovereignty—who belongs and how we belong—is central to the interpretation of

Indigenous arts" (400). Using theories of the gaze, audience reception, and "blood memories," Mithlo analyzes the political tropes at play in the work of Chippewa filmmaker Marcella Ernest and Ho-Chunk photographer Tom Jones in their goal of radically restructuring the field of art (392): "Blood memories are powerful political tropes mobilized to call attention to the legacies of colonialism in contexts as diverse as battle fields, boarding schools, and sacred sites" (393).

In "The Oppositional Consciousness of Yolanda M. López," Karen Mary Davalos examines the work of artist Yolanda López and argues that it articulates the multivocal, polyvalent identity consciousness developed by US Third World feminists. She asserts that this work enacts oppositional consciousness—a methodology and praxis described by Chela Sandoval. One of her primary goals is to demonstrate the conceptual, deconstructivist, and semiotic approach López takes to challenge overlapping systems of subordination and control. She focuses on the ways in which López's political activism is suffused throughout her work, noting that "Within one aesthetic project, López can voice cultural nationalism and simultaneously outline its limitations for women" (425).

Section V is a fitting final coda as it returns to the themes of social movements, justice, and politics that led to the formation of the ethnic studies at UCLA and nationwide. Social justice covers a multiplicity of political and social activity, as evidenced in this book. In the first chapter of this section, Jorge Marsical traces the relationship between representations of César Chávez and the various sectors of the Chicano movement during the Vietnam War. He examines Chávez's own self-fashioning, his public statements and actions, and journalistic, artistic, and literary representations of the leader as well as critiques from the political right and left. Marsical argues that "just as the Movimiento is inconceivable without the UFW [United Farm Workers], the most dramatic successes of the UFW are inconceivable without the Movimiento in its emergent stages within the broader radicalized condition of US society, especially among youth. For many non-Latino activists, the efforts of the UFW embodied a utopian project composed of diverse ethnic groups and classes" (433).

Social activism and social justice necessarily manifest both utopian and pragmatic goals. The next chapter, authored by Paul Ong, Melany De La Cruz-Viesca, and Don Nakanishi, utilizes statistics to offer a corrective to the mainstream media's 2008 discussion of Asian Americans in voting and in American politics. The authors contend that the mainstream analysis lacked an in-depth understanding of Asian Americans, citing commentaries that claimed that a large majority of California's Asian American voters supported Hillary Clinton "because of racial bias" (459). However, the authors counter that misconception by demonstrating that many Asian Americans supported Barack Obama in Hawai'i's primary election" (460). Drawing on the 2006 American Community Survey (ACS) and the 2006 November Current Population Survey (CPS), the authors provide accurate assessments of the absolute and relative size of the Asian American population, key demographic characteristics, their participation in electoral politics, the barriers they encounter, and future prospects in an attempt to correct misrepresentations of Asian American voters.

A relatively recent movement in Indigenous studies is examined in Devon Mihesuah's discussion of food sovereignty. She unpacks the meaning of the term and addresses many of the challenges tribes face in creating self-sufficient food systems and reconnecting tribal members with their traditional foodways. She cites examples from Oklahoma—which with its thirty-eight tribal nations and its multifaceted history evinces many of the problems encountered throughout Indian country, including environmental problems, uneven food quality, poor Indigenous health, intratribal factionalism, racism, and the glaring dichotomy of affluence and extreme poverty. According to Mihesuah, a "food sovereign" tribe ideally has the right to control its food production, food quality, and food distribution; supports tribal farmers and ranchers by supplying machinery and technology needed to plant and harvest; and is not answerable to state regulatory control. One challenge to attaining food sovereign status is to determine what the traditional foodways are and whether members agree on what is "traditional" (470).

The final chapter of this book, taken from the Million Dollar Hoods project, breaks down the price of bail paid in Los Angeles County by race. The statistics it cites shows that Latinos pay the most, followed by African Americans and then whites, both of whom pay less than half of what Latinos pay. Citing a report indicating that women bear the brunt of paying these costs, it concludes that "the money bail system demands tens of millions of dollars annually in cash and assets from some of LA's most economically vulnerable persons, families, and communities" (490). Not only does the report find the bail system to be deeply inequitable, it also finds that many "are too poor to pay the price for freedom" (492).

In commemorating fifty years, *Knowledge for Justice*, in representing a small sample of the collective scholarship of the UCLA ethnic studies centers, speaks to the present and future as well as the past. There is of course no possible way that a single volume, even double or triple the length of this reader, could possibly capture the depth and richness of the creativity, energy, and community that have been so intertwined with our centers. Accordingly, we have attempted to offer some glimpses with the hope that these writings will serve as reminders and spark new conversations and debates as they relate to our contemporary contexts. In addition, these authors in their collective wisdom can provide frames of reference for thinking critically about what lies ahead.

## NOTES

1. Haily Branson-Potts, "No Group Exempt from Hate Crime Surge," *Los Angeles Times*, September 29, 2016: B2, https://search.proquest.com/latimes/docview/1824139528/C3C3247A4AF8468CPQ/%201?accountid=14512; Jaweed Kaleem, "Attacks on Religious and Racial Minorities Fueled Sharp Rise in Hate Crimes in 2017, FBI Says," Los Angeles Times (Online), November 13, 2018, https://search.proquest.com/latimes/docview/2132796011/C3C3247A4AF8468CPQ/2?accountid=14512 .

2. Johnnella E. Butler, "Ethnic Studies as a Matrix for the Humanities, the Social Sciences, and the Common Good," in *Color-Line to Borderlands: The Matrix of American Ethnic Studies*, ed. Johnnella E. Butler (Seattle: University of Washington Press, 2001), 21.

3. Philip J. Deloria, "Broadway and Main: Crossroads, Ghost Roads, and Paths to an American Studies Future," *American Quarterly* 61:1 (March 2009): 10.

4. Ibid., 14.

5. Kimberlé Crenshaw, "Demarginalizing the Intersection of Race and Sex: A Black Feminist Critique of Antidiscrimination Doctrine, Feminist Theory and Antiracist Politics," *University of Chicago Legal Forum*, Iss. 1, Article 8 (1989), http://chicagounbound.uchicago.edu/uclf/vol1989/iss1/8.

6. David K. Yoo, Pamela Grieman, Charlene Villaseñor Black, Danielle Dupuy, and Arnold Ling-Chuang Pan, eds., *Knowledge for Justice: An Ethnic Studies Reader* (Los Angeles: Los Angeles: UCLA American Indian Studies Center Press, UCLA Asian American Studies Press, UCLA Chicano Studies Research Center Press, and the Ralph J. Bunche Center for African American Studies, 2019), 3. Subsequent references will be inserted parenthetically in the text.

# I.

# LEGACIES AT FIFTY

ORIGINS

# A MESSAGE TO OUR READERS

DON T. NAKANISHI AND LOWELL CHUN-HOON

There are not many things that we're sure about as we send this first issue of the *Amerasia Journal* to press. We do know, that some very generous people have thought enough of the idea of a national journal on Asians in America to help us finance this first issue, and that some people have felt sufficiently committed to write the articles and poems that appear on the following pages. We also know that many people are sincerely concerned about the fate of Asian American communities and are trying very hard to see if they can make the lives of their immigrant brothers and those who live in ethnic communities a little bit better. But, aside from these things, we are not quite as certain as we would like to be.

We realize that there have been numerous perceptions that others in this nation have had about Asian Americans, as well as a myriad of self-perceptions that each Asian American has embodied. At one time, we were perceived as a "heathen" race to be dealt with forcibly and with little concern for our basic human rights, while at other times, as a successful minority that should be emulated by others. At the same time, there was once a period when our ancestors considered themselves sojourners with a definite concern to return to their homelands, while others perceived themselves as legal members of this society and sought to establish a meaningful life here. Our purpose in initiating this journal resulted from these seemingly contradictory perceptions and self-images during various phases in the Asian American experience. As a result, we set three goals: an attempt to accurately assess our past, to attain a clear knowledge of our present situation, and to pose plausible, well-defined visions of our future. In this first issue, we are far from attaining any of the three original goals.

We were fortunate, though, to have the privilege of interviewing Warren Furutani, national Japanese American Citizens League (JACL) community involvement coordinator, and to exchange our own views with this sincerely dedicated individual on various matters such as the plight of Asian American communities, Asian American studies, and

Don T. Nakanishi (1949–2016) was the founding publisher of *Amerasia Journal.* He was professor of education and Asian American studies at UCLA, as well as the director of the UCLA Asian American Studies Center. Lowell Chun-Hoon was the founding Editor of *Amerasia Journal.* He is an attorney based in Honolulu, Hawai'i.

possible visions for the future. We thank him most gratefully for this opportunity. But, at the same time, we have made mistakes. In interviewing Mr. Chin Ho of Honolulu, Hawai'i, a remarkably successful Hawaiian businessman and an international figure in his own right, our tape recorder failed us. As a result, we can only offer our readers and Mr. Ho our apologies for the loss of a similar provocative conversation about Asians in America and the absence of a complete article concerning Asian Americans in Hawai'i. We lament the fact too that we were not able to get an article about Korean Americans for our first issue, or more than simply a poem on the Filipino-American experience.

In the end, though, the *Amerasia Journal* is not our journal. It belongs to our readers. We exist as a journal to collect and publish the best and most provocative material we can find on Asians in America. If our judgment or our goals are inadequate, we hope they get corrected. If there are others who would like to work with us, they are welcome to join us. Also, if there are people who can do what we're trying to do better than we can by themselves, they have our sincerest best wishes. For in the end, it will be our readership that sustains or deserts us. Unless we or our goals are relevant to their needs, concerns, and aspirations, we're simply shouting loud and listening to the echoes of our own voices in a closed room. We'd like *Amerasia Journal* to be more than a soliloquy, and we need your assistance. Please let us know what you think.

## NOTE

Reprinted with permission from Lowell Chun-Hoon and Don Nakanishi, *Amerasia Journal* 1:1 (1971): iii.

# AMERICAN INDIAN CULTURE CENTER: BEGINNINGS

## EDITOR'S NOTE

The UCLA American Indian Studies Center (AISC) was founded in 1969 as a research institute dedicated to addressing American Indian issues and supporting Native communities. The AISC serves as a hub of activities for Indigenous students, staff, faculty, alumni, and community, as well as serving as a bridge between the academy and indigenous peoples locally, nationally, and internationally. We foster innovative academic research by students and faculty, publish leading scholarship in the field of American Indian Studies, and support events and programming focused on indigenous issues.

Under the directorship of Shannon Speed (Chickasaw), the Center also works in collaboration with some of the country's most influential and respected scholars writing and teaching in American Indian Studies today, who have made UCLA one of the highest ranked and most respected universities in the field.

The core objectives of the AISC are to:

- facilitate and disseminate research about indigenous peoples;
- strengthen graduate and undergraduate education;
- seek extramural funds to support student and faculty research; and
- carry out university and public service programs related to the Center's mission.

To accomplish these aims, the AISC maintains a reference library; publishes books as well as the *American Indian Culture and Research Journal*; organizes symposia, conferences, film screenings, and other events; supports academic programs in American Indian Studies and administers postdoctoral and predoctoral fellowships and research awards through the Institute of American Cultures.

The Center serves as a focal point for scholars, staff, students, and community members. Our research focus is broad and encompasses topics ranging from the contemporary urban Indian experience to issues unique to reservation communities. We seek to balance a local, national, and international focus, with special attention given to California Indian nations. Foundational to our mission is a commitment to facilitating indigenous peoples' distinct social, cultural, economical, political, and legal needs by virtue of their status as native nations.

The rest of this chapter is taken from the first issue of the *American Indian Culture Center Journal* (now called the *American Indian Culture and Research Journal*).

## INTRODUCTION

Today, the American Indian Culture Center (AICC) is nothing less than the beginnings of the realization of a dream on the part of Indian people, both in this state and across the nation. What we have called a dream is in actuality a strongly expressed desire from our Indian communities that our people have a decisive voice in the determination of our own educational programs and needs. With what we hope is a realistic appreciation of and insight into the values of a self-determined educational process, we see the American Indian Culture Center as the initial step toward full self-determination in all institutions that encompass Indian life and society.

Traditionally, education among Indian people has been largely a hit-and-miss affair, a chancy process with misdirection to the real needs and goals of Indian people. The American Indian Culture Center exists as an attempt to correct this situation, particularly within that realm of activities and sphere of influence which UCLA exercises as a major institution of higher education.

This journal will attempt to answer some questions frequently asked about the American Indian Culture Center. To attempt to answer such questions is to describe AICC: its current objectives and commitments, its present status, and its future goals. What has continually impressed us is the very real difficulty in articulating a precise definition of AICC in terms of a static role and structure. Perhaps this is because we see AICC as the embodiment of the desires and efforts of all those who have had a hand in its formation and growth. This is to say, AICC exists in the energy, struggles, and commitments of those people creatively involved in it and who have struggled and worked for countless years for Indian self-determination.

## INFORMATION AND DEVELOPMENT

### *Origin*

In December of 1968, AICC became a reality on the UCLA campus. At that time the University was proposing the formation of an "Institute of American Cultures." In essence, this institution was to be an umbrella structure to accommodate the formation of various American Ethnic Group Cultural Centers on campus. Prior to this time the black and Chicano students and community people had convinced the University of the wisdom and appropriateness of instituting their respective "Ethnic Study Centers" within and supported by the University.

The University committed itself to such efforts because it recognized the essential justness and necessity of special efforts on the part of major educational institutions to support the thrust of ethnic communities to achieve full participation in American life. Seen as essential to such full participation was the attainment of a strong tradition of higher education to sustain the various ethnic communities' efforts toward full self-determination.

The University conceived the proposed Institute to be an administrative convenience which would also accommodate American Indian and Asian components. The Indian community and students were then approached in this venture. While the idea of Ethnic Studies Centers was not a new one, there had not yet been an organized effort on the part of Indian students in this direction because of their relatively small number on campus. On January 16, 1969, a "Southern California Indian Leadership Meeting" was held on the UCLA campus with approximately fifty participants. There were community representatives, students, and University personnel present. The idea of instituting an Indian Cultural Center on campus was discussed as well as alternative organizational patterns, objectives, and long-term goals of the Center. It was decided that the policy and objectives of the Culture Center would be determined by a Steering Committee made up of representatives from the Indian community, Indian students, and university faculty. A temporary Steering Committee was then selected from those present at the meeting and co-chairmen were elected.

As a first step, the Center was named the American Indian Culture Program. It was understood that the Program was to eventually attain the status of a Center. The first order of business was the formulation of a comprehensive proposal which would outline exactly what the center was, its goals and organization, and a working budget. The proposal, as a communal effort, would then be submitted for approval to the Committee on Educational Policy of the Academic Senate of the University. Upon approval, the Program would then be granted official recognition and status as an ethnic cultural center: a permanent component of the University with a defined role and function.

## *Initial projects and activities*

Interim staff were also appointed at the initial Steering Committee meeting: director, research assistant, and administrative assistant/secretary. During the remainder of the meeting, participants discussed alternative ways the Center could serve as mediator between the needs of the community and the resources of the University. The formation of an Institute for the Preservation of Indian Resources (i.e., land and water), curricula development that would integrate the history of the American Indian with Anglo-American history, and work on establishing an urban cultural and recreational facility were typical suggestions made during early Steering Committee meetings.

As the year progressed, the staff of AICP began to explore the possibilities for AICP involvement. It was found that their primary role was the coordination of efforts being made by community people and students on a wide range of projects. A vocational school, a newsletter, a recreation center, a library, colloquiums, etc., were all projects brought to the attention of AICP, and the staff found themselves involved in supporting, assisting where they could, and trying to keep abreast of all activity that touched the campus and the community. The Steering Committee underwent a succession of different chairmen and members.

AICP soon began to focus its efforts primarily on three major areas:

1. The recruitment and increased enrollment of Indian students on the UCLA campus.
2. The adequate formulation of a proposal which would be the basis of AICP existence and justification for permanent staff, and eventually, the attainment of Center status.
3. Preparations for hosting the six-week summer Institute on Contemporary Indian Studies to be sponsored by NIYC (National Indian Youth Council) on the UCLA campus.

### *Proposal and staff recruitment*

A proposal was submitted to the Academic Senate, rejected and resubmitted, rejected and submitted again. During this process, the Steering Committee and staff of AICP were experiencing an evolution and refinement of their own conception of what AICP should be and how this might be expressed in the proposal.

During the summer of 1969, the staff intensified its recruitment efforts within the national Indian community to obtain a highly qualified individual to fill the position of permanent director of AICP. It was recognized that they had a difficult task in finding someone of Indian background who had the academic qualifications to be eligible for faculty status at the University with the additional attributes of leadership ability and administrative experience that would equip him for the role. Late in the summer, several applicants were interviewed. Mr. Roger Buffalohead, a Ponca Indian, doctoral candidate and ethno-historian, was selected. Mr. Buffalohead ably provided needed leadership for AICP during a six-month period before he had to resign because of serious health problems. In February of 1970, Mr. Emmett Oliver was appointed as Interim Director to head the program through June of 1970. In mid-June, Mr. Anthony Purley, a Laguna Indian with substantial administrative experience, was selected as permanent director who assumed duties on July 20, 1970.

Illustrative of the spirit of the proposal and the conception of the Center's role is the following excerpt from the proposal submitted to the University, which will serve as AICP's charter upon acceptance:

> In twentieth-century America, when the whiteman's folly has finally caught up with him in a spoiled land and a polluted environment, nothing less than revolutionary change in all phases of life will provide the leadership and the thought necessary to undertake the recovery which must occur, if the Indians are to save themselves from their white friends and the shortcomings of the dominant society. Convinced of this basic premise of a rational regeneration, we believe a small part of that change can be stimulated and perhaps even directed and evaluated with the establishment of a viable, flexible, effective, and meaningful American Indian Studies Center at the University of California at Los Angeles . . . The function of institutions or agencies designed to serve the needs of Indian people must be completely re-evaluated. While the philosophical aims of these institutions may be well-intentioned, they nevertheless deny or ignore the cultural integrity and validity of Indian people. The criteria of success in this "custodial" office seem to be measured by how fast Indian people can be estranged from their tribal group and brought into a so-called "mainstream culture." Individual and collective Indian failures to respond to present policies and programs are judged as inherent Indian faults rather than as institutional and philosophical inadequacies . . . The creation of an American Indian Studies Center must be judged on the basis of what it is: the first step in the right direction toward the solution of conflicts rooted deeply in the past and without easy amelioration. An intelligent and determined thrust must be made to develop a pattern of relationship between the Indian and the non-Indian communities which will lead to success for the Indians in the multi-cultural, multi-lingual, and multi-national environment of

modern American society. Any lesser aim would be a disservice to Indian people as well as to the University and to the nation.

### *Student recruitment efforts*

Indian students at UCLA involved in the early developments of AICC found themselves with a unique opportunity to consolidate their common interests and for the first time began to function as a unified group. An optional ethnic survey issued to all UCLA students during the fall registration of 1968 indicated that there were seventy-six American Indian students on campus at that time. Indian students active in the development of AICC conducted a thorough follow-up and turned up only seven students who were American Indians. These seven students, working with an already existent Special Education Program (SEP) through which the University was sponsoring special efforts to recruit promising minority students to the campus, were successful in securing a commitment on the part of the University to establish a separate Indian Component to the High Potential Program (HPP). An Indian staff would be hired to work with fifty Indian students in an entry-level program aimed at preparing Indian students to compete in the University system. Through the efforts of the American Indian Student Association, which was formed by these seven students, the enrollment of American Indians at UCLA had grown to ninety at the beginning of the winter quarter of 1970.

It was felt that these and other efforts at expanding the educational opportunities available to Indian students at the University were most consistent with the goals of AICC and its role as an organizational structure supporting Indian-initiated projects on campus.

### *Summary*

Over the course of the previous year and a half AICC has been in a developmental stage; those involved have found that it has not been an easy process. Less than half of the original Steering Committee remained as active members and none of the original staff. Those remaining have experienced the evolution of AICC, which is perhaps only an inevitable price of flexibility, meeting the need of change. In role and function, AICC is more of a process than an organizational unit, more of an active involvement of people than an administrative entity.

## AMERICAN INDIAN CULTURE CENTER TODAY

### *Present status*

Recognizing the inadequacy of simply explaining that AICC is administratively designed as a research unit within the University structure, we turn to the objectives as stated in the AICC charter:

1. To join in participation with the American Indian communities as an essential means of fostering active relationship of the larger society's institutions with those of the Indian people.

2. To stimulate the development of programs which marshal and focus the resources of the University on the problems of the American Indian.
3. To assist in the development of curricula and scholarly materials concerned with the rich legacy of art, music, literature, religion, crafts, inventions, history, and other features of past and contemporary Indian life.
4. To encourage and support research in all areas of knowledge relevant to the American Indian.
5. To develop University and community resources to accomplish the above objectives.

From its origin, AICC was so structured as to be able to rely on the collective wisdom and guidance represented in those individuals comprising the Steering Committee as is aptly stated in the proposal:

> The Steering Committee will have the responsibility of determining the direction and content of the American Indian Studies Center. Its composition has been designed to combine the talents and skills of both the Indian and academic communities. Such a committee it is hoped, will produce an imaginative and creative approach in drawing upon and applying the resources of the University to the needs of Indian people.
>
> The Indian orientation will be provided by representation from the complex and heterogeneous "Indian Community" of California and the Indian students at UCLA. An Indian perspective of this kind is essential if the concept of Indian self-determination is to become more than empty rhetoric. The academic community will be represented by faculty and administrative officials of the University whose primary responsibility will be to assist the committee in the utilization of University resources.

In late spring, the staff of AICC was reduced and until June 11, 1970, consisted of only the director and administrative assistant. During this period, the staff devoted its full time and efforts to the coordination of project activities and in sponsoring independent Indian student and community ventures consistent with broad goals of AICC.

## *Project involvement*

Talent Search. The US Office of Education approached AICC requesting them to submit a proposal to participate in the Educational Talent Search Program. The purposes of the Talent Search Program are:

1. To identify qualified youth of economically disadvantaged backgrounds who have the potential and desire for post-secondary school training.
2. To locate financial assistance for these students.
3. To encourage high school or college dropouts of demonstrated aptitude to re-enter post-secondary programs.

The broad goals of the Talent Search Program are to contact Indian youth throughout Southern California in an intensive counseling, guidance and recruitment effort. Consequently, while AICC submitted a proposal to the US Office of Education, the

Center has already begun to implement its own Talent Search Project. Robert Chiago, an Indian who has a Master's degree, administrative experience, and experience working with Indian students, is the Talent Search Director. He is in the process of following up initial research work begun by Tom Nelford, a graduate student temporarily employed by AICC. As of July 2, 1970, the following has been accomplished:

> We have identified all elementary, junior, and senior high schools in the Talent Search area which have Indian students enrolled. We are compiling a list which will include the school districts within each county, the schools within each school district and the number of American Indian students enrolled within each school.
>
> We are designing a comprehensive questionnaire which will allow for numerous variables pertinent to the research of American Indian students.
>
> We have written approximately 300 letters, the bulk of which were to Indian newspapers (nationwide), community colleges (statewide), and business concerns (Southern California area). These letters contained a generalized description of the Talent Search Project, a request for knowledge of opportunities available such as educational, vocational, or employment, and also any information which might be helpful to our Project.
>
> We have had numerous trivial tasks, such as meetings, calls, letters, telephone conversations, etc.
>
> We have contacted and informed various Indian organizations of the Talent Search Project.
>
> We are in the process of exploring possible funding for the Talent Search Project. We are rewriting the proposal to fit the guidelines of these other funding sources.

It is hoped that the Talent Search Program will prove to be one of the most valuable projects in which AICC is involved. This is particularly so in terms of the long-range impact we expect to exert on the Indian youth approached, the Educational Institutions worked with and, most importantly, the Indian communities with which we hope to establish a dialogue.

Curriculum Development and Research. The Indian individual, as he makes his way through the processes of American higher education is largely forced to conclude that even the present University curricula does little to correct the misunderstanding which prevails in general society about the American Indian. Indeed, that stereotypes of the Indian continue to permeate all levels of society.

In the proposal, now chartered for AICC, a long list of course offerings, including American Indian History, Literature, Art and Music, Indian languages, Religions and Philosophies, will be earmarked as future topics for concentrated research and curriculum development. AICC will prepare a "Handbook on American Indian Studies." The Center will soon contract the research involved in this handbook. Treating such areas as "The Origin of American Indians, US Indian Policy, Indians in Contemporary Society, and California Indians," the foreword of the proposal reads:

> In recent years there has been an upsurge of interest in studying the problems of minority groups. Perhaps the most significant aspect of this trend is that the people

themselves are concerned about the image that is being cast upon history and upon contemporary society.

The American Indian has long been subjected to numerous studies from almost every academic discipline, as well as from hopelessly inept amateurs. Anthropologists, educators, sociologists, psychologists, historians, and journalists have all had their day.

A very real problem one faces when attempting to do research on American Indians is the vast amount of vindictive, condescending, and inaccurate, or hopelessly superficial material encountered as a result of so many studies.

At this time it is most important that materials be made available for the study of the American Indian, based on scholarly work, which will reflect the Indian point of view.

The primary objective of this book is to provide a guide of relevant readings and references about American Indians for secondary school use. This task has been undertaken with the practical concern in mind that classroom teachers usually do not have the time available to seek out, sift through, and categorize the massive amounts of information which is available on American Indians. This reader has been prepared as a tool which will be readily accessible to the teacher and the student, and hopefully will make the study of the American Indian both meaningful and relevant.

It is hoped that this book will represent the filling of an educational and cultural void which has existed for too long in the teaching of American History.

Presently, Patricia Locke, educational specialist, in conjunction with working on curriculum development, is developing plans for an Indian Studies Symposium proposed to be held at the Lake Arrowhead Conference Center in September, 1970.

Library Services and Facilities. Sporting a calendar on the wall published by the Indian community on Alcatraz and decorated with such lively stickers as "Custer Died for Your Sins," or "Indians Discovered America" and "Indians Died for Peace," the present library facility of AICC is a relaxed and attractive area used by the Indian students as a study and sometimes social area. In a very concrete way, the present library is a substantial beginning in the direction of achieving its objectives as outlined in the Charter. Beyond the present physical facility, and the 100 select volumes collected along with numerous Indian periodicals as of this date, the library is envisioned as an extensive research unit in itself. To excerpt from current AICC correspondence to the incoming librarian:

> The American Indian Cultural Center Library is planned as a collection of between three and four thousand books which will duplicate for the Center the basic resources in the field in the University Research and College Libraries, supplemented by a unique collection of such auxiliary materials as pamphlets, bibliographies, journal articles, clippings, photographs, audio tapes, maps, and microfilm. The scope of the library will cover all aspects of the history and culture of the Indians of North America, as well as studies of present-day conditions of Indian life. Special emphasis will be given to building a valuable in-depth collection on the Indians of California. Materials will be organized and catalogued by patterns set in UCLA's other libraries, in order to facilitate referrals in both directions. The library will be housed in a

separate room adjacent to the Center in Campbell Hall, and, while intended primarily for the Center's own faculty and students, will be available on a regular schedule of open hours to the whole campus community.

Barbara al-Bayati, a highly qualified librarian, is presently working with AICC on a half-time basis while working on an advanced degree and promises to contribute her excellent background to the task of organizing a library such as proposed.

Seminars and Colloquiums. Sponsored by AICC, Mr. N. Scott Momaday, a Kiowa Indian and Pulitzer Prize-winning author, spoke on "The American Indian in Conflict: Tribalism in Modem Society" at the University. As the latest in a series of prominent Indian speakers brought to the campus by AICC, Mr. Momaday's appearance exemplifies the efforts the Center will continue to exert as a service to primarily the Indian students and the University at large. Particularly gratifying has been the presence of community Indian people at some of the more well-publicized seminars which AICC has attempted to present on a regular basis.

Publications. Because of budgetary problems AICC has not been as active in this area as was hoped. While numerous ideas were put forth, the considerable time, effort, and expense involved in publishing a newsletter has unfortunately not been available to AICC staff. For the coming year, a portion of the budget has been set aside for a quarterly journal to be published under AICC's auspices. This present edition is our initial effort at a journal. It is hoped that future editions can be devoted to a wide variety of topics of timely and vital interest to the Indian community at large.

Educational Opportunities for Indian Students. The text of the following letter from the Chairman of the American Indian Student Association has been submitted to us for publication in the journal. We feel it speaks eloquently and explicitly for the students.

The American Indian Student Association is composed entirely of American Indians enrolled at UCLA. Our membership includes full-time High Potential, undergraduate, and graduate students. Our organization in its present form has been in existence since February of 1969.

We have watched with concern as our Indian brothers and sisters enter college. We know well the many problems they will face. We have faced the loneliness and isolation. We have felt our identity slipping away as we are made but one in many. Helping our fellow Indians overcome these difficulties is one of the Student Association's major goals.

We have formulated additional goals for our Indian Studies Program here:

1. The purpose of this department should be to instruct Indians and help them further their education.
2. A second purpose of equal import should be to educate all non-Indians about Indians.
3. A third goal is to develop a liaison with other Indian students across the country.
4. A further goal is that this program will develop and create employment opportunities for all Indians.

A large percentage of the Indian students presently attending UCLA are in either the Educational Opportunities Program (EOP) or make up the Indian component of the High Potential Program (HPP), a component of SEP. The American Indian component was established in the fall of 1969 with fifty High Potential students. Since Los Angeles is one of the melting pots for American Indians, tribes from throughout the nation are represented in the Program. Twenty-three additional HPP students and eight more EOP students were admitted in the winter quarter of 1970. As explained in the recruiting brochure distributed by the High Potential staff:

> There are many bright young Indians, who if given an opportunity, could succeed at a major university such as UCLA. Under traditional admission standards, however, many Indian students have not been accepted either because of a poor high school record and/or because the high school they attended did not properly prepare them for higher education. A poor high school record does not always mean that a student has a low aptitude. It could mean that a student's interests were not met and that he was poorly motivated in his classes. Some of these students would be good candidates for the UCLA High Potential Program. The program would help a student to identify and evaluate his interests and also strengthen the necessary skills that he is weak in. In order for the High Potential Program to successfully prepare a student for the regular UCLA curriculum, he or she must have a strong desire to succeed and must be willing to work hard and make a sacrifice.

Potential HPP applicants are screened by an Indian Selection Committee primarily interested in the student's real desire for a college education and aptitude. A close working relationship exists between AICC and the staff of HPP. While there is no official administrative connection between the two programs, this relationship has grown as a natural consequence of their mutual interest in serving the Indian students.

As an essential counterpart to its recruitment efforts, AICC has continued to serve as a focal point of information on all aspects of educational opportunities available to Indian students at UCLA. Other programs such as the "Teaching Credentials and Masters' Education Opportunity Fellowship Program" offered by the Graduate School of Education, the "Legal Education Opportunity Program" participated in by the School of Law and "UCLA Minority Urban Program and Development Program" are but a few examples.

Communication with Other Indian Studies Programs. In recent years, we have witnessed the rapid growth of interest in the American Indian on a national scale. One measure of this has been the institution of such programs as AICC at universities and colleges throughout the country. The goals, activities, and interests which the Center mutually shares with other Indian Studies Programs are obvious and need no elaboration. Recognizing that there is much to be learned from their counterparts, the staff of AICC has attempted to share ideas and maintain a liaison with the other centers. Consequently, along with other efforts at maintaining communication, the center has made it a regular practice to send representatives to the other institutes as the occasion demands, usually drawing on various members of the student body or staff. Representatives are responsible for submitting a report on the conference, meeting or seminar attended at the regular steering committee meeting and keeping the Center informed as necessary.

## SUMMARY AND EVALUATION

The admittedly brief outline of projects in which the Center has maintained an active involvement is not meant to be an exhaustive account but only to give the reader some idea of the kinds of things the Center has been able to support. Perhaps even this involvement, if measured in an atmosphere of militant activism, would fall short of being called revolutionary change. It has been our experience, however, that talk is easy while those imaginative and creative efforts AICC hopes to continue to support remain a hard and trying task. The rewards for such a contribution lie not in a self-pleasing approbation but in seeing people succeed in making available real opportunities and in satisfying real needs. It is these factors which we hope constitute a true measure of the Center's contribution.

As this journal was compiled, we were struck by the realization of how little we have been able to convey the real spirit and day-to-day immediacy that is so much a part of AICC's involvement. At the outset, we were aware that this journal was to be necessarily limited in scope and content. Our aim has simply been to inform the reader in a limited way about those events leading up to the creation of the Center, to give some idea of our rationale and motivation, to give an account of what AICC is doing today and what we hope to do. With regrets we acknowledge our inability to tell the very human story of the personalities, drama and costly struggles that were involved in bringing AICC to its present status.

And finally, at this stage, we question whether the institution of AICC has been justified by the real human costs that have been involved, whether the Center can continue to exist within the confines of the University without becoming just another white institution in the eyes of the Indian people. We question whether this is ultimately the right path for the future or whether there is a wiser choice. These are difficult questions that strike at the essence of AICC's existence. In the end, we can only conclude that as long as AICC continues to engage in a real dialogue with the Indian community and remains attuned to those needs then the future will tell the tale. Whether the Center and those involved in it will fulfill its promise to make a lasting and meaningful contribution to the future of the American Indian people and their struggle for regeneration, will only be known in time

## AMERICAN INDIAN STUDIES PROGRAM- INTERIM STEERING COMMITTEE

**Community**

Elijah Smith, CIEA
Wanda Adamson, CIEA
Sandra Johnson, ITC
Illace Lavato, CIEA
Mary Boles, UAIC
Tim Wapato, UAIC
Francis Allen, UAIC
Charles Narcho, Indian Welcome House

Robert Banages, Long Beach State College
Charles Curo, Groumont
Frank Mazzetti, Rincon
Jim Olguin, UAIC
Emmett St. Marie, Morongo

**Faculty**
Dr. Jerome Cohen, Professor of Social Welfare, UCLA
Mr. Donald Roberts, Assistant Professor, Environmental Design, UCLA
Dr. Elwin V. Swenson, Director, Overseas Program, UCLA

**Administration**
Dr. David Saxon, Vice-Chancellor

**Students**
Dennis Jennings, Undergraduate Educational Opportunity Program
Kenneth Harwood, Undergraduate Public Services
Arch Henry White, Undergraduate Social Services
Carl Schildt, Undergraduate Public Services

**High Potential Program**
Karen Jacobson, Teacher, High Potential Program

## AMERICAN INDIAN CULTURE CENTER 3221 CAMPBELL HALL

**Staff**
Emmet S. Oliver, Interim Director
Doreen Pond, Administration Assistant II
Robert K. Chiago, Associate Director

## HIGH POTENTIAL PROGRAM 1235 CAMPBELL HALL

**Staff**
Anita T. Brown, Coordinator
Theresa Thomas, Secretary

**Teachers**
Karen Jacobson, Pre-Subject A
Art Zimiga, History
Patricia Locke, English

## NOTE

Reprinted with permission from *American Indian Culture Center Journal* (Spring 1970): 5–12.

# RALPH J. BUNCHE CENTER FOR AFRICAN AMERICAN STUDIES

The Ralph J. Bunche Center for African American Studies, founded in 1969 as the Center for Afro-American Studies (CAAS), was renamed after Nobel Prize winner, scholar, activist, and UCLA alumnus Ralph J. Bunche in 2003, in commemoration of the centenary of his birth.

The Bunche Center is the result of the struggle by black students at UCLA to have their history and culture recognized and studied. While the fight to have African American Studies acknowledged as a legitimate field of study was taking place all over America during the 1960s, it took on special significance at UCLA when two Black Panthers were killed at Campbell Hall in January 1969 after a clash over who would lead the center.

Alprentice "Bunchy" Carter and John Huggins, leaders in the Los Angeles chapter of the Black Panther Party, were shot and killed. Two brothers, who were members of the rival Black power group, the US Organization, were convicted of the murders, but escaped from prison in 1974. One of the brothers surrendered to authorities in South America many years later.

UCLA students had written a proposal for the center in 1968 and 1969 that documented the need for black Americans to be educated about their history and culture, to lessen their vulnerability to the "corrosive effects of American racism," and to give them the tools required to "understand and control the forces and attitudes presently shaping their lives."

The Bunche Center was established as an Organized Research Unit (ORU), with the mission to develop and strengthen African American Studies through five primary organizational branches: research, academic programs, library and media center, special projects, and publications.

The Center supports research that (1) expands the knowledge of the history, lifestyles, and sociocultural systems of people of African descent and (2) investigates problems that have bearing on the psychological, social, and economic well-being of persons of African descent. Research sponsored and conducted by the Bunche Center is multidisciplinary in scope and spans the humanities, social sciences, fine arts, and several professional schools.

The Center also administers three competitive scholarship programs—the Julian "Cannonball" Adderley Memorial Scholarship, the John Densmore Scholarship, and the Roxanne Chisholm and Jeanette Chisolm Moore Endowed Scholarship—which fund students majoring in Afro-American Studies and other disciplines.

The Bunche Center Library and Media Center (LMC) provides specialized information services to UCLA faculty, students, and staff and to researchers in the Southern California area at large. In so doing, it supports the academic programs and research projects in African American Studies and complements the resources of the UCLA library system.

The Special Projects division is responsible for the development and presentation of cultural and scholarly programming designed to enrich the experiences of the UCLA and off-campus communities. Among its notable activities is the annual Thurgood Marshall Lecture on Law and Human Rights. The Special Projects unit also interacts with businesses, cultural organizations, and other academic institutions to foster a better understanding of the Bunche Center mission, and the Special Projects staff plays a key role in fundraising efforts.

The Bunche Center is housed within the Institute of American Cultures (IAC), which was established in 1969 to promote the development of ethnic studies at UCLA by providing a structure for coordination of the four ethnic studies centers on campus (Bunche Center, Chicano Studies Research Center, Asian American Studies Center, and American Indian Studies Center). Through each center, the IAC awards annual predoctoral and postdoctoral fellowships, as well as faculty and student research grants.

Every day the Center works to live up to the goals set forth by the founders and "provide a creative arena for educational development relevant to the lives and existence of African Americans."

# DIRECTOR'S NOTE

CHON A. NORIEGA

The UCLA Chicano Studies Research Center emerged in the midst of social protest against profound disparities in educational access for the Mexican-descent population in the United States. It was originally named the Mexican American Cultural Center (1969–71). The name was changed to the Chicano Studies Center in 1971 and then to the current Chicano Studies Research Center in 1980. In its first two years its administration consisted of an Executive Committee that reported to a "Mesa Directiva" composed of students, faculty, and administrators. In 1971 the directorship was created, and the Mesa Directiva and the Executive Committee were combined into a Steering Committee. Since 1973 the CSRC has had an annually appointed Faculty Advisory Committee (FAC) per the requirements for a University of California Organized Research Unit (ORU).

From the first issue in spring 1970, the CSRC's journal, *Aztlán: A Journal of Chicano Studies,* has been dedicated to scholarly research relevant to or informed by the Chicano experience. The journal has also always undertaken the even more difficult task of defining—or even deconstructing—that experience. Little could be taken for granted; and, in fact, great effort has been necessary in order to bridge the disciplinary border between the social sciences and the humanities and the sociopolitical border between the academy and the community. Why? Internal differences—particularly of class, region, language, gender, and sexuality—have had a profound impact on the development of Chicano studies.

In 1969, the founders of *Aztlán* were graduate and even undergraduate students at UCLA, including: Juan Gómez-Quiñones, Deluvina Hernández, Reynaldo Macías, Teresa McKenna, and Roberto Sifuentes. These and other students came together across disparate fields—history, sociology, education, English, Spanish, political science, and theater arts—as an extension of their involvement in the Chicano student movement and the early formation of Chicano studies. Over the next fifteen years, the founding editors would bring out an impressive range of scholarship that both shaped and legitimized a multidisciplinary field. Meanwhile, these scholars moved from student to professor, often taking up the necessary but daunting task of institutional reform, program development, and mentorship within the university. Today they are recognized as the founding generation of Chicano studies.

Chon A. Noriega is the director of the UCLA Chicano Studies Research Center, professor in the UCLA Department of Film, Television, and Digital Media, and consulting curator of Chicano and Latino art at the Los Angeles County Museum of Art. He is the author of *Shot in America: Television, the State, and the Rise of Chicano Cinema* (2000) and co-author of *Home—So Different, So Appealing* (2017).

## AZTLÁN EDITORS, 1970 TO THE PRESENT

Juan Gómez-Quiñones, Roberto Sifuentes,
Jaime Sena, Alfredo Cuéllar .............................. Spring 1970–Fall 1971

Juan Gómez-Quiñones, Roberto Sifuentes ........................ Spring 1971

Juan Gómez-Quiñones, Reynaldo Flores Macías,
Andrés Chávez, Deluvina Hernández....................... Fall 1971–Fall 1974

Juan Gómez-Quiñones, Reynaldo Flores Macías,
Teresa McKenna ..................................... Spring 1975–Fall 1984

Raymund A. Paredes, Manuela Miranda,
Carlos P. Otero ...................................... Spring 1985–Fall 1986

Raymund A. Paredes, Edit E. Villarreal,
Carroll B. Johnson ................................. Spring 1987–Fall 1996

Chon A. Noriega ................................. Spring 1997–Spring 2016

Charlene Villaseñor Black .................................. Fall 2016–present

## ORIGINAL MISSION STATEMENT AND EDITORIAL STAFF AND INAUGURAL POEM FROM *AZTLÁN* 1:2 (FALL 1970)

AZTLAN introduces a vital self-sustaining analytical and philosophical dialogue on issues involving Chicanos.

### *Sponsor*

The Chicano Cultural Center was opened in June 1969. Its stated objectives are (1) to encourage and support research in all areas of knowledge relevant to the Chicano community, (2) to assist in developing programs and research focusing the unique resources of the University on problems of the Chicano community, (3) to assist in developing new curriculum and bibliographical materials dealing with the culture, history, and problems of the Chicanos, (4) to actively engage in furthering the involvement of the University of California with the Chicano community. As coordinator between the Chicano community and institutions of higher learning, and as a research and bibliographical resource, the Center seeks to promote an active quest for solutions to the problems of the barrios of America. AZTLAN is an extension of these goals, reaching out nationwide to reinforce this quest.

### *Objective*

First in the United States to focus scholarly discussion and analysis on Chicano matters as they relate to the group and to the total American society, AZTLAN will serve as an authoritative and credible information source for the general public, and as a publishing outlet and a meaningful classroom resource for teachers at all educational levels. It will contribute to the understanding of intergroup problems and intergroup relations.

### *Scope*

AZTLAN provides a forum for the publishing of scholarly writings on the Chicano community. Editorial responsibility rests with the editorial staff. AZTLAN invites scholarly papers and rigorous, thorough, original research and analysis in the social sciences and the arts. Its broad interdisciplinary context stimulates discussion of social, economic, political, historical, philosophical and literary matters involving Chicanos. The Editorial Staff is comprised of concerned scholars in various disciplines who are indigenous to the Chicano community.

### *Associate Editors*

Juan Gómez-Quiñones, History, UCLA
Roberto Sifuentes, Spanish, UCLA

### *Assistant Editors*

Reynaldo Flores Macías, Education, UCLA
Andrés Chávez, Political Science, UCLA
Deluvina Hernández, Sociology, UCLA

### *Contributing Editors*

Jesus Chavarria, History, University of California at Santa Barbara
Carlos Muñoz, Political Science, University of California at Irvine
Carlos Blanco, Spanish, University of California at San Diego
Ramón Eduardo Ruiz, History, University of California at San Diego
Carlos Cortes, History, University of California at Riverside
Carl Vasquez, Political Science, Stanford University, Palo Alto, California
Jaime Sena, Sociology, Claremont College
Alfredo Cuéllar, Political Science, Claremont College
Armando Valdez, La Causa, Inc., Oakland, California
Romeo Flores Caballero, Colegio de México, México D.F.

### *Technical Editor*

Vicente Aceves Madrid, Theater Arts, UCLA

### *Artist*

Judithe Hernández, Otis Art Institute
Cover design: *La lechuza de antaño en el presente*

Cover of *Aztlán* 1:2 (Fall 1970), with Judithe Hernández's *La lechuza de antaño en el presente.*

## NOTES

"Director's Note" draws from Chon A. Noriega, "The Dissension of Other Things," in *The Chicano Studies Reader: An Anthology of Aztlán, 1970–2015*, edited by Chon A. Noriega, Eric Avila, Karen Mary Davalos, Chela Sandoval, and Rafael Pérez-Torres (UCLA Chicano Studies Research Center Press, 2016). Reprinted with permission.

The list of editors was compiled by Charlene Villaseñor Black.

The mission statement, the 1970 editorial staff, and the inaugural poem were published in *Aztlán: Chicano Journal of the Social Sciences and the Arts* 2, no. 1 (Fall 1970): iii–vii.

# REMEMBERING ALCATRAZ:
## Twenty-Five Years After

TROY JOHNSON AND JOANE NAGEL

In the early morning hours of November 20, 1969, eighty-nine American Indians landed on Alcatraz Island in San Francisco Bay. Identifying themselves as "Indians of All Tribes," the group claimed the island by "right of discovery" and by the terms of the 1868 Treaty of Fort Laramie which gave Indians the right to unused federal property that had been Indian land previously. Except for a small caretaking staff, Alcatraz Island had been abandoned by the federal government since the early 1960s, when the federal penitentiary was closed. In a press statement, Indians of All Tribes set the tone of the occupation and the agenda for negotiations during the nineteen-month occupation:

> We, the native Americans, re-claim the land known as Alcatraz Island in the name of all American Indians . . . [W]e plan to develop on this island several Indian institutions: 1. A CENTER FOR NATIVE AMERICAN STUDIES. . . . 2. AN AMERICAN INDIAN SPIRITUAL CENTER. . . . 3. AN INDIAN CENTER OF ECOLOGY. . . . 4. A GREAT INDIAN TRAINING SCHOOL. . . . [and] an AMERICAN INDIAN MUSEUM. . . . In the name of all Indians, therefore, we reclaim this island for our Indian nations. . . . We feel this claim is just and proper, and that this land should rightfully be granted to us for as long as the rivers shall run and the sun shall shine. Signed, INDIANS OF ALL TRIBES.[1]

In the months that followed, thousands of protesters and visitors spent time on Alcatraz Island. They came from a large number of Indian tribes, including the Sioux, Navajo, Cherokee, Mohawk, Puyallup, Yakima, Hoopa, Omaha. The months of occupation were marked by proclamations, news conferences, powwows, celebrations, "assaults" with arrows on passing vessels, and negotiations with federal officials. In the beginning months of the occupation, workers from the San Francisco Indian Center gathered food and supplies on the mainland and transported them to Alcatraz. However, as time went

Troy Johnson (d. 2013) was emeritus professor of history and American Indian studies at California State University, Long Beach. Joane Nagel is chair of the Anthropology Department and a professor of sociology at the University of Kansas, Lawrence.

by, the occupying force, which generally numbered around one hundred, confronted increasing hardships as federal officials interfered with delivery boats and cut off the supply of water and electricity to the island, and as tensions on the island grew.

The negotiations between Indians of All Tribes and the federal government eventually collapsed, and Alcatraz Island was never developed in accordance with the goals of the Indian protesters. In June 1971, the dozen or so remaining protesters were removed by federal marshals, more than a year-and-a-half after Indians of All Tribes first took over the island. Despite their failure to achieve their demands, Alcatraz represented a watershed moment in Native American protest and resulted in an escalation of Indian activism around the country.

The occupation, which caught the attention of the entire country, provided a forum for airing long-standing Indian grievances and for the expression of Indian pride. Vine Deloria noted its importance, referring to the occupation as a "master stroke of Indian activism"[2] and recognizing its impact on Indian ethnic self-awareness and identity: "Indianness" was judged on whether or not one was present at Alcatraz, Fort Lawson, Mt. Rushmore, Detroit, Sheep Mountain, Plymouth Rock, or Pitt River. . . . The activists controlled the language, the issues, and the attention.[3]

The Alcatraz occupation and the activist events that followed it offered firm evidence to counter commonly held views of Indians as powerless in the face of history, as weakened remnants of disappearing cultures and communities. In contrast, the events on Alcatraz and the activism that spread in its wake fueled American Indian ethnic pride and strengthened Native individuals' sense of personal empowerment and community membership.

For example, Wilma Mankiller, now principal chief of the Cherokee Nation of Oklahoma, visited the island many times during the months of occupation. She describes the personal impact of the event as "an awakening that ultimately changed the course of my life."[4] The life-changing impact of the Alcatraz occupation emerged as a recurrent theme in our interviews with Native Americans who participated in or observed the protests of that period:

> **George Horse Capture**. In World War II, the marines were island-hopping; they'd do the groundwork, and then the army and the civilians would come in and build things. Without the first wave, nothing would happen. Alcatraz and the militants were like that. They put themselves at risk, could be arrested or killed. You have to give them their due. We were in the second wave. In the regular Indian world, we're very complacent; it takes leadership to get things moving. But scratch a real Indian since then, and you're going to find a militant. Alcatraz tapped into something. It was the lance that burst the boil.[5]
>
> **John Echohawk**. Alcatraz just seemed to be kind of another event—what a lot of people had been thinking, wanting to do. We were studying Indian law for the first time. We had a lot of frustration and anger. People were fed up with the status quo. That's just what we were thinking. Starting in 1967 at the University of New Mexico Law School, we read treaties, Indian legal history. It was just astounding how unfair it was, how wrong it was. It [Alcatraz] was the kind of thing we needed.[6]

**Leonard Peltier**. I was in Seattle when Alcatraz happened. It was the first event that received such publicity. In Seattle, we were in solidarity with the demands of Alcatraz. We were inspired and encouraged by Alcatraz. I realized their goals were mine. The Indian organizations I was working with shared the same needs: an Indian college to keep students from dropping out, a cultural center to keep Indian traditions. We were all really encouraged—not only those who were active, but those who were not active as well.[7]

**Frances Wise**. The Alcatraz takeover had an enormous impact. I was living in Waco, Texas, at the time. I would see little blurbs on TV. I thought, These Indians are really doing something at Alcatraz. . . . And when they called for the land back, I realized that, finally, what Indian people have gone through is finally being recognized. . . . It affected how I think of myself. If someone asks me who I am, I say, well, I have a name, but Waco/Caddo—that's who I am. I have a good feeling about who I am now. And you need this in the presence of all this negative stuff, for example, celebrating the Oklahoma Land Run.[8]

**Rosalie McKay-Want**. In the final analysis, however, the occupation of this small territory could be considered a victory for the cause of Indian activism and one of the most noteworthy expressions of patriotism and self-determination by Indian people in the twentieth century.[9]

**Grace Thorpe**. Alcatraz was the catalyst and the most important event in the Indian movement to date. It made me put my furniture into storage and spend my life savings.[10]

These voices speak to the central importance of the Alcatraz occupation as the symbol of long-standing Indian grievances and increasing impatience with a political system slow to respond to Native rights. They also express the feelings of empowerment that witnessing and participating in protest can foster. Loretta Flores did not become an activist herself until several years after the events on Alcatraz, but she eloquently describes the sense of self and community that activism can produce:

> The night before the protest, I was talking to a younger person who had never been in a march before. I told her, "Tomorrow when we get through with this march, you're going to have a feeling like you've never had before. It's going to change your life." Those kids from Haskell (Indian Nations University) will never forget this. The spirits of our ancestors were looking down on us smiling.[11]

The impact of the Alcatraz occupation went beyond the individual lives and consciousnesses it helped to reshape. The events on Alcatraz marked the beginning of a national Indian activist movement, sometimes referred to as "Red Power," that kept national attention on Indian rights and grievances. The founding of D-Q University in California, the Trail of Broken Treaties, the takeovers of the BIA, the siege at Wounded Knee, the Longest Walk: All of these followed in the wake of Alcatraz.

Despite its influence, the occupation of Alcatraz Island has largely been overlooked by those who write or speak today of American Indian activism. Much has been written about the battles fought by Indian people for their rights regarding access to hunting and fishing areas reserved by treaties in the states of Washington and Oregon, the continuing struggles for those same rights in Wisconsin and Minnesota, and the efforts of the Six Nations to secure guaranteed treaty rights in the northeastern United States. The 1972 takeover of the Bureau of Indian Affairs (BIA) headquarters in Washington, DC, and the 1973 occupation of Wounded Knee are well known as well, as is the killing of an Indian man, Joseph Stuntz, and two FBI agents on the Pine Ridge Reservation in 1975. Yet it is to the occupation of Alcatraz Island twenty-five years ago that one must look to find the genesis of modern-day American Indian activism. The movement began in 1969 and continues to this day.

A large number of occupations began shortly after the November 20, 1969 landing on Alcatraz Island. Most scholars and the general public who follow Indian issues frequently and incorrectly credit this new Indian activism to the American Indian Movement (AIM). AIM was founded on July 28, 1968 in Minneapolis, Minnesota, by Dennis Banks, George Mitchell, and Vernon and Clyde Bellecourt. Although AIM became a central actor in and organizer of much Native American protest during the 1970s and after, in 1969, at the time of the Alcatraz occupation, AIM was largely an urban movement concerned with overcoming discrimination and pervasive abuse by police, and its membership was not directly involved in the Alcatraz occupation. Only after visiting the Indians on Alcatraz Island and realizing the possibilities available through demonstration and seizure of federal facilities did AIM actually enter into a national activist role.

AIM leaders recognized the opportunities when they met with the Indian occupiers on Alcatraz Island during the summer of 1970 and were caught up in the momentum of the occupation. On a broader scale, they realized the possibilities of a national activist movement. Additionally, AIM leaders had seen firsthand, during their visit to Alcatraz, that the bureaucracy inherent in the federal government had resulted in immobility: No punitive action had been taken against the Indian people on the island. This provided an additional impetus for AIM's kind of national Indian activism and was congruent with the rising tide of national unrest, particularly among young college students. AIM's first attempt at a national protest action came on Thanksgiving Day 1970, when AIM members seized the Mayflower II in Plymouth, Massachusetts, to challenge a celebration of colonial expansion into what then was mistakenly considered to be a "new world." During this action, AIM leaders acknowledged the occupation of Alcatraz Island as the symbol of a newly awakened desire among Indians for unity and authority in a white world.

## BACKGROUND OF THE ALCATRAZ OCCUPATION

The 1960s and early 1970s was a time of urban unrest across the nation. The United States was deeply involved in an unpopular war in Vietnam. The civil rights movement, Black Power, the rise of La Raza, the Latino movement, the stirring of the new feminism, the rise of the New Left, and the Third World strikes were sweeping the nation, particularly college campuses. While US armed forces were involved in the clandestine invasion and bombing of Cambodia, the announcement of the massacre of innocent civilians in a hamlet in My Lai, Vietnam, burned across the front pages of American newspapers.[12] Ubiquitous campus demonstrations raised the level of consciousness of college students. People of all ages were becoming sensitized to the unrest among emerging minority and gender groups, who were staging demonstrations and proclaiming their points of view, many of which were incorporated by student activists. White students faced with the draft and an "unjust" war ultimately empathized with minority populations, thus adding numbers and support to their causes. Sit-ins, sleep-ins, teach-ins, lockouts, and boycotts became everyday occurrences on college campuses. And from these college campuses—specifically the University of California, Santa Cruz; San Francisco State University; the University of California, Berkeley; and the University of California, Los Angeles—emerged the Native Americans who would comprise the first occupation force on Alcatraz Island.

Latino, black, white, and Native protests each had different sources and goals. The roots of American Indian activism were buried in centuries of mistreatment of Indian people. The latest was the federal government's relocation program of the 1950s and 1960s, which promised to move reservation residents to major urban areas for vocational training and to assist them in finding jobs, adequate housing, and financial assistance while training was underway. More than one hundred thousand Indian people were relocated as a result of this process. The training, which generally was supposed to last three months, often lasted only three weeks; the job assistance was usually one referral, at best; the housing was 1950s and 1960s skid row; and the financial support ran out long before the training was started or any hope of a job was realized. The history of the San Francisco Bay Area relocation effort is replete with examples of Indian people—men, women, boys, and young girls—who sat for days and weeks at bus stations, waiting for the government representative who was to meet them and start them on the road to a new, successful urban life.[13]

Another group of Indian people who relocated to the Bay Area were those who had served in the military during World War II and then chose to settle in urban areas after the war. These veterans often brought their families with them. The majority of the thirty thousand Indians who served in the armed forces during the war had left the reservation for the first time in their lives to join up. During the war, they got used to regular employment and regular paychecks; in addition, they became accustomed to living with electricity, modern appliances, and hot and cold running water. These conveniences, taken for granted in non-Indian homes, were rare or nonexistent on Indian reservations. It was only natural that, once exposed to such basic services, Indian veterans would want to establish a more modern lifestyle for themselves and their families. Their relatives, too, sought the "good life" offered in the urban areas. Many Indian people wanted to see what was available in the cities that older brothers or uncles talked about as a part of their military experience. With relatives now living in urban areas such as New York, San Diego, Los Angeles, and San Francisco, many relocated and some found employment, but most returned home to the reservation.

Still other Indian people migrated to the Bay Area in the war years to work in defense industries, and they remained there. Because of the industrial need fed by the war and in keeping with the policy of termination of tribal groups and assimilation of Indians into non-Indian society, the government also relocated thousands of Indian workers to San Francisco.

In the Bay Area—one of the largest of more than a dozen relocation sites—the newly urban Indians formed their own organizations to provide the support that the government had promised but failed to provide. Generally, these groups were known by tribal names such as the Sioux Club and the Navajo Club, but there were also sports clubs, dance clubs, and the very early urban powwow clubs. Eventually, some thirty social clubs were formed to meet the needs of the urban Indians and their children—children who would, in the 1960s, want the opportunity to go to college and better themselves.[14]

By the early 1960s, a growing and increasingly organized urban Indian population, dissatisfied with the federal relocation program and with conditions both on the reservations and in the city, began to search for a means to communicate their concerns and grievances. Alcatraz Island appeared to be a promising site for launching an information and protest campaign.

## THE OCCUPATIONS

In actuality, there were three separate occupations of Alcatraz Island. The first was a brief, four-hour occupation on March 9, 1964, during which five Sioux Indians, representing the urban Indians of the Bay Area, occupied the island. The event was planned by Belva Cottier, the wife of one of the occupiers. The federal penitentiary on the island had been closed in 1963, and the government was in the process of transferring the island to the city of San Francisco for development. Meanwhile, Belva Cottier and her Sioux cousin developed plans of their own. They recalled having heard of a provision in the 1868 Sioux treaty with the federal government that stated that all abandoned federal lands reverted to ownership by the Sioux people. Using this interpretation of the treaty, they encouraged five Sioux men to occupy Alcatraz Island and claim it for the Sioux people. They issued press releases claiming the island in accordance with the 1868 Sioux treaty and demanded better treatment for urban Indians. Richard McKenzie, the most outspoken of the group, pressed the claim for title to the island through the court system, only to have the courts rule against him. More importantly, however, the Indians of the Bay Area were becoming vocal and united in their efforts to improve their lives.

The 1964 occupation of Alcatraz Island was a forewarning of the unrest that was fermenting, quietly but surely, in the urban Indian population. Prior to the 1964 occupation, the Bay Area newspapers contained a large number of articles about the federal government's abandonment of the urban Indian and the state and local government's refusal to meet their needs. The social clubs that had been formed for support became meeting places for Indian people to discuss the discrimination they were facing in schools, housing, employment, and health care. They also talked about the police, who, like law officers in other areas of the country, would wait outside of Indian bars at closing time to harass, beat, and arrest Indian patrons. Indian centers began to appear in all the urban relocation areas and became nesting grounds for new pan-Indian, and eventually activist, organization.

The second Alcatraz occupation came out of the Bay Area colleges and universities and other California college campuses where young, educated Indian students joined with other minority groups during the 1969 Third World Liberation Front strike and began demanding that colleges offer courses that were relevant to Indian students. Indian history written and taught by non-Indian instructors was no longer acceptable to these young students, who were awakened to the possibility of social protest to bring attention to the shameful treatment of Indian people.

Among the Indian students at San Francisco State was a young Mohawk named Richard Oakes. Oakes came from the St. Regis Reservation, had worked on high steel in New York, and had traveled across the United States, visiting various Indian reservations. He eventually had wound up in California, where he married a Kashia Pomo woman, Anne, who had five children from a previous marriage. Oakes worked in an Indian bar in Oakland for a period of time and eventually was admitted to San Francisco State. In September 1969, he and several other Indian students began discussing the possibility of occupying Alcatraz Island as a symbolic protest, a call for Indian self-determination. Preliminary plans were made for a symbolic occupation to take place in the summer of 1970, but other events caused an earlier execution of the plan.

The catalyst for the occupation was the destruction of the San Francisco Indian Center by fire in late October 1969. The center had become the meeting place for the Bay Area Indian organizations and the newly formed United Bay Area Indian Council, which had brought the thirty private clubs together into one large council headed by Adam Nordwall (later to be known as Adam Fortunate Eagle). The destruction of the Indian center united the council and the American Indian student organizations as never before. The council needed a new meeting place, and the students needed a forum for their new activist voice.

After the fire, the second occupation of Alcatraz Island was planned for November 9, 1969. Richard Oakes and the other Indian college students, along with a group of people from the San Francisco Indian Center, chartered a boat and headed for Alcatraz Island. Since many different tribes were represented, the name Indians of All Tribes was adopted for the group.

The initial plan was to circle the island and symbolically claim it for Indian people. During the circling maneuver, however, Richard and four others jumped from the boat and swam to the island. They claimed Alcatraz in the name of Indians of All Tribes and left the island after meeting with the caretaker, who asked them to leave. Later that same evening, Oakes and fourteen others returned to the island with sleeping bags and food sufficient for two or three days; they left the island the following morning without incident.

In meetings following the November 9 occupation, Oakes and his fellow students realized that a prolonged occupation was possible. It was clear that the federal government had only a token force on the island and that no physical harm had come to anyone involved. A new plan began to emerge.

Following the brief November 9 occupation, Oakes traveled to UCLA, where he met with Ray Spang and Edward Castillo and asked for their assistance in recruiting Indian students for what would become the longest Indian occupation of a federal facility to this very day. Spang, Castillo, and Oakes met in UCLA's Campbell Hall, now the home of the American Indian Studies Center and the editorial offices of the

*American Indian Culture and Research Journal,* in private homes, and in Indian bars in Los Angeles. On November 20, 1969, the eighty Indian people who occupied Alcatraz Island included seventy Indian students from UCLA.

The occupation of Alcatraz would last nineteen months and would bring together Indian people from across the United States, Alaska, Canada, Mexico, and South America. Most importantly, Alcatraz would force the federal government to take a new look at the situation faced by urban Indian people, the long-forgotten victims of a failed relocation program.

## LIFE ON THE ROCK

Once on the island, the people began to organize themselves immediately. An elected council was put into place. Everyone was assigned a job: security, sanitation, day care, housing, cooking, laundry. All decisions were made by unanimous consent of the people. Sometimes meetings were held five, six, seven times per day to discuss the rapidly developing occupation.

The federal government, for its part, insisted that the Indian people leave and placed an ineffective coast guard barricade around the island. Eventually, the government agreed to the Indian council's demands for formal negotiations. But, from the Indians' side, the demands were nonnegotiable. They wanted the deed to the island; they wanted to establish an Indian university, a cultural center, and a museum; and they wanted federal funding to establish all of these. The government negotiators turned down their demands and insisted that they leave the island.

It is important to remember that, while the urban Indian population supported the concept of an occupation and provided the logistical support, the occupation force itself was made up initially of young, urban Indian college students. The most inspiring person, if not the recognized leader, was Richard Oakes, who is described as handsome, charismatic, a talented orator, and a natural leader. Oakes was strongly influenced by an Iroquois organization known as the White Roots of Peace, which had been revitalized by a Mohawk, Ray Fadden, and an Iroquois holy man, Mad Bear Anderson. The White Roots of Peace was an old Iroquois organization that taught Iroquois traditions and attempted to influence Mohawk youths to take up leadership roles in the Mohawk Longhouse. This was an effort to revive and preserve Iroquois traditional life.

In the autumn of 1969, Jerry Gambill, a counselor for White Roots of Peace, visited the campus of San Francisco State and inspired many of the students, none more than Oakes, with whom he stayed. Gambill found a willing student and later a student leader in Richard Oakes. But Oakes's position as leader on the island, a title he himself never claimed, quickly created a problem. Not all of the students knew Oakes, and, in keeping with the true concepts underlying the occupation, many wanted an egalitarian society on the island, with no one as their leader. Although this may have been a workable form of organization on the island, it was not comprehensible to the non-Indian media. Newspapers, magazines, and television and radio stations across the nation sent reporters to the island to interview those in charge. They wanted to know who the leaders were. Oakes was the most knowledgeable about the landing and the most often sought out and identified as the leader, the "chief," the "mayor of Alcatraz."

By the end of 1969, the Indian organization on the island began to fall into disarray. Two groups rose in opposition to Richard Oakes, and, as the Indian students began returning to school in January 1970, they were replaced by Indian people from urban areas and reservations who had not been involved in the initial occupation. Where Oakes and the other students claimed title to the island by right of discovery, the new arrivals harked back to the rhetoric of the 1964 occupation and the Sioux treaty, a claim that had been pressed through the court system by Richard McKenzie and had been found invalid. Additionally, some non-Indians now began taking up residency on the island, many from the San Francisco hippie and drug culture. Drugs and liquor had been banned from the island by the original occupiers, but they now became commonplace.

The final blow to the early student occupation occurred on January 5, 1970, when Richard Oakes's twelve-year-old stepdaughter fell three floors down a stairwell to her death. Yvonne Oakes and some other children apparently had been playing unsupervised near an open stairwell when she slipped and fell. Following Yvonne's death, the Oakes family left the island, and the two remaining groups maneuvered back and forth for leadership. Despite changes of leadership, however, the demands of the occupiers remained consistent: title to Alcatraz Island, the development of an Indian university, and the construction of a museum and cultural center that would display and teach the valuable contributions of Indian people to the non-Indian society.

By this time, the attention of the federal government had shifted from negotiations with the island occupants to restoration of navigational aids to the Bay Area—aids that had been discontinued as the result of a fire on Alcatraz Island and the discontinuance of electrical service. The government's inability to restore the navigational aids brought criticism from the coast guard, the Bay Area Pilot's Association, and local newspapers. The federal government now became impatient. On June 11, 1971, the message went out to end the occupation of Alcatraz Island, which had begun on November 20, 1969.

The success or failure of the Indian occupation of Alcatraz Island should not be judged by whether the demands for title to the island and the establishment of educational and cultural institutions were realized. If one were to make such a judgment, the only possible answer would be that the occupation was a failure. Such is not the case, however. The underlying goals of the Indians on Alcatraz were to awaken the American public to the reality of the plight of the first Americans and to assert the need for Indian self-determination. In this they were indeed successful. Additionally, the occupation of Alcatraz Island was a springboard for Indian activism, inspiring the large number of takeovers and demonstrations that began shortly after the November 20, 1969 landing and continued into the late 1970s. These included the Trail of Broken Treaties, the BIA headquarters takeover in 1972, and Wounded Knee II in 1973. Many of the approximately seventy-four occupations that followed Alcatraz were either planned by or included people who had been involved in the Alcatraz occupation or who certainly had gained their strength from the new "Indianness" that grew out of that movement.

## REMEMBERING ALCATRAZ

This special edition of the *American Indian Culture and Research Journal* [published in 1994] celebrates the twenty-fifth anniversary of the Alcatraz occupation and presents a unique collection of articles focusing on Alcatraz as a watershed in contemporary American Indian history. Alcatraz was a defining moment in the lives of the American Indian people who participated either directly or in support of those on the island. Many of the individuals who were involved in the occupation have gone on to become prominent leaders in Indian education, law, and tribal government. The articles in this collection are authored by some of those people. The first six papers are written by persons who were directly involved with the occupation, including LaNada Boyer, the only person who was involved in the occupation from the first day until the last. The next three articles present reflections and analyses of the occupation itself and of Indian activism as a broader social movement. They include a recollection and assessment by Vine Deloria, Jr., and John Garvey's detailed examination of the federal government's reaction to the Alcatraz occupation. The final four authors focus on long-term assessments and consequences of the occupation and the activist period, including Karren Baird-Olson's focus on American Indian activism in the mid-1970s and Zug Standing Bear's discussion of the community reconstruction and cultural renewal that have occurred in the decades since the occupation.

Alcatraz Island remains a strong symbol of Indian activism and self-determination, and a rallying point for unified Indian political activities. On February 11, 1978, Indian participants began the "Longest Walk" to Washington, DC, to protest the government's ill treatment of Indian people. That walk began on Alcatraz Island. On February 11, 1994, AIM leaders Dennis Banks, Clyde Bellecourt, and Mary Wilson met with Indian people to begin the nationwide "Walk for Justice." The walk was organized to protest the continuing imprisonment of Leonard Peltier as a result of the June 26, 1975 shootout between AIM members and FBI agents on the Pine Ridge Reservation in South Dakota. That walk also began on Alcatraz Island. On Thanksgiving Day of each year since 1969, Indian people have gathered on Alcatraz Island to honor those who participated in the occupation and those who continue the struggle for Indian self-determination. In the final analysis, the occupation of Alcatraz Island was a major victory for the cause of Indian activism and remains one of the most noteworthy expressions of renewed ethnic pride and self-determination by Indian people in this century.

## NOTES

Reprinted with permission from Troy Johnson and Joane Nagel, *American Indian Culture and Research Journal* 18:4 (1994): 9–23.

1. Peter Blue Cloud, ed., *Alcatraz Is Not an Island* (Berkeley, CA: Wingbow Press, 1972), 40–42.

2. Vine Deloria, Jr., "The Rise of Indian Activism," in *The Social Reality of Ethnic America*, ed. R. Gomez, C. Collingham, R. Endo, and K. Jackson (Lexington, MA: D.C. Heath, 1974), 184–85.

3. Ibid. In 1993, Deloria reflected on the longer-term impact of the Red Power movement. This era will probably always be dominated by the images and slogans of the AIM people. "The real accomplishments in land restoration, however, were made by quiet determined tribal leaders. . . . In reviewing the period we should understand the frenzy of the time and link it to the definite accomplishments made by tribal governments" (correspondence with the editors, 1993).

4. Telephone interview, Tahlequah, Oklahoma, 27 November 1991.

5. Telephone interview, Fort Belknap, Montana, 24 May 1994.

6. Telephone interview, Boulder, Colorado, 9 July 1993.

7. Telephone interview, Leavenworth, Kansas, 1 June 1993.

8. Telephone interview, Oklahoma City, Oklahoma, 24 August 1993.

9. Rosalie McKay-Want, "The Meaning of Alcatraz," quoted in Judith Antell, "American Indian Women Activists" (Ph.D. diss., University of California, Berkeley, 1989), 58–60.

10. Grace Thorpe, interview by John Trudell, *Radio Free Alcatraz*, 12 December 1969.

11. Citation missing in the original.

12. The Nixon presidential archives make no mention of the invasion of Cambodia, since it was largely a secret operation (though poorly kept) at this time. President Nixon and his staff make direct analogies between the Indian people on Alcatraz and My Lai and the shootings at Kent State. It was agreed that the American people would not stand by and see Indian people massacred and taken off Alcatraz in body bags.

13. Native American Research Group, *American Indian Socialization to Urban Life Final Report* (San Francisco, CA: Institute for Scientific Analysis, revised 1975).

14. Joan Ablon, "Relocated American Indians in the San Francisco Bay Area: Social Interaction and Indian Identity, in *Human Origination* 23 (Winter 1964): 297.

# ALCATRAZ, ACTIVISM, AND ACCOMMODATION

VINE DELORIA, JR.

Alcatraz and Wounded Knee 1973 have come to symbolize the revival of Indian fortunes in the late twentieth century, so we hesitate to discuss the realities of the time or to look critically at their actual place in modern Indian history. We conclude that it is better to wrap these events in romantic notions and broker that feeling in exchange for further concessions from the federal government; consequently, we fail to learn from them the hard lessons that will serve us well in leaner times.

Activism in the 1950s was sporadic but intense. In 1957, Lumbee people surrounded a Ku Klux Klan gathering in North Carolina and escorted the hooded representatives of white supremacy back to their homes sans weapons and costumes. In 1961, a strange mixture of Six Nations people and non-Indian supporters attempted a citizens' arrest of the secretary of the Interior, and, sometime during this period, a band of "True Utes" briefly took over the agency offices at Fort Duchesne. The only context for these events was the long suffering of small groups of people bursting forth in an incident that illustrated oppression but suggested no answer to pressing problems. In 1964, the "fish-ins" in the Pacific Northwest produced the first activism with an avowed goal; continual agitation in that region eventually resulted in *U.S. v. Washington,* which affirmed once and for all the property rights of Northwest tribes for both subsistence and commercial fishing.

Indians benefited substantially from the civil rights movement of the 1960s and the ensuing doctrines concerning the poor, which surfaced in the Economic Opportunity Act and more particularly in its administration. The civil rights movement had roots in a hundred small gatherings of concerned attorneys brought together by Jack Greenberg and Thurgood Marshall to determine the legal and philosophical basis for overturning *Plessy v. Ferguson.* Concentrating on the concept of *equality,* a series of test cases involving access to professional education in the border states cut away the unexamined

VINE DELORIA, JR. (1933–2008) was an acclaimed scholar and a professor in the Department of History, University of Colorado at Boulder.

assumption that separate facilities for higher education automatically meant equality of treatment and equality of the substance of education.

In 1954, *Brown v. Topeka Board of Education* stripped away the cloak of indifference and hypocrisy and required the dismantling of segregated schools. By extension, if schools were to be integrated, why not lunch counters and buses, and why not equality under the law in all public places and programs? The *Brown* strategy was created on behalf of the oppressed multitudes of African Americans but did not involve the rank and file people until the movement went into the streets and lunch counters of the South. With the announcement of "Black Power" by Stokely Carmichael and SNCC in 1966—made possible in some measure by the insistence of federal War on Poverty administrators that the "poor" knew better than anyone else what poverty was and how to combat it—the civil rights movement became a people's movement.

A people's movement has many benefits—the mass of minority groups are involved, and political strength increases dramatically—but it also has immense vulnerability in that goals that can be seen, articulated, and achieved are surrendered in favor of symbolic acts that illustrate and demonstrate the suffering and frustrations of the people. Symbolic acts demand attention from an otherwise unaware general public, but they also fail to articulate the necessity of specific actions that can and must be taken by the government at the local, state, and federal levels to alleviate the crisis. Consequently, the choice of remedy is given to the institutional structure that oppresses people and to the good and bad politicians and career bureaucrats who operate the institution.

The Poor People's March of 1968 best exemplifies the problem of a people's movement unable to articulate specific solutions and see them through to completion. Organized partially in memory of the slain Martin Luther King and partially as an effort to secure increases in the funding of social programs, the march floundered when participants spent their time harassing members of the cabinet about problems that had no immediate solution and demanding sympathy and understanding from federal officials who could not translate these concerns into programmatic responses. Smaller protests had maintained a decent level of funding for poverty programs in past years, but, this time, the march faced the bitter reality of the Vietnam War and the impossibility of continuing to expand the federal budget into unrealistic deficits.

It is important to note that, while the Indian fishing rights struggle maintained itself with measurable goals, Alcatraz represented an Indian version of the Poor People's March. The proclamation presented by the first invaders of the island demanded a bewildering set of responses from the federal government, focusing on transfer of the island's title to an Indian organization and the funding of an educational center on the island for the thousands of Indians who had made the Bay Area their home. The popular interpretation of the occupation was that Indians were entitled to own the island because it was federal surplus property and therefore qualified under a provision of the 1868 treaty of Fort Laramie.

Unfortunately, the treaty provision was a myth. Red Cloud had simply remained in the Powder River country until the government withdrew its troops from the Bozeman Trail and then, satisfied that the trail was closed, arrived at Fort Laramie in November 1868 to sign the treaty. During the Alcatraz occupation, when White House staff and Department of Interior lawyers looked at the treaty, they could find no phrase that justified returning the island to the Indian occupants; consequently, they were blocked from using any executive powers to resolve the crisis.

The initial group of Indian occupants was composed of students from Bay Area colleges and universities, but, as the occupation continued, these people were replaced with enthusiastic recruits from across the nation and with unemployed people who had nowhere else to go. The mood of the occupants was that they should use the press as often as possible; thus the goal of the movement quickly became confused, with various spokespeople articulating different philosophies on different occasions.

The difference between Alcatraz and the fishing rights fight, and between the *Brown* litigation and the Black Power movement, should be made clear: Behind the sit-ins and the fish-ins was the almost certain probability that, should activists be convicted at the trial court level, they would have their convictions overturned by a higher court and/or the object of their protest would be upheld at a higher level of litigation. *Brown* and the Medicine Creek fishing rights treaty were already federal law before people went out to protest; the protests were made on behalf of impartial enforcement of existing law. This foundation of legality did not exist for either the Poor People's March or the occupation of Alcatraz. Therefore, in legal terms, these activities meant nothing.

My role in Alcatraz was sporadic and, in a few instances, not welcomed by some of the activists on the Rock. While I was director of the National Congress of American Indians (NCAI), I had worked for several years with people in the Bay Area as part of the NCAI's concern for relocated Indians. I entered law school in the fall of 1967 and, by the time of the occupation, had already written *Custer Died for Your Sins,* which was released in early October 1969. Some years before, Richard MacKenzie and others had briefly landed on Alcatraz, and, in the years since that first invasion, Bay Area activists such as Adam Nordwall had disrupted Columbus Day celebrations and, with some modest successes, generally tried to focus the attention of Bay Area politics on urban Indian problems. Ironically, some of the people who were now shouting "Red Power" into every microphone they could find had called me a communist the year before for doing a Frank McGee NBC news interview that advocated Red Power.

Adam Nordwall saw that the occupation would flounder unless it was tied to some larger philosophical issue that could be seen by the American public as important to their own concerns for justice. During the fall of 1969, I was asked several times to come out to Alcatraz to discuss how the people on the island could transform the occupation into a federal issue that could be resolved by congressional action. I favored announcing that not only did Indians want the island, we wanted a federal policy of land restoration that would provide a decent land base for small reservations, return submarginal lands to tribes that had them, and, in some cases, restore original reservation boundaries.

On Christmas Eve 1969, I flew out to California to discuss the land issue with people on the island, but the meeting never got off the ground. Instead of listening to our presentation on land restoration, the activists began quarreling about who was in charge of the operation. Richard Oakes had many supporters, but he also had many rivals. Adam and I were considered intruders because we had not been in the original invasion. About all we got out of the meeting was the sneer that the activists had the whole world watching them, and they were in control of Indian policy. We pointed out that a sensible program had to be articulated so that the administration could act, but we got no positive response.

In January 1970, hoping to highlight a land and treaty issue, I invited Merv Griffin to come out to Alcatraz and do part of a show from there. Unfortunately, many of the people on the Rock had not moved forward in their thinking; Merv got the old response of how the island belonged to Indians under the 1868 treaty and how they wanted to establish an educational and vocational training facility on the island.

In the spring of 1970, a group of us held a national urban Indian conference on Alcatraz in another effort to provide a context for securing the island. In November 1969, this same urban group had held its conference the weekend before the San Francisco Indian Center burned, but now, under different leadership, we were trying to focus everything on the Bay Area in the hope of defining an issue that the public would embrace. The meeting was not long underway when a man and woman began to scream at each other across the room, viciously and seemingly without any provocation. Every time anyone would propose a course of action, one or the other would jump up and let loose a string of curses designed to infuriate everyone. Most people sat there politely listening to the nonsense, but eventually the meeting just dissolved. Later, we discovered they were a husband and wife who went through this performance at every meeting they attended.

While our meeting was being held, we learned that Richard Oakes and his supporters had been thrown off the island the day before and that they were likely to confront us when we returned to the mainland. We met only one sullen young man who warned us that he was going to remember our names and faces. Later that evening, as we sat around trying to figure out what to do, we hit on a plan. We had someone call Oakes's headquarters and, in his best reservation English, relate that he was supervising two buses of Navajo boys who were traveling to the Hoopa Bear Dance and wanted to be housed for the night. The Oakes contingent immediately tried to enlist these Navajo as a force to help Oakes recapture the island. They gave us directions for finding their headquarters, and we promised to come help them. A few minutes after hanging up the phone, we decided it would be even better to include buses of Navajo girls, so we had a rather prominent Indian woman call the headquarters and pretend that she was matron over two busloads of girls from Navajo Community College who were looking to make contact with the Navajo boys. This phone call created a dilemma for us and for Oakes's people. They wanted to get the two busloads of girls and lose the boys; we wondered how long we could continue to drive four phantom buses around the Bay Area.

Our pretend Navajo man then called Oakes's people back and said he had gotten lost and was in Oakland, and we got new directions for reaching their headquarters. Our woman then got back on the phone and told Oakes's group that the girls' buses were only a few blocks away. Their response was that they would go out and buy food and get ready to welcome the girls, apparently forgetting that the boys' buses would be along shortly also. We hung up and pondered the situation we had created. The consensus was that we should call back and confess the whole thing before everyone was inconvenienced. We were just about to confess when one of our group said, "Wait a minute! Real Indians would just go their own way and not say a word; we are thinking like responsible, educated Indians." So we just went back to our hotel to bed.

The next morning, as we embarked for Alcatraz to finish the meeting, we were greeted by two surly Oakes supporters. They told us to go ahead and visit the island, but they assured us that we would not stay long because they had reinforcements of four hundred Navajo arriving momentarily and we would be thrown off the Rock along with the anti-Oakes people. Needless to say, our meeting went well, and the Navajo never did arrive. I will not mention the names in our little group, but I can confess that they are still prominent, responsible, national Indian leaders.

The occupation of Alcatraz lingered on. A rougher group of people occupied the island, and it became useless to try to make sense of the occupation. Increasingly, it became a hazard to go out there. Eventually, many of the buildings were burned, and feeble, nonsensical ultimatums were issued by the declining population on the Rock. Finally, the government swooped down and took the remaining people away. I visited the island about a decade later and heard a surprisingly mild and pro-Indian explanation of the occupation from a Park Service guide. I walked around the grounds and remembered some of the difficult meetings we had held there and how, several times, we almost had a coalition that could have affected land policy. Unfortunately, most of the people involved in the occupation had no experience in formulating policy and saw their activities as primarily aimed at awakening the American public to the plight of Indians. Thus a great opportunity to change federal programs for Indians was lost.

*The Trail of Broken Treaties* came along in the fall of 1972. By that time, the activists had devised the Twenty Points, which, in my opinion, is the best summary document of reforms put forth in this century. Written primarily by Hank Adams, who supervised the fishing rights struggle until the Supreme Court ruled in favor of Indians, it is comprehensive and philosophical and has broad policy lines that can still be adopted to create some sense of fairness and symmetry in federal Indian policy.

Then came the Wounded Knee occupation, with its aftermath of trials and further violence. Indians were well represented in the media from the Alcatraz occupation through the Wounded Knee trials, but, unfortunately, each event dealt primarily with the symbols of oppression and did not project possible courses of action that might be taken to solve problems.

The policy posture of Indians at Alcatraz was part of a historical process begun during the War on Poverty when people demanded action from the government but failed to articulate the changes they wanted. With the incoming Nixon administration in 1969, we clamored for an Indian to be appointed as commissioner. Because we failed to support Robert Bennett, who was already occupying the office, the inept Louie Bruce was installed. Bruce's chaotic administration produced an era in which résumés were enhanced and job descriptions were watered down so that the respective administrations could appoint Indian puppets to symbolize the presence of Indians in the policymaking process. Today the government, under Ada Deer, is at work trying to create a new set of categories—"historic" and "nonhistoric" tribes—so that benefits and services can be radically reduced. When Indians do not clearly articulate what they want, the government feels free to improvise, even if it means creating new policies that have no roots in anything except the fantasies of the creator.

Alcatraz was more than a protest against the oppressive conditions under which Indians lived. In large part, it was a message that we wanted to determine our own destiny and make our own decisions. That burden is still upon us and weighs heavily when contemporary tribal chairpeople are consulted about policy directions. Almost always, immediate concerns or irritating technicalities are regarded as important in the consultative process, and, consequently, it is increasingly difficult to determine exactly where people think we are going. Like the activists at Alcatraz, we often mill around, keenly aware that we have the ears of the public but uncertain what to do next. Until we can sketch out realistic scenarios of human and resource goals, we continue to resemble those occupants of the Rock a quarter of a century ago: We want change, but we do not know what change.

## NOTE

Reprinted with permission from Vine Deloria, Jr., *American Indian Culture and Research Journal* 18:4 (1994): 25–32.

# BETWEEN JAPANESE AMERICAN INTERNMENT AND THE USA PATRIOT ACT

## The Borderlands and the Permanent State of Racial Exception

SCOTT MICHAELSEN

## FIRST REGISTER: THE INTEGRITY OF THE BORDER: WIRE, SEARCHLIGHTS, PIT, DIRT

3. Wire fence.
4. We travelled along the fence, walking.
5. We entered here. 1 block. Borde. This whole part of El Borde has lights and searchlights . . .
10. This is the street where those of the *migra* constantly pass by.
11. This that I mark over with the pen is a pit where you have to cross practically on all fours . . .
14. Police car.
15. Dirt road. Here we had to throw ourselves down so they wouldn't grab us. And when the car passed we were off to the races.
16. This was all running, to the point I couldn't bear my legs anymore.
17. Here we jumped into the gully because the *migra* saw us there and told us to stop.
18. When we jumped I fell because someone grabbed me and it was a fat potbellied guy. I got myself up thanks to another guy who urged me on.
19. Here we left to enter this fucking country.

(Notes for a map or sketch of the geography of a Tijuana border crossing, in a letter from Lety Martínez González of Los Angeles to Argelia Gonzáles Morales of Oaxaca, Mexico, June 4, 1990)

Scott Michaelsen is professor of cultural studies at Michigan State University, where he teaches classes in literature of the Americas, popular culture, and philosophy and theory in relation to literature and society. He is co-author of *Anthropology's Wake: Attending to the End of Cultural Analysis* (Fordham University Press, 2009), author of *Border Theory: The Limits of Multiculturalism* (University of Minnesota Press, 1999), and co-editor of *CR: The New Centennial Review*.

As a first requirement for continued thinking after 9/11, an entire conversation taking place in the United States needs to be displaced. On one side of this conversation lies the argument that we must be very alert in the wake of 9/11 so as not to repeat the mistakes of the past, and in particular the experience of the Japanese American internment camps of World War II. It is still within the realm of modern or living memory that constitutional rights were suspended along racial lines—and this must never happen again. Art Gutman, for example, following President George W. Bush's rhetoric, says that we must be "'vigilant' but not 'vigilantes'" (2002). On another side of this conversation is the argument that freedom comes with sacrifice, and that a time of war mandates certain costs in the realm of liberty. Chief Justice of the US Supreme Court William Rehnquist has written, for example, that "It is neither desirable nor is it remotely likely that civil liberty will occupy as favored a position in wartime as it does in peacetime. . . . The laws will . . . not be silent in a time of war, but they will speak with a somewhat different voice" (1998, 224–25). On yet a third side of this conversation is the assertion that the new, post-9/11 era is a better one and that we have crossed the racial boundaries of the past. As one anonymous Internet posting from 2001 put it, "We've come a long way in 50 years, from 'Japs bombed Hawaii, so we'll intern everyone who looks like that' to 'The enemy of America is not our many Muslim friends. It is not our many Arab friends'" (DeCandido 2001).

But all sides of this conversation forget something that Neil Gotanda (1991), Andrew Kull (1992), and others of various political stripes have asserted for some time: that the US Constitution has never been "color-blind" and that indeed, as Charles W. Mills points out, the entire history of the philosophy of universalist social contractarianism is linked to what Mills calls the exclusionary "racial contract" (1997).

This essay first revisits the two best-known examples of racialized law in the twentieth-century United States—the law that legalized the Japanese American internment camps during World War II and the USA PATRIOT Act, enacted during the post-9/11 "war on terror"—in order to come to terms with what might be called *the permanent state of racial emergency*, or *the permanent state of legal racial exception*, as exemplified by the US-Mexico borderlands.[1] The borderlands has been for generations (and for decades in constitutional law) a zone without normal, traditional, or equivalent Fourth Amendment protections against "unreasonable" search and seizure.[2] Generalized "foreignness," thought to its limit, here has long been associated with criminality, and documented Mexican nationals, undocumented Mexicans, and Chicanos all have shouldered the burden.[3] The US-Mexico borderlands is a race surveillance camp, a zone where the full measure of the Bill of Rights is permanently suspended, and the significance of this remains to be examined when considering the implications of race and law in the United States.[4] The borderlands, as a primary site for declaration of the permanent racial emergency, supersedes the more celebrated race law examples of Japanese American internment and the USA PATRIOT Act. They simply *belong* to this permanent polity, rather than pose strange exceptions to the rule of color-blindness.[5]

A rereading of the two key Supreme Court decisions regarding Japanese American treatment during wartime, *Hirabayashi v. United States* (320 US 81 [1942]) and *Korematsu v. United States* (323 US 214 [1944]), makes clear that the suspension of constitutional rights along racial lines is not an extraconstitutional matter.[6] Indeed, racially based exceptionalism lies at the core of the US version of the doctrine of sovereignty. Justice Stone's lead opinion in *Hirabayashi* asserts:

> Because racial discriminations are in most circumstances irrelevant and therefore prohibited, it by no means follows that, in dealing with the perils of war, Congress and the Executive are wholly precluded from taking into account those facts and circumstances which are relevant to measures for our national defense and for the successful prosecution of the war, and which may in fact place citizens of one ancestry in a different category from others. "We must never forget, that it is a constitution we are expounding," "a constitution intended to endure for ages to come, and, consequently, to be adapted to the various crises of human affairs." . . . The adoption by Government, in the crisis of war and of threatened invasion, of measures for the public safety, based upon the recognition of facts and circumstances which indicate that a group of one national extraction may menace that safety more than others is not wholly beyond the limits of the Constitution and is not to be condemned merely because in other and in most circumstances racial distinctions are irrelevant. (320 US 100–01)

In *Korematsu*, Justice Frankfurter's concurrence makes a similar point:

> Action is not to be stigmatized as lawless because like action in times of peace would be lawless. To talk about a military order that expresses an allowable judgment of war needs by those entrusted with the duty of conducting war as "an unconstitutional order" is to suffuse a part of the Constitution with an atmosphere of unconstitutionality. (323 US 224–25)

The cited passages braid together three crucial themes: emergency/crisis/public safety, the law of white supremacy, and what Carl Schmitt refers to as the sovereign exception to the existing legal order ("Sovereign is he who decides on the exception" [Schmitt 1985, 5]). Important to note here is the fact that the racialized suspension of legal rule is theorized as within the shell of constitutionalism. Justice Stone's argument is that precisely because the US Constitution is a *constitution*—meant on its face to be preserved in its constituted-ness—therefore *nothing* that preserves the Constitution, including the abrogation/nullification of its inner logics and rights, can be "wholly beyond the limits of the Constitution."[7] Race law, according to Stone, is not typical constitutional law, but neither is it unconstitutional. And Frankfurter's seconding is even clearer: a war need, in principle, cannot be "an unconstitutional order." At the limit of the Constitution, it is constitutional for sovereignty to order the disembowelment of the US Constitution. To say this another way: it is constitutional (it is within the boundaries, and among the inner possibilities, of the Constitution) to suspend the Fourteenth Amendment's seeming color-blindness.

As Carl Schmitt reminds, sovereignty is a "borderline concept," or one that pertains to the "outermost sphere" of a legal system or order (1985, 5). In a related modality, Richard K. Ashley defines the proper exploration of the problem of sovereignty as "neither domestic nor international. It is the 'nonplace' defined in terms of the ever problematical difference between the two" (1989, 285).[8] Sovereignty is an "inner" possibility of any constitutional order, yet its application necessarily crosses this border and traces the outline of both inside and outside. The definition of the word "citizen," according to Justice Taney's decision in the infamous *Dred Scott v. Sandford* (60 US 393 [1856]), is simply this: "a member of the community who form a sovereignty" (60 US 422). Sovereignty's first interest will always be, therefore, the border between the inner and outer, between the domestic and the international, between the citizen and all that is not the citizen: the citizen-from-elsewhere, the noncitizen, the second-class citizen, the alien and the undocumented, the refugee. It is "here" that the exception will become, in effect, the rule, under cover of emergency (or, at least, heightened need or special exigency). The law can be racially inflected, always and in every way imaginable, at the "nonplace" where sovereignty makes its primary mark—at the border, or precisely neither inside nor outside the sovereign territory. This, in a nutshell, is one way of grounding and phrasing the argument that *structurally* the US Constitution is not fundamentally color-blind. At its limit, the US Constitution incessantly and necessarily thinks racial ordering and domination.

Indeed, the foundation of American polity and American sovereignty is exceptional white supremacy. One way this can be demonstrated is through the entire body of case law in affirmative action matters, which is grounded on a reading of the *Korematsu* and *Hirabayashi* decisions. Closely reading Justice Powell's lead decision in the "reverse discrimination" case of *Regents of University of California v. Bakke* (438 US 265 [1978]), which to date defines the permissible boundaries of affirmative action, one finds that

> the logic of the state of emergency in *Hirabayashi* and *Korematsu* will be applied to California-Davis in order to ascertain whether the State of California's racial hierarchies justify the emergency measure of quota-based affirmative action. For Powell, of course, California does not meet the test. Thus, the same standard which *permits* the Japanese concentration camps *denies* the need for affirmative action. But this is more than the mere application of some clear and determinate standard in two separate cases. By thinking these two instances together as a coherent political strategy, one can conclude that the logic of the limit in *Bakke* is double: *Affirmative action can only proceed so long as it does not disturb white privilege, while at the same time the Constitutional protection of raceless citizenship extends also only to the point where white privilege senses its disturbance.* (Michaelsen and Shershow 2002, 16)[9]

The court system's idea of "rigid scrutiny," when applied to race-based law, examines the "state of emergency." To determine a "state of emergency," in reverse, is to open the door to race-based and racially inflected suspension of a color-blind Constitution.

It is, perhaps, an open secret that the USA PATRIOT Act (2001), passed by Congress in the wake of 9/11, partly operates much like the earlier Antiterrorism and Effective Death Penalty Act (1996)—the so-called secret evidence law—in that it "selectively" subjects "Arab immigrants" to "Star Chamber treatment" (Cole and Dempsey 2002, 128).[10] Though facially neutral (that is, neither act makes reference to race as such), the racialized applications of these acts have yet to meet successful challenge along the lines of *Yick Wo v. Hopkins* (118 US 356 [1886]), the lead case for the overturning of a facially neutral law designed to be executed along racial lines.[11] Nor is it clear that a successful challenge is possible, given that *Yick Wo* merely involved laundrymen's buildings and routine city ordinances, while the secret evidence and PATRIOT acts concern "national security."

In the first test of a crucial portion of the USA PATRIOT Act, the racial application of the act was legitimated through reference to the precedent of the US-Mexican border. This founding piece of case law regarding the USA PATRIOT Act is a product of the secret court system established by the Foreign Intelligence Surveillance Act (FISA) of 1978, and the decision was handed down on November 18, 2002, by the United States Foreign Intelligence Surveillance Court of Review (USFISCR 2002). It is worth explaining that the FISA court system consists of two bodies: the Foreign Intelligence Surveillance Court (USFISC), which is a thirty-member body that rules on Department of Justice requests for "foreign intelligence" surveillance, and the Foreign Intelligence Surveillance Court of Review (USFISCR), a three-member panel that met in 2002 for the very first time in order to consider the US government's appeal of an earlier USFISC ruling.[12]

The case is an extremely complex one, turning on questions of whether the Justice Department, and in particular the FBI, is constitutionally required to set up an intelligence firewall between its domestic crime-solving and international intelligence-gathering units in order to prevent Fourth Amendment violations that might result from criminal intelligence obtained during foreign intelligence gathering.[13] The Department of Justice under Attorney General John Ashcroft sought and received a ruling from USFISCR that in effect dismantled the firewall and also went several steps further, facilitating, among other things, criminal surveillance without probable cause.[14] This has prompted at least one commentator to quip, "The Fourth Amendment isn't dead, but no one will insure it" (Osher 2002).

The USFISCR, in making its decision in favor of the government and the USA PATRIOT Act, explicitly invokes the US-Mexico border. The review court argues that we should not simply "jettison Fourth Amendment requirements in the interest of national security" (USFISCR 2002, 51). Instead, we must carefully "balance" the "government's interest against individual privacy interests" (52). In particular, the government has "special needs, beyond the normal need for law enforcement" in certain situations (53). "Apprehending drunk drivers and securing the border constitute such unique interests," according to the court (53). The court suggests that the "integrity of the [US-Mexico] border" (54) is the sort of ongoing, permanent "emergency" (55) that lays the constitutional foundation for the USA PATRIOT Act and a rule of law in which traditional "Fourth Amendment warrant standards" are not precisely met, but "certainly come close" (56). Here, an inch is as good as a yard, and the important point is that a discrepancy in color-blind constitutionalism appears ("certainly come[s] close"), however small it may seem at first glance. Measuring the extent of the damage, it is critical to be alert to a nexus of metaphorics that judge the figure of the "foreign"—the figure who will have the law applied to her or him in this differential manner—to be inherently "criminal." The FISA review court asserts that there is no real or sustainable distinction between the gathering of "foreign intelligence" and the investigation of crime, for the simple reason that "the definition of an agent of a foreign power, if it pertains to a U.S. person . . . is closely tied to criminal activity" (10), and again, "the definition of an agent of a foreign power—if he or she is a U.S. person—is grounded on criminal conduct" (11). Therefore, and following a Department of Justice argument, "the supposed pre-PATRIOT Act limitation in FISA that restricts the government's intention to use foreign intelligence information in criminal prosecutions is an illusion" (7). Indeed, in the USA PATRIOT Act, "the statute's definitions of foreign intelligence and foreign agent are actually cast in terms of criminal conduct" (17). The looseness and conceptual flexibility of the categories "foreign intelligence information" and "agent of a foreign power" should be noted: the former simply means, at its maximum limit, any "clandestine intelligence activities" undertaken by the latter, which is defined, again at its maximum limit, as "a foreign-based political organization not substantially composed of United States persons" (9). These definitions, it should go without saying, cast a very wide net. As the Electronic Frontier Foundation, a watchdog group, makes clear, an "agent of a foreign power" would include "a British national who works for the British embassy in the United States" (Tien 2001). And "clandestine intelligence activities" likely would be subject to Cole and Dempsey's droll formulation of the problem of sovereignty: "terrorism is whatever the Secretary of State decides it is" (2002, 119). "Clandestine intelligence activities," for example, might theoretically include videotaping a city skyline, reading documents in a library, or surfing the Internet.[15]

To repeat: The example of the US-Mexico border undergirds the first substantial court review of the USA PATRIOT Act with regard to constitutionality and the Fourth Amendment and permits the general criminalization of that which is deemed foreign. Ultimately, the USA PATRIOT Act's constitutionalism is grounded on the logic of a series of 1970s US Supreme Court decisions regarding the US Border Patrol and its permanent checkpoint, temporary checkpoint, and "roving patrol" or car-stop operations. All roads from the USA PATRIOT Act, in other words, lead back to the border. The key cases in this regard, discussed in more detail in the next section, are *Almeida-Sanchez v. United States* (413 US 266 [1973]), *United States v. Peltier* (422 US 531 [1975]), *United States v. Ortiz* (422 US 891 [1975]), *United States v. Brignoni-Ponce* (422 US 873 [1975]), and *United States v. Martinez-Fuerte* (428 US 543 [1976]). The last of these is the case that the FISA review court twice directly cites. In these cases, the *permanent state of racial emergency* is theorized and the permanent *exception* to colorblind constitutionalism is codified.[16]

## SECOND REGISTER: THE VISIBILITY OF CRIMINALITY: LANDSCAPE, DOG, BOY

> The first day in February, I was walking to a downtown Chevron station to pick up my car. On the corner of Prospect and Upson, a green car was parked—just sitting there. A part of my landscape. I was walking on the opposite side of the street. For some reason, I knew they were going to stop me. My heart clenched like a fist; the muscles in my back knotted up. *Maybe they'll leave me alone. I should have taken a shower this morning. I should have worn a nice sweater. I should have put on a pair of socks, worn a nice pair of shoes. I should have cut my hair; I should have shaved. . . .*

The driver rolled down his window. I saw him from the corner of my eye. He called me over to him—*whistled me over*—much like he'd call a dog. I kept walking. He whistled me over again. *Here, boy.*

—Benjamin Alire Sáenz, "Exile El Paso Texas"

While it is all well and good to talk about wartime exceptionalism, the simple truth of the matter is that for 2,000 miles of border, and for one hundred miles interior to the United States, the exception is the rule.[17] The borders or "exterior boundaries of the country" are, according to Supreme Court Justice White, a "zone, not a line," and this zone is approximately 200,000 miles square (413 US 294). Internal checkpoints are, therefore, according to Justice Stewart, "functional equivalents" of the actual border (413 US 272). In this zone, Stewart says, the government has "extraordinary responsibilities and powers" (413 US 272). It is not practical to secure a warrant in the border, for example, with cars whizzing by (413 US 281). Fourth Amendment warrants and matters of probable cause have a "less precise" "locus" in the borderlands—with "less precise" meaning that there is a more generalized and disseminated sense of probable cause and far less (or even no) need for conventional warrants, in the zone. According to Justice Powell, the border zone is an "unconventional problem" or a "novelty" that needs a "reasonable" solution in order to meet the "legitimate need of Government" (413 US 284–85). And Justice White agrees in principle: there are special "practicalities" to "border-area law enforcement" that cannot be properly judged from the "vantage point" of the Potomac (413 US 295).

So how does the system work, in legal terms? Virtually all of these cases ended up being decided in favor of the Mexican American defendants, and yet, incrementally and ironically, this body of cases slowly removed and eliminated Fourth Amendment protections in the borderlands. All of these cases turn on the question of whether, where, and how the Border Patrol can stop and search vehicles that appear to contain "Mexicans." In *Almeida-Sanchez*, the Court determined that roving patrols that stop vehicles without probable cause violate the search and seizure protections.[18] Justice Stewart's lead opinion, however, judged that, theoretically, such stops might be "warrantless" and still meet the conditions of probable cause (413 US 269). And Justice Powell's concurring opinion argued, in cascading fashion, that car stops are a "far less intrusive" Fourth Amendment problem than the searching of persons or buildings; that "appropriate limiting circumstances" would legitimate roving stops; and that, as an example, one such "limiting circumstance" would be "experience with obviously nonmobile [impassable] sections of a particular road" (413 US 279, 279, 281). In short, this first Border Patrol case provided an intellectual foundation for a form of always available "probable cause" for car stops based on knowledge of what occurs typically in the surrounding geography.

In *Peltier* (the one case in this sequence that was decided against the Mexican American defendant), the Supreme Court refused to apply *Almeida-Sanchez* retroactively.[19] The Court suggested that future application of the exclusionary rule would depend on the "knowledge" of the Border Patrol officer (422 US 542), a decision that Justices Brennan and Marshall predicted would apply eventually to all search and seizure cases, thus making Fourth Amendment protections an entirely "subjective" matter (422

US 552, 553). In *Ortiz*, fixed checkpoint searches were forbidden without probable cause, but probable cause was widened to include numerous factors.[20] In *Brignoni-Ponce*, a roving patrol case, the Court determined that "reasonable suspicion," rather than probable cause, should guide Border Patrol cases (422 US 882).[21] The "limited nature of the intrusion," according to Justice Powell's lead opinion, sets a reasonableness standard that depends upon "specific and articulatable facts" "taken together with rational inferences from these facts" (422 US 880).[22] Finally, in *Martinez-Fuerte*, another checkpoint case, Powell again wrote for the Court in determining that checkpoint car stops may take place merely "on the basis of apparent Mexican ancestry" (328 US 563 ).[23]

Thus, the state of the legal art at the border, since the 1970s, turns on two seemingly separate standards. At the border "itself," or at its "functional equivalent" (the checkpoint set up at least twenty-five, and no more than one hundred, miles away from the border), simply looking Mexican is judged inherently suspicious and a sound reason for interference. Internal checkpoints are the equivalent of an "'area' warrant," and "some quantum of individualized suspicion" is an unnecessary precondition for a stop and search (428 US 561). Roving patrols, on the other hand, must continue to meet a standard of "reasonable suspicion," and looking Mexican is not quite enough in this regard: "The likelihood that any given person of Mexican ancestry is an alien is high enough to make Mexican appearance a relevant factor, but standing alone it does not justify stopping all Mexican Americans to ask if they are aliens" (422 US 886–87). But reasonable suspicion regarding the presence of undocumented Mexicans includes, in Ortiz, "the number of persons in the vehicle, the appearance and behavior of the driver and passengers, the inability to speak English, the responses they give to officers' questions, the nature of the vehicle, and indications that it may be heavily loaded" (422 US 897). *Brignoni-Ponce* goes on at great length in expanding this possible list:

> Officers may consider the characteristics of the area in which they encounter a vehicle. Its proximity to the border, the usual patterns of traffic on the particular road, and previous experience with alien traffic are all relevant. . . . They also may consider information about recent illegal border crossings in the area. The driver's behavior may be relevant, as erratic driving or obvious attempts to evade officers can support a reasonable suspicion. . . . Aspects of the vehicle itself may justify suspicion. For instance, officers say that certain station wagons, with large compartments for fold-down seats or spare tires, are frequently used for transporting concealed aliens. . . . The vehicle may appear to be heavily loaded, it may have an extraordinary number of passengers, or the officers may observe persons trying to hide. . . . The Government also points out that trained officers can recognize the characteristic appearance of persons who live in Mexico, relying on such factors as the mode of dress and haircut. . . . In all situations, the officer is entitled to assess the facts in light of his experience in detecting illegal entry and smuggling. (422 US 884–85)

Therefore, probable cause does not exist merely on the basis of people looking as if they are of "Mexican descent," but the visualization of Mexicanness coupled with any other factor at all (poverty, place, and the general and finally unverifiable "experience" of the officer) provides more than enough warrant for each and every stop, as Justice Douglas's concurring opinion in *Brignoni-Ponce* makes clear (422 US 890). While all Mexicans, Mexican Americans, and Chicanos are not treated identically by the Border Patrol, and the marks of a bourgeois life typically move one from the category of suspicion to that of indifference, it doesn't take much for suspicions to rise again. When Ben Sáenz was accosted on foot, walking in a neighborhood close to the border, he merely happened to look "wrong." As everyone knows in the borderland, being left to mind one's own business can be a matter of a shave, a shower, a haircut, or a clean sweater. Markers of class and/or poverty are crucial in practice; but, in reverse, as the Supreme Court has sustained, the Border Patrol's claim regarding any such marker is more than enough.

All of this, of course, is not simply a matter of accepting the annoyance of stops and questions, because the stop is the first step toward entry into the criminal justice system. For example, soaring, wildly inequitable rates of charging, convicting, and incarcerating Chicanos are directly related to the daily, racially profiled stops (Guinier and Torres 2002, 254–67).[24] This in turn fits within a larger context concerning the on-again, off-again racialization of the Mexican American population in the United States. Menchaca (2001, 215–76), for example, relates the nineteenth-century portion of this story, but it is the Supreme Court decision in *Hernandez v. Texas* (347 US 475 [1954]) that federally determines that persons of Mexican descent are, at least in certain geographic spaces, such as Jackson County, Texas, "a separate class . . . distinct from 'whites'" (347 US 479). Yet in *San Antonio School District v. Rodriguez* (411 US 1 [1973]), a case that granted the state of Texas freedom to look the other way when it comes to the underfunding of heavily Mexican American public school districts, Rodriguez was deemed simply a member of the "poor," which is not, according to the Court, a discernible or definable class (411 US 19). When it comes to the integrity of the border, on the other hand, the Supreme Court has no trouble recognizing a "Mexican" when it sees one.

## THIRD REGISTER: MERELY "BEING THERE": VOMIT, EARTH

> I vomit verses
> In green trousers when la Migra
> asks where I was born,
> being the color of the earth.
>
> —José Antonio Burciaga, "Green Nightmares"

The question before us in the wake of 9/11 and the USA PATRIOT Act—the question of a racial/national discrepancy in Fourth Amendment rights—involves not *something new* that has invaded our legal system, but a simple extension (into wiretapping, for example) of a system of racialized surveillance long considered the rule in the borderlands. This is, as noted already, merely a portion of the larger story that Mills refers to as the "racial contract," and a careful look at Mills's influential argument and prescription will clarify how progressive praxis and activism might proceed from here. Mills, as suggested, belongs to a long line of scholars who attempt to trace the historical foundations of white supremacy in the United States. On the one hand, this essay could not have been written without the type of work that Mills, Gotanda, Kull, and others have undertaken. On the other hand, what must be rethought, from here forward, is whether such work goes far enough in its claims. Such historically based work will always miss the structural impediment to the overturning of white supremacy, and therefore it always advocates a too-easy and hence only partial (or tactically and temporarily pragmatic) fix for what lies before us.

Mills's *Racial Contract* begins from the proposition that "racism . . . is itself a political system," and that one must reinvestigate the origins and trajectory of social contract theory in order to comprehend it (1997, 3). According to Mills, three contracts come into being simultaneously when the social contract is instituted: the "political contract" proper, which is "an account of the origins of government and our political obligations to it"; the "moral contract," which is "the foundation of the moral code established for society"; and, finally, the "racial contract," which establishes "epistemological" "norms of cognition" along racial lines (9–11). The first two such contracts are blurred and overlapping: the distinction between "political obligations" and a "moral code" is not an obvious one, especially since Mills goes on to define the moral contract as encompassing a complex of beliefs and obligations (with the latter defined as belonging to the political contract): "a schedule of rights, duties and liberties that shape citizens' moral psychology, concepts of the right, notions of self-respect, etc." (10). Mills goes on to argue that the moral contract has taken precedence over the political contract in recent theorizations of social contract theory, such as that of John Rawls, and that, therefore, social contract theory today is honed down to a core of moral theory (10).

The racial contract, in contrast, is a separate matter, and one that is linked to the political/moral contract historically and therefore in a merely happenstance manner:

> [Carole] Pateman thinks contractarianism is necessarily oppressive . . . whereas I see domination within contract theory as more contingent. For me, in other words, it is not the case that a Racial Contract had to underpin the social contract. Rather, this contract is the result of a particular conjunction of circumstances in global history which led to European imperialism. And as a corollary, I believe contract theory can be put to positive use once this hidden history is acknowledged. (Mills 1997, 136–37)

Again, according to Mills, "the 'Racial Contract' is simply realist—willing to look at the facts without flinching, to explain that if you start from *this*, then you will end up with *that*" (102). With the racial contract understood, then, as merely historical and contingent (rather than structural and necessary), and the analysis of it a merely realist position (rather than theoretical, for example), the transcendence of the racial contract involves simply a reversal of historical amnesia (77) and a choice by whites to quit it, in the manner of race traitorism (107, 126). Once this is accomplished, we would be left with a moral contract cleansed of the business of race.

Two progressive positions, perhaps, are possible here. Either whites will recognize what they have done to persons of color (demoted them to subpersons) and will disavow this exclusive position (23). Or whites, caught up in the generalized dissemination of the racial contract, will opt out because of self-interest. With regard to this second option, for example, one might want to note that the border is an inherently unstable figure (neither inside nor outside) and one that constantly threatens to engulf all sides. Whites sometimes suffer from the surveillance of the borderlands camp in the US Southwest and from the fact that the same system has begun to emerge in the North in the wake of 9/11. For example, in November 2002 internal checkpoints and car stops were implemented in Michigan, especially in the Detroit-Dearborn-Toledo corridor (Audi 2002). One could further note that in *Whren v. United States* (517 US 806 [1996]), search, seizure, and "temporary detention" of anyone suspected of any sort of traffic violation was constitutionally authorized, even as Justice Scalia recognized that "everyone is guilty of violation" of traffic laws on a routine basis and that the decision may well end up "permitting the police to single out almost whomever they wish for a stop" (517 US 818).[25]

The FISA court's dismantling of the firewall between foreign intelligence and domestic crime-solving, too, necessarily subjects whites to wiretapping without probable cause, and to subsequent prosecution, when they knowingly or unknowingly associate with those who are deemed "foreign." And in perhaps the furthest imaginable extension of the suspension of the most basic and fundamental constitutional privileges, a post-9/11 secret presidential order permits military-style execution of US citizens, as the assassination of Kamal Derwish in Yemen on November 3, 2002, proved. The drone aircraft that launched the missile might be pointed at any of us, in theory. (Regarding this event, then national security advisor Condoleezza Rice announced that it fell "well within the bounds of accepted practice. . . . I can assure you that no constitutional questions are raised here.") One could well argue, in other words, that since 9/11 we have entered an era in which not a single US citizen is guaranteed the right to anything but potential slaughter.[26] Constitutional exceptionalism theoretically reigns over everyone, and perhaps, following Mills, whites will attempt to scale back the racial contract when they recognize that everyone potentially has become a "Mexican," an "Arab," and "foreign" to the rights of citizenship.

But as Justice White argued in *Delaware v. Prouse* (440 US 648 [1979]), the government cannot and should not subject "every occupant of every vehicle on the roads to a seizure" (440 US 661).[27] And, one should add, *likely will not, given the racially profiled nature of the majority of such car stops*. The choice that will be made concerns whether everyone now is a "Mexican," or whether every place now operates like the border when it comes to persons of color. The latter, I am suggesting, is far more likely than the former. *Delaware v. Prouse* explicitly prevented the Border Patrol's random car-stop policy from expanding out toward everyday police work nationwide. And as David A. Moran writes, with reference to *Whren*: "In practice, many Americans, particularly those who are not members of racial minorities or other groups likely to be singled out for police harassment, may never realize that their rights have been diminished" (2002, 837). The new northern version of Border Patrol roving stops primarily exists to monitor and intimidate the large Arab American and Arab immigrant population in southern Michigan and northern Ohio. Derwish, not surprisingly, was Arab American.

But suppose Mills's dream did come to pass, and whites repudiated the racial contract for whatever reason: one then is left with the problem of the moral contract, and one must determine whether the moral contract can supersede the violence of the racial contract. Mills needs to be read closely here: the white racial contract, he writes, "categorize[s] the remaining subset of humans as 'nonwhite' and of a different and inferior moral status, subpersons" (1997, 11). This is the key to understanding the racial contract: "a category crystallized over time in European thought to represent entities who are *humanoid* but not fully *human* ('savages,' 'barbarians') and who are identified as such by being members of the general set of nonwhite races" (23). But the problem that Mills does not acknowledge, and apparently cannot see, is that the crucial discrimination for comprehending the racial contract is in fact *the same* discrimination that undergirds the totality of the moral contract. The moral contract, through and through, turns upon the divide between those who are fully human and those who are less so. The moral contract is guaranteed only by the labor or elevation of the citizen. Thomas Hobbes, writing in 1651 in *De Cive* (The Citizen), could not be clearer on the problem of the limited and severe moral capacity for citizenship:

> All men, because they are born in infancy, are born unapt for society. Many also, perhaps most men, either through defect of mind or want of education, remain unfit during the whole course of their lives; yet have they, infants as well as those of riper years, a human nature. Wherefore man is made fit for society not by nature, but by education. Further, although man were born in such a condition as to desire it, it follows not, that he therefore were born fit to enter into it. For it is one thing to desire, another to be in capacity fit for what we desire. (1991, 110)

Rousseau, too, in *The Social Contract* (1762), makes precisely the same point, albeit in seemingly more inclusive and inviting terms. The citizen's

> faculties are exercised and developed, his ideas enlarged, his sentiments ennobled, his entire soul elevated to such an extent, that if the abuses of this new condition did not often degrade him to beneath the condition he has left, he should ceaselessly bless the happy moment which wrested him from it forever, and out of a stupid and bounded animal made an intelligent being and a man. (1997, 53)

It is the moral contract, in the first place, that, *before deciding on race*, secures rights to citizens only on the basis of their having lifted themselves toward an identity that is fully human. It is the moral contract, in the first place, that establishes a threshold for judgment of that which is not yet "ennobled," "elevated," "intelligent" (Rousseau), of that which lacks the "education" (Hobbes) to manage its affairs in a moral manner. Cheryl I. Harris notes, with reference to US republicanism, that "rights were for those who had the capacity to exercise them, a capacity denoted by racial identity" (1993, 1745). It is important to disentangle the two halves of her formulation; the racial decision to make whiteness supreme modifies or concretizes the prior moral decision regarding beings with/without the "capacity" to properly exercise rights. Different or additional concretizations are theoretically possible, all built upon an original and exclusive moral foundation.

Mills's dream is that everyone should be deracialized and considered a full "person" under the social contract (1997, 55). And, in terms of sovereignty, Mills has postulated political *decision* without *division*. But he also acknowledges, without further comment, that the category of "persons" is "necessarily related to subpersons. For these are identities as 'contrapuntal ensembles,' requiring their opposites" (58). In other words, no matter how universalized the granting of personhood, the figure of the "subperson" continues to lurk as an available, and necessary, related category. In principle, the moral contract cannot escape the fatal problem that it depends upon a judgment of a certain achievement or labor in the form of development or elevation. The decision to enact the most minimal social contract, in other words, cannot but divide and exclude: the moral contract is *an inherently exclusive form and necessarily provides the purchase for the categories of race, ethnicity, nation, and the like.*

To say this is to force Mills's judgment of the racial contract's contingent nature back to the terrain of structural exclusion. While one certainly might yearn for the optimism of Mills's formulation of the problem, and might wish that racial exceptionalism could be voided, Schmitt reminds that exceptionalism in principle cannot be dismantled or disempowered:

> If measures undertaken in an exception could be circumscribed by mutual control, by imposing a time limit, or finally, as in the liberal constitutional procedure governing a state of siege, by enumerating extraordinary powers, the question of sovereignty would then be considered less significant but would certainly not be eliminated. (1985, 12)

Why is this so? One might think of the question of the legal order and its relationship to the sovereign exception as akin to the structure and agency problematic, for example. Strong structure necessarily first depends on, and secondarily produces, agency (the two related halves of Ferdinand de Saussure's *Course in General Linguistics* [1965] make this clear). Jacques Derrida's several interventions into the question of the foundations of any legal order continually make this point: that any such founding political moment necessarily involves an agential "coup de force" that cannot be squared with mere order and that both "gives itself and signs its own law" (2002, 50, 53). Caught up in the question of the performative, the legal order necessarily fails to conceal the sort of violent and exclusive "autonomy" that brought it into being and that necessarily continues to cohabit its terrain/territory, at its limit (53). Relatedly, and perhaps counter-intuitively, Aristide R. Zolberg demonstrates the ways in which the polis or state produces, in the first place, the figure of the refugee: the "inherent dynamics" of the founding political decision marks "certain groups as obstacles to the successful formation of a nation-state" (1983, 29–30). And if exceptionalism cannot be eliminated, and if a legal order always must think, first at the moment of its founding and incessantly thereafter, about the question of its own interiority/exteriority, then the question of "race" and its many analogues (such as "anarchy" and "terror," to name just two) remain in play. No state sovereignty can escape it, because it is the sovereign voice that produces such figures (Ashley 1989, 267).

The question before us, then, is one of state sovereignty and citizenship in general, and the limit of their inclusivity—their endless invention/proliferation of lesser beings in the form of second-class citizens, noncitizens, and refugees. Here, José Antonio Burciaga's "Green Nightmares" (1992) provides a clue toward an edgewise thought, in the form of an excluded figure whose posture is one of absolute refusal. When Burciaga vomits "verses in green trousers" in response to questions from *la migra*, decked out in their green uniforms, he parodies and postulates mere corporeal *being there* ("being the color of the earth") as the only legitimate standard (a standard that would not amount to a standard or threshold) for the bearing of rights. His vomiting involves a practice of both absolute disgust and "insolence," "which doesn't respect anybody or anything" (Bataille 1988, 13). It is, instead, a signal of being's extrusion from itself, its distance from and deferral of its own presence and representability, and its stubborn inability to be contained by legal strictures such as borders.[28] This is, in a Bataillean vocabulary, the figure of the "formless," a limit figure that "has no rights in any sense and gets itself squashed everywhere, like a spider or an earthworm" (1985, 31). This messy and "squashed" figure has a necessarily collective aspect to it, forecasting a "universe" of connectedness that "is something like a spider or spit," according to Bataille. One might note here, for example, that during the first weekend of the war in Iraq, in March 2003, San Francisco protesters used a strategy that they called "shock and hurl," parodying the Pentagon's strategy of Baghdad bombing that would "shock and awe" Iraqis. These activists staged a "vomit-in," upchucking collectively onto government property and producing their own limit version of a (non) community of spit (*WorldNetDaily* 2003).

So what can be done with such a figure? Too rapidly, perhaps, one can suggest that Burciaga's strange position concerning the nonexclusivity of mere being permits one to begin to reimagine the question of justice in relation to sovereignty. Burciaga's figure is strictly undecidable in relation to sovereignty because no law could institutionalize it. It signals a relationship among beings of "infinite right," "owed to the other . . . before any contract" (Derrida 1992, 22, 25).[29] This is another way of saying that, in vomiting, Burciaga attempts to show the "nonplace" of sovereignty and, in doing so, attempts to leave something excessively *un-stated.*

But this does not mean that it therefore remains foreign to law, judgment, and sovereignty. Indeed, it remains possible, always, to pass sovereign decisions through this figure in order to take account of the problem of justice (Derrida 1992, 22–23). Doing this would necessitate that sovereignty take up the burden of the *unworking* of sovereignty, in an infinite and unending praxis. Sovereignty, for example, would have to take account of race in such a way as to each time freshly broach the question of deracialization, rather than use its powers unendingly and unthinkingly to repeat and repromulgate the foundational designs of white supremacy. Since there will continue to be sovereign decisions, such decisions would have to start shifting the rules of the national and global legal-racial game to *the limits of their foundations.*

No one would suggest, today, that such a possibility is easy to imagine or institute, and it is certainly true that the political activism necessary to bring it about seems herculean. But only this option avoids the traps of liberal political philosophy and its inability to think both the exclusivity of all constitutionalism and the intractable problem of sovereignty. This possibility shall remain, then, Burciaga's open challenge and invitation.

## NOTES

Reprinted with permission from Scott Michaelsen, *Aztlán: A Journal of Chicano Studies* 30:2 (2005): 87–111.

1. To be perfectly clear: the USA PATRIOT Act is only one part of the "war on terror," a project that involves numerous international and domestic legal inventions on the part of the US government.

2. Johnson (2002, 910) refers to this as the "border exception" doctrine.

3. This is not to suggest that these populations are not endlessly differentiated within themselves by the reach, scope, and application of border law. Most importantly, as this essay will show, the current law governing the border patrol is implicitly prejudiced against visible signs of poverty.

4. See Agamben (2000, 36–44) on the definition of the "camp." "The camp is a piece of territory that is placed outside the normal juridical order. . . . The camp is the structure in which the state of exception is permanently realized" (39).

5. I note in passing that the law allowing for immigration raids by the Immigration and Naturalization Service (INS) is a significant related matter. While I cannot do justice to this topic in these pages, one might begin by reexamining the Supreme Court cases of *Immigration and Naturalization Service v. Lopez-Mendoza* (468 US 1032 [1984]) and *United States v. Verdugo-Urquidez* (494 US 259 [1990]), both of which turn on Fourth Amendment matters. Also relevant are some of the materials gathered by Sedillo Lopez (1995), which examine the constitutionality of such raids and the status of the Fourth Amendment in relation to the INS and undocumented workers.

6. In *Hirabayashi*, the Supreme Court upheld Gordon Hirabayashi's conviction for violation of an order to report to a Japanese American internment camp. In *Korematsu*, Fred Korematsu's conviction for violating Exclusion Order No. 34 was upheld. The order mandated that all persons of Japanese ancestry must vacate "military areas," including San Leandro, California.

7. The quotations within Stone's opinion are from *McCulloch v. Maryland* (1819), the famed National Bank case, which turns on the affirmation of the necessary means of the federal government to accomplish its objectives.

8. See Bartelson (2001, 149–81) for a thoughtful reading of Ashley's and others' contributions, in the 1980s and 1990s, to the retheorization of the problem of sovereignty.

9. While this essay does not explore the question of sovereignty and exceptionalism as applied to blacks or African Americans, see the first half of Michaelsen and Shershow (2002), devoted to affirmative action, for an example of how such an analysis might proceed.

10. Also see Akram and Johnson (2002) on the racial nature of the secret evidence law.

11. In *Yick Wo*, the Supreme Court reversed the conviction of a San Francisco laundryman who had violated an ordinance outlawing wooden laundry buildings. The Supreme Court decided that the ordinance itself was not discriminatory, but its application was.

12. See the *Memorandum Opinion* (USFISC 2002), which was handed down by the PISA court on May 17. See also *American Civil Liberties Union et al.* (2002), a friend of the court brief from six organizations outlining the firewall problem.

13. See Osher (2002) for a lawyer's reading of the USA PATRIOT Act's significance for the Fourth Amendment and search and seizure.

14. The FISA review court ruling was challenged by the American Civil Liberties Union, among others, and appealed to the Supreme Court, where it was turned down without comment on March 24, 2003 (see Greenhouse 2003). Because the review court permits only the government to appear as a party in its proceedings, it was unlikely that the ACLU's challenge would succeed. In effect, the FISA review court is its own "supreme" court.

15. See Gonzales and Rodriguez (2003) on a disturbing instance of a post-9/11 FBI investigation at the border of what one might call FWM, or "Filming While Mexican": '"The informant

who reported this tip was concerned because you're dark,' the agents say." Gonzales and Rodriguez, nationally known columnists whose work is syndicated by Universal Press Syndicate, had been filming images of the fence between Mexico and the United States in order to make a documentary about migration and immigration.

16. It should be noted that both jurists and other scholars have made the connection between the border patrol and Japanese American internment; see Braber (2002). Also see "Driving While Mexican" (2003, 58), which is an edited version of Judge Jacques L. Weiner's dissent in a border patrol car-stop case that reached the US Court of Appeals 5th Circuit in 2000: "Shame on us. At least the war that prompted the Supreme Court to condone the internment of Japanese Americans was a full-fledged, Congressionally-declared, 'shooting' war." Even though each so-called minority group in the United States has its own legal history relative to exclusion, it also is true that all such groups are legally threaded together through the problem of sovereignty. I also want to make clear a fact that should be obvious: while the USA PATRIOT Act is directed against Arabs and South Asians in the United States, its provisions can and are being brought to bear against Latinos (and other groups as well), compounding the original border exception doctrine.

17. For a brief summary of the legal situation in the borderlands from *The Nation*, see Silko (2003).

18. In an apparent Fourth Amendment victory, the Supreme Court invalidated a warrantless search of Almeida-Sanchez's car by a roving Border Patrol vehicle, twenty-five miles from the border. The search had uncovered marijuana, leading to Almeida-Sanchez's arrest.

19. The *Peltier* case, similar to *Almeida-Sanchez*, involved a man randomly stopped by a roving Border Patrol vehicle seventy miles from the border. Upon discovery of 270 pounds of marijuana in the vehicle, an arrest took place. The Supreme Court permitted the search of Peltier's car, arguing that the case pre-dated *Almeida-Sanchez*.

20. *Ortiz* involved a car stop at a traffic checkpoint near San Clemente, California; three undocumented aliens were found in the trunk of Ortiz's car. The Supreme Court invalidated the search of the trunk on the basis of probable cause.

21. *Brignoni-Ponce* involved the same checkpoint as *Ortiz*. In this case, the questioning of vehicle occupants regarding their citizenship and immigration status was invalidated by the Court because the Border Patrol officers had relied entirely on the appearance of Mexican ancestry.

22. Luna (2002, 759) writes: "As Fourth Amendment scholars have noted, 'reasonableness' may well be the law's favorite weasel word, beyond hard definition, simple in application and sufficiently elastic to reach nearly any result."

23. Three combined cases involving the San Clemente checkpoint all concerned the questioning of occupants regarding citizenship and immigration status. In each case, undocumented aliens were apprehended. For other readings of these cases, sometimes at odds with my theoretical account, but generally in concert regarding their pragmatic implications, see Sosa (1990), Johnson (2000), and Lopez (2001/2).

24. Johnson (2002, 900) cites general police numbers that indicate that blacks, Chicanos/Latinos, and Asians are subjected to car stops at a rate eight to ten times that of whites.

25. See Moran (2002) for a reading of the *Whren* decision, which upheld the detention of a motorist believed to have committed a civil traffic violation. After the drafting of Moran's article, the Supreme Court ruled in *Illinois v. Lidster* (2004) that a highway checkpoint designed to ask motorists about a hit-and-run accident was legal. Lidster was arrested for driving while intoxicated when he was stopped at this checkpoint. A reading of *Martinez-Fuerte* undergirds this decision.

26. There was very little US news reporting on the Derwish assassination. On these points, see Vann (2002), Associated Press (2002), and Lumpkin (2002).

27. In this nonborder case, a patrolman stopped a vehicle to check the driver's license and registration, and ended up arresting him for possession of marijuana.

28. "Human life, distinct from juridical existence, existing as it does on a globe isolated in celestial space, from night to day and from one country to another—human life cannot in any way be limited to the closed systems assigned to it by reasonable conceptions" (Bataille 1985, 128).

29. The future of thinking rights demands, according to Levinas, that one think "a right of the other man above all": the "charity, mercy and responsibility for the other, and already the possibility of sacrifice in which the humanity of man bursts forth, disrupting the general economy of the real in sharp contrast with the perseverance of entities persisting in their being" (1999, 48).

## WORKS CITED


Agamben, Giorgio. 2000. *Means without End: Notes* on *Politics.* Translated by Vincenzo Binetti and Cesare Casarmo. Minneapolis: University of Minnesota Press.

Akram, Susan M., and Kevin R. Johnson. 2002. "Migration Regulation Goes Local: The Role of States in U.S. Immigration Policy." *New York University Annual Survey* of *American Law* 58, no. 3: 295–355.

American Civil Liberties Union et al. 2002. *In Re Appeal from July 19, 2002 Opinion of the United States Foreign Intelligence Surveillance Court.*" No. 02-001 in the United States Foreign Intelligence Surveillance Court, September 19. Brief on Behalf of *Amici Curiae* American Civil Liberties Union, Center for Democracy and Technology, Center for National Security Studies, Electronic Privacy Information Center, Electronic Frontier Foundation, and Open Society Institute in Support of Affirmance. http://news.findlaw.com/hdocs/docs/terrorism/fisaapp091902amicus.pdf.

Ashley, Robert K. 1989. "Living on Border Lines: Man, Poststructuralism, and War." In *International/Intertextual Relations*, edited by James Der Derian and Michael J. Shapiro, 259–321. Lexington, MA: Lexington Books.

Associated Press. 2002. "CIA Allowed to Kill Americans in al-Qaida: Citizens Overseas Can Be Targets, Officials Say." *Lansing State Journal*, December 4, 1A.

Audi, Tamara. 2002. "Traffic Checks: Random Stops Begin Today in Michigan." *Detroit Free Press* online edition, November 12.

Bartelson, Jens. 2001. *The Critique of the State.* New York: Cambridge University Press.

Bataille, Georges. 1985. *Visions of Excess: Selected Writings, 1927–1939.* Edited and translated by Allan Stoekl, with Carl R. Lovitts and Donald M. Leslie Jr. Minneapolis: University of Minnesota Press.

———. 1988. *Guilty*. Translated by Bruce Boone. Venice, CA: Lapis Press.

Braber, Liam. 2002. "Korematsu's Ghost: A Post-September 11th Analysis of Race and National Security." *Villanova Law Review* 47, no. 2: 451–90.

Burciaga, José Antonio. 1992. "Green Nightmares." In *Undocumented Love/Amor Indocumentado: A Personal Anthology of Poetry*, 104–5. San Jose, CA: Chusma House.

Cole, David, and James X. Dempsey. 2002. *Terrorism and the Constitution: Sacrificing Civil Liberties in the Name of National Security*. Revised edition. New York: New Press.

DeCandido, Keith R. A. 2001. "Some Thoughts on George W. Bush's Declaration of War Against the al Qaeda." *SSF Net*, September 20.

Derrida, Jacques. 1992. "Force of Law: The 'Mystical Foundations of Authority'." In *Deconstruction and the Possibility of Justice*, edited by Drucilla Cornell, Michael Rosenfeld, and David Gray Carlson, 3–67. New York: Routledge.

———. 2002. "Declarations of Independence." In *Negotiations: Interventions and Interviews, 1971–2001.* edited by Elizabeth Rottenberg, translated by Tom Keenan and Tom Pepper, 46–54. Stanford, CA: Stanford University Press.

De Saussure, Ferdinand. 1965. *Course in General Linguistics.* Edited and translated by Wade Baskin. New York: McGraw-Hill.

"Driving While Mexican vs. the 4th Amendment." 2003. In *Puro Border: Dispatches, Snapshots, and Graffiti from La Frontera,* edited by Luis Humberto Crosthwaite, John William Byrd, and Bobby Byrd, with Jessica Powers, 57–58. El Paso: Cinco Puntos.

Gonzales, Patrisia, and Roberto Rodriguez. 2003. "The Knock on the Door." *Column of the Americas* (distributed by Universal Press Syndicate), March 14.

Gotanda, Neil. 1991. "A Critique of 'Our Constitution Is Color-Blind.'" *Stanford Law* Review 44, no. 1: 1–68.

Greenhouse, Linda. 2003. "Group Loses Challenge to Government's Broader Use of Wiretaps." *New York Times* online edition, March 24.

Guinier, Lani, and Gerald Torres. 2002. *The Miner's Canary: Enlisting Race, Resisting Power, Transforming Democracy.* Cambridge, MA: Harvard University Press.

Gutman, Art. 2002. "On the Legal Front: Implications of 9/11 for the Workplace." *Industrial-Organizational Psychologist* 39, no. 3: 35–40.

Harris, Cheryl I. 1993. "Whiteness as Property." *Harvard Law Review* 106, no. 8: 1707–91.

Hobbes, Thomas. 1991. *Man and Citizen.* Edited by Bernard Gert. Indianapolis: Hackett.

Johnson, Kevin R. 2000. "The Case against Race Profiling in Immigration Enforcement." *Washington University Law Quarterly* 78, no. 3: 675–736.

———. 2002. "U.S. Border Enforcement: Drugs, Migrants, and the Rule of Law." *Villanova Law Review* 47, no. 4: 897–919.

Kull, Andrew. 1992. *The Color-Blind Constitution.* Cambridge, MA: Harvard University Press.

Levinas, Emmanuel. 1999. "The Rights of Man and Good Will." In *The Politics of Human Rights,* edited by Obrad Savic, translated by Michael B. Smith, 46–49. New York: Verso.

Lopez, Alberto B. 2001/2. "Racial Profiling and *Whren:* Searching for Objective Evidence of the Fourth Amendment on the Nation's Roads." *Kentucky Law Journal* 90, no. 1: 75–122.

Lumpkin, John J. 2002. "American Killed in Yemen Attack Identified as Alleged Buffalo al-Qaida Leader." *Anchorage Daily News* online edition, November 12.

Luna, Eric. 2002. "Drug Exceptionalism." *Villanova Law Review* 47, no. 4: 753–807.

Martínez González, Lety. 1990. Letter to Argelia Gonzáles Morales, Oaxaca, Mexico, June 4. Reprinted in *Between the Lines: Letters Between Undocumented Mexican and Central American Immigrants and Their Families and Friends,* edited by Larry Siems, 5. Hopewell, NJ: Ecco Press, 1992.

Menchaca, Martha. 2001. *Recovering History: Constructing Race: The Indian, Black, and White Roots of Mexican Americans.* Austin: University of Texas Press.

Michaelsen, Scott, and Scott Cutler Shershow. 2002. "Practical Politics at the Limits of Community: The Cases of Affirmative Action and Welfare." Postmodern Culture 12, no. 2. Project MUSE, doi:10.1353/pmc.2002.0002.

Mills, Charles W. 1997. *The Racial Contract.* Ithaca, NY: Cornell University Press.

Moran, David A. 2002. "The New Fourth Amendment Vehicle Doctrine: Stop and Search Any Car at Any Time." *Villanova Law Review* 47, no. 4: 815–38.

Osher, Steven. 2002. "Privacy, Computers and the PATRIOT Act: The Fourth Amendment Isn't Dead, But No One Will Insure It." *Florida Law Review* 54, no. 3: 521–42.

Rehnquist, William H. 1998. *All the Laws But One: Civil Liberties* in *Wartime.* New York: Knopf.

Rousseau, Jean-Jacques. 1997. *The Social Contract* and *Other Later Political* Writings. Edited and translated by Victor Gourevitch. New York: Cambridge University Press.

Sáenz, Benjamin Alire. 1992. "Exile El Paso Texas." Prologue to *Flowers for the Broken*. Seattle: Broken Moon Press.

Schmitt, Carl. 1985. *Political Theology: Four Chapters on the Concept of Sovereignty*. Translated by George Schwab. Cambridge, MA: MIT Press.

Sedillo Lopez, Antoinette, ed. 1995. *Latino Employment, Labor Organizations, and Immigration*. New York: Garland.

Silko, Leslie Marmon. 2003. "The Border Patrol State." In *Puro Border: Dispatches, Snapshots, and Graffiti from La Frontera,* edited by Luis Humberto Crosthwaite, John William Byrd, and Bobby Byrd, with Jessica Powers, 72–78. El Paso: Cinco Puntos.

Sosa, Steve. 1990. "An Introduction to Search and Seizure under the Immigration Reform and Control Act of 1986." *Chicano Law Review* 10, no. 1: 33–46.

Tien, Lee. 2001. "Foreign Intelligence Surveillance Act: Frequently Asked Questions (and Answers)." Electronic Frontier Foundation, San Francisco, September 27.

USFISC (United States Foreign Intelligence Surveillance Court). 2002. *Memorandum Opinion (as Corrected and Amended)*. May 17.

USFISCR (United States Foreign Intelligence Surveillance Court of Review). 2002. In re: Sealed Case No. 02-001, consolidated with 02-002. On Motions for Review of Orders of the United States Foreign Intelligence Surveillance Court, nos. 02-662 and 02-968. November 18.

Vann, Bill. 2002. "White House Defends CIA Killing of US Citizen in Yemen." *World Socialist Web Site*, November 12. http://www.wsws.org/en/articles/2002/11/yem-n12.html.

*WorldNetDaily*. 2003. "Anti-War Protest Strategy: Shock and Hurl." March 20. http://www.wnd.com/2003/03/17856/.

Zolberg, Aristide R. 1983. "The Formation of New States as a Refugee-Generating Process." *Annals of the American Academy of Political and Social Science* 467, no. 1: 24–38.

## CASES CITED

Almeida-Sanchez v. United States, 413 US 266 (1973)
Delaware v. Prouse, 440 US 648 (1979)
Dred Scott v. Sandford, 60 US 393 (1856)
Hernandez v. Texas, 347 US 475 (1954)
Hirabayashi v. United States, 320 US 81 (1942)
Illinois v. Lidster, 540 US 419 (2004)
Immigration and Naturalization Service v. Lopez-Mendoza, 468 US 1032 (1984)
Korematsu v. United States, 323 US 214 (1944)
McCulloch v. Maryland, 17 US 316 (1819)
Regents of University of California v. Bakke, 438 US 265 (1978)
San Antonio School District v. Rodriguez, 411 US 1 (1973)
United States v. Brignoni-Ponce, 422 US 873 (1975)
United States v. Martinez-Fuerte, 428 US 543 (1976)
United States v. Ortiz, 422 US 891 (1975)
United States v. Peltier, 422 US 531 (1975)
United States v. Verdugo-Urquidez, 494 US 259 (1990)
Whren v. United States, 517 US 806 (1996)
Yick Wo v. Hopkins, 118 US 356 (1886)

# "STIRRIN' WATERS" 'N BUILDIN' BRIDGES:
## A Conversation with Ericka Huggins and Yuri Kochiyama

YURI KOCHIYAMA, ERICKA HUGGINS, AND MARY UYEMATSU KAO

[*Editor's note:* Yuri Kochiyama passed away in 2014.]

August 8, 2008 was the first time Yuri and Ericka had a conversation together. Ericka requested a joint interview with Yuri for her contribution to this special issue of *Amerasia*, in the spirit of bridging the African American and Asian American communities. I [Mary] was awestruck with the task at hand in the presence of these two women who embodied the historic moments of the shooting deaths of Malcolm X and Bunchy Carter and John Huggins (Ericka's deceased husband). Yuri and Ericka have remained steadfastly loyal to the causes of human rights for all human beings. Their lifetime struggles against injustice in all of its forms continue to inspire people from all walks of life.

## BACKGROUND HISTORY

Yuri Kochiyama is the most famous Asian American human rights activist who emerged out of the 1960s Black Liberation Movement, and will forever be remembered for holding Malcolm X's head in her lap as he lay dying from over a dozen gun shot wounds at the Audubon Ballroom on February 21, 1965. *Passing It On: A Memoir* by Yuri Kochiyama recounts many of the important political revelations she has experienced in her life. [At the time of this writing, she was eighty-eight] and living in an assisted living facility in downtown Oakland, California.

In January 1969, John Huggins and Bunchy Alprentice Carter were gunned down in Campbell Hall, home of four newly formed ethnic studies centers at UCLA. From May 1969 to May 1971, Ericka Huggins, along with Bobby Seale, was sequestered in prison on framed-up charges in another one of Cointelpro's attempts to destroy the

Yuri Kochiyama (1921–2014) was a human rights activist prominent for bringing together Asian American and African American communities. She is best known for holding Malcolm X as he was assassinated on February 21, 1965. Ericka Huggins is an educator and activist, who held a leadership position in the Black Panther Party. She was a professor in Women and Gender Studies at California State University-East Bay at the time of this interview. Mary Uyematsu Kao is an activist and artist. She was the designer and production manager of *Amerasia Journal* and a staff member at the UCLA Asian American Studies Center, retiring in 2018.

Black Panther Party. The campaign to "Free Bobby Seale, Free Ericka Huggins" became an international rallying call against the treachery U.S. imperialism. This happened at the height of influence of the Black Panther Party, and Ericka had just organized the New Haven Chapter of the Black Panther Party.

Ericka stands out as the only woman to hold a leadership position in the Black Panther Party for fourteen years. She was the director of the Oakland Community School from 1973–1981, which was created by the Black Panther Party, and was one of the first community-run child development and elementary schools in the nation. In the late 1970s she taught Hatha Yoga and meditation to internees in the California state and country prison system through the Siddha Yoga Prison Project. She taught herself meditation when she was in prison as a means of survival. In 1990, Ericka was the first woman to be a volunteer support coordinator for the Shanti Project, developing programs for women and children with HIV in the Tenderloin and Mission districts of San Francisco. She is currently a professor in Women's Studies at California State University-East Bay.

## INTERACTIONS IN HISTORY, AS TOLD BY YURI KOCHIYAMA

There has been much history where people have interacted without violence and bloodshed; exchanged resources through friendly and peaceful relationships; especially between China and Africa from about the eleventh century. This story is not well known.

True history has often been hidden, obscured, lied about, distorted. It is up to students, progressive scholars, and truth seekers to "dig into history" and find the gems. It will be an exciting task. And many young people, filmmakers and researchers are doing it.

Several years ago I had the good fortune to run into Steve Wong who once owned the People's Bookstore in San Francisco, and who graciously let me borrow two eye-opening books. *"Smoked Yankees"* has letters from black soldiers in all of America's wars. The section about black soldiers who were sent to the Philippines and how they felt is enlightening. The other book is the *Star Raft: China's Encounter with Africa* about the time before Christopher Columbus. Yes, history is important!

Remember, Malcolm X used to admonish: "Study history. Learn about yourselves and others. There's more commonality in all of our lives than we think. It will help us understand one another." But history, according to the way it is told, can be used as a weapon to divide us further.

The East African slave trade was the slavery of Africans and Asians on European ships in the Indian Ocean, carrying trade that took Asian slaves from Bengal, South India, Sri Lanka, the Indonesian archipelago, the Philippines, China and Japan to Dutch and Portuguese possessions in Asia and Africa.

Between 1870 and 1890, when Congress was debating the infamous Chinese Exclusion Bill, black leaders like Frederick Douglass and Augustus Straker spoke out against it. They declared that opponents of the Chinese were opponents of blacks. One lone courageous senator, Blanche K. Bruce, the only African American senator, challenged the bill on the Senate floor. He voted against limiting the rights of the Chinese.

At the turn of the century, there arrived in the US from Japan, a man by the name of Sen Katayama. He is considered the first Asian who attended a black college in the South. Together with the highly acclaimed black writer of the Harlem Renaissance period, Claude McKay, they organized the Communist Party in New York. And they went to Moscow together. Katayama made an indelible mark on the history of ethnic laborers in the US, but is sadly unknown even among Asian Americans.

By 1920, another Asian arrived, interacted with blacks, and in the course of his own nation's liberation struggle, rose to international fame. He was Ho Chi Minh. Ho lived in the ghettoes of both Chicago and Harlem, became an admirer of the formidable black leader, Marcus Garvey, and supported him. He wrote probably one of the earliest books on racism in the US, and racism in Africa, both printed in the Soviet Union in the 1920s. Considered one of the world's greatest leaders, Ho struggled unrelentingly for the independence of his nation. He was forced into self-exile for thirty years, but he became the inspiration for anti-Vietnam War activists around the world in the 1960s and 1970s.

In the 1930s, another giant, a black man, W.E.B. Du Bois, historian, writer, teacher, political leader, this time crossed the water traversing the other way to Asia. He visited China, Manchuria, and Japan. DuBois met Mao and other Chinese leaders. Other famous black Americans have visited the People's Republic of China—Langston Hughes, Vickie Garvin, Robert Williams, and several members of the Black Panther Party. Asian American activists who traveled with the Black Panthers to China and North Korea were Pat Sumi, who passed away, and Alex Hing, still an activist in New York.

In the early 1940s, one of the black leaders who was sent to jail because he would not support the war against Japan was Elijah Muhammad of the Nation of Islam. He and other NOI leaders were all sent to prison. Some years after Elijah Muhammad came out of prison, a wealthy Japanese businessman by the name of Seiho Tajiri was so impressed with Elijah that he joined the Nation of Islam. Tajiri opened two offices called the Japanese/African American Society, one in Chicago and the other in Atlanta, for the purpose of friendship and commercial cooperation between the two people.

One of the most significant events in modern history was the 1955 Bandung Conference, led by Ahmad Sukarno, head of Indonesia. It was the first conference of its kind, attended by Third World leaders, predominantly Africans and Asians, on a diplomatic level. The US government was irked not being invited, but many prominent blacks attended, like Adam Clayton Powell, Bill Worthy, and Margaret Cartwright, who was the first black reporter assigned at the UN. Malcolm held him in high esteem because Sukarno would not accommodate himself to the white man. Sukarno flung out the words, "To hell with US aid!" The US had Sukarno ousted in a coup. Sukarno never regained his position of power, but he brought about the converging of Africans and Asians on world issues.

Also in the 1950s, just as America became embroiled in the Korean War, which the US called a "police action," a distinguished, charismatic black spokesman, Paul Robeson, declared at a rally at Madison Square Garden that "it would be foolish for African Americans to fight against their 'Asian brothers'." (Yes, he called the Koreans his "Asian brothers.") He urged blacks to resist being drafted for the Korean conflict, adding that if we don't stop our armed adventures in Korea today, tomorrow it will be Africa. "The place for the Negro people to fight for their freedom is at home." Despite Robeson's multi-gifted talents and dynamism as a football hero, lawyer, actor, singer, speaker of world renown, Robeson became a threat to the US. Robeson was a lover of humanity; precursor to the revolutionary black internationalists of the '60s. You can see why he became such a target for red-baiting and vindictive assaults. And sure enough, there are American troops in Africa today.

The 1960s brought many pertinent events. One that received media attention was the declaration of support for blacks in America in their struggle by none other than Mao Tse-tung, the highly recognized leader of the emerging People's Republic of China. During the 1968 riots, he publicly declared: "On behalf of the Chinese people, I hereby express resolute support for the just struggle of the Black people in the US."

The most charismatic black leader who made an impression on Asian Americans was Malcolm X. His universal appeal was his love and pride of his race, respect for all peoples of color, his strength in his conviction for self-determination, his pursuit for equality, human rights, human dignity, and truth. Young Asian Americans of the '60s were as much in awe of Malcolm as were other Third World activists.

We must break down barriers and phobias; building working relationships; but also understanding, recognizing that each ethnic group has its own primary issues, and need ethnic privacy and leadership. However, as a united force, together, we can challenge the system where those with wealth and political power live high off the toil and desperation of the marginalized.

We must see one another as friends and neighbors and sincerely be concerned of one another's plights and problems. If we want to change society, we can first begin by transforming ourselves; learning from one another about one another's history, culture, dreams, hopes, personal experiences. We'll find that we seek the same lofty principles and values and visions of the best in society. We must become one for the future of society.

In this conversation, the following abbreviations will be used for the sake of brevity: EH—Ericka Huggins; YK—Yuri Kochiyama; MK—Mary Kao; and JK—John Kao. While the beginning of the conversation may seem somewhat abrupt, it took no longer than a few minutes for Yuri to get down to business.

YK: I guess when your husband, and . . . what's the other brother's name?

EH: Bunchy . . .

YK: The Black Panther Party must have been shocked . . .

EH: Yeah, shocked and sad and ready to retaliate. However, there was really no one to retaliate against. Because though it looked like it was US organization, it was the FBI, and they admitted to it later. In writing.

YK: Yeah, the FBI, they're . . .

EH: Aren't they crazy?

YK: They're treacherous . . .

EH: And American taxpayers . . . we're paying for it. We were all very sad and angry. And we decided that the best way was to keep going.

YK: There have been many times that Asians and Africans have linked up. From as far back as 1100, Asians and Africans have had connections with each other. Back in 1882, it was only blacks who opposed the Chinese Exclusion Act. The only black senator at that time, Blanche K. Bruce, spoke out against the Exclusion Act. He was angry too because he said, "This could have happened to black people. And they would lose their civil rights." The Chinese were very surprised and grateful that the black speakers spoke in support for them. In 1889, when Theodore Roosevelt took his Rough Riders, the white US Army, to the Philippines . . . and killed a million Filipino civilians—the black soldiers that were with the Rough Riders were shocked at the brutality of American soldiers massacring the Filipinos. The highest officer for the blacks shouted to his men, "We're fighting on the wrong side. We should be with the Filipinos." He took the black soldiers into the mountains, and hooked up with the Filipino guerillas. This true story must never be forgotten. It shows that ordinary soldiers have shown courage to confront and fight corrupt officers.

EH: And we can assume that women were involved in all that, right? The question Mary is asking is "Why don't we know their names, when we speak of Du Bois . . . what about Shirley Graham DuBois? The women were always there. You're an example of that—because you were always there. There were women there. Why do you think we don't hear about the women?

YK: Well, the only woman that really stands out, and so many people, even movement people don't know. The black woman that's the most outstanding in history is Vicki Garvin.

EH: Oh, I vaguely read a short little something. Tell us about her.

YK: Vicki Garvin would be the most well-known woman leader. But she didn't live in the US during the Civil Rights Movement. She lived in Africa a lot. In 1964, when Malcolm went to Ghana, she introduced Malcolm to the international community there. And the Chinese ambassador was so impressed meeting Malcolm, that he invited Malcolm to China. He said that China should know about Malcolm and what he's doing for blacks here. But he couldn't go; he had too many commitments. Malcolm asked Vicki Garvin to go to China. And she thought maybe she would stay a few weeks or several months. She stayed ten years. And she taught English to the Chinese. And she was a social activist. She had been doing a lot of work in Africa. She worked with people like Du Bois. She's worked with every black leader of that time. Yet Vicki Garvin wasn't that well known because she was in Africa—in Nigeria; and then in China for ten years. So by the time she came back to the US, she was older and maybe not in such good health. She married a white communist in China.

EH: See, that's exactly what we're talking about. There should be a way, not that it's good or bad, right or wrong any more . . . let's just make it good, let's make it right, by putting these faces and names out there.

Like when Richard Aoki was doing his work in the '60s, there had to be women who were also doing the same work. Who are they? What's their names? Can we call them forward? I know they were there.

In every part of the movement, there were women doing all the organizational work, and all the programmatic work, and keeping offices running . . . and truth be told, in the Black Panther Party—keeping men happy. I don't mean happy in a "wife-y" kind of way, but uplifting almost every situation.

There's a woman in the entertainment industry who's working on a film called "Growing Up Panther." And it's interesting—the premise is there are women who did a lot of the work. Who are they? Can we name them? And she did man-on-the-street interviews. Do you know that out of the ten people she spoke to, only one of them could name one person. And the one person she named was Angela Davis.

YK: Was she in the Black Panther Party?

EH: Sure she was. John Huggins invited her into the Black Panther Party. But mostly we know her with the Communist Party. She wanted to be in both the Communist Party and the Black Panther Party and the Black Panther Party said, "No, choose one or the other." And well, can't do that—and so she stayed with the Communist Party.

MK: But she was with the Panthers for a while, wasn't she?

EH: Yeah, in Los Angeles. And it was before John and Bunchy were killed. That's where I met her . . . I met her in 1968 in Los Angeles.

YK: You mean, that was before your husband was killed . . .

EH: Yeah, we were all friends. When John was killed, they arrested all of us at my house to get us off the streets. And then they let us go. Well, they let me go on bail, so I could take John's body back to New Haven, Connecticut, where he was from. The person waiting for me when I got out of the women's prison was Angela. It was really wonderful.

But anyway, in this film idea that my friend is doing, people couldn't remember names of any women in the Black Panther Party. That's ridiculous. They could come up with Angela, and two people named Elaine Brown. But then she had in her little film footage a whole scroll of names, because I gave her the names. I can call them off from the top of my head. And I know what they did. And they weren't just wives and girlfriends. They made sure all the party programs thoroughly survived and were maintained and managed well, and took care of everything, including more military things. But you have to dig around and find it, and I think the reason is that we live in a very male-dominated society.

MK: But it's also a very short-term memory society. People do not know history. They probably mention Elaine because . . .

EH: She ran for office . . .

MK: She wrote a book . . .

EH: She ran for city council and she wrote a book. But a book isn't the only reason why because if Angela Davis never wrote a book, everybody would still know about her. Why did the media put Angela out there? They put her out there because she was an African American member of the Communist Party. And she was a threat. Furthermore, they wanted to make people dislike her. There was another guy doing a BET special on a show called "The American Gangster," and he was pointing out how the FBI/ COINTELPRO was a gang, they were thugs. And their principle was to call forward anyone who proposed themselves to be a Messiah. They listed Martin Luther King, Malcolm X and the Black Panther Party: " . . . make certain that they don't rise to fame."

And so they made it their business to set up the circumstances where people would be harmed, or jailed, or at worst, killed. When they describe the US organization and the Black Panther Party, the FBI says, "We'll send letters and we'll draw cartoons demeaning each of the organizations, and we'll send it from the other organization." Then they said, "We'll let nature take its course." Isn't that something?

YK: The US is so conniving and slimy . . .

EH: Yes, it is. And yet, this is where we live.

YK: But you know, in the Asian Movement, one of the first Asian American groups was Triple A, Asian Americans for Action. And they were mostly elderly Asians, like Kazu Iijima, Mary Ikeda, Min Matsuda, but what happened was all the young people didn't like having older Asian women on top of them. So they left and went to Chinatown and joined I Wor Kuen.

MK: Especially the young guys.

YK: Yeah, the guys all left.

MK: Because it was their mothers in the group—a lot of them were actually families.

EH: And what does culture and tradition say about that? Even if they weren't their mothers. We experienced this in the Black Panther Party too, when Huey went to Cuba, and left Elaine to run the Black Panther Party, which she did for a year. And as a result, all the programs blossomed, group connections were made. But when she did this . . .

YK: The Black Panther Party agreed to that?

EH: The men in the Party would agree with anything Huey said. But when he was in Cuba, and Elaine would try to make decisions, they would try to ignore them, because she was a woman. There wasn't any other reason. But after a while, when they realized it wasn't going to change, they began to respect her because she was very honest about how it was going to work and how it wasn't going to work.

We live in a global society that says the people who birth the children are not good enough to take care of important matters in the world. And that's so far from practical reality. It's all these old notions that come from women being the property of men. It goes way way way back. So women in the movement need to be talked about because it helps to unpack the system that's in place that says "It's okay if people of color are in a position of deciding their destinies but it's not okay if women do."

YK: But then women just wanted to have organizations with just women. Third World Women's Alliance just became an all women's group. They realized they had no power whenever there were men in the group. So they left and did their own thing.

MK: That wasn't really true of Triple A—it was run by older Nisei women. And they were powerhouses. And even though you say that all the young people left, there were still other young people coming through Triple A, working with Triple A—they [Triple A] had national respect in the Asian American Movement. Like in LA, it was like—"These are heavy ladies. And they're our mothers' age, and they're more political than all of us."

YK: That's like Kazu Iijima, who was way ahead of us. She was like our mentor. The women in Triple A were amazing. There was Mitzi Fromartz, Taxi Wada . . . and then we had all kinds of Asian men from all different ethnic backgrounds, like Mr. Mukherji from India and Mr. Mok from Cambodia.

MK: But your husbands were also in the group.

YK: Yeah . . .

MK: And they were fine. They were very quiet. They let the women do their thing, and they were very quiet.

EH: Because they knew it was uplifting for the whole community. And the Third World Women's Alliance was the same way.

MK: Was Third World Women's Alliance national?

EH: The Third World Women's Alliance wasn't national. I remember it in California.

YK: New York, it was very mixed.

EH: I do notice that when women see suffering, they want to respond to it immediately. And I remember working with the Third World Women's Alliance on the high rates of infant mortality in Oakland. In the late 1970s, Oakland had the second highest infant mortality rate to Sub-Sahara in Africa.

YK: Really!!!

EH: And the Allen Temple Baptist, the largest Black Baptist church in Oakland, held a press conference and put this out. I called the Third World Women's Alliance and said we have to develop a coalition. This can't happen in our city. We have to call Highland Hospital on the carpet, and find out why their prenatal care is so poor, because that was at the root of it. And we worked with some clinics in East Oakland, but the Third World Women's Alliance and the women of the Black Panther Party created the coalition to fight infant mortality. And we took pregnant women and women with babies to the Alameda County Board of Supervisors and complained about Highland, where a woman could give birth on a bench in the waiting room. Well, it shifted. It shifted because of that coalition of mostly Asian, Latino, and African American women.

I was also thinking back to a group of women of color, primarily African American women, but I think there were some other women in there. My mother lives in an assisted living facility—

YK: In New York?

EH: She lives in Oakland . . . she's blind, and her memory is really poor because she had a stroke—she's ninety now. But I made friends with a woman there who's almost ninety-four who helped start an organization called "Black Women Stirring the Waters."

YK: Black Women Stirring the Waters? That's a good name . . .

EH: Virginia Rose, and her husband was an Oakland City Council person way back when—Joshua Rose. Virginia says that they started Black Women Stirring the Water because they wanted black women to come together and discuss issues and take action on them. And at the time they did that, they were mid-aged women. Well, I said, "Where did you get that name Black Women Stirring the Waters?" And she said Sojourner Truth, in this speech, says, "If the waters of change are already moving, then we may as well step in and keep them stirred." I paraphrased it, but that's the gist of it. And I just loved it. And she's my friend to this day. When I first met her, her spirit is just so bright. And so I went to introduce myself to her and I couldn't get my name out. And the ninety-one-year-old woman said, "You don't have to introduce yourself. I know who you are!"

["Wows" all around]

EH: She's just like Yuri, she's still doing what she can do. And she's even in a wheelchair, but she's always stirring something up. And remember Irene Hernandez? She was one of the women in Black Women Stirring the Waters, and a whole bunch of other really well-known names of women in the Bay Area, activists of every kind. It's kind of phenomenal to think that there's so many wonderful women and so few of them are known.

YK: And then on the East Coast, there was a group B.W.E., Black Women Enraged, and they were mostly older women, but very very active. I mean, they were active in other kinds of community work. Vida Gaynor was the head of it.

EH: That name sounds familiar, I don't know why. But going back to the bridging you described between the Asian American and African American community, and even Asia and Africa, I think this is just so important because when Richard Aoki was part of the Black Panther Party—it just felt normal. When we had Latinos that were part of the Black Panther Party, it felt normal. It didn't feel like it was some different people. We believed that all of us should work together. And did you know that there were Asian women in the Black Panther Party as well? And Latin women . . . I can't remember all their names. And there was one Armenian women who was a Black Panther Party member, and two or three white women and men—who were actually members. We just believed that if people really wanted to fight for justice on behalf of all oppressed people, which was our perspective, then if they weren't coming with a lot of guilt and shame and fear, or they wanted a husband or a wife, then fine. And these people stayed around and did their work, and it's all history now.

JK: Yuri was beginning to get into the history of the Triple A, the membership, the strong women that were working in the Triple A . . . maybe you could expound a little more on that, and also Triple A's participation in the Black Liberation Movement, in the Civil Rights Movement . . .

YK: Triple A didn't actually work with black organizations or black issues. But Triple A worked with all kinds of Asians. We had male East Indians—Mukherjee, who was a well-known Indian—we had Thais, we had Vietnamese. It was just that our young Asians didn't like the idea that older Asian women were more or less the force behind that group.

EH: Did Triple A support the end to the war in Vietnam?

YK: Oh, Triple A was very active in that. But it is strange now that I think of it. One-by-one the men left, and only a few were left in Triple A. And people just took it for granted that it was a women's group. I'm just wondering if I remember seeing my husband there towards the end. Well, my husband was getting active in other things—you know, 442 stuff.

EH: But you know when there's a man's organization, when men are running it—we never think that's a man's organization.

YK: Right, right . . . it's just an organization.

EH: Isn't that interesting? I'm not, as they say, "bitching about it." I'm just stating facts. That is how systems keep things in place because we start believing that an organization equals a man's organization—it's normed. We believe that's normal. So then we believe that when women are running an organization, it's abnormal somewhere in there.

MK: Or it's only for women.

EH: And of course that wasn't the case. I never heard of Triple A before today. I can tell it wasn't a women's organization, it was an organization run by women. That's a totally different story. I can tell you about women's organizations, like the very first lesbian organization in the Bay Area—the Daughters of Bilitus. No men were allowed in there, and only certain women were allowed in there. That's different. Triple A was for the uplifting of humanity, and specifically Asian Americans. That makes sense. And the Black Panther Party was run by women. I can't stress that enough. And it is not a secret. David Hilliard, Huey Newton if he was alive, Bobby Seale, all the men in leadership of the party will tell you that women ran it. But the books are written by men. And who very rarely mention women. Our history is not there for people to analyze or look at. It's like Mary Magdalene, who was written out of the Bible.

YK: Oh, was she?!

EH: It's a beautiful story. My mother loved the Bible. She's blind, so I read to her from the Bible. Do you know that Mary Magdalene was the only one courageous enough to say "Hey wait a minute. Jesus' body is in that tomb, and nobody's going to claim that body?" And the other disciples said to her, "You could get killed." And she basically said, "So what. That's my master, that's my teacher." And she claimed his body. Well, whether we believe in it or not, why was she written out of the Bible?

YK: Well, how come people know about Mary Magdalene?

EH: Because there's all these people interested in the resurgence of the sacred feminine which is just like what we're talking about today. Why do women keep getting written out of history? If I was a man I would want to know this. It's not just because I'm a woman, I'm a sociologist. I have to wonder why you would write out all these wonderful women if you weren't trying to hold something for yourself, hold something in place. There's a whole different theory: the reason why she was written out is because actually Jesus wasn't celibate, that Mary and Jesus were lovers, and they have children. So the theory is the Christian elite tried to cover her lineage. That's what the whole Da Vinci Code thing is about. But there are other books before the Da Vinci Code about these clandestine Christian male-only clubs, sects, their whole purpose is to cover Mary Madgalene's tracks. Isn't that interesting?

YK: It certainly is! I don't think many people know . . .

EH: And I'm so intrigued, whenever I see where women are written out of history, my first question is, "Why? What was the reason?" And with the Black Panther Party, I think the media just so jumped on top of young handsome black men with guns and black berets, their gender bias and sexist notion of a woman couldn't fit in there. Because the women in the Black Panther Party dressed and behaved exactly like the men in the Black Panther Party in those early days.

MK: And what were the women doing—there was the Free Breakfast Program, all of these really positive things . . .

EH: Not only that, we were doing all the other things that men were doing.

MK: But it was those images the press didn't really care to play up . . .

EH: Even when the media showed the breakfast program, they would show men feeding the children. Which is true, they did. But you didn't see the women until you saw some beautiful caricature of a woman that looked like a combination of Angela and Kathleen, with a gun. I call her Angeleen. You know, it's like just some pop culture idea of a woman. No, it wasn't like that. You know, we didn't have a new pair of shoes for years. The best thing we could say about any of our clothing is that it was clean. We weren't your typical women in any way, shape or form. We sacrificed—I don't mean it in a negative way, but we sacrificed all that. We said, "We're going to serve the people." But we never bragged about it. But now that our history has become so important to everybody, it really does an honor for the history of those women, some of whom are dead. To act like it didn't occur, that would be acting like the Party started and not mentioning Huey and Bobby. As a matter of fact, I remember in the mid- to late 1970s, a group of women, I was one of them, went to Huey Newton, and said, "You know, women run everything and always have. How come there's no women on the Central Committee of the Black Panther Party?

YK: Oh, there wasn't?

EH: Uh-huh. We were all in leadership but not on the Central Committee. It was all men. I often wondered what they did.

[Everybody busting up in laughter]

EH: It sounds funny, but things were not changing that needed to change in our party. So we went to Huey, a bunch of us, and said there should be women on the Central Committee. Huey said, "Alright comrades. Well, who?" We gave him a long list of people, and within like a few months, there were six women on the Central Committee. Huey was really open like that. He also spoke a lot about sexism in the Party. If the women came with complaints, he was the first to respond—up until the time he got severely addicted and then he didn't respond to anything. I remember how dreadful it was for a man to hit a woman, a beater—which is common in our society because society says men own women, the ownership thing, that it was okay. But it wasn't okay in the Black Panther Party. If you hit somebody, you're gonna get hit, simple as that. So don't do it. And we felt the same way about children. No children should be harmed. If you harmed a child, you got harmed.

I remember him telling me one time that he was envious of the relationships that women have with each other . . . because they're so honest and so real. And he wished that men were able to express that kind of honesty. They had it, but society says, "No, you can't express it. You can't be that intimate with another man." People don't even know that the men even cared about the women in the Party—and they did.

MK: There's a book that came out fairly recently, going back to the history and trying to go back to what the women's role was in the Party, and so they're starting to speak to this.

EH: Charles Jones wrote a book called *The Black Panther Party Reconsidered.* You would think he was one [Black Panther], which is what I think he wants people to think. He's a nice guy, but he doesn't check his sources. And so I called him one day and told him "You know Charles, your book is really wonderful, but did you know that this was inaccurate? I'm not hard to find." But in the academic world, people get ensconced in their notion of what something ought to be written like . . . and forget the living sources that you might want to check with them.

MK: Academia is like that—from the books, and they think the real sources might be subjective, but then the written stuff is just as subjective . . .

EH: I'm working on an anthology called, *Ya Wanna Make a Revolution: Women in the Black Revolt.* And at this conference, I met Diane Fujino, because Diane Fujino presented about you at the conference. And I go "Whoa, that's Yuri she's talking about."

She has a famous picture of you holding Malcolm. And she talked about your life and how your home was always open to the entire community. I think she said that each weekend there were always people coming over to your house. And a lot of them were African American people. And you always believed there has to be a bridge between the communities that suffer.

The presentation made me think about the chapter for that book that my friend Angela Ernest and I are writing. She's a scholar who was responsible for the Black Panther Party archives when it first came to Stanford University. We decided to write a chapter from the standpoint of the Oakland Community School, because that's where you see the power of the women—in terms of young children's revolutionary education. It was called Oakland Community School Revolutionary Model for Education.

So how is it that I'm writing for this book since I'm not considered a scholar? I'm considered a source. When Angela called me and said, "How do you feel about me writing a chapter on the Oakland Community School?" I said, "Fine. Find out if I can write it with you." And she said, "What a great idea. I don't think that's ever been done before." The bridge between the live source and academia. And the professor that's putting the anthology together said, "That's fine as long as it's unbiased."

[Outburst from everybody]

EH: That really is that crap because everything that comes out of academia is so biased. This book is on women in the black revolt from the '30s to now. But the whole conference, each presentation—I was floored by how much I do not know about women in the movement. And I know many many women in the movement. For instance, I met the first black woman to write in *Freedomways* magazine. Esther something Johnson, Esther Cooke Johnson, something like that. And she came. Her life was being presented. She's ninety-three and she came. Her husband was stalked during the McCarthy Period and was put in jail. These are some of the earliest black members of the Communist Party USA. It was phenomenal. It was such an educational experience.

Can you talk some more about why you chose to be connected to the Black Liberation Movement?

YK: Well, I lived forty years in Harlem. So I got to meet and hear some of the best speakers—well everybody came to Harlem at some time. So you couldn't help but meet them. Whether it was Stokely Carmichael, who became Kwame Ture, and there was Mandela—he did come once. The whole 125th Street was just jam-packed. People were even sitting in the trees. It was fantastic. But I mean, Fannie Lou Hamer, all of them came to Harlem at some time.

EH: How did you end up living in Harlem?

YK: Just by luck. We started out with one kid in a two-bedroom apartment. But before we knew it we had six children and then a place opened in Harlem. And I think they wanted the Harlem housing project not just to be black but mixed, so if you were not black you had a better chance of getting in. And so we got in the project in Harlem, Manhattanville. And it was just a perfect time, 1960. And all sorts of things were going on then. So many people were going down south, you know, to the Civil Rights Movement in Alabama and Mississippi . . . and then, after meeting Malcolm, he said would you like to come to the meetings—the OAAU. And all the blacks were there—they didn't stop anyone, I met a couple of Japanese from Japan, and they were going to meetings, Malcolm's meetings.

EH: So what made you go to that speech that day to hear Malcolm? Why were you there that day?

YK: The day that he was killed?

EH: Uh-huh.

YK: Well, most of us who were going to Malcolm's meetings, we went every time Malcolm spoke.

EH: Did you think about it when you ran up on the stage or did you just go?

YK: Well, once things started, you know, two guys jumped up in the middle of the auditorium. One screamed, "Get your hands out of my pocket." And they started fighting. And everybody's attention was on these two. And Malcolm was at the podium.

EH: Of course, that was the whole point, wasn't it?

YK: Yeah, and they didn't know it was so well planned. They had three guys, these guys were doing the distraction. And even Malcolm's guards were sucked in. Everybody was looking at the two. But the two guys, they had guns. But there were three guys in front with shotguns. And Malcolm came from behind the podium. He was the perfect target. He was shot many times. I think they said there were thirteen bullets in him.

EH: So you just ran up there?

YK: Well, a guy passed me, and I was hoping he was a security for Malcolm. None of us knew how to get up on that stage. So I followed him. He must have been security. He did the right thing. He didn't go to Malcolm. He went to the curtain and pulled the curtain to see if anyone was hiding there. And Malcolm just fell back, and I put his head on my lap. But he didn't say a word. People say, "What did he last say?" He was just having a hard time breathing.

EH: And then he died.

YK: It was sad. You know, Malcolm knew that something was going to happen.

EH: So did John Huggins. So did I. John went to UCLA that morning, but he forgot to take his house keys. So he knocked on the door. And I knew his knock. So I ran to the door, and before he could even get inside the door I grabbed him, and I said, "they took you away, they took you away. I'm so glad you're back." I was so in that place where I was trying to figure out if it was a dream. And he just had to peel my hands away from him for me to let him go. He said, "Where's the baby?" That was his response. And a shiver went through my heart because he didn't say, "Oh, it's just a dream." He didn't say, "Oh, you're being silly." Then he said, "Where's the baby?" I said, "She's in the room sleeping." And then I stopped crying. And he said, "I'm here now."

He walked about an hour with the baby. He knew he was going to die. I'm so sure of that. I didn't cry for a really long time because I already knew he was going to die, and it was just a matter of time. And so when the police came to take us away, I didn't cry. Well, they arrested all of us and handcuffed us and took us away. But they didn't handcuff me—they had some common sense that I had to hold the baby.

YK: Oh, there was you and the baby . . .

EH: They put all the other women in one police car, and two carloads of men, all party members that had converged at my house after John and Bunchy were killed. And I think what saved our lives that day was that it was daytime, and also the whole community came out and just stood out in the parking lot. They had me in the car separate from everybody else with the baby. And a woman police officer riding in the backseat with me. And we stopped at the morgue. The two cops leaned back, joking with one another, and they said, "That fuckin' baby looks Chinese . . . who'd you sleep with Huggins, Mao Tse-tung?"

YK: Oh my god! Oh my goodness!

EH: "You want to see his body? We're sure it's him . . ." You know the first thing I thought of when they talked that way, I thought about what my mother would say. She'd say, "Sugar, they just have no home training. They weren't raised right." And that kind of kept me in an amused place so I wouldn't fall apart because John was dead. Bunchy was dead. They were the two dearest people to me. And they took us to 77th Street Police Station. But yeah, "Who'd you sleep with, Mao tse-tung?" There you go again, Asians and blacks . . .

MK: That's [because] of the Red Book . . .

EH: Of course. Of course . . . You have to understand that those connections that the party made was all these organizations of poor people of all colors, that scared the mess out of the United States. They couldn't say it was just the Red Book. Or Russia influencing us. Or we believed Fidel was great. We were actually working together. They hated it because they couldn't just call us black militants. The papers kept saying that. And they kept saying that we hated white people. That was so far from the truth. That wasn't where we were coming from. We hated the behavior of the police, which we called fascist. And we hated the behavior of people who were racist. But we didn't hate all white people. Some of our greatest supporters were white.

But the one thing that I remember so strongly is how people know when their life is ending. They have a sense that they are nearing an end. And I've watched this with many other people who didn't die violently like that. But John definitely knew. And so it took me all that day and night before I allowed myself to cry, because it wasn't a dream. It was real. So I've often wondered how you felt sitting there with Malcolm. And I felt that way when Diane showed the photograph. And she kept the slide behind her while she was talking for a really long time. And so we all got to stare at it, and I was looking at your face and his head, and I was wondering, "Wow, what happened in those moments?" Did that make you want to continue to do more of what you're doing?

YK: I think it did for everyone who was there. That they have to commit themselves deeper because when Malcolm died, what he was teaching everybody was the government was so threatened by . . .

EH: You should see the FBI papers on Malcolm X. I cannot believe that it was the Nation of Islam . . . just the Nation of Islam. It was so well orchestrated.

YK: It was that well choreographed.

EH: Yes, yes they did. And John and Bunchy's was choreographed like that as well. They created an incident with Elaine Brown, which some people blame her for. But two guys came and called her a name and pulled on her clothing—to create a scene, because they knew that John and Bunchy would be annoyed. And they went to find these two men. And when they walked into that room in Campbell Hall, the shots were fired. It was orchestrated. The FBI said a few months later it wasn't supposed to happen like that—they started the circumstances to make them at odds with one another, but nobody was supposed to die.

My students today don't know any of this. My Asian immigrant students know absolutely nothing about American history. My students ask, "What was the 1960s like?" in my sociology class. And when we talk about social movements and social change, they talk about, "Okay, there was an Asian organization, there was a Latino organization, there was a Native American organization, there was a black organization, there was a women's organization, a gay organization . . . " And I say, "Wait a minute. There was an actual time of the 1960s during which I lived that we actually worked together." And they go, "No way, didn't you fight?" Sure we fought. We didn't like each other for anything sometimes. But mostly we agreed that we had power in being together. We talked through our differences, unless an organization was just bizarre and just a wild card. We were able to work together and put aside our differences because it was so important that we show a united front. There were even organizations called United Front. There were conferences called "United Front Against Fascism," remember that? And all the students sit there like, "That really happened?" They can't imagine it because the regular history books just delete whole parts of history.

We have a long ways to go, and so, it's important that in the *Amerasia* magazine, or in any other written documents, we keep talking about how we worked together, because for instance in Southern California where you are, the stratification between the African American and Asian community is terrible. Not only that, the Korean storeowner that killed the black girl. Step in the shoes of the Korean storeowner, and then step in the shoes of the girl—you got to if you look at history. Just look at the systems in place that will allow for that, and continue to allow that—and I just think it's important that we keep talking together out loud. People of different cultures, and even ideologies, talking for the purpose of bringing together a united front.

MK: Do you think it's easier for, this is going to sound feminist—the women of the different communities to make stronger bridges than the men . . . . I don't know, the men have some . . . gender issues . . .

EH: Even Webster's Dictionary says that feminism is the belief in the social, economic, and political equality of the sexes. So if you say you're a feminist, then we can run the spectrum from the most simple way of looking at life all the way over to women who sequester themselves on an island somewhere—in their own island where their children are at. But, yeah, I do find that when we're talking about bridging, women are able to stay in the conversation longer. I also have men in my women's studies classes who are so aware, clear, and pleasant with their own feelings that they can stay in that conversation too. I just think we have to keep on talking. What do you think, Yuri?

YK: I think you're right. We have to keep talking. We have to keep reaching out into other ethnic groups and . . . and . . .

EH: . . . and make the conversation easy enough for men to stay involved. Sometimes the edge that we bring to something creates more angles and edges. If we're soft around the edges and strong at the same time, everybody feels safe enough to be in the conversation. I've learned this teaching women's studies on a state university campus with lots of men in the classes, that they have as a general education requirement . . . and they come in afraid that I'm going to, or somebody in there is going to bash them. I never do that. I wouldn't allow that. That would be contrary to my political, social and spiritual beliefs to do that. So as a result, the men will come into the conversation, and do you know how they do it? They start talking about their mothers and aunts—grandmothers, and great-grandmothers, and sisters raise them, because so much these days kids don't have any fathers. They don't have any fathers! And men are just as bitter about it as the women but society says that it's not okay for men to talk about how they feel about anything. So I made my classroom a safe place for men to talk, and sometimes they come in and they bash, because they're so angry and they never have an open forum for anything. There is room for lots of ideas to flourish. I think humanity is teetering on a precipice right now—where anything could create more war, and more poverty, and more famine . . . and more atrocity. And that it's up to us, those of us that are living, whatever age we are, to shift it.

MK: Yuri, let me try and get you to talk about special concerns for women involved in movements? Because you know, you've been in plenty of movements . . .

YK: I think there are new issues, especially like lesbians and gays.

MK: LGBT . . .

YK: That issue wasn't around forty years ago.

EH: It was around but it wasn't talked about.

YK: So the new target would be those people plus still, the poor people will always be targets and people of color, and blacks will be treated worse . . . this country is so color . . . what's the word?

EH: Struck . . .

YK: Yeah, color struck! Do you think its gotten a little better—racism, or no?

EH: I think young people are more willing to cross lines that were considered abnormal now. And what I see of young people today is hopeful, because they're choosing partners, choosing to love someone outside their culture, or choosing to love someone of the same sex—I'm just saying that all these things are social constructs . . . and have no meaning when it comes to the heart. We don't have any meaning in someone's heart—it's what society says is okay or not okay. So in that way I see some improvement, because as you well know, it once was a crime punishable by arrest and jailing for white and Asian people or white and black people to cohabitate or get married. It was the law, and that law ended way too late in history. But the law ended against miscegenation, and I also think the vast holdout—even stronger than lesbian and gay—the last holdout is between women and men.

And the reason I say that is because that old history that says women are owned by men . . . that may be gone, but can women take complete control of their lives? And it be seen as okay? Nobody really talks in communities of color about rape and incest in the communities of color. We'll talk about racism of whites and people of color, but incest? We try not to talk about things that just add another layer of depressive, oppressive memory to it. But it's true, if women just had total control of their own independence—and it's sexually, socially, economically, it's politically, then there would be a greater chance at ending racism. Do you follow me?

YK: Yeah . . .

EH: It's all intertwined, like a huge spider web. And wherever the spider puts pressure on the web, everything moves. So—gender is a huge part of that web. And I think sometimes in the social movement, we deny this exists. We act like it doesn't, or that women have to walk on eggshells about it. That's how I feel.

MK: So what do you think are the most important things that you learned from the 1960s–1970s movement that you want to share with young people today? What do you feel you've learned from all your past involvements?

YK: Maybe I'm going off the track, but there's so much that people don't know—how Asian and Africans have interacted through history. I mean, China sent 13,000 workers to Africa, to work with 36,000 Zambians to build a TanZam Railway [also known as the Uhuru Railway]. North Korea sent workers to Zimbabwe and they built Heroes Acres. Chinese workers help construct the National Sports Stadium, the largest athletic stadium in Africa. Asian and Africans have interacted, and most people don't even know those things that happened. We have to let them know from the beginning that—especially the Chinese and Africans have come together way way back. And I don't know why they don't have those things in the history book.

EH: The resentment is set up because of the model minority myth, the resentment between the black and Asian communities. A young black woman came to me one day in my "Women of Color in the United States" class—she waited till everyone was gone. And she came to me with tears in her eyes and she said, "I am so sorry. I never knew Asian women suffered. I thought they had it made. I believed that they're just good in school, they get the best jobs, and moved to the best homes." That was one of those times where the Vietnamese women in the class were sharing their after-war family stories. Oh, it was hard to hear. So this woman said, "I'm so sorry I had all those stereotypes, all the backward beliefs that Asian women, especially Asian women like white women, just have it made." And you're right, Yuri, the history just isn't there. People don't even know the history of the internment camps.

YK: Parents don't ever tell their kids. The Japanese were ashamed they were sent to, as people called them, "concentration camps."

EH: That's right, that's right. I have a friend who still flies the flag in his front window . . . the American flag, because he's so ashamed. So we all are battling our demons, let's say. But one thing about demons, if you shine light on them, they'll run away. So talking about them out loud is very important.

EH: Did you know that he [Malcolm X] and Martin Luther King were working on plans to combine the movements?

YK: No, I didn't know.

EH: Yeah, there's a play called "The Meeting" about that. And the Martin Luther King Research and Education Institute has the letters between the two of them. And you've seen the picture of the two of them together, right? That was real. They really were wanting to merge.

YK: Yes, I think it was going to happen, but the US didn't allow it. The US wanted both assassinated.

EH: Orchestration, orchestration . . . I'm going to give you a hug. Thank you for being who you are.

YK: Thank you! I'm so pleased I got to meet you!

EH: Yeah, it was fun!

MK: You're going to be late . . .

EH: Yeah, it's okay. It was worth it!

## NOTE

Reprinted with permission from Yuri Kochiyama, Ericka Huggins, and Mary Uyematsu Kao, *Amerasia Journal* 35:1 (2009): 140–167.

# 2017 HOLLYWOOD DIVERSITY REPORT:
## Setting the Record Straight

DARNELL HUNT, ANA-CHRISTINA RAMÓN, MICHAEL TRAN, AMBERIA SARGENT, AND VANESSA DÍAZ

## EXECUTIVE SUMMARY

This is the fourth in a series of reports to examine relationships between diversity and the bottom line in the Hollywood entertainment industry. It considers the top 200 theatrical film releases in 2015 and 1,206 broadcast, cable and digital platform television shows from the 2014–15 season in order to document the degree to which women and minorities are present in front of and behind the camera. It discusses any patterns between these findings and box office receipts and audience ratings.

The following highlights emerge from this year's analysis:

1. *Minorities.* Constituting nearly 40 percent of the US population in 2015, minorities will become the majority within a few decades. Since the previous report, people of color have posted gains relative to their white counterparts in five of the industry employment arenas examined (i.e., film leads, broadcast scripted leads, broadcast reality and other leads, digital scripted leads, and broadcast scripted show creators). Minorities

Darnell Hunt is dean of Social Sciences and professor of sociology and African American studies at UCLA. He has written extensively on race and media, including numerous scholarly journal articles and popular magazine articles. He has also published four books about these issues: *Screening the Los Angeles "Riots": Race, Seeing, and Resistance* (Cambridge University Press, 1997), *O. J. Simpson Facts and Fictions: News Rituals in the Construction of Reality* (Cambridge University Press, 1999), *Channeling Blackness: Studies on Television and Race in America* (Oxford University Press, 2005), and (with Ana-Christina Ramón) *Black Los Angeles: American Dreams and Racial Realities* (NYU Press, 2010). Prior to his positions at UCLA, he chaired the Department of Sociology at the University of Southern California (USC). Over the past two decades, Dr. Hunt has worked on several projects exploring the issues of access and diversity in the Hollywood industry. Ana-Christina Ramón is the director of research and civic engagement for the Division of Social Sciences at UCLA. She is a social psychologist trained in quantitative and qualitative methods. For more than a decade, she has worked on social justice issues related to equity and access in higher education and the entertainment industry. She manages the Hollywood Advancement Project and its graduate research team and is co-author (with Dr. Hunt) of the past five Hollywood Diversity Reports. She is currently the managing editor of the e-forum LA Social Science for the Division of Social Sciences at UCLA. She co-edited a book (with Dr. Hunt) titled *Black Los Angeles: American Dreams and Racial Realities* (New York University Press, 2010).

**Table 2: Underrepresentation Factors, by Arena, Minorities and Women, 2014-15***

| Arena | Minorities | Women |
|---|---|---|
| Film Leads (2015) | < 3 to 1 | < 2 to 1 |
| Film Directors (2015) | < 4 to 1 | > 6 to 1 |
| Flm Writers (2015) | > 7 to 1 | < 4 to 1 |
| Broadcast Scripted Leads | > 3 to 1 | < Proportionate |
| Cable Scripted Leads | > 2 to 1 | < 2 to 1 |
| Broadcast Reality/Other Leads | < 2 to 1 | > 3 to 1 |
| Cable Reality/Other Leads | > 2 to 1 | > 2 to 1 |
| Digital Scripted Leads | > 3 to 1 | < 2 to 1 |
| Broadcast Scripted Creators | < 5 to 1 | > 2 to 1 |
| Cable Scripted Creators | 5 to 1 | > 2 to 1 |
| Digital Scripted Creators | < 7 to 1 | > 2 to 1 |

***Gains since the previous report highlighted in green, losses in red.**

lost ground in four of the eleven arenas (i.e., film directors, film writers, cable scripted leads, and digital scripted show creators) and merely held their ground in the other two (i.e., cable scripted show creators and cable reality and other leads). They remained underrepresented on every front in 2014–15:

- Nearly 3 to 1 among film leads
- Nearly 4 to 1 among film directors
- Greater than 7 to 1 among film writers
- Greater than 3 to 1 among broadcast scripted leads
- Greater than 2 to 1 among cable scripted leads
- Nearly 2 to 1 among broadcast reality and other leads
- Greater than 2 to 1 among leads for cable reality and other shows
- Greater than 3 to 1 among digital scripted leads
- Nearly 5 to 1 among the creators of broadcast scripted shows
- Nearly 5 to 1 among the creators of cable scripted shows
- Nearly 7 to 1 among the creators of digital scripted shows
- Nearly 3 to 1 among the credited writers for broadcast scripted shows
- Greater than 3 to 1 among the credited writers for cable scripted shows and digital scripted shows

2. *Women.* Relative to their male counterparts, women posted gains in all Hollywood employment arenas since the previous report, with the exception of two—broadcast reality and other leads and cable reality and other leads—where they fell further behind. Still, like minorities, they remained underrepresented on every front in 2014–15:

- Nearly 2 to 1 among film leads
- More than 6 to 1 among film directors
- Nearly 4 to 1 among film writers

- Less than proportionate representation among broadcast scripted leads
- Nearly 2 to 1 among cable scripted leads
- Greater than 3 to 1 among broadcast reality and other leads
- Greater than 2 to 1 among cable reality and other leads
- Less than proportionate representation among digital scripted leads
- Greater than 2 to 1 among the creators of broadcast scripted shows
- Greater than 2 to 1 among the creators of cable scripted shows
- Greater than 2 to 1 among the creators of digital scripted shows

3. *Accolades.* In 2015, minority-directed films and those with minority leads lost ground at the Oscars relative to those led by white directors or that featured white leads. While films featuring women leads gained some ground at the Oscars in 2015, those directed by women failed to win a single Oscar. At the Emmys, broadcast scripted shows created by minorities gained ground relative to those initiated by white show creators, while shows created by women continued to lose ground relative to those created by men. Meanwhile, not one of the cable scripted shows created by minorities won an Emmy that year (matching the previous three years), and cable shows created by women continued to lose ground relative to those created by men.

4. *Gatekeeping.* Since the last report, the three dominant talent agencies have maintained (and in some cases increased) their combined, dominant shares of the film directors, film writers, film leads, broadcast scripted show creators, broadcast scripted leads, and cable scripted leads credited for the theatrical films and television shows examined in 2014–15. Minorities remain woefully underrepresented on the rosters of these powerful gatekeepers.

5. *Diversity Initiatives.* The most prominent industry diversity initiatives are writers' programs (film and television) and grant programs (film). These programs are highly competitive, offering opportunities for networking and financing to a relatively small number of the thousands of potential, diverse candidates. Initiatives focused on developing diverse creative executives—an area highlighted in earlier reports as in dire need of improvement—are even less readily available.

6. *The Bottom Line.* Consistent with the findings of earlier reports in this series, new evidence from 2014–15 suggests that America's increasingly diverse audiences prefer diverse film and television content.

- Films with relatively diverse casts enjoyed the highest median global box office receipts and the highest median return on investment
- Minorities accounted for the majority of ticket sales for five of the top-ten films in 2015 (ranked by global box office)
- Relatively diverse films excelled at the box office between 2011 and 2015, regardless of genre

Median 18–49 viewer ratings (as well as median household ratings among whites, blacks, Latinos, and Asian Americans) peaked during the 2014–15 season for broadcast scripted shows featuring casts that were greater than 40 percent.

Minority

- Social media engagement peaked for broadcast scripted shows with casts that reflected the diversity of America
- Median black household ratings peaked for cable scripted shows with casts that were majority minority in 2014–15
- For Asian American and Latino households, median ratings peaked in the cable scripted arena for shows with casts that were from 31 to 40 percent minority
- For white households and viewers 18–49, the peak interval in the cable scripted arena contained shows with casts that were from 11 to 20 percent minority
- Social media engagement peaked for cable scripted shows with casts that were from 21 to 30 percent minority

## HOLLYWOOD DIVERSITY: TAKE FOUR

> "What do you do when someone says, 'Your color skin is not what we're looking for?'"
>
> —America Ferrera

> "Having your story told as a woman, as a person of color, as a lesbian, or as a trans person or as any member of any disenfranchised community is sadly often still a radical idea."
>
> —Kerry Washington

The previous report in this series examined theatrical films released in 2014 and broadcast, cable, and digital shows airing or streaming during the 2013–14 season. The goal was to assess the degree of racial and gender diversity in front of and behind the camera. For the various film and television arenas examined (e.g., lead roles, film director, film writer, television writer, and show creators), last year's report (as its two predecessors) found that underrepresentation was the norm for people of color and women. All too often, as America Ferrera exclaims in the quote above, industry decision makers (typically white men) have green–lighted projects for which people of color are both marginal to the story and excluded from the creative work behind the scenes.

The current report extends the analyses presented in prior reports in the Hollywood Diversity Report series. This section examines theatrical films released in 2015 and broadcast, cable, digital platform and syndicated shows airing or streaming during the 2014–15 season in order to identify any meaningful trends in minority and female access to industry employment. The following headlines summarize the most significant findings.

### *Film*

**1. *Minority Share of Lead Roles*[1] *Stagnant in Film***

Figure 12 shows that the minority share of lead roles in the top films examined peaked at 16.7 percent in 2013. Since the last report, the minority share has stayed more or less flat, 12.9 percent in 2014 versus 13.6 percent in 2015. Because minorities collectively accounted for 38.4 percent of the US population in 2015, they were underrepresented by a factor of nearly 3 to 1 among lead roles in the films examined for that year. Still, this was an improvement over minorities' share of lead film roles in 2011 (10.5 percent), which corresponded to underrepresentation by a factor of nearly 4 to 1. Films

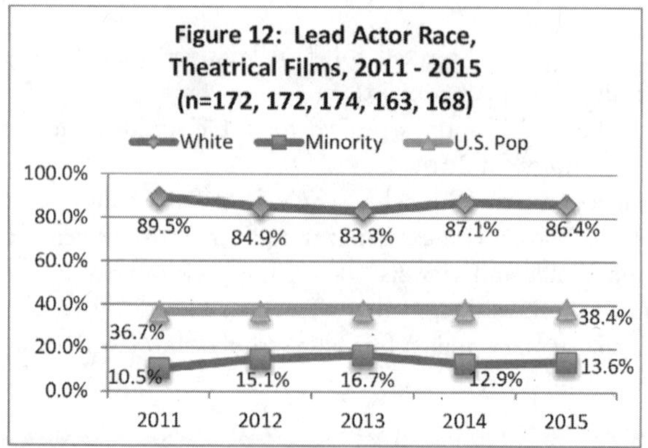


with minority leads in 2015 include *Furious 7, San Andreas, Straight Outta Compton,* and *Concussion.* From the trend line evident in figure 12, it now appears as if 2013—dubbed by some as a "breakout year for black film"[2]—was *not* the beginning of a rising trend in minority-led films.

### 2. *Women Gain Ground among Lead Roles in Film*

Women claimed the lead roles in 29 percent of the 168 top films examined for 2015 (see fig. 13), up from just 25.8 percent the previous year. Still, the female share of lead roles was below the peak, 30.8 percent share observed in 2012. Because women constitute slightly more than half of the US population, they were underrepresented by a factor of a little less than 2 to 1 among leads for the films examined in 2015. Films that featured female leads that year include: *Cinderella, American Ultra,* and *Fifty Shades of Grey.*

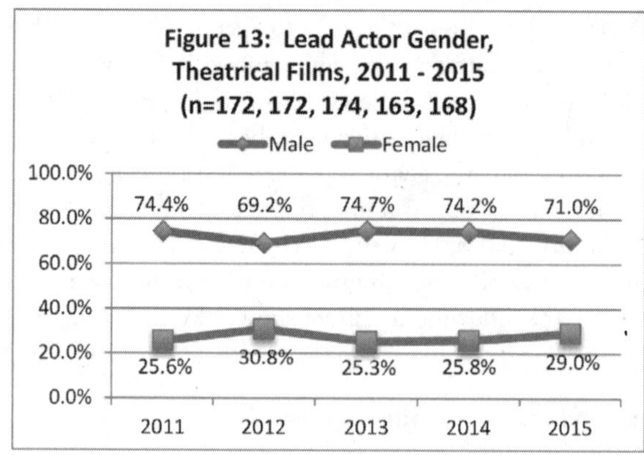


### 3. *Overall Cast Diversity*[3] *in Film Continues to Decrease*

Figure 14 reveals that films with casts that are 10 percent minority have increased their share of the top films since the last report, from 34 percent in 2014 to 38.5 percent in 2015. In other words, top films with relatively little cast diversity have actually increased their plurality share. At the same time, the share of films with majority-minority casts

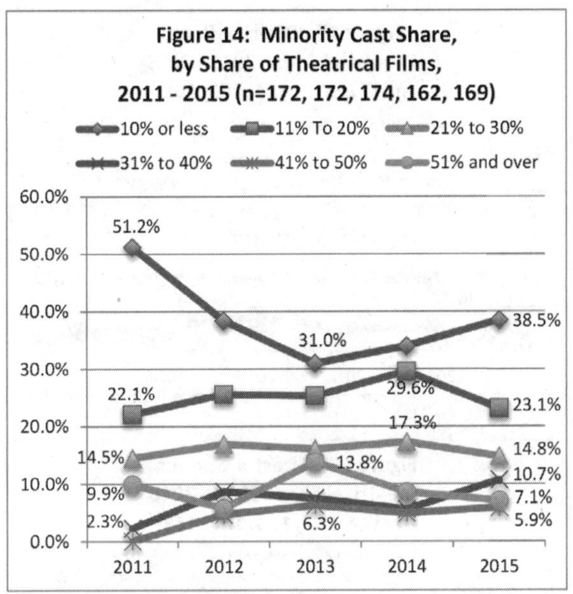


declined over the period, from 8.6 percent in 2014 to just 7.1 percent in 2015. Titles in this category include *Furious 7*, *Straight Outta Compton*, *Creed*, and *The Perfect Guy*.

By contrast, it's worth noting that the share for films with casts from 31 percent to 40 percent minority—the interval containing the minority share of the overall population—nearly doubled since the last report (from only 5.6 percent to 10.7 percent of the total). Finally, figure 14 shows that the peak year for film cast diversity was 2013, when majority-minority films accounted for 13.8 percent of the total and the least diverse films "only" 31 percent. As discussed above, of course, 2013 was also the so-called "breakout year for black film."

### 4. *Minorities Continue to Lose Ground among Film Directors*

Minorities directed only 10.1 percent of the 168 films examined for 2015 (see fig. 15), down from 12.9 percent in 2014. The figure for 2015 is the lowest on record over the report series. As minorities accounted for 38.4 percent of the population in 2015, their degree of underrepresentation within the corps of film directors increased to a factor of nearly 4 to 1. The minority share of directors peaked in 2013 at 17.8 percent, which suggests that the progress identified on the director front in earlier reports was more of an aberration than the beginning of an upward trend. Examples of minority-directed films from 2015 include *Furious 7*, *Straight Outta Compton*, *Creed*, and *Dope*—films that also featured minority leads.

### 5. *Women Gain Ground among Film Directors*

Throughout this report series, women film directors have had the dubious distinction of claiming the highest degree of underrepresentation for any group in any arena. Figure 16 shows that women directed 7.7 percent of the top films examined for 2015, which

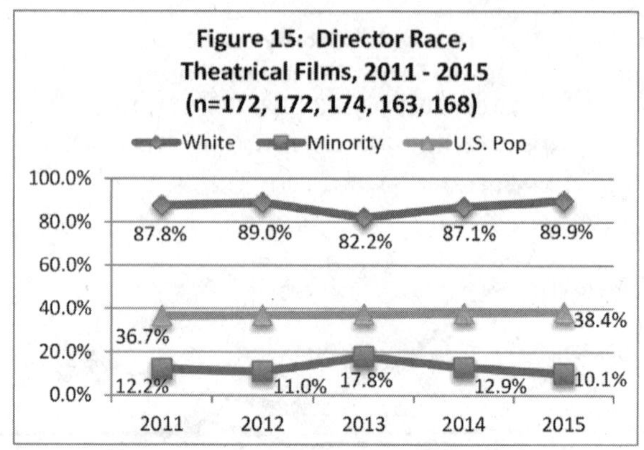


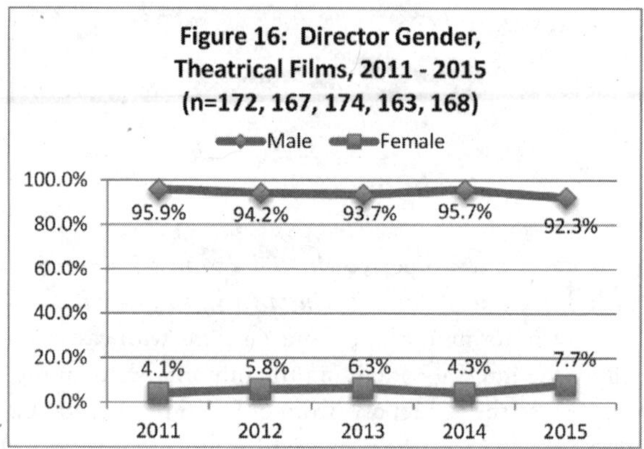


is more than a 3 percentage-point increase over 2014 and the highest share on record for the group. Still, as a little more than 50 percent of the population, women remained woefully underrepresented among film directors in 2015, by a factor of nearly 7 to 1. Films directed by women in 2015 include *Fifty Shades of Grey*, *Pitch Perfect 2*, *The Intern*, and *Jupiter Ascending*.

**6. *Minorities Continue to Lose Ground among Film Writers*[4]**

Consistent with findings above about the losses minorities have endured since the previous report in their share of film directors, minorities have also lost ground within the corps of film writers. Figure 17 shows minorities wrote just 5.3 percent of the 168 films examined for 2015, down from 8 percent in 2014. The minority share of writers—like the group's share of leads and directors—had peaked at more than double this figure, 11.8 percent, in 2013. Relative to the minority share of the population, minorities were underrepresented by a factor of more than 7 to 1 among film writers in 2015. Films from 2015 that featured minority writers include *Creed*, *The Perfect Guy*, *Dope*, and *The Visit*.

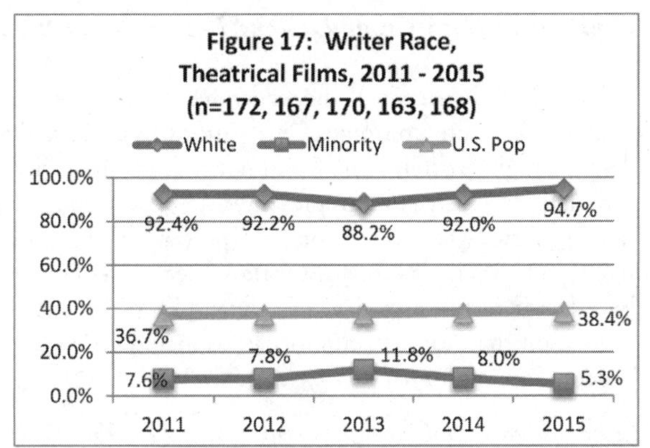


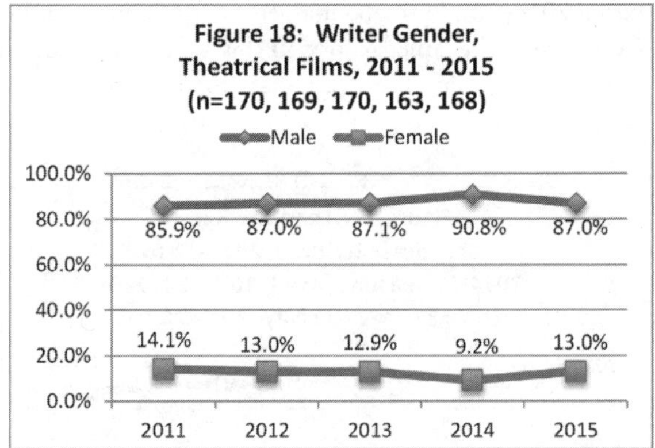


### 7. *Women Gain Ground among Film Writers*

Figure 18 shows that women received writing credits in 13 percent of the 168 films examined for 2015, up from the 9.2 percent figure the group posted in 2014. The 2015 share matches the share the group claimed in 2012 and 2013, but is still about a percentage point below its 14.1 percent share for 2011. Despite the gains noted above for women film directors, the group still fared better as writers in film in 2015 than as directors, an arena in which they were "only" underrepresented by a factor of about 4 to 1. Examples of films written by women in 2015 include *Fifty Shades of Grey, Terminator: Genisys, Pitch Perfect 2,* and *Kingsman: The Secret Service.*

## *Television*

### Leads

Lead actors are significant figures in the television arena because, more often than not, the storytelling from week to week revolves around their characters. As discussed throughout this report series, people of color and women have been underrepresented among television leads traditionally, raising questions about audience engagement with the images of American society in circulation.

**1. *Minorities Continue to Gain Ground among Lead Roles in Broadcast Scripted Shows***

Minority actors claimed 11.4 percent of the lead roles in broadcast scripted programming during the 2014–15 season, up from the 8.1 percent figure posted for the 2014–15 season (see fig. 19). Though the trend line for minority leads has a clear upward trajectory, minorities remain seriously underrepresented in this broadcast scripted arena. That is, given that minorities accounted for 38.4 percent of the population in 2015 (gray line), their 2014–15 share of broadcast scripted lead roles corresponds to underrepresentation by a factor of more than 3 to 1. Examples of broadcast scripted shows from the 2014–15 season that featured minority leads include *Black-ish* (ABC), *Jane the Virgin* (CW), *Empire* (Fox), and *Fresh Off the Boat (ABC).*

**2. *Minorities Continue to Lose Ground among Leads in Cable Scripted Shows***

Figure 20 shows minority actors accounted for 15.8 percent of the lead roles in cable scripted shows during 2014–15, down about a percentage point from the 2013–14 figure (16.6 percent). Consistent with earlier reports in this series, this share remains considerably larger than the corresponding broadcast share for minorities, due to the fact that

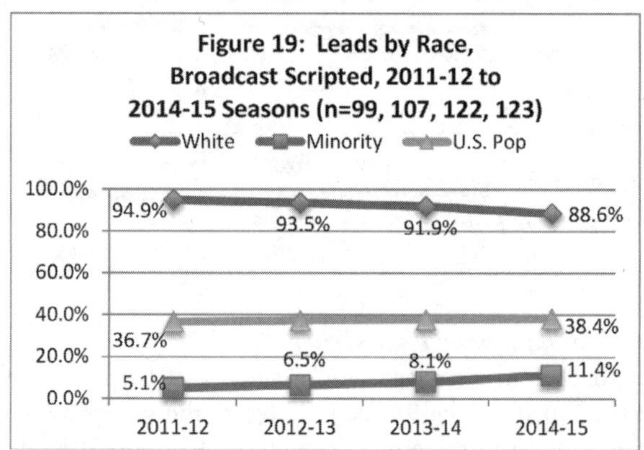


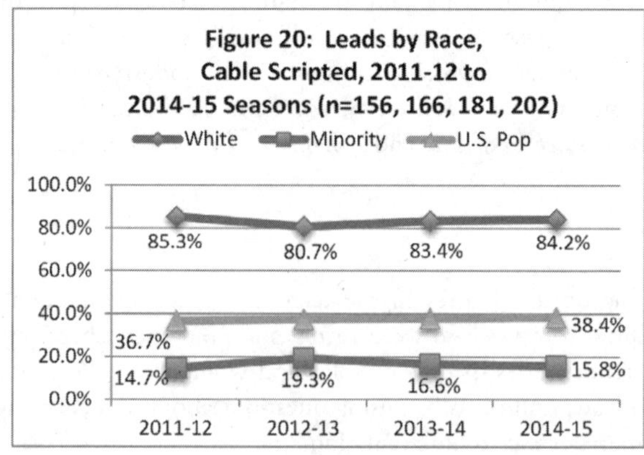

several cable networks market primarily to minority (or "urban") audiences. Still, minorities were underrepresented by a factor of more than 2 to 1 among cable scripted leads during the 2014–15 season. The following titles are among cable scripted shows that featured minority leads in 2014–15: *Being Mary Jane* (BET), *Devious Maids* (Lifetime), *From Dusk Till Dawn: The Series* (El Rey), *Ballers* (HBO), and *Power* (Starz).

**3. *Women Gain a Little Ground among Lead Roles in Broadcast Scripted Shows***

Women accounted for 38.2 percent of the lead roles in broadcast scripted shows during the 2014–15 season, up from the 35.8 percent figure the group posted for 2013–14 (see fig. 21). Earlier reports in this series document that women had approached proportionate representation among leads in the arena, before losing considerable ground relative to their male counterparts by 2013–14. The gains since the last report are relatively modest in light of the overall pattern charted in figure 21. Examples of broadcast scripted shows with women leads in 2014–15 include *2 Broke Girls* (CBS), *Grey's Anatomy* (ABC), *How to Get Away with Murder* (ABC), and *Jane the Virgin* (CW).

**4. *Women Gain a Little Ground among Leads in Cable Scripted Shows***

Figure 22 shows women accounted for 35.6 percent of the lead roles in cable-scripted shows in the 2014–15 season, up from the 33.2 percent share posted a season earlier.

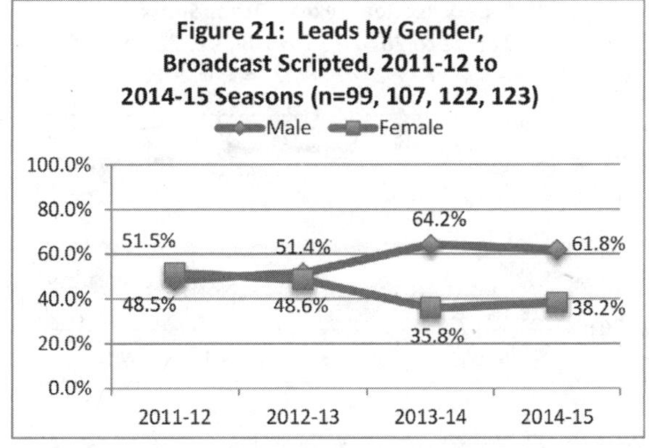


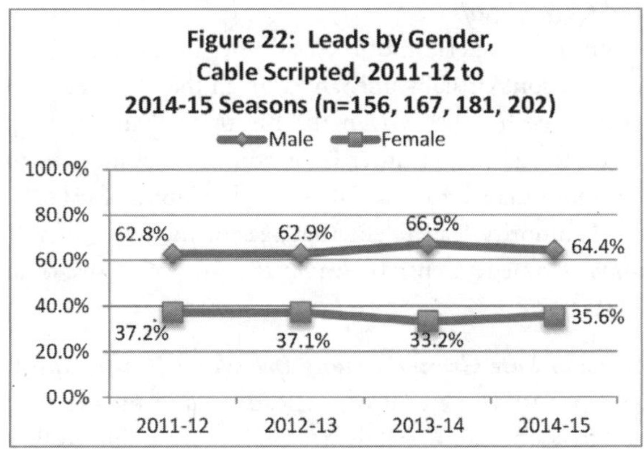

As in the previous report, women did only marginally better in the broadcast scripted arena than in the cable scripted arena, a notable change from the first two reports showing women fared much better as leads in broadcast. At a little more than half of the US population, women would have to increase their share of lead roles by about 15 percentage points in order to achieve proportionate representation in scripted cable television. Cable scripted shows featuring women as leads in 2014–15 include *Bates Motel* (A&E), *American Horror Story* (FX), *K.C. Undercover* (Disney), and *Veep* (HBO).

**5. *Minorities Gain Ground among Leads in Broadcast Reality and Other Shows***

Figure 23 shows minorities accounted for 24 percent of the broadcast reality and other leads during the 2014–15 season, up more than 7 percentage points from the 16.7 percent figure posted in 2013–14. Relative to their share of the population, minorities remained underrepresented in the arena, though the figure for the 2014–15 season was the highest on record. Broadcast reality and other shows that credited minorities as leads in 2014–15 include the following: *America's Got Talent* (NBC), *Tavis Smiley* (PBS), and *America's Next Top Model* (CW).

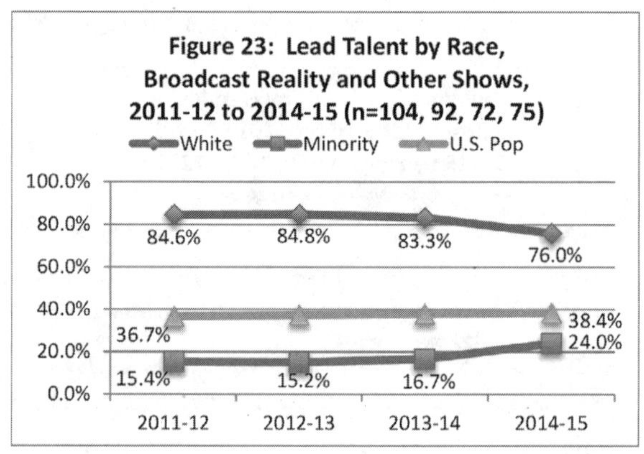


**6. *Minorities Remain Underrepresented by a Factor of More than 2 to 1 among Cable Reality and Other Leads***

Minority talent claimed 16.1 percent of the lead roles on cable reality and other shows during the 2014–15 season, virtually unchanged from the 15.9 percent share the group claimed in 2013–14 (see fig. 24). Given the minority share of the population, the minority share of cable reality and other leads still corresponded to underrepresentation by a factor of more than 2 to 1 in 2014–15. Examples of cable reality and other shows that featured minority lead talent that season include *Gabriel Iglesias Presents Stand-Up Revolution* (Comedy Central), *Iyanla Fix My Life* (OWN), and *Love & Hip Hop: Hollywood* (VH1).

**7. *Women Continue to Lose Ground among Broadcast Reality and Other Leads***

Women accounted for just 16 percent of the lead roles in broadcast reality and other shows during the 2014–15 season, nearly a 5 percentage-point decline from the 20.8

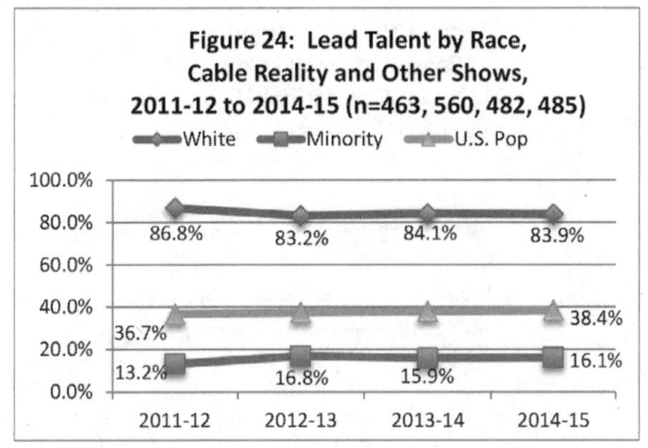


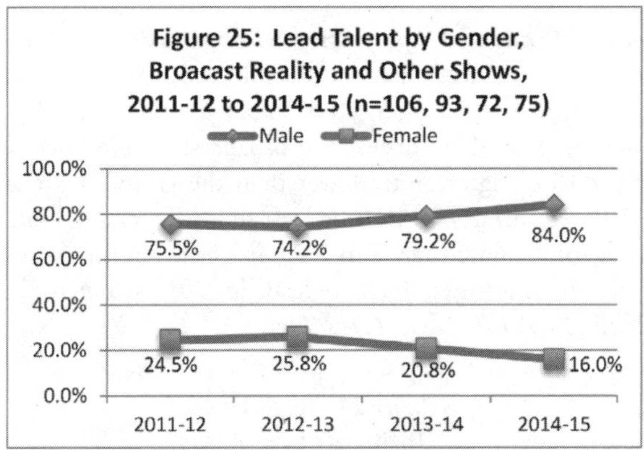


percent share the group posted in 2013–14 (see fig. 25). At a little more than half of the population, women were underrepresented by a factor of more than 3 to 1 among broadcast reality and other leads in 2014–15. Examples of broadcast reality and other shows that featured women leads that season include *20/20* (ABC), *America's Next Top Model* (CW), *The View* (ABC), and *The Talk* (CBS).

**8. *Women Continue to Lose Ground among Cable Reality and Other Leads***

Figure 26 shows a steady, downward trend in women's share of lead talent in cable reality and other programming. Women accounted for just 21.7 percent of the lead roles in this arena during the 2014–15 season, a 3.2 percentage-point decrease from the 24.9 percent share the group claimed during the 2013–14 season. Women would thus have to more than double their share of lead roles in cable reality and other programming in order to reach proportionate representation in this arena. The following titles are among the cable reality and other shows that credited women as leads in 2014–15: *Ellen's Design Challenge* (HGTV), *Little Women: LA* (Lifetime), *Girl Code* (MTV), and *Livin' Lozada* (OWN).

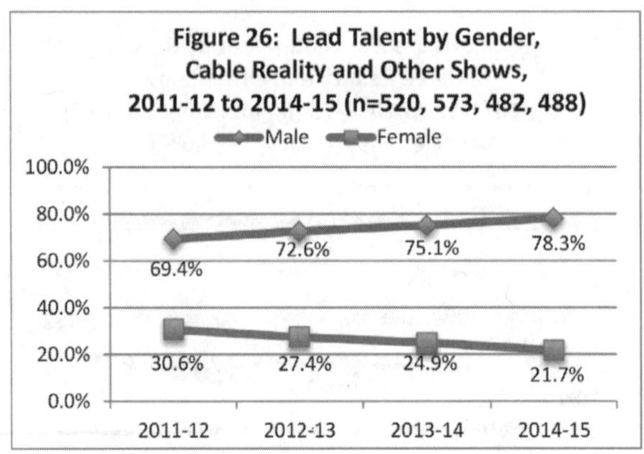


**9. *Minority Share of Leads on Digital Scripted Shows Mirrors Broadcast Scripted***

Figure 27 shows minorities accounted for just 11.1 percent of lead roles in digital scripted shows for the 2014–15 season, up from 9.1 percent in 2013–14. This figure is comparable to the minority share of leads in broadcast scripted programming for the season (11.4 percent) but significantly lower than the group's share in cable scripted programming (15.8 percent). As in the broadcast scripted arena, minorities were under-represented by a factor of more than 3 to 1 among leads on these shows. Examples of digital scripted shows that featured minority leads for 2014–15 include *Sense8* (Netflix), *East Los High* (Hulu), and *Club de Cuervos* (Netflix).

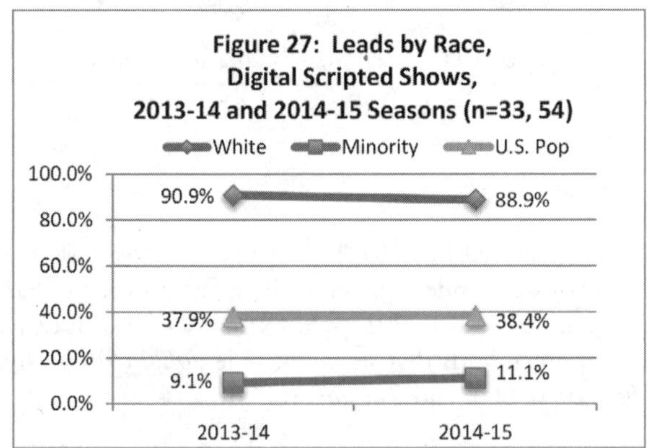


**10. *Women's Share of Digital Scripted Leads Stagnant***

Figure 28 shows women accounted for 35.2 percent of the lead roles in digital scripted programming during the 2014–15 season, virtually unchanged from a season earlier. The latest digital arena figure is nearly identical to 35.6 percent share the group posted in the cable scripted arena for the 2014–15 season. Examples of digital scripted shows that featured women leads that season include *Grace and Frankie* (Netflix), *Orange is the New Black* (Netflix), and *The Hotwives of Orlando* (Hulu).

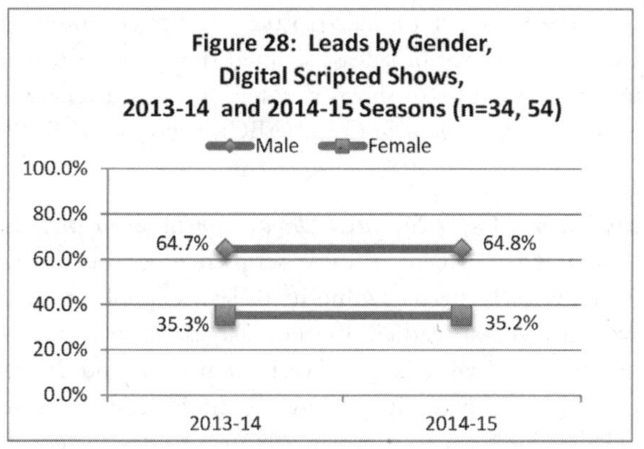


Overall Cast Diversity

**1. *Share of Majority-Minority Broadcast Scripted Shows More Than Doubles***

Overall cast diversity for broadcast scripted shows has increased a bit over the last two reports. Figure 29 illustrates that 26.8 percent of shows in the 2014–15 season had casts that were only 10 percent minority or less, down from 28.1 percent in 2013–14. Shows with casts that were from 11 percent to 20 percent minority became the plurality among the cast diversity intervals that season, 27.6 percent of all shows. Meanwhile, the share of majority-minority shows more than doubled since the last report, increasing from just 3.3 percent of all shows in 2013–14 to 8.9 percent in 2014–15. It's worth noting there were no majority-minority broadcast scripted shows as recently as the 2012–13 season. The diversity interval containing the 38.4 percent

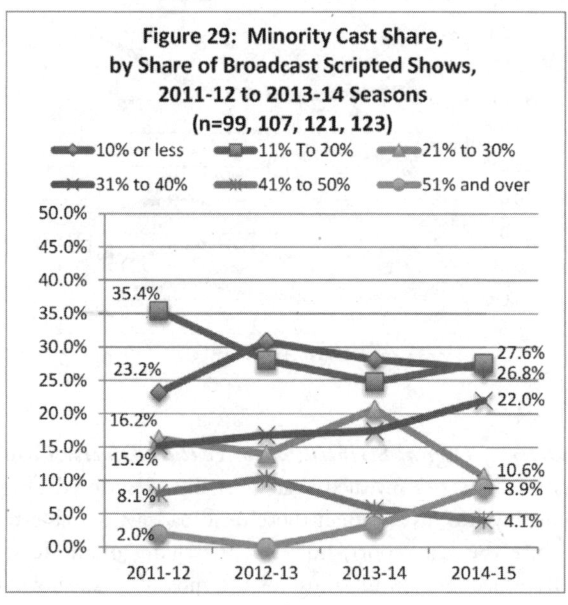

minority share of the US population in 2015 (i.e., 31 percent to 40 percent) also saw a notable increase in its share of broadcast scripted shows between reports, from 17.4 percent to 22 percent. Examples of shows that fell into this diversity interval in 2015 include *2 Broke Girls* (CBS), *American Crime* (ABC), *Chicago Fire* (NBC), *Bones* (Fox), and *The Flash* (CW).

**2. *Share of Least Diverse Cable Scripted Shows Continues to Increase***

Figure 30 shows that 45.1 percent of cable scripted programs during the 2014–15 season had casts that were 10 percent minority or less, a sizable increase from the 36.7 percent share evident a season earlier. The next largest share of the programs—17.8 percent—consisted of those with casts between 11 percent and 20 percent minority. Meanwhile, cable scripted shows with majority–minority casts increased only slightly, from 9 percent of all cable scripted shows in 2013–14 to 9.9 percent in 2014–15. The diversity interval containing the 38.4 percent minority share of the US population in 2015 (i.e., 31 percent to 40 percent) contained 9.4 percent of the shows in 2014–15, down from 13.6 percent of the total in 2013–14. Shows that fell into this latter interval in 2014–15 include *Fear the Walking Dead* (AMC), *Major Crimes* (TNT), *Suits* (USA), *Looking* (HBO), and *Jessie* (Disney).

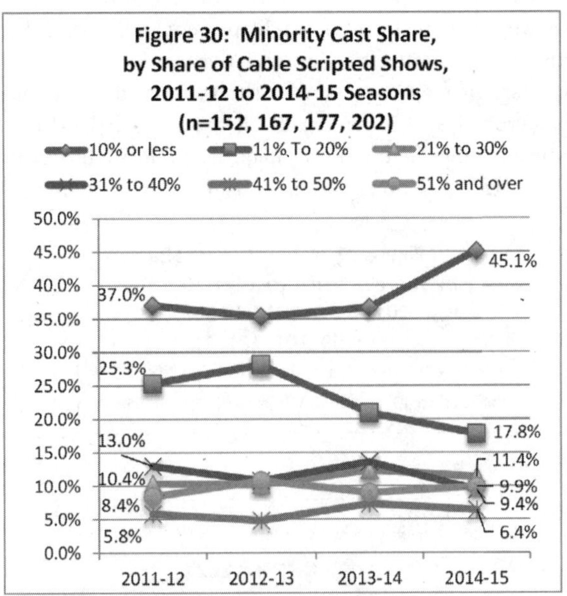


**3. *Nearly a Quarter of Digital Scripted Shows Feature Diverse Casts***

Previous reports in this series revealed that most digital scripted programs had casts that were considerably less diverse than those on broadcast or cable television. Figure 31 shows that since the last report, however, the shares of the least diverse digital scripted shows have declined, while those of the most diverse shows have increased.

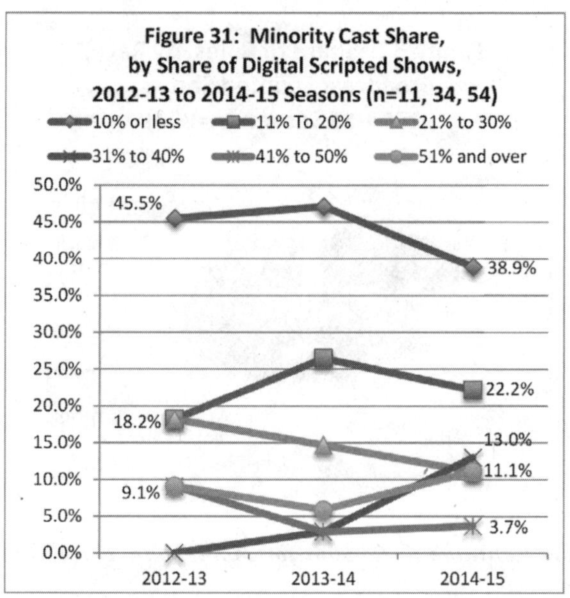


That is, only 38.9 percent of digital scripted shows featured casts that were 10 percent minority or less during the 2014–15 season, down from 47.1 percent a season earlier. While another 22.2 percent had casts that were only from 11 to 20 percent minority, this figure too was down from the 26.5 percent figure posted in 2013–14. By contrast, the share of majority-minority digital scripted shows nearly doubled since the last report—increasing from just 5.9 percent of the total in 2013–14 to 11.1 percent in 2014–15. Similarly, the share of digital scripted shows that fell into the diversity interval containing the minority share of the US population (i.e., 31 percent to 40 percent) nearly quadrupled between reports (from 2.9 percent to 13 percent). Shows that fell into this latter diversity interval in 2014–15 include *Orange Is the New Black* (Netflix), *Sense8* (Netflix), *and South Beach* (Hulu).

### 4. *Dominant White Share of Broadcast Scripted Roles Declines*

Figure 32 reveals white actors claimed 76 percent of the 806 roles examined in broadcast scripted programming during the 2014–15 season, down a bit from the 80 percent share the group posted a season earlier. Meanwhile, minorities combined for 24 percent of all roles, up from the 20 percent share evident in 2013–14. Minorities would have to increase their 2014–15 share of these roles by more than 50 percent to reach proportionate representation. Breakdowns for specific minority group shares that season include: black, 13 percent; Latino, 5 percent; Asian American, 4 percent; Native Americans, 0 percent; and mixed, 2 percent. Constituting nearly 18 percent of the US population in 2015, Latinos remained the most underrepresented among the minority groups, by a factor of more than 3 to 1.

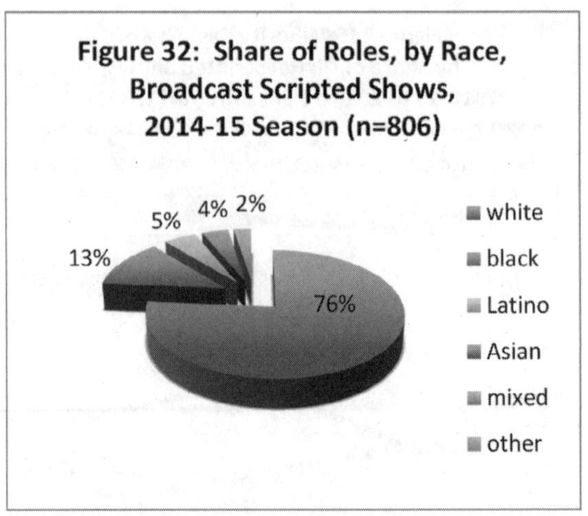


**5. *White Actors Continue to Account for More Than Three Quarters of Cable Scripted Roles***

Figure 33 presents the percentage distribution of cabled scripted roles by race during the 2014–15 season. It shows white actors claimed 79 percent of the 1141 cable scripted roles, while minorities combined for 21 percent. These white and minority shares were nearly identical to those documented in the previous report for the 2013–14 season. African American actors accounted for more than half of all minority roles in scripted cable shows in 2014–15. Claiming 11 percent of the roles in this arena, the group nearly matched its share of the US population. The shares of cable scripted roles claimed by other minority groups were similar to the small shares observed in broadcast scripted programming (4 percent for Latinos, 3 percent for Asian Americans, 3 percent for mixed actors, and 0 percent for Native Americans).[5]

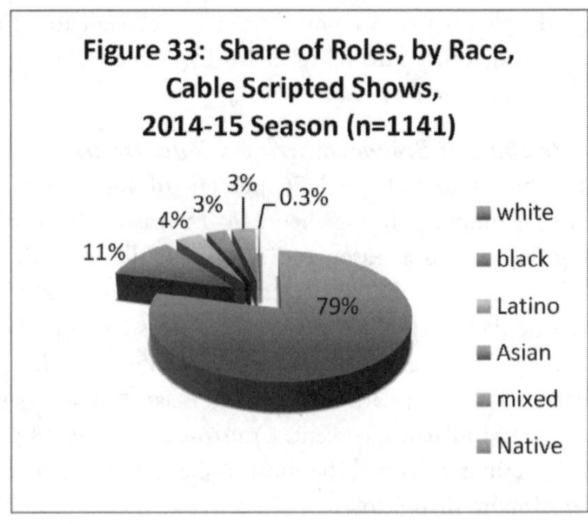

**6. *Male Actors Maintain Majority Share of Broadcast Scripted Roles***
Figure 34 shows male actors accounted for 57 percent of the 807 roles examined in broadcast scripted programming for the 2014–15 season, virtually matching the 56 percent share posted a season earlier. Women claimed 43 percent of the roles in 2014–15.

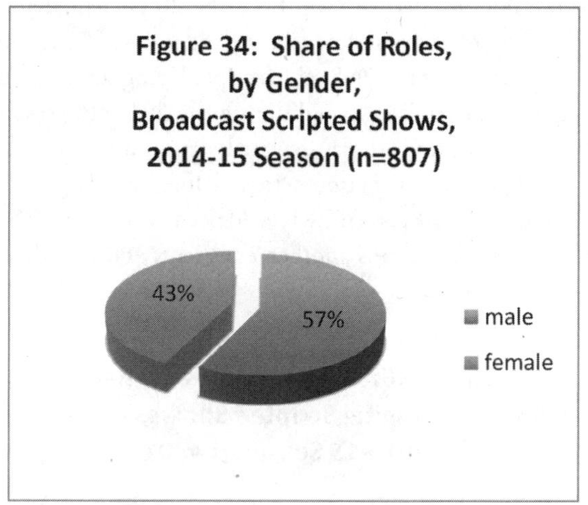


**7. *Male Actors Maintain Majority Share of Cable Scripted Roles***
As in previous reports, the advantage enjoyed by male actors continued to be more pronounced in the cable arena than it was in broadcast. Figure 35 shows male actors accounted for 59 percent of the 1141 roles examined in cable scripted programming for the 2014–15 season, exactly matching the figure from a season earlier. Women claimed just 41 percent of the roles.

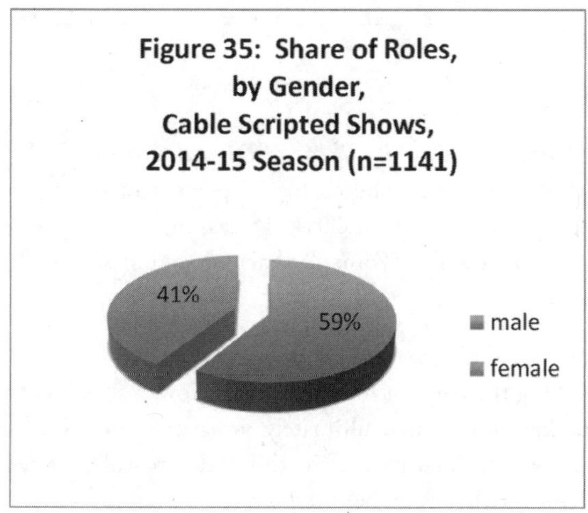

**8. *Minority Actors Increase Share of Digital Scripted Roles***

Figure 36 presents the percentage distribution of digital scripted roles by race during the 2014–15 season. It shows white actors claimed 74 percent of the 301 scripted roles examined in digital platform programming during the 2014–15 season, down from the 80 percent figure posted a season earlier. Accordingly, minorities combined for 26 percent of the roles in 2014–15, up from the 20 percent share they claimed in 2013–14. The white/minority breakdown in digital scripted programming is similar to that for both broadcast scripted and cable scripted programming, though minority actors fared slightly better overall in digital during the 2014–15 season. But the distribution of specific minority group shares deviated significantly from those observed in other arenas. In the digital arena, Latino actors claimed the largest share of the roles among the minority groups, 10 percent, while African Americans accounted for just 7 percent of the roles, Asian Americans another 7 percent, and mixed actors 2 percent.

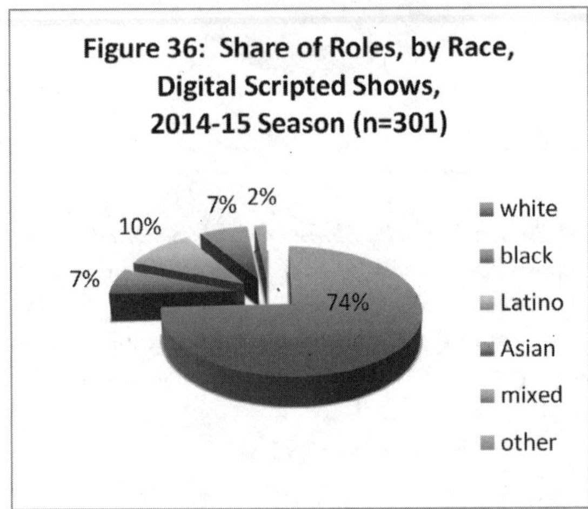


**9. *Male Actors Maintain Majority Share of Digital Scripted Roles***

Figure 37 shows male actors accounted for 57 percent of the 301 roles examined in digital scripted programming for the 2014–15 season, virtually identical to their 57.5 percent share a season earlier. Women's share of digital scripted roles in 2014–15 was 43 percent.

Show Creators

By successfully selling the concept for a television show, a show's creator sets in motion a host of production choices that ultimately impact the degree of diversity in writer staffing and casting. Previous reports in this series reveal that television's corps of creators have been overwhelming male and white.

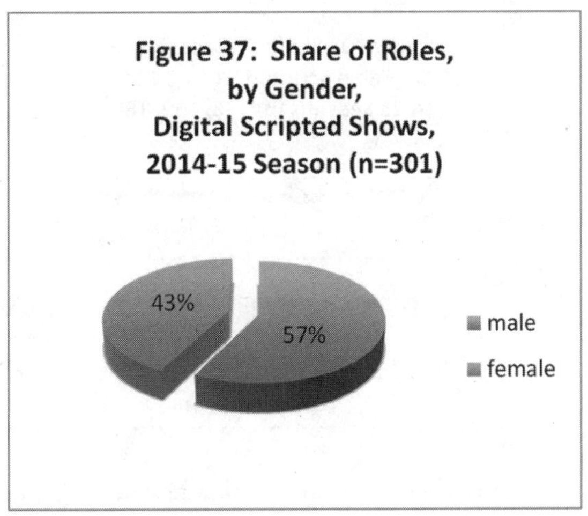


**1. *Minorities Gain among Creators[6] of Broadcast Scripted Shows***

Figure 38 reveals minorities were credited as creator for 8 percent of the broadcast scripted shows examined for the 2014–15 season, more than double the 3.3 percent share posted in 2013–14. Nonetheless, minorities were underrepresented by a factor of nearly 5 to 1 among the ranks of show creators in broadcast scripted programming that season. It's worth noting that six of the ten broadcast scripted shows with minority creators aired on a single network: *American Crime* (ABC), *Black-ish* (ABC), *Cristela* (ABC), *Grey's Anatomy* (ABC), *Scandal* (ABC), and *The Whispers* (ABC). The other four shows from 2014–15 with minority creators are *Sleepy Hollow* (Fox), *The Carmichael Show* (NBC), *The Millers* (CBS), and *The Mindy Project* (Fox).

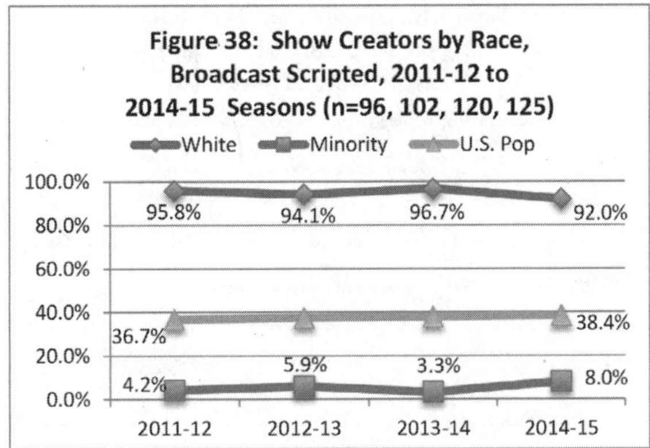


**2. *Minorities Tread Water among Creators of Cable Scripted Shows***

Minorities were credited as creator in just 7.5 percent of cable scripted shows for the 2014–15 season (see fig. 39), a figure virtually identical to the 7.8 percent share the group posted a season earlier. However, because the majority share of the US population

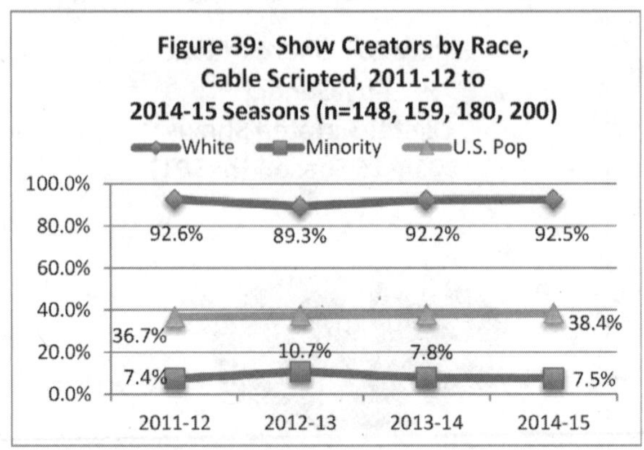


grew by about half a percentage point since the last report, the group's degree of underrepresentation among cable scripted creators also grew—to a factor of more than 5 to 1. Examples of cable scripted shows for which minorities were credited as show creator in 2014–15 include *Being Mary Jane* (BET), *Black Jesus* (Adult Swim), *The Haves and the Have Nots* (OWN), and *From Dusk Till Dawn: The Series* (El Rey).

### 3. *Minorities Tread Water among Creators of Digital Scripted Shows*

Minorities constituted 5.6 percent of the creators of digital scripted shows during the 2014–15 season (see fig. 40), nearly matching the share claimed by the group a season earlier (6.2 percent). As a result, minorities remained underrepresented by a factor of nearly 7 to 1 in this arena. Digital scripted shows with minority creators in 2014–15 include *East Los High* (Hulu) and *Club de Cuervos* (Netflix).

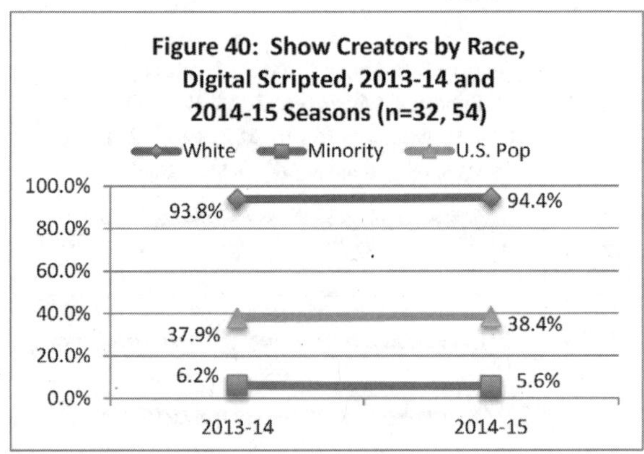


### 4. *Women Tread Water among Creators of Broadcast Scripted Shows*

Figure 41 shows that 22.4 percent of the creators of broadcast scripted shows were women during the 2014–15 season, which approximates the 21.5 percent figure posted a season earlier. As a result, women remained underrepresented among these important industry players by a factor of more than 2 to 1 for the 2014–15 season. Among

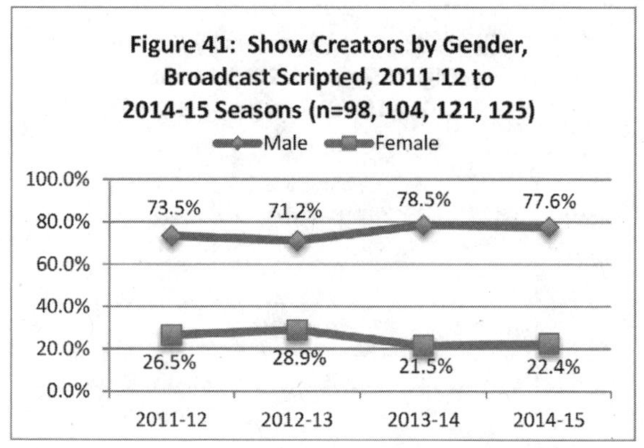


broadcast scripted shows that credited women as show creator in 2014–15 are the following: *Beauty and the Beast* (CW), *Grey's Anatomy* (ABC), *Scandal* (ABC), *New Girl* (Fox), and *The Mindy Project* (Fox).

**5. *Women Make Little Headway among Creators of Scripted Shows in Cable***

Women were credited as creator in 20.9 percent of cable scripted shows for the 2014–15 season, up slightly from the 18.2 percent share posted a season earlier but virtually unchanged from the share observed for the 2011–12 (see fig. 42). Underrepresented by a factor of more than 2 to 1, women were nearly as likely to create scripted shows in cable as they were in broadcast during the 2014–15 season. Among cable scripted shows that credited women as show creator in 2014–15 are the following titles: *The Missing* (Starz), *Finding Carter* (MTV), *Masters of Sex* (Showtime), *Girls* (HBO), and *Lost Girl* (Syfy).

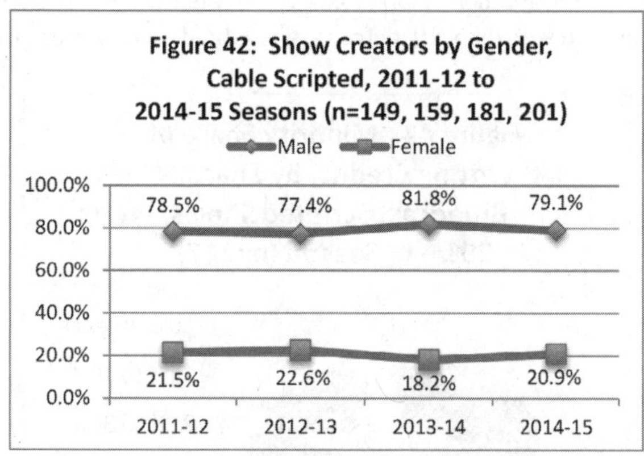


**6. *Women Post Gains among Creators of Digital Scripted Shows***

Figure 43 shows that 20.4 percent of the 54 digital scripted shows examined for the 2014–15 season were created by women, up from just 15.6 percent a season earlier.

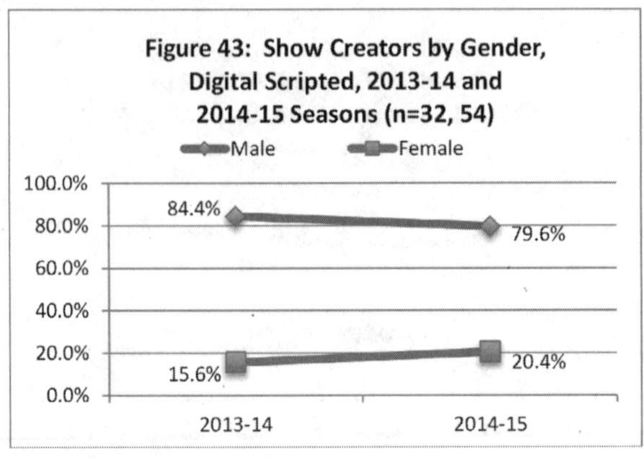


As a result, women were underrepresented by a factor of less than 3 to 1 in 2014–15. Examples of digital scripted shows created by women in that season include *Orange Is the New Black* (Netflix), *Grace and Frankie* (Netflix), *Transparent* (Amazon), and *Difficult People* (Hulu).

### TV Writers

Television is all about the storytelling, and this important process, of course, starts with the writing. One of the key takeaways from earlier reports in this series is that—more often than not—diverse writers' rooms are the ones that have diverse showrunners at the helm. But studies also have consistently found over the years that Hollywood's writing rooms are far from diverse.[7] Though there appears to be some movement on this front recently, data from the 2014–15 television season still echo these findings.

**1. *Minorities Gain Ground among Credited Writers for Broadcast Scripted Shows***

As figure 44 shows, for about half of broadcast scripted programs from the 2014–15 season (52 percent), fewer than 10 percent of credited writers were minorities. That

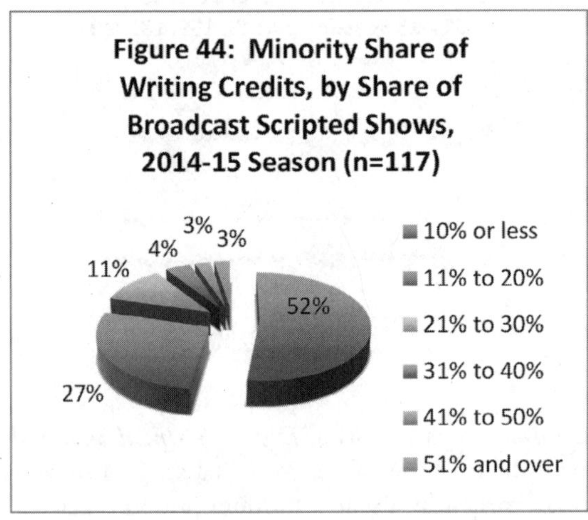

is, the share of shows with the fewest credited minority writers declined 9 percentage points since the last report, from 61 percent in the 2013–14 season. For the next largest share of shows, 27 percent, minorities constituted between 11 and 20 percent of the credited writers for the season. It is worth noting that for only 4 percent of the shows were minorities between 31 percent and 40 percent of the credited writers—the diversity interval containing the minority share of the population in 2015 (i.e., 38.4 percent). Three of the five shows in this latter interval aired on ABC, including *Revenge* (ABC), *Scandal* (ABC), and *Secrets & Lies* (ABC); the other two shows in the interval were *Criminal Minds* (CBS) and *Gracepoint* (Fox). Meanwhile, for 3 percent of the broadcast scripted shows from 2014–15, minorities constituted the majority of credited writers. There were no such shows in 2013–14. Shows in which a majority of credited writers were minority in 2014–15 include *American Crime* (ABC), *Empire* (Fox), and *Fresh Off the Boat* (ABC). The overall minority share of credited writers for broadcast scripted shows for 2014–15 was 13.4 percent, up nearly 4 percentage points from the 9.7 percent share minorities claimed the previous season. Minorities were underrepresented by a factor of nearly 3 to 1 among these writers, an improvement over previous seasons.

**2. *Minority Share of Credited Writers Remains 10 Percent or Less for Two Thirds of Cable Scripted Shows***

Figure 45 shows that for 66 percent of cable scripted shows from the 2014–15 season, the minority share of credited writers was 10 percent or less. This figure is virtually unchanged from the previous season. By contrast, the minority share of credited writers was more than 50 percent for only 5 percent of the cable shows that season, a figure that also approximates the one from a season earlier (4 percent). The 5 percent share of cable scripted shows for which minorities constituted the majority of credited writers, of course, largely mirrored those with minority show creators and majority-minority casts in 2014–15. Indeed, all but two of the shows for which the majority of credited writers were minorities were black-oriented sitcoms and dramas airing on networks that cater to significant African American audiences. These latter shows include *Being Mary*

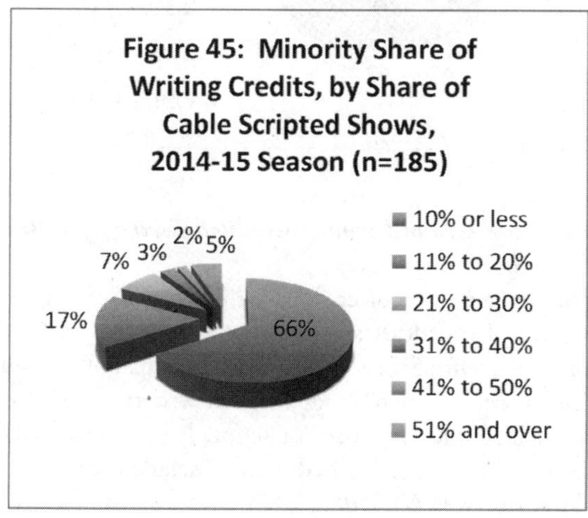

*Jane* (BET), *Real Husbands of Hollywood* (BET), *The Haves and the Have Nots* (OWN), and *Tyler Perry's For Better or Worse* (OWN).

The overall minority share of credited writers for cable scripted shows in 2014–15 was 10.6 percent, up a bit from 9.1 percent the previous season. As a result, minorities were underrepresented in this arena by a factor of more than 3 to 1.

**3. *Minorities Gain a Little Ground among Credited Writers for Digital Scripted Shows***

As figure 46 illustrates, the minority share of credited writers was 10 percent or less for 73 percent of digital scripted shows in 2014–15, which was unchanged from a season earlier. Meanwhile, for 15 percent of digital scripted shows from 2014–15, between 11 and 20 percent of credited writers were minorities. The remaining 12 percent of digital scripted shows featured corps of credited writers that were more diverse. These shows included the following: *Club de Cuervos* (Netflix), *Blue* (Hulu), and *East Los High* (Hulu). The overall minority share of credited writers for digital scripted shows in 2014–15 was 10.8 percent, up 2 percentage points from the 8.8 percent figure a season earlier. As a result, minorities were underrepresented by a factor of more than 3 to 1 in this arena.

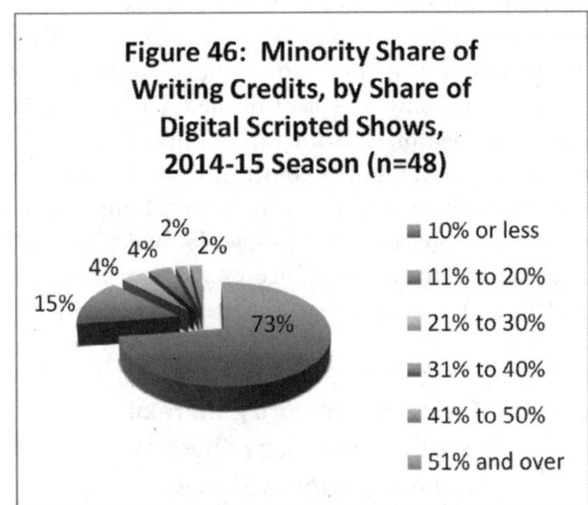


**4. *Women Gain a Little Ground among Credited Writers for Broadcast Scripted Shows***

Figure 47 shows the female share of credited writers was between 31 percent and 40 percent for 26 percent of broadcast scripted shows in 2014–15, between 41 percent and 50 percent for 17 percent of the shows, and greater than 50 percent for 17 percent of the shows. Women were 10 percent of credited writers or less for only 8 percent of shows that season. Examples of broadcast scripted shows from 2014–15 for which women constituted the majority of credited writers include the following: *2 Broke Girls* (CBS), *Jane the Virgin* (CW), *Nashville* (ABC), and *The Middle* (ABC). The overall

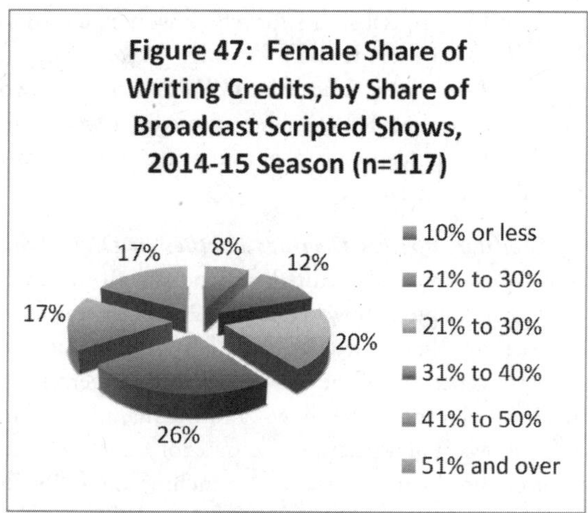

**Figure 47: Female Share of Writing Credits, by Share of Broadcast Scripted Shows, 2014-15 Season (n=117)**

female share of credited writers for broadcast scripted shows in 2014–15 was 35.9 percent, up more than 3 percentage points from the 32.5 percent figure observed for 2013–14. By contrast, you will recall, women were credited as writer for only 13 percent of the theatrical films released in 2015 and 9.2 percent of the films released in 2014.

**5. *Writing Credits Remain Less Gender Diverse in Cable Than in Broadcast***

The female share of credited writers was greater than 30 percent for about 42 percent of cable scripted shows in the 2014–15 season (see fig. 48)—a figure that matches the one from the previous two reports and that is considerably lower than the 50 percent share of shows for which this was true in the broadcast scripted arena in 2014–15. That is, women were between 31 percent and 40 percent of the credited writers on 16 percent of the shows in 2014–15, between 41 percent and 50 percent of the credited writers for 14 percent of the shows, and the majority of the credited writers for just 12 percent of

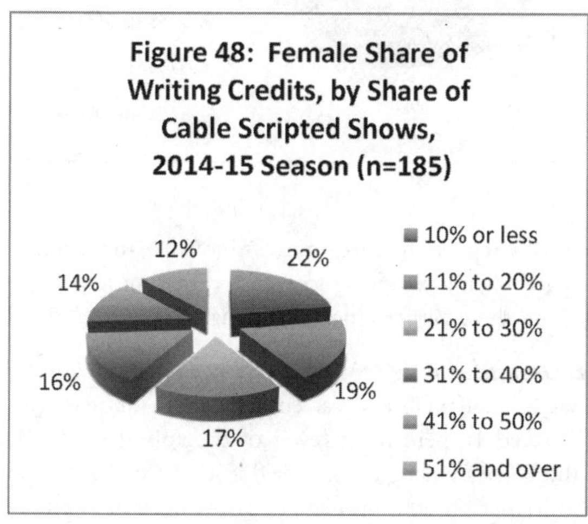

**Figure 48: Female Share of Writing Credits, by Share of Cable Scripted Shows, 2014-15 Season (n=185)**

the shows. Examples of cable scripted shows for which women constituted the majority of credited writers in 2014–15 include the following: *Masters of Sex* (Showtime), *Hot in Cleveland* (TV Land), *Being Mary Jane* (BET), *Nurse Jackie* (Showtime), and *Pretty Little Liars* (Freeform). The overall female share of credited writers for cable scripted shows in 2014–15 was 30.6 percent, up 3 percentage points from the 27.6 percent figure the group posted a season earlier.

**6. *Female Share of Credited Writers Declines Further in Digital Scripted Shows***
Figure 49 shows the female share of credited writers was greater than 30 percent for only 32 percent of digital scripted shows from the 2014–15 season, down from 46.2 percent the previous season. That is, women were between 31 percent and 40 percent of the credited writers for 6 percent of the shows, between 41 percent and 50 percent of the credited writers for 13 percent of the shows, and the majority of the credited writers for 13 percent of the shows. Digital scripted shows for which women writers constituted the majority of credited writers that season include the following: *Orange Is the New Black* (Netflix), *The Hotwives of Orlando* (Hulu), and *Grace and Frankie* (Netflix). The overall female share of credited writers for digital scripted shows in 2014–15 was 27.3 percent, down slightly from 28.1 percent in 2013–14 and lower than the shares posted in either the broadcast scripted or cable scripted arenas in 2014–15.

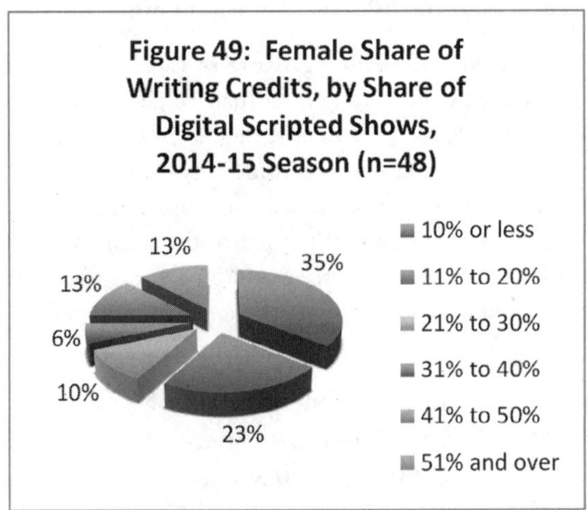


## TV Directors

As noted in the previous reports in this series, minorities and women have faced an uphill battle in the past when attempting to secure directing jobs in television. Below we update findings from these earlier reports by considering the 2014–15 season.

**1. *Minorities Gain Ground among Directors of Broadcast Scripted Shows***
Figure 50 shows that for half of broadcast comedies and dramas from the 2014–15 season, minorities directed 10 percent or fewer of the episodes. This is a considerable improvement over the 68 percent figure observed a season earlier. By contrast, minorities directed between 31 percent and 40 percent of the episodes—the diversity interval

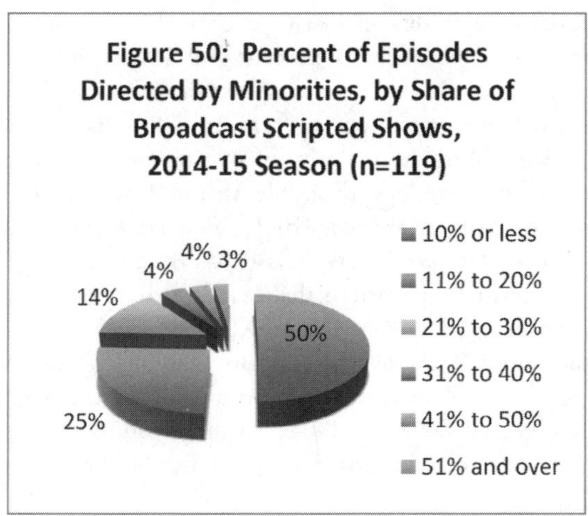


containing the 38.4 percent minority share of the US population in 2015—for only 4 percent of broadcast scripted shows, which is unchanged from 2013–14. Examples of shows in this interval include *Grey's Anatomy* (ABC), *The Mentalist* (CBS), *Last Man Standing* (ABC), and *Bad Judge* (NBC). For 3 percent of the shows in 2014–15, minorities directed the majority of the episodes, up from no shows a season earlier. Examples of these shows include *American Crime* (ABC) and *Empire* (Fox). The overall minority share of directors for broadcast scripted shows in 2014–15 was 13.9 percent, up more than 5 percentage points from the 8.6 percent figure observed a season earlier. Nonetheless, minorities were underrepresented by a factor of nearly 3 to 1 among the directors of broadcast scripted shows in 2014–15.

**2. *Minority Directors Remain Concentrated on Minority-Oriented Shows in Cable***

Figure 51 shows that for 70 percent of the cable scripted shows during the 2014–15 season, minorities directed 10 percent or fewer of the episodes. By contrast, minorities

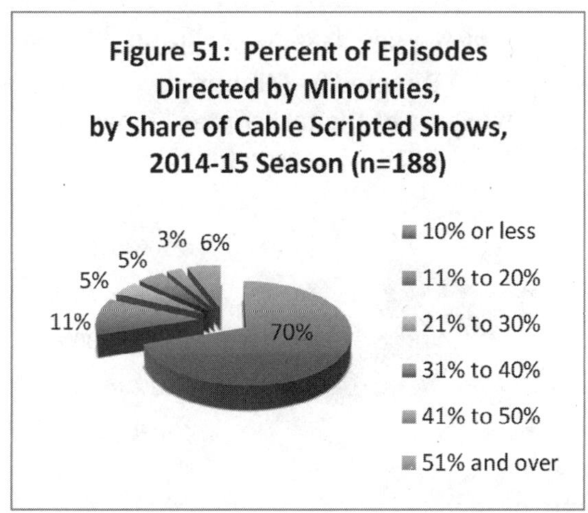

directed the majority of episodes on just 6 percent of the shows—an increase over the previous season—and between 41 percent and 50 percent of the episodes for only 3 percent of the shows. It's worth noting that the cable scripted shows for which minorities directed the majority of episodes in 2014–15—like those observed above for which minorities received the majority of writing credits—were typically black-oriented shows airing on networks with sizable African American audiences. Examples of these shows include *Being Mary Jane* (BET), *Real Husbands of Hollywood* (BET), *The Game* (BET), *The Haves and Have Nots* (OWN), and *Tyler Perry's For Better or Worse* (TBS). Exceptions to this pattern that season were *From Dusk Till Dawn: The Series* (El Rey Network) and *Lab Rats* (Disney XD), for which minorities also directed the majority of the episodes. The overall minority share of directors for cable scripted shows in 2014–15 was 13.4 percent, up more than 4 percentage points from the 9.1 percent figure observed for 2013–14. As in the broadcast arena, minorities were underrepresented by a factor of nearly 3 to 1 among the directors of cable scripted shows in 2014–15.

### 3. *Minorities Gain among Directors of Digital Scripted Shows*

Minorities directed 10 percent or fewer of the episodes on 74 percent of digital scripted shows in 2014–15 (see fig. 52). This is a considerable improvement over the 88 percent figure observed a season earlier. Similarly, minorities directed a majority of the episodes for 8 percent of digital scripted shows in 2014–15, which exceeded their corresponding shares in either the broadcast or cable arenas for the season. Digital scripted shows for which minorities directed more than half the episodes in 2014–15 include the following: *Blue* (Hulu), *Club de Cuervos* (Netflix), *East Los High* (Hulu), and *Narcos* (Netflix). The overall minority share of directors for digital scripted shows in 2014–15 was 12 percent, a significant increase over the 3.4 percent share claimed by the group in 2013–14. As a result, minorities were underrepresented in this arena by a factor of more than 3 to 1 in 2014–15.

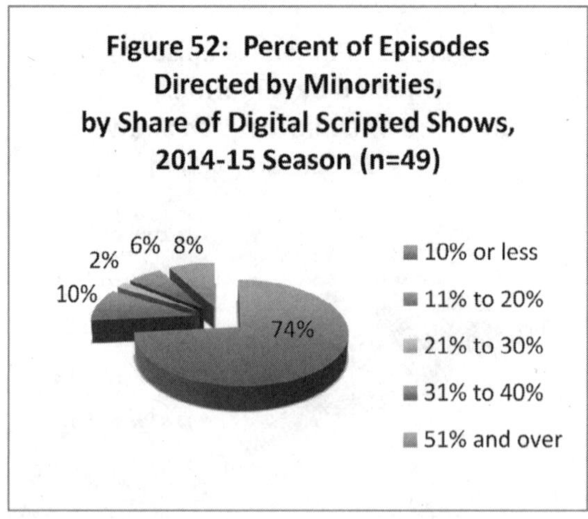

Figure 52: Percent of Episodes Directed by Minorities, by Share of Digital Scripted Shows, 2014-15 Season (n=49)

### 4. *Women Gain among Directors of Broadcast Scripted Shows*

While previous studies document that women have had a harder time securing directing employment in television than their male counterparts,[8] their directorial prospects in television have far exceeded those in theatrical film. This trend continued in 2014–15. Recall that women directed only 7.7 percent of the films examined in 2015, up from the paltry 4.3 percent share observed for 2014 films. Figure 53 shows that for the 2014–15 season, women directed 10 percent or fewer of the episodes for 43 percent of broadcast scripted shows—a sizable improvement over the 57 percent figure from a season earlier—and between 11 and 20 percent of the episodes for 27 percent of the shows. Meanwhile, women directed more than 20 percent of episodes that season for 30 percent of broadcast scripted shows, which includes the majority of episodes for six shows: *Call the Midwife* (PBS), *American Crime* (ABC), *The Middle* (ABC), *Jane the Virgin* (CW), *The McCarthys* (CBS), and *Downton Abbey* (PBS). The overall female share of directors for broadcast scripted shows in 2014–15 was 17.1 percent, up considerably from their 12.5 percent share for 2013–14. As a result, women were underrepresented among the directors of broadcast scripted shows by a factor of about 3 to 1 in 2014–15.

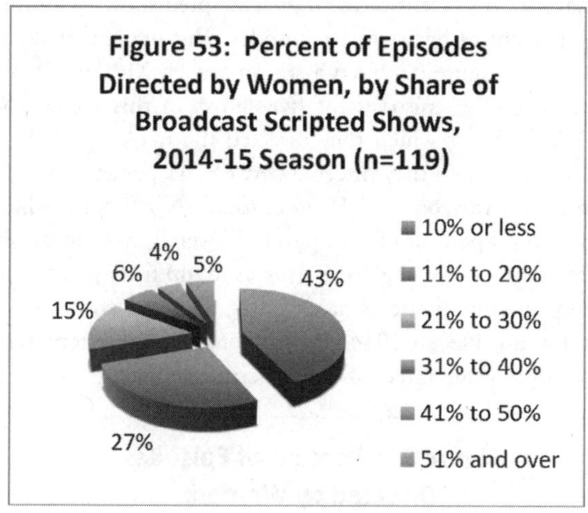


### 5. *Women TV Directors Continue to Fare Worse in Cable than in Broadcast*

Figure 54 shows that for 55 percent of the cable scripted shows examined in 2014–15, women directed 10 percent or fewer of the episodes. This is an improvement over the 62 percent figure observed for 2013–14. Meanwhile, women directed the majority of the episodes for just 2 percent of the cable scripted shows examined in 2014–15, unchanged from a season earlier. Examples of these shows include *Veep* (HBO), *Married* (FX), and *Austin & Ally* (Disney). The overall female share of directors for cable scripted shows in 2014–15 was 12.4 percent, up a bit from the 10.9 percent posted in 2013–14. For the 2014–15 season, women were underrepresented among the ranks of cable scripted directors by a factor of more than 4 to 1.

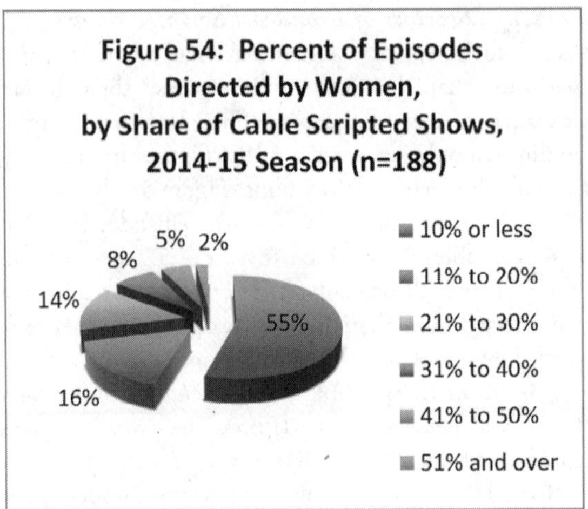


**6. *Women TV Directors Continue to Fare Worst in Digital, Despite Gains***

Figure 55 shows that for 74 percent of the digital scripted shows examined in 2014–15, women directed 10 percent or fewer of the episodes. This figure actually compares unfavorably to the 64 percent figure observed a season earlier. Meanwhile, women directed more than 30 percent of the episodes for five shows in this arena—*Sense8* (Netflix) and *Transparent* (Amazon), for which they directed the majority of the episodes; *High Maintenance* (Vimeo), for which they directed between 41 percent and 50 percent of the episodes; and *Good Work* (Amazon) and *House of Cards* (Netflix), for which they directed between 31 percent and 40 percent of the episodes. Overall, women directed 9.1 percent of the digital scripted episodes for the 2014–15 season, up from just 5.6 percent a season earlier. Despite the gain, this figure remains lower than the corresponding figures for women in broadcast and cable. In 2014–15, women were underrepresented by a factor of more than 5 to 1 among the ranks of digital scripted directors.

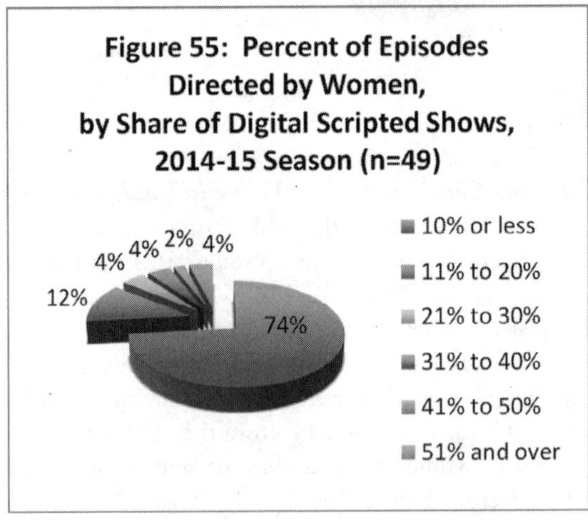

### Summary

Table 2 summarizes the various film and television arenas examined for 2014–15 (e.g., lead roles, director, writer, and show creators) by degree of underrepresentation for minorities and women (see Appendix). It shows that across all arenas, for both minorities and women, pronounced underrepresentation is still the norm. Minorities gained a little ground among film leads, broadcast scripted leads, broadcast reality and other leads, digital scripted leads, and broadcast scripted show creators. They lost ground among film directors, film writers, cable scripted leads, and digital scripted show creators. They held their ground among cable scripted show creators and cable reality and other leads.

Meanwhile, women posted gains in all areas except two—broadcast reality and other leads and cable reality and other leads. Still, they too remained underrepresented on every front in 2014–15.

## NOTES

Reprinted with permission from Darnell Hunt, Ana Christina Ramón, Michael Tran, Amberia Sargent, and Vanessa Díaz (Los Angeles: Ralph J. Bunche Center on African American Studies at UCLA, 2017), https://bunchecenter.ucla.edu/wp-content/uploads/sites/82/2017/04/2017-Hollywood-Diversity-Report-2-21-17.pdf/.

1. These films included the top 200 theatrical 2015, ranked by worldwide box office, minus foreign films.

2. The 2014–15 season is defined as television programming that originally aired between September 1, 2014 and August 31, 2015.

3. Total numbers for the various analyses in this report may deviate from the overall total for the number of films or television shows considered due to focused analyses on a subset of the data (noted below) or missing values for some cases (e.g., many reality shows do not identify a cast, directors, or writers).

4. Household ratings (HH) are defined as the percentage of the universe of households tuned to a particular TV program during the average minute of the program. This includes incremental viewing to programs watched at the time of the telecast as well as watched in DVR playback that occurs within seven days of the original telecast. The HH ratings presented by race are based on the race of the head of household, while 18–49 ratings are based on individual viewers. Social media ratings consist of tweets and unique authors, which are measures of relevant US Twitter activity from three hours before through three hours after a broadcast, local time. "Tweets" are ascribed to a linear TV episode, while "unique authors" refer to unique Twitter accounts that have sent at least one tweet ascribed to a specific TV episode.

5. Theatrical Market Statistics: 2014, MPAA (2014), p.2.

6. These figures include films that received any domestic box office in a given year. Ibid, p. 19.

7. Ibid., pp. 12–13

8. Genres were derived from the keywords *The Studio System* identified for each film.

# CRITICAL REFLECTIONS ON 4/29/1992 AND BEYOND

## A UCLA School of Law Roundtable

DEVON CARBADO, CHERYL I. HARRIS, JERRY KANG,
SAÚL SARABIA

Jerry Kang (JK): It's hard to believe that it's been almost twenty years since what Koreans call Sa-I-Gu—4/29—when Los Angeles burned, and I'm excited about being able to have a conversation with some of my closest colleagues on the two decades having passed. Let me introduce my guests and then we'll start the conversation. We have Devon Carbado, who's a professor of law at UCLA. We have Cheryl Harris, who's also professor of law, and the Rosalinde and Arthur Gilbert Professor of Civil Liberties and Civil Rights. We have Saúl Sarabia, who is the program director of the Critical Race Studies (CRS) concentration at UCLA and also a lecturer in law. I'm Jerry Kang, professor of law with also a courtesy appointment in the department of Asian American Studies. I am also the inaugural chair of the *Korea Times/Hankook Ilbo* Chair in Korean American Studies.

We're all good friends and scholars working on race, and the goal here is to think hard about what we remember about Sa-I-Gu and what has happened in the past twenty years. I think it would be interesting to start off just by remembering where we

Devon Carbado is professor of law at the UCLA School of Law and recently served as Vice Dean of the Faculty. Former director of the Critical Race Studies Program at UCLA Law, Carbado has published in critical race theory, employment discrimination, criminal procedure, constitutional law, and identity, and is co-editor of *Race Law Stories*. Cheryl I. Harris is Rosalinde and Arthur Gilbert Professor of Civil Rights and Civil Liberties at the UCLA School of Law. Teaching in the areas of constitutional law, civil rights, employment discrimination, and critical race theory, Harris is well known for her influential writings in Critical Race Theory, particularly the widely cited piece "Whiteness as Property." Jerry Kang is professor of law at the UCLA School of Law and holds the inaugural *Korea Times/Hankook Ilbo* Chair in Korean American Studies in the UCLA Asian American Studies Department. Kang specializes in civil procedure, critical race studies, and communications law. He is the author of numerous influential articles on various subjects, including implicit bias, and Asian American jurisprudence. He is the author of *Communications Law and Policy: Cases and Materials* (4th ed., 2012) and co-author of *Race, Rights, and Reparation: The Law and the Japanese American Internment* (2001). Saúl Sarabia focuses on community-based social justice advocacy, strategizing with community residents to include their voice in law-making and public policy reform. He served as the director of the Critical Race Studies Program at the UCLA School of Law from 2005–12, teaching Critical Race Theory and Latinos/as and the Law.

were. There are certain moments in American history about which you can ask people "Where were you?"—for example, when JFK was shot, when Lennon died, maybe when Michael Jackson passed away. So what happened to you and your life when Los Angeles burned on April 29th 1992? What do you remember of it, if anything? Devon, tell us your story to begin.

Devon Carbado (DC): I was in law school at the time, my first year of law school, so I actually remember the moment quite well and [how] it felt from a distance; I was back east. But in some ways, it also felt near because I had lived in the area where all this occurred, which is to say, the West Adams district of Los Angeles on 23rd Street—so think of where Arlington intersects with Adams and that's basically where I had lived prior to attending law school. And for people who don't know Los Angeles, that's probably five or six blocks south of Koreatown, I think.

So in some sense I was far. In another sense, it was near because I was about to return literally to that scene three weeks later, and in fact did and remember that it felt kind of like a war zone, or at least how I imagine a war zone might feel, since I've never been in one. I don't mean to suggest that it was therefore race war, but the scene, the aftermath, felt like something really big had happened—and physical destruction was everywhere.

The only other thing I would say is that it happened at the time that I was taking criminal law. As you might imagine, then, the event figured prominently in our discussions and provided a very concrete way for the class to explore the intersection of race and policing, particularly in the context of urban space.

JK: Let's go around and just get a sense of where we were geographically and what was our psyche at the time. Then we can probe deeper. Cheryl?

Cheryl Harris (CH): I was living in Chicago and I had just started teaching law two years before. So I guess I would say that it did feel very distant. I had no connections to Los Angeles at the time really. I had family here, but had not visited them in a long time and didn't really have an understanding of Los Angeles as a space.

But I will say that from the vantage point of what I could see, there was just a huge sort of [what] I would call double disjuncture. So the first thing was that I could not understand how the jury had acquitted the LAPD officers who beat Rodney King. What I had seen leading up to the trial was simply the tape of his beating and the fact that the jury had acquitted them seemed to just be a radical disjuncture, a sort of complete mismatch between the picture and the story. Right? . . . Speaking of criminal law, you think about evidence; the evidence of the tape itself was evidence of a crime and the fact that these police officers had been acquitted, I mean, I wasn't naive. I'd certainly been around long enough to see police officers be acquitted before in circumstances where the evidence dictated otherwise, but this seemed to have been just a complete sort of disjuncture between the picture and the story.

When the unrest started, the other thing that was sort of a complete shock to me was another kind of disjuncture between the picture and the story. So the picture was basically of a multiracial civil unrest. Meaning, I was looking at pictures of Latino people, of black people sort of pouring in and out of neighborhoods. They were on fire and the story was all about a sort of black-Korean race war. So it was a very confusing moment for me trying to understand how this picture that was actually up on the screen was mapping on to the story. It was clear to me that there was a lot more going on than the story that was being told, but I couldn't make sense of it from where I was. I didn't actually come to Los Angeles until two years later when some of the debris had been cleared away and there was indeed this narrative of a black-Korean race war that had sort of mapped on to what I have subsequently come to learn was a far more complicated picture.

JK: Sure, and just that topic, the way you framed it—about the picture we see mediated through video cameras, through broadcast versus the underlying reality—and when it matches and when it doesn't is something that we definitely will talk about more.

CH: Yeah, and just to mention the other thing was, I remember in particular there was one juror from the trial that was interviewed who kept saying race had nothing to do with it. This was all about whether or not the police are able to use reasonable force. Race has nothing to do with it. So it was again just sort of complete mismatch between the picture and the story.

JK: It was surreal in all kinds of ways and the war zone aspect of it made it seem surreal. I think we're, without intention, moving geographically from the east to the west . . .

Saúl Sarabia (SS): That's right. I was actually here at UCLA, where we are doing this filming. I was a student in my fourth year and it is actually interesting to hear the story of someone who was as far east as Devon and in the middle of the country [as Cheryl] say they felt distant yet close, because I was in West LA and felt like I could've been on the east coast when it all happened. And really, it's such an LA story, because the images that I have of the immediate aftermath once it became obvious that there was some civil unrest happening are the images mediated by cars and television. TV and cars, they're the things I remember the most of that first evening.

The campus was shut down early and people were asked to make their way home and, at that time, the initial flashpoint was Florence and Normandie, which was obviously south of Koreatown and closer to the heart of South LA, but not quite as south as Watts. It kept creating enough anxiety that the university issued this notice to people to go home. I was at that time a staff member for one of the minority student publications on campus, which actually meant that the space in which I was engaging as a student was this multiracial, progressive, youthful space, working alongside the future leaders from various communities. We were watching this happen, also not surprised entirely by the larger dynamic of the legal system declaring the innocence of police officer[s] accused of brutality against a person of color, but certainly by the extremity of the verdict and the extremity of what was happening on the streets to know something big was happening.

By the time I made it through central campus to the central parking lot, all the cars were stuck; they couldn't go anywhere because so many people were trying to leave at the same time. So I was happy to be on foot because the talking heads that were on the campus televisions suggested that there was this imminent threat that was spreading everywhere and this was why people needed to go home. Of course, I lived in the apartments not too far from the campus. By the time I made it there, dark had come down on the city and it was clear that we were not going to be allowed to move around freely. There was talk already about bringing in the National Guard. That didn't happen until the next day. I don't remember if classes were canceled, but I do remember that we moved freely on the campus the next day and, by dusk the second day, there were tanks here in Westwood.

JK: Really . . .

SS: Primarily around the shops in Westwood, obviously prepared for any kind of potential move westward. And the thing that struck me the most about my experience at that point of what was happening in the city in which I grew up was that if I wanted to be with my people or go further east . . . I couldn't, I was being locked into the Westside. For folks who are not from LA, UCLA is in West LA, basically between Bel Air and Beverly Hills, and that's where I was, ironically, watching all this happen.

What I remember staying with me the most that second night was the image of the tanks in Westwood, which was cleared out and where there was nothing going on. If anyone was going to dare to threaten those shops, they were going to have no luck. But then coming home and watching all these Korean American merchants and their children and their neighbors having to protect themselves from what was happening with the fires and the looting, I was wondering, "How could it be that there's nothing going on here and we have full protection and these people are unprotected by the state?"

I also remember the image of having students who are not from LA huddled in their living rooms, literally locked down by what the news was telling them was this imminent threat, people with maps mapping out the next fire that was being reported. This was not just a multiracial unrest, but also that it was actually [happening in] multiple locations. It quickly spread out of Florence and Normandie, and yet the story on the news was still this narrative of "this is some version of Watts and the rest of the city." Yet people were sitting there with maps wondering whether the fires were getting close enough to them to be scared.

JK: I'm struck by, as you describe it, how different the underlying communication technologies were back then, right? So as you're walking to the parking lot, you're not checking your smart phone then . . .

SS: No.

JK: That's not what we had at the time. People now would be mashing up Google maps with news reports trying to figure out where the fires are . . .

DC: No tweets.

JK: No tweets, which raises interesting questions, like how information travels and the rise of social media. Consider their impact, if it happened all over again. Would people have a different account of it from different kinds of first-person perspectives?

As for me, I wasn't even teaching here, so I'm with Devon out in Cambridge on the east coast. So this is what I remember—and I have generally a poor memory, but certain things stand out very, very powerfully. I was in Cambridge. I remember distinctly I was working in the *Harvard Law Review* office. It's in a separate building, Gannett House, and in that building there was a small black-and-white television set in the lounge for the editors. I remember my eyes being glued to the TV set, seeing what I thought was completely surreal? So it's a war zone. I can't believe this is happening—how can you see the cops beating the hell out of this guy no matter what he did, how could you go that medieval on a person, and then not be held accountable? And then to witness the reaction, what was in some ways predictable, and then to see that there were no police or no security to help them.

I was transfixed. I want to share, I guess, something a little bit more personal. Because in many ways all I could think was the saying "There but for the grace of God go I." My parents . . . I'm an immigrant, my parents are immigrants, my parents don't have any education, and even if they did, they would have suffered the economic dislocation upon immigration that could have led them to be merchants. My dad is self-employed. They fit exactly the economic class of the people who were running those shops. If we had settled in Los Angeles instead of Chicago and Skokie, I would have been right there. I didn't know LA, I didn't even know that I would end up clerking here afterwards, but I knew that I could have had exactly that life.

Then to see what was happening, and to see first-hand what the pain could be, because I know what my parents are like, I know how hard they work, I know what they would have been feeling to see everything that they had built up burned down. I also know the imperfections of my parents and that generation, and I know how racism and prejudice and fear and anxiety, all of that, work. There's no one who's innocent and no one who's perfect and no one's who's guiltless. But as I saw people who looked like me, people who looked like my parents basically being put out to what looked like essentially a "state of nature," into a conflagration they had no chance of getting out. I just remember tears welling up in, of all places, this very elite bastion back at the Harvard Law School?

The other thing I want to share is that about a year earlier, the Asian American Law Students Association, AALSA, and the Black Law Students Association had actually held an event where we actually tried to deal with some of the conflict between African American customers and Korean merchants, and we had a little conference, at a time when things were crazy . . .

CH: So had the Latasha Harlins [shooting happened] . . .

JK: Yes, it had just happened a month earlier. It had just happened, but before that, there had been enough of the boycotts with angry consumers both in New York as well as LA going after Korean merchants, sometimes for good reasons, sometimes not. There were politics everywhere. Almost as an act of building up goodwill, we jointly created a venue where we invited people from the Black-Korean Alliance—we got people out from LA, we got people from New York, to talk about how we can deal with this problem and to what extent it's a genuine problem, to what extent it was media-fueled, all those things. Latasha Harlins had been shot just a month before, and we were talking about those [issues] and we were trying to figure out what, if anything, we could do—all the while recognizing how supercilious it was to think that a bunch of Harvard law students could do anything from that kind of distance. And yet, we had that conference, so I knew what the build-up was. And when I saw Los Angeles burning, I have to admit it was very hard to keep back the tears, and it was deeply emotional.

Yet again, it was the Koreans or the Asians who were getting run over. No people are perfect—certainly Korean immigrants of that first generation are far from a perfect people, and yet again they're being screwed over. That's what I thought—screwed over by circumstances, by politicians, by white power sources, including the police and the National Guard who had them very low on any list to protect. I was thinking "riots" not "civil unrest." I was thinking "riots" not "rebellion," and the politics of naming are obviously difficult. I'm describing how I felt then, not necessarily thinking about what name is the best in the contemporary context. At some point, we should talk about the difficulties of even naming and why Koreans are most comfortable calling it Sa-I-Gu as a unique name. And it wasn't as if I was clueless about structural problems; I understood what happened with Watts in '65.

And yet what enraged me was the fact that Koreans weren't given voice, outside of maybe Angela Oh on *Nightline* and a few people. It was almost always white people or African Americans—even Latinos had almost no voices, it seemed to me, on mainstream mass media, and certainly not Koreans. I have told my friends that I was not necessarily meant to be a race scholar, but it was an event like Sa-I-Gu that changed me much more as I went through law school and thought about what it meant and what obligations I had as a Korean American, as an immigrant, who thought about race, who might have a venue later on, such as this one, to talk about these things.

So I wanted to share my emotional affect. It was very much about rage, rage against impotency, right? Not having the power to say anything and to be heard anywhere. And I wonder if it would be different if people could blog now, or if there were tweets that would catch on. But the consolidation of media power and what that allowed—because I know how the black-Korean merchant conflict was being constructed. How they were playing the Latasha Harlins shooting video over and over again in saturation coverage, intentionally cutting off the first ten, fifteen seconds of the video that showed her being shot. Nothing excuses someone shooting a child, but the full video shows how the escalation happened, the physical punching that happened before, and one could see the craziness that could have happened at the moment. But what the media showed constantly was the last few seconds of the clip where you saw an innocent child being shot from the back. That just made the stakes higher. So I was just angry.

DC: Well, I guess I would just start where you ended in a way, because it's interesting to think about the disjunction that you describe, Cheryl, which is the fact of this video, on the one hand, and the jury's response to it, on the other. Because one could say that, to some extent, from a mass media perspective, there was a story about why perhaps we should have paid less attention to what we saw, given that we don't know what preceded it, right? In this respect, there's some continuity between the controversy surrounding the King beating and the controversy surrounding the shooting of Latasha Harlins.

With respect to the latter, remember that many people raised questions about what had transpired before the shooting, just as people were raising questions about what had transpired before the Rodney King beating.

My own sense of that is it's difficult to think about this moment and not think about the extent to which anger was a part of the emotional reaction. Indeed, if I go back to my criminal law class for a minute, I remember black students, one after the other, expressing what that moment meant for them in terms of what it said about police violence and the extent to which the police can engage in it with a certain kind of impunity or at least with no obvious accountability.

On the other hand, there was another kind of disconnect, I mean, a disconnect having to do with how one manages that anger on an individual and community level. Because as a foreigner myself, I wondered about whether directing that violence within the community, including against Koreans and Korean Americans, made sense. So response—which included but was certainly not limited to mass destruction of property, looting, and violence—engendered a kind of disconnect for me as well, notwithstanding that I obviously understood the history of quote-unquote race riots in the US more generally. I couldn't quite understand that moment emotionally, even as I could understand it intellectually and politically and presumably we'll talk about that in a minute. Emotionally the moment was hard.

CH: Yeah, so I think, emotionally, I guess, the word I would feel is frustrated. I was both angry and frustrated, angry because I had been somewhat aware more from the east coast narrative than from a west coast one, one regarding the sort of black-Korean tensions which had already manifested themselves in Ice Cube's "Black Korea," and had already manifested itself in the boycotts in Brooklyn.

And just to sort of bring it all around here, I was actually just scrolling through some clips of things before this meeting just to remind myself of some of those media images that I was telling you about, that I was seeing. I ran across a clip of an interview with Tupac Shakur, who was being asked about his reactions to this and one of the things he said was, "You know, I hate to say it, but I told you so." "I told you so," and I was seeing he had a very conflicted reaction. He said on the one hand [he] was seeing a kind of beautiful energy coming out—he didn't use the word energy—but he referred to the youth as beautiful. But at the same time, he's saying [he] was anxious because [he] was worried we were going to lose a lot of people. So the interviewer asked him, well, what does this say about how Hollywood portrays people of different races and is it a time for Hollywood to sort of assess itself? Tupac said it's time for America to ask itself how it views different people of different races, because we're in a country where you live or die by the stereotype.

I thought in a way that that really captured some of my frustration; that is to say, the stereotype of black criminality which was inscribed onto Rodney King, meant that as he was lying on the ground—he still represented a mortal threat, such that it justified, as you said, Jerry, going medieval on you. By the same token, the stereotype of the sort of insular, unassimilable model minority Korean meant that they weren't even on the radar screen to be cared about. Nor were Latinos seen as subjects in any of this in any way, they were just nameless bodies moving across the screen and so . . .

JK: Ambient.

CH: Yeah, ambient, exactly. So the point of it all was our frustration regarding the inability, it seemed, to break out of a particular narrative, and actually understand what was happening or talk about what was happening. And fast forwarding to Katrina—[it] reminded me of the way the media constructs or narrates a particular event. Here, one could sense that there was both an aspect of revolt against a kind of systemic police violence, as well as the way complete economic dislocation was fueling things. But that story got retold as a kind of simple competition between blacks and Koreans. Because, you know, I'm old enough . . .

DC: . . . the law and order narrative . . .

CH: And the law and order narrative comes back into play to take back control. The analogy to Katrina that I would draw is that you have this moment where racial subordination is revealed by Katrina—why it is that all these black and poor people are homeless, with nowhere to go and literally left to drown? This moment the national gaze is transfixed and everyone is forced to look at something that is for the most part kept underground. Quickly, in a matter of days, [it] gets transformed into a story about black animality and disorder and chaos that has to be controlled by the state. So it was just incredibly frustrating to me to look at the situation and realize that there was something important happening, but that the story was somehow just completely submerged. I honestly, when I think about it, did not think about the Korean merchants in a way much different than I had seen the merchant class in these kinds of civil unrest before, and you could go back . . .

JK: Like the Jews in the '60s.

CH: You could go back to even Caribbean merchants in certain places, or in places like Detroit, Arab merchants. So I'm saying there's a certain kind of circularity—what I mean by this is to say that civil unrest, when it expresses itself in this way, is always the ethnic merchant class that is structurally located in that place for a particular set of reasons that becomes the first target. And the question that you put on the table, though, is why are they left defenseless and why are they left voiceless. And that, I have to honestly say, that didn't come into my consciousness until I actually came here, right? I mean, I understood that they were targeted in a particular way, but the absence of police protection for them was just not visible for me until I actually got here and saw some of the devastation that Devon talked about, which was still around by the time I arrived two years later.

SS: So I can share some of the same feelings and emotions, but I am thinking through what exactly was going through my mind or what was the main emotion then. I have to say I was outraged about a lot of the pieces that were unfolding, the obvious larger story of the role and complicity of a legal system where the race problem was already embedded in conversations about colorblindness, which insists racial oppression is not part of what this country is about. And yet, we all knew otherwise, we being everyone on the planet that was looking at the images for a year because the police beating video had circulated internationally for a long time before this happened. Wherever you went—my relatives in Mexico, wherever you were—people got that there is something about an authority that is unmistakably white and that's embedded with structural power being exposed in that moment in its injustice against communities of color. I think that there was outrage obviously about the verdict at the beginning, but then there was—once you had that filter of an injustice that mapped on to the stratification in the hierarchies that we all recognize, but were locked into a national discourse that insists they don't really exist when the news is presenting all these images—was incredibly frustrating.

I remember the shift in frames by the newscasters, who were first talking [to] the folks who were arriving and burning stuff down almost sympathetically, at first saying, "you know people are pissed off for a reason, look at these images and we don't know what else to say about it," but this is the frame. But then you kept seeing all these brown, not black, looters and you kept seeing places that were not South LA, and they finally had to figure out a way to describe a multiracial experience. This quote from Shakur is so telling because I remember when a newscaster finally shifted the frame by commenting about an image that was on the screen of Latinos taking property out of a shop, saying "many of these people look to me to be undocumented . . . "

JK: By racial inspection.

SS: Yes, by racial inspection and it was just another moment in which the frustration of knowing that he or she who controlled the media [took] this position of white authority to filter where our sympathies are supposed to lie. I felt outraged when I saw Reginald Denny, the white trucker pulled out of his truck and beat up, just in the way that I felt in the moment that I realized these Korean merchants and folks who probably weren't even store owners were just there trying to defend what was going on, as much as I felt for Rodney King. I mean, all these questions around racial innocence, right, once it started to come together around the lens of the type of authority that the legal system, that the media, have to say what is really a claim to innocence or an infraction and what is not, all started to come together in this way. But that was also partnered with this sense that nothing was going to be the same again. That the invisibility would not go unchallenged and that there was going to be a moment in which the obvious invisibility of certain groups, and its consequences, would have to be addressed.

So for Latinos, there were a lot of Central American neighborhoods and it was obvious that they couldn't find a Central American authoritative voice to put on camera. They just kept calling in people to try to provide analysis, deportations started, or arrests started to happen, martial law started to happen and all of these questions exposed that there was far more complexity to all the various groups in the city. It basically pushed back on the liberal racial sensibility that we had of ourselves in this multiracial city, and that it brought to the foreground fault lines around which there were long grievances with no name and that called for more voices. Certainly, this is something that happened afterwards. But at that moment, it was just that not having a voice, as you [Jerry] were just describing, I think, which was was pissing me and other people of color off the most.

JK: Yes.

CH: You know it's interesting you should say that, Saúl, because I was thinking about the fact that in a way the appearance of Latinos as sort of central in this, as central but voiceless figures in the story really confounded things. To put this simplistically, sometimes it seemed as though the newscasters were struggling with, well, what were they mad about?

SS: Yes, they were.

CH: Right. It's kind of like we get why the black people might be mad because Rodney King got beaten, but what are they mad about? Not that I'm saying that it was an effort to justify black rage, but I'm saying . . . It's like [the Latinos] are just sort of cruising or may be even piggy backing or free riding or something—it was a strange kind of narrative.

DC: And what's particularly ironic about the newscaster who says, for example, that they looked like they were undocumented, is that they were actually articulating a legal standard—"Mexican appearance" can, as a matter of law, function as a basis for undocumented status, or to put [it] the way courts do, as a basis for determining whether a person is an "illegal alien."

JK: So we've talked about lots of different topics. In addition to discussing where we were and how we felt, we've talked about lots of things that dance around causation. It might be crazy for us to even ask about what caused the riots in any deep sense. But as critical scholars, what we want to do is to make that which is invisible visible, right? The easiest explanations are at a one-to-one, individual level. They are the easiest explanations because they are the most transparent, thinking there are bad people who overresponded or overreacted and did so for self-interested reasons. And that in many ways reflects the most conservative law-and-order perspective. You need law and order because you have a culture of poverty or undocumented people who are lawless to begin with, by their essential nature. In some sense, they are here just taking an opportunity to express their bad values because law-and-order, the pressure that usually keeps them at bay, was suddenly lifted for whatever reasons. Thus, you get anarchy, you have a state of nature, and you have the crazies going crazy. That is, in some ways, the simplest explanation, and it is at the level of individual bad actors. It essentializes an individual as good or bad with good values or bad values, and they do what they do.

But there are deeper explanations that are harder to describe and therefore get less traction within sound bytes or media discourse. I'm going to trot out a couple of causes, different ways to think about causes. One idea that is often times emphasized is the *cultural* one, that the reason why there was tension between blacks and Koreans is that there were cultural misunderstandings. If we all had more cultural sensitivity—and understood why Koreans might not beam or smile at you and look at you eye-to-eye, or not leave change in your hand, or why their speech might sound staccato if they are not fluent English speakers—that if we had just greater cultural sensitivity, then none of this would have happened. It's a cultural story.

A second set of explanations are much more *economic*, which is about what's going on in places like South Central. Who's got jobs, what kind of hope is there, and what kind of life is there? And when you've got that much depression, economic and psychological, it is a powder keg that will explode in all kinds of ways. And as Cheryl described, there is always a middleman layer that's usually an ethnic minority that comes in a particular way, jumps the queue, in some sense, over a longstanding population of African Americans. And this layer acts as almost the sponge that soaks up the anger and the resentment of people who are at the bottom of this hierarchy, and that structure won't change. So there is a cultural explanation, and there's an economic explanation. I know this list is overly stylized, but I wanted to put them out there.

A third set of reasons is *ideological*. It's about values, and one can tell an ideological story that is, I think, a nationalist one. Like from a black nationalist's prospective: "This is our space. Who the hell are you, foreigner, to come in? I don't know where you are getting the money. I want to start up a shop. I can't start up a shop. You are getting money from some place, starting up a shop, selling to our people, not hiring us, disrespecting us constantly, right, maybe shooting one of us. Who are you to invade our territory, our space, our turf, and treat us like that? What do you expect to happen?" And we can also tell a Korean nationalist story, the Korean story about what it means to survive and come over here and to be desperately concerned about maintaining something like a Korean identity for their children, to survive in a place that they didn't really expect to see?

So the ideological story could be a nationalist story, but then again, it could be a straight-up racism or prejudice story, right? Koreans received racial stereotypes through American media, through military bases that have been in Korea for quite some time after the Korean War, about the hierarchy of white over black. Let's also not forget how Asians are depicted as constantly unfair competitors, who are inscrutable, inassimilable? This started way back from the late 1800s, the early 1900s, that constant refrain of the Asian as the sojourner who never wants to actually set up roots. So it could be racism, right? And everyone is potentially both the target and the holder of racist beliefs.

And the fourth cause that I want to put out there is the *media gone wild*. It's completely expected that you want to get hot video that's always playing, and you show it because people want to see it, and it just appeals to their interest. As K.W. Lee, a famous Korean American journalist, described it, he calls what happened to Los Angeles the first media-inspired pogrom, and he blames white mainstream media for it, full stop. And so I want to hear your views about the causes of Sa-I-Gu. Was it a cultural thing? Was it pure economics? Was it ideological? Was it media? Of course, it's all these things and none of these things, but is there something that you want to point out as being really important to describe what really happened, why it happened?

SS: I'm not sure if this is one of the four or one dimension that contains elements of each, but I think of Sa-I-Gu, ultimately, as a political failure. It's important to capture the big picture of what was circulating at the time. The political discourse and structures that were supposed to hold together a burgeoning city in a moment of deep demographic change and deep economic change in which the middle-class infrastructure had fallen out simply failed.

The central actor, in this explanation, is the police force, which is supposed to maintain order in that context and how it engages all of these various communities. It was being indicted, targeted as the on-the-ground representative of the legal and political institutions that had failed, the same system and the same dynamics that produce the disjuncture between that image and the verdict. Its paradigmatic face was Daryl Gates, a man who had been unapologetic about the use of chokeholds that had killed black people over and over in South LA, a man who led an institution that understood itself to protect the rest of the city from the brown east side and black south side of the city, particularly from black and brown male youth. And at that time, we had an African American mayor who was also a former LAPD police officer, who, in the narrow constraints of the liberal discourse of the time, didn't have something like the citizen's commission that came afterwards to regulate and have as a tool to handle what by all accounts, from a racial perspective, a renegade and oppressive white law enforcement agency. It was largely perceived to be the responsible agent in poor communities of, not all the things that you describe, but certainly of the indignity that comes with being pulled over by the police for not being able to afford registration tags, of being presumed of being a criminal because of the way that you dress, and a whole host of aggressions not recognizable to the rest of the city.

So I think, first and foremost, the political infrastructure that was in place to mediate and to make sense to the people around the city of its new economic dynamics, these multiracial dynamics, had failed. I have to say that in addition to outrage, there was a widespread feeling of, "finally, it happened." There was a collective sense that a legitimate expression against the way in which we are being asked to insert ourselves as people with group identities, whether we like it or not, into a project that is by definition built on competition, built on racialized hierarchy, that has failed. A new solution to that, a new set of discourses had to emerge after that.

I [can] tell one story that I wouldn't have known then, but I learned later when I went to work in South Central as a community organizer after law school. For a year before the unrest, residents in South Los Angeles were trying to do something about the crack epidemic, which scholars had studied—I think one of the most brilliant pieces around what happened was Melvin Oliver's piece on the character of the unrest, describing [how] you had the '80s divestment of public money for things like high schools in South LA, you had the falling of the price of crack, and you had mass unemployment. Jobs were taken by corporations out of neighborhoods like that to other countries. And then you had a moment in which the crack epidemic emerges and, again, a whole set of public policies that are about criminalizing people who became addicts and about using the carcereal system . . . not to fix those problems but making them worse. And so what happens in neighborhoods like South LA, you had the limited opportunities for economic self-actualization, whether it's a Korean immigrant or local African American or even Mexican American US-born folks, in that context.

The group I ended up working for years after the unrest, the Community Coalition, had convened community residents during the year before the verdict and unrest to look at the issue of the crack epidemic, from the perspective of its root causes, and the residents insisted on studying the question of how do you get so many liquor outlets in a place like South LA. Many of them [were] run by this merchant class—but somebody, some state agency, has to issue the permit to have three liquor stores on four corners, right? And what these residents learned is that there were more liquor outlets in South Central LA than in eleven states, that per capita there was more liquor in that community than any other part of the city. So, they began to engage this African American mayor about the possibility of doing something to reduce the number of liquor outlets, one year before this happened.

The day before the verdict, there was a community town hall with the mayor in which the response of the city, which is what any city does when disenfranchised residents point to structural inequities, [was] to create a blue ribbon commission with the task of figuring out how to solve this problem with other experts, whomever they are. The next day, the verdict happened and over the next three days, people burnt down half of those liquor stores, in three days. I'm not saying it was justified, and I'm not saying that people weren't harmed in the process, but structurally speaking, stepping back away from that political dynamic and thinking about what that says about how people felt, what the injustice of the verdict created as an opening to speak back against, I think it tells volumes about the political failure that led up to this.

JK: But just on that point about zoning—a huge number of Korean American stores and shops, a thousand or more, were harmed, destroyed, or burned. And when they tried to rebuild, and tried to get loans and the permits to rebuild the stores, it was difficult for them. Many organizations tried to stop the relicensing of liquor stores. Even if you think structurally and think that for this area, having that many liquor stores doesn't make sense, consider the perspective of the particular owner trying to rebuild, who doesn't know anything else to do. He says to himself, "Well, it's not as if I'm selling liquor just because I'm invested in selling liquor. It's because that's where you get the highest mark up." If they didn't sell liquor at these stores, then maybe they couldn't survive.

So many individuals couldn't rebuild. There was a huge exodus of Koreans, and we might think about what it means after a disaster whether or not the people can return, right? I'm thinking about Cheryl's great work on Katrina and what a right of return looks like. You might think from this disaster, something better should come for the entire community including the people who were victimized, right? But sometimes there's no easy answer . . .

CH: What this has to do, I think, really both with the cause—and you ask about causation—and there's also something about looking in the aftermath, what we can see both about the cause and the consequence. I guess, for me, I very much agree with Saúl's analysis and would just add that it was both the political failure and the ideological retooling. What I mean by that is the fact that—and I'm borrowing here from David Roediger's idea—[there is a] way in which the economic and racial ideological structure always has to have a kind of management, racial management plan, if you will, just to simplify it. And it has to do with how both labor and capital are racially stratified. So the point that you make about the Korean merchant then, okay, so he or she is in a structural position where the easiest thing to get is the liquor license? From the aspect of the neighborhood, what might be needed is a grocery store. But that becomes structurally, I guess I would say, off the table, because of the overall economics, right?

And so, from both sides of the fence, then it becomes a way in which a neighborhood is stripped both of infrastructure as well as access to the basic things that we think of as needed to live. A particular class is allowed to step into that breach, but only in a limited capacity, only in, because, of course, liquor is the most heavily regulated [product]. I guess I would say it's the easiest thing to lose, a liquor license.

JK: But those stores also had groceries . . .

CH: But that's what I'm saying. I'm saying that they then become the delivery mechanism for food into the communities. And still today, these communities look very much the same in terms of limited access to the things that we think of as being necessary to even constitute a livable space. And so my point is to say is that, in some ways 4/29 marked a crisis point. That is to say, that the old pressure cooker, the old management system having reached its limits in terms of what it could do, and so all these things then form a confluence in which it erupts. What consolidated afterwards, however, was a new narrative. Not so new, really, but a sort of retooled ideological narrative about the failure of multiculturalism. So it then doesn't become an analysis of any of the underlying causes, it just becomes the cultural story, a racism story, in which it's these people have embedded differences and it's just an unfortunate consequence. This then gets translated into a black-brown, or a black-Asian conflict.

JK: Right, which is in some ways much more salient now . . .

CH: It was the model for that, right? I mean, it was already in motion, but I'm saying it has been rolled out. It also got rolled out in the wake of Katrina. Embedded cultural differences. And now, I don't want to overstate the point, which is to say I don't want to ignore the fact that there are, in fact, cultural chasms that have to be bridged. But the point that I'm trying to make is that this is a political and ideological crisis but it was retold in a particular way such that basic information even regarding what happened in the moment in 4/29 is still not easily accessible now today, right? But the images still are easily accessible. And that standard narrative is easily accessible, which is that it's all about the fact that we just can't get along.

JK: Devon, what do you think?

DC: I don't think I have much to add to that. I do think that all of the factors that you described can be expressed through a structural frame—deindustrialization, joblessness, police abuse, and the very fact that this quote-unquote merchant class can emerge in a particular space is itself structural. There's a reason we don't see a merchant class, or a kind of middle minority, on the Westside; we see it in a particular space. To put this another way, it's not simply a result of individual preferences why a merchant class would emerge in the inner city, it's a result of where the points of entries might be for a particular kind of market activity and how that itself becomes racialized in the way that Cheryl expressed via her points about race and capital coming together.

So it's not that I would diminish concerns about cultural differences, it's not that I would diminish agency, I would simply say that one has to start with the kind of political failing, the structural dynamics, including police abuse, and how people understand themselves in relation to those structural dynamics. I don't think it would be inaccurate to say, for example, that the way some black constituencies reacted reflected an iteration of the yellow peril threat. To say that that perceived racialized threat operated the way that it has historically *vis-à-vis*, for example, the internment of people of Japanese descent or Chinese exclusion, would be an overstatement, but clearly there were discourses about economic competition, about foreignness, about un-Americanness, that track historically antecedent discourses about a "yellow" menace.

But to talk about that in a way that completely elides the broader structural dynamics would be a mistake.

As a parallel to the "Yellow Peril" threat that some African Americans perceived, some Koreans and Korean Amercans perceived African Americans in terms of criminality, violence and cultural pathology. Here, too, there are structural forces at play that at least partially explain why Korean Americans would trade on those ideas. The challenge, going forward, is to find a way to talk about the structures, preexisting racial narratives, agency and political accountability. Because I do think there's a political accountability piece that we cannot lose sight of, but we have to think about political accountability in relationship to structures. Otherwise, it really just becomes "Can we all get along?," and we all know that that can't be the real question.

JK: So I'm going to try to look forward a little bit and try to figure out what have we learned in the past twenty years. We have identified a theme to remember that some things happen not simply because of chance or bad luck, but because the structures incline bad things to happen to particular types of people in particular ways. And that's an important lesson to keep in mind, how these very factors interrelate in a particular structure that makes, again, certain bad things more likely than not to happen.

But what else have we learned in two decades—and I want to suggest that maybe we've learned nothing, right? I mean, we're academics, and we could talk about these things in fancy ways, but arguably there is a huge historical amnesia. Even at ground zero. I don't know what people have learned. I don't know whether people who are walking through K-Town now—many parts of which look radically different, reconfigured into huge shopping malls—are we, including Korean Americans, struck with amnesia? Maybe we've just refused to talk about it, either out of depression or repression. What have we learned in the law about a conflagration like that? Did we learn anything from Sa-I-Gu that was used or useful for Katrina or other kinds of crises?

Maybe a sharp way to put this point is to ask could it happen again? So think about what is happening in Europe, think about what Occupy Wall Street means, think about unemployment, in certain areas, structural unemployment being unbelievably high for certain types of people, right? Think about anger, with the idea that there's no hope for a better life. Could it happen again? And could it happen again along ethnic lines? Could Los Angeles burn again for three to four days, and if it can, what, if anything, have we learned? I want to know whether you're optimistic or pessimistic. Where are you now on this?

DC: This is one of those questions that is difficult to answer except on a somewhat abstract level in the following sense. Can it happen again? Sure, it can happen again. Am I thinking that it's going to happen again tomorrow, I don't know? I guess as I think about it, it seems as though what we saw in the moment was a hard predicate, there has to be a predicate, a trigger, something that taps into a preexisting set of concerns. Some might be legitimate, some might not be. The key is that the predicate becomes the basis for some kind of social expression.

What will be the predicate today? That's one question. Do I think the kind of economic deprivation you mentioned, the protest about Wall Street greed? We could talk about the war on terror, the ongoing war—I mean, are those the necessary predicates? Could be, I'm not sure . . .

JK: It could be someone shot on BART, right, or at the Metro.

DC: Well, someone was shot on BART and so . . .

JK: That's right, bring that possibility to LA.

DC: Well, we could just say bring it to some city, including where it occurred, San Francisco. And, to be clear, there were massive organizational efforts around this issue in Northern California. But something like what we saw in Los Angeles . . . could that happen again? Presumably the answer is yes; Cheryl and Saúl's comments about the ongoing structural problems help to explain why. But maybe part of the problem relates to community building. If I were to ask myself, do I think that the idea of political community among and between quote-unquote people of color is much more than an articulated idea? Much more than? Maybe not much more than that, and so what does that mean if you don't have preexisting political communities, on the one hand, that could manage something were it to happen again, on the other. And how do we talk about the structural dynamics which continue to shape how we experience our lives and our sense of our social and political connections with others? I mean, if it's the case that it's always a story about agency and social responsibility, then I don't think we are any better situated today . . .

JK: Think about the financial crisis. Can we talk about that structurally?

DC: I don't know . . .

CH: But you know, I would just say it's interesting to think about the picture of the city now and even that area now as compared to then, and what does that suggest. So the first thing I want to note is the fact that this remains a sort of completely unmarked historical event in many ways, in the context of the city and the story of the city itself. In other words, the reconstruction that happened of Koreatown in the wake of this event is a reconstruction which leaves out the merchants that you are talking about, but allows for the expression of new shopping malls and very fancy places to emerge in Koreatown, which maps on to a story about the triumph of individual effort, capital, and all the rest.

It seems to me that, at this juncture, this really is the problem. That is, we haven't taken it seriously as an event that was an expression of a lot of things that are still very much in place in the city today. The difference that I would note—and I guess I would say, yes, of course it can happen again—but I think that the way in which it comes about is, for me, going to be more complex, because we also have the emergence of a kind of politics in which groups that have traditionally been on the outside now have symbolic membership. So we have, for example, Villaraigosa as mayor, we have a black president, we have a symbolic kind of access to political power and all of the attendant groups and official structures that they stand upon.

JK: But no Koreans?

CH: But no Koreans, right. And so the question is how then does that play out now, what are the triggers, and how does the system itself respond to the potential of this kind of unrest, given that now ostensibly there's a certain strata that has been given more of a stake in the structure? So there is no Daryl Gates is what I'm saying, sitting at the head of the police department. It's a much more, I would say, complex question. That said . . .

DC: West Adams is no longer, I don't think, predominantly black . . .

CH: Yeah, right, exactly, and very few areas of the city actually are predominantly black anymore. So one of the things that I think is an interesting question is if, in fact, 4/29 marked the emergence of a new form of civil unrest, meaning that it looked different from 1965, what would the form look like now, what would its expression be? I don't think it will be an exact replica of that.

JK: Yeah.

CH: But I do think it's possible.

JK: Saúl, how are you feeling about this?

SS: I'm optimistic. I feel like it is true that the racial project and the economic project of the country is inherently unstable and that some version of this, I think, has to happen in certain periods of time. I'm not saying we know what the particular manifestations of the outcry of subordinated groups will be or of what groups will be positioned in what way, but we do know that vulnerability has been structured in the way that we've talked about in 1992. So, it will not be the same in 2015, 2030, but I do see it as a built-in part of how these unstable ideological projects, which are inherently racialized in a way that people experience them on the ground, that there is no reason to think it won't happen again. The structures that should be responsive are actually getting more exclusionary, such as the education system in this state, which has become more exclusionary in terms of the people from the poorest communities and certain racial groups being represented.

I want to point out for, example, in terms of the legal field, the American Bar Association, has a committee on racial diversity that was established after 4/29. Every institution that represents the elite structure of the country decided they needed to do something to respond to what happened, right? This was such an indictment of the status quo that how could you not? Our profession decides to survey communities of color across the country to see how they feel about the legal system. Overwhelmingly, all the communities of color they engaged said it does not represent us in any meaningful way and it's racist. This was basically the response that our profession got and what we did to try to speak to that was is to create a subcommittee on diversity, that did, for example, some work to address the issues around Katrina, Cheryl was discussing, which is how I came to know of their work.

One can make an argument that more meaningful structural changes, putting lawyers in these communities where people could actually have solution to the kinds of issues that they are facing, such as foreclosures during the economic crisis and all the things that people are living through right now—the profession did not do that, and it's not actually educating and producing more lawyers necessarily in those communities. At the same time, and we know this to be true of any unstable project, this moment created openings, and like you [Jerry] described in your own trajectory, a rise of a consciousness so that individual agency resides everywhere.

And so you have individual Korean American leaders who are not necessarily symbolic leaders in the way that Mayor Villaraigosa or President Obama are having to be to shepherd in an obviously new moment in the larger project, but who are out there doing community building and who've created a very self-conscious political awareness and discourse within the Korean American community that says "we need to understand what multiracial literacy is, we need to understand what multiracial coalition building looks like and how to make it happen, and we need to actually engage that work in a way that takes into account the particularities and the specificity of our immigrant experience, of our experience as a second generation or 1.5 generation people, and as people of color in an economically stratified and racially ordered society." And they are the actors that I think that have more promise than the symbolic agents because the political institutions and the larger structure that I am describing always give the same response to pressing community needs, as we saw in the liquor store example. And I think that is far more promising than anything else.

JK: You know, if I have a glimmer of hope, it is driven by really remarkable community NGOs [Non-Governmental Organizations]. And they don't always agree, and again there's politics everywhere, there's competition for both recognition and funding, but there are organizations that were created in the crucible of the remains of Sa-I-Gu, like the Korean American Coalition. And if you think about the work that the KYCC, which is now the Koreatown Youth Community Center instead of the Korean Youth Community Center and…

SS: KIWA [Koreatown Immigrant Workers Alliance] . . .

JK: KIWA, right. If you think about these organizations and what they do, day in and day out. They serve a clientele, a base, a community that goes way beyond what it means to be just Korean.

SS: Right . . .

JK: It's about Koreatown, it's about the people there. Could be huge Latino community. And when I see that work . . . which is the kind of work that does not fit into a model minority trajectory. Korean immigrants who come over, suffer social and economic dislocation, are not telling their kids to grow up to do that kind of work, right? Instead, they are telling their kids to become professionals, get a job, make sure you have money, take care of your kids. And yet I see lots of people who have options, who still go back into that kind of community building work. That's the kind of work I see and in many ways fundamentally admire. Those NGOs on the ground do make me think that something better could happen.

Then again, as much as we emphasize structure, we have to emphasize agency, and that's in each of us. I know each one of us—even as insignificant as academic life or ivory tower life might be—when we make choices, when our lives are hard, we intentionally make choices to build bridges across different communities, across different, not only academic disciplines, but areas of focus and knowledge. When you [Devon] write about the Supreme Court case *Ozawa* [*v. United States* (1922)], when we participate in events about post-9/11 racial profiling of South Asians, when I write about the Japanese Americans, we are all in some sense deciding to vote with our hours, with our hands, with our minds in a particular way to stand next to each other. Because when we break bread and cooperate with each other, even when things get awful, then we have a kind of reserve that we can draw upon that is so important. I guess that is something that makes me a little bit more optimistic.

I guess the final thing I want to emphasize, which is both agency as well as structure, is that there's a cadre of Korean American attorneys in LA, like hundreds of them now who are bright—they might be working in corporate law firms, serving corporate clients, doing nothing especially connected with the community. But when push comes to shove, I mean, it would be a different voice out there. If *Nightline* needs desperately to find some Korean looking person who doesn't speak with an accent, they would have more options.

CH: Well, you know, I guess the only friendly amendment that I would offer is not to say that the work of academics is always relevant. But I do think that the work we do in academic institutions around these questions is absolutely critical. You know, it is a space that is itself engaged in knowledge production. And in terms of both shaping future generations as well as shaping the body of knowledge around which we can then make interventions, it becomes crucial.

And so the very things that we struggle for both in terms of access to the institution, access to its resources, who gets in the door, what kind of training they have—these are tremendous political questions and responsibilities that I think we have. I would never make the argument that everything that we do is important simply because we are doing it in an academic space. But my friendly amendment would be to say that it is not trivial at all. There is a reason why the doors that Saúl was talking about are hard to get into, and it is because of the recognition of what a place or what an academic institution does, what it is, what its job is. To the extent that we can in our own practices try to challenge ourselves around these issues, I think it becomes more than just symbolic or trivial.

DC: And indeed, I think one could say, in that respect, that academics have not completely done their part. I mean, one of the things that we talked a little bit about earlier is just the absence of a very thick, robust accounting of A., what happened; B., how it has shaped the city; and C., what that might mean for Los Angeles going forward. So whether you're thinking about that in sociological terms, whether you are thinking about that in legalistic terms, it just seems to me that there is an awful lot of work that one can still do to better understand what that moment means for the city of Los Angeles and, indeed, for the nation at large.

JK: Well, Devon Carbado, Cheryl Harris, Saúl Sarabia, thank you very much for an honest and insightful conversation.

## NOTE

Reprinted with permission from Devon Carbado, Cheryl I. Harris, Jerry Kang, and Saúl Sarabia, *Amerasia Journal* 38:1 (2012): 1–28.

# FORMATIONS AND WAYS OF BEING

# INTRODUCTION

## (*BLACK FOLK HERE AND THERE*: AN ESSAY IN HISTORY AND ANTHROPOLOGY)

ST. CLAIR DRAKE

*Black Folk Here and There* is written from a point of view that, in recent years, has been frequently referred to as a "black perspective"—reality as perceived, conceptualized, and evaluated by individuals who are stigmatized and discriminated against because they are designated as "Negroes" or "Blacks." The tradition of vindicationist scholarship referred to in the preface has, of course, always embodied that perspective whether those specific words were used to characterize it or not. Nevertheless, not all research and writing from a black perspective has racial vindication as its raison d'être. Some of it is purely expressive with no instrumental ends in view, as, for instance, much of the poetry and fiction.

The adoption of a black perspective in history, philosophy, or the social sciences deliberately restricts the frame of reference within which people and events are observed and evaluated. The focus is narrowed so as to concentrate on the Black Experience, with full awareness, of course, that social class, nationality, ethnicity, tribal affiliation, and/or religious orientation all make the experience different from person to person. In addition, the broader sociocultural context conditions it profoundly. But the derogation of "blackness" creates a residual common perspective despite the variations, and it is one example of what Karl Mannheim described as a "partial perspective" when he developed his theory of the sociology of knowledge in *Ideology and Utopia*. He writes, "perspective signified the manner in which one views an object, what one perceives in it, and how one construes it in his thinking . . . not only do the concepts in their concrete contents diverge from one another in accordance with differing social positions, but the basic categories of thought

St. Clair Drake was a pioneer in black studies who was the first permanent director of Stanford University's African and Afro-American Studies program. A professor emeritus of sociology and anthropology, Drake was an early researcher on black Americans. His works included *Black Metropolis: A Study of Negro Life in a Northern City*, an acclaimed 1945 work written with Horace R. Cayton. The book studied segregation, poverty, and discrimination in Chicago's South Side ghetto of Bronzeville. Drake was a founder of the American Society for African Culture and of the American Negro Leadership Conference on Africa, the author of many books and articles, and the recipient of many awards, including honorary degrees.

may likewise differ."[1] Such partial perspectives are not an obstacle in the pursuit of truth about social situations; in fact, they are necessary in order to know the *entire* truth. An approximation to total knowledge is impossible if data are not available that reflect ethnic, racial, national, class, and age- and gender-related special experiences. Some things can be known only by those who have experienced them in these social roles.

People who view reality from a partial perspective, if they have the will to do so, with some training, can communicate the content, the meanings, and the feeling tone of their experiences to others. Insofar as this is true, research from a black perspective has a vindicationist potential. It can serve as a corrective to biases, conscious or unconscious, that persist in studies of black people produced from other perspectives.

When a black perspective has vindicationist aims, it tends to assume a polemical tone. However, even when it is neither vindicationist nor polemical, mainstream historians and social scientists have, traditionally, looked askance at it. Scholars who utilized it were frequently dismissed as "biased" and charged with violating scholarly norms of objectivity and detachment. During the past decade, however, increasing self-criticism has laid bare the hidden agendas of so-called "objective" social science. These developments, along with dialogue initiated by professors and students from subordinated ethnic groups, as well as by feminists, Marxists, and Third World historians and social scientists, have contributed to a restructuring of professional norms. With the sanction of the now-respectable sociology-of-knowledge frame of reference, validity has been conceded to a black perspective as well as to a number of other intellectual points of view.

Such validity was conceded by sociologists in the United States during the late 1960s and early 1970s. For example, in 1973 the American Sociological Association, for the second time, presented a Du Bois-Frazier-Johnson award at its annual meeting. The recipient (who was, incidentally, the author of this book) was cited for "sustained and vigorous efforts as teacher-scholar-essayist to advance the intellectual liberation of college and university students in the United States, Africa, and the islands of the Caribbean." This Pan-Africanist orientation being cited with approval was more characteristic of the scholar-activist Dr. W. E. B. Du Bois than it was of the other two black sociologists whom the award also honored: Dr. Charles S. Johnson and Dr. E. Franklin Frazier. The willingness to include Dr. Du Bois along with the two sociologists in establishing an award, and to include the politically charged word "liberation" in the 1973 citation, indicated a profound change in attitude on the part of the leaders of the American Sociological Association. In the past Du Bois had been considered too much of a partisan in his attacks on racial discrimination to be a "good" social scientist, even though *The Philadelphia Negro*, published in 1896, was generally recognized as a piece of outstanding pioneer work in urban sociology, and his publications while holding the chair in sociology at Atlanta University could not be ignored. Unfortunately, Du Bois was no longer living when the institution of the ASA award bestowed Establishment legitimacy on his intellectual contributions.

Frazier and Johnson, as protégés of Robert E. Park, founder of the Chicago School of sociology, won the respect of their peers between 1920 and 1960 through the high quality of their research and because of their contributions to an understanding of the dynamics of social and cultural change with special reference to race relations. These men were in continuous demand as consultants to governmental and private agencies on problems involving relationships between white Americans and their black fellow citizens. (Du Bois, meanwhile, was associated with organizations exerting pressure for change.) Although Frazier and Johnson were expected to interpret the black perspective to others, it was understood that, as social scientists, their scholarly writings would maintain a neutral and objective tone. They, like most other black scholars prior to the 1970s, did not question the wisdom of working within the parameters set by the academic disciplines within which they had done their graduate work. (There were no interdisciplinary degrees in Black Studies in those days.) Each aspired to make some contribution to his discipline while, at the same time, carrying out research and publication on the Black Experience in such a way that it would, at least indirectly, contribute toward what a chapter heading in Drake and Cayton's *Black Metropolis* (1945) referred to as "Advancing the Race."

Among some Afro-American scholars who won academic distinction through this nonpolemical, discipline-oriented approach to the study of the Black Experience were Horace Mann Bond in the field of education; Allison Davis in social anthropology and social psychology; Ralph Bunche in political science; and Abram Harris and Robert Weaver in economics. Vindicationists made effective use of the work of such scholars in their own polemical writing (for example, Frank Snowden's outstanding contribution to Greco-Roman classical scholarship, *Blacks in Antiquity*). *Black Folk Here and There* is closer in tone to the style of Du Bois than was *Black Metropolis*, coauthored with Horace Cayton. That book was more similar to the Johnson-Frazier type of research, and to that of the above-mentioned group of discipline-oriented scholars.

In one field, however, in addition to such discipline-oriented scholars as Dr. John Hope Franklin, a group of Afro-American historians, under the leadership of Dr. Carter G. Woodson, developed what Engerman and Fogel in *Time on the Cross* refer to as "The Negro School." From 1915, when they established the Association for the Study of Negro Life and History, this group of historians frankly stated an explicit vindicationist aim: to challenge, correct, and supplement what was erroneously claimed to be the truth about Negroes, and to do it from a black perspective, using both detached scholarship and polemics. Their monographs and their periodical forum, the *Journal of Negro History*, won the respect of their peers. *Time on the Cross* points out that they made solid contributions through methodological innovations in historiography, although they were always considered marginal to the mainstream in the field of American history.

A survey of the great outpouring of works written from a black perspective during the 1960s and 1970s suggests certain pitfalls to be avoided when trying to set the historical record straight. Among these is the presentation of highly plausible possibilities as though they were "facts," and the imputing of racist motivations to individuals who lived in the remote past and whose actions that were disadvantageous to blacks might be more appropriately explained in some other way. A few very race-conscious historians turned concepts such as Negritude and Black Power into mirror images of White Racism, a development as indefensible as it was extreme. However, when pursued with caution, vindicationist efforts need not be unscholarly although they may be unconventional. For instance, the criteria of relevance used in research from a black perspective will often lead to emphasis upon facts and personalities that others deem unimportant or even trivial. These may be crucial to a full understanding of the Black

Experience; and, when integrated into meaningful patterns, even those who initially questioned their usefulness may recognize their value.

Emphasizing the Black Experience sometimes involves the idiosyncratic treatment of data. For instance, the more popular works of the self-trained historian Joel A. Rogers (e.g., *Sex and Race*) sometimes used photographs to "prove" the Negro ancestry of various important personalities in a manner that cannot be defended—as in the case of Beethoven. On the other hand, much of Rogers's work depends upon meticulous documentation to establish his claims. Thus the work of this particular vindicationist is valuable but must be used with caution. Other black scholars, such as Cheikh Anta Diop in *African Origins of Civilization* and Yosef Ben-Jochannan in *Black Man's Religion*, use unconventional approaches that those unsympathetic with their points of view will find disconcerting. When I am writing from a black perspective, I, too, occasionally indulge in peculiarities that might be proscribed in a publisher's manual of style, and are in contrast to the more conventional stance I assume in other contexts. For instance, in order to emphasize previously neglected themes and facts I am not averse to the use of a more liberal sprinkling of capitalized and italicized words than conventional stylists prefer. In this book, however, I have refrained from anything so idiosyncratic as the device, used by Dr. Du Bois in *Black Reconstruction*, of appending to each carefully researched and soberly presented chapter a paragraph or two of passionately rhetorical opinion or judgment. I do, however, frequently mention the race of authors or participants in events, whereas presentation from some other perspective would make such designations unnecessary or even inappropriate.

This work is designated, as was Du Bois's *Black Folk Then and Now*, an "essay." This format allows for expression of opinion as well as the presentation of fact, and permits peculiarities of style that would not be acceptable in a scientific monograph. The book is called "an essay in history and anthropology." Scholars in both fields will, no doubt, decide that it has only a dubious connection with either discipline. If so, it will be because of my inadequate workmanship, not because the designation is unjustified. The late E. E. Evans-Pritchard, one of the founding fathers of British functional anthropology, noted upon one occasion that "Maitland has said that anthropology must choose between being history and being nothing." Evans-Pritchard pushed the point further by saying, "I accept the dictum, though only if it also be reversed—history must choose between being social anthropology and being nothing."[2] My view is closer to that of the distinguished American anthropologist Sidney Mintz, who wrote, "we need not accept the assertion that anthropology would ultimately be history or else it would be nothing at all in order to discover that the usefulness of history for anthropology, and of anthropology for history, is genuine and important." He warned, however, that "most of us who plunge today into problems that require the skills of both disciplines for their solution continue to feel with justice rather like the blind men charged with describing the elephant."[3] Yet, in his own work on the African impact on New World societies, Sidney Mintz has proved to be a craftsman of high merit in the development of concepts and methods for utilizing historical materials in anthropological investigations.

The use of the comparative method in analyzing historical data for an exercise in macrosociology or macroanthropology—as *Black Folk Here and There* is—becomes an especially hazardous intellectual enterprise when the anthropologist is, as I am, untrained in historiography. The result of such a venture runs the risk of being either superficial and anecdotal on one hand, or too heavily documented and ponderously pretentious on the other. If this work avoids either extreme and turns out to be at all significant, it will be, in large measure, the result of the fine work of specialists whose scholarship I have drawn upon. I have used written documents in place of the participant-observer notes usually brought back from anthropological fieldwork. My use of what some might consider excessive quotation from secondary sources is an attempt to adapt one of some anthropologists' preferred techniques of presentation, in which excerpts from interviews with informants are woven into the text. The authors of these authoritative works here act as my informants. I like to have them speak for themselves; I try to make it possible for the reader to savor some of the flavor of their words. This book, like Du Bois's *Black Folk Then and Now*, was not designed as a project that would examine primary source material. It is, rather, a critical review of a wide range of existing published data—text and photographs—that have relevance to the Black Experience, and an integration of such data into what I consider an interpretative pattern.

The claim of *Black Folk Here and There* to an affiliation with anthropology cannot rest upon the manner in which the raw data are assembled, analyzed, and presented. It is based instead upon the selection of concepts for organizing the data. These have been the study of acculturation under conditions of conquest, and of behavior and symbols associated with social stratification. The entire study might be considered an exercise in symbolic anthropology, broadly conceived. On another level the study deals with the traditional anthropological concern for the relationship between race and culture in human societies and the implications of studies of prehistory and physical anthropology for the Black Experience. Anthropology tempers ethnic chauvinism by insisting upon an attitude of cultural relativism prior to passing judgment upon cultures different from our own.

One of the aims of this book is to give the reader an initial acquaintance with some relevant and potentially interesting published data that are not widely known and sometimes not readily accessible. One of its purposes, too, is the integration of familiar data into new patterns of relevance. Suggestions are included for additional reading and for possible future research, since some matters discussed herein remain obscure or confused while others merit more in-depth discussion and analysis. If, in addition to satisfying curiosity and answering a few previously unanswered questions, the book also has the effect of stimulating research that leads to an occasional master's thesis or doctoral dissertation, it will have more than justified the time and effort that went into it.

*Black Folk Here and There* deals with the Black Experience before White Racism emerged as a dogma to support a system of institutionalized practices designed to justify the transatlantic African slave trade and Western Hemisphere slave systems. Later, White Racism developed to reinforce colonial imperialism in Africa, Asia, and Oceania. The author has been working for several years on a book manuscript, entitled *Africa and the Black Diaspora*, that analyzes the forces which brought White Racism into being and the counterforces which emerged concurrently in various parts of the world. *Black Folk Here and There* conceptualizes *slavery*, *skin-color prejudice*, and *racism* as three quite distinct phenomena, each of which had existed separately from the other prior to the period of the great European overseas explorations but which became intertwined and mutually interdependent in the African diaspora of the Western Hemisphere.

The empirical evidence presented here supports the view that prejudice and discrimination based upon skin color existed for several centuries before the beginning of European overseas expansion but were not accompanied by any systematic doctrines of racial inferiority and superiority, that is, "racism" as we define it for the purposes of this study. Nor were color prejudice and discrimination institutionalized as structural principles defining systems of slavery, caste, or class. Slavery is a phenomenon that has existed in many times and places without any connection with either skin-color prejudice or racism. *Africa and the Black Diaspora* will consider in detail the relatively recent unique phenomenon of the institutionalization of skin-color prejudice in the form of *racial slavery*. It will also describe factors in the emergence of doctrinal supports for such a system, based upon theology and pseudoscience. From the outset *racial slavery* was systematically undermined by economic and noneconomic factors within the Western capitalist societies which gave birth to it. After it disappeared in the Americas during the nineteenth century, slavery *not* based upon racial discrimination continued to exist in various parts of Asia, the Middle East, and Africa.

Chapters 1 and 2 of this volume present the basic concepts that guide the examination of the empirical data in the chapters to follow. A distinction is drawn between generalized skin-color prejudice and prejudice against Negroes and Negroidness. The most crucial conception is the proposition that beliefs, attitudes, and behavior of others toward Negroes must always be understood as operating in relation to certain domains within any specific society. These are *esthetic*, *erotic*, *status conferring*, *moral-mystical*, and *utilitarian* (such as economic, military, and political). One or several of these domains may be dominant, insofar as skin-color evaluation is concerned, within a specific social situation. Though others exist, they are of lesser importance. Seemingly contradictory forms of belief and behavior with regard to skin color may exist side by side within a single society.

As the study developed, it became clear that a distinction must be made between the following three objects of evaluation when contrasts between black and white, blackness and whiteness, are made: (1) nonhuman objects and abstract ideas; (2) human beings defined as "colored" or "nonwhite"; and (3) human beings who have a Negro facial configuration associated with dark skin-color. "Blackness" is often a term that really means "Negroidness"; nevertheless, it is possible for societies to incorporate highly pejorative stereotypes and attitudes about "Negroes" without having similar reactions to other dark-skinned people, however "black" they may be. In formulating questions to be addressed in the examination of empirical data, these have assumed priority:

1. Is the tendency universal to make the color black symbolic of undesirable objects, situations, and emotional or psychological states?
2. Does the devaluation of the color black within the symbol system of a specific society necessarily lead to the expression of negative prejudices against people defined as "black" within that society?
3. If negative stereotypes are held, and negative attitudes are expressed, against people defined as "black" within a society, does this necessarily result in discriminatory behavior toward them?

From a mass of secondary source material an attempt is made here to answer the above questions for each of several situations. The extent to which this is possible varies greatly with time and place. In many situations the data are not present in the written record to attempt an answer. The complexity of the problem extends beyond considerations of time and place, since the study of the record left by literates gives us an inadequate view of what the nonliterate segment of many populations felt—or how they acted, in instances where their alleged racial stereotypes and attitudes are presented by others. An attempt is made, however, to infer popular attitudes and behavior patterns from folklore, proverbs, and by analogy, comparing ancient situations with contemporary ones of similar societal type.

In addition to the three questions noted above, special attention is given to the following questions: *When, where, and why did pejorative connotations originally become attached to a specific kind of black person—the Negro physical type? Did these connotations diffuse to other areas and, if so, how and why? Did such connotations ever originate again independently and, if so, where and under what circumstances?* Scholars have given considerable attention to the question of why dark skin color is frequently denigrated. Virtually none has attempted to explain why "Negroidness," prior to the transatlantic slave trade, bore the brunt of skin-color prejudice in some parts of the Mediterranean world and the Middle East.

All of the chapters, where the data are available, also try to address two other questions: (1) What are the factors that have been decisive in changes of attitude and behavior toward black people in various times and places? and (2) What are the factors that have been decisive in the change of attitude and behavior of black people toward themselves in various times and places?

*Black Folk Here and There* is presented in two volumes, the first of which includes the theoretical introduction to the analysis of cases as well as one such analysis. The strategy for presenting the empirical data in a comparative frame of reference entails beginning with a chapter on the Black Experience in the ancient Nile Valley, the case presented in volume l. Egypt provides the longest continuous documented record of relations between a variety of racial groups, including those defined as "Negro" by anthropologists and by customary usage. At times blacks had military and political dominance in Egypt and in the upper Nile Valley, known to the ancient Greeks as Ethiopia. A study of the interaction between Egypt and Ethiopia provides valuable data for examining the self-concepts of diverse black groups when in contact with each other prior to periods of domination by lighter-skinned peoples. In addition, special emphasis is placed upon ancient Egypt because of the significance of that civilization in all vindicationist writing, past and present.

The need continues for correcting numerous errors that operate to obscure the role of the Negro people in the development of Egyptian civilization. Chapter 3 attempts to deal with some of these problems, which were posed in Dr. Du Bois's book *The Negro* in 1915 and have more recently been the subject of discussion at a symposium convened by UNESCO. In addition to the correction of errors, it is important to treat in some detail certain aspects of Egyptian-Ethiopian history that have often been neglected in discussing relations between black and white people. One such theme is the close relations between the ancient Jews and the Nile Valley peoples.

The second volume consists of chapters 4, 5, and 6 and a concluding epilogue. Chapter 4 presents data on relations between black and white people in the Mediterranean world and the Middle East prior to the rise of Islam in the seventh century AD. Emphasis is placed upon the fact that, after the sixth century BC, two distinct Jewish traditions emerged—Palestinian and Mesopotamian—the former retaining historic connections with the Nile Valley peoples, the latter developing relations with Negroes from inner Africa through slaves imported into the Tigris-Euphrates Valley, and with Persian religious thought. The importance of the rabbinic scholars of the Mesopotamian diaspora in the development of myths about blackness and black people is examined and contrasted with the biblical tradition of Palestine. This latter tradition was close to that of the GrecoRoman world in its relatively favorable attitude toward the people whom the Greeks called "Ethiopians." Since European and American literate culture evolved from a synthesis of the Greco-Roman and the Judaic tradition as it took shape in early Christianity, the attitudes of the church fathers toward blackness in the Christian symbol system and toward Ethiopians is examined. Propositions about the transfer of color symbolism to social relations and to persons are considered in the light of data from the Mediterranean and Middle Eastern cultures. This is where the "roots," so to speak, of medieval Christendom are to be found. (A thorough examination of skin color as it functions in the societies of the Indian subcontinent would be instructive, but this is not done because of limitations of time and space and in order to keep the focus on "Negroidness.")

Chapter 5 is entitled "The Black Experience in the Muslim World." Between the seventh century AD and the beginning of the Crusades in the eleventh century, the religion of Islam, drawing its initial impulse from Judaism and Christianity, became the most important social and political force throughout the Middle East and the African and European Mediterranean coasts, as well as in Spain and Portugal. Because the followers of Islam were in intimate contact with Negroes from below the Sahara and from the coasts of East Africa, and because of widespread misunderstanding about Muslim attitudes and behavior toward blacks as compared with those of Christians, it was considered important to devote a chapter to the status of black people throughout the area in which Christianity had been dominant for five centuries but was replaced to a large extent by Islam, a new religion.

The data in chapter 5 confirm the proposition that widespread and deep-seated prejudice against Negroidness may prevail in some domains within a culture, even though there is no strong derogation of blackness in the abstract or of non-Negro black peoples. The conclusion also emerges that if slavery in a social system is not racial slavery, and if institutionalized racism does not exist, prejudice against Negroes will not necessarily prevent a considerable degree of individual mobility based upon talent in some domains and upon the existence of favorable stereotypes in others.

Chapter 6 contrasts the Black Experience in European Christendom between the eighth and fifteenth centuries with that in the Muslim world during the same period. The key variable is slavery, which was omnipresent under Islam but absent from most of European Christendom after the tenth century AD. In both cultures positive and negative values were associated with Negroidness. In neither were all slaves Negro. By examining the differences between the Iberian Peninsula and the British Isles on the eve of the sixteenth-century European expansion around the Atlantic basin, a baseline is set for studying the contrasting forms that racial slavery and White Racism took in areas settled by the British on one hand and those settled by the Spanish and the Portuguese on the other. Volume 2 ends with an epilogue entitled "The End of an Epoch in Black History," which discusses the historic turning point in black/white relations that occurred during the sixteenth century AD, when the Black Diaspora into the Western Hemisphere began.

## NOTES

Reprinted with permission from St. Clair Drake, *Black Folk Here and There: An Essay in History and Anthropology* (Los Angeles: Ralph J. Bunche Center for African American Studies at UCLA,1987), 1–11.

1. Karl Mannheim, *Ideology and Utopia: An Introduction to the Sociology of Knowledge* (New York: Harcourt, Brace and Co., 1936), 244, 246.

2. E. E. Evans-Pritchard, *Social Anthropology and Other Essays* (New York: The Free Press, 1962), 152.

3. Sidney W. Mintz, "History and Anthropology: A Brief Reprise," in Stanley L. Engerman, Eugene D. Genovese, and Alan H. Adamson, eds., *Race and Slavery in the Western Hemisphere: Quantitative Studies* (Princeton: Princeton University Press, 1975), 477–494; quotation from p. 479.

# NILE VALLEY BLACKS IN ANTIQUITY

ST. CLAIR DRAKE

The continent of Africa, 11,759,000 square miles of land, largely savannah and desert but also including extensive high plateau and mountain areas and a small amount of equatorial rain forest (so-called jungle), is inhabited by over 300 million people of many colors, tongues, and tribes (see map 1). Most of them, however, would be classified as "black" according to American convention. Africa provides a crucial case in examining the Degler-Gergen proposition that the color black is always contrasted negatively with *white*, that such evaluations carry over to social relations, and that all people everywhere—including black people themselves—are prejudiced against dark skin color. Archaeological evidence and written documentation covering several millennia of contact between Negroid and Caucasoid people in the northern portion of the contingent are available, and these data can be utilized in the study of these important questions.

As the Nile Valley provides us with the oldest documented cases of cooperation and conflict involving "Negroes" and other races, that region is of great importance in examining the reactions of black people to themselves and to other people. Furthermore, the Blumer and Cox generalizations about the linkages between race relations and various kinds of social situations can be examined utilizing Nile Valley data from long time spans, as can changes in the significance of skin-color differences. This chapter therefore concentrates upon the Nile Valley portion of the continent.

The Nile Valley, as one of several geographical locations chosen for discussing "black folk here and there," not only provides data of importance for anthropology and comparative history; it also constitutes a specific portion of Africa that Afro-American religious, political, and educational leaders invested with great significance during the nineteenth century and that still carries high symbolic import. These leaders wrote and spoke to slaves and their descendants, whose African backgrounds lay in western and central Africa, where people had been captured in raids, shackled, stripped naked for the voyage across the ocean, and then sold on the auction block after being inspected like animals. Their captors thought of them as immoral savages whose customs included exotic (and erotic) rituals frequently connected with the worship of "idol gods." They were heathens. Nudity, bodily scarification, and occasional cases of cannibalism and human sacrifice were cited as evidence of a general degradation of black people that justified their enslavement by a "more advanced

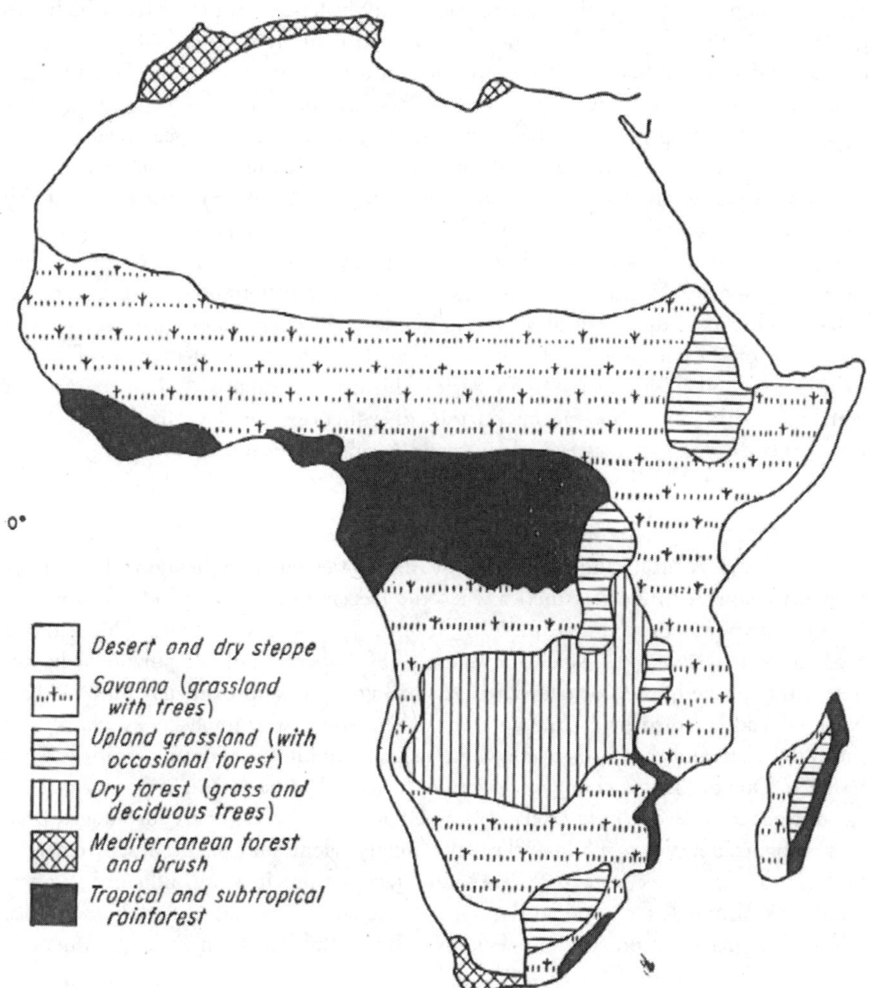


**Map 1.** Vegetation Zones of Africa. Reprinted, by permission, from George Peter Murdock, *Africa: Its Peoples and Their Culture History.* Copyright © 1959 by McGraw-Hill Book Company.

race." By the beginning of the nineteenth century, without denying the existence of some of these practices, which they too considered deplorable, Afro-Americans who had managed to secure some education questioned whether *all* tribes *everywhere* in Africa exhibited any or all of these characteristics. They sought satisfying nonracist explanations for the presence and distribution of traits and practices that Westerners disapproved of. They expressed confidence in the ultimate triumph of "civilization" and Christianity in what Europeans called the "Dark Continent," but which was their Ancestral Homeland, however unsavory its reputation or deplorable some aspects of its reality. "Blackness" referred to a sociocultural condition as well as to the color of their bodies. Their self-esteem was at stake.

This chapter begins with examples of an ambivalence toward Africa, which was generated by the constant derogation of the continent from which Afro-Americans could not dissociate themselves, however uncomfortable the association. Some leaders assumed the role of defending Africa against its detractors and developed that genre of speaking and writing which has been referred to as "vindicationist" (see preface).

We then move on to the critical "test case" of Egyptian history, which is discussed with an emphasis on the declining role that black elites played after conquests by Assyrians, Persians, Greeks, Romans, Arabs, and Turks. Some attention is given to the controversy over whether or not any Egyptians—and even some prominent Ethiopians—were "Negroes." Copious use is made of illustrations so that readers can make judgments of their own in some crucial cases. The chapter also includes a general discussion of the meaning of "blackness" in ancient Egypt. The Kingdom of Meroe in Ethiopia, and its implications for African history, are discussed. And the chapter concludes with some observations on the consequences, for the African psyche, of repeated confrontations between Africans and Asians and Europeans.

## AMBIVALENT EXILES

About 697,000 Africans and individuals of African descent were being held in slavery by white colonists in North America when the Declaration of Independence from the British crown was proclaimed in 1776. Thomas Jefferson, who drafted it, included a preamble that spoke of inalienable rights to life, liberty, and the pursuit of happiness, although he himself owned slaves. A small group of approximately 60,000 "Free Negroes" had emerged by 1776, and among them were a few intellectuals who shared the enthusiasm and the hopes of the white radical republicans and took their promises seriously. One of them, a young woman from Senegal, had been bought as a slave at the age of eight by a devout New England family. Fortunately, her owners encouraged what they recognized as young Phillis Wheatley's literary talent, and she eventually emerged as America's first black poet to receive public recognition. It is not difficult to understand why, although she opposed slavery, she held such an image of herself and Africa as is here expressed in one of her poems, "On Being Brought from Africa to America":

> 'Twas mercy brought me from my *Pagan* land,
> Taught my benighted soul to understand
> That there's a God, that there's a *Saviour*, too;
> Once I redemption neither sought nor knew,
> Some view our sable race with scornful eye,
> "Their color is a diabolic die."
> Remember, *Christians*, *Negroes*, black as Cain,
> May be refined, and join th' angelic train.[1]

This African girl, reared in a New England household, rejected Africa, although she stated her opposition to slavery in other poems. For thousands of slaves, on the other hand, nostalgic memories of the Africa from which they had been forcibly carried away were a source of pleasant contemplation. Indeed, for some of them, life in Africa seemed preferable to life in North America. For instance, two years before the

Declaration of Independence was signed, a group of North American Negroes of such mind sent a petition to the British governor of Massachusetts. They asked to go back to Africa, and they complained of being "held in a state of Slavery within the bowels of a free and Christian country," stating that they had been "unjustly dragged by the cruel hand of power from our dearest friends and sum [sic] of us stolen from the bosoms of our tender Parents and from a Populous Pleasant and plentiful country."[2] Unlike Peter Salem, Prince Hall, and other Free Negroes who fought at Lexington, Concord, and Bunker Hill, these were native-born Africans existing as slaves in an alien land. They wanted to go home. In contrast to them Phillis Wheatley identified with the Free Negro supporters of the Revolution and wrote a poem extolling George Washington!

After the revolutionary war, slavery was not abolished by the new nation. Free Negroes were denied citizenship and equal rights. They were able to maintain a sense of positive identity only by calling themselves "African" and giving their churches and societies such names as *African* Methodist, Free *African* Society, *African* Lodge 459 of the Prince Hall Masons. At the same time, they decisively rejected African *culture* and the idea of emigrating to Africa. In fact, they began sending missionaries to convert their kinsmen, just as the white churches did.[3]

About 150 years after Phillis Wheatley wrote the poem about her "pagan" fatherland, another black poet, Countee Cullen, who grew up in an African Methodist Episcopal Church (AME) parsonage as an adopted child, expressed a very different attitude in his poem "Heritage." First, he raised a pertinent query:

> What is Africa to me Copper sun or scarlet sea,
> Jungle star or jungle track,
> Strong bronzed men, or regal black,
> Women from whose loins I sprang
> When the birds of Eden sang?
> One three centuries removed
> From the scenes his fathers loved,
> Spicy grove, cinnamon tree,
> What is Africa to me?

The poet then bemoaned his being forced, as a Christian, to "Quench my pride and cool my blood." He wrote this lament:

> My conversion came high-priced
> I belong to Jesus Christ. . . .
> Not yet has my heart or head
> In the least way realized
> They and I are civilized.[4]

Ambivalence toward Africa has been characteristic of literate black people throughout the Western Hemisphere diaspora. The poems cited above represent polar extremes of feeling about African cultures that have existed in North American Afro-American communities for over 350 years. During some periods shame about the Ancestral Homeland has been the dominant mood among intellectuals as well as among devout Christians. In other periods negative attitudes have been challenged by romanticists in revolt against Puritan values and bourgeois norms of behavior, to which they counterposed other values, such as those expressed in the concepts of Negritude and soul.[5]

The persistence of this ambivalence merits study as a source of the desire for "vindication." One of the most insidious aspects of the system of slavery as it developed in the Western Hemisphere was the concerted and deliberate attempt to convince black people that they were inferior "by nature" and an "ugly" variety of mankind. Remnants of these ideas still exist. Within the last two decades, in the midst of the black struggle against such "brainwashing," some "friends of the Negro" have begun to suggest that dark skin color generally, and black skin color in particular, are *universally* considered undesirable. They consider this "natural" and a burden that blacks must face up to. These "Modern Manicheans," as chapter 2 points out, insist that *Africans themselves dislike (and perhaps despise) dark skin color, even when they themselves are dark, and they assert that all Africans idealize "whiteness," both at the level of abstract symbolism and as a preferred "somatic norm image."* Objective examination of the generalizations that Africans dislike dark skin color and experience negative associations with "blackness" in the abstract did not become historically urgent until after the fifteenth and sixteenth centuries, when European invaders for the first time exercised White Power, in their relations with Africans and Western explorers invaded Africa as well as the Americas and Oceania.

There have been ideological reasons for popularizing the conception that "colored" natives were welcoming white men as long-expected supernatural beings. Many discoverers and explorers also inflated their own egos and justified their abuse of "native" women by convincing themselves that they were the ideal lovers whom the women preferred to their own men. They may have been honestly self-deluded in some cases; in others it was quite likely that some of their trusted informants during the period of initial contact told the white foreigners what they thought these powerful newcomers wanted to bear. Yet, while some Europeans were stressing the advantage they assumed their "whiteness" gave them, others reported that they had made contact with Africans who conceived of the "Devil" as white and who preferred their own black skins, flat noses, and kinky hair to the European norms of beauty.[6] No satisfactory explanation of these contradictory accounts has yet appeared in the literature on race relations and the black self-concept. What seems clear is that when Europeans (i.e., "white" people) exhibited superiority in firepower and other technical developments during their expansion after the fifteenth century, some of the peoples of Africa, Asia, the Americas, and Oceania (i.e., "colored" people) were overawed. A mystique of whiteness sometimes developed, but what it meant and how long it lasted varied from time to time and from place to place.

In seeking to explain the presence of skin-color prejudices in some parts of the world, there is no need to invoke theories about a primordial dislike for dark skin. Specific historical and anthropological studies suggest alternative explanations. Instead of speculating, as the Degler-Gergen propositions do, about human propensities to contrast light and dark, black and white, or the universality of early life experiences that lead to the derogation of "blackness," a reassessment of the empirical evidence, based on cultural comparisons, is necessary.

Africa is the logical place to begin such a comparative study. Is it true, for instance, that all Africans, even those not influenced by contact with white people, dislike "blackness" in the abstract and idealize a lighter body image than their own? If so, has this been true in all historical periods? This is a matter for historical and anthropological research, with special attention given to early periods and with an emphasis upon the "Negro" as a physical type, because "Negroes" have been most viciously derogated.* The questions of when and where so-called Negroes first appeared in human history and what relations they had with other people at the time are relevant to such an enquiry.

## NEGRO ORIGINS AND AFRICAN PREHISTORY

Vindicationist scholars welcomed the increasing consensus among anthropologists during the second half of the twentieth century that it was neither in Java nor in China that the first true men, as distinct from other anthropoids, had appeared during the process of evolution.[7] The idea that mankind originated in eastern or southern Africa seemed, to the vindicationists, to have a strong antiracist potential. They soon had to contend with the suggestion from some physical anthropologists, however, that this did not necessarily mean that the early men were dark skinned, and it certainly did not prove that they were "Negroes."[8]Although some cogent reasons have been cited for believing that *Homo habilis* and other African hominids *were* dark skinned, the oldest human fossils do not meet the anthropometric criteria for Negroes, or any variety of modern man, for that matter.[9] As to where and when the Negro type first appeared with the distinctive combination of skin color, facial features, lip form, and hair type used to distinguish it from the Caucasoid and Mongoloid stocks, modem physical anthropologists have no certain answer. Nor do they offer any convincing explanations about why similar physical types exist today in what must be some very old societies in Oceania and Southeast Asia.

Most anthropologists lean toward the view that the Negro physical type appeared late in the process of evolution in Africa, as a variation on a more generalized, probably dark-skinned human type.[10] The oldest fossils classified by anthropologists as "Negro" are approximately 10,000 years old, these coming from both the eastern and western Sahara regions, where they were associated with bone harpoons and fishhooks. These are the remains of people who lived in this area before it became a desert—when it was well watered, lush, and green. The ultimate origin, in time and place, of this oldest known "Negro" type is unknown. Such people may certainly have lived in other areas where soil and climate did not permit fossilization of bones.[11]

British Africanists Roland Oliver and John Fage present the prevailing theory of a late emergence of the Negro physical type in Africa in their widely used *Short History of Africa*. At the same time, the authors stress the point that "in *pre*-historic times—at least through all the long millennia of the paleolithic or 'Old Stone Age'—Africa was not even relatively backward; it was in the lead." In speaking of the elaboration and spread of improved tool styles, Oliver and Fage maintain that *"there is little doubt that throughout all but the last small fraction of this long development of the human form, Africa remained at the center of the inhabited world* [italics added]"; and with regard to the earliest type of stone tools, "the centre of their distribution appears to be the woodland savannah region of tropical Africa." Since Oliver and Fage believe in a late date for the appearance of Negroes in Africa, this scenario presumably places the dynamic early African prehistory sometime before the emergence of any Negroes![12]

Polemicists who stress what they believe to be distinctive inherited mental and temperamental traits that differentiate one race from another usually postulate an early divergence of white and black people from a common ancestor. The late Carleton Coon, an American anthropologist, achieved the same end by arguing that Negroes emerged late from an ancestral line that began developing separately over 200,000 years ago. Moreover, this separate line certainly was not "in the lead." Few of his colleagues took him seriously, then or later, when he wrote in his book *The Origin of Races* (1962) that "as far as we know now, the Congoid [i.e., Negro] line started on the same evolutionary level as the Eurasiatic ones in the Early Middle Pleistocene and then stood still for half a million years, after which Negroes and Pygmies appeared as if out of nowhere."[13] An anthropologist of liberal persuasion, Ashley Montagu, in a critical analysis of *The Origin of Races*, commented:

> Since according to Coon, the Negroes were the last of the subspecies of Homo erectus to be transformed into *sapiens* (pp. 655–666), the level of civilization attained by them is "explained." They simply do not have as long a biological or genetic history as sapiens, as we whites or Caucasoids.[14]

A theory of late emergence could, logically, mean either that Negroes are the most highly evolved or that they are "retarded," depending upon what one has to say about their progenitors. Oliver and Fage, who believe in a late appearance, do not concern themselves with this argument between "racists" and "vindicationists."

With such little fossil evidence on hand, discussion of the *late prehistory* and *early history* of Africa's Negroes is more rewarding than arguing about early prehistory. That portion of the Negro African population living on the savannah land south of the desert and in the Nile Valley certainly participated in and contributed to the great food-producing revolution of about 7,000 or 8,000 years ago, based upon the domestication of grain, sheep, goats, pigs, and cows. This agricultural revolution led to a population explosion of both the Caucasian and black populations that occupied northern Africa. The rest of the continent remained sparsely populated for several thousand years, although some of its peoples gradually increased in number as they adopted new sources of food, or as they domesticated some plants themselves. Extensive migration of the expanding northern populations into central and southern Africa occurred after iron tools made it possible to clear forests and as new crops suited to new ecologies became available (map 2). Oliver and Fage expressed the dominant view among Africanists in the fifties when they wrote:

> Six or seven thousand years ago . . . at the end of man's purely parasitic existence as a hunter and gatherer . . . Africa was already inhabited by the ancestors of the four main types recognized as indigenous in historical times [i.e., Caucasian "Hamite," Bushman, Pygmy, and Negro]. . . . *The Negro appeared on the scene even later than the other three types, and his present predominance was certainly achieved during the modern food-producing period* [italics added].[15]

This food-producing period began with what some archaeologists call the Neolithic Revolution in the Middle East. The major technical advances of that "revolution" involved the domestication of plants and animals, innovations that made possible the substitution of settled village life for existence in hunting and gathering bands, and thereby laid the foundation for the emergence of cities and the "civilization" associated with them. (Some groups continued to prefer a nomadic existence but it was now based upon pastoralism.) The Middle Eastern Neolithic began in the highlands of eastern Africa and southwestern Asia when some innovative peoples domesticated various cereal grains, small animals, cattle, a few vegetables, and some fruits. Coffee is regarded by American anthropologist George Peter Murdock as one of the contributions of the East African highlands. The "Southwest Asiatic food complex" and the "East African food complex" were transferred to the Tigris-Euphrates river valley,[16] to the Fertile Crescent between that area, and to the Nile Delta, as well as into the Nile Valley itself (map 3).

Improved nutrition and sedentary patterns of living led to population explosions in some areas. The food cultivators in the Nile Valley and the savannah of northern Africa soon outnumbered the hunters and fishers in these areas and later displaced the Pygmies and Bushmanoid peoples farther south. Oliver and Fage here comment on an ongoing controversy:

> There are those who would argue the case for an original and independent invention of agriculture in this sub-Saharan region [i.e., "the light woodland savanna which stretches from Senegal to the upper Nile"]. Against this, however, there is at present a lack of any firm archaeological evidence for the existence of truly cultivating communities to the south of the Sahara earlier than the end of the second millennium B.C.[17]

The first to argue that case, George Peter Murdock, saw no need to rest his case on archaeology. He used a sophisticated method of analysis, developed by the Russian botanist Vavilov, to demonstrate that certain wild strains of plants had first been domesticated by Mandespeaking Negroes in the area near the big bend of the Niger River, in what is now the Mali Republic.

Murdock insists that while North Africa was borrowing the crops of the Southwest Asian food complex, first introduced into Africa through the Egyptian delta by immigrants from the Fertile Crescent of Asia Minor, and while some of these crops were being adopted by oasis dwellers in the desert, a West African food-producing revolution may have been under way in the area near the present-day city of Timbuctoo.

Murdock assigns a date of about 5000 BC for the time when these innovations began to spread eastward toward the Nile Valley. In what he calls the "Sudanic food complex" were included several types of yams, one variety of rice, and watermelon; but, above all, there was cotton, which had previously been considered an Indian contribution.[18]

Although Murdock espouses his point of view with crusading fervor and dedicates the book in which he presents his evidence to "Americans of African Descent," a leading Afro-American Africanist, Professor Joseph Harris, has advised caution regarding Murdock's vindicationist conclusion, noting that "support for [his] position is minimal because the confirming evidence is slight." Since Harris wrote, however, some

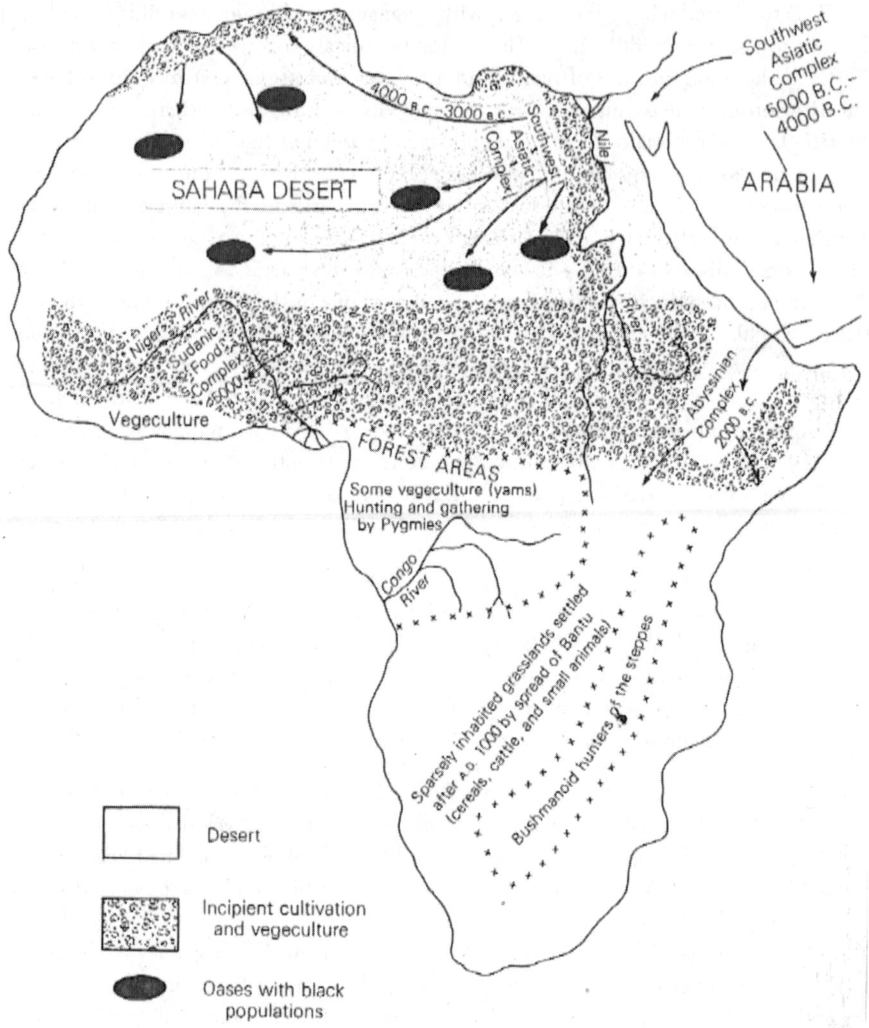


**Map 2.** Diffusion of Food Complexes in Africa. Cartography based on a concept by the author.

experts whose opinions cannot be discounted have rallied to the support of portions of Murdock's argument.[19] Murdock insists that racism prevented earlier recognition of "West African Negroes as one of mankind's leading creative benefactors." He is convinced that early anthropologists fell victim to "the vulgar assumption, widespread among Asiatics as well as Europeans, that the Negro is an inferior race incapable of making any substantial contribution to civilization," and that "all complex manifestations of culture in Africa south of the Sahara must have emanated from some other and 'higher' race like the Caucasoid 'Hamites'."[20]

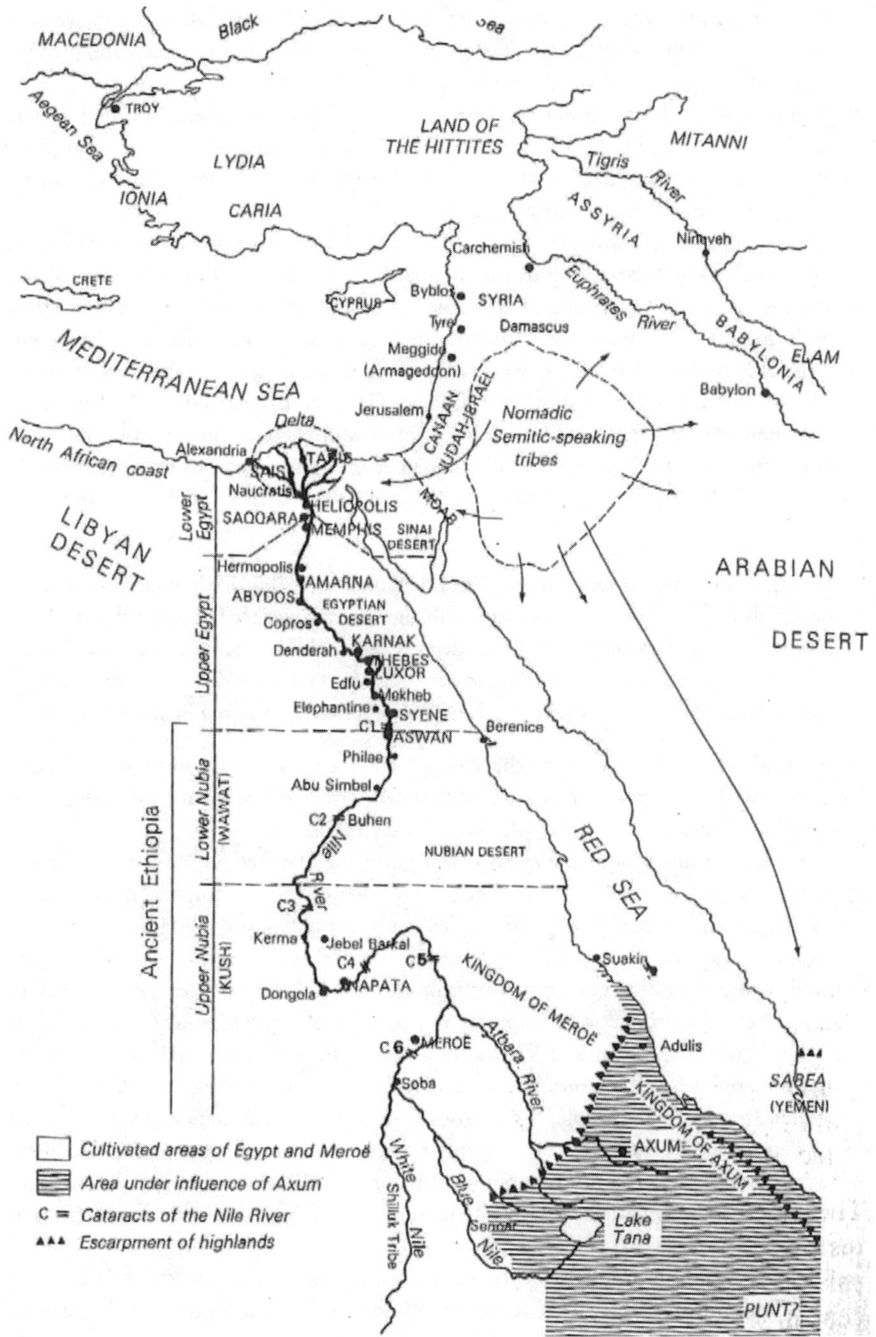


**Map 3.** Ancient Settlements and Political Divisions in the Nile Valley. Cartography based on a concept by the author.

The population explosion among the Negroes of the savannah lands in western Africa between 8000 and 5000 BC, resulting from the adoption of agriculture, precipitated a population spread throughout central and southern Africa into territory occupied by Pygmies and Bushmen. Some of these hunters and gatherers were absorbed; others retreated into inaccessible forest, desert, and mountainous areas to become "marginal" peoples. A cattle-keeping people with some Bushmanoid and Negroid affinities evolved into the Hottentots of South Africa (see map 2).

During the massive movements of peoples in Africa in response to climatic and demographic changes extending over a long period of time, small, previously isolated groups were thrown into contact with one another. When such groups met, they not only fought one another occasionally but also mixed genetically. This is evident from the archaeological record as well as from the physical appearance of the existing populations of central and southern Africa.[21] They borrowed cultural traits from one another, too. For example, the "clicks" of Bushmen and Hottentots occur now in Bantu speech. Alan Lomax, the distinguished musicologist, came to a surprising conclusion after an exhaustive comparative analysis of African and Afro-American musical styles:

> As Negro tribes moved east and south into the jungle, they displaced, often absorbed, or established symbiotic relationships with the African Hunter bands, at the same time, acquiring their musical style. Evidence is everywhere at hand to support this notion. . . . *This Negro-Pygmy style was kept alive by the black slaves in America and now forms the baseline for the entire Afro-American [musical] tradition* [italics added].[22]

Large numbers of Africans from the Congo-Angola region were brought to North America as well as to the West Indies and Latin America and were probably the culture bearers of this musical style that links Africa and the diaspora.

We know nothing about the extent to which color or other physical traits symbolized ethnicity or group solidarity for the people involved in the migrations of African prehistoric times. Rock paintings in the Sahara and predynastic artifacts in Egyptian tombs reveal a keen awareness of differences in physical type, but what meanings were attached to them—esthetic, erotic, mystical, or status allocating—we have no way of knowing.[23] If relations between some of the peoples of contemporary eastern Africa (e.g., the Watutsi, Wahutu, and Watwa, or Ba-Twa, pygmies) are studied for clues to the past, relative height emerges as a status attribute of considerable antiquity.[24] There are legends, too, of "red" people, the Bachwezi, who came as invaders and were invested with mystical significance. However, among other people in the same region, "redness" was considered within the normal ethnic range of a number of tribal populations, not as evidence of miscegenation with Caucasians. And "red" was not a word that signified superior esthetic status.[25]

"Prehistoric" times for most of the peoples of Africa existed until Islamic penetration after the ninth century AD; for some, "prehistory" ended only after the massive invasion by Europeans in the sixteenth century. Some Africans never saw white people until World War I! Attitudes toward skin-color differences can only be inferred from relations observed after conflict began, or from folklore and legend or sociolinguistic analysis. Objective research of this type has been neglected, but a group of British racist anthropologists confused the situation during the late nineteenth century by elaborating the "Hamitic myth," which has played the same role in African studies as the "Aryan myth" has played in European pseudohistory. They assumed that wherever lighter-skinned "Hamitic" Africans met darker-skinned Africans, the former scorned the latter and made serfs or slaves of them, and that the blacks, an inferior breed biologically, deferred to these lighter-skinned peoples. That myth has almost been destroyed, but remnants of it linger in the literature on eastern and southern Africa. The term "Hamitic" is still used by Africanists whose attempts to purge it of racist implications have not yet been entirely successful.[26]

The Nile Valley alone, of all the regions of the Ancestral Homeland, provides an ideal situation for examining race relations in the earliest historic periods of the continent. The vast expanse of North Africa now occupied by the Sahara, Libyan, and Egyptian deserts was well watered and grassy up to about 2500 BC and was occupied by Negroes and Bushmanoid peoples as well as pastoral Caucasians. As desiccation began after 2500 BC in response to climatic changes, many of these people, with their cattle, small animals, and rudimentary agricultural practices, moved southward into the savannah, with some of the blacks remaining on the oases as agriculturalists or cultivators of date palms. Others of this racially mixed Sahara population wandered eastward into the fertile Nile Valley, augmenting an agricultural population already there and adding new racial elements to a basically Negro indigenous population. Increases in population density created a challenge to the ingenuity of the political leaders of the Nile Valley to bring new land into cultivation through expansion of irrigation schemes. A similar process of concentration of population resulting from desiccation was taking place in the Tigris Euphrates Valley.[27]

The two river valleys became centers where "civilization" developed under the aegis of priestly hierarchies. That is, a type of society emerged with writing, a calendrical system, mathematics and astronomy, religious cults administered by a priesthood, and property relations that resulted in the emergence of wealthy leisured classes existing on a share of the surplus provided by serfs, slaves, and taxable peasant-freemen. Armies used for defense and conquest grew up as an integral part of these systems of "civilized" living. Immediately south of Egypt several Kushitic, or Ethiopian, kingdoms developed also as a part of the Nile Valley "civilized" complex, surrounded on both sides by the barbarian peoples of the desert. The early Nile Valley civilizations have always been considered important in vindicationist arguments (see map 3).

## *The Roles of Egypt and Ethiopia in Black History*

By the time the interracial abolition movement was organized in the United States in 1831, Afro-American leaders had developed a network of institutions devoted to self-help, aid to runaway slaves, and protest against slavery and racial discrimination suffered by Free Negroes. In their speeches, sermons, tracts, newspapers, and books, they referred frequently to Ethiopia, and the ministers made their congregations familiar with the prophecy in Psalms 68:31: "Princes shall come out of Egypt and Ethiopia shall soon stretch forth her hand unto God."

In February 1829, one Robert Alexander Young applied for a copyright for his pamphlet entitled *The Ethiopian Manifesto, Issued in Defense of the Black Man's Rights in the Scale of Universal Freedom*. The next year the most militant of the pamphleteers, David Walker, in his *Appeal . . . to the Coloured Citizens of the World*, wrote: "Though our cruel oppressors and murderers may (if possible) treat us more cruel, as Pharaoh did the children of Israel, yet the God of the Etheopeans, has been pleased to hear our moans in consequence of oppression; and the day of redemption from abject wretchedness draweth near." Later, despite his denunciation of the oppressive pharaoh, he wrote of other Egyptians who were "wise legislators," and produced pyramids, also "turning the channel of the Nile." He called them "sons of Africa or of Ham, among whom learning originated, and was carried thence into Greece where it was improved upon and refined."

Young and Walker were Free Negroes who had read widely and knew something of history and geography.[28] The less sophisticated slaves did not fix their attention on Ethiopia and had little reason to admire Egypt which, for them, was the country where lived the pharaoh who had oppressed "God's chosen people." When the spirituals grew up on the plantations, some of them expressed identification with Moses and "the mixed multitude" that he led "out of the house of bondage," with an Ethiopian wife at his side. The Egyptian pharaoh who pursued the Jews fleeing slavery was the villain. The slaves sang: "Go down Moses; / Way down in Egypt's Land; / Tell Ol' Pharaoh / Let my people go." They exulted in his defeat as Jehovah showed his hand, singing, "Oh, Mary don' you weep; I Oh Mary, don' you moan; / Pharaoh's army got drownded." It was only after Emancipation that Egypt could become a master symbol in Afro-American liberation mythology and racial advancement ideology.

Both slaves and Free Negroes knew that Egypt and Ethiopia were said to be in Africa, the place where some of them had been born and from which some of the ancestors of all of them had come. Those who became familiar with the Bible knew that both places were somewhere in the vicinity of "the Holy Land." (The Creation story referred to a "river of Ethiopia" as being one of the boundaries of the Garden of Eden.) But the exact geographical location of Ethiopia, prior to the late nineteenth century, was never a matter of much concern to Afro-Americans. Ethiopia was both the name of a place-whose location somewhere in Africa was vague—and a metaphor for a widely scattered diaspora people, as was the term "Israel." However, by the end of the nineteenth century, better-educated Afro-Americans were becoming interested in the fate of the specific areas in Africa referred to by Jews, Greek, and Romans as Ethiopia, the land inhabited by "the people with the burnt faces." In the 1980s, the old historic Arab name, "Abyssinia," and "Ethiopia" were both being applied to the kingdom in the East African highlands that had fought off the Muslims and remained Christian in the sixteenth century and that defeated Italy in 1896 at the Battle of Adowa, thus preserving its independence during the European "scramble for Africa." Black people everywhere identified with the victor in that battle, and some thought that prophecy was being fulfilled—that Ethiopia was now about to "stretch forth her hand unto God."

By the middle of the nineteenth century, most literate black leaders in the United States were aware that the ancient Greeks and Romans had made favorable remarks about Ethiopians, since abolitionists, black and white, used quotations from the *Iliad* and the *Odyssey*, from Herodotus, Dioscorus, and Strabo to defend black people when involved in polemics about their inborn capabilities.[29] Some knew that Dioscorus had repeated stories told to him by Egyptians who said that their country was originally a colony of Ethiopia. Most who knew this knew that ancient Ethiopia was in the Nile Valley. They were also, no doubt, familiar with a statement by Herodotus that, in some translations, described Egyptians as having black skin and kinky hair.[30] They did not begin confidently to claim Egypt as part of the black world, however, until they became familiar with the findings of some of the French Egyptologists that appeared in the early nineteenth century. After that, Egypt became a cherished symbol for many vindicationists, along with Ethiopia. Devout Afro-American churchgoers were ambivalent, however, because their image of cruel and blasphemous pharaohs, gleaned from the Bible, tarnished the image of Egypt and made it difficult for them to embrace Egypt with pride. The more sophisticated black intellectuals had no such conflict. It satisfied them that Egypt had been powerful.

The transatlantic African slave trade and the use of black slaves in the Western Hemisphere were practices being challenged by the growth of humanitarian sentiment in Britain and France at the same time that Egyptology was coming into being as a serious discipline. The first scholars to describe the Egyptian antiquities noted that some of the high-status individuals had Negroid features.[31] Some apologists for slavery accepted these reports but insisted that an unfortunate Negro infusion into a fine white strain of Egyptian leaders had caused Egyptian civilization to decline, and they warned against letting such miscegenation occur in the United States. Others argued that these Negroid Egyptians were not really "True Negroes" of the type brought to the New World as slaves but were a different, more intelligent breed of dark-skinned people.

The founding fathers of the American School of Ethnology, Josiah C. Nott and George R. Gliddon, became involved in this discussion in the 1840s, giving legitimacy to a recently published book, *Crania Egyptica*, written by physician S. G. Morton, that reported on the author's hobby of collecting skulls. Combining Morton's amateur anthropometry with biblical folklore, Nott and Gliddon suggested that the Egyptians were gifted *dark-skinned Caucasians* descended from Noah's son Ham. These people had developed writing, mathematics, astronomy, and lofty philosophical conceptions, and with tautological naïveté Nott and Gliddon pointed out that this would have been impossible had they been Negroes. They claimed that later, however, Egyptian civilization was debased by miscegenation with Negroes, who came from a quite different Noaic line of descent and who were also the ancestors of the blacks enslaved in the American South. Unless the United States preserved a rigid color line in its dealings with enslaved and Free Negroes, they argued, Anglo-Saxon civilization would disappear as pharaonic civilization had.[32] Such ideas were widespread until the 1930s, and Afro-American leaders felt duty-bound to combat them.

Egyptology thus became a crucial arena in the persisting struggle between anti-black racists and those black intellectuals who considered themselves to be vindicationists. The latter were not prepared to leave the arguments of the Notts and the Gliddons unchallenged. One of their basic strategies was to call attention to the fact that the early dynasties of Egypt, including some of the most creative ones, included a number of pharaohs who would be considered "Negroes" by white Americans if they were asked to judge their race on the basis of photographs not designated as "Egyptian." But black scholars were not the first to point out this similarity to New World Negroes.

Among the first Europeans to reflect upon the race of ancient Egyptians was Count Constantine de Volney (1757–1820), who visited Egypt between 1783 and 1785. He wrote of the brown-skinned Christian Copts, who formed a great part of the nonurban population, that "all have a bloated face, puffed up eyes, flat nose, thick lips; in a word, the true face of the mulatto." The count was surprised and puzzled at finding in Egypt this physical type with which he was familiar in Europe, where it had resulted from matings between white people and Africans or blacks from the Caribbean. After viewing the Sphinx, he was convinced that a similar process of miscegenation had been at work in Africa, but with blacks as the majority population and whites the minority in the initial mixture. This led him to write about the Sphinx in words that were disconcerting to the proslavery forces of his day:

> On seeing that head, typically Negro in all its features, I remembered the remarkable passage [of Herodotus]. . . . The ancient Egyptians were true Negroes of the same type as all native-born Africans. That being so, we can see how their blood mixed for several centuries with that of the Romans and Greeks, must have lost the intensity of its original color, while retaining nonetheless the imprint of its original mold. . . . What a subject for meditation, to see the present barbarism and ignorance of the Copts, descendants of the alliance between the profound genius of the Egyptians and the brilliant mind of the Greeks! Just think that this race of black men, today our slave and the object of our scorn, is the very race to which we owe our arts, sciences, and even the use of speech! Just imagine, finally, that it is in the midst of peoples who call themselves the greatest friends of liberty and humanity that one has approved the most barbarous slavery and questioned whether black men have the same kind of intelligence as Whites![33]

This sounds like a volley being shot at one of the count's famous contemporaries, Thomas Jefferson, the American politician-intellectual. The count is, of course, including mulattoes and quadroons and octoroons in his concept of "Negroes" and "blacks," as did the Sage of Monticello when it suited his purposes to do so.

Baron Vivant Denon, a contemporary of Count Volney, who accompanied Napoleon's army to Egypt as an artist making sketches, wrote of his journey to Cairo:

> I had only time to view the Sphinx, which deserves to be drawn with a more scrupulous attention than has ever yet been bestowed upon it. Though its proportions are colossal, the outline is pure and graceful, the expression of the head is mild, gracious and tranquil; the character is African; but the mouth, the lips of which are thick, has a softness and delicacy of execution truly admirable [see plates 1 and 2].[34]

Following Volney and Denon, a century of savants tried to prove that Egyptians were, and always had been, white! There were always a few Egyptologists, however, who took an objective position and claimed that some pharaohs were Caucasian, some Negro, and some mixed; and that the average degree of admixture within the general population varied from period to period, but was, in a general sense, "mulatto."

Black vindicationists, as did Volney and Denon, used the Sphinx as a symbol of the Negro presence in Egypt. Believed to have been modeled on the head of a prominent pharaoh from Old Kingdom times, when the basic outlines of Egypt's future greatness were set, the Sphinx evoked the following comment from the distinguished Afro-Caribbean nineteenth-century scholar who is sometimes called the "Father of Black Cultural Nationalism," Edward Wilmot Blyden:

> Her [*sic*] features are decidedly that of the African or Negro type, with "expanded nostrils." If, then, the sphinx was placed here looking out in majestic and mysterious silence over the empty plain where once stood the great city of Memphis in all its pride and glory, as an "emblematic representation of the king"—is not the inference clear as to the peculiar type of race to which that king belonged?[35]

In commenting on the Sphinx, the contemporary Afro-American historian Chancellor Williams, of Howard University, here refers to Pharaoh Chefren [Khafre], who is reputed to have had the monumental sculpture carved from a rock in the desert:

> As though he intended to settle the question of biracial identity for all ages to come, he had his African features so boldly and clearly carved into a portrait statue that not even a fool could seriously doubt that this mighty monarch was a "Negro."[36]

Arthur Weigall, an Englishman, former inspector general of antiquities for the Egyptian government and a distinguished Egyptologist, agrees that the Sphinx portrays Pharaoh Chefren and states that "the features of the face bear a decided resemblance to those of the statues of about this period."[37] However, comparison of the Sphinx with the most widely publicized portrait statue of Chefren reveals the latter as presenting less Negroid features.[38] But this fact itself has significance in examining the Degler-Gergen propositions, for it reveals no reluctance on the part of the pharaoh to have whatever degree of Negroidness he did possess emphasized in a highly public situation on the borders of the Delta, the most non-Negroid part of Egypt, gateway to the country. Since the Sphinx signified wisdom, it follows that neither Egyptians nor foreigners saw anything incongruous in symbolizing wisdom by Negroidness. Egyptologist Weigall, certainly no partisan of Negro Africans (a chapter in one of his books refers to the Twenty-fifth Dynasty as "an astonishing era of nigger domination"),[39] suggested the following about the Sphinx:

> Probably it was originally an actual representation of the Pharaoh Khafre [i.e., Chefren] in his aspect as an incarnation of the sun -god, and gradually it came to be regarded as the embodiment of the collective Pharaonic spirit.[40]

Racism has put such blinders on people of the contemporary Western world that most tourists visiting Cairo today can take their camel rides around the Sphinx without ever noticing what struck Volney and Denon so forcefully, namely, that an ancient pharaoh of Egypt was physically the same type of person as the slaves who toiled on plantations in the Americas and the Caribbean. If these tourists were to relate what they saw to their own experience, they would notice that the pharaoh was the same type of man who today walks the streets of Kingston, Harlem, Birmingham, and the South

Side of Chicago. Likewise, most of the Arab population of Egypt is probably unaware that millennia before their ancestors arrived on the scene after AD 700, most of the Egyptians resembled the Sphinx, and that blacks, not Arabs, were once the dominant type in Egypt. Today Aswan, far up the Nile, or even Khartoum in the Sudan, presents a more accurate picture of early Egypt's population than does Cairo.

Count Volney was somewhat less than scientific in inferring from the Sphinx alone that the entire population of Egypt had been Negro during the Old Kingdom. (Perhaps only the ruling class, or a portion of it, was Negro!) Volney ignored the fact, too, that ancient Egypt included barbarities to match those of the southern planters. Nevertheless, his scholarly intuitions were more soundly based than those of Thomas Jefferson, who refused to accept evidence from either the Bible or the classics, both of which he knew well, that refuted the argument that no black person at any time, anywhere, had ever shown intellectual capacities equivalent to those of whites. Almost a century later, W. E. B. Du Bois commented that, "in recent years, despite the work of exploration and interpretation in Egypt and Ethiopia, almost nothing is said of the Negro race. Yet that race was always prominent in the valley of the Nile."[41] He tried to fill in this gap with his own writing, publishing a book, *The Negro*, in 1915, in which he summarized, in an accurate and clear manner, all that was then known about the role of various racial groups in ancient Egypt. Twenty-five years later he published *Black Folk Then and Now*. Du Bois evaluated the data objectively, in an effort to set the record straight about the participation of blacks in the building of Egyptian civilization, but made only modest claims for their contributions.

During the years between Count de Volney's visit to Egypt and Dr. Du Bois's book, a mass of data had accumulated, for Egyptology had emerged as a professional discipline based in a few European and American university departments and museums. French academics kept tight control of the Cairo Museum under an agreement with the Turkish rulers. In discussing his sources, Du Bois wrote, "The works of Breasted and Petrie, Maspéro, Budge, and Newberry and Garstang are the standard books on Egypt. They mention the Negro but incidentally and often slightingly."[42]There were as yet no black Egyptologists in either Africa or the diaspora. (Including a few Egyptians, there are less than a dozen even today.) However, these men, and another, Arthur Weigall, not mentioned by Du Bois, despite their biases, were enthusiasts for preserving antiquities and were industrious scholars who learned to decipher hieroglyphics. Thus they provided the necessary "raw materials" that vindicationists needed for fashioning a more acceptable account of Egyptian history.

Du Bois attempted to evaluate the classical Greco-Roman sources and the material published by Egyptologists—translations of texts, reproductions of temple frescoes, photographs of sculpture—and came to a conclusion that, with some minor modifications and reservations, is surprisingly close to that of contemporary mainstream Egyptology:

> Of what race, then were the Egyptians? They certainly were not white in any sense of the modem use of that word—neither in color nor physical measurement, in hair nor countenance, in language nor social customs. *They stood in relationship nearest the Negro race in earliest times, and then gradually through the infiltration of Mediterranean*

*and Semitic elements became what would be described in America as light mulatto stock of Octoroons or Quadroons.* This stock was varied continually: now by new infiltration of Negro blood from the south, now by Negroid and Semitic blood from the east, now by Berber types from the north and west [italics added].[43]

What Du Bois called a "light mulatto stock of Octoroons or Quadroons" has been dubbed "Hamite" when found in Africa but is classified as "Negro" or "black" in the United States, and is treated accordingly. It is a matter of taxonomical irony that, by the time Du Bois wrote *The Negro*, anthropologists had taken a word that was used during the period of slavery to mean "an inferior breed of humanity descended from Ham, that is, a Negro," and transformed it to mean "a light-skinned African with Caucasian features, definitely *superior* to darker Africans, especially Negroid ones." Du Bois assailed the use of the term "'Hamite,' under cover of which millions of Negroids have been characteristically transferred to the 'white' race by some eager scientists."

Black Americans with an interest in this issue asked two perfectly logical questions that drew evasive answers from physical anthropologists, wrapped up in technical jargon: "Why are people who look like us called 'white' or 'Hamite' if they live in Egypt but 'Negroes' if they live in this country?" and "Why, if someone of that type turns up among the Egyptian pharaohs is he classified 'white,' but if he lived in Mississippi he'd be put in the back of the bus?" Du Bois and other vindicationists were led to adopt a simple basic strategy. *They called for consistency in the use of the term "Negro." They pointed out that failure to do so automatically removed virtually all of Egypt's achievements from the realm of the Black World.* They challenged Egyptologists to face up to the inconsistencies of their terminology and to realize the racist uses to which their inconsistencies were being put. Some did, and were Du Bois now living, he would be pleasantly surprised at some of the modem publications on Egypt. But the inconsistency still remains unresolved—and usually unrecognized—particularly among historians who have not yet assimilated the latest results of research in Egyptology.

The attack on semantic sleight of hand reached its peak during the sixties in the work of Dr. Cheikh Anta Diop, a professor at the University of Dakar in Senegal, West Africa. This French-trained African savant had specialized in history, linguistics, Egyptology, and the use of scientific tests for determining the approximate age of some archaeological finds. The leading vindicationist was now an African, not a diaspora black. He was also a scholar who could meet the Egyptologists on their own ground.

During the 1960s, Diop and a group of African scholars convinced UNESCO that it should sponsor the research for, and the writing and publication of, a definitive history of Africa, most of which would consist of contributions by African scholars but would also include the work of non-Africans approved as collaborators by an editorial committee with an African majority. The first two volumes of what is to be a nine-volume work appeared in 1981, published jointly by UNESCO, the University California Press, and Heinemann of London. Some of the historical articles deal with Egypt and Ethiopia. Several explicitly consider the question of the race of the early Egyptians, including an annex that summarizes the discussions that took place in 1974 at a conference that had been arranged at the urging of Diop. Dr. G. Mokhtar, editor of volume 2 of *A General History of Africa*, called attention in an overview to the implications of that conference:

> Already in 1874 there was argument about whether the ancient Egyptians were "white" or "black." A century later a UNESCO-sponsored symposium in Cairo proved that the discussion was not, nor was likely soon to be closed. It is not easy to find a physical definition of "black" acceptable to all.

Mokhtar, himself an Egyptian, had put his finger on the crux of the problem.

The official report of the 1974 symposium stated that much of the activity turned out to involve a "successive and mutually contradictory monologue" between individuals opposing Diop's views and either Diop himself or a Congolese linguist and historian, Dr. Theophile Obenga, who supported him. Only these two scholars and a Sudanese represented "Negro Africa," as contrasted with six Egyptians, one Canadian, one representative from the United States, and eight from Europe. No one from England participated. The most vocal and energetic opponents of Diop's views were Professors Jean Vercoutter and Serge Sauneron, both French Egyptologists. The rapporteur stated that the "disagreement was profound" on the question of whether or not the ancient Egyptians were Negroes, but some unity was achieved on three other issues: (1) desire to see careful studies made of the relationship between the ancient Egyptian language and other African languages; (2) support for more thorough studies of Egyptian mummies; (3) desire for clarification of terminology and methodology used by anthropologists in racial classification. Egyptians objected to the obvious enthusiasm of Diop to see the point firmly established that the ancient Egyptians were "black." The Sudanese participant said he "did not think it important to establish whether the ancient Egyptians were black or negroid; what was most remarkable was the degree of civilization they had achieved." The Sudanese scholar had a lively exchange with Diop on linguistic methodology and on the proper semantic values to place on linguistic methodology and on the proper semantic values to place on ancient Egyptian words sometimes translated as "black people." Professor Jean Leclant, a French savant, leaned a bit toward Diop's view that the ancient Egyptians were not Caucasians, but was inclined to say they were "neither white nor negro." It was obvious that much of the polarization at this conference came because Diop and Obenga insisted upon a definition of "Negro" that included a very wide range of skin color and features, whereas the other participants clung to a concept of "Negro" that was essentially a holdover from traditional physical anthropology. Those who used the narrow definition did not deny that such physical types had been present in every period of Egyptian history, but they questioned their predominance at any given period. In considering ancient Egyptian populations, they also refused to call "brown" (or "red") and "yellow" people "black," as Diop, using North American criteria, insisted upon doing. Maurice Glele, a program specialist in the Division of Cultural Studies, UNESCO, remarked that

> if the criteria for classifying a person as black, white or yellow were so debatable, and if the concepts which had been discussed were so ill-defined and perhaps so subjective or inseparable from habitual patterns of thought, this should be frankly stated and a revision should be made of the entire terminology of world history in the light

of new scientific criteria, so that the vocabulary should be the same for every one and that words should have the same connotations, thus avoiding misconceptions and being conducive to understanding and agreement.

Diop and Obenga insisted upon using the current physical anthropological data, along with iconographic inquiry and linguistic analysis, to characterize the ancient Egyptians as "black" in both a technical anthropological sense and in terms of popular usage. The rapporteur states that Diop dismissed his critics summarily as being so conditioned that they could not face facts:

> He was, therefore, in no doubt: the first inhabitants of the Nile valley belonged to the black race, as defined by the research findings currently accepted by specialists in anthropology and prehistory. Professor Diop considered that only psychological and educational factors prevented the truth of this from being accepted. . . .Professor Diop was not in favor of setting up commissions to verify patent facts which, at the present time, simply needed formal recognition.

None of the participants other than Diop and Obenga was willing to accept the "Negroness" of the early Egyptians as a "patent fact." Instead of "formal recognition" of what were regarded as "facts" by Diop and Obenga, other participants did recommend the establishment of several commissions to study the problem in more detail. Most insisted that the Egyptian populations had been "mixed" from the earliest times. They did not discuss whether such "mixed" populations would be characterized as "black" or "Negro" if current social definitions in Europe and North America were used; nor did they discuss usage in other contexts where political ends would be served thereby. For Diop, these were crucial questions that were ignored by the symposium.[44]

In Mokhtar's summation of the findings of the symposium, he noted that while some of Diop 's arguments had been adopted as expressing the consensus of the group, there had been no unanimous agreement upon any point except that what laymen or political personalities mean by "race" is not what geneticists and most contemporary anthropologists mean. Diop's rejoinder was that specialists should remember that laymen do not react to genotypes and blood types but to phenotypes, that is, to what old-fashioned anthropologists call "races." Diop argued that the question we must answer is, "Did Egyptians resemble what ordinary people, today, call 'Negroes'?" not "What do skull measurements and blood types show?"[45]

Some scholars lash out at those who write about Egypt from a black perspective, with displays of amazing insensitivity to motivation. Fortunately, this did not occur at the symposium. However, one of the most distinguished contemporary British Africanists, Roland Oliver, of the London School of Oriental and African Studies, previously quoted and cited, in reviewing the chapter by Diop entitled "The Origins of Ancient Egypt" in the UNESCO *General History of Africa for the Times Literary Supplement,* dismisses this highly trained scholar as being not "serious" and ridicules him for having "made a life-long hobby of the thesis that the Ancient Egyptians were black." The disagreement between Oliver and Diop, in part, involves the issue of how broad a definition of "black" or "Negro" should be used by scholars. Yet, since the British scholar felt impelled to deride the African savant as a " rumbustious Senegalese museum director," and to dismiss his work by saying that "of sixty-odd contributions there is only one which is a total nonsense," we can only assume that the emotion behind the contemptuous tone suggests that more than semantics is involved.[46] Diop's occasional overstatement of his case and his tendency sometimes to treat folklore as fact, as well as his use of oral tradition without fully adequate controls in a previous work, had been criticized by a French university professor. But that scholar did so in a temperate tone and accorded some respect to a learned African colleague. In fact, Diop published these criticisms along with his answers to them. There was far less for a conventional scholar to quarrel with in the 1981 article criticized by Oliver than in the earlier work that brought on the controversy with the French scholar. Yet Oliver seemed more inclined to "destroy" Diop than to "correct" him.

Oliver also accused Diop of flogging a dead horse, commenting that "Edward Wilmot Blyden held the same view but that was a century or more ago." Then, in trying to argue that some Negroid admixture in the Egyptian population is now generally accepted (introduced through slavery, according to him), he states that it is ridiculous to call the ancient Egyptian people as a whole "black." Here Oliver revealed the gulf between a British liberal academic perspective and a black perspective. He missed Diop's whole point, since black scholars see inconsistency (if not hypocrisy) in the English practice of calling the children of African and West Indian fathers and British mothers "black" but sneering at those who use the same designation for similar types among the ancient Egyptians. These black scholars have never been willing to accept a definition of "Negro" or "black" that includes a wide range of physical types when Anglo-Africans, Afro-Americans, or Afro-West Indians are classified, but uses totally different criteria of classification for Egyptians.

A portion of Diop's book, *The African Origin of Civilization*, argues for a definition of "Negro," in dealing with ancient and modern Africa, that would include the same range of physical types represented in the Afro-American population of the United States. He argues that no Egyptian term for "black race" existed that would be equivalent to "Negro," and that the word *Nehesi*, frequently translated as "Negro," actually means "people of the south." A wide range in color and physical type existed among these Nehesi, who lived above the first Nile cataract.[47] Within the Egyptian population, classifications on the basis of skin color do not seem to have been the custom. The only foreigners who were so classified seem to have been some of the inhabitants of the African area west of Egypt, who were referred to by a term that meant "Yellow" and who were usually called "Libyans" by the Greek historians.[48] There is some evidence that the Egyptians called themselves "black," that is, *khem*, although some scholars insist this word meant "people who live on the black land," not "people with black skin." Despite the acceptance of people of all colors as Egyptians, there was undoubtedly a somatic norm image. It may or may not have been the same as that *conventionally* represented in the painting of males as dark reddish-brown or red and females as very light brown or lemon color, but it was not so dark as that of Negroes among the Nehesi. After the Eighteenth Dynasty, artists frequently attempted to portray various physical types of foreigners by showing a wide range in skin color and facial features, but the written record makes no reference to the significance of the differences.[49] Prisoners of war are shown bound and beaten without regard to race or color. The somatic norm image seems to have changed over a long span of time from "Negro" to brown with Caucasoid features.

Although Du Bois's assessment of the racial situation in ancient Egypt foreshadowed the progressive modern view, his statement about the culture stressed external influences to an extent that has been abandoned by most Egyptologists. Du Bois wrote of Egypt that

> *like all civilizations it drew largely from without and undoubtedly arose in the valley of the Nile, because that valley was so easily made a center for the meeting of men of all types and from all parts of the world. At the same time Egyptian civilization seems to have been African in its beginning and in its main line of development, despite strong influences from all parts of Asia* [italics added].[50]

The statement that Egypt "drew largely from without" was the standard view when Du Bois wrote. This is no longer the consensus among Egyptologists. There was some borrowing of ideas and technology, but the emphasis today is on the point that the "main line of development" was African. *The best of the modern Egyptologists consider the Egyptian culture a specialized, refined variant of Nile Valley cultures, which in turn are a variant of a broader continental African type.*

Recent research supports the vindicationist argument that the early Egyptians did not "borrow" or "adopt" a basic culture from blacks to the south—that is, from "Negroes"—but were themselves part of a continuous Negro population extending from the mouth of the Nile up beyond the sixth Nile cataract into what is now the Republic of Sudan. Both the physical type of the people and the details of the culture in the portion of the Nile Valley that is now Egypt changed over many millennia, but the basic "Negroidness" of both is discernible despite miscegenation and acculturation.

Egyptian religious systems and ethical codes were elaborations and refinements of a common core of African beliefs and practices that were widespread south and east of Egypt. Students of the Book of the Dead point out that beneath the esoteric symbolism and the residue of magical spells from predynastic times, the versions of the text used during the Fourth and Fifth Dynasties—indubitably Negroid dynasties—contain philosophical ideas and ethical codes that are alien neither to the Judeo-Christian values cherished by Western civilizations nor to Indian, Chinese, or Persian religious values. Passages such as the following—in the Book of the Dead—from the so-called Negative Confession, existed long before the Ten Commandments, Buddha's Sevenfold Aryan Path, or the Confucian maxims:

> I have not committed evil in the place of truth.
> I have not defrauded the poor man of his goods.
> I have allowed no man to go hungry.
> I have made no man to weep. I have slain no man.
> I have not encroached upon the fields of others.
> I have not taken away the milk from the mouth of the babes.[51]

## PERSPECTIVES FOR VIEWING EGYPTIAN HISTORY

The reconstruction and interpretation of Egyptian history is always carried out from some socially conditioned perspective. The basic data have been gathered by professional Egyptologists, and their ethnic and racial biases are often evident in their presentation and analysis of results. These researches have not, however, seriously affected the traditional scheme of periodizing Nile Valley history that was written down by the Egyptian priest-scholar Manetho for the benefit of Greek enquirers between 300 and 200 BC. He recorded that the northern portion of the Nile Valley (see map 3), below the first cataract, had been ruled by thirty-one "dynasties" or "royal families." Each ruler was known as a "pharaoh," and Manetho provided a list of these sovereigns. With the advent of professional Egyptology in the late eighteenth century, the process began of examining the validity of Manetho's scheme against archaeological data and written records, of reconciling contradictory bits of evidence, and of assigning dates to the dynasties and the periods during which specific kings reigned. Egyptian chronology then had to be coordinated with Near Eastern and continentwide African chronology as it slowly became clear from the archaeological record.[52]

The result of nearly 200 years of research is now a substantial measure of agreement among Egyptologists to use some date between 3200 and 3000 BC as the approximate time when the first Egyptian dynasty was established. Furthermore, the first two dynasties are usually called the Early Dynastic, or Archaic Period, ending between 2600 and 2800 BC, after which four dynasties form the Old Kingdom, followed by four more, usually called the First Intermediate Dynasties, and then a Middle Kingdom. After another Intermediate, or "low," period, the New Kingdom begins. It includes the Ramesside kings. The New Kingdom, or New Empire, was followed by six other dynasties preceding foreign conquest by Persians, Greeks, and Romans. (See chart 3 for a summary of some of the significant events during the first twelve dynasties.)

The thousand-year period prior to the rule of the First Dynasty is referred to as the Predynastic period, behind which the Chalcolithic, Neolithic, and Paleolithic periods, in that order, stretch far back into the past. "Prehistory" ends and "history" starts sometime between 3500 and 3000 BC, when scribes and priests began to make written records, with the Egyptians being, perhaps, the first people in human history to do so in a systematic fashion.[53] Over the next 500 years a civilization was emerging in the Nile River Valley and the Nile Delta concurrently, with similar developments in the Tigris-Euphrates Valley and the Indus River Valley. *This anthropological frame of reference is of value to students of Egyptian history regardless of their political or ethnic perspectives.*

From *a black perspective*, three periods of Egyptian history have special significance: dynasties three and four of the Old Kingdom (2750 BC-2200 BC); dynasty eighteen of the New Kingdom (1550 BC-1305 BC); and dynasty twenty-five, sometimes referred to as the Ethiopian, or Kushitic, Dynasty (715 BC-656 BC), also of the New Kingdom. The first high point of Egyptian creativity occurred during dynasties three and four, and since Negroid pharaohs, priests, and intellectuals were prevalent then, these dynasties are important for vindicationist purposes. What is sometimes called the "Glorious Eighteenth" is discussed herein as "The Eighteenth Dynasty: Leaders of a

National Renaissance." It has been selected because, according to North American social criteria, it was a "Negro" dynasty. The Ethiopian, or Kushitic, Twenty-fifth Dynasty was composed of pharaohs from above the first cataract of the Nile and ruled Egypt and Kush as a single empire for seventy years. The significance of this dynasty from a black perspective is obvious, and it is therefore considered in some detail.

There is still some debate among Egyptologists about the setting of dates for important events in ancient Egyptian history, including those that mark the beginning and end of specific dynasties and pharaonic incumbencies. What might be called a revised standard chronology was presented in 1980 by Cyril Aldred in *Egyptian Art in the Age of the Pharaohs.* Most Egyptologists are in general agreement with his scheme. The dates used throughout this book (including chart 3), however, are those presented by the scholars who produced volumes 1 and 2 of UNESCO's *General History of Africa*, published in 1981. This represents the first attempt by African scholars, and Egyptologists in whom they reposed confidence, to establish a system of periodization and dating that is satisfactory from a black perspective. Therefore, it seems appropriate to use their dates in this book. Those scholars accepted the standard periodization but, in some instances, have chosen dates that vary slightly from those put forth by Aldred. I have not adopted their most striking deviation, which involves substituting a minus sign (-) for BC and a plus sign (+) for AD. This was done out of deference to those Africans who are Traditionalists or Muslims, and for whom Anno Domini ("Year of our Lord") is both ethnocentric and offensive, with Before Christ ("the Anointed One") conferring a status upon Jesus that they do not concede. (Some Jewish and UNESCO publications use BCE—Before the Common Era, and C.E.—Common Era, to achieve this same, less ethnocentric, result.) At the risk of being considered insensitive, I have retained the more familiar BC and AD, recognizing at the same time why the usage has been abandoned by some scholars. No insult is intended nor any ethnocentric claim for the superiority of the Christian religion made. I have discussed the matter at some length because it is essential to an understanding of the only important revision in periodization that this particular black perspective entails.

From *the perspective of students of interracial relations,* all of the dynasties are useful for examining attitudes toward "Negroidness" and for testing Blumer's theory of race relations as well as the DeglerGergen propositions. However, the period of the seven dynasties that existed between the end of the Ramesside Age (between 1085 and 1070 BC) and the conquest of Egypt by the Romans in 31 BC presents a crucial case of a situation likely to generate racial prejudice. For the first time since an earlier invasion by Southwest Asians, Egyptians were dominated by an alien ruling class that differed from them by being "white" in skin color. This period of domination came after they had themselves operated as an imperialist power in the Middle East. Resentment against the invaders was strong and conflict frequent. The extent to which the dominant foreigners used the difference in color to justify their rule, or the Egyptians used it to justify rebellion, merits study. The extent to which the somatic norm image of the conqueror influenced the self-concept of the Egyptians, as Hoetink's theory suggests it would, can be observed during this period.

| Time-Periods and Dynasties | Significant Internal Events | Relations with Asians and Europeans | Relations with Peoples of Wawat and Kush (i.e., ancient Ethiopia) |
|---|---|---|---|
| Middle Kingdom—Dynasties Eleven through Twelve 2150–1780 B.C. | Theban princes from Upper Egypt re-unify nation. | Widespread trade relations with Crete and Asia Minor. | "Nehesi" repulsed; then Nubia invaded in search for gold. Temple of Amon erected at Cataract Four. |
| First Intermediate Dynasties—Seven through Ten 2200–2150 B.C. | Monarchy weakened by local feudal lords during sixth led to disorder. | Asian nomads, taking advantage of disorders, infiltrate delta provinces. | While Asians are harassing the delta, the "barbarian" Blacks attack at Cataract One, but trade continues. |
| Old Kingdom—Dynasties Three through Six 2750–2200 B.C. Era of "The Pyramid Builders" and great intellectual growth | Petrie says Fourth Dynasty is "of Nubian origin." King as "god" who unifies and is also symbol of Osiris, the culture hero and god. Building in stone after Dynasty Two. | No invasions from Asia; fruitful trade and exchange of ideas with Mesopotamia. Some danger of nomadic invasion from north after Dynasty Five. | "Barbarian Blacks" impel "civilized" Egyptian Blacks to counterattack and erect a barrier at Cataract One against incursions by the "Nehesi" (southerners). Tradition of Punt as "the sacred land" being recorded on walls of some tombs. |
| Early Dynastic Period—One, Two 3000–2750 B.C. Beginning of writing | Upper and Lower Kingdoms united by Menes (Narmer) under Red and White crowns. | Archaeology indicates indicates trade with Mesopotamia. | Limited amount of trade with people in Nubia beyond Cataract One. |
| Predynastic Period—Before 3000 B.C. | Teter-Neter, and the Anu, march down the Nile from Theban area. | Asians bring domesticated plants and animals into delta area. | West Africans introduce food crops near Cataract VI; people from Punt (Somalia?) probably entering Nile Valley. |

**Chart 3.** Ethnic Interaction during Predynastic Period and Dynasties One through Twelve

## EGYPT BEFORE THE PHARAOHS

### *Race and Color in Predynastic Egypt*

Since Egypt is generally regarded as one of the two "cradles of civilization," Mesopotamia being the other, students of the black Experience have continually raised questions about the extent of Negro participation in the Neolithic "food-producing revolution" that preceded "civilization." What kind of people were the original Egyptians? Were the first Egyptians who practiced agriculture blacks or Asians? Did the Egyptians domesticate plants and animals themselves, or did they borrow the techniques and the crops from the peoples of the Fertile Crescent? Is it possible that the Mesopotamian peoples and the Arabians were themselves black, and therefore that borrowing from these areas meant one black group borrowing from another? Is it possible that several different racial groups have lived together in Egypt from prehistoric times? These matters, except for the last question, are still in dispute.

Egyptologists, in studying predynastic Egypt, rely heavily upon archaeology, in addition to drawing conclusions from myths, folklore, and oral tradition. There is no way to assess the "race" of human remains found in the various sites without playing the "numbers game" that anthropologists play. When Dr. Du Bois wrote *The Negro* in 1915, both the racists and the antiracists had been at each other hammer and tongs for decades citing figures on cephalic indices, cranial capacities, skull shape, facial angles, nasal structure, and so on. The rules of the game involved accepting some fundamental ideas about the meaning of cranial statistics, of which the most relevant was: "The greater the degree of alveolar prognathism (i.e., forward projection of the lower face), the more Negroid the skull" (fig. 1). A certain combination of skeletal measurements was used to define an ideal type, the "True Negro," among living Africans; when bones approximating this norm were found, the fossil was assessed as "Negro," despite the absence of skin and hair. Skeletal material, particularly cranial, was defined as "white" in a similar fashion. Limbs and pelvis measurements were also used.

In carrying on the dialogue, most black scholars have not criticized the entire field of anthropometry. The majority of them have preferred, rather, to accept the premises and to argue within them, although the assumptions and techniques themselves are vulnerable.[54] However, after two decades of using anthropometric data to substantiate his arguments about the race of predynastic Egyptians, Cheikh Anta Diop, writing in 1981 in UNESCO's *A General History of Africa*, revealed his feeling of frustration:

> The arbitrary nature of the criteria used, to go no farther, as well as abolishing any notion of a conclusion acceptable without qualification, introduces so much scientific hair-splitting that there are times when one wonders whether the solution of the problem would not have been nearer if we had not had the ill luck to approach it from this angle.

Yet he proceeded immediately to say, "Although the conclusions of these anthropological studies stop short of the full truth, they still speak unanimously of the existence of a negro race from the most distant ages of prehistory down to the dynastic period."[55]

Diop was careful not to say that the only race detectable among ancient Egyptian fossil finds and mummies was "Negro," as anthropologists use the term. He presents statistics he had used in earlier works to give a generalized summary based upon available studies of about 2,000 predynastic skulls. These indicated that Egyptologists had classified 36 percent as "definitely Negroid," 33 percent as "Mediterranean," and 11 percent as " Cro-Magnon." (An earlier study had suggested that only 25 percent were Negroid.)[56] In view of the fact that the "Mediterranean Race" was called the "Brown Race" by Sergi, the Italian anthropologist who first described it, Diop would be on firm ground if he merely argued that most of this skeletal material was *probably* covered by an integument that would have led to the individuals' being classified as "nonwhite" or " colored."[57] But since such "brownness" in populations of African descent in Europe and the United States is enough to define them as "Negro," Diop insisted upon doing so as well. In addition, since adding the Mediterraneans to the group of skeletons defined as "Negro" increases the proportion of blacks and browns to 56 percent of the total, he felt justified in calling the entire population "Negro." The African, Diop, would seem to have as much justification for doing this as a British Egyptologist had for describing the predynastic population without mentioning a possible Negro component.[58]

The pro-Negro American anthropologist George Peter Murdock avoids a definitive statement about these predynastic fossils found in Egypt by making the matter contingent upon the racial assessment of data from subsequent periods. He wrote of the Egyptian Neolithic cultures that they were "borne by people indistinguishable in physical type from the later dynastic Egyptians," whom he calls "Caucasoid."[59] Although Murdock is aggressively antiracist, he uses a very narrow definition of "Negro" in his book *Africa*. For example, a number of black ethnic groups are classified as "Caucasian" because their skeletal traits are similar to those of Europeans. In dealing with fossils, Murdock, like all the other archaeologists and anthropologists, has only bones—without any skin or hair—to work with in deciding whether or not a fossil is "Negro." The term "Caucasoid" cannot be equated automatically with "white," but the skeletal features in this case preclude calling the fossils "Negro."

In his 1981 UNESCO article, Diop challenged Egyptologists, as he had done previously, to use a system he had devised for measuring the amount of melanin present in the skin of mummies. However, because predynastic mummified remains are so rare, the method would be of limited use for that period.[60] In any event, it could determine only the degree of "blackness," not the extent of "Negroidness." The predynastic Egyptians could have been black but more similar in features to the Dravidian and Veddoid peoples of India than to the people of Central Africa. (Indeed, portraits of some dynastic Egyptians have the "Indian look.")[61] Arguments about fossils and mummies, like arguments about the living, revolve as much around the question of how broadly the term "Negro" or "black" should be extended as they do about the collection, manipulation, and evaluation of empirical data.

The question of the race of the early Egyptians is bound up with the question of where predynastic movement toward civilization in the Nile Valley began. Some anthropologists think the archaeological evidence supports a theory of direct evolution of the dynastic regimes out of a predynastic civilization that grew up among the Delta peoples. They assert that this advanced culture, like the practice of agriculture, diffused north to south, up the Nile. Diop argues against this view by pointing out that there was no delta until near historic time, the Mediterranean coast, before then, extending almost as far inland as the city of Memphis is today. Diop also cites archaeologists who have presented impressive data to support the position that the valley civilization originated in Neolithic cultures of southern Egypt, near the border with Nubia or perhaps in Nubia itself.[62]

All students, despite these differences of opinion, agree that a relatively high level of efficient cultivation was necessary to sustain the emergent kingdoms, and that by 3100 BC this foundation had been laid by predynastic people living in small groups on both sides of the Nile, from its mouth southward through an area extending beyond the first cataract into Nubia. They cultivated some crops that were first domesticated in

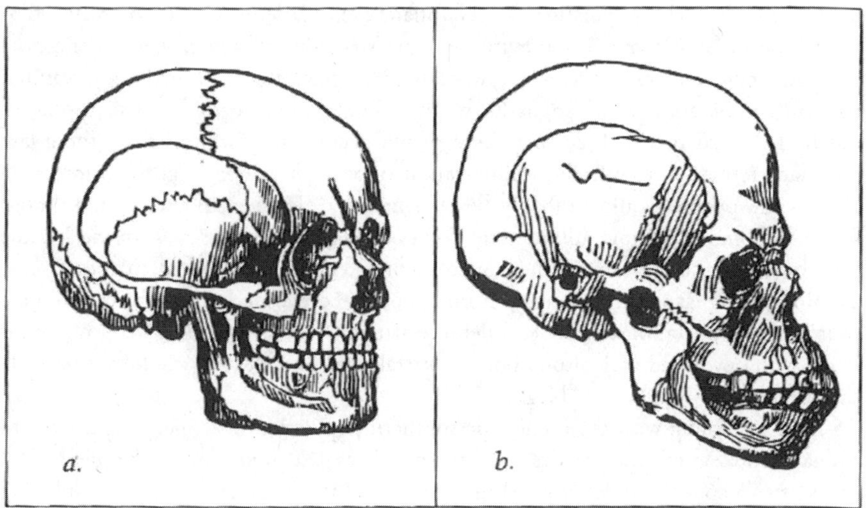


**Fig. 1.** Alveolar Prognathism in Two Skulls. Reprinted from Nott and Gliddon, *Types of Mankind* (1855). *a.* Greek Specimen. *b.* West African Specimen

Southwest Asia—wheat, barley, and a variety of fruits, melons, and vegetables. They also used animals from that area—goats, asses, and cattle. From the East African highlands came plants supplying essential oils such as castor and safflower, and from West Africa they received cotton, gourds, and watermelon. The flax used for linen they probably domesticated themselves. These predynastic Egyptians were thus participants in what archaeologists began to call the "Neolithic Revolution" in the early post-World War II years, or, alternatively, the "food-producing revolution."[63] The Nile Valley was not one of the centers in which the domestication of plants and animals occurred at the beginning of the Neolithic Revolution, but it provided a fertile area for the new economies to take root.

Because the northern area (Lower Egypt) was the region where crops and animals introduced from Southwest Asia first appeared, there has been considerable discussion about the probable race of the inhabitants. Were they immigrants from the Fertile Crescent or an indigenous Nile Delta population that adopted innovations from beyond their borders? Or were they a mixed racial group coming in from the deserts? A number of northern sites containing skeletons and artifacts have been excavated. Given the emphasis that physical anthropologists have placed upon alveolar prognathism as a diagnostic trait in assessing a skull as "Negro," it is significant to note that Sir Arthur Keith (who, incidentally, believed in the innate inferiority of black people) found "prevalence of alveolar prognathism" in the so-called Natufian type that some scholars feel was the first to cultivate plants and animals in northern Egypt. This was the same breed of man who had made the basic innovations of the Neolithic Revolution somewhere in the Middle East.

If the early Delta population was Natufian, even Carleton Coon, an anthropologist whose racist statements sometimes embarrassed his colleagues, would concede a Negroid tinge. On one occasion he wrote of Natufians that "the wide, low vaulted nose, in combination with prognathism, gives a somewhat negroid cast to the face." But he hastened to conclude that these people were really "white," that "these late Natufians represent a basically Mediterranean type with minor Negroid affinities."[64] These same people would probably be classified as "Negroes" in the United States, where such *minor* Negroid affinities are always enough to tip the scales. In the Middle East, however, they remain "white." Such inconsistencies have evoked charges against the professional taxonomists ranging from hypocrisy to racism, by those blacks who are aware of their operations. They see a definite attempt to insist that the Neolithic innovators who developed agriculture, pottery, metallurgy, and weaving could not possibly have been what we now call "Negroes."

Even in dealing with the prehistoric southern population of Upper Egypt, close to Nubia, Coon was reluctant to designate the people as "Negroid" despite the presence of trait s usually considered definitive. Thus he writes of the Badarian Neolithic people that "while the prognathism and nose form would suggest a negroid tendency, this cannot be established since the hair form is definitely not negroid." (In this case mummified remains were available.) Coon referred to the Sebilians in the southern area with esthetic approval as being of "a fine Mediterranean type," although in another context he notes that "Mediterranean proper often carries a slight Negroid tendency." As to the Naqada skeletons, which had "less prognathism than the Badarians," it was Coon's opinion that they represented people similar to the contemporary Coptic population in Egypt, who "probably represent the ancient Egyptian type more faithfully than the Muslim population."[65] This was the type that Count Volney compared with the Sphinx and decided that ancient Egyptians had Negro features. Thus Coon uses the words *somewhat, minor, and slight tendency* to minimize the importance of traits that he himself calls "negroid" in the prehistoric southern population of Egypt and its probable descendants. These are the people whom black scholars consider most crucial in assessing possible Negro contributions to early Egyptian civilization. (It might be noted that Coon used similar language to minimize the extent of "Negroidness" in Natufian fossils.)

Those who consider the North—Lower Egypt—to be the important center of prehistoric innovations usually stress the probability of an Asian origin for the inhabitants. But they, too, have to contend with traits anthropologists call Negroid in the fossilized or mummified human remains, whether they be Natufian or the so-called "Northern Race" that came later. Thus, as late as 1964, one of the most eminent of the American Egyptologists argued for the superiority of some presumably non-Negroid populations that were assumed to have been present in Lower Egypt; and he hinted, during a period when most anthropologists had abandoned the idea, that intelligence was correlated with cranial traits:

> The early northern Egyptian, wherever we encounter him—Merimda, El-Omari, Maadi North, Maadi South, and Heliopolis—appears to have been somewhat taller and more sturdily built than his Upper Egyptian contemporary and to have been endowed with a broader and better formed skull and a generally greater cranial capacity.[66]

Despite the fact that most anthropologists usually pounced upon prognathism as almost conclusive evidence of "Negroidness," this scholar did not wish to admit that the "purity" of a Northern Race he sought to define was compromised, although he had to concede that it might be: "The prognathism observed in the skulls from Maadi South and Heliopolis may or may not indicate the infiltration of a negroid strain into the northern region."[67] He was anxious to draw a sharp line between the inhabitants of Lower Egypt, near the Mediterranean, and those farther south:

> Generally speaking, however, the prehistoric northerner seems to represent a type distinct in race and physique as well as in culture from the people of the south. In him, rather than in some intrusive group of outlanders, we may perhaps recognize, with Junker, the ancestor of the so-called Dynastic Race, or Giza type, of Early Dynastic and Old Kingdom times.[68]

Arnold Toynbee, an erudite British scholar, in describing what he calls the Egyptiac Civilization in his monumental work, *A Study of History*, was more inclined to accept the idea of a racially mixed population as the originator of Egyptian civilization than some hypothetical special northern "Dynastic Race." Nevertheless, explicitly antiracist though he was, Toynbee was not able to break out of his conservative British intellectual mold. The result was ambiguity about racial terminology and reliance upon a narrow range of sources. In the final analysis, his thought-provoking work is flawed. Toynbee argues cogently against those who would explain the origin of *any* civilization in terms of some genetic predisposition or theory of racial superiority. Yet he unwittingly lends support to the racist camp by restricting the term "Black Race" to "Australian Blackfellows, the Papuans and Melanesians, the Veddahs of Ceylon and the Todas of Southern India, as well as the Negro population of Africa south of the Sahara." After presenting this definition, he makes the categorical statement that "*the only one of the primary races... which has not made a creative contribution to any one of our twentyone civilizations is the Black Race*"; and, in another context, "*the Black Race has not helped to create any civilization* [italics added]." These sweeping conclusions about the unique lack of creativity on the part of black people, slightly modified in phrasing, received very wide dissemination in the Book-of-the-Month Club abridgment of Toynbee's nine volumes.[69] They must have confirmed the prejudices of thousands of Americans and reinforced stereotypes about their neighbors.

Toynbee's argument that black people did not even "help" in the development of the one African civilization he analyzes—the "Egyptiac"—is predicated upon excluding all mixed-blood Egyptians from the category "black" and ignoring the contributions of individual full-blooded Negroes who appeared throughout Egyptian history and who were particularly prevalent during the late predynastic period and the first four dynasties, when Egyptian civilization took form and flowered. He accepted the standard view of Egyptologists that both Caucasoid and Negroid genetic strains were represented in the Egyptian population; but, in repudiating biological explanations of creativity, he did not consider this mixture important except as an index to the fact that Egyptians, unlike most other Africans, had not been isolated from people bearing other cultures.

Sometimes Toynbee seems to be referring only to contributions made by entire ethnic groups, not isolated individuals, meaning that no groups of relatively unmixed Negroes in Africa had developed civilizations or "helped" to originate artifacts and ideas that went into them. Thus, in discussing why blacks had made no contributions in Africa, he proceeds to discuss inhabitants of specific geographical areas. He quotes French anthropologist Maurice Delafosse, in order "to suggest certain features in the Negro's circumstances which convincingly account for his failure to take an active part in the enterprise of Civilization during these first five or six thousand years."

Neither scholar imputes any genetic deficiency to Negroes, but Delafosse, who was an expert on West African societies, stressed a single factor: isolation from Mediterranean cultural innovations that were carried into Europe, through force and persuasion, by Roman legions and, later, by Roman Catholic priests. As Delafosse phrases it, "the Gauls, our ancestors," were constantly in contact with "more evolved" peoples, while "the unfortunate Negroes were during the same period almost completely isolated from *the rest of humanity* [italics added]."[70] The enthnocentrism in the Delafosse statement is revealed in the word *unfortunate.* The fortunate people were those conquered by Roman troops. Delafosse ignores the Negroes of eastern Africa, where the kingdom of Meroë developed between the fourth and sixth Nile cataracts. His isolation theory is certainly somewhat less applicable there. Delafosse ignores also the role of these Negroes in the development of Egyptian civilization over many centuries and misconstrues their choice to disengage from the Mediterranean power struggles. Rome was not able forcibly to "civilize" Meroë, although it had treaty relations and diplomatic intercourse with this black kingdom.

Europe was conquered and Mediterranean civilization was imposed upon it. Meroe, in contrast, preserved its independence and seems to have borrowed more from India and Persia than from the Greeks and Romans. In any event, the crucial issue raised by historian Toynbee does not concern the period with which the Delafosse quotation deals. It concerns, rather, the fourth and third millennia BC, before the Roman "civilizers" of Europe had themselves been "civilized" by the Greeks. It deals with a period in which important ideas in philosophy, mathematics, and religion were developed in Egypt, ideas for which both Greeks and Romans would later admit they were indebted to the Egyptians. Even Toynbee's sources indicate black participation in these developments. And despite Toynbee's insistence that blacks did not "help" to create any civilization—including the "Egyptiac"—he presents a quotation from an archaeologist that demolishes the foundation of his own argument. V. Gordon Childe was his authority for a remark pointing out that the ancient Egyptians resembled a group of contemporary Africans: "*On the upper Nile there dwell today people allied to the oldest Egyptians in appearance, stature, cranial proportions, language and dress* [italics added]." The reference was to the Shilluk, a very Negroid people whether judged by the criteria of the anthropologist or the layman! Perhaps the learned British historian did not know this, or was using such a narrow definition of Negro as to exclude the Shilluk.[71]

The beginnings of Egyptian civilization can be discerned from artifacts found in a late predynastic village called Naqada, just south of Thebes in Upper Egypt. The culture, of which Naqada was part, extended across the border into Lower Nubia as far as the second cataract of the Nile. It was in contact there with another culture, which the specialists call Nubian-A, that extended as far as the sixth cataract. There were no sharp differences at that time in either the physical type of the people or the cultures in what became the border area between Egypt and Nubia in dynastic times. In fact, there is increasing evidence that these two cultures, Nubian-A and Naqada, shared many traits and that the peoples were essentially of the same physical type.

The question immediately arises as to why the Naqada people developed what Toynbee calls "Egyptiac civilization" between 4000 BC and 3000 BC, whereas the Nubian-A people, in what later became Kush, did not. Their "civilization" emerged much later, only after extensive Egyptianization. Aspects of Toynbee's "challenge and response" theory are more relevant than the isolation hypothesis in explaining why one segment of a black group on the Nile developed a "civilization" whereas a closely related group did not.

Some Egyptologists make the plausible suggestion that as desiccation became more widespread on both sides of the Nile large masses of people moved into the fertile valley north of the first cataract, where their existence depended upon working out the technical and social problems posed by the annual flooding of the Nile. The more sparsely populated areas south of the first cataract, especially where pastoralism rather than agriculture provided the main subsistence mode, did not make such demands upon the leadership. What we call "civilization" emerged as an adaptation in the former situation, where ecological pressures dictated technological and social innovation.

In the Egyptian case, as in Mesopotamia, a priesthood received a portion of the agricultural surplus in return for knowledge and leadership in the development of irrigation and flood control, as well as the religious sanction it provided to the government. These religious ideas were shared by people living in areas between the first cataract and beyond the sixth, but there was no pressure in that region for religious leaders to supply social leadership. Recent archaeological excavations in Nubia confirm the existence of burial customs similar to those in predynastic Egypt, and Egyptian tradition points to the "uncivilized" black lands as the source of Egypt's religious concepts and rituals. Students of the Book of the Dead see hints of an older stratum of beliefs shared with inner Africa embedded in the Pyramid Texts.

Speaking of the similarity of the cultures in southern Egypt and northern Nubia at approximately 5000 BC, Aldred notes that

> the essentially African culture of the early Predynastic period might have remained sterile at this level as it did apparently in the Sudan, where a Badarian type of culture persisted for a much longer time, if it had not been fertilized by contacts with a different civilization coming from Asia. . . . All these innovations, however, have no appearance of having been imposed by conquests.[72]

Not all scholars accept the "fertilization" theory, but most do. Undoubtedly the factor that made the crucial difference in the late Predynastic Period between black cultures above the first cataract of the Nile and those below it was that the latter group, living in Egypt, adopted or invented metallurgical techniques for working copper and gold, and that they developed mathematical systems and writing. Some Egyptologists are inclined toward the view that the stimulus, and perhaps the models, were supplied through contact with peoples from Mesopotamia, and that these contacts were useful in solving the problem of developing a system of agriculture in the Nile Valley. The significant fact, however, is not that these Africans borrowed ideas and techniques from outside, if they did, but that they reworked them, integrated them into their own distinctive cultural matrix, and used them to serve their own cultural values. They added to the stock of common knowledge in such a way that aspects of Egyptian thought were eventually incorporated into the intellectual heritage of Europe by way of the Greeks. Egyptian history is consistent with Toynbee's theory that civilization flowers when cultures meet. His blind spot lay in an unwillingness to concede the black contribution to the process that occurred in the Nile Valley.

Diop has pointed out traditions among the Egyptians themselves concerning the adoption of metallurgy that indicate the technology came from outside of the valley culture. One of the oldest legends refers to a group of metal workers in predynastic times who came to the Nile Valley as "invaders" and proceeded to build forges from the first cataract to the edge of the Delta. The southern Egyptian version of the story, recorded on the walls of a temple at Edfu after the Greek conquest of Egypt, speaks of the god Harmachis, who reigned in Nubia, presiding over conquest of the valley by his son Horus, who settled his companions, the "blacksmiths," with him throughout the valley. The Egyptologist Gaston Maspéro accepted the legend as reflecting a historic event and referred to the innovators as "Negro blacksmiths." A French Egyptologist, Alexandre Moret, cited by Diop, interprets the legend in one of its other versions as indicating that the smiths began their journey in the north and carried the innovation to the southland. Regional pride, as well as changes in the prestige of Kush, may account for the variations in the story. The contradictory legends may, however, represent two distinctly different events widely separated in time: one being the adoption of metallurgy involving gold, copper, and silver from the Middle East; the other the adoption of iron-working techniques, possibly introduced centuries later, during late dynastic times, from Meroë, near the sixth cataract of the Nile.

The problems in interpreting these stories about the smiths are compounded by the ambiguity concerning the meaning of the hieroglyphics. Does the glyph translated as "blacksmiths" mean "workers in iron" or "black" (i.e., Negro) smiths? Diop has insisted upon the latter interpretation. Both versions of the legend, however, derive the rituals presided over by the priests at Heliopolis in the north from the impact of smiths, for whom the worship of Re, the sun-god, was important. Professor Vercoutter, writing in 1981, states that copper, gold, and silver were diffused widely throughout the Nile Valley before the pharaonic era. No theory of an outside origin of metallurgy is necessary to account for the use of these metals. However, only meteoric iron was used until the eighth century BC. After that time, iron was mined and smelted and tools, weapons, and technique diffused widely from Meroë.[73]

The pioneer among British Egyptologists, Sir Flinders Petrie, who excavated in the Thebaid, was convinced that the basic elements of Egyptian predynastic cultural development came into Egypt from the southeast, near the Red Sea, but that the rulers of the highly creative Old Kingdom dynasties were of Nubian origin.[74] If this view is accepted, the question still remains of precisely where the predynastic migrants came from and how long they had been settled within the borders of Egypt before political unification of the area between the Red Sea and the first cataract occurred. Archaeologists now know that fine ceramics were being made near the sixth cataract of the Nile just prior to the dynastic period and societies based upon cattle breeding and mixed agriculture were in existence there, but no movements northward from this area have yet been traced.[75] Nor have population movements been traced from Nubian areas closer to Egypt during the period when desiccation was probably forcing people into the valley and then northward as the area between the first and third cataracts—Lower Nubia—became less habitable.

Two locations were considered "holy" from late predynastic times on into later Egyptian history. One was the Thebaid, the area from the vicinity of the city of Thebes southward to the first cataract. The shrine of Hathor, the Nubian mother-goddess, was at Denderah, and that of Hapi, the god of the Nile, at the first cataract itself. The other sacred spot, "God's Land," or the "Holy Land," was located vaguely somewhere to the south. From there, it was said, the original Egyptians came and the rituals for worshiping the gods originated. This was "the land of the ancestors." By the time the Greeks first visited Egypt, Ethiopia was being referred to by the priests as "that sacred land of origin," but its boundaries were stated with imprecision. At an earlier period, God's Land was called the "Land of Punt" and because of the crops grown there, the oils and incense characteristic of the country, early Egyptologists assumed the reference was to the area around the Red Sea near what is now Somalia, or even across the sea in southern Arabia.[76] When the priests told Greek and Roman enquirers that Egypt was a colony of the Ethiopians, European and American scholars have usually assumed that they must have meant the less Negroid areas in the Horn of Africa. The ancient Greeks and Romans, however, took for granted that they were referring to the Kingdom of Meroe, up the Nile.

Petrie was one of the Egyptologists who was convinced that the people who established the predynastic civilizations were invaders from Arabia or Mesopotamia who, coming across the Red Sea at some point, moved over to the Nile Valley near Thebes and then marched northward to Memphis (near present-day Cairo). Diop notes that the proponents of this view refer to a specific group of people, the Anu, following a specific culture bearer, Teter-Neter, as the "civilizers" marched down the Nile from the south. He has reprinted from Petrie portraits of Teter-Neter, the predynastic leader of the Anu, and Narmer, who is by tradition considered the founder of the first dynasty. Both had physical characteristics that anthropologists call "Negroid." Thus, regardless of whether the Anu migrated from Asia or were an indigenous African people coming in from eastern Africa or from areas farther up the Nile, the archaeological evidence suggests that their leader was Negroid.

The possibility that the "civilizing thrust" spread down the Nile northward into Egypt and eastward into Somalia and Arabia should not be ruled out. There is increasing archaeological evidence to support this view. In considering the location of the area referred to as the Egyptian ancestral land or the sacred land, it should be remembered that the entire landscape between the Nile Valley and the Red Sea may have been very different during the millennium prior to 3000 BC, when the first dynasty of kings emerged in Egypt. What is now desert between the Nile and the Red Sea may have been grassland across which people moved easily, just as they moved freely deep into what is now the Sahara Desert. Links by water southward around the Ethiopian highlands to the Red Sea may even have existed. These lands may not have been as impassable as they are today.[77]

In any event, recent archaeological work reported by scholars from the Oriental Institute at the University of Chicago suggests that viable and prosperous Nubian kingdoms may have existed between the fourth and sixth Nile cataracts, that is, between the old capital of Kush and the later one at Meroë prior to the development of the first Egyptian kingdoms.[78] This lends some credence to stories preserved by priests that Egypt, in late predynastic times, was established as a colony of the Ethiopians—that people were moving northward beyond the first Nile cataract carrying the rudimentary elements of what would become Egyptian civilization. According to this reconstruction, changes in climate and terrain between the first Nile cataract and the third later broke the connection between the Ethiopian "mother kingdom" and Egypt. The Ethiopians being isolated from contact with Mesopotamia and the countries of the Fertile Crescent did not have the stimulus that comes from intensive intercultural contact. A few black scholars have suggested that Ethiopia during this period may have been the "civilizer" of both southern Arabia and the Nile Valley below the first cataract. Some Arabian and Jewish legends, in fact, suggest that conquering armies from Ethiopia wandered about in Arabia and other eastern lands in remote antiquity.[79] The question of predynastic cultural origins remains in the realm of speculation, possibility, and probability, not irrefutable fact.

Black vindicationists have never concentrated their efforts on trying to explain why Nubians did not develop advanced mathematics and calendrical systems as their kinsmen below the first cataract of the Nile did; or why they did not develop the common stock of religious beliefs into elaborate metaphysical and cosmological systems as the priests in Thebes, Memphis, and Heliopolis did. Most, including Du Bois, have taken satisfaction from the fact that Negroes were well represented in the populations of the Egyptian dynasties of great accomplishment, and were, therefore, "helping" to create a civilization, to use Toynbee's word. Others, such as Diop, have argued that the early Egyptians *were* Negroes and, therefore, that Egyptian civilization of the first four dynasties was a black civilization. The basic problem with Toynbee's argument lay in his neglect of evidence, which was at hand when he wrote, indicating that many of the Egyptians of the Predynastic and the Early Dynastic periods in Egypt were, in fact, "Negroes" as anthropologists use the term, and many more were Negroes or "black" in the broader sense of the term, as it is employed by custom in the United States. However, insofar as the valley absorbed populations from what are now the Libyan and Sahara deserts, Bushmanoid and Caucasoid types, as well as "Hamites" and Negroes, were all represented in the Nile Valley population. The proportions of one physical type as compared with another varied over time, and from place to place, and in relation to the size of the component groups.[80]

The rock paintings of the Sahara Desert leave no doubt that one dark, but non-Negroid, population coexisted there with a considerably darker variety of mankind during the millennium preceding the emergence of dynastic Egypt. It is assumed that both of these physical types, as well as more Caucasoid peoples, drifted into the Nile Valley as desiccation gradually took place, producing the Sahara and Libyan deserts.

Petrie refers to a painted tomb at Hierankopolis that portrays "combats of black men overcoming red men." He is convinced that this painting, as well as a scene carved on an ivory knife handle, support archaeological evidence that early settlements in Egypt were "the result of the mixture of half a dozen races fighting for supremacy." Diop considers all of these early peoples to be within the normal range of variability of a basic Negro physical type. In these dynastic scenes some observers see post-Neolithic "racial" conflict between "Libyans" and "blacks," but whether the antagonists conceptualized their relations as "interracial" we have no way of knowing. There are scenes, too, of early Egyptian kings exulting in victory over people whose beards mark them out as "Asiatics."[81] Did these conflicts result in prejudice structured along a color line? Most Egyptologists are inclined to say no, because in later periods such conflicts were never written about by Egyptians in terms of race and color.

In later periods physical traits distinguishing groups of captives from one another are depicted on numerous victory monuments. Modern conventional wisdom would suggest that over a period of time skin color and physical features would emerge as cues eliciting unfavorable attitudes and generating stereotypes. But if we try to specify the nature of conflicts, especially for periods so remote as the predynastic, we run the risk of reading our own customary reactions back into ancient Egypt.

Whether evaluations of blackness in general and dark skin color in particular differed in dynastic times from such evaluations in predynastic times we shall never know. . . .

## NOTES

* Although "Afro-American" and "black" are currently the terms preferred in referring to North Americans of African descent, the term "Negro" has a specialized meaning in the anthropological literature that requires its use in the discussion of African populations in this book.

Reprinted with permission from St. Clair Drake, *Black Folk Here and There: An Essay in History and Anthropology* (Los Angeles: Ralph J. Bunche Center for African American Studies at UCLA, 1987), 115–171. This chapter is an excerpt from the original and has omitted certain passages.

1. *Memoirs and Poems of Phillis Wheatley*, 3d ed. (Boston: 1838; reprinted by Mnemosyne Publishing Co., Miami, Fla., 1969), p. 48.

2. The full text of this petition is presented in Herbert Aptheker, ed., *A Documentary History of the Negro People in the United States* (Secaucus, N.J.: Citadel Press, 1973), vol. 1., pp. 8–9.3

3. For a list of churches bearing the designation ''African" and a discussion of the reasons for the shift away from the practice of naming organizations in this manner after 1817, with the word "colored" being preferred, see St. Clair Drake, "Negro Americans and the 'Africa Interest'," in *American Negro Reference Book*, ed. John P. Davis (Englewood Cliffs, N.J.: Prentice-Hall, 1966), pp. 669–673. This chapter also includes a discussion of Afro-American reinterpretations of the doctrine of Providential Design, which some white Christians used to explain why a benevolent deity permitted Africans to be enslaved. They believed that slavery was a means of exposing them to Christianity and II civilization, 11 so that some of them could be prepared to return to Africa to "redeem" and "uplift" their kinsmen.

4. Countee Cullen, *On These I Stand* (New York: Harper and Brothers, 1947), pp. 24–28.

5. See St. Clair Drake, " 'Hide My Face?' On Pan-Africanism and Negritude," in *Soon One Morning*, ed. Herbert Hill (New York: Knopf, 1963), pp. 78–105; and LeRoi Jones, "The Myth of a 'Negro Literature,'" in *Home* (New York: Morrow, 1966), 105–115.

6. Winthrop Jordan, *White Over Black* (Baltimore: Penguin, 1969), p. 258.

7. An American anthropologist, writing in the 1950s, stated that Africa was probably the "cradle of mankind, 11 and that "for several decades hardly a year has passed without some exciting new evidence of early man or of manlike apes in East or South Africa to strengthen this conclusion" (George Peter Murdock, *Africa: Its People and Their Culture History* [New York: McGraw-Hill, 1959), p. 7). For an article by the British archaeologist whose research in East Africa revealed some of the earliest hominids, see L. S. B. Leakey, "Adventures in the Search for Man," *National Geographic Magazine* (January 1963), pp. 132–152. Note also J. Desmond Clark, "The Prehistoric Origins of African Culture, *11 in Papers in African Prehistory*, ed. J. D. Fage and R. A. Oliver (Cambridge: Cambridge University Press, 1970), pp. 3–4. See also "Why Is East Africa Important?" Preface to G. L. Isaac and R. McCown (Menlo Park, Calif.: W. A. Benjamin, 1976).

8. For an article emphasizing the non-Negroid character of fossils of early man in the area where it is thought mankind originated, see Sonia Cole, ''The Stone Age of East Africa," in *History of East Africa*, vol. 1, ed. R. Oliver and G. Mathew (Oxford: Oxford University Press, 1963), pp. 23–57 (especially pp. 42, 48, and 53–54).

9. The belief that the first men and women were dark skinned is based upon the assumption that melanin provided protection against the ultraviolet rays of the tropical sun. But knowledge that African higher apes have a wide range of skin color, and speculation that hominids might have originated in less torrid subtropical Africa, or that cultural and economic factors could be more important than climate in the selection for skin color within a gene pool where variation was great have led to some questioning of the older general assumption about the dark skin color of the earliest humans. For a discussion of these points, see John Buettner-Janusch, Origins of Man (New York: Wiley, 1966), pp. 366–377; David Pibeam, The Ascent of Man: An Introduction to Human Evolution (New York: Macmillan, 1972), p. 83; Harold F. Blum, ''Does the Melanin Pigment of Human Skin Have Adaptive Value?" in Man in Adaptation: The Biosocial Background, ed. Yehudi A. Cohen (Chicago: Aldine, 1968), p. 143; and J. F. Downs and H. K. Bleibtreu, Human Variation (Beverly Hills, Calif.: Glencoe Press, 1969), pp. 181–188. For an excellent popular exposition see Montagu, *What We Know about "Race."*

10. A strong statement in favor of the theory of a late appearance of the Negro in human evolution is included as part of a discussion entitled "Early Man in Man in Africa," Harry A. Gailey, Jr., *History of Africa from Earliest Times to 1800* (New York: Holt, Rinehart and Winston, 1970), p. 19. Carleton Coon, in *The Origin of Races*," states the minority view, viz., that the Negro type is very old and is evolutionarily retarded" by about 250,000 years. A distinguished Berkeley prehistorian is convinced that ''by the end of the Pleistocene, the Bush physical stock was already present in South Africa and it may be postulated that, similarly, by selective processes, the Negroid and Erythriote [i.e., the so-called Hamitic] types had also made their appearance. . . . Because of their blood group relationships, the man and the Negro must be derived from the same African ancestral stock." An "unspecialized Negroid ancestral type" is spoken of as living in the Congo river basin during "the Later Stone Age," but "there is reason to suppose that the gin of the Negro physical stock and its distribution in Africa is linked with the forest and woodland savannah region" (J. Desmond Clark, "Origins of African Culture," pp. 19–20, 25).

11. For a discussion of climatic changes over long time spans in the Sahara, and of fossils found there that seem to be Negroid, see Clark, ''Origins of African Culture," p. 18–20. See also some observations to the point that "mystery surrounds the origin of the true Negro," in Roland Oliver and J. D. Page, *A Short History of Africa* (Baltimore: Penguin, 1962), pp. 20–22. For an excellent

description of the oldest fossils classified as "Negro" and "Negroid," see Frederick S. Hulse, *The Human Species* (New York: Random House, 1963), pp. 237–239.

12. Oliver and Fage, *Short History of Africa*, pp. 14–16.13

13. Coon, *Origin of Races*, p. 658.

14. "On Coon's *The Origin of Races*," in *The Concept of Race*, ed. Ashley Montagu (New York: Collier Books, 1964), pp. 228–241 (especially p. 234).

15. Oliver and Fage, *Short History of Africa*, pp. 21–22.

16. Murdock, Africa, chapter 4, "Economy," especially pp. 22– 24. This discussion of a Middle Eastern Neolithic period adopts a useful but oversimplified frame of reference from V. Gordon Childe, *Man Makes Himself* (New York: Mentor, 1951), chapter 5, "The Neolithic Revolution." See also V. Gordon Childe, *What Happened in History* (Harmondsworth, England: Penguin, 1967), chapter 3, "Neolithic Barbarism," and chapter 4, "The Higher Barbarism of the Copper Age." A standard account, which argued the case for the introduction of the food-producing revolution into the Nile Valley by Caucasoid people from the Middle East, may be found in Oliver and Fage's *Short History of Africa*. Another scholar examines the arguments of those who oppose this view and gives reasons for his adherence to it (Glyn Daniel, *The First Civilizations* [New York: Crowell, 1968), chapter 1, "Savagery, Barbarism and Civilization"). For a revisionist argument suggesting the possibility that "the agriculture of tropical Africa is original and that of the Middle East derivative," see Christopher Wrigley, "Speculation on the Economic Prehistory of Africa," in *African Prehistory*, ed. Fage and Oliver, pp. 59-74. The late R. Porteres did not discuss priority in innovation but concluded that "recent research has confirmed the importance of the Fertile Crescent in the history of world agriculture." He warned, however, against neglecting the roles of other areas, including several in Africa (R. Porteres and J. Barrau, "Origins, Development and Expansion of Agriculture," in *A General History of Africa*, vol. 1, ed. J. Ki-Zerbo [Berkeley: University of California Press, 1981], pp. 687–705.)

17. Oliver and Fage, *Short History of Africa*, p. 28.

18. Murdock, *Africa*. A chart comparing the cultivated plants of West Africa with those of Ethiopia, Southwest Asia, Southeast Asia, and America is presented on page 23. A full discussion of Murdock's theory of a separate West African center of plant domestication is presented on pages 64–72, along with an indictment of those who fail to recognize or admit that "the assemblage of cultivated plants ennobled from wild forms in Negro Africa ranks as one of the four major agricultural complexes evolved in the entire course of human history" (pp. 64–65).

19. Joseph Harris, professor of history at Howard University, made these remarks in his excellent *Africans and Their History: A Major Work of Historical Re-evaluation* (New York: Mentor, 1972), p. 30. [This Afrocentric volume serves as a fine complement to Oliver and Fage's Eurocentric *Short History of Africa*.) Professor Porteres, in the scholarly article referred to in note 16, does not call Murdock by name but concedes that "in addition to the Abyssinian centre and the African portion of the Mediterranean centre, there existed also a West African centre, and an East African one" (pp. 693–694). For another scholar who gives some credibility to Murdock's argument, see Wrigley, "Economic Prehistory of Africa," in *African Prehistory*, ed. Fage and Oliver, pp. 61–63. J. Desmond Clark, in his article "The Spread of Food Production in Sub-Saharan Africa" in the same volume, comments that "the archaeological record as yet provides no confirmation for the belief that an independent centre of cereal crop domestication existed in West Africa as suggested by Porteres and Murdock" (p. 33). Clark does not discuss the other crops that Murdock contends were domesticated by the Mande Negroes, including cotton and watermelon.

20. Murdock, *Africa*, p. 64. This kind of entrenched attitude can be found in Sir Harry H. Johnston's long and learned article "A Survey of the Ethnography of Africa," *Journal of the Royal Anthropological Institute of Great Britain and Ireland* 43 (1913), pp. 375–421. Sir Harry insisted

that iron smelting must have been imported into sub-Saharan Africa, for "I myself require very convincing proof that the pure blooded Negro ever originated anything" (p. 418). The tautological character of the Hamitic argument is illustrated by the comment of an anthropologist about one African ethnic group that "the rude character" of some of their pottery suggests that they were "well tinctured with Negro blood." Such inference of race from inferior craftsmanship where the physical traits are not Negro occurs less frequently than the explaining of "inferior" culture by the presence of Negroid traits (C. G. Seligman, "Some Aspects of the Hamitic Problem in the Anglo-Egyptian Sudan," *Journal of the Royal Anthropological Institute* 43 [1913], p. 592).

21. For some excellent photography showing a wide variety of African physical types, accompanied by a group of authoritative articles written by experts for laymen, consult the second volume in the Danbury Press Peoples of the Earth series, Africa from the Sahara to the Zambesi, published in 1972. Issues of National Geographic containing articles on Africa are excellent for getting acquainted with the wide range of physical types within the African population. These types are the products of millennia of miscegenation operating concurrently with the processes of geographical and social isolation to produce and stabilize a variety of subtypes. Two excellent articles appear as chapters in volume 1 of the *UNESCO General History of Africa*, one by the African editor, J. Ki-Zerbo, "Editorial Note on the 'Races' and History of Africa," and the other by Russian Africanist D. Olderogge, entitled "Migrations and Ethnic and Linguistic Differentiation." Ki-Zerbo concludes that "Today, except for a few dissenting voices, the large majority of scholars agree on the basic genetic unity of peoples south of the Sahara" (p. 268). Cheikh Anta Diop also insists that Africans themselves view this mass of people as one population despite the wide range in color and physical features, as do Afro-Americans, West Indians, and Latin Americans when dealing with the descendants of the African slaves in the New World (see Diop, *The African Origin of Civilization: Myth or Reality* [New York: Lawrence Hill, 1974], pp. 48–49). A wide range in color and features, and two types of hair ("smooth" and "frizzy") are considered normal to "Negro" African populations according to Diop. Professional anthropologists insist upon a narrower definition that makes facial architecture crucial (especially degree of prognathism) and does not accept "smooth" or "straight" hair as a Negro trait. Incidentally, Herodotus spoke of "smooth"- and "woolly"-haired Ethiopians.

22. Alan Lomax, "The Homogeneity of African-Afro-American Musical Style," in *Afro-American Anthropology: Contemporary Perspectives*, ed. Norman E. Whitten and John F. Szwed (New York: Free Press, 1970), pp. 191, 193.

23. That skin color, along with other physical differences, was recognized in early times is apparent in rock paintings, incised portrayals, and drawings. The nature of the social sentiments associated with the recognition of physical differences, however, is not clear. See Henri Breuil, *The Rock Paintings of South Africa* (London: Trianon Press, 1955); Henri Lhote, *The Search for the Tassili Frescoes: The Story of the Prehistoric Rock Paintings of the Sahara* (London: Hutchinson, 1959); and Jean D. Lajoux, *Rock Paintings of Tassili* (New York: World, 1963).

24. Jacques Maquet, *The Premises of Inequality in Ruanda* {London: Oxford University Press, 1960). This anthropologist analyzes the dynamics of a caste-like system that evolved with Pygmies at the bottom. See also Marcel D'Hertefelt, "The Rwanda of Rwanda," in *Peoples of Africa*, ed. James L. Gibbs, Jr. (New York: Holt, Rinehart and Winston, 1965), pp. 403–440. It is difficult to make a plausible guess about the nature of the system of social ranking among Pygmies, Bushmen, and similar hunting and gathering people before they came in contact with agricultural Negroes. These groups today do not have slaves and do not make internal color distinctions. Whether this was true in the remote past we do not know. The study of marginal peoples who have fled into refuge areas is instructive however and such groups studied in East Africa do not have slaves or classes."

25. There are legends among the Bun yoro-Kitara people of Uganda that a tall, "red" people called the Bachwezi, who had supernatural powers, came to Uganda. After the reign of a few

Bachwezi kings, they disappeared from the area. When the Europeans arrived, some people thought the Bachwezi were returning. See J. W. Nyakatura, *Anatomy of an African Kingdom* (Garden City, N.J.: Doubleday, 1973), chapter 1, "Abachwezi Rule," pp. 21–49, for a careful piecing together of the oral tradition. Among the Kikuyu, light-brown people are sometimes referred to as "red" and as coming from a specific area. They are "Fort Hall Kikuyu." Variations in physical type are wide within this Kenyan ethnic group, however.

26. The first effort at scholarly demolition of the Hamitic theory, accompanied by the charge that it was being used in a racist manner, was carried out by an American anthropologist, Joseph Green berg. See his *Studies in African Linguistic Classification* (Evanston, Ill.: Northwestern University Press, 1955). For a sophisticated recent critique by another American scholar, see Wyatt MacGaffey, "Concepts of ' Race in the Historiography of Northeast Africa," *Journal of African History* 7, 1 (1966): 99–115. Greenberg dropped the term entirely in his work. Murdock, however, clung to it for use in classifying languages only, not for designating entire cultures. He then used the term "Cushitic" to apply to some of the Caucasoid peoples who had previously been called Hamites, thus compounding confusion since most scholars and interested laymen use the term "Cushite" to apply to Negroid peoples. Dr. J. Ki-Zerbo, in his introduction to volume 1 of the *UNESCO General History of Africa*, states that "the excesses of racially prejudiced physical anthropology are now rejected by all serious authors. But the Hamites and other brown races invented to fit the purpose [are] still to be found in the mirages and fantasies produced by otherwise scientific minds" (pp. 21–22). P. Diagne, in the same volume (p. 245), states that the term "Hamite," despite the work of modem linguists and ethnologists, "has still continued to be used as a criterion for discriminating between certain black peoples who are regarded as superior beings, and the rest." The authors in volume 2 of the *General History*, who occasionally use the term, assume that readers take for granted their absence of racist intent. The history of the use of the term "Hamite" merits thorough study. The article that first gave the Hamitic theory respectability in English-speaking circles was Charles Seligman's "Some Aspects of the Hamitic Problem in the Anglo Egyptian Sudan," *Journal of the Royal Anthropological Institute of Great Britain and Ireland* 43 [1913]: 593–704, especially pp. 679–680. Seligman later gave wide currency to the British theory of Hamitic superiority in his book Races of Africa (London: Butterworth, 1930). Even the revision of this work in 1957 perpetuated the Hamitic myth and retained a number of offensive passages. The most derogatory statements about "Negroes" as compared with "Hamites" in the British anthropological literature appear in the works of a missionary who became an "expert" on East Africa: John Roscoe (see "Immigrants and Their Influence in the Lake Region of Central Africa" in The Frazer Lectures, 1922–1932, ed. Warren R. Dawson [London: Macmillan, 1932], pp. 25–46, and "Bahima: A Cow Tribe of Enkole," *Journal of the Royal Anthropological Institute of Great Britain and Ireland* 37 [1907]: 93-118. A Belgian anthropologist, Emil Torday, made the first challenge to this group of British scholars in a sarcastic attack on Seligman and his followers that is reprinted in the Introduction to the 1930 edition of Herbert Spencer's Descriptive Sociology, published by the Herbert Spencer Trust, London . A very restrained criticism of the Hamitic formulation as being tautological was made by one of Seligman's students after he had become one of Britain's most distinguished anthropologists, E. E. Evans-Pritchard, in his chapter "Ethnological Survey of the Sudan" in The Anglo-Egyptian Sudan from Within, ed. J. A. de C. Hamilton (London: Faber and Faber, 1935), pp. 79–93. For more recent discussions see St. Clair Drake, "Destroy the Hamitic Myth," Presence Africaine 24–25 (February–May 1959), pp. 228–243, special issue, English edition; and Edith S. Sanders, "The Hamitic Hypothesis: Its Origins and Functions in Time Perspective," Journal of African History 10, 4 11969): 521–532.

27. "At present the arable lands of Egypt and Western Asia are embedded in large tracts of desert. But it seems that in the Ice Age the pressure of cold air over Europe compelled the Atlantic rain storms to travel east by a more southerly track, so that the whole area from the west coast of

Africa to the Persian mountains was a continuous belt of park and grassland. . . . [A] change of climate, which started in the Old Stone Age, continued in the New, and very gradually changed living conditions throughout the Near East. . . . Progressive desiccation marked the period from perhaps 7000 BC onwards, turning the plateau from grassland into steppe, and, 'ultimately, into desert, and making the valleys of the great rivers inhabitable" (Henri Frankfort, *The Birth of Civilization in the Near East* [Bloomington: Indiana University Press, 1954], pp. 33–34). Oliver and Fage, in their *Short History of Africa*, state that "early Egyptian cultivators of the valley margin soon began to suffer from the steady desiccation of, the climate during the late fifth and early fourth millennia. It was the encroaching drift sand of the desert which stimulated the Tasians and Badarians of Mickdie Egypt to move down and clear the flood-plain, with results so startling for the, history of the world. From that moment onwards the remains of the Predynastic period indicate a phenomenal growth of population" (p. 26).

28. Young's Ethiopian Manifesto can be found in Sterling Stuckey, *The Ideological Origins of Black Nationalism* (Boston: Beacon Press, 1972), pp. 30–38. See Stuckey, *Ideological Origins*, pp. 40 and 58, for references to Ethiopia in Walker's *Appeal*. Black plantation religious symbols emphasized the Jewish slave experiences in Egypt, with the Exodus, Jordan, and Jericho appearing in songs, sermons, prayers, and testimonials. In contrast, Free Negro ministers, as members of a literate clergy elaborated the retrospective and prospective myth of "Ethiopianism" based on the prophecy of ultimate vindication for Egypt and Ethiopia in the Psalms. Note St. Clair Drake's *Black Religion and the Redemption of Africa* (Chicago: Third World Press, 1971); and Albert J. Raboteau's *Slave Religion: The "Invisible Institution" in the Antebellum South* (New York: Oxford University Press, 1978).

29. References to ancient Egypt and Ethiopia appeared in a book published in England but read by Free Negroes in the United States, *A Tribute for the Negro, Being a Vindication of the Moral, Intellectual, and Religious Capabilities of the Coloured Portion of Mankind, with Particular Reference to the African Race* (Manchester, 1848), by William Armstead. "Part First" was entitled "An Inquiry into Claims of the Negro Race to Humanity, and a Vindication of Their Original Equality with the Other Portions of Mankind" and included among the subtopics the following: "Their Origin and Noble Ancestry-Ethiopians and Egyptians Considered." The author, after discussing "this noble ancestry, said that "all Africans" were "fully entitled to claim [it] as their own" (pp. 120–123).

30. Herodotus wrote that he considered the people of the colony of Colchians near the Black Sea to be Egyptians, "'because they are black-skinned and have wooly hair," as were the inhabitants of "several other nations." The fact that they also practiced circumcision clinched the matter of their Egyptian origin for him. Frank Snowden, in *Blacks in Antiquity* (Cambridge, Mass.: Harvard University Press, 1971), p. 290, cites a fellow classicist to support the idea that Herodotus meant precisely "black skin and kinky hair": P. T. English, "Cushites, Colchians, and Khazars," *Journal of Near Eastern Studies* 18 (1959): 49–53. Others claim the passage means only "dark skinned and curly haired," not "black and kinky haired."

31. When Egyptian antiquities were first discovered by the scholars who accompanied Napoleon, there was a tendency to credit Negroes with the founding of the Egyptian nation and with its early advances toward civilization. A quick reversal of this view took place, partly because of pressure from proslavery interests (see Diop, *African Origin*, pp. 45–57).

32. J. C. Nott and George R. Gliddon, *Types of Mankind or Ethnological Researches* (Philadelphia: Lippincott, 1855), chapter 5, "African Types"; chapter 8, "Egypt and Egyptians."

33. Quoted in Diop, *African Origin*, pp. 27–28.

34. Vivant Denon, *Travels in Upper and Lower Egypt*, vol. 1 (New York: Arno Press, 1973), pp. 271–272; reprinted from the 1803 edition published by Longman and Reese of London.

35. Quoted from Blyden's *From West Africa to Palestine*, in W. E. B. Du Bois's *The Negro* (London: Oxford University Press, 1970; republication of the original edition published by Henry Holt, 1915), p. 19. Blyden wrote these words after a visit to Egypt.

36. Chancellor Williams, *The Destruction of Black Civilization* (Chicago: Third World Press, 1974), p. 73.

37. Arthur Weigall, A History of the Pharaohs, vol. 1 (London : Thornton Butterworth, 1925), p. 177.

38. Note "King Khephren-side view" and "King Khephren-front view," in Cyril Aldred, *The Development of Ancient Egyptian Art from 3,200 to 1,315 B.C.* (London: Alec Tiranti, 1952), plates 17, 18.

39. Arthur Weigall, *Personalities of Antiquity* (Garden City, N.J.: Doran and Co., 1928), chapter 24, "The Exploits of a Nigger King," p. 186.

40. Weigall, *History of the Pharaohs*, vol. 1, p. 177 .

41. Du Bois, *Black Folk Then and Now: An Essay in the History and Sociology of the Negro Race* (New York: H. Holt and Co., 1939, 1940).

42. Ibid., p. 148.

43. Ibid., pp. 9, 17.

44. The quotations from the 1974 UNESCO conference are taken from G. Mokhtar, ed., *A General History of Africa*, vol. 2 (Berkeley: University of California Press, 1981), "Introduction," pp. 14, 59–78.

45. Cheikh Anta Diop, "Origin of the Ancient Egyptians," in *General History of Africa*, vol. 2, ed. G. Mokhtar, pp. 50–51.

46. Roland Oliver, "The African Rediscovery of Africa," *Times Literary Supplement* (March 20, 1981), p. 29.

47. Modem Egyptologists occasionally point out that to translate "Nehesi" as "Negro" is misleading. Older Egyptologists invariably did so, thus giving the impression that the Egyptians drew a racial distinction between themselves and the people of Kush. In fact, Nehesi was applied to a number of physical types living south of Egypt, including some blacks, most of whom were Negroid, but not all. It was never applied to Egyptians with Negro facial characteristics. There is some evidence that from the Eighteenth Dynasty on, the "typical" Nehesi was thought of as being a Negro although the word was applied to any southerners regardless of physical type. See Diop, *African Origin*, pp. 46–49.

48. Snowden points out, *in Blacks in Antiquity* (p. 112), that Latin writers spoke of both Leucaethiopes and Melanogaetuli in the Sahara, that is, light-skinned Ethiopians and "dark-skinned members of the Gaetuli tribe." They also referred to "Libyans resembling Ethiopians." This suggests that a wide range of physical types were living in "Libya," the vaguely defined area stretching west of Egypt. Some Egyptian paintings portrayed "Libyans" (called Libou, Temehou, Tehenou, and Meshwesto) as "yellow skinned" with distinctive dress and hair styles. Some scholars use the wide range of Negro types portrayed during the Eighteenth Dynasty and after as evidence that Egyptians had not had contact with Blacks above the sixth Nile cataract before that time.

49. One Egyptologist states that, in painting, "Flesh tones were determined more by convention [than by the natural color of the person], the skin of Egyptian men being painted red-brown and that of their womenfolk pale ochre . . . nevertheless there are some departures from these norms, some women being depicted with yellowbrown skins." His statement that "Nubians and Negroes were usually represented as black" ignores the fact that some Egyptians, male and female, were sometimes portrayed as black, too. The conditions under which the conventional representation of Egyptians was ignored is relevant to our inquiry but not discussed (Cyril Aldred, *Egyptian Art in the Days of the Pharaohs*, 3100–320 B.C. [London: Oxford University Press, 1980], p. 30).

50. Du Bois, *The Negro*, p. 17. For a critical analysis of contemporary views about the origins of Egyptian culture, see G. Mokhtar's introduction to *General History of Africa*, vol. 2, p. 21, in which he concludes that "an invasion of civilizing element from the outside, notably from Mesopotamia, rests only on the flimsiest evidence."

51. Quoted in E. A. Wallis Budge, *Osiris and the Egyptian Resurrection* (New York: Dover, 1973), pp. 338–339.

52. An important research breakthrough occurred in the first quarter of the twentieth century when the British inspector-general of antiquities of the Egyptian government, Arthur Weigall, reconstructed a text of the annals written on a large stone tablet possessed by an Italian museum. He was able to fill in gaps by translations from a fragment of this Palermo Stone that remained in Cairo, and from several fragments located elsewhere. He then correlated the Palermo Stone dynasties with those of Manetho as well as king lists deciphered from the Turin Papyrus and the Abydos List. Even a layman can share the excitement of this scholarly detective work as reported by the man who carried it out (Weigall, *History of the Pharaohs*, vol. l, The First Eleven Dynasties, pp. xi– 42).

53. Ethnocentric partisanship has led to disputes over the question of whether writing was invented first in Egypt or in Mesopotamia. Childe, in *Man Makes Himself*, does not address himself directly to this question but implies independent invention. (See chapter 8, "The Revolution in Human Knowledge"; see especially p. 147, where he states, inter alia, that by 2950 BC the Egyptian system of writing was "already more mature than that of the oldest Sumerian documents"). Frankfort, however, is convinced that writing was a Mesopotamian invention borrowed by Egyptians (*Birth of Civilization*, pp. 105–108).

54. Professor Frank Snowden, for instance, hews close to the anthropometrists' line in classifying sculptured and painted images according to race (see pp. 7–11 of his *Blacks in Antiquity*). Diop, in *African Origin* and "Origin of the Ancient Egyptians" (pp. 27–57), takes anthropometry seriously, although in the latter work he expresses some doubt about its value in deciding whether the original Egyptians were "Negroes."

55. Diop, "Origin of the Ancient Egyptians," p. 28.

56. Ibid., p. 29.

57. See Giuseppe Sergi, *The Mediterranean Race: A Study of the Origin of European Peoples* (New York: Scribner's, 1901). The entire work is an argument for the fundamental homogeneity of a "Brown Race" living on both sides of the Mediterranean and in parts of the Middle East. General shape of the skull viewed from various positions, rather than minute measurements taken on the skull, as well as skin color in the living, were used in defining the Brown Race.

58. Aldred, *Old Kingdom*, pp. 16, 22.

59. Murdock, *Africa*, pp. 101, 106.

60. Diop, "Origin of the Ancient Egyptians," "Melanin Dosage Test," p. 35.

61. See the National Geographic Society publication *Ancient Egypt* (1978), color plates on pp. 128–129, 132–133.

62. Diop, *African Origin*, p. 93, and chapter 5.

63. Childe, *Man Makes Himself*, chapter 5, "The Neolithic Revolution," pp. 59–86. (See note 16.)

64. Carleton S. Coon, *The Races of Europe* (New York: Macmillan, 1939), p. 62.

65. Ibid., pp. 92, 95.

66. William C. Hayes, *Most Ancient Egypt* (Chicago: University of Chicago Press, 1965), p. 135.

67. Ibid.

68. Ibid.

69. Arnold J. Toynbee, *A Study of History*, vol. 1 (London: Oxford University Press, 1939), pp. 233, 238. An abridgement of the six-volume *A Study of History*, was published by D. C. Somervell, under auspices of the Royal Institute of International Affairs, in 1947. This was a Book-of-the-Month Club selection. (See p. 54 of the abridged version.)

70. Toynbee, *Study of History*, vol. 1 (1939), pp. 233–235. This is a translation from the French quotation in Toynbee's book taken from M. Delafosse, *Les noirs de l'Afrique* (Paris: Payot, 1922), pp. 156–160. This same idea is expressed in Maurice Delafosse, *The Negroes of Africa: History and Culture*, translated from the French by F. Fligelman and published by an affiliate of the Association for the Study of Negro Life and History, The Associated Publishers, Washington, D.C., 1931.

71. This reference to the Shilluk appears in both editions of *Study of History*, a surprising concession in view of the stress Toynbee places on the Egyptians' not being black during their early creative period. (See pp. 312–315 in the 1939 edition, from which the quote used by Childe was taken, and pp. 71–72 in the 1947 abridged edition.) For a discussion of the Shilluk, using extensive photographic documentation, see E. E. Evans-Pritchard, *"Shilluk-Sudan" in Africa from the Sahara to the Zambesi*, ed. Tom Stacey (New York: Danbury Press, 1972), pp. 46–53.

72. Aldred, *Old Kingdom*, pp. 31, 34. See also Frankfort, *Birth of Civilization*, pp. 100–111, "The Influence of Mesopotamia on Egypt Towards the End of the Fourth Millennium B.C."

73. Diop, *African Origin*, pp. 87–89. For a discussion of the metallurgy question, based on the available archaeological data and without reference to folklore, see J. Vercoutter, "Discovery and Diffusion of Metals and Development of Social Systems up to the Fifth Century before Our Era," in *General History of Africa* vol. 1, ed. J. Ki-Zerbo, pp. 634–655, 706–729.

74. Flinders Petrie, *The Making of Egypt* (London: Sheldon Press, 1939), chapter 8, "The Dynastic Conquest," pp. 65–68; chapter 12, "The Pyramid Age," pp. 105–112.

75. David O'Connor, "Nubia before the New Kingdom," in *Africa in Antiquity: The Arts of Ancient Nubia and the Sudan*, vol. 1 (Brooklyn: Brooklyn Museum, 1978), pp. 52–53, touches briefly upon the factors that inhibited diffusion northward from Kush, or what is referred to as Upper Nubia. See also the discussion of pottery in volume 2, pp. 38–39.

76. See, e.g., Wilson, *Burden of Egypt*, p. 176. By an ingenious deduction from Eighteenth Dynasty records, one unconventional scholar has attempted to prove that Judea was "Punt" and "God's Land" and that Hatshepsut was the Queen of Sheba who visited both (Iramanuel Velikovsky, *Ages in Chaos* [Garden City, N.J.: Doubleday, 1952], pp. 114–129).

77. It has been suggested that in the period prior to the post-Makalian dry phase, which began in the fourth millennium BC, the swamps of the Bahr-al-Ghazal and the arid land between the upper Nile and Ethiopia had not cut off the people of the southern Sudan from the civilization of the Nile Valley (Wrigley, "Economic Prehistory of Africa," p. 71).

78. Boyce Rensberger, "Nubian Monarch Called Oldest," *New York Times* (March l, 1979), pp. Al, Al6. See also Bruce Williams, "The Lost Pharaohs of Nubia," *Archaeology* 33, 5 (1980): 12–21.

79. John G. Jackson, *Introduction to African Civilization* (Secaucus, N.J.: Citadel Press, 1974), chapter 2, "Ethiopia and the Origin of Civilization." See chapter 19, "The King of Ethiopia," in Angelo S. Rappaport and Raphael Patai, *Myth and Legend of Ancient Israel*, vol. 2 (New York: KTAV, 1966), pp. 244–249.

80. Petrie, *Making of Egypt*, chapter 8, "The Dynastic Conquest." Petrie begins with a subtitle, "Conflict of Races." He visualizes the Negroid Anu (or Aunu) invading from Asia, subduing Caucasoid and Negroid peoples already there making conquests in Libya and Nubia. Illustrations of sculptured images of Narmer and Teter-Neter are presented. Both have Negroid traits. See reprints of these photographs in Diop, *African Origin*.

81. Ibid., pp. 21, 65, 67. Petrie describes in some detail the conflicts that he interprets as racial. See also Diop, *African Origin*, pp. 131–132, 164–167.

# SETTLERS OF COLOR AND "IMMIGRANT" HEGEMONY

## "Locals" in Hawai'i

HAUNANI-KAY TRASK

> For a colonized people the most essential value, because the most concrete, is first and foremost the land: the land which will bring them bread and, above all, dignity.
>
> —Frantz Fanon, *The Wretched of the Earth*[1]

> The world's indigenous peoples have fundamental human rights of a collective and individual nature. Indigenous peoples are not, and do not consider themselves, minorities. . . . Self-determination of peoples is a right of peoples . . . Under contemporary international law, minorities do not have this right.
>
> —Sharon Venne, *Our Elders Understand Our Rights: Evolving International Law Regarding Indigenous Rights*[2]

> The indigenous Hawaiian people never directly relinquished their claims to their inherent sovereignty as a people or over their national lands to the United States, either through their monarchy or through a plebiscite or referendum.
>
> —US Public Law 103-150, the "Apology Bill"[3]

As the indigenous people of Hawai'i, Hawaiians are Native to the Hawaiian Islands. We do not descend from the Americas or from Asia but from the great Pacific Ocean where our ancestors navigated to, and from, every archipelago. Genealogically, we say we are descendants of Papahanaumoku (Earth Mother) and Wakea (Sky Father), who created our beautiful islands. From this land came the *taro,* and from the *taro,* our Hawaiian people. The lesson of our origins is that we are genealogically related to Hawai'i, our islands, as family. We are obligated to care for our mother, from whom all bounty flows.

Haunani-Kay Trask is a Native Hawaiian nationalist, professor of Hawaiian Studies at the University of Hawai'i, and author of *From a Native Daughter: Colonialism and Sovereignty in Hawai'i.*

## HISTORY AND SETTLER IDEOLOGY

After nearly two thousand years of self-governance, we were colonized by Euro-American capitalists and missionaries in the eighteenth and nineteenth centuries. In 1893, the United States invaded our nation, overthrew our government, and secured an all-white planter oligarchy in place of our reigning *ali'i,* Queen Lili'uokalani.[4]

By resolution of the American Congress and against great Native opposition, Hawai'i was annexed in 1898. Dispossession of our government, our territory, and our legal citizenship made of us a colonized Native people.

Today, modern Hawai'i, like its colonial parent the United States, is a settler society. Our Native people and territories have been overrun by non-Natives, including Asians. Calling themselves "local," the children of Asian settlers greatly outnumber us. They claim Hawai'i as their own, denying indigenous history, their long collaboration in our continued dispossession, and the benefits therefrom.[5]

Part of this denial is the substitution of the term "local" for "immigrant," which is, itself, a particularly celebrated American gloss for "settler." As on the continent, so in our island home. Settlers and their children recast the American tale of nationhood: Hawai'i, like the continent, is naturalized as but another telling illustration of the uniqueness of America's "nation of immigrants." The ideology weaves a story of success: poor Japanese, Chinese, and Filipino settlers supplied the labor for wealthy, white sugar planters during the long period of the Territory (1900–1959). Exploitative plantation conditions thus underpin a master narrative of hard work and the endlessly celebrated triumph over anti-Asian racism. Settler children, ever industrious and deserving, obtain technical and liberal educations, thereby learning the political system through which they agitate for full voting rights as American citizens. Politically, the vehicle for Asian ascendancy is statehood. As a majority of voters at midcentury, the Japanese and other Asians moved into the middle class and eventually into seats of power in the legislature and the governor's house.[6]

For our Native people, Asian success proves to be but the latest elaboration of foreign hegemony. The history of our colonization becomes a twice-told tale, first of discovery and settlement by European and American businessmen and missionaries, then of the plantation Japanese, Chinese, and eventually Filipino rise to dominance in the islands. Some Hawaiians, the best educated and articulate, benefit from the triumph of the Democratic Party over the *haole* Republican Party. But as a people, Hawaiians remain a politically subordinated group suffering all the legacies of conquest: landlessness, disastrous health, diaspora, institutionalization in the military and prisons, poor educational attainment, and confinement to the service sector of employment.[7]

While Asians, particularly the Japanese, come to dominate post-statehood, Democratic Party politics, new racial tensions arise. The attainment of full American citizenship actually heightens prejudice against Natives. Because the ideology of the United States as a mosaic of races is reproduced in Hawai'i through the celebration of the fact that no single "immigrant group" constitutes a numerical majority, the post-statehood euphoria stigmatizes Hawaiians as a failed indigenous people whose conditions, including out-migration, actually worsen after statehood. Hawaiians are characterized as strangely unsuited, whether because of culture or genetics, to the game of assimilation.

Of course, the specific unique claims of Native Hawaiians as indigenous peoples are denied through the prevailing ideology of "power sharing." Here, power sharing refers to the spoils of the electoral system, which are shared, in succession, among "ethnic groups." Politically, "power sharing" serves to reinforce the colonial position that Hawaiians are just another competing "ethnic group" waiting their turn for political dominance. Disguising the colonial history and subordinated position of Natives, while equating Natives and non-Natives, the ideology tells a false tale of just desserts. Empirically, of course, subjugated peoples cannot willingly share anything. In the case of Hawaiians, we have nothing left to share. Our lands and resources, taken at the overthrow and transferred at annexation to the American government and later to the State of Hawai'i are, literally, not under our control. But the utility of the propaganda of "power sharing" is that it begs the question of *why* Natives should share power, while reinforcing the refrain that those in power have justly earned their dominant place. Given that Hawaiians are indigenous, that our government was overthrown, and that we are entitled, as a nation, to sovereignty, the argument that we should share power with non-Natives who benefit from the theft of our sovereignty is, simply, grotesque.

When the centenary of the American invasion of Hawai'i, overthrow of the Native government, and forcible annexation of the archipelago are commemorated by thousands of protesting Natives in 1993 and 1998, anti-Hawaiian sentiment among growing numbers of Asians and *haole* is already a political reality. One recent example of this new form of prejudice is the assertion of a "local nation."[8]

Ideologically, the appearance of this "local nation" is a response to a twenty-year-old sovereignty movement among Hawaiians. Organized Natives, led by a young, educated class attempting to develop progressive elements among Hawaiians, as well as to create mechanisms for self-government, are quickly perceived as a threat by many Asians uneasy about their obvious benefit from the dispossession and marginalization of Natives. Arguing that Asians, too, have a nation in Hawai'i, the "local" identity tag blurs the history of Hawai'i's only indigenous people while staking a settler claim. Any complicity in the subjugation of Hawaiians is denied by the assertion that Asians, too, comprise a "nation." They aren't complicit in maintaining institutional racism against Natives, nor do they continue to benefit from wholesale dispossession of Native lands and sovereignty. In truth, "local" ideology tells a familiar, and false, tale of success: Asians came as poor plantation workers and triumphed decades later as the new, democratically elected ruling class. Not coincidentally, the responsibility for continued Hawaiian dispossession falls to imperialist *haole* and incapacitated Natives, that is, not to Asians. Thus do these settlers deny their ascendancy was made possible by the continued national oppression of Hawaiians, particularly the theft of our lands and the crushing of our independence.

This intra-settler competition between *haole* and Asians is a hallmark of colonial situations. Such contests serve, especially if severe, to mask even further the dispossession and marginalization of Natives. Asians—particularly the Japanese—like to harken back to the oppressions of the plantation era, although few Japanese in Hawai'i today actually worked on the plantations during the Territory (1900–1959). But at the threshold of a new century, it is the resilience of settler ideology which facilitates and justifies non-Native hegemony: "immigrants" who have struggled so hard and for so long *deserve* political and economic supremacy. By comparison, indigenous Hawaiians aren't in power because they haven't worked (or paid their dues) to achieve supremacy. In more obviously racist terms, Hawaiians deserve their fate. We suffer the same categorical character flaws as other Native peoples. To wit, we are steeped in nostalgia or cultural invention; we yearn for the past instead of getting on with the present. Or we are, as a collective, culturally/psychologically incapable of learning how to bend our energies toward success in the modern world.

Against this kind of disparaging colonial ideology, Hawaiians have been asserting their claims as indigenous people to land, economic power, and political sovereignty for at least the last twenty years. Hawaiian communities are seriously engaged in all manner of historical, cultural, and political education. *Halau hula* (dance academies), language classes, and varied resistance organizations link cultural practice to the struggle for self-determination. In this way, cultural groups have become conduits for reconnection to the *liihui,* or nation. Political education occurs as the groups participate in sovereignty marches, rallies, and political lobbying. The substance of the "nation" is made obvious when thousands of Hawaiians gather to protest the theft of their sovereignty. The power of such public rituals to decolonize the mind can be seen in the rise of a new national identification among Hawaiians. After the 1993 sovereignty protests at the Palace of our chiefs, Hawaiians, especially the youth, began to discard national identity as Americans and reclaim indigenous identification as Natives. Re-forming a *lahui* that had allegedly disappeared in 1893 continues to serve the process of decolonization on at least two levels. The first is one of throwing off colonial identification as Americans. The second is understanding our Native nation as eligible in both international law and American law for inclusion in policies of Native sovereignty. Hawaiian resistance today is anchored in the increasing knowledge that Hawaiians once lived under their own national government as citizens of the Hawaiian rather than the American nation. Thus, the citizenship of our Native people and the territory of our nation, that is, the land base of our archipelago, are the contested ground. *The struggle is not for a personal or group identity but for land, government, and international status as a recognized nation.*

The distinction here between the personal and the national is critical. Hawaiians are not engaged in identity politics, any more than the Irish of Northern Ireland or the Palestinians of occupied Palestine are engaged in identity politics. Both the Irish and the Palestinians are subjugated national groups committed to a war of national liberation. Hawaiians, although not in the stage of combat, are nevertheless engaged in a kind of national liberation struggle. The terrain of battle now involves control of lands and natural resources, including water and subsurface minerals. Any negotiations over settlements other than land involves millions of dollars. By these actions is the *liihui* seen to be, and experienced as, a palpable national entity.

If Hawaiians have a pre-contact, pre-invasion historical continuity on their aboriginal territories—that is, on the land that had been ours for two thousand years—"locals" do not. That is, "locals" have no indigenous land base, traditional language, culture, and history that is Native to Hawai'i. Our indigenous origin enables us to define what and who is indigenous, and what and who is not indigenous. We know who the First Nations people are since we were, historically, the first people in the Hawaiian archipelago. Only Hawaiians are Native to Hawai'i. Everyone else is a settler.

Local Asians also know, as we do, that they are not First Nations people. But ideologically, Asians cannot abide categorization with *haole.* Their subjugation at the hands of *haole* racism, their history of deprivation and suffering on the plantations, demand an identity other than settler. Faced with insurgent Hawaiians on the left, and indifferent or racist *haole* on the right, young Asians politicize the term "local." Primarily a defense against categorization with *haole,* especially *haole* from the American continent, "local" identification has been strengthened in response to "Native" insurgency. As the sovereignty front gains ground and as more Hawaiians assert an indigenous primacy, defensive Asians begin to concoct a fictitious socio-political entity based in Hawai'i. Hence the strangely disconnected idea called "local nation."[9]

The projection of a "local nation" as but the latest ideological evolution of "local" Asian identity is a telling illustration of how deeply the threat of Hawaiian nationalism has penetrated the fearful psychologies of non-Natives. Various ethnic groups in Hawai'i are fronting their "local" claims to residency and political ascendance in our aboriginal homeland precisely at the time when organized political power on the part of Natives is emerging. Challenging the settler ideology that "we are all immigrants," Native nationalism unsettles the accustomed familiarity with which *haole* and Asians enjoy their dominance in everyday Hawai'i. Behind their irritation, however, Asians sense a real political threat. They know the stakes in the various organized sovereignty initiatives are substantial.

The Japanese American Citizens League-Honolulu (JACL-Honolulu) is a recent example of how settlers front their alleged support of Hawaiian sovereignty (the JACL-Honolulu passed a lukewarm sovereignty resolution) while attacking Hawaiian leaders who represent the sovereignty movement.[10] In fall of 1999, the local Honolulu dailies had a field day attacking Hawaiian sovereignty leader and Office of Hawaiian Affairs (OHA) Trustee, Mililani Trask, because she referred to Senator Daniel Inouye as the "one-armed bandit" in an OHA meeting. Trask explained the nickname was originally given to Inouye by his own Japanese army comrades in the second World War. (It was also the nickname commonly used for him by his good friend and former Hawai'i governor, Jack Bums, among others.) The nickname referred to Inouye's admitted theft of jewelry from dead wartime noncombatants. The arm on which he wore the jewelry was later blown off, a fate his war buddies named "*bachi,*" roughly translated as "bad karma," what we Hawaiians might call "*holm,*" or getting one's just desserts for a bad deed.[11]

Release of Trask's use of the term was done by OHA trustees on the Inouye dole. These were the same trustees Trask had criticized for supporting Inouye's longstanding refusal to include Hawaiians in the federal policy on recognized Native nations. The local newspapers, particularly the right-wing, missionary-descended *Honolulu Advertiser,* ran a biased news story without comment from Trask and a racist cartoon with her cut-off right leg stuck in her mouth.[12]

Never mind, of course, that the "one-armed bandit" epithet was given to Inouye by his own comrades, nor that the substantive issue was Inouye's twenty-five-year lock on all federal funding for Hawai'i which, following Democratic Party procedure, has gone only to Inouye favorites, none of whom support Hawaiian control of Hawaiian lands and entitlements.

In the end, the issue of Inouye's interference in the sovereignty process, including his massive funding to compliant Hawaiian friends, received little coverage in the press. Trask's detailed reply to the *Advertiser* went unreported until Trask called her own press conference to release all information regarding Inouye's control of the sovereignty process. The *Advertiser* then admitted they had received her reply via email but claimed it "wasn't retrieved" by press time. Trask finally paid to have the details of Inouye's political interference printed in the OHA paper.[13]

The JACL-Honolulu, meanwhile, played their customary reactionary role, targeting Trask and successfully obscuring her analysis. In the public controversy which followed, the anti-Hawaiian politics of the JACL were never addressed. The JACL and its spokesperson Clayton Ikei published a letter in the *Hawai'i Herald,* and copied it to other media, asking Trask to avoid "future resort to divisive racial and ethnic characterizations" of Inouye.[14]

Neither Ikei nor the membership of the JACL showed any interest in the substance of Trask's criticism of Inouye, namely that he was interfering in a Native process. Following their usual practice, the JACL, like the Japanese membership of the Democratic Party, obscured the issue of their control over Hawai'i politics and Native resources by vilifying a Native leader who criticized non-Native interference by Inouye and his friends.

Politically, the JACL, the Honolulu dailies, and Dan Inouye had once again teamed up to disparage and berate a Hawaiian leader. The JACL continued the familiar role of the Japanese in Hawai'i by opposing Hawaiian control over Native lands, water, and political representation. Inouye's twenty-year refusal to introduce federal legislation recognizing Hawaiians as Native peoples eligible for inclusion in the federal policy on recognized Native nations was never mentioned, let alone criticized by any of the involved parties in the controversy, including the JACL. Clearly and swiftly, the JACL had acted to support the power of the Japanese-controlled Democratic Party while disparaging a Hawaiian leader who sought to analyze and expose that same control.

This collaborationist role of the JACL is in stark contrast to the critical support given to Trask and the sovereignty movement in general by a new group, Local Japanese Women for Justice (LJWJ), formed as a result of the Inouye-Trask controversy. Comprised entirely of local Japanese women led by Eiko Kosasa and Ida Yoshinaga, the group published a lengthy piece in the *Honolulu Advertiser* (and later in the Japanese newspaper, *Hawai'i Herald*) criticizing both the *Advertiser* and the JACL for attacking a sovereignty leader. The anti-sovereignty role of certain Japanese leaders in Hawai'i, like Inouye, was also analyzed, as was the role of the JACL in supporting Japanese internment during the Second World War.[15]

The response of the JACL, written by Bill Hoshijo and David Forman, to their Japanese sisters was swift and nasty. They defended internment of their own people, while simultaneously arguing that the war years were a complex and difficult time for all. Refusing to acknowledge their collaborationist role in continuing Hawaiian subjugation, they also once again defended the record of Dan Inouye. True to form, the JACL failed to counter any of the substantive positions their Japanese sisters had argued.[16]

This critical exposure of the JACL frightened their supporters and other Japanese leaders, including one Eric Yamamoto, a professor at the University of Hawai'i Law

School. For the past several years, Yamamoto has been busy publishing scholarly articles supporting "reconciliation" between Hawaiians and some of the Christian churches who benefited from missionization in Hawai'i, including theft of Native lands and complicity in the overthrow of the Hawaiian government.[17] Yamamoto and JACL leaders, like David Forman, view the JACL as a friend to Hawaiians despite their attack on Trask and her supportive Japanese sisters in LJWJ.

Of course, as a law professor, Yamamoto knows full well that no amount of alleged "reconciliation" can equal the return of lands, money, and self-government to the Hawaiian people. Moreover, substantive "reconciliation" would mean Hawaiian control of the sovereignty process from beginning to end. Such Native control, however, is opposed by the JACL and their fellow non-Native travelers.

The role of groups such as the JACL, as well as other Asian supporters, like Yamamoto, has clearly been to organize Asians against a nationalist Hawaiian agenda while arguing that everyone in Hawai'i must participate in the sovereignty process.

Of course, the notion that settlers should participate in any form in the sovereignty process is ludicrous. In principle and in practice, Native sovereignty must be controlled by Natives. Just as federally recognized tribes on the American continent do not allow non-Natives to represent their peoples, so Hawaiians should not allow non-Natives to determine our strategies for achieving sovereignty. Simply put, "Native" sovereignty is impossible when non-Natives determine the process.

The current task forces appointed by Senator Daniel Akaka and charged with considering the relationship between Hawaiians and the state and federal governments have sitting non-Native members, including David Forman and Eric Yamamoto. Because of non-Native participation, the principle and practice of Native self-determination is violated. As with the findings of past task forces and commissions, nothing will be recommended which advances Native control over land and waters now enjoyed by the state and federal governments and non-Native citizens of Hawai'i.

There are other Asians, not on the task force, who have decided that the role of a "go-between" is essential to the relationship of Asians and Hawaiians. Predictably, this role highlights the activities of the self-styled and self-appointed mediator, rather than the sovereignty issue itself, as critical to any resolution of conflict. In practice, the "go-between" is a double agent. While professing private support to Hawaiians, such double agents actually lobby our few Asian allies to stay within the Japanese fold, that is, to refrain from publicly criticizing Asians who attack Hawaiian leaders.

Jill Nunokawa, civil rights counselor at the University of Hawai'i, is one among many young Asian professionals who, when asked, refused to lend public support to Local Japanese Women for Justice (LJWJ). According to Eiko Kosasa, co-chair of LJWJ, Nunokawa expressed the concern that a public defense of Mililani Trask was bad for the Japanese since Trask was not only criticizing Inouye but Japanese power in general, including their control of Hawaiian lands and entitlements. Nunokawa told Kosasa that Hawaiians were "going down the race road," and she did not wish to join them there. Tellingly, the Hawaiian sovereignty movement, that is, justice in the form of self-determination was represented by Nunokawa as the "race road." Here, Native control of Hawaiian lands, waters, entitlements, and above all, representation at the national level is thus characterized as a "race" issue.

But the real "race" issue to those who control our lands is not the assertion of Hawaiian claims but the loss of Japanese control. In other words, the fear Nunokawa expressed is a pervasive fear Japanese feel about Hawaiian sovereignty since current Japanese control of Hawaiian lands and waters through their control of the state apparatus is directly challenged by Native sovereignty. The Japanese know that they have, as a group, benefited from the dispossession of Hawaiians. Justice for us would require, among other things, an end to Japanese Democratic Party control over Hawaiian lands and waters. Given that the Japanese as a political block have controlled Hawai'i's politics for years, it is obvious that substantive Hawaiian sovereignty requires that Japanese power brokers, specifically, Senator Dan Inouye, the JACL, and the rest of the Japanese-dominated Democratic Party, would no longer control Hawaiian assets, including land and political representation.

When movement Hawaiians remark that "Japanese can't be trusted" in the struggle, they are thinking of false friends like Nunokawa, Yamamoto, and the JACL. No matter their much-touted support in resolutions, articles, and personal statements, these alleged Japanese supporters always come down on the side of the reigning Democratic party since they are direct beneficiaries of its continuing power. As history proves, power is never freely relinquished by those who wield it.

The women in LJWJ, meanwhile, are themselves under attack by Japanese politicos in Hawai'i. Because these women dared to speak publicly against continued Japanese control over Hawaiian lands, resources, representation, and sovereignty, they have been isolated and severely criticized by the Japanese community. Even members of their families have carried out harsh retribution against them.

Such retribution points up the need for larger and larger groups of critical-thinking Asians to support a form of Hawaiian sovereignty created by Hawaiians, rather than the state or federal governments or non-Hawaiians. Truly supportive Asians must publicly ally themselves with our position of Native control over the sovereignty process. Simultaneously, these allies must also criticize Asian attempts to undermine sovereignty leaders. Until young Japanese leaders, such as Nunokawa, are willing to stand publicly with Hawaiian leaders such as Mililani Trask and her Japanese female supporters in Local Japanese Women for Justice, the antisovereignty, anti-Hawaiian effect of groups like the JACL will continue to grow.

While settler organizations like the JACL continue to stir up hatred against Native leaders, the real issue of justice for Hawaiians is intentionally obscured. As enunciated in the Ka Uihui Master Plan, this justice would mean a "federally-recognized" Native Hawaiian land base and government that would establish a nation-to-nation relationship with the American government as is the case today with nearly five hundred American Indian nations. Such a relationship would mean plenary powers for the Hawaiian nation over its territories. At present, these territories are controlled by the state and federal governments which regulate public use.

Once Hawaiians reclaim these lands, public and private relationships between Natives and non-Natives will be altered. For example, settlers will have to pay taxes or user fees to swim at Native-owned beaches, enjoy recreation at Native-owned parks, drive on Native-owned roads, fly out of Native-owned airports, educate their children at public schools on Native-owned lands, and on, and on. Above all, non-Natives will have to live alongside a Native political system that has statutory authority to exclude, tax, or otherwise regulate the presence of non-Natives on Native lands. The potential shift here frightens non-Natives because it signals the political and economic ascendance of Natives. At the least, Native power means no more free access by non-Natives to Native resources.

## INDIGENOUS PEOPLES AND MINORITIES IN INTERNATIONAL LAW

The growing tensions between Asians and Hawaiians in Hawai'i have a corollary in the development of indigenous peoples' human rights in international law. In Article 1 of the United Nations Charter, peaceful relations between nations are seen to depend upon the principles of equal rights and self-determination of peoples. The question that has occupied the Working Group on Indigenous Populations (first convened in 1982 at the United Nations in Geneva) has been the definition of indigenous peoples and the elaboration of their rights. The primary document here is the Draft Declaration on the Rights of Indigenous Peoples. A product of twenty years' work by indigenous peoples themselves as well as human rights lawyers and jurists, the Draft Declaration is the most complete international document on the rights of indigenous peoples.

The Declaration was preceded by two major studies conducted by the Sub-Commission on the Prevention of Discrimination and Protection of Minorities by UN Rapporteurs Espiell (1974) and Deschenes (1985), as part of the broad concern regarding the definition and therefore rights of both minorities and indigenous peoples.[18]

In Hector Gros Espiell's study "peoples" were to be considered as, and treated as, categorically different from "minorities." He based his distinctions on UN language regarding rights to self-determination and decolonization. He concluded that, under international law, self-determination is a right of peoples and not minorities. The critical link for Espiell was the presence of colonial and alien domination. In addition to being a principle of international law, then, self-determination is a right of "peoples" under colonial domination.

In 1985, a Canadian, Justice Jules Deschenes, submitted a report on minorities to the Sub-Commission. His discussion of "minority" clarified the relationship between a minority and a majority as critical. He defined "minority" as:

> A group of citizens of a State, constituting a numerical minority and in a non-dominant position in that State, endowed with ethnic, religious or linguistic characteristics which differ from those of the majority of the population, having a sense of solidarity with one another, motivated, if only implicitly, by a collective will to survive and whose aim is to achieve equality with the majority in fact and in law.[19]

At the same time, Deschenes was conducting his study another Rapporteur, Martinez Cobo, was undertaking a project on indigenous peoples for the Sub-Commission. His definition of indigenous peoples aided in the clarification of exact differences between minorities and indigenous peoples:

> Indigenous communities, peoples and nations are those which, having a historical continuity with pre-invasion and pre-colonial societies that developed on their territories, consider themselves distinct from other sectors of the societies now prevailing on those territories, or part of them. They form at present nondominant sectors of society and are determined to preserve, develop, and transmit to future generations their ancestral territories, and their ethnic identity, as the basis of their continued existence as peoples, in accordance with their own cultural patterns, social institutions, and legal system.[20]

In Rapporteur Martinez Cobo's final report, the identification of indigenous peoples received a great deal of clarification. For example, Cobo argued that indigenous peoples must be recognized according to their own conceptions of themselves. No attempt should be accepted which defines indigenous peoples through the values of foreign societies or the dominant sections of societies. Artificial, arbitrary, or manipulatory definitions, Cobo argued, must be rejected by indigenous peoples and the international human rights community. Finally, Cobo emphasized that the special position of indigenous peoples within the society of nation-states existing today derives from their rights to be different and to be considered as different.

Part of that difference inheres in the *critical identification of historical continuity*. Cobo listed several kinds of historical continuity into the present, including the following:

> a) Occupation of ancestral lands;
> b) Common ancestry with original occupants of these lands;
> c) Culture, in general, including dress, religion, means of livelihood, forms of association, membership in traditional communities;
> d) Language.[21]

Finally, Professor Erica-Irene Daes, the Chairperson-Rapporteur of the Working Group on Indigenous Populations, has written that "acknowledging the significance of 'territory' may be necessary to address another major logical and conceptual problem: differentiating 'indigenous peoples' and 'minorities.' A strict distinction must be made between 'indigenous peoples' rights' and 'minority' rights. Indigenous peoples are indeed peoples and not minorities."[22]

This is a primary distinction because, under international law, "minorities" do not have the right to self-determination. The rights of indigenous peoples have also concerned governments whose countries contain a large percentage of indigenous peoples, such as Greenland. In 1991, the Parliament of Greenland argued for a clear distinction between the rights of minorities and the rights of indigenous peoples.

> the world's indigenous peoples have fundamental human rights of a collective and individual nature. Indigenous peoples are not, and do not consider themselves, minorities. The rights of indigenous peoples are derived from their own history, culture, traditions, laws and special relationship to their lands, resources and environment.[23]

Finally, Justice Deschenes referred to his country's distinctions between indigenous peoples and minorities in the Constitution Act of Canada, arguing that the United Nations should take guidance from Canada's example and define indigenous peoples and minorities separately.

Specific aspects of the Draft Declaration bear directly upon the differences between indigenous peoples and minority populations. Indigenous peoples are defined by precontact, aboriginal occupation of traditional lands. They are not minorities, no matter their number. In other words, the numbers of indigenous peoples do not constitute a criterion in their definition.

While the Declaration covers many areas of concern, certain rights are critical to the distinction that must be made between Natives and minorities. In Article 3 of the Draft, indigenous peoples have the right of self-determination (which minorities do not), and by virtue of that right indigenous peoples can determine their political status.

Political self-determination is tied to land rights and restitution. The doctrine of discovery by which the Americas, the Pacific, and so many other parts of the world were allegedly "discovered" is repudiated. The companion doctrine of *terra nullius* is identified as legally unacceptable. Thus, aboriginal peoples have a position from which to argue that traditional lands should be restored to them. In Article 26, indigenous peoples have the right to own, develop, control and use the lands and territories . . . they have traditionally owned. . . . This includes the right to the full recognition of their laws, traditions, and customs, land-tenure systems and institutions for the development and management of resources, and the right to effective measures by States to prevent any interference with, alienation of, or encroachment upon these rights.[24]

In Part VII, Article 31, the Declaration states that "Indigenous peoples, as a specific form of exercising their right to self-determination, have the right to autonomy or self-government."[25] Interestingly, these rights are considered in Part IX, Article 42, to "constitute the minimum standards for the survival, dignity, and well-being of the indigenous peoples of the world."[26] The Draft Declaration is a document still in formation. As the world's indigenous peoples make their expensive and arduous trek to Geneva each summer when the Working Group on Indigenous Populations convenes, the struggle for recognition and protection of the claims of Native peoples is strengthened. Whole lifetimes are expended on the process of attempting to move the existing powers of the world to acknowledge and protect indigenous peoples. This process has changed the consciousness of indigenous peoples all over the globe, including Hawai'i. Indigenous peoples can now cite the UN Draft Declaration on Indigenous Human Rights in the struggle for protection of their lands, languages, resources, and most critically, their continuity as peoples.

On the ideological front, documents like the Draft Declaration are used to transform and clarify public discussion and agitation. Legal terms of reference, indigenous human rights concepts in international usage, and the political linkage of the non–self-governing status of the Hawaiian nation with other non-self-governing indigenous nations move Hawaiians into a world arena where Native peoples are primary, and dominant states are secondary, to the discussion.

## KA UIHUI HAWAI'I

On the international stage, the vehicle which has represented Hawaiians most effectively is Ka Uihui Hawai'i. Because it is the frontline organization of Hawaiian sovereignty, Ka Uihui Hawai'i serves as the indigenous party representing Native, as opposed to settler, interests. Through its Master Plan, Ka Uihui Hawai'i has given concrete policy shape to Native political aspirations. Mental decolonization has led to a first stage of political decolonization. Countering settler American ideology, the Plan depends for much of its argument on Native cultural understanding of Hawaiian history, politics, and economics. Like other embodiments of nationhood, the Ka Uihui Master Plan is both an enunciation of principles and an agenda for political action.[27]

Relying, in part, on international legal standards, the Master Plan endorses the rights and principles contained in four major international documents. These are the Charter of the United Nations, the International Covenant on Civil and Political Rights, the International Covenant on Social, Economic, and Cultural Rights, and the Draft Declaration on the Rights of Indigenous Peoples at the United Nations. Specifically, the rights to self-determination and to self-development are cited in the Master Plan as critical to Hawaiian sovereignty.

In terms of policies regarding the United States, the Plan rejects the current status of Hawaiians as wards of the State of Hawai'i, pointing out that wardship is usurpation of Hawaiian collective rights to land and political power, as well as a violation of Native human and civil rights. Moreover, wardship classifies Hawaiians with children and the incompetent, revealing the racist intent of the classification.

Critically, the Plan rejects American nationality by asserting that self-determination means jurisdiction over lands and territories, and internal and external relationships, including the following: the power to determine membership; police powers; the power to administer justice; the power to exclude persons from National Territory; the power to charter businesses; the power of sovereign immunity; the power to regulate trade and enter into trade agreements; the power to tax; and the power to legislate and regulate all activities on its land base, including natural resources and water management activities and economic enterprises.

The current policy of state wardship for Hawaiians whereby the state controls Hawaiian lands and waters is repudiated. Given that the State of Hawai'i has maintained a policy of non-recognition of the indigenous peoples of Hawai'i and has consistently acted as the Native representative despite an extensive record of state neglect and mismanagement of the Native trusts, the Ka Uihui Master Plan calls for termination of this policy.

Citing the 1993 Apology Bill passed by the US Congress, the Plan notes the Apology acknowledges that "the indigenous Hawaiian people have never directly relinquished their inherent sovereignty as a people or over their national lands to the United States, either through their monarchy or through a plebiscite or referendum."[28]

Therefore, the goals of Ka Uihui Hawai'i are simple: final resolution of the historic claims of the Hawaiian people relating to the overthrow, state and federal misuse of Native trust lands (totaling some two million acres) and resources, and violations of human and civil rights. Resolution of claims will be followed by self-determination for

Hawaiians; federal recognition of Ka Lahui Hawai'i as the Hawaiian Nation; restoration of traditional lands, natural resources, and energy resources to the Ka Lahui National Land Trust.

The burden rests with the United States and the State of Hawai'i to inventory and restore the lands of the Native trusts, both federally and state-held, and to remedy all federal and state breaches of the trust relating to these assets. The federal and state governments must segregate the trust lands from other public and private lands. The United States must allocate not less than two million acres of land (that is, all the ceded lands) drawn from state-controlled and federally controlled lands to the National Land Trust.

In the area of the National Land Trust, Ka Uihui identifies the land and natural resource entitlements of indigenous Hawaiians within the entire archipelago. These entitlements include state-held trust lands, that is, Hawaiian homes, lands, and ceded lands; marine resources and fisheries; surface and ground water rights, and submerged lands; lands and natural resources under the federal government; energy resources such as ocean thermal and geothermal sources; minerals, airspace and the trust assets of the private trusts.

Although the Master Plan has many other specific areas relating to various concerns, such as the private Hawaiian trusts, the Plan also delineates an international relationship. Citing Chapter XI, Article 73, of the United Nations Charter, the Plan notes that the United States, as Hawai'i's "administering agent" accepted as a "sacred trust" the obligation "to assist the inhabitants of the territory of Hawai'i in the progressive development of their free political institutions."[29]

In 1953, the Fourth Committee of the UN General Assembly passed Resolution 742 requiring that the inhabitants of territories be given several choices in achieving self-government. These choices include free association, commonwealth, integration (statehood), and independence, or "other separate systems of self-government."

The United States never allowed decolonization in Hawai'i under the United Nations process, nor did it allow the inhabitants of the territory their right to choose options identified in Resolution 742. The plebiscite in 1959 allowed only one choice—Statehood—other than Territorial status. By not including other choices, the United States violated international human rights law as well as the human rights of Hawaiians.

Given that Hawai'i was removed at the request of the United States from the United Nations list of Non-Self-Governing Territories in 1959, the position of Ka Lahui Hawai'i is reinscription of Hawai'i on that list, thereby recognizing Hawaiians as still eligible for self-determination. In the meanwhile, Ka Lahui has chosen to develop a culturally appropriate "separate system of self-government," which incorporates Hawaiian values and traditions. As part of this assertion, Ka Lahui has called for segregation of Hawaiian trust lands and assets from the State of Hawai'i. Additionally, a record of extensive civil and human rights abuses of Hawaiians by the state and federal governments must be established and strenuous advocacy of Hawaiian rights and claims must proceed.[30]

## NATIVES AND "LOCALS"

Apart from its embodiment of Native aspirations, the Ka Lahui Hawai'i Master Plan can be read as a perfect illustration of the distance between Natives and "locals" in Hawai'i. The issues before Hawaiians are those of indigenous land, cultural rights, and survival as a people. In contrast, the issues before "locals" have merely to do with finding a comfortable fit in Hawai'i that guarantees a rising income, upward mobility, and the general accoutrements of a middle-class "American" way of life. Above all, "locals" don't want any reminder of their daily benefit from the subjugation of Hawaiians. For them, history begins with their arrival in Hawai'i and culminates with the endless retelling of their allegedly well-deserved rise to power. Simply said, "locals" want to be "Americans."

But national identification as "American" is national identification as a colonizer, someone who benefits from stolen Native lands and the genocide so well-documented against America's Native peoples. Here, "identity" is not, as often asserted in Hawai'i, a problem for Hawaiians. It is, rather, a problem for non-Natives, including Asians. We are engaged in decolonizing our status as wards of the state and federal governments and struggling for a land base.

Asians and *haole* have been thrown into a cauldron of defensive actions by our nationalist struggle. Either they must justify their continued benefit from Hawaiian subjugation, thus serving as support for that subjugation, or they must repudiate American hegemony and work with the Hawaiian nationalist movement. In plain language, serious and thoughtful individuals, whether *haole* or Asian, must choose to support a form of Hawaiian self-determination created by Hawaiians.

The position of "ally" is certainly engaged in by many non-Natives all over the world. Support organizations, like the Unrecognized Nations and Peoples Organization, for example, work on a global level to give voice to Native peoples at international forums, and even in their home countries. A few groups in Hawai'i primarily comprised of non-Natives (e.g., Local Japanese Women for Justice) serve the same function.

But the most critical need for non-Native allies is in the arena of support for Hawaiian self-determination. Defending Hawaiian sovereignty initiatives is only beneficial when non-Natives play the roles assigned to them by Natives. Put another way, nationalists always need support, but they must be the determining voice in the substance of that support and how, and under what circumstances, it applies.

Of course, Hawaiians, like most colonized peoples, have a national bourgeoisie, that is, a class that ascends due to collaboration with the state and federal governments. This class serves to counter indigenous nationalist positions. Often, potentially "supportive" locals complain about the confusion surrounding the many sovereignty positions. But the easiest and most defensible position is the one which follows the Ka Uihui Master Plan. No matter the future leadership of Ka Uihui, the Plan will remain as the clearest document of this period in Hawaiian history. Non-Natives who support the Plan are, in effect, supporting all the struggles of indigenous peoples which created the Draft Declaration at the United Nations.

Finally, it must be recalled that history does not begin with the present nor does its terrible legacy disappear with the arrival of a new consciousness. Non-Natives need to examine and reexamine their many and continuing benefits from Hawaiian dispossession. Those benefits do not end when non-Natives begin supporting Hawaiians, just as our dispossession as Natives does not end when we become active nationalists. Equations of Native exploitation and of settler benefit continue. For non-Natives, the question that needs to be answered every day is simply the one posed in the old union song, "which side are you on?"

## GLOSSARY

*ali'i*: chief
*haole*: originally all foreigners, now only white people
*halau hula hula*: is the traditional dance of the Hawaiian people; *hiilau hula* are dance academies that are currently enjoying a revival
*lahui*: people, race, nation
*taro*: starchy tuber that is the staple of the Hawaiian diet; metaphorically, *taro* is the parent of the Hawaiian people

## NOTES

Reprinted with permission from Haunani-Kay Trask, *Amerasia Journal* 26:2 (2000): 1–24.

1. Frantz Fanon, *The Wretched of the Earth* (New York: Grove Press, 1968), 44.

2. Sharon Helen Venne, *Our Elders Understand Our Rights: Evolving International Law Regarding Indigenous Rights* (Penticton, British Columbia: Theytus Books, Ltd., 1998), 82 and 77

3. S.J. Res. 19, (U.S. Public Law 103-150), 103d Congress, 1st Session, 107 Stat. 1510 (November 23, 1993).

4. See US President Grover Cleveland's message to the U.S. Congress in the "The President's Message Relating to the Hawaiian Islands," December 18, 1893, *House Ex. Doc. No. 47, 53rd Congress, Second Session, 1893,* 445–58; called the Blount Report.

5. See Daniel K. Inouye, *Journey to Washington* (Englewood, NJ: Prentice-Hall, Inc., 1967); George R. Ariyoshi, *With Obligation to All* (Honolulu: Ariyoshi Foundation, 1997); Ronald Takaki, *Pau Hana: Plantation Life and Labor in Hawaii, 1835-1920* (Honolulu: University of Hawaii Press, 1983) and *Strangers from a Different Shore: A History of Asian Americans* (New York: Penguin Books, 1989).

Also see various materials published to commemorate 100 years of Japanese settlement in Hawai'i: Roland Kotani, *The Japanese in Hawaii: A Century of Struggle* (Honolulu: Hawaii Hochi Ltd., 1985); Franklin Odo and Kazuko Sinoto, *A Pictorial History of the Japanese in Hawai'i,1885–1924* (Honolulu: Bishop Museum Press, 1985); Dennis Ogawa and Glen Grant, *To a Land Called Tengoku: One Hundred Years of the Japanese in Hawaii* (Honolulu: Mutual Publishing of Honolulu, 1985).

6. For a detailed investigation of Chinese and Japanese political ascendancy as a class in post-Statehood Hawai'i, see George Cooper and Gavan Daws, *Land and Power in Hawai'i* (Honolulu: University of Hawai'i Press, 1985).

7. For statistics on Hawaiian population, housing, land, education, health, prisons, and employment, see Office of Hawaiian Affairs, *Native Hawaiian Data Book, 1998* (Honolulu: Office of Hawaiian Affairs, Planning and Research Office, 1998).

8. Candace Fujikane, "Between Nationalism: Hawai'i's Local Nation and Its Troubled Racial Paradise," *Critical Mass: A Journal of Asian American Cultural Criticism* 1, no. 2 (1994): 23–57.

9. For an early discussion of the term "local," see Eric Yamamoto, "The Significance of Local," in *Social Process in Hawai'i* 27 (1979), 101–15. For later discussions, see Jonathan Okamura, "Aloha Kanaka me ke Aloha 'Pdna: Local Culture and Society in Hawai'i," *Amerasia* 7, no. 42 (1980); Eric Chock, "The Neocolonialization of Bamboo Ridge: Repositioning *Bamboo Ridge* and Local Literature in the 1990s," *Bamboo Ridge* 69 (1996): 11–25. Fujikane now appears to have some doubts about her earlier assertion of a "local nation." See "Reimagining Development and the Local in Lois-Ann Yamanaka's *Saturday Night at the Pahala Theater*," *Social Process in Hawai'i* 38 (1997): 40–62.

10. Japanese American Citizens League Resolution, "Reaffirming Support for the Restoration of Human, Civil, Property and Sovereign Rights of Hawai'i's Indigenous People," adopted at the 1992 JACL National Convention.

11. For the initial news coverage, see *Honolulu Advertiser,* Nov. 10–13, 1999. In a 1989 interview with Mike Tokunaga, Democratic Party insider from the 1950s, Tokunaga recalled a 1959 story where Jack Burns identified Inouye as the "one-armed bandit." Center for Oral History, "Oral History Interview with Mike Tokunaga by Larry Meacham and Daniel W. Tuttle on September 12, 1989" in *Hawai'i Political History Documentation Project, Vol. III* (Honolulu: Center for Oral History, University of Hawai'i at Mānoa, 1996), 1233. In the *Advertiser* story of November 11, 1999, Inouye's Japanese war comrades said they never used the term "one-armed bandit" to describe Inouye. In fact, as pointed out by Richard Borreca in a *Star-Bulletin* column on November 17, 1999, the nickname was used by John Burns when Inouye was first running for the US Senate. Borreca claims that Burns used the term "jokingly" when asking why Inouye was planning to run for the Senate rather than the House of Representatives. The source for Borreca's article was Tokunaga's oral history.

In truth, the oral history reveals that Burns was angry at Inouye because the Party plan was for Inouye to run for the House. Why Burns could call Inouye "the one-armed bandit" without assault by the press is explained by the simple observation that critics of the Democratic Party, in this case, one Mililani Trask, are dangerous to continued Japanese control of the Party, and most critically, dangerous to the monumental power that the Democratic Party and the state apparatus wield over Hawaiian resources.

Trask's use of the "one-armed bandit" phrase was a false issue. The real issue was and remains Inouye's control over the sovereignty process. In this instance, the issue was lost amidst the well-orchestrated attack on Trask. In fact, the *Advertiser* story and vicious cartoon were perfectly timed to appear before, during, and immediately after Veterans' Day.

In a paid advertisement (titled, appropriately, "Inouye's Legacy to Hawaiians") printed in the 17, no. 2 (Feb. 2000) issue of the OHA newspaper, *Ka Wai Ola,* Trask detailed the *Advertiser* campaign to disparage her and to prevent the airing of critical issues regarding Inouye's interference in the sovereignty process. Needless to say, her side of the story was never printed in the two Honolulu dailies. Significantly, the issue of Inouye's interference in the sovereignty process which Trask had severely criticized, never saw the light of day.

12. Dick Adair, Cartoon, *Honolulu Advertiser,* Nov. 12, 1999, A: 12.

13. "OHA Trustee Won't Back Down," *Honolulu Advertiser,* Nov. 11, 1999, A: l; Mililani Trask, "Inouye's Legacy to Hawaiians," *Ka Wai Ola 0 OHA* 17, no. 2 (February 2000): 20–21.

14. Clayton C. Ikei, representing the JACL. See November 22, 1999 letter to Mililani Trask and the media, reprinted in the local Japanese American community newspaper. Clayton C. Ikei, "JACL Opposes Trask's Comments to Inouye," *Hawai'i Herald,* Dec. 3, 1999, A-7 and Pat Omandam, "AJA Group Asks Trask Not to Be Ethnically Divisive," *Honolulu Star-Bulletin,* Nov. 25, 1999, A:3.

15. Ida Yoshinaga and Eiko Kosasa, Local Japanese Women for Justice, "Local Japanese Should Understand Inouye's Real Agenda," *Honolulu Advertiser,* Feb. 6, 2000, Focus Section I, and reprinted as "Understanding Inouye's Real Agenda," *Hawai'i Herald,* Mar. 3, 2000, A-4.

16. Bill Hoshijo and David Forman, Japanese American Citizens League, "JACL Fights Against Racism, No Matter Where It Comes From," *Honolulu Advertiser,* Feb. 27, 2000, Focus Section: 1, and reprinted as "JACL Speaks Out to Clear the Record," *Hawai'i Herald,* Mar. 3, 2000, A-4.

17. See Eric Yamamoto, "Rethinking Alliances: Agency, Responsibility and Interracial Justice," *UCLA Asian Pacific American Law Journal* 3 (33): 33–74. Yamamoto discusses the participation of Hawai'i-based Asian American churches in the public apology by the United Church of Christ (U.C.C.) made to Hawaiians concerning the participation of the churches in the 1893 overthrow of the Hawaiian monarchy. The apology was made by Paul Sherry, president of the United Church of Christ, before some 15,000 people on the centenary of the overthrow at the Palace of our Chiefs, on January 17, 1993. In discussions with Hawaiian leaders preceding the apology, Paul Sherry responded to my criticism that such apologies were useless to the Hawaiian people. I suggested the U.C.C. return some of the lands the churches controlled in Hawai'i in lieu of an apology. Sherry responded that I was criticizing the church for attempting to receive what he called "cheap grace," an easy forgiveness achieved for very little. Given that reparation monies (totaling over a million dollars) from the church hierarchy went to Hawai'i churches rather than to Native Hawaiians, my conclusions were that while the U.C.C. attained their "cheap grace," we Hawaiians, as usual, received nothing. Also see Eric Yamamoto, *Interracial Justice: Conflict and Reconciliation in Post-Civil Rights America* (New York: New York University Press, 1999).

18. See the discussion of these two studies in Venne, *Our Elders,* 77–83.

19. Ibid., 80.

20. Ibid.

21. Ibid., 88.

22. Ibid., 146.

23. Ibid., 82.

24. Ibid., 212.

25. Ibid., 213.

26. Ibid., 215.

27. Ka Uihui Hawai'i, *Ho'okupu a Ka Lahui Hawai'i: The Master Plan, 1995* (Honolulu: Ka Uihui Hawai'i, 1995).

28. U.S. Public Law, 103rd Congress.

29. Ka Uihui Hawai'I, *Master Plan*, 5.

30. Ibid., 6–8.

# THE IDEAL IMMIGRANT

THERESA DELGADILLO

We've been explaining ourselves to ourselves and to others for a long time.
—Rubén Martínez

The public discourse about Latina/os, migration, and immigration in the United States has long been fraught with xenophobia and racism. In the aftermath of 9/11, moreover, the immigration issue has been firmly tied to national security in both governmental policy and the public imagination. In this recent period, the state has asserted extraordinary controls over immigrants and citizens that affect not only the discourse of immigration but also the notion of citizenship itself. Although civil rights legislation has enhanced Latina/o inclusion in the nation, this has always been tempered, as historian David G. Gutiérrez (1995) observes, by US immigration discourses and policies that facilitate the entry of Latina/o workers while limiting their incorporation in the society (6, 40, 147, 154, 211).[1] Whereas scholars such as Otto Santa Anna (2002), Leo R. Chavez (2001, 2008), and Rachel Rubin and Jeffrey Melnick (2006) have examined how Latina/os are constructed by others in media coverage and popular culture, this essay examines ethnic self-representation in documentary books and interrogates the image of Latina/os sutured to discourses of immigration, citizenship, and security in these photographic and prose narratives.

Of particular interest here is the relationship between the figure of the "ideal immigrant" in the mythos of the United States and Latina/o nonfictional narratives of migration, self, and community in an era of virulent anti-immigrant discourse. Although most people in the United States either came here from other parts of the world or are descended from those who did, it is not this fact that the popular mythos of an immigrant America addresses. As many have observed, the mythos masks the historical tensions, inequalities, and violence between and against the varied ethnic and

Theresa Delgadillo is professor of comparative studies and director of the Latina/o Studies Program at The Ohio State University. Her research in Chicanx and Latinx studies includes religion and spirituality, the Midwest, and Afro-Latinidad. She has published *Latina Lives in Milwaukee* (University of Illinois Press, 2015) and *Spiritual Mestizaje: Religion, Gender, Race, and Nation in Contemporary Chicana Narrative* (Duke University Press, 2011), and she is the editor of *Latinx Talk*.

racial groups that came to form the US populace. Moreover, this mythos generally refers only to those ethnicities that arrived in the nineteenth and early twentieth centuries: the Irish, Italians, and Poles are often cited as examples, while the founding fathers are not. The insistence on the universality of this trope muddles the difference between native, settler, slave, refugee, and exile. It also displaces African Americans, Native Americans, and Mexican Americans from the status of "true" citizen, since they are not originally immigrants. Equally important is the fact that this mythos underwrites US exceptionalism, with no small impact on domestic and foreign policies. The converse of the stereotyped and racist views of Mexican and Latina/o migrants in the nation's imaginary is a figure produced by this national mythos: the "ideal immigrant." This figure is typically understood as a hardworking, heterosexual, white ethnic male. Given entry at Ellis Island, he lifts himself and his family up by virtue of his own efforts, and as a result his descendants enjoy considerable wealth and privilege. The ideal immigrant might also be a refugee from a fascist, dictatorial, or communist regime, but again, he is typically imagined as a white male heterosexual who follows the well-trodden immigrant path of social and economic mobility. So ingrained is this idealized, racialized, and gendered image of the immigrant, whose sexuality is always normative, that we often have a difficult time recognizing those who do not fit this profile as immigrants.[2]

How do Latina/os enter into this prevailing narrative, with its idealized imagery? How does this mythos of the United States affect Latina/o self-representations? How does the desire to contest the damaging discursive representations of Latina/os in the media and society affect self-representation? How do Latina/o self-definitions compete for dominance in the popular imaginary, particularly in the aftermath of September 11, 2001? This essay critically examines three nonfiction trade publications that intervene in the construction of Latina/os in the popular imaginary in an era dominated by anti-immigrant public discourse and the expansion of draconian homeland security measures. The pressure of this context often leads, in these texts, to a reification of Latina/os that undercuts the contestatory power of their self-representation, as when the visual celebration of Latina/o humility, anonymity, and hard work obscures Latina/o labor rights. At other times the narrative attempt to site Latina/os within the nation itself betrays the enduring tensions surrounding their incorporation. *Americanos: Latino Life in the United States/La Vida Latina en los Estados Unidos* (Olmos, Ybarra, and Monterrey 1999) and *Mexican Chicago* (Jirasek and Tortolero 2001) are photographic narratives of, respectively, contemporary Latina/o life in the United States and the historical presence of Mexicans in Chicago. *The New Americans* (Martínez 2004) chronicles the journeys of recent immigrants from Palestine, Nigeria, the Dominican Republic, and Mexico to the United States. All three books remember in a way that Paul Ricouer (1999) describes as "telling otherwise"—revealing knowledge that is otherwise obscured, unknown, marginal, or ignored (9). *Americanos* and *Mexican Chicago*, with their explicit aim of deepening the incorporation of Latina/os in the fabric of the nation, resonate with Susan Sontag's (1977) suggestion that the photograph is "mainly a social rite, a defense against anxiety, and a tool of power" (8–9). In these texts, photos remember and record Latina/o lives to ensure they will not be forgotten and to document and prove Latina/o contributions to the United States.[3]

These collections thus constitute a testimony of identity and belonging, a defense against erasure, and a tool for claiming citizen and human rights for Latina/os in a nation increasingly hostile to them. But what understandings of Latina/os do they project into the popular imaginary? What and how these images signify is particularly important in an era when, as Ali Behdad (2005) argues, "the figure of the immigrant-foreigner" that underwrites the curtailment of civil liberties after 9/11 is emblematic of a national historical amnesia with regard to immigration (170) and when we are witnessing the resurgence of a nativist scapegoating and othering of Mexican migrants that, as David Gutiérrez (1995) notes, has long influenced US immigration policy and Mexican American–Latina/o unity.

Following Roland Barthes's (1981) methodology for reading photographs, we must consider the differential punctums—idiosyncratic points of meaning—that these images may give rise to among different individuals and groups. John Berger's assertion that the photograph is essentially ambivalent, evidence of something in the past but requiring interpretation (Berger and Mohr 1982, 88), requires us to attend, as well, to the interpretations offered and implied in the collections themselves. This reading considers each of these elements, very much in line with Gregory Stanczak's (2007) argument that making meaning of photographs requires us to pay attention to technical choices and temporal and spatial editing constitutive of this medium, to discern photographic aim, and to understand a context for the photograph (79). Locating these three texts at the juncture of immigration debate, institutionalization of Latina/o histories and literatures, and contemporary politics, this essay unpacks the construction of the "ideal immigrant" in Latina/o visual and literary representations. It finds that Latina/o constructions of this idealized figure inject more-expansive transnational notions of citizenship into the public debate but frequently reinscribe the discourses of exclusion at its core.

## IMMIGRANTS AND AMERICANNESS

> Choices made about immigration policy in the 1920s—and the reasons for those decisions—played a fundamental role in shaping democracy and ideas about group rights in the United States. By establishing barriers to immigrants, the policy-makers privileged an Anglo-Saxon conception of US identity, thereby rejecting the claims of other traditions in the nation.
>
> —Desmond King, *Making Americans*

As this quote from Desmond King's (2000) study of immigration history and policy demonstrates, contemporary debates on immigration—both public and governmental—continue to reverberate with the prior constructions of citizenship and "Americanness" that have been embedded, in myriad ways, in the social, political, educational, and economic life of the United States. The template for the Anglo-American as model citizen was fashioned by the founding fathers and repeatedly reinscribed in the centuries to follow.[4] Behdad (2005) argues that as an "illusory retrospective narrative, the myth of immigrant America needs to deny the historical context of its formation while ignoring the horrendous disciplining and criminalizing of aliens that is happening around us today." This narrative overlooks, among other historical realities, the "colonialist will" for westward expansion that was at the heart of nineteenth-century immigration policies (8). Informed by this myth, both liberals and conservatives enshrine images and stories of an ideal immigrant whose presence, according to political scientist Bonnie Honig, validates or reaffirms the nation in a capitalist way by promoting the belief in the universal possibility of economic advancement, in a communitarian way by re-creating family and community units, in a traditional way by bringing patriarchal models of family back to the nation, and in a liberal democratic way by choosing citizenship and validating the nation (Behdad 2005, 13–14; Honig 2001, 74–75).

King (2000) notes that early immigration policies with respect to Mexicans were largely designed to facilitate migrant labor. Mexicans were a useful source of inexpensive manpower for US farms and industries—though their usefulness was seen as temporary, as evidenced by forced repatriations in the 1930s and 1950s (233). But Mexicans were not exempt from the eugenicist notions that underpinned early twentieth-century immigration policy. The government's desire to admit only "appropriate" and "assimilable" immigrants (and potential citizens) drove the debates over national origin quotas in US immigration policy during the 1920s (163, 166, 224). Because the 1924 Immigration Act, which defined favorable national origins for immigrants, ignored African Americans, American Indians, Mexicans, and Asians (already barred from citizenship), it underscored just how irrelevant all of these groups were to notions of citizenship and Americanness (224). In this period, the conception of the ideal immigrant and citizen expanded beyond the Anglo-American to include other European backgrounds, but it still excluded those with non-European backgrounds.

David G. Gutiérrez (1995) finds that far from enjoying unrestricted access to the United States, Mexican migrants were carefully policed from the late nineteenth century onward. They were subject to head taxes, literacy requirements, labor restrictions under the Bracero Program, limitations on unions, discrimination, segregation, and summary deportation "regardless of [their] character, length of stay in the United States, employment record, or familial relationship to bona fide American citizens" (44, 47, 52, 211). These measures were accompanied by discriminatory and denigrating attitudes toward Mexicans and Mexican Americans, anxiety about their incorporation into the nation, and violent, extraordinary, and inhumane policies against Mexican migrants. These attitudes, which persist today, have been invoked in insidious ways to fuel divisions between US workers and to limit or roll back social programs. In his study of the increased hostility toward immigrants, for example, David M. Reimers (1998) speculates, without evidence, that black resentment of Hispanics fueled riots in 1980 and 1989 and that Hispanics were displacing blacks and unions from the employment arena (36, 91). In contrast, reporter Julia Preston (2009), writing about the impact of the recent economic downturn on immigrant, black, and white workers, quotes a career center administrator as stating, "We don't have anyone that has any beefs with the Latino population that I've seen come and go through here." Instead, white and black workers worry about either finding employment comparable to what they had before or continuing to receive benefits. While there are tensions among marginalized ethnic and migrant groups in the United States, these tensions are not the primary source of the current hostility toward migrants.

The emergence of a divisive public discourse around migrants, Mexicans, and Mexican Americans and the linguistic mechanisms underpinning this discourse take center stage in Santa Ana's (2002) analysis of media coverage of the anti-immigrant legislative initiatives of the 1990s in California. Proponents of the measures cast migrants as freeloading dependents of the state.[5] Santa Ana uncovers the dehumanization of migrants in the discourse surrounding Proposition 187, which sought to deny undocumented workers access to public services; Proposition 209, which dismissed affirmative action as a form of "special treatment" for minorities; and Proposition 227, the "English for the Children" referendum, which curtailed or eliminated bilingual education. Santa Ana demonstrates how anti-migrant discourse around Proposition 187 created a climate in which the anti-"special treatment" stance of Proposition 209 became more palatable, in turn opening the way for the English-only rhetoric of Proposition 227. His study of these events brings into focus how reportage promoted wedges between disenfranchised groups, to the eventual detriment of all those groups.[6]

The September 11 attacks and the US government's response to them served to dial up anti-immigrant rhetoric still higher, focusing now on the imagined equation of immigrants with terrorists. The linkage between terrorism/national security and immigration/border control took firm hold on the public imagination in the post-9/11 period. But these connections are not new. Ronald Reagan, in 1986, explicitly linked border control to the threat of foreign terrorism and asked Congress for the "authority to declare 'immigration emergencies' of up to 120 days, during which time the border could be sealed by the military and aliens deemed threats to national security could be rounded up and detained without warrant" (Massey, Durand, and Malone 2002, 87). It is hard to imagine that Reagan had the nation's airports and seaports in mind when he referred to sealing the border; more likely he meant the US-Mexico land border. Congress did not give Reagan the authority he sought, but fifteen years later, following 9/11, Congress readily granted such extraordinary powers to President George W. Bush. Behdad (2005) notes that "brown-skinned immigrants and citizens are now routinely subjected to surveillance, interrogation, incarceration, and deportation as the perception of the foreigner as a threat to democracy has been rapidly codified into such discriminatory laws as the USA Patriot Act," signed into law on October 26, 2001 (9).

Latina/os' longtime struggle for inclusion in an unwelcoming nation is my frame for analysis of the visual and textual narratives examined in this essay. It is one that differs from the "nation of immigrants" framework often employed in considering migrant stories. Indeed, the latter notion surfaces in both *Americanos* (Curry Rodríguez 1999, 70–72) and *The New Americans*, though Rubén Martínez (2004) tempers it by offering evidence that nativism and anti-immigrant sentiment have been equally a part of US culture since the nation's founding (7). While the US self-conception as a "nation of immigrants" may provide some political and ethical support for less discriminatory policies toward migrants, it also sustains a mythos that ignores violence and inequalities in the making of the nation through its immigration policy. I suggest that the Janus-faced nature of this national mythology, following Martínez, or ambivalence, following Behdad, are more useful frameworks from which to examine Latina/o visual and literary self-representations of community and migration.

## SPEAKING WHERE NO ONE HAS SPOKEN BEFORE

> But the force of photographic images comes from their being material realities in their own right, richly informative deposits left in the wake of whatever emitted them, potent means for turning the tables on reality—for turning *it* into a shadow. Images are more real than anyone could have supposed.
>
> —Susan Sontag, *On Photography*

As photographic collections, *Americanos* and *Mexican Chicago* share some similarities. Both strive to represent Latina/o cultures and populations in the United States in a period when demographic shifts are placing these populations on the US agenda in new and often troubling ways. Both combine photographs with essays and/or extensive captions, and both put forward a story or series of stories—sometimes implicit but more often quite explicit—about their subjects. In this they follow in the tradition of the documentary book, that combination of photo essay and words first introduced in England in 1873 by John Thomson and continued in the United States by Jacob Riis, Lewis Hine, and others who expanded on the form in the twentieth century (Rothstein 1986, 116). A number of well-known documentary books in early or midcentury focused on the poor or working classes as subjects, though later texts took on a wider cross-section of US society (115). To the extent that photographs pay homage to their subjects, they become extensions of those subjects (Sontag 1977, 155). The photographs in these two volumes are no different, synecdochically linked to the Latina/o subjects they represent. As photographs assume the capacity to function as evidence of a history, Walter Benjamin (1985) notes, they "acquire a hidden political significance" (226). It is this significance that the editors and authors of both collections exploit. The photos collected in *Americanos* and *Mexican Chicago* perform a productive memory work, or what some might call countermemory, against the discursive erasure of Latina/o populations. The documentary photographic approach used in both books, with its goal of informing, educating, and influencing viewers, underscores the ideological, social, and political aims of both works, though they differ aesthetically (Rothstein 1986, 18; Sontag 1977, 63). We can locate these aims in each volume by examining the selection of photographs and their composition, the sequencing and juxtaposition of photographs, as well as the captions and essays.

The two works, however, also diverge in significant ways. *Americanos* is part of a multimedia effort that includes a traveling photographic exhibition organized by the Smithsonian Institution, an HBO documentary film, related music products by Warner Music Group, and book-signing events around the country with Edward James Olmos, one of three principal organizers of the project and the author of the book's preface. *Americanos* makes extensive use of large color photographs, mainly contemporary images created by professional photographers. It also features work by professional writers, academics, and artists, and design by an advertising and marketing firm. With few exceptions, all participants in assembling the project are Latina/o, a testament to the occupational and class diversity and professional accomplishment of Latina/os. We must, therefore, weigh the involvement of major publishing and media corporations in creating a multimedia commodity against the significance of Latina/o involvement in every aspect of the *Americanos* project.

*Mexican Chicago*, in contrast, is published by a small commercial publishing house that specializes in popular photographic histories of particular neighborhoods, towns, urban enclaves, and ethnic communities in its series Images of America. Books in this series are usually created by a collaborative group that includes both professionals and community members. In recent years Arcadia has also published *Pioneros: Puerto Ricans in New York City 1892–1948* (2001), *Latino Milwaukee* (2006), *Latinos in Pasadena* (2009), and *Central Americans in Los Angeles* (2010), among others—books which, like *Mexican Chicago*, narrate the story of a specific Latina/o community in a specific city from arrival to the present. *Mexican Chicago* was edited by Carlos Tortolero and Rita Arias Jirasek of Chicago's Mexican Fine Arts Center Museum with the help of museum staff. It incorporates the family and personal photographs of the city's Mexican residents along with images from the archives of several Chicago-area historical societies. Except for sixteen pages of color reproductions, the images in *Mexican Chicago* are black-and-white, most dating to the first half of the twentieth century. The lengthy captions present historical information and quote recollections from community members.

Despite the proliferation of photography books that Sontag notes in *On Photography* (1977, 75), few of these books have taken Latina/os as their principal subject matter. In this way both *Americanos* and *Mexican Chicago* break new ground. Each text articulates a concern with the issue of visibility: Jirasek and Tortolero note in the preface to *Mexican Chicago* that the history represented in the photos they offer is not "easily available to the general public," while Olmos writes in the preface to *Americanos* that "this book shows both that which we see and take for granted as well as that which is unseen or ignored," suggesting that the book provides an antidote to two kinds of invisibility (Jirasek and Tortolero 2001, 7; Olmos, Ybarra, and Monterrey 1999, 10).

The distinction made by the editors of *Mexican Chicago* between what Mexican communities might see and know about themselves and what the general public knows suggests autonomous organization not visible in or erased from the public record. *Americanos*, on the other hand, situates Latina/o readers alongside all other readers as recipients of the text. This reflects another fundamental difference between these books: *Mexican Chicago* focuses on one Latina/o group, Mexican Americans, while *Americanos* is a pan-ethnic volume, covering multiple national-origin groups broadly termed "Latino." In the latter book, Olmos observes that disparate groups such as Chicanos in California or Puerto Ricans in New York are not always aware of each other's stories (Olmos, Ybarra, and Monterrey 1999, 10). Accordingly, the photos, captions, and essays take note of intra-Latina/o diversity.

These varied aims—to share a Mexican American history, created by those who lived it, with a broader public; to educate a general readership about contemporary Latina/o life; to deepen Latina/o self-knowledge; and to showcase Latina/o talent and culture—require different visual and literary techniques. *Mexican Chicago* provides public documentation and validation of a longstanding community and its participation in the life of a specific city. The editors tap into the existing archive of photos taken by members of Chicago's Mexican American community to commemorate their lives and activities; the collection and careful preservation of these photos suggests communal cohesion and pride. These are private archives of public lives. *Americanos*, in contrast, employs Latina/o professional photojournalists to show a more intimate side of contemporary life and culture than that which is displayed on the streets or in the news. It features "insider" photos of Latina/os engaged in play, work, love, worship, or civic activities. These are public archives of private lives, and they are also the artistic expressions of Latina/o photographers whose skill and expertise are on display in this volume. Including photos from the 1970s forward along with a few older images, *Americanos* focuses on the vibrant present—the doing, the action, the building. It is concerned with what uniquely defines this large ethnic group, but it also responds to an overarching discourse of exclusion, evident when Olmos (1999) states, "We, and especially our children, need to see that we are an integral and equal part of U.S. society" (9).

Each of these texts emphasizes visibility, which is not the same as transparency. Therefore, in the context of contemporary debates about immigration and post-9/11 anti-foreigner paranoia, let us consider how Chicana/os and Latina/os in these texts, both subjects and photographers, choose to frame themselves, what aspects of their experiences and their pasts they choose to memorialize, and which fragments of their histories—histories that can never be represented in their entirety—they reveal. Through this reading, we can locate Latina/o efforts to resist both exclusion from the United States and the economic effects of globalization in the narrative construction of transnational and transcultural subjectivities; yet we can also "see" how these narratives are simultaneously influenced by the mythos of an immigrant America and framed by discourses of citizenship.

## HEMISPHERIC BELONGING AND NATIONAL EXCLUSION

*Americanos* is not merely a response to uninformed stereotypes of Latina/os; it is also an assertion of hemispheric belonging that challenges the primacy of US national citizenship in determining "legitimacy." The title itself situates Latina/os within and beyond the borders of the United States, asserting a hybrid transnational identity. Key essays by Olmos, David Hayes-Bautista, and Carlos Fuentes position Latina/os as intrinsically American by virtue of hemispheric belonging, deep roots within the United States, and contributions to US economy, life, and culture. Visually this assertion is embodied in photos of an elderly Tejano holding a very old photo of a loved one, a small child riding a bike past a mural of mariachis in Boyle Heights, three children dancing in a Miami restaurant, a group of dancers in indigenous dress in Chicago, and a member of an indigenous dance troupe in California caught in mid-dance. Together these images recall historic sites of Spanish, Indian, and Mexican settlement in the Americas that predate Anglo-American settlement, but they also carry an affective charge as images of love, joy, reverence, sadness, and energy.

As the set of opening images demonstrates, the photographs collected here document the variety of Latina/o life all over the United States, in Florida, New York, Illinois, Texas, Washington, California, and other states. *Americanos* disrupts stereotypical assumptions about this ethnic group with attention to its multiracial character, regional differences, and varied national backgrounds. In contrast to the visual images of anonymous crowds or criminals prevalent in the media, *Americanos* presents photographs of individuals and small groups, generally from the full frontal perspective with details of faces, dress, and person clearly visible. This approach tends to grant, though it does not guarantee, greater agency to its subjects.

The volume also includes more photos of Latina/o professionals than generally seen in the media, though not to the exclusion of working-class people. Equally important, as noted above, is the fact that the volume features the work of Latina/o photographers and essays written by accomplished Latina/os in a variety of fields. This showcase of professional and artistic talent for a mass or mainstream audience itself contributes to another important aim of *Americanos*: advocating the fuller inclusion of Latina/os in the nation.

*Americanos* is in some ways a response to what Frances Aparicio and Susana Chávez-Silverman (1997) identify as the hegemonic tropicalizations of Latina/os—that is, the intersecting set of discourses through which Anglo fear defines Latinidad. This is one reason why, for example, Hayes-Bautista's essay in the volume begins in this way: "Far from representing a threat to society, the Latino presence is strengthening the basic institutions of society: the family, work, and education" (1999, 40). Photographs of religious, family, educational, and work life support Hayes-Bautista's assertion. In this way, documentary photography, political argument, and affect are mobilized to present a case for Latina/o belonging that nonetheless betrays the anxieties of exclusion.

Despite its earlier assertions, *Americanos* appears to offer a nationalist rather than hemispheric argument for inclusion. Its brief allusions to a hemispheric history remain metaphoric, as in the suggestion that "the faces, the bodies, the movements of the men and women hark back to the great dawn of North America . . . the grand memory of the past" (Fuentes 1999, 12). In its celebratory leveling of multiple cultural, ethnic, and racial experiences, this view falls short of a conception of race or ethnicity capable of disrupting exclusionary paradigms.[7] This essentialism reverberates in Carlos Fuentes's discussion of both working-class and professional Latina/os, described as either laborers whom readers depend on or as ethnics who bring color to contemporary life. The now-familiar defense of Latina/o migrants that Fuentes repeats here—"Without them, prices would rocket, inflation would inflate, and food would be scarce"—highlights the US reliance on their labor and the benefits derived from it. Yet like other aspects of the argument here, it also reinscribes a difference that authorizes exclusion—in this case in the form of low wages and poor working conditions (15).

Although the book introduces readers to the work of Latina/o photographers, the overwhelming use of beautiful, colorful, contemporary photographs that lack dates and sometimes names suggests that photography as art overwhelms the documentary impulse in this work. This type of photography denies its subjects a history and thereby weakens the text's assertion of Latina/o agency and hemispheric belonging and its challenge to nativist and anti-foreigner discourses.[8] Here photography as art presents a series of nonthreatening ethnographic images of ceremonial and celebratory events that veer toward turning their subjects into attractive objects for the consumption and pleasure of the viewer. This approach turns even grimy, demanding physical labor into appealing images, as, for example, in a Pedro Pérez photo of Emma Velázquez, Saúl Sandoval, and Gerardo Rodarte shucking oysters, or a photo by Timothy González of Luis Estrada working in a tulip field. Both compositions feature vivid colors and textures. Indeed, the latter image is reminiscent of Diego Rivera's famous paintings of flower vendors at market, and deliberately so, I believe, as a recasting of an image with which North American audiences would already be favorably acquainted. These and other photographs of Latina/os engaged in labor-intensive work, though elegantly framed by the camera, hide from us the real conditions of labor and remuneration that the workers face. Sontag warns that images like these, by "smoothing out, making aesthetic," create a danger that can only be tempered through interpretation.[9] In our interpretation, we must attend to the messy oyster evisceration off-center, the specks of shellfish visible on the arm and apron, the dirt under the fingernails of the flower picker, the faint pursing of lips and the line of the muscle in one and the knitted brow in the other to understand that all is not as it seems.

*Americanos* evokes the narrative of exceptionalism embodied in the American dream of opportunity at the beginning of the book, before any essays, with two photographs that show anonymous Latina/o workers who metaphorically represent this mythos of upward mobility. Patriotic feeling for the United States displaces the claim of hemispheric belonging and appears to underwrite an uncritical celebration of tradition, family, and ethnic unity. The first image shows a ladder towering over a tree and reaching toward the sky. The ladder is held by a worker poised to climb it, his back to the camera. The second photo shows the hands of a woman, identified in the caption as Bernadine Mendoza, sewing an enormous US flag on an industrial sewing machine. These images reveal both the labor that Latina/os perform in the United States and the anonymity of that labor—an invisibility that the book seeks to counter. They also metonymically reference the mythos of immigrant America, a nation whose fields and garment factories were once worked by immigrant Europeans.[10] As opening images, they convey some of the central concerns of this text: visibility, nation building, patriotism, and inclusion in the United States.

Janet Jarman's photos of one Mexican family contrast with most images in *Americanos* in that they convey the toll of immigration on some Latina/os. Marisol's mother appears isolated on the factory floor, a small figure visually contained within the workplace; Marisol stands alone and apprehensive on her first day of school in the United States; Marisol and her siblings bathe in an outdoor tin, appearing to resist the gaze of the camera by closing their eyes, turning, or running away in ways that call attention to their poverty. Although subjects are frequently photographed in profile in *Americanos*, the full-frontal view is more common, and rarely are subjects caught unaware or avoiding the camera's gaze, as they are in the Jarman images. This is one reason why Jarman's photographs stand out, starkly revealing vulnerabilities absent from many of the other images in this text.

Published in 1999, *Americanos* was in preparation, and appeared in print, as an increasingly hostile anti-immigrant and anti-Latina/o discourse unfolded across the nation. Propositions 187, 209, and 227 had all passed in California. The public debate surrounding Propositions 187 and 209 included large mass demonstrations against the proposed legislation in communities throughout California, yet there are no photos of this in *Americanos*. Indeed, of two hundred photos in the book there are only three, spread over four pages, that portray public protests: one of César Chávez leading United Farm Workers strikers and two others of women and children marching against drugs and violence. Though largely absent from political organizing or protests, Latina/os are present in *Americanos* as veterans of US wars in eight photographs spread over six pages. These are an important corrective to the general lack of recognition that has been afforded Latina/o veterans; however, the way that *Americanos* foregrounds patriotic military service to the nation over democratic participation in the political process, or even dissent, suggests a self-silencing intended to fit Latina/os into the mold of the ideal immigrant. The rhetorical violence of casting Latina/os as foreigners and outsiders and thereby silencing their demands and inhibiting their rights appears to force *Americanos* to prove its patriotism. Yet the emphasis on military service, in the absence of other images, veers toward the stereotypes of this ethnic group as silent, humble, and submissive to authority, dedicated to family and home.[11]

Although *Americanos* includes photographs of single mothers, working women, professional women, and women artists, as well as an essay by Lea Ybarra countering popular stereotypes of Latinas as passive and submissive, *Americanos* also reinscribes traditional gender roles. For example, the section on religious participation reveals men in possession of religious iconography or sacred objects, standing or preaching, while women are generally pictured listening, kneeling, or sitting. In the section on Latina/os at work, there are thirty-two images featuring men at work versus nineteen featuring women at work.[12] This pattern is even more pronounced in the athletics section, where girls appear in only two of the seventeen photos of people engaged in baseball, water polo, boxing, soccer, surfing, roller derby, and rodeo. In the section on family, equal numbers of photographs show fathers or brothers with children and mothers with children, but the men appear more actively engaged—pushing a child on a swing or cuffing an arm around the neck in a protective gesture, while the women most often simply stand next to or hold children, suggesting nurture. Finally, the text's focus is primarily on the heteronormative family; while some images might show single parents, *Americanos* does not acknowledge gay and lesbian Latina/os or families.

What are we to make of these aspects of the text, especially since it is a text committed to correcting superficial and popular images of Latina/os and educating Latina/os about ourselves? I suggest that the ethnic self-representation of *Americanos* may, indeed, add positively to mainstream perceptions of Latina/os and to our self-perceptions precisely because it refutes degrading stereotypes with visual evidence of contribution, accomplishment, and social cohesion. Moreover, to the degree that we read these images as Latina/os representing themselves, we must recognize the subjectivity and agency of those pictured, for, following Rey Chow, their images attest to a witnessing gaze that exists prior to any othering that occurs in the taking of the image (1993, 50–52). Yet this collection also suggests that Latina/os live under constant pressure to prove their citizenship and patriotism, their hard work and gratitude. Where the text surrenders to such demands, it disarms Latina/o efforts to achieve equality, educational opportunity, labor and civil rights, and gender parity. Despite staking out the important claim of hemispheric belonging, *Americanos* primarily stages an already familiar story of a group whose hard work, family values, traditional gender roles, and religious submission make them candidates for the role of "ideal immigrant" in the twenty-first century. *Americanos*, in its desire for acceptance, reproduces a national mythos that erases the inequalities and violence constitutive of national formation as well as the struggles and organization that made many of the accomplishments depicted in its pages possible.

## OPENING OUR ARCHIVE TO YOU: *MEXICAN CHICAGO*

While *Americanos* focuses on individuals and families, the photos collected in *Mexican Chicago* emphasize community gatherings and migratory and social movements. Rita Arias Jirasek and Carlos Tortolero, in the preface to *Mexican Chicago*, describe their project as "the first step in creating a body of work that begins to document and preserve the history of Mexican communities in Chicago and to promote a more comprehensive understanding of the Mexican experience in the Midwest" (2001, 7). The editors note that amid increasing attention to the history and experience of Latina/os in the Midwest, *Mexican Chicago* offers a native account, stories told in "the voices of those who lived and are living the history that these photographs document" (7). The book thereby asserts the presence and longstanding history of multiple Mexican neighborhoods in a US city not typically associated with Mexicans, either in the popular imagination or in earlier scholarship.[13] In this text, the stories and photos of Mexican Chicagoans provide a composite picture and narrative of the migration, immigration, and settlement through which their communities came into being and flourished. Yet the book also self-reflexively signals the particular social locations of community members participating in the construction of this visual/literary narrative, allowing readers to glean the rich and multiple stories and even alternative narratives only partially revealed in this text.

Three aspects of the text are particularly important in this regard: the multiple sources of the photographs included in the book, the brief chapter introductions, and the captions that accompany the photos. The photographs presented in *Mexican Chicago* were culled from the files of community photographers and archivists, local museums and newspapers, and family albums. Taken by many different photographers on many different occasions, they reflect different reasons for photography. Captions explain why the photographs were taken and what they meant to their intended audiences, often going beyond simple names and dates to present details of family, individual, or organizational histories, building and street changes, political viewpoints, observations by or about those pictured, and explanations of cultural rituals. Many of the captions include anecdotes about the events or individuals that are suggestive of larger stories, such as this caption accompanying a formal photo of two couples (fig. 1):

> This photograph of the *compadres*, parents and co-parents of Susie Gómez, illustrates the seriousness of this relationship. They are posed in a formal family portrait. Susie's early life was spent on the West Side of the city. Susie Gómez recalls, "When my father first came, he was standing on the corner of Wabash and Harrison looking for Mexicans. He stopped the man who would become my godfather, Benites, who helped him. They lived at 1130 South Halsted on the second floor of a building that was torn down." Susie took part in activities both at Hull House and Marcy Center. She is a respected community elder. (Jirasek and Tortolero 2001, 23)

The image reveals two couples in formal dress, the parents and godparents of the woman quoted in the caption. Her words provide a glimpse of early twentieth-century Chicago life for Mexicans. The caption identifies Gómez as a participant in well-known social reform and service movements of that era. Like this caption, the brief

**Figure 1.** Two couples/*compadres* on the West Side of Chicago in the 1920s. Reprinted by permission from *Mexican Chicago* by Rita Arias Jirasek and Carlos Tortolero (Charleston: Arcadia Publishing, 2001).

narratives that accompany many photographs convey the sense that there is much more to be mined here.

*Mexican Chicago*'s formal chapters, organized around areas of social engagement such as "political activism," "spirituality," and "cultural organizations," make full use of materials from multiple sources. The photos in this collection are, in general, visually flatter than those in *Americanos*. Black-and-white formal portraits, family pictures, and group photos predominate, with two or more photos typically printed on each page in contrast to the full-page, full-color, artful photos of *Americanos*. But the photos in *Mexican Chicago* may convey the agency of those pictured more forcefully because, as photos mostly created by the subjects themselves, they combine both image and witnessing gaze—being seen and seeing and, following Rey Chow, confirming their own existence (1993, 51). In identifying the specific experiences of one ethnic group at particular sociohistoric moments, *Mexican Chicago* invites readers to consider how Mexicans interacted with others in the city and how their experiences resembled or differed from those of other Latina/o and non-Latina/o ethnic groups. Telling the story of one ethnic group in one Midwestern city, *Mexican Chicago* appears to have a narrower focus than *Americanos*, but by situating members of that group in relation to both their adopted city and their former homeland, it conveys a vibrant transnational community. Reproductions of migration documents, photos sent as tokens of affection to relatives in another country, and contemporary photos of Mexican president Vicente

Fox parading through Chicago are just a few of the images that suggest that living between and in two countries is a central feature of this community.

A sepia-toned class communion photograph from 1938 graces the cover of *Mexican Chicago*, revealing a group of young Mexican Americans standing on what appears to be the steps leading up to an altar to Our Lady of Guadalupe, whose enormous image hovers above them. Most of the children look straight into the camera, but several gaze off in different directions. They hold certificates of completion, candles, and prayer cards, and one girl holds up the visual image on the face of what looks to be a prayer card. The children are varied in phenotype and skin tone. A second photo on the inside cover combines Mexican and American elements in the image of a *charro* on horseback, stepping along a concrete roadway in a parade and holding the US flag. The rider's face is not visible to us, only his form and elaborate charro costume on the horse, emphasizing the fusion of cultural elements over individual traits. The visual economy of these images aptly conveys the ethos of *Mexican Chicago*'s visual and literary narrative: an emphasis on documenting the long history of self-formation of a specific, heterogeneous, and transnational ethnic community in the Midwest. Religion and patriotism figure quite strongly in opening this book, though the focus here is less on religious institutions than on religious community, devotions specific to Mexican Americans, diversity of community, and hybrid identities.

In general, *Mexican Chicago* deploys a critical gaze in telling the story of this community, advancing a historically specific rather than mythic narrative. In chapter 1, titled "The Road to Chicago," readers "see" the record of Mexican immigration to the United States in the copy of an "alien head-tax receipt," with the names of the El Paso Electric Railway and the US Department of Labor stamped upon it; the back of the receipt shows a handwritten description of a woman and child and the notation of re-entries in 1925 and 1941 (fig. 2). This is not simply a benign image of an immigrant's documents, a record of her journey, but instead a self-reflexive consideration of citizenship. A critique emerges from the combination of the word "alien," the remembrance of fluctuations in border policies, particularly those through which Mexican labor was exploited, and the way that this image makes visible the cataloging and commoditization of immigrant bodies. These documents served to legitimize Mexican immigrants by entering them in a system of information and thus of control.[14] Placing the image of the alien head-tax receipt at the beginning of this volume, with a 1917 photo of Mexican workers clearing fields in Illinois on the facing page, provides "proof" of legal migration and affirms that the contemporary, urban Mexican American community has a long history in the region. It also foregrounds a history of immigration policies in which the needs of business outweighed those of migrants and citizens.[15] *Mexican Chicago* does not, therefore, advance a vision of America as the land of opportunity or as a dream; instead it offers evidence of the social and economic forces, and the negotiation of structures of domination, that drove the multiple border crossings and the formation of Mexican Chicago in the early part of the twentieth century. The images of both sides of this immigration document also suggest the ethos of this volume, which pieces together the documents, voices, and photos at hand to create a more complete narrative, one that might resist control via self-definition.

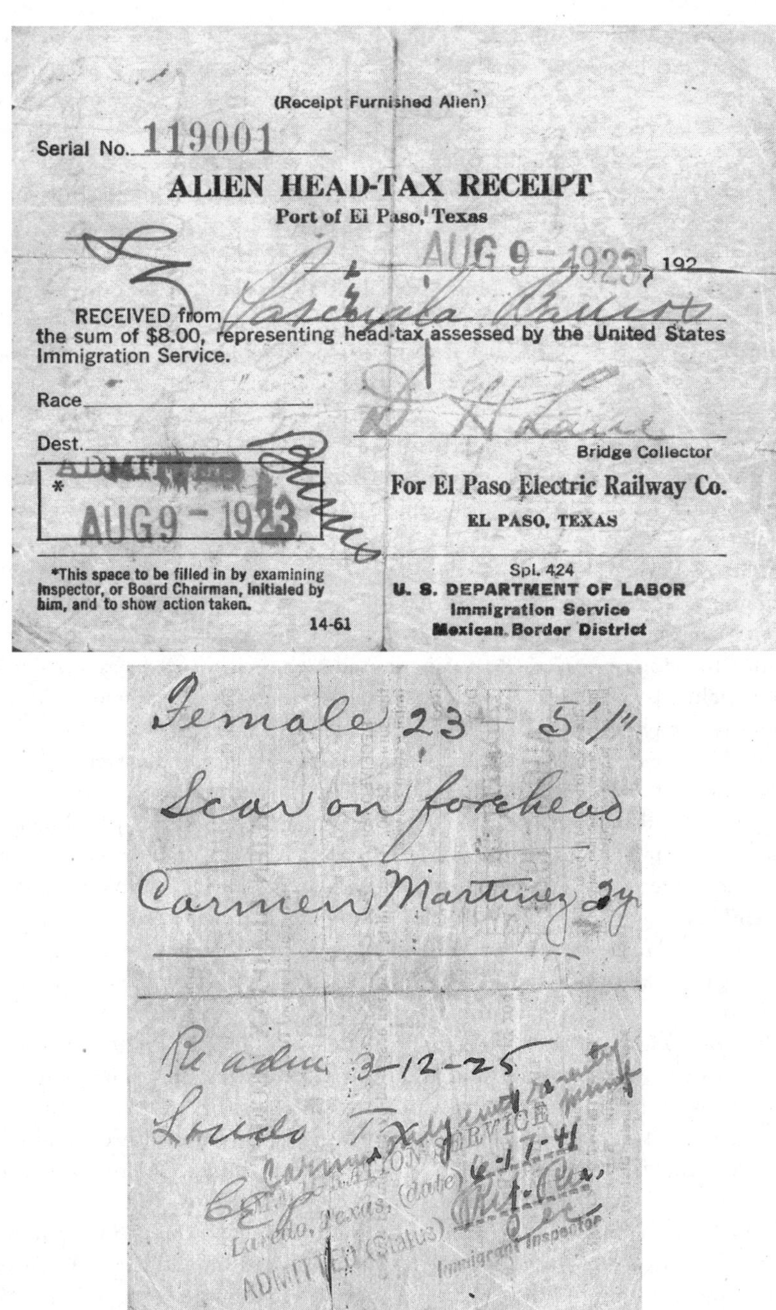

(Receipt Furnished Alien)

Serial No. 119001

**ALIEN HEAD-TAX RECEIPT**

Port of El Paso, Texas

AUG 9 - 1923, 192

RECEIVED from

the sum of $8.00, representing head-tax assessed by the United States Immigration Service.

Race

Dest.

Bridge Collector

For El Paso Electric Railway Co.

EL PASO, TEXAS

ADMITTED
*
AUG 9 - 1923

*This space to be filled in by examining Inspector, or Board Chairman, initialed by him, and to show action taken.

14-61

Spl. 424

U. S. DEPARTMENT OF LABOR

Immigration Service

Mexican Border District

Female 23 5'1"

Scar on forehead

Carmen Martinez

Re adm 3-12-25

Laredo Tx

IMMIGRATION SERVICE

Laredo, Texas, (date) 6-17-41

ADMITTED (Status)

Immigrant Inspector

**Figure 2.** An alien head-tax receipt from 1923. Reprinted by permission from *Mexican Chicago* by Rita Arias Jirasek and Carlos Tortolero (Charleston: Arcadia Publishing, 2001).

Images of the railroads that carried many Mexicans to Chicago appear quite early in this narrative, establishing both the livelihoods and the modes of transportation that made these migrations possible. Among the photographs of Mexican workers on railroads and families traveling by rail, a particularly suggestive image is that of worker Calixto Arroyo posed in front of a massive railroad engine. Although dwarfed by the machine, he is seemingly leading rather than being led by it. The photo aptly conveys both the opportunity presented by industrial mechanization and its grip upon Mexican workers. The caption tells us that he worked and lived in New York, California, and Ohio before settling in South Chicago. The photo thus testifies to an extensive migratory history and suggests an unexplored record of Mexican communities and interethnic encounters in a variety of sites, but it also hints at the difficulty of many migrations. This is one of several photos in *Mexican Chicago* that represent the complexities of the industrial work experience of Mexican Americans, including moments when its effect on community may have been a destructive one.

In a similar vein, many of the photos in *Mexican Chicago* focus on the immigrant subject engaged not in a "traditional" cultural event but in the everyday processes of transculturation, creating new Mexican and American transnational communities in the United States. In the color photo section, a group photo of participants in Casa Aztlan, a community service center, aptly conveys this duality, showing participants beneath a Spanish-language banner hung in front of their Chicago headquarters. The caption states that the group organizes "Mexicans around such social concerns as immigration, workers' rights, and political issues impacting Mexicans both here and in Mexico." Captions to the photographs of well-known murals in Chicago's Mexican community explicitly link their creation to the influence of the Mexican mural movement, yet the murals convey ideas and depict individuals and events specifically relevant to Mexican Chicagoans. Another photo, taken at the inauguration of the first Spanish-language television program in Chicago, shows Mexican actor German Valdez alongside prominent Mexican Americans. Among those pictured is José Chapa, a television broadcaster who later became the first Mexican in Chicago to become a dual citizen of both Mexico and the United States. In contrast to *Americanos*, *Mexican Chicago* concretely situates Mexicans in the history of the city, documenting the organization, accomplishment, struggle, transformation, and contributions of this varied community.

*Mexican Chicago* often references previous ethnic immigrants to the city, contrasting their experiences to those of Mexican Americans and acknowledging the tensions between the various groups that have shaped Chicago. This is not a volume that presents its subjects as fitting neatly into the already established mold of the ideal immigrant. In these images the communities of Mexican Chicago demonstrate their cultural traditions, patriotism, family loyalties, religious affiliations, and hard work. However, the book also shows those traditions in flux. People in the photos are involved in political and social movements, including antiwar and labor protests, and in autonomous community organization, making cross-border connections. While typical extended families are shown, the images also refute gender stereotypes by including activist and athletic women and religious men. The biggest shortcoming here is the exclusion of Mexican and Mexican American gays and lesbians. Only one photo in the collection, of a community educational event on HIV/AIDS, suggests the existence of Latina/o gay and lesbian communities. *Mexican Chicago*'s focus on the heteronormative family, particularly in the many images of church-related social and family events, continues an exclusion of gays that undermines the book's demand for inclusion and recognition.

In sum, although it presents the images and stories of some individuals who appear to adopt the mythos of immigrant America, particularly upwardly mobile business-people, *Mexican Chicago* goes far in disrupting popular perceptions and images of Mexicans and Latina/os and in creating a complex narrative of migrant transnational communities that cannot easily be fit into the ideal immigrant box. Sadly, it does not go quite far enough.

## NEW AMERICANS OR IDEAL IMMIGRANTS?

Published in 2004, *The New Americans* is a companion book to a PBS video documentary series. Not merely the transcribed text of the video documentary, *The New Americans* is Rubén Martínez's meditative re-creation of the journeys of individual migrants, framed by broader economic and political events of the time and considered from the perspective of a second-generation Latino immigrant. This volume differs from both *Americanos* and *Mexican Chicago* in several ways. It is primarily a literary rather than a visual narrative; it focuses on migrants of various ethnicities rather than exclusively on Latina/os; and it is primarily concerned with telling the stories of individuals rather than of communities in the United States. Moreover, unlike the other two, *The New Americans* appeared in print well after the events of September 11, 2001. However, its employment of the mythos of immigrant America makes it highly relevant to this essay's analysis, and for that reason I include a brief discussion of it here.

*The New Americans* contains five essays describing five different immigrant experiences. Naima Saddeh, a Palestinian woman, is a recent university graduate who marries a Palestinian American and moves with him to Chicago, pleased to escape the dire situation of her homeland and pursue teaching in the United States. Nigerians Israel and Ngozi Nwidor spend two years in a refugee camp and then gain asylum in the United States, relocating to Chicago. The Nigerian essay also features Barine Wiwa-Lawani, sister of slain activist Ken Saro-Wiwa, who is resettled with her daughters as refugees in Chicago. Though Israel was a petrochemical engineer and Barine a successful entrepreneur in Nigeria, they end up working in factory and hotel service jobs in Chicago. Dominican baseball players Ricardo Rodríguez and José García are top prospects from small, impoverished towns who win spots on the Los Angeles Dodgers' single-A minor league team in Great Falls, Montana. Pedro Flores is a Mexican worker who secures visas for his wife, Ventura, and their children Nora, Lorena, Maribel, Juliana, Juana, and Pedro Jr. to join him in the United States, where Pedro, his wife, and the older children work in the fields. Newlyweds Anjan Bacchu and Harshini Radhakrishnan migrate from India to Silicon Valley, where Anjan is hired to work in the computer industry.

Each of these essays is accompanied by another, shorter essay, a "narrative of exile," about a prominent individual—an artist, activist, musician, or filmmaker—who hails from the same country as the migrants profiled. These mini-narratives of exile are generally more charged with emotion, expressed in the art or activism of these prominent individuals, than the stories of the migrant workers. Here, too, Martínez's autobiography intersects with those of his subjects. The focus on exile requires an engagement with the interlocking political, social, and economic structures that create the conditions that require exile, and the exiles profiled have frequently resided in several countries, not only the United States. Differences between exile and migrant that emerge in *The New Americans* include more extensive mobility in the case of the former, persecution versus choice in leaving one's homeland, class status, and the way that these circumstances inform perceptions of exiles and migrants. As legal labels, these terms indicate differential status and frame individuals in particular ways. As Madelaine Hron notes, "Neither refugee nor immigrant can complain about life after immigration lest they be accused of blaming others for their choice or being ungrateful" (2009, 8). The inevitable result, as Hron reminds us, is that immigrant suffering is silenced, a dangerous undercurrent that Martínez negotiates throughout these essays. However, exiles by definition are compelled to leave one place for another, and this secures from society authority for greater expression of one's interior life and distress. In the counterpoint between the narratives of immigration and the narratives of exile in this volume, each sheds light on the other and furthers the projects of thinking global citizenship.

*The New Americans* departs from, or rather, alters the typical immigrant narrative in significant ways. Unlike *Americanos* and *Mexican Chicago*, it provides a detailed story of complex individual decisions, and it is the only one of the three to explicitly critique the mythos of immigrant America. Although the focus is on assimilation in the United States, the essays provide extensive contextualization, a detailed backstory of the economic, political, and social situations of the migrants in their home countries, indicating the circumstances that gave rise to their flight and hinting at the involvement of the United States in these global events. In this way the volume endows its subjects with lives and agency prior to their arrival in the United States rather than casting them as the typical homeless immigrants ready to be remade. This aspect of the narratives also makes the workings of economic and political globalization evident in ways that heighten our awareness of the relationship between global capitalism and migration. The emphasis on flight to a US refuge allows readers to maintain faith in US exceptionalism, though the full stories here complicate that faith. *The New Americans*, therefore, remains wedded to the national narrative of the United States as a nation of immigrants, but it enacts an update of the mythos in keeping with global political, economic, and social shifts.

Latina/os enter this revised mythos through the accounts of Dominican baseball players Ricardo Rodríguez and José García, Mexican migrant Pedro Flores and his family, and Martínez's own family story. The author's frequent comparison of his family's migrant experience with that of the migrants and exiles he writes about discursively creates a common ground among disparate groups, as for example when he writes of Naima Saddeh's mother: "Um Mujahid reminds me of my own Mexican grandmother." He prefaces his profile of the filmmaker Mira Nair with a story comparing his cousin's wedding in Guatemala, where he felt both "suffocated and liberated" by family, with the Indian wedding depicted in the film *Monsoon Wedding*, and he compares his mother's efforts to communicate with family back in El Salvador in the 1950s with that of contemporary Nigerians sending VHS tapes home. Martínez's story, woven through the stories of his subjects, ties these disparate experiences together into a common story, positively suggesting more similarity than difference among varied migrant groups. This is theme that the book's front cover design suggests in its basket-weave pattern.

In contrast to his previous work, *Crossing Over: A Mexican Family on the Migrant Trail* (2002), which focused on the undocumented and transnational, this latest work by Martínez embraces the mythos of the United States as an immigrant nation in order to revise it. His rhetorical move is to naturalize more recent migrants as part of the fabric of the nation, as participants in its long history as a nation of immigrants. He re-ethnicizes the figure of the ideal immigrant from white ethnic to Latina/o, African, and Palestinian with in-depth coverage of these individual stories, though maintaining the focus on individual migrants. It is not an uncritical reproduction of this mythic narrative, but an intervention in shaping the popular imaginary about "Americanness" through the strategic invocation of this mythology, a kind of sly mimicry that attempts to destabilize reigning exclusions.[16]

*The New Americans* highlights the degree to which transnational connections are severed rather than maintained in the lives of migrant workers. The "different space and belonging" across national boundaries that migrants construct, according to Alicia Schmidt Camacho (2008), recedes here, replaced by an emphasis on the journey to a land of opportunity and efforts to assimilate to a new reality in the United States. This shift in interpretive lens becomes even more evident in Martínez's oft-repeated references to the distinctions between "old world" and "new world." The heightened sense of deep division between the United States and the rest of the world that emerges in Martínez's essays corresponds to the actual legal and physical barriers against migrants that the United States erected after 9/11. It also appears to reaffirm the discourses of nation, patriotism, and assimilation that are deployed with renewed vigor in the same period with little room for dissent. Yet, a frame for understanding migrants that relies on both these discourses and the related mythos of the ideal immigrant is not without its costs. As Arjun Appadurai observes, "This incapacity of many deterritorialized groups to think their way out of the imaginary of the nation-state is itself the cause of much global violence because many movements of emancipation and identity are forced, in their struggles against existing nation-states, to embrace the very imaginary they seek to escape" (1996, 166). Because of these contradictions, *The New Americans* presents an opportunity to consider what kind of critical intervention in the reigning mythos of an immigrant American might succeed.

In *The New Americans* the ideal immigrant is legal. Each of the five stories involves people who travel to the United States with permission, either as legal migrants or as refugees. Indeed, the process of securing this permission—by winning selection from a refugee camp, gaining financial guarantees of sponsorship, or entering the types of employment for which legal migration is readily granted—proves to be a key part of each immigrant's story and a factor in determining the opportunities to which each will have access in the United States. Martínez's effort to unite the varied concerns of migrants from the West Bank, Africa, India, and Latin America in a new mythos, to suggest that the new face of immigration is not only Latina/o and that the difficulties facing Latina/o migrants confront all migrants, runs up against this differential in migrant status and employment. This emphasis on legal status is striking, particularly since these essays appeared just two years after Martínez's *Crossing Over*, a compelling story of Mexican undocumented migrants whose transnational existence raises new questions about borders, borderless economies, and citizenship. Just a few years apart and yet worlds away, *Crossing Over* is a pre-9/11 text, while *The New Americans*, which opens with Martínez's account of being questioned by federal agents as a suspicious character in the immediate aftermath of the September 11 attacks, is clearly a post-9/11 text. Although the later volume works to revise the myth of immigrant American into a more inclusive one, to expose our blind spots with respect to the history of immigration policy, and to advance a global rather than national context for a consideration of migration, the pressure to reproduce the myth and demonstrate patriotism leads *The New Americans* to inadvertently reproduce the rhetoric of "them/old world" and "us/new world," and to erase the undocumented.

## CONCLUSION

> Neither popular nor academic thought in this country has come to terms with the difference between being a land of immigrants and being one node in a postnational network of diasporas.
>
> —Arjun Appadurai, *Modernity at Large*

David G. Gutiérrez and Pierrette Hondagneu-Sotelo note that "while the institution of national citizenship has long been broadly accepted as an emancipatory institutional feature of liberal democracies, recent scholarship has raised a number of serious questions about this premise" because of the exclusionary function of citizenship (2008, 506). The three volumes discussed here appear to intuit this. Whereas a certain kind of legibility is granted to the subjects of *The New Americans*, who have arrived as legal and grateful migrants to a land of opportunity, or at least a land largely shielded from extreme poverty, war, harassment, torture, and death, this cannot obscure what appears to be an arbitrary difference between them and others—the illegible, those not granted legal status. Neither can it temper the isolation they face once here. These stories, as well as those of *Mexican Chicago*, reveal various forms of regular and routine exclusion, often without regard to legal status, that raise questions about the freedom of citizenship as well as the meaning of democracy. All three of the volumes suggest frustration with the bounds of the nation-state and a yearning for a form of civic belonging more adequate to contemporary migratory flows.

Yet they all, also, reinscribe exclusionary discourses in different ways. To engage the present to the exclusion of the future or past, especially in troubling times, encourages us to trade memory for acceptance. To embrace an uncritical nationalism or pan-nationalism, whether of the US, Latina/o, or Mexican variety, simplifies the historic complexity of peoples as well as the relations within and between Latina/o, Latin American, and US communities. *Mexican Chicago* and *The New Americans* resist the traditional figure of the ideal immigrant in unique ways, and the latter offers the sharpest explicit critique of the mythos of immigrant America. But the first leaves out gay and lesbian Latina/os and the latter leaves out the undocumented from their reconfigured national communities, while *Americanos* subordinates political participation and dissent, labor rights, gender equality, and homosexuality in its construction of the Latina/o ideal immigrant.

These three books manifest the contemporary pressures toward conformity that reproduce dangerous discourses, particularly in a post-9/11 era when the loaded discourse of "them" versus "us," paranoid fear of foreigners, economic instability, and the unprecedented expansion of state power over individual and group liberties have become the norm. Insofar as these texts adopt the rhetoric of inclusion in a multicultural nation-state, they appear to undermine efforts by Latina/os and migrants generally to fully secure their democratic rights and achieve well-being. However, to the degree that these texts bring into focus global conditions, transnational networks, and hemispheric contexts, they go far in revealing Latina/o realities and suggesting new narratives of the US relation to the world.

## NOTES

*Opening epigraph:* Rubén Martínez, foreword to *Chicano: A Novel,* by Richard Vasquez (New York: HarperCollins, 2005). *Figure 2: Mexican Chicago,* by Rita Arias Jirasek and Carlos Tortolero, is available online from Arcadia Publishing at http://www.arcadiapublishing.com. Reprinted with permission from Theresa Delgadillo, *Aztlán: A Journal of Chicano Studies* 36:1 (2011): 37–67.

1. Schmidt Camacho observes that "the Bracero Program ultimately cemented the vision of Mexican migrants as temporary workers in the United States, to the detriment of both migrants' labor autonomy and Mexican American civil rights" (2008, 63).

2. Catherine Ceniza Choy gives an example of this in *Empire of Care*: "In 2001, Cheri A. Nievera, president of the Philippine Nurses Association of Greater St. Louis, wrote to the *St. Louis Post Dispatch* about an article the paper had recently published on newly recruited Filipino nurses at Barnes-Jewish Hospital. The article referred to the Filipinos as 'mail-order nurses.' Nievera critiqued this representation: 'Last I checked, people who moved to the United States . . . were called immigrants, then citizens and, most importantly, members of a thriving, a diverse community. Who knows? One day you may wake up to see a "mail-order nurse" at your bedside taking excellent care of you. Filipino nurses are professionals, and we deserve respect, not belittlement'" (2003, 189).

3. *Americanos* states, "The face of America should include us" (Olmos, Ybarra, and Monterrey 1999, 9). *Mexican Chicago* cites an 1850 census identifying Mexicans in Illinois as proof that Mexican Americans have been a part of life in Chicago for longer than popularly recognized (Jirasek and Tortolero 2001, 8).

4. Behdad, in the first chapter of *A Forgetful Nation* (2005), discusses the views of Alexander Hamilton and John Quincy Adams on immigration, while Rubén Martínez takes up the views of Hamilton and Ben Franklin in the prologue to *The New Americans* (2004).

5. This highly charged and gendered discourse introduced expressions such as "anchor baby," obscuring the labor contributions of migrants.

6. Desmond King, citing Claire Jean Kim, describes this as "racial triangulation," in which the "dominant group valorizes subordinate group B relative to subordinate group C" in order to dominate both groups and maintain inequality between them and dominant whites (2000, 289). Charles Ramírez Berg, in *Latino Images in Film* (2002), also refers to the phenomenon of triangulation to maintain domination in the act of stereotyping, abstracting from the work of Murray Bowen in *Family Therapy in Clinical Practice* (1978) on triangulation among families.

7. A formulation of race as embodied memory that presents greater opportunity for altering existing racial projects has been offered by Rafael Pérez-Torres in "Racial Memory and the Modern Borders of the Nation-State" (2009).

8. In *On Photography*, Sontag states: "Socially concerned photographers assume that their work can convey some kind of stable meaning, can reveal truth. But partly because the photograph is, always, an object in a context, this meaning is bound to drain away; that is, the context which shapes whatever immediate—in particular, political—uses the photograph may have is inevitably succeeded by contexts in which such uses are weakened and become progressively less relevant. One of the central characteristics of photography is that process by which original uses are modified, eventually supplanted by subsequent uses—most notably, by the discourse of art into which any photograph can be absorbed" (1977, 106).

9. "A photograph is completely neutral. Unless one has a capacity to interpret it or can interpret it with help from the photograph itself. If a certain consciousness is not there, then the experience isn't even photographed. Therefore, for example, there are no photos from the Korean War which would be comparable to those from the Vietnam War—simply because the consciousness changed" (Sontag 1995, 92–93).

10. Willa Cather's 1918 novel *My Antonia*, a fictionalized portrait of recently arrived poor European immigrants at work in Midwestern agriculture, exemplifies this association, as does the well-known and iconic history of the formation of the International Ladies' Garment Workers' Union among European immigrant women employed in New York's garment industry.

11. Anthropologist Arlene Dávila (2008), examining contemporary corporate marketing of and to Latina/os, notes that the supposed characteristics of an undifferentiated Hispanic mass—conservatism, communalism over individualism, family values, religion, tradition, patriotism—are widely touted by both business and political sectors.

12. Photographs with both men and women working are counted in each category, so the total number in my count exceeds total number of photographs on work in the text. Photos of veterans are excluded from these figures.

13. Scholarship on Latina/os in the Midwest has been steadily growing, with important work in this area by Julian Samora, Zaragosa Vargas, Dennis Valdez, Gabriela F. Arredondo, and Jorge Chapa. For research on Latina/o literature in the Midwest, see Norma Alarcón, Theresa Delgadillo, Amelia Montes, and Theresa Melendez.

14. Sontag notes, "Through being photographed, something becomes part of a system of information, fitted into schemes of classification and storage . . . thereby providing possibilities of control that could not even be dreamed of under the earlier system of recording information: writing" (1977, 156).

15. David G. Gutiérrez notes that Congress imposed head taxes and other restrictions on "undesirable" immigrants between 1882 and 1917 in response to nativist and racist movements. The laws requiring head taxes were among "the first of what would become a long series of increasingly exclusionary immigration statutes" (1995, 52).

16. See Bhabha (1994) for discussion of sly mimicry.

## WORKS CITED

Aparicio, Frances R., and Susana Chávez-Silverman, eds. 1997. *Tropicalizations: Transcultural Representations of Latinidad*. Hanover, NH: University Press of New England.

Appadurai, Arjun. 1996. *Modernity at Large: Cultural Dimensions of Globalization*. Minneapolis: University of Minnesota Press.

Barthes, Roland. 1981. *Camera Lucida: Reflections on Photography*. New York: Hill and Wang.

Behdad, Ali. 2005. *A Forgetful Nation: On Immigration and Cultural Identity in the United States.* Durham, NC: Duke University Press.

Benjamin, Walter. 1985. *Illuminations: Essays and Reflections.* New York: Schocken Books. Orig. pub. 1955.

Berger, John, and Jean Mohr. 1982. *Another Way of Telling.* New York: Pantheon.

Bhabha, Homi. 1994. *The Location of Culture.* New York: Routledge.

Bowen, Murray. 1978. *Family Therapy in Clinical Practice.* Northvale, NJ: Jason Aronson.

Chavez, Leo R. 2001. *Covering Immigration: Popular Images and the Politics of the Nation.* Berkeley: University of California Press.

———. 2008. *The Latino Threat: Constructing Immigrants, Citizens, and the Nation.* Palo Alto, CA: Stanford University Press.

Chow, Rey. 1993. *Writing Diaspora: Tactics of Intervention in Contemporary Cultural Studies.* Bloomington: Indiana University Press.

Choy, Catherine Ceniza. 2003. *Empire of Care: Nursing and Migration in Filipino American History.* Durham, NC: Duke University Press.

Curry Rodríguez, Julia E. 1999. "Immigrant Contributions." In Olmos, Ybarra, and Monterrey 1999, 70–72.

Dávila, Arlene. 2008. *Latino Spin: Public Image and the Whitewashing of Race.* New York: New York University Press.

Fuentes, Carlos. 1999. "Introduction." In Olmos, Ybarra, and Monterrey 1999, 12–14.

Gutiérrez, David G. 1995. *Walls and Mirrors: Mexican Americans, Mexican Immigrants, and the Politics of Ethnicity.* Berkeley: University of California Press.

Gutiérrez, David G., and Pierrette Hondagneu-Sotelo. 2008. "Introduction: Nation and Migration." *American Quarterly* 60, no. 3: 503–21.

Hayes-Bautista, David. 1999. "Latino Contributions." In Olmos, Ybarra, and Monterrey 1999, 40.

Honig, Bonnie. 2001. *Democracy and the Foreigner.* Princeton, NJ: Princeton University Press.

Hron, Madelaine. 2009. *Translating Pain: Immigrant Suffering in Literature and Culture.* Toronto: University of Toronto Press.

Jirasek, Rita Arias, and Carlos Tortolero, eds. 2001. *Mexican Chicago.* Images of America Series. Charleston, SC: Arcadia.

King, Desmond. 2000. *Making Americans: Immigration, Race, and the Origins of the Diverse Democracy.* Cambridge, MA: Harvard University Press.

Martínez, Rubén. 2002. *Crossing Over: A Mexican Family on the Migrant Trail.* New York: Picador.

———. 2004. *The New Americans: Seven Families Journey to Another Country.* Photographs by Joseph Rodriguez. New York: New Press.

Massey, Douglas S., Jorge Durand, and Nolan J. Malone. 2002. *Beyond Smoke and Mirrors: Mexican Immigration in an Era of Economic Integration.* New York: Russell Sage Foundation.

Olmos, Edward James, Lea Ybarra, and Manuel Monterrey, eds. 1999. *Americanos: Latino Life in the United States/La Vida Latina en los Estados Unidos.* Boston: Little, Brown.

Pérez-Torres, Rafael. 2009. "Racial Memory and the Modern Borders of the Nation-State." Paper presented at conference on "Migration, Border, and Nation-State," Texas Tech University, Lubbock, Texas, April 9–11.

Preston, Julia. 2009. "A Slippery Place in the U.S. Work Force." *New York Times,* March 22, A1.

Ramírez Berg, Charles. 2002. *Latino Images in Film: Stereotypes, Subversion, and Resistance.* Austin: University of Texas Press.

Reimers, David M. 1998. *Unwelcome Strangers: American Identity and the Turn against Immigration.* New York: Columbia University Press.

Ricouer, Paul. 1999. "Memory and Forgetting." In *Questioning Ethics: Contemporary Debates in Philosophy*, edited by Richard Kearney and Mark Dooley, 5–11. New York: Routledge.
Rothstein, Arthur. 1986. *Documentary Photography.* Boston: Focal Press.
Rubin, Rachel, and Jeffrey Melnick. 2006. *Immigration and American Popular Culture: An Introduction.* New York: New York University Press.
Santa Ana, Otto. 2002. *Brown Tide Rising: Metaphors of Latinos in Contemporary American Public Discourse.* Austin: University of Texas Press.
Schmidt Camacho, Alicia. 2008. *Migrant Imaginaries: Latino Cultural Politics in the U.S.-Mexico Borderlands.* New York: New York University Press.
Sontag, Susan. 1977. *On Photography.* New York: Farrar, Straus and Giroux.
———. 1995. "Does a Photograph of the Krupp Works Say Anything about the Krupp Works?" Interview by Fritz J. Raddatz. In *Conversations with Susan Sontag*, edited by Leland Poague, 88–96. Literary Conversations Series. Jackson: University Press of Mississippi. Orig. pub. in *Die Zeit*, 1978.
Stanczak, Gregory C. 2007. *Visual Research Methods: Image, Society, and Representation.* Thousand Oaks, CA: Sage.

# REFIGURING AZTLÁN

RAFAEL PÉREZ-TORRES

One image central to Chicano/Chicana intellectual and social thought has been the figure of Aztlán. Too often, the name of this mythic homeland is either dismissed as part of an exclusionary nationalist agenda or uncritically affirmed as an element essential to *chicanismo.* In refiguring Aztlán, we move toward a conceptual framework with which to explore the connections between land, identity, and experience. Significantly, these connections become centrally relevant as the political, social, and economic relationships between people and place grow ever more complicated and fluid. The problems posed by Aztlán as a site of home and dispossession represent the types of discursive engagements many different constituencies have, in their own idiom, undertaken. Beyond the dynamic issues posed by the questions of national origin—one in four people living in California today, for example, was born outside the US national border—are the issues of shifting genders and sexualities, the interrogation of national identification, and the investigation of indigenous ancestry, all areas interrogating the relation between locality and identity.

Within a Chicana/o context, Aztlán as the mythic Aztec homeland has served as a metaphor of connection and unity. During the nearly thirty years of its modern incarnation, Aztlán has come to represent a nationalist homeland, the name of that place that will at some future point be the national home of a Chicano people reclaiming their territorial rights. It has also come to represent the land taken by the United States in its nineteenth-century drive to complete its manifest destiny. The current controversy over border control in the Southwest is, then, but the latest battle in the retaking of Aztlán, a retaking represented by the migration and immigration of Latinos to the United States through both legal and extralegal means. Aztlán also stands as an index within Chicana/o cultural production as the grounds of contested representations: a site of numerous resistances and affirmations. These multiple significances of Aztlán indicate

Rafael Pérez-Torres, professor of literatures in English at UCLA, has published numerous articles on Chicana/o literature and culture, postmodernism, multiculturalism, and contemporary American literature. He is the author of *Movements in Chicano Poetry* (Cambridge, 2005) and *Mestizaje: Critical Uses of Race in Chicano Culture* (University of Minnesota Press, 2006) and co-author of *To Alcatraz, Death Row, and Back* (University of Texas Press, 2005).

its durability. Locating the source of this durability, naming that which energizes it, forms one of the central tropes in discussions of Aztlán. The present essay is no exception. It seeks to trace some of the historical, literary, and intellectual discourses on the meanings of Aztlán. The object is not to conclude that one of these discourses serves to better describe or locate Aztlán. Rather, I argue that at stake is not so much the worth of Aztlán as cultural/critical signifier as its role in shifting the horizon of signification as regards Chicana/o resistance, unity, and liberation. As the following discussion serves to illustrate, Aztlán remains significant precisely because it functions as an empty signifier. I briefly elaborate this point at the close of the essay.

To call Aztlán an empty signifier is not to say that the term is vacuous or meaningless. On the contrary, if anything, Aztlán is overly meaningful. From a historical perspective, for example, three moments of contestation are evoked in the naming of Aztlán: the Spanish invasion of the Aztec Empire, the appropriation of Mexican lands by the United States in the nineteenth and early twentieth centuries, and the immigration to (or reconquest of) the US Southwest by Mexicanos and Central Americans in the contemporary era. But to be fair, for many in the Chicano "community," Aztlán signifies little; it is the political, social, and cultural Chicana/o elite of a particular stripe for whom Aztlán resonates as an icon imbued with some historical meaning. Five hundred years of European presence in the Americas is contested by an assertion of the indigenous, by an affirmation of native civilizations, by the recollection of Aztlán.

Even though it does not quite add up as a political or cultural metaphor, the lure of Aztlán seems irresistible to the Chicano intelligentsia. The term inevitably calls up difficulties in relation to itself, difficulties that lead the reclamation of Aztlán to take on numerous forms. From a literary and cultural critical position, Daniel Alarcón argues that Aztlán can best be understood as a palimpsest, as "a trope that allows a more complex understanding of cultural identity and history" given that "Aztlán has been used to obscure and elide important issues surrounding Chicano identity, in particular the significance of intracultural differences" (1992, 35–36). Cherríe Moraga has rearticulated the nationalist concerns associated with Aztlán, expanding its metaphorical qualities to reconnect it to different forms of social struggle. Thus Aztlán as a metaphor for land stands as an overdetermined signifier: "For immigrant and native alike, land is . . . the factories where we work, the water our children drink, and the housing project where we live. For women, lesbians, and gay men, land is that physical mass called our bodies. Throughout Las Américas, all these 'lands' remain under occupation by an Anglo-centric, patriarchal, imperialist United States" (1993, 173). From a sociological position, Mario Barrera describes Aztlán as a locus of difficulty, the site of struggle for Chicano equality and community. This struggle forms the catalyst driving Chicano political activism and, consequently, the engine leading to an accelerated assimilation "seen most dramatically in the overwhelming loss of fluency in Spanish by the third generation [of Mexican immigrants . . . but also seen] in the trend toward residential dispersion and the rising rate of intermarriage" (1988, 5).[1] I, too, elsewhere have argued that Aztlán has shifted from signifying a homeland to signaling a complexity of multiple subjectivities called the borderlands.[2]

Each of these positions regarding Aztlán is limited in its scope and can be contested at numerous turns. Viewing Aztlán as a place of *mestizaje*, of multiple and simultaneous subjectivities, elides the way in which notions of the borderlands change depending on their contextualization: whether from a historiographic, sociological, cultural, or ethnographic position. Arguing that assimilation is the problematic result of political engagement erases the de-indigenization undergone historically by mestizos and overlooks the dynamic sociocultural contributions made by continuous migration and immigration to the United States. To recast Chicano nationalist concerns within a larger framework of indigenous rights does not fully address the historical and cultural specificities enacted within different localities of political struggle. Understanding Aztlán primarily as a trope does little to address the specificities of Aztlán as a contestation of power.

## AZTLÁN AND THE PLAN

In large part, the elusive and powerful quality of Aztlán as a signifier has to do with the history of its production. Aztlán was introduced to Chicana/o discourse with "El Plan Espiritual de Aztlán," drafted in March 1969 for the Chicano Youth Liberation Conference held in Denver, Colorado. The question in regard to "El Plan Espiritual de Aztlán" is how it enacted Chicana/o self-affirmation and determination. Aztlán marks a matrix where at least two seemingly contradictory strands of Chicano thought meet. On the one hand, the term "Chicana/o" signifies an identification with struggles for change within or the transformation of socioeconomic and political systems that have historically exploited Mexicans and people of Mexican ancestry. The focus along this trajectory is on the transformation of material conditions, on gains in a real economic and political sense.[3] On the other hand, the term "Chicana/o" identifies a subjectivity marked by a heritage and culture distinct from and devalued by Euro-American society. The interplay between these two meanings of the term Chicana/o is complex and not at all resolved. Although the claims for Chicano cultural agency have been to a greater or lesser degree effective, their translation into social empowerment has been largely unsuccessful. This tension between the social and cultural polarities within Chicana/o activism is made evident in the various articulations of the term Aztlán.

Aztlán as a signifier marking the completion or return of the Chicano to a homeland suggests both cultural and social signification.[4] As the representation of place, Aztlán makes claims to a political and economic self-determination not dissimilar to those asserted by indigenous populations throughout the world. As a symbol of unity, Aztlán indicates a type of cultural nationalism that is distinct from—though meant to work hand-in-hand with—social activism. The sense of a double signification resounds in "El Plan Espiritual de Aztlán":

> Brotherhood unites us and love for our brothers makes us a people whose time has come and who struggle against the foreigner "Gabacho," who exploits our riches and destroys our culture. With our heart in our hands and our hands in the soil, We Declare the Independence of our Mestizo Nation. We are a Bronze People with a Bronze Culture. Before the world, before all of North America, before all our brothers in the Bronze Continent, We are a Nation, We are a Union of free pueblos, We are Aztlán. (1972, 403)

Against the Euro-American, the *gabacho,* the plan condemns he who "exploits our riches" and simultaneously "destroys our culture." These two spheres in which violence occurs are—within the logic of the plan—equitable but not identical. One represents the riches of land and labor, commodities within sociopolitical and economic systems of exchange. The other manifests self-identity and cultural independence. The tension between cultural and political autonomy makes itself felt in the image of the Chicano community as at once affirming culture ("With our heart in our hands") and nation ("and our hands in the soil"), both coming together in the formation of a "Mestizo Nation." What this nation consists of—beyond the essentializing and vague vision of a "Bronze People" with a "Bronze Culture" forming a "Union of free pueblos"—remains unspoken.

There are those who want to claim Aztlán as the embodiment of a successful unity between the cultural and political. As a student of both religious studies and legal discourse, Michael Pina argues that Aztlán represents the successful union of the spiritual and social:

> On one level Chicano nationalism calls for the re-creation of an Aztec spiritual homeland, Aztlán; on another, it expresses the desire to politically reconquer the northern territories wrested from Mexico in an imperialist war inspired by American "Manifest Destiny." These two mythic narratives merged to form the living myth of Chicano nationalism. This myth spanned the diachronic chasm that separates the archaic contents of cultural memory from the contemporary struggle for cultural survival. (1989, 36)

In effect, Pina argues that the evocation of Aztlán bridges "the diachronic chasm" between past indigenous identity and contemporary social activism as well as spanning the gap between cultural and political agency. Rather than evoke a bridge beyond history, I would argue that Aztlán reveals the discontinuities and ruptures that characterize the presence of Chicanos in history. Although it evokes a Chicano homeland, Aztlán also foregrounds the construction of history within a Chicano context. The difficult articulation of Chicana/o history—a history that speaks of dispossession and migration, immigration and diplomacy, resistance and negotiation, compromise and irony—remains ever unresolved.

## AZTLÁN AND THE DIASPORA

Aztlán can at times be articulated as a rather quaint dream, a fantastical delusion:

> Through Aztlán we come to better understand psychological time (identity), regional makeup (place), and evolution (historical time). Without any one of these ingredients, we would be contemporary displaced nomads, suffering the diaspora in our own land, and at the mercy of other social forces. Aztlán allows us to come full circle with our communal background as well as to maintain ourselves as fully integrated individuals. (Anaya and Lomelí 1989, iv)

Despite such assertions, in action Aztlán marks less a wholeness than a heterogeneity of the subject position Chicana/o in terms of identity, geography, history, psychology, spirituality, and nationality. It is impossible to ignore the nomadic role Chicanos and Mexicanos have played within a diasporic history of the United States.

While invoking the diasporic in relation to the Chicano/Mexicano, one might want to tread lightly. From a political scientific perspective, William Safran argues that the concept of diaspora should be expanded to include more than that segment of a people living outside their homeland. His focus is primarily on the contemporary diaspora of "third world" people into Europe. He suggests that the term be applied to expatriate minority communities whose members share a memory of, concern with, and desire for a return to their homelands. As such, Safran notes—in a move that resonates with the conclusions drawn by Mario Barrera—the "Hispanic (or Latino) community in the United States has not generally been considered a diaspora. The Mexican Americans, the largest component of that community . . . are assimilating at a steady pace." More importantly, for the purposes of his argument, Safran argues that "Mexican Americans do not cultivate a homeland myth . . . perhaps because the homeland cannot be easily idealized. The poverty and political corruption of Mexico (which is easy enough to observe, given the proximity of that country) stand in too sharp a contrast with conditions in the United States" (1991, 90). This is quite a reversal of that favorite Mexican saying: "Poor Mexico. So far from God and so close to the United States." Given the means of mass communication and relative ease of international travel, it is not clear how the physical closeness of Mexico to the United States significantly affects the comparative de-idealization of it as a homeland in the minds of its diasporic population. More centrally, Mexico—as a national or cultural icon—does at many levels remain significant for most individuals self-identified as Chicano or Mexicano or Mexican American.

More to the point, the evocation of the diasporic or nomadic indicates that there is no one ideal subject that encapsulates the multiplicity of Chicana/o subjectivities. One cannot assert the wholeness of a Chicano subject when the very discourses that go into its identity formation—be they discourses surrounding the mutability of gender identity, sexuality, class and cultural identification, linguistic and ethnic association—are incommensurably contradictory. It is illusory to deny the nomadic quality of the Chicano/Mexicano community, a community in flux that yet survives and—through survival—affirms its own self.

This is not to dismiss either the political significance of Aztlán or the social relevance of "El Plan Espiritual." The plan does—owing much to Frantz Fanon—articulate an ambitious (if ambiguous) nationalism suggesting that the spiritual longing and physical needs of the subaltern "native" are inexorably bound together. Although Fanon argues in *The Wretched of the Earth* that the immediate effects of a cultural nationalism are difficult to gauge—"I am ready to concede that on the plane of factual being the past existence of an Aztec civilization does not change anything very much in the diet of the Mexican peasant today"—he goes on to argue that "this passionate search for a national culture which existed before the colonial era finds its legitimate reason in the anxiety shared by native intellectuals to shrink away from that Western culture in which they all risk being swamped" (1968, 209). By Fanon's argument, the search for an "other" space proves not to be simply an escape from the present. On the contrary, since colonial processes wish to impose rule upon the past as well as the present and future of a colonized people, the quest for a past proves to be a great act of resistance and self-affirmation: "The native intellectuals, since they could not stand wonderstruck before the history of today's barbarity, decided to go back further and to delve deeper down; and, let us make no mistake, it was with the greatest delight that they discovered that there was nothing to be ashamed of in the past, but rather dignity, glory, and solemnity" (210). The affirmation of a glorious past becomes the condemnation of a repressive present.

Evoking a similar sentiment, "El Plan Espiritual de Aztlán" declares:

> In the spirit of a new people that is conscious not only of its proud historical heritage, but also of the brutal "Gringo" invasion of our territories: We, the Chicano inhabitants and civilizers of the northern land of Aztlán, from whence came our forefathers, reclaiming the land of their birth and consecrating the determination of our people of the sun, declare that the call of our blood is our power, our responsibility, and our inevitable destiny. (1972, 402–03)

The plan hearkens back to the "forefathers" as a basis for reclamation, a tenuous position at best given the diverse indigenous past of actual Chicanos. The plan, though influenced by Fanon's thought, strikes wide of the mark in relation to Fanon's final point about national culture:

> A national culture is not a folklore, nor an abstract populism that believes it can discover the people's true nature. It is not made up of the inert dregs of gratuitous actions, that is to say actions which are less and less attached to the ever-present reality of the people. A national culture is the whole body of efforts made by a people in the sphere of thought to describe, justify, and praise the action through which that people has created itself and keeps itself in existence. (1968, 233)

In evoking the quaintly and faintly recalled past, the plan fails to clearly articulate that which has best served Chicanos and Chicanas in the preservation of self. It does, however, help highlight a sense of historical consciousness—"the brutal 'Gringo' invasion of our territories"—that forms a central trope in Chicana/o cultural criticism. History, after all, has proved to the Chicano that US society has no patience or respect (when it has time to take notice at all) for people of Mexican ancestry, US citizens or not. Employing Aztlán as signifier, Chicano activists, artists, and critics constantly write and rewrite history.

The invocation of ancestry by the plan reclaims a position and a heritage that lays claim to integrity and agency. This claim suggests, through the "call of our blood," an essentialized and biologically determined nationalism that proves finally untenable. So problematic is this essentialization that, a decade after the plan, the poet Alurista felt compelled to defend it in his explanation of Chicano cultural nationalism. Alurista was—along with Rodolfo "Corky" Gonzales—one of the plan's drafters and masterminds. Luís Leal notes in "In Search of Aztlán" that "before March, 1969, the date of the Denver Conference, no one talked about Aztlán. In fact, the first time that it was mentioned in a Chicano document was in 'El Plan Espiritual de Aztlán,' which was presented in Denver at that time. Apparently, it owes its creation to the poet Alurista who already, during the Autumn of 1968, had spoken about Aztlán in a class for Chicanos held at San Diego State University" (Leal 1981, 20). As a principal player in the articulation of Aztlán, Alurista in 1981 argues that the plan "clearly stated that 'Aztlán belonged to those who worked it' (not only Xicano workers) and that no capricious frontiers would be recognized—an important point which, in the fervor of an exclusivist narrow nationalism, was quickly overlooked" (1981, 25). Alurista disavows what could be interpreted as the most exclusivist elements of nationalism evident in the plan. At the same time, he insists upon a type of transnational "nationalism," a cultural nationalism distinct from the "exclusivist narrow nationalism" of strict political delineation.

This distinction helps explain the tension between two (ultimately contradictory) veins of Chicano "nationalism" strongly influential in subsequent movements of cultural and political identification. Aztlán variously seems to signal a rationally planned nationalist movement and a mythopoetic cultural essence. Although the drafters of the plan, after Fanon, seem to view a cultural nationalism as simultaneous with a political nationalism, Aztlán came to be the hotly disputed terrain on which either one or another type of nationalism was ostensibly founded. Elyette Labarthe, discussing the development of Aztlán, notes the importance of these disputes in the early development of Chicano self-identity: "On one side an oracular voice crackled over that of reason, on the other side a dispassionate voice piped up above that of the inspired poet, but could not quite blot it out" (1990, 79). Militant factions in the Chicano movement, Labarthe points out, viewed Alurista's nationalism as a hollow and romanticized vision that subverted real claims to Aztlán, real political-nationalist interests. The tensions between the locally political and the universally cultural form one series of the fault lines that run through the terrain of Chicano cultural articulations.

## AZTLÁN AND NATION

Jorge Klor de Alva implies that this rupture between cultural and political nationalisms influenced the breakdown of leadership among Chicano communities. With the eye of an anthropologist, he notes:

> On one side are leaders with a humanist bent, often schooled in literature or fine arts, who tend to focus on cultural concerns while emphasizing the cultural autonomy of the individual. Their naive cultural nationalism is ultimately too chauvinistic to promote the unification efforts needed to overcome the divisive forces of monopoly capitalism and the seductiveness of modern fragmenting individualism. On the other side are those primarily trained in the social sciences, whose research is delimited by a preoccupation with economic and political issues, and whose eyes are fixed on social structures and the work force. The radicals among them disparage the importance of culture and nationalism while focusing primarily on the significance of class. (1989, 137)

Although Klor de Alva goes on to elaborate that this schema is "deceiving in its simplicity," it nevertheless reflects a distancing between "two valuable and necessary camps" (138). The schisms between "the political" and "the cultural" within Chicano discourses run deeply. They spread out over a larger historical and geographic terrain not divided neatly into camps like "political" versus "cultural," or "historical" as opposed to "mythical." The fissures involved in Chicano nationalist claims derive from a number of different historical sources: the nationalist movements—American Indian and Black—current in the political climate of the late 1960s; the Third World struggles for national sovereignty of the 1950s; the "nationless" status of Chicanos who, after fighting in World War II, returned to a country where they were still considered foreigners in the 1940s; the institutionalization, following the Mexican Revolution, of Mexican national culture in the 1920s and 1930s; the usurpation of Mexican territorial rights in 1848; the continuous migrations of Mexicans before, during, and after the US-Mexican War; the struggle for Mexican independence from Spain begun in 1810. All these form influential trajectories that cross at the matrix of Chicano nationalism.

The influence of the Mexican Revolution on Chicano thinking in particular should not be minimized. As Leal and Barrón note, "Immigration from Mexico to the United States from 1848 to 1910 was negligible. After 1910, however, and especially during the critical years of the Mexican Revolution (1913–1915), which coincided with the outbreak of World War I and the consequent expansion of American industry and agriculture, large numbers of immigrants crossed the border" (1982, 20). The influences on the economic and social conditions of Chicano life in the United States certainly changed as a result of the revolution. Not the least of these changes was the backlash against Mexicans that came—among other times—in the 1920s.[5]

The indigenism so valued by Chicano cultural discourses clearly draws its influence from the construction of postrevolutionary Mexican nationalism. Thus events following the Mexican Revolution—especially the institutionalization of "revolutionary" ideology—have significantly influenced the articulation of Chicana/o identification. The affirmation of native roots in the cultural identification of the Mexican begins with José Vasconcelos's service as minister of education under President Alvaro Obregón (1920–1924). Other movements toward Chicano empowerment are prefigured in the Mexican postrevolutionary world as well. In the politico-cultural realm, one finds a strong conflict between Mexican intelligentsia who wish to ally themselves with an international Marxism and those seeking to discover the true character of Mexico. Samuel Ramos undertook *Profile of Man and Culture in Mexico* in 1934 as a personality study of Mexico, and Jorge Cuesta's anthology of modern Mexican poetry from 1928 serves as an investigation into the meaning of Mexican cultural tradition. Octavio Paz notes: "They both reflect our profound desire for self-knowledge. The former represents our search for the intimate particulars of our nature, a search that was the very essence of our Revolution, while the latter represents our anxiety to incorporate these particulars in a universal tradition" (1985, 162). Of course the work of Paz himself has been extraordinarily influential, both as an affirmative point of reference and a sore point of rejection. Of Mexico, Paz argues: "Ever since World War II we have been aware that the self-creation demanded of us by our national realities is no different from that which similar realities are demanding of others. The past has left us orphans, as it has the rest of the planet, and we must join together in inventing our common future. World history has become everyone's task and our own labyrinth is the labyrinth of all mankind" (173). The embrace and rejection of the type of universalism that so interests

Paz in this passage (and throughout his writing) forms a strong trajectory in the movement of Chicano cultural construction.

These strong intellectual and cultural associations with Mexico, according to Genaro Padilla, arise from a profound sense of disconnection experienced by Chicana/o writers and thinkers. They have, Padilla argues,

> a nostalgia for the Mexican homeland, especially as it has been imagined in that mythical realm of Aztlán. This impulse has manifested itself intensely in the last two decades, a period during which the Chicano, feeling deeply alienated from the foster parent United States, wished to maintain a vital spiritual link with Mexico, the model of language, culture and social behavior. This explains, in part, why Chicano cultural nationalists not only appropriated the pre-Columbian mythology of Mexico, but also its Revolutionary heroes—Benito Juárez, Emiliano Zapata, Pancho Villa—and affected a kinship with Mexico's common people and their history. (1989, 126)

While the longing described in Padilla's discussion might best seem to apply within a New Mexican cultural context, the kinship his argument asserts as central does inform the construction of Chicano cultural nationalism across the nation, especially as regards a nationalist alliance to progressive economic, social, and political agendas. What specific course those agendas should take—and the role that the culture should play in relation to those agendas—forms part of the discontinuity apparent in the realm of Aztlán.

Aztlán stands as that region where the diverse political, geographic, and cultural concerns gripping the Chicano imagination meet. Alurista, as we have seen, views Aztlán as a sign whose referent is unproblematically present. From Alurista's view, the conflation of a nation and a culture seems to provide no tension. Thus, he can assert that Chicano literature "is a national literature, and will have to reflect all the levels that our nation implies, all that IS our people" (Bruce-Novoa 1980, 284). Aztlán as a Chicano nation, from this perspective, stands as an ontological certainty. The literature that will emerge from it will reflect the same nationalist concerns as any other national literatures. There is a curious elision of nation, literature, and people in Alurista's configuration of Aztlán. The term comes to represent not just the fact of sovereignty, but the fact of existence, the very being that is the Chicano—a reflection of the essentializing moves manifested by this strain of Chicano cultural articulation, an essentialization that Alurista seems elsewhere to speak against.

In "In Search of Aztlán," Luís Leal looks upon the idea of Aztlán, and the "Plan Espiritual" specifically, from a more historical perspective. He traces the effects and traditions of Aztlán, most particularly by documenting "the rebirth of the myth in Chicano thought" (1981, 20). "El Plan Espiritual de Aztlán" forms an important document and turning point in the articulation of Chicano consciousness. In it, Leal argues, the Chicano "recognizes his Aztec origins" as well as "establishes that Aztlán is the Mexican territory ceded to the United States in 1848" (20). The plan articulates the affirmation of origins, both indigenous (though reified in the form of the "Aztecs") and nationalist. He goes on to note that "following one of the basic ideas of the Mexican Revolution, it recognizes that the land belongs to those who work it," making explicit the connection between Aztlán and the cultural history that enables its articulation. Leal's comments thus point toward the historical loci and salient components that make up the discursive practices associated with Aztlán. This historical perspective quickly dissolves in his essay into something else.

Leal concludes with the admonition "whosoever wants to find Aztlán, let him look for it, not on the maps, but in the most intimate part of his being" (22). His discussion, which begins as a historical project, turns into a rhetorical one. Aztlán ceases to exist except as a vague search for spiritual centering. Sylvia Gonzales makes a similar discursive move six years before Leal, eliding the historical ground of Aztlán with an essential and ultimately romantic notion of universal "culture." In her essay "National Character vs. Universality in Chicano Poetry," Gonzales begins by articulating a sociohistorically bound notion of Aztlán: "In recognition of our oppression, the Chicano people . . . searched for identity and awareness as a group, as a nation within a nation. This became the cultural, psychological, philosophical and political nation of Aztlán" (1975, 15). Aztlán thus represents a contested, resistant site. Not specifically bound to a geographic reclamation, Aztlán in Gonzales's view is a discursive construction arising out of political necessity. However, her argument quickly moves from a project of political resistance to one of eschatological dimensions. Her vision of Aztlán leaves a messianic vision of cultural universality: "The world awaits the appearance of a disciple capable of propounding the message, interpreting the underlying language of their work, which has already been proscribed. That disciple will have to be a priest, a magician or a poet" (19). This articulation of Aztlán moves from issues of self-determination to a dream of cultural salvation.

## LINES OF FLIGHT

In the end, the terrain termed Aztlán comes to represent both specific geographic locales and the means of a counter-discursive engagement. In either case its efficacy in terms of political-institutional transformation remains questionable. When compared with the other plans marking El Movimiento, "El Plan Espiritual de Aztlán" does not leave as distinct a political legacy. Elyette Labarthe argues that the power of "Aztlán" lies in its imaginative conceptualization of Chicano unity: "The socioeconomic debate was to be awarded a spiritual dimension and a dynamism that were sadly lacking. The symbol of Aztlán had the power to legitimize the struggles, to cement the claims. It was a compensatory symbolic mechanism, fusing poetico-symbolic unity to sociocultural concerns. The Chicanos who were divided by history, found in it an ancestral territory and a common destiny" (1990, 80). Its compensatory function served to make it a lasting image. But, as a compensatory strategy, its political effects proved less than prepossessing.

Finally, as the arguments by Gonzales and Leal indicate, the function of Aztlán was to pronounce a minority position that staked claims for legitimacy through a cultural and ancestral primacy. In immediate terms, however, as Juan Gómez-Quiñones argues, the plan "was stripped of what radical element it possessed by stressing its alleged romantic idealism, reducing the concept of Aztlán to a psychological ploy, and limiting advocacy for self-determination to local community control—all of which became possible because of the plan's incomplete analysis which, in turn, allowed its language concerning issues to degenerate into reformism" (1990, 124). The political vagueness of the plan allowed it to dissipate its energies along the small fault lines of numerous cultural discourses. And this dispersal, although causing tremors in the cultural terrain of Euro-American society, did little to shake the walls and bring down the structures of power as its rhetoric so firmly proclaimed.

Aztlán as a supposed "common denominator with the claims to the *vatos locos, pochos, pachucos, cholos* and other *mestizos*" (Labarthe 1990, 80) fails. Purportedly invoked as a politically unifying metaphor, Aztlán becomes something quite different. Although politically and ideologically vague, "El Plan Espiritual de Aztlán" does help establish the discursive habits by which Chicano culture asserts its autonomy. Aztlán thus forms not a national but a critical region for El Movimiento. At its most efficacious moments, it comes to represent a cultural site by which to express pride in origins and heritages. The investigation of the past, the reclamation of history, the pride of place embodied in Aztlán manifests itself in the idea of chicanismo.

The poet José Montoya explains: "*chicanismo* is a basic concept which embodies both the Indio and the Spanish aspects of our heritage. As Chicano people we now accept the Indio side of our heritage. We somehow never had too much of a problem with our Hispanitude one way or the other. But to be considered an Indio!" (1986, 25). The mestizaje of Montoya's exclamations forms a nexus of cultural and personal identity that first gained currency in the nationalist movements of postrevolutionary Mexico. Although the impetus for the celebration of *indigenismo* emerges from the nationalist discourses of Mexico, hegemonic views on race and culture die long and agonized deaths. Despite the ideological valorization of mestizaje, the racism present in both US and Mexican societies certainly circulates in the "Mexican American" communities. In a North American context, this means that the members of these communities are under pressure to assimilate particular standards—of beauty, of identity, of aspiration. In a Mexican context, the pressure is to urbanize, modernize, and Europeanize. Which is to say that in order to belong to larger imagined communities of the nation—particularly in the United States—"Mexican Americans" are expected to accept anti-indigenous discourses as their own.

In this respect, Aztlán has allowed for a subjectivity that reclaims the connection to indigenous peoples and cultures. Although it does not offer a viable political platform that would allow for a reclamation of a nation, it has in varied ways provided an alternate national consciousness. It has in problematic ways allowed for another way of aligning one's interests and concerns with community and with history. This may prove to be the most lasting legacy of Aztlán. In crystallizing a sense of rightful place and identity, it has sought to enable a newfound agency. Though hazy as to the precise means by which this agency will emerge, Aztlán has valorized a chicanismo that reweaves into the present previously devalued lines of descent.

These lines of descent do not come to us without problematic implications. Reimaginings of the past—Mexican, indigenous, Aztec, pure—are understood as true. Their revivification can, however, only be enacted through their manifestation in a conflicted present. Aztlán thus becomes a terrain of discontinuity, of disjuncture. An infatuation with tradition and the "native" represents the type of fetishization of Aztec and Mayan themes and icons critiqued by Jorge Klor de Alva: Chicanos "have consistently emphasized the form over the content of native ideology and symbolism by oversimplifying both to the point of caricaturing the intricate and enigmatic codes that veil the meanings of the original texts" (1986, 24). While an infatuation with historical "accuracy" is of course suspect, so, too, an easy manipulation of cultural iconography must be critiqued. In this regard, Daniel Alarcón's redeployment of Aztlán as a palimpsest is very instructive. Aztlán as a cultural/national symbol represents a paradox: it seeks to stand as a common denominator among Chicano populations, yet it divides rather than unifies; it maintains cultural traditions while promoting assimilation into Anglo-American culture; it affirms indigenous ancestry while simultaneously erasing the very historical, cultural, and geographic specificity of that ancestry. Consequently, Alarcón astutely maintains: "Unless Aztlán is understood in all of its layers, all its complexity, it will never be an attractive model to the diverse culture its leaders seek to encompass within its borders, borders that have been and will continue to be fluid" (1992, 62). Aztlán represents not a singular homeland, but rather borderlands between sites of alliance.[6] The borderlands mark a site of profound discontinuity between regions delimiting racial, sexual, gender, and economic identities.

To think of Aztlán as a signifier of the borderlands does not negate its historical significance. It still reaches out to the geography of the American Southwest and attempts to represent its distinct material qualities. Yet, it is also true that conceptions of the borderlands refute Aztlán as a fixed entity. Partly, the refutation of the nationalist dreams of the Chicano movement results from the conflicted message in which revolutionary rhetoric articulated what quite quickly became reformist demands. These reformist positions ultimately offered neither genuine self-determination nor universal liberation. Partly, the refutation of nationalist demands is because Latinos, as the fastest growing minority in the United States, have, in a sense, already reclaimed the Southwest. Partly, there remains the unshakable belief that the Southwest was never lost. Thus Aztlán as borderlands marks a site that both belongs to and has never belonged to either the United States or Mexico.

The tumultuous histories informing constructions of the US Southwest mark the impossible interstices between imagination and history. In its negative recollection of repressive social forms, Aztlán as signifier marks how historically grounded Chicano consciousness is. This historical perspective serves to acknowledge the fluid mending and blending, repression and destruction of disparate cultures making up chicanismo. A tempestuous sense of motion therefore marks that region termed the "borderlands." Neither a homeland, nor a perpetuation of origin, the borderlands allude to an illimitable terrain marked by dreams and rupture, marked by history and the various hopes that history can exemplify. The borderlands represent the multiplicity and dynamism of Chicana/o experiences and cultures. It is a terrain in which Mexicans, Chicanos, and mestizos live among the various worlds comprising their cultural and political landscapes.

Sergio Elizondo, among others, seeks to give voice to the idea of the borderlands. He discusses a relationship to land that Chicana/o culture has often sought to express:

> We understand now the Border between the United States of America and the Estados Unidos Mexicanos; now we would do well to consider that Borderlands might be a more appropriate term to designate the entire area over which the Chicano people are spread in this country. In so doing, we would come also to understand that the mere physical extension between the US-Mexico border and, let

> us say, Chicago, is a fact of human dispersion, and not a diaspora of the Chicano people. It is not static for us, but rather it has always been a dynamic and natural motion motivated by laws and processes common to all cultures. Our migrations north of the old historical border have extended the geography and social fabric of Aztlán northward in all directions; we have been able to expand our communal life and fantasies. (1986, 13)

Elizondo speaks to a number of the issues that emerge as central to the Chicano cultural imagination. The problematization of heritage and tradition, the relation between Chicano cultural and social experiences, the significance of land and nation, the expansion of "homeland" and "fantasies," all inform the various movements of contemporary Chicano culture. It is interesting that Elizondo suggests the movement of Chicanos through the United States is "motivated by laws and processes common to all cultures." The desire to make Chicana/o identity "universal" still finds a voice. Nevertheless, Elizondo's statement indicates that the notion of Aztlán has given way to a broader and more diverse vision of Chicano cultural terrain. This cultural terrain expands the realm of desire for Chicanas/os, moving it as it does across the entire face of the United States and beyond; but it also closes a chapter on Chicano cultural identity. No longer grounded exclusively in the Southwest or border region, the borderlands expand the territorial claims of Chicanos. Elizondo portrays this expansion as simply the extension of "the geography and social fabric of Aztlán." His conceptualization does not address at all what that sign "Aztlán" signifies.

As with the articulations of Chicano nationalism, Elizondo's view of Aztlán fails to perceive the multiplicity and discontinuity evident in the histories and geographies encompassed by the signifier "Aztlán." The discussion to this point should serve to indicate that as a place, or even as a unifying symbol or image, any fixed significance ascribed to Aztlán erases the vast differences that inform the terms "Chicana" and "Chicano." The histories of Mexicans in this country are marked by a series of tensions and ruptures—cultural, linguistic, political, sexual, economic, and racial—that cut across bounded terrains, that cut across ways in which one can and cannot call one's location "home." The interstitial becomes the liminal where the living between becomes a way of moving through such definitions as Other, native, foreign, gringo, pocho, etc. The performance artist Guillermo Gómez-Peña addresses the multiplicity that makes up identity in the borderlands:

> My "identity" now possesses multiple repertories: I am Mexican but I am also Chicano and Latin American. At the border they call me *chilango* or *mexiquillo*; in Mexico City it's *pocho* or *norteño*; and in Europe it's *sudaca*. The Anglos call me "Hispanic" or "Latino," and the Germans have, on more than one occasion, confused me with Turks or Italians. My wife Emily is Anglo-Italian, but speaks Spanish with an Argentine accent, and together we walk amid the rubble of the Tower of Babel of our American postmodernity. (1988, 127–28)

The identities Gómez-Peña exposes lead to a decentering of subjectivity accompanied by loss—of country, of native language, of certainty. But this leads as well to gain: a multifocal and tolerant culture, cultural alliances, "a true political conscience (declassicization and consequent politicization) as well as new options in social, sexual, spiritual, and aesthetic behavior" (129–30).[7] The desire to rediscover a homeland within the current climate of Chicano culture coexists with a much more complex and extensive reclamation. Demands for home are made simultaneously with calls for a reclamation of all that is cast between, all that is devalued by other nationalist identities. An interstitial Chicano culture traces "lines of flight," movements toward deterritorialization.[8] Chicana/o writers and critics most powerfully enable this type of cultural configuration as they have sought to articulate the deficiencies of a nationalism that presumes the centrality of heterosexual male subjectivity. Their experiences suggest a textured and multifaceted sense of self.

## HYBRID WORLDS

In this context, no Chicana author is associated with the borderland more than Gloria Anzaldúa. Caught between the worlds of lesbian and straight, Mexican and American, First World and Third World, Anzaldúa's writing seems to exemplify and reflect the condition of the interstitial and liminal—of being simultaneously between and on the threshold. In the poem "To Live in the Borderlands Means You," the speaker visits the various characteristics of the borderlands. The title reads as the first line of the poem, a device immediately signaling a transgression of borders and marking the thematics of the poem. The title also allows for a shifting in syntactical meaning. Taken alone the title signals a conflation between the "you" the title addresses and the borderlands of which it speaks. Melding into the poem, the title also signals the mestizaje inherent in the borderlands:

> To live in the Borderlands means you
> are neither hispana india negra española
> ni gabacha, eres mestiza, mulata, half-breed
> caught in the crossfire between camps
> while carrying all five races on your back
> not knowing which side to turn to, run from.
> (1987, 194)

The borderlands in the poem become a zone of transition and not-belonging. You are not Hispanic, Indian, black, Spanish, or white, but mestiza. Identity emerges from the racial, cultural, and sexual mixture. It is a land of betrayal where "*mexicanas* call you *rajetas*" and "denying the Anglo inside you / is as bad as having denied the Indian or Black." A mestizaje of linguistic and sexual identity emerges in the borderland as well: "*Cuando vives en la frontera* / people walk through you, the wind steals your voice, / you're a *burra* [donkey], *buey* [mule], scapegoat / . . . / both woman and man, neither— / a new gender." The poem's interlingual expression and evocation of interstitial spaces represents the power of transgression. The borderlands do not represent merely a cultural or national transgression. As the imagery evoked by the poem suggests, sexual and gender identities give way before the transformative forces of a true mestizaje. To live in the borderlands means transgressing the rigid definitions of sexual and racial, national and gender definitions.

The battles of the borderlands finally are fought on a ground in which enemies are not without. In the borderlands "you are the battleground / where enemies are kin to each other; / you are at home, a stranger, / the border disputes have been settled / the volley of shots have shattered the truce." There is a discontinuity inherent in the borderland. From this perspective, Elizondo is right in conflating Aztlán with the borderland; they meld one into the other as regions of rupture where self and other perpetually dance around and through one another.

Although one enemy remains—the homogenizing elements of society that seek to erase any trace of "race," the mill that wants to "pound you pinch you roll you out / smelling like white bread but dead"—these enemies do not stand wholly without. These are the lessons internalized through the racism and violence that mark the borderlands. The borderlands represent a home that is not home, the place where all the contradictions of living among and between worlds manifests itself. Anzaldúa articulates the difficulties and problems inherent to this realm of discontinuity. Not offering a vision of another land as the utopian hope for peace or justice, all the poem can offer is advice on how to negotiate through the ruptured terrain of the borderlands: "To survive the Borderlands / you must live *sin fronteras* / be a crossroads." To live without borders means that the subjectivity to which Anzaldúa's poetry points constantly stands at the intersection of various discursive and historical trajectories. The crossroads that subjectivity becomes allows as well for the self to venture down various roads, follow trails that lead across numerous—often discontinuous, often contradictory, often antithetical—regions: European, Indian, Mexican, American, male, female, homosexual, heterosexual. The quest suggested by Anzaldúa's sense of the borderlands is not toward a fixed or rigid identity. The Chicana/o becomes a fluid condition, a migratory self who reclaims not merely the geographic realm of Aztlán. Instead, Chicanos/as come to be seen as transfiguring themselves—moving between the worlds of indigenous and European, of American and Mexican, of self and other.

## FILLING THE VOID

The transformation of "Aztlán" from homeland to borderlands signifies another turn within Chicana/o cultural discourse. It demarcates a shift from origin toward an engagement with the ever-elusive construction of cultural identity. As the US-Mexican border represents a construction tied to histories of power and dispossession, the construction of personal and cultural identity entailed in any multicultural project comes to the fore in Chicana/o cultural production. The move represents at this point a liberating one that allows for the assumption of various subject positions. The refusal to be delimited, while simultaneously claiming numerous heritages and influences, allows for a rearticulation of the relationship between self and society, self and history, self and land. Aztlán as a realm of historical convergence and discontinuity becomes another source of significance embraced and employed in the borderlands that is Chicana/o culture.

The tendency in these figurations and refigurations of Aztlán recast it variously as an ontological reality or an epistemological construction. Aztlán thus is repositioned and refigured as a shifting, and thus ambiguous, signifier. Ambiguity suggests—problematically—a sense of equivalence. Rather than think of Aztlán as ambiguous signifier, we might consider it "empty," a signifier that points, as Ernesto Laclau argues, "from within the process of signification, to the discursive presence of its own limits" (1996, 36).[9] This shift does not help us fix the significance of the term Aztlán. It does, I hope, help sketch some ideas that unravel the bind to which the continued discussions of Aztlán attest. There can be two explanations why we have not, so to speak, arrived at Aztlán. On the one hand, the plan to get to Aztlán—representing nation, unity, liberation—has not been adequately articulated as yet. (This implies that the proper configuration of Aztlán is still to be enacted at some future utopian date.) Or, on the other hand, all the different articulations of Aztlán are equally valid and so we each live our own little atomized Aztlán. The first position is obfuscatory, the second hopeless. Both run counter to that which Aztlán seeks to name.

As an empty signifier, Aztlán names not that which is or has been, but that which is ever absent: nation, unity, liberation. The various articulations of Aztlán have sought to make these absences present in the face of oppressive power based on: racial grounds and the Chicano emergence from the indigenous; historico-political grounds and the struggles over land most clearly indexed by the US-Mexican War of 1846–1848; economic grounds represented by the exploitation of laborers and most specifically farmworkers; sexual and gender grounds formed by the colonization of female and queer bodies; and cultural grounds invoked by references to indigenous, folk, and popular arts. Whatever its premise, the term "Aztlán" consistently has named that which refers to an absence, an unfulfilled reality in response to various forms of oppression.

This does not help us understand why the signifier Aztlán has so haunted Chicana/o critical thought. Perhaps the ways in which Aztlán has been used in contestations of power explain something of its sustained attraction. The discourses surrounding Aztlán present themselves as the incarnation of the term: the articulation of unity, of nation, of resistance to oppressive power. Each articulation offers its particular understanding of Aztlán as its fulfillment. This is precisely the reason that Aztlán never adds up. As a sign of liberation, it is ever emptied of meaning just as its meaning is asserted, its borders blurred by those constituencies engaged in liberating struggles named by Aztlán. This simultaneous process of arrival and evacuation does not mark a point of despair, nor in describing it do I mean to disparage Aztlán. On the contrary. We cannot abandon Aztlán, precisely because it serves to name that space of liberation so fondly yearned for. As such, it stands as a site of origin in the struggle to articulate, enact, and make present an absent unity. Aztlán is our start and end point of empowerment.

## NOTES

Reprinted with permission from Rafael Pérez-Torres, *Aztlán: A Journal of Chicano Studies* 22:2 (1997): 13–41.

1. This argument of linguistic loss is complicated by the resurgence of interest in the learning and use of Spanish by second- and third-generation Mexicans. See Gonzales (1997).

2. See especially chapter 3 of my book *Movements in Chicano Poetry*, "From the Homeland to the Borderlands, the Reformation of Aztlán." There is an implied teleological argument in that discussion I now reject. Consequently, the present essay attempts to draw upon, elaborate, and clarify my previous analysis. The incisive comments offered by the readers of the journal *Aztlán* have helped me greatly in this venture and I thank them. All errors, misrepresentations, and slips of logic remain stubbornly mine.

3. Here one finds a dichotomy. As Juan Gómez-Quiñones notes, Chicano leaders of the 1960s were impeded by the contradictions between their assertive, often separatist, rhetoric and their conventional reformist demands involving educational reform and voter registration drives (1990, 141–46).

4. Thus Douglas Massey and his associates (1987) draw upon the signifier to name their study of transnational Mexican migration *Return to Aztlán*.

5. See Acuña (1988, 130–43) and Ralph Guzmán (1974, 21–22) for examples of Euro-American reactions and ensuant legislation to "stem the tide" of Mexican immigration.

6. In this respect we might think of Chela Sandoval's discussion of US feminists of color in the 1970s. She notes that feminists of color began to identify common grounds upon which they formed coalitions across boundaries of cultural, racial, class, and gender differences. Their position in the borderlands of feminism enabled a crossing across difference, a recognition of sameness amid difference, a recognition of other countrywomen and countrymen living in a similar and sympathetic psychic terrain. The differences between these men and women—differences signifying struggle, conflict, asymmetry, differences implying dislocation, dispersal, disruption—were never erased. Rather, a fuller process of recognition occurred (1991, 11).

7. Of course, this articulation is complicated by Gómez-Peña's privileged position as a member of an international artistic elite capable, economically and politically, of crossing borders with relative ease.

8. The term "line of flight" from Deleuze and Guattari (1983, 1986) is meant to suggest escape from binary choices. The line of flight is formed by ruptures within particular systems or orders. It allows for third possibilities—neither capitulation to regimes nor unconditional freedom from them. The line of flight is a way out, a means of changing the situation to something other.

9. Laclau's discussion of empty signifiers has helped me think through some of the thorny dilemmas set in motion by the various articulations of Aztlán. While I sympathize with his political project, I do not fully ascribe to his view that modern democracy will begin as "different projects or wills will try to hegemonize the empty signifiers of the absent community" (1996, 46). His analysis of the empty signifier itself, however, I find insightful.

## WORKS CITED


Acuña, Rodolfo. 1988. *Occupied America: A History of Chicanos*. 3rd ed. New York: Harper & Row.

Alarcón, Daniel Cooper. 1992. "The Aztec Palimpsest: Toward a New Understanding of Aztlán, Cultural Identity and History." *Aztlán* 19, no 4 2: 33–68.

Alurista. 1981. "Cultural Nationalism and Xicano Literature During the Decade 1965–1975." *MELUS* 8 (Summer): 22–34.

Anaya, Rudolfo A., and Francisco Lomelí, eds. 1989. *Aztlán: Essays on the Chicano Homeland.* Albuquerque: Academia/El Norte Publications.

Anzaldúa, Gloria. 1987. "To live in the Borderlands means you." In *Borderlands/La Frontera: The New Mestiza,* 194–95. San Francisco: Spinsters/Aunt Lute.

Barrera, Mario. 1988. *Beyond Aztlán: Ethnic Autonomy in Comparative Perspective.* Notre Dame, IN: University of Notre Dame Press.

Bruce-Novoa, Juan. 1980. *Chicano Authors: Inquiry by Interview.* Austin: University of Texas Press.

Cuesta, Jorge. 1928. *Antología de la poesía mexicana moderna.* Mexico: Contemporaneos.

Deleuze, Gilles, and Félix Guattari. 1975. *Kafka: For a Minor Literature.* Translated by Dana Polan. Minneapolis: University of Minnesota Press.

———.1972. *Anti-Oedipus: Capitalism and Schizophrenia.* Translated by Robert Hurley, Mark See, and Helen R. Lane. Minneapolis: University of Minnesota Press.

Elizondo, Sergio D. 1986. "ABC: Aztlán, the Borderlands, and Chicago." In *Missions in Conflict: Essays on US-Mexican Relations and Chicano Culture,* edited by Renate von Bardeleben, 13–23. Tübingen: Gunter Narr Verlag.

"El Plan Espiritual de Aztlan." 1972. First presented at the Chicano Youth Liberation Conference in Denver, Colorado, March 1969. In *Aztlan: An Anthropology of Mexican American Literature,* edited by Luis Valdez and Stan Steiner, 402–06. New York: Knopf.

Fanon, Frantz. 1961. *The Wretched of the Earth.* Translated by Constance Farrington. New York: Grove Press.

Gómez-Peña, Guillermo. 1988. "Documented/Undocumented." Translated by Rubén Martínez. In *The Graywolf Annual Five: Multi-Cultural Literacy,* edited by Rick Simonson and Scott Walker, 127–34. St. Paul, MN: Graywolf Press.

Gómez-Quiñones, Juan. 1990. *Chicano Politics: Reality and Promise, 1940–1990.* Albuquerque: University of New Mexico Press.

Gonzales, John M. 1997. "Relearning a Lost Language." *Los Angeles Times,* 26 May 1997.

Gonzales, Sylvia. 1975. "National Character vs. Universality in Chicano Poetry." *De Colores* 1: 10–21.

Guzmán, Ralph. 1974. "The Function of Anglo-American Racism in the Political Development of Chicanos." In *La Causa Política: A Chicano Politics Reader,* edited by Chris F. García, 19–35. Notre Dame, IN: University of Notre Dame Press.

Klor de Alva, J. Jorge. 1989. "Aztlán, Borinquen and Hispanic Nationalism in the United States." In *Aztlán: Essays on the Chicano Homeland,* edited by Rudolfo Anaya and Francisco Lomelí, 135–71. Albuquerque: Academia/El Norte Publications.

———. 1986. "California Chicano Literature and Pre-Columbian Motifs: Foil and Fetish." *Confluencia* 1 (Spring): 18–26.

Labarthe, Elyette Andouard. 1990. "The Vicissitudes of Aztlán." *Confluencia* 5 (Spring): 79–84.

Laclau, Ernesto. 1996. "Why Do Empty Signifiers Matter to Politics?" In *Emancipation(s),* 36–46. New York: Verso.

Leal, Luís. 1981. "In Search of Aztlán." Translated by Gladys Leal. *Denver Quarterly* 16 (Fall): 16–22.

Leal, Luís, and Pepe Barrón. 1982. "Chicano Literature: An Overview." In *Three American Literatures,* edited by Houston A. Baker Jr., 9–32. New York: Modern Language Association.

Massey, Douglas S., Rafael Alarcón, Jorge Durand, and Humberto González. 1987. *Return to Aztlán: The Social Process of International Migration from Western Mexico.* Berkeley: University of California Press.

Montoya, José. 1986. "Chicano Art: Resistance in Isolation 'Aquí Estamos y no Nos Vamos.'" In *Missions in Conflict: Essays on US-Mexican Relations and Chicano Culture,* edited by Renate von Bardeleben, 25–30. Tübingen: Gunter Narr Verlag.

Moraga, Cherríe. 1993. "Queer Aztlán: The Reformation of Chicano Tribe." In *The Last Generation,* 145–74. Boston: South End Press.

Padilla, Genaro. 1989. "Myth and Comparative Cultural Nationalism: The Ideological Uses of Aztlán." In *Aztlán: Essays on the Chicano Homeland,* edited by Rudolfo Anaya and Francisco Lomelí, 111–34. Albuquerque, NM: Academia/El Norte Publications.

Paz, Octavio. 1985. *Labyrinth of Solitude.* Translated by Lysander Kemp, Yara Milos, and Rachel Phillips Belash. New York: Grove Press.

Pérez-Torres, Rafael. 1995. *Movements in Chicano Poetry: Against Myths, Against Margins.* New York: Cambridge University Press.

Pina, Michael. 1989. "The Archaic, Historical and Mythicized Dimensions of Aztlán." In *Aztlán: Essays on the Chicano Homeland,* edited by Rudolfo Anaya and Francisco Lomelí, 14–48. Albuquerque: Academia/El Norte Publications.

Ramos, Samuel. 1962. *Profile of Man and Culture in Mexico.* Austin: University of Texas Press.

Safran, William. 1991. "Diasporas in Modern Societies: Myths of Homeland and Return." *Diaspora* 1, no. 1: 83–99.

Sandoval, Chela. 1991. "U.S. Third World Feminism: The Theory and Method of Oppositional Consciousness in the Postmodern World." *Genders* 10 (Spring): 1–24.

# IN THE EYES OF THE BEHOLDER:

## Understanding and Resolving Incompatible Ideologies and Languages in US Environmental and Cultural Laws in Relationship to Navajo Sacred Lands

SHARON MILHOLLAND

Meeting the legal requirement and moral imperative to protect both the physical and spiritual integrity of sacred lands depends on applying traditional indigenous philosophies and bodies of knowledge. Although important progress is evident in US environmental and cultural laws written to acknowledge the needs, rights, and interests of Native peoples in the management of sacred lands, a significant amount of work remains. Native peoples still face working within a body of federal law that imposes values, concepts, and languages of the dominant Western society and barely recognizes the traditional Native knowledge systems and values necessary for meaningful protection and access to sacred lands. Consequently, the legal tools intended to protect sacred lands often conflict with traditional indigenous values relative to land and religious practices, privilege the values of the dominant society, erode tribal identity and sovereignty, and leave sacred lands vulnerable to desecration or destruction.

In the United States, federal and state environmental, cultural, and religious freedoms protection laws mandate cooperation and consultation with Native peoples to protect effectively, and permit access to, sacred places on federally held lands. The federal government is charged with a legal trust duty to tribal governments to exercise the highest standards of good faith and integrity in order to protect Indian lands, resources, and cultural heritage. Regardless of this substantial legal framework, Native nations across the United States have repeatedly expressed concerns that consultation and collaboration efforts with state and federal land-management agencies are inconsistent and inadequate.[1] They believe that land management prescriptions and practices are unilaterally determined, geographically limited in scope, and not culturally

Sharon Milholland is a private consultant in Tucson, Arizona. She earned a PhD in American Indian studies from the University of Arizona and has fifteen years of experience managing cultural resources on federal lands in the southwestern United States.

compatible.[2] Native nations complain that various forms of industrial, commercial, and recreational development continue to threaten essential sacred places.[3]

For example, in the state of Georgia, the Muscogee people are battling proposed interstate highway expansion that threatens to restrict access to, and damage, mound temples and historic villages in the Ocmulgee Old Fields.[4] In Nevada, the Western Shoshone Nation is fighting to protect its sacred Yucca Mountain from transformation into this country's central repository for nuclear waste.[5] Southeastern California is the stage for the Quechan tribe's struggle to halt the permit for an open-pit gold mine that threatens to obliterate sacred sites and a sacred trail network in Indian Pass.[6] In the Pacific, Native Hawaiians are fighting telescope development on top of their elder ancestor, Mauna Kea. This volcano on the island of Hawai'i is the highest point in Pacific Polynesia and is the "highest portal to the Hawaiian Universe."[7] In Alaska, the Gwich'in are fighting proposed oil drilling in the National Arctic Wildlife Refuge. These grounds are sacred because they are habitat for caribou, the very source of Gwich'in subsistence and nationhood.[8]

To Native peoples, compliance with existing environmental and cultural laws by itself does not result in meaningful and effective sacred lands protection and access. Intent and interpretation of the language of existing environmental and cultural laws are at issue. Effective strategies for sacred lands protection and access are those that scrutinize existing law and management practice for incompatible and hegemonic ideologies and languages. Resolving the problem of incompatible ideologies and languages in laws treating sacred lands can include tribal governments working with Congress to integrate traditional indigenous worldviews directly into the law. More importantly, resolution depends on cultivating a willingness among legislators, public land managers, project proponents, and stakeholders to commit to the practice of fulfilling sacred lands' protection needs according to traditional indigenous philosophies prior to drafting new legislation or implementing negotiations or environmental evaluations mandated in existing US law.[9]

In this article, I raise a few examples of incompatible concepts and languages in US federal environmental and cultural laws affecting the management of indigenous sacred lands. I explain these examples by describing the management of a selection of Navajo (Diné) sacred places and elsewhere. Through fundamental concepts rooted in postcolonial theory and critical race theory, I suggest an intellectual framework for understanding why traditional indigenous values and knowledge are marginalized and why incompatible Western values have been privileged and enshrined in US law and policy in relationship to the management of Native sacred lands. Finally, I want to introduce you to *hozho*, the Navajo philosophy of harmony and natural beauty, which is intimately related to the Navajo orientation to their land.[10] This is an abstract, complex, highly spiritual doctrine of Navajo philosophy and spiritual practice. The environmental and cultural laws and policy of the United States are not inclusive of the philosophy of *hozho*. By considering the Navajo traditional philosophy of *hozho*, I discuss how incorporating traditional indigenous values and knowledge in sacred lands management can resolve values conflict for Native peoples, as well as raise some complex issues regarding the introduction of traditional cultural and spiritual concepts into the language of tribal or federal law.

## INCOMPATIBLE IDEOLOGIES AND LANGUAGES BETWEEN US ENVIRONMENTAL OR CULTURAL LAWS AND TRADITIONAL NAVAJO VALUES AND KNOWLEDGE

Native worldviews regarding the sacredness of the land are essential when making decisions about the land. Certain distinctive landscapes are valued as an essential and vital part of Indian being, and a moral duty to protect these places exists in order to secure the future survival of the earth, sun, stars, and all forms of life.[11] "A culture's vitality is literally dependent on individuals [living] in community with the natural world."[12] The land's features, and the sense of place and kinship they create, are central to the identity of a Native individual and a people.[13]

> The land with its water, plants, and animals is a spiritual creation put into motion by the gods in their wisdom. These elements are here to help, teach, and protect through an integrated system of beliefs that spell out man's relationship to man, nature, and the supernatural. To ignore these teachings is to ignore the purpose of life, the meaning of existence.[14]

> The importance Native Americans traditionally place on "connecting" with their place is not a romantic notion that is out of step with the times; instead, it is the quintessential ecological mandate of our time.[15]

### *Navajo Sacred Lands and Traditional Philosophy*

Sacred places, belief systems, and spiritual practices are unique to each Native culture. To the Navajo, sacred lands generally include locations mentioned in oral tradition, places where something supernatural has happened; plants, minerals, and healing waters may be collected; or humans communicate with the supernatural world by means of prayers and offerings.[16] A special type of sacred place is the "built" Anasazi site, such as masonry pueblos, burial areas, or rock image panels.[17] Because warfare was an important part of Navajo life, ceremonial sites connected to battle are also sacred.[18] In terms of their physical form, most sacred places are distinctive features on the natural landscape.

The Navajo people describe the perimeter of their homeland, or the Diné Bikeyah, with four sacred mountains. The mountains are where the natural and spiritual universes join, and they embody the values that are most pervasive in Navajo life: "healing the sick, protecting the people and their goods, bringing rain for crops and livestock, and insuring tranquility in life."[19] These mountains are essential to Navajo being and a significant source of food, water, medicinal plants, and places of worship.[20] The four sacred mountains marking the terrestrial boundaries of their traditional territory are the most powerful of the Navajo sacred landscapes.[21]

> Our Navajo spiritual and social laws are represented by the sacred mountains, as well as the four seasons and the four parts of the day. The foundations of our rules and laws for our lives are within our sacred mountains, the four seasons and the four parts of the day. The sacred mountains were placed here to give us the understanding

of our strength and courage. They shield us from evil, harm, and danger. . . . We think of them as our home, as the foundation of our hogan and our life.[22]

## *Traditional Indigenous Values and Knowledge Are Marginalized*

The complex environmental and cultural legislative and regulatory framework governing indigenous sacred places that are in the stewardship of the United States does not always recognize the Native system of moral values, elegantly expressed as "the quintessential ecological mandate of our time," as an obvious and justifiable source of guiding principles. Rather, environmental and cultural protection laws embody the ideologies and languages of Western science and property law. Legislators defined sacred places, religious objects, and American Indian human remains as "historic property" or "cultural resources." They also defined Western scientists as the most qualified authorities to understand and care for this property through laws like the 1906 Antiquities Act, the 1966 National Historic Preservation Act (NHPA), and the Archaeological Resources Protection Act.[23]

At the time Congress enacted these statutes, legislators did not take into account the unique values and philosophies of Native peoples, such as *hozho*, in the treatment of this cultural property.[24] In the United States, property law is defined in accordance with the dominant society's values, and the ability to hold property is consistent with the ability to wield power.[25] Consequently, decision makers for federal land-management agencies largely privilege scientific, recreational, and economic values over indigenous traditional values in managing cultural property. Whether by deliberate or inadvertent decisions or actions, the federal government has culturally constructed, socially sanctioned, and legally legitimized the removal of the voices and values of Native peoples from the management of their cultural property. In the end, the legal tools designed to manage sacred lands conflict with traditional indigenous values relative to land and religious practice, privilege the values of the dominant society, erode tribal identity and sovereignty, and leave sacred lands vulnerable to desecration or destruction.

## *Postcolonial Theory, Critical Race Theory, and Indigenous Sacred Lands*

To understand why traditional indigenous values and knowledge are marginalized, and why incompatible Western values have been privileged and enshrined in US law and policy in relationship to the management of Native sacred lands, I examine this legal architecture under the lens of critical theory. Postcolonial theory and critical race theory can be linked together to form an intellectual framework for analysis of American Indian affairs because the subjects of race and political standing for indigenous peoples are unavoidably intertwined.[26] American Indians are a distinct racial group that entered into formal treaties with the US government on a nation-to-nation basis. Understanding how social, political, and legal institutions in the United States create and maintain hierarchical power structures with Native governments, and then fail to resolve power and values conflicts, can be explained through central tenets emerging in these two bodies of theory.

Postcolonial theory is a rapidly evolving field of scholarship generally sharing skepticism about value neutrality in Western institutions. The term *postcolonial* is inclusive of a wide spectrum of definitions of power-holding Western institutions and ideologies in societies having colonial histories. Although "post" colonialism suggests that colonial practices and ideologies are erased, colonized lands and peoples actually have residual colonial institutions, including government, courts, education, mass media, and the church, that continue to shape national identity even in a postcolonial political era.[27] Exploring the nature and degree of how the institutions in power sustain and legitimize their political positions is one focus of postcolonial theory.[28] The concept of incommensurability is the condition in which dominant Western institutions construct concepts and languages are so incompatible with non-Western values and goals that these are leveraged into the margins, and the dominant society maintains power in order to privilege its own values and goals.[29]

Critical race theory is another rapidly evolving intellectual tradition expanding across multiple disciplines that essentially questions the existence of neutral principles of constitutional law. *Black's Law Dictionary* defines it as "a reform movement within the legal profession . . . whose adherents believe that the legal system has disempowered minorities. Critical race theorists observe that even if the law is couched in neutral language, it cannot be neutral because those who fashion it have their own subjective perspective that, once enshrined in law, has disadvantaged minorities and even perpetuated racism."[30] Critical race theory emerged in the mid-1970s among legal scholars who built on the insights of critical legal studies and feminism in response to a need for a new theory to address racism occurring after the civil rights era of the 1960s. Critical race scholars argue that the practice of relying on precedent in civil rights litigation lacks effectiveness in securing rights for people of color in any sustained way. Critical race scholars also claim that arguments for rights for minorities have procedural solutions focused on the appearance of equality rather than substantive solutions focused on actual equality. Further miring equal rights advancement for minorities, those rights are usually limited when they conflict with the interests of the powerful.[31]

The first assumption of critical race scholarship is that for people of color racism is commonplace and can be encountered in aversive or deliberate form.[32] Second, critical race theory holds that the concept of race is a social invention and that these social concepts of race are enshrined in the law.[33] Third, critical race theory recognizes the "voice of color" as a unique collection of personal stories of individuals who have been ignored or alienated by the dominant institutions.[34] Critical race theorists posit that progress to eradicate racism occurs only when it is to the advantage of the dominant society to do so, a concept known as *interest convergence*.[35] The concept of interest convergence emerged from the work of Derrick Bell, one of the intellectual founders of critical race theory.[36] In his analysis of the 1954 US Supreme Court ruling in *Brown v. Board of Education*, he asserts that civil rights advances always coincide with the self-interest of the dominant society.[37] Conversely, impediments to civil rights advancement can also be rationalized by the self-interest of the dominant society.

### *Incommensurability, Interest Convergence, and Indigenous Sacred Lands*

The concepts of incommensurability and interest convergence are evident in US environmental and cultural protection laws relative to the preservation of indigenous sacred places. A very broad example of incommensurability in this body of law is the distinction between the cultural environment and the natural environment, rather than considering them as integrated. This body of law also transforms spiritual responsibilities and "the quintessential ecological mandate of our time" to a set of bureaucratic procedures often just giving the appearance of adequate treatment. One of the most important specific demonstrations of incommensurability and interest convergence in the legal language of sacred lands management is the codification of the fundamental term *sacred land*.

Indigenous sacred lands have generally been described as natural features such as rivers, waterfalls, springs, mountains, buttes and spires, or built features such as burial areas, rock image panels (pictographs or petroglyphs), medicine wheels, vision quest monuments, dance arbors, sweat bath enclosures, and gathering areas where sacred trees, plants, stones, water, or other natural materials are collected.[38] Lawmakers have seized on the physical place and the built environment in order to create a single legal definition that is narrow in scope and not necessarily consistent with how Native peoples regard sacred or holy places. The Sacred Sites Executive Order 13007 (24 May 1996) directs agencies administering federal lands to accommodate access to, and ceremonial use of, Indian religious sites to the "extent practicable" as determined at the discretion of a land manager. This order defines *sacred site* in the following manner: "'Sacred site' means any specific, discrete, narrowly delineated location on Federal land that is identified by an Indian tribe or Indian individual determined to be an appropriately authoritative representative of an Indian religion, as sacred by virtue of its established religious significance to, or ceremonial use by, an Indian religion, provided that the tribe or appropriately authoritative representative of an Indian religion has informed the agency of the existence of such a site."[39]

Another effort to codify the term *sacred* occurs in the Native American Sacred Lands Act (H.R. 2419).[40] This bill strives to enact Executive Order 13007 into law and provide authority to place federal land into trust for the benefit of the Indian tribe or tribes for which the land is considered sacred.[41] The latest draft of this bill was motivated in direct response to the Quechan tribe's fight against the development of an open-pit gold mine in Indian Pass, California. In general, the bill intends to protect indigenous sacred sites from aggressive energy development. Additionally, this bill provides authority for federal land managers to enter into cooperative agreements with tribes in order to manage a sacred landscape on federal land and any lands adjacent to sacred places.[42] The bill also underscores the importance of Native science and oral history as valid lines of evidence supporting the definition and significance of sacred sites. It also provides a more accurate definition of *sacred land*. "The term 'sacred land' means any geophysical or geographical area or feature which is sacred by virtue of its traditional cultural or religious significance or ceremonial use, or by virtue of a ceremonial or cultural requirement, including a religious requirement that a natural substance or product for use in Indian tribal or Native Hawaiian organization ceremonies be gathered from that particular location."[43]

Important criticism remains, however, regarding the sufficiency of this definition and the appropriateness of attempting to codify definitions of the sacred.[44] Arguably, a single statutory definition cannot capture the grand multiplicity of perspectives on what is "sacred." The concept of "sacred" is broad, abstract, and imbued with such deep personal spiritual meaning transcending the physical and the metaphysical, that the notion of creating a single definition of *sacred* extends beyond incommensurable and approaches impossible. Native peoples are qualitatively different from each other in cultural and spiritual heritages. Definitions of what constitutes "sacred" are accordingly particular. The meaning of the sacred, or sacred lands, is relative to individual geographical areas; individual cultures or tribes, bands, clans, or societies within the tribe; or men and women within the tribe.

The "sacred" also embodies a tribe's unique experience and language. Different groups of people may see the same phenomenon as either sacred or secular. Sacredness of a place can derive from human actions of great significance, nonhuman actions of great significance, or from higher powers having revealed themselves to human beings.[45] Stories about places without any obvious physical definitions may still encompass sacredness.[46] Tribal philosophers and scholars who have compared Native faiths and the concept of sacred have concluded that tribes have some general spiritual ideas and practices in common, and that these generalities are more appropriate for secular discussion.[47] For example, a generally accepted broad description of *sacred*, rather than a legal definition, is "something special, something out of the ordinary, and often it concerns a very personal part of each one of us because it describes our dreams, our changing, and our personal way of seeing the world. The sacred is also something that is shared, and this sharing or collective experience is necessary in order to keep the oral traditions and sacred ways vital. . . . Having a guiding vision in common as a people and maintaining it with renewals, ceremonials, rituals, and prayers."[48]

The National Environmental Policy Act of 1969 (NEPA) is one of the most significant pieces of environmental legislation enacted in the United States.[49] It requires rigorous assessment of the ecological and cultural impacts of federal undertakings and preservation of important historical, cultural, and natural aspects of our national heritage. This law contains concepts and language that are incommensurable with Native worldviews on sacred lands management. For example, indigenous cultures and spirituality are intertwined with the land, and the effects of an action on the land also impacts Native culture, spirituality, and sovereignty. Yet the NEPA does not adequately consider the effects of proposed projects on indigenous societies and cultures in a way that is meaningful to Native peoples. Specific examples of concepts and language central to the NEPA in which Indian people must participate and integrate their values, understandings, and bodies of knowledge are *social impact assessment* and *mitigation.*

Social impact assessment is a part of the environmental impact analysis required by the NEPA. Social impact includes "the consequences to human populations of any public or private action—that alter the ways in which people live, work, play, relate to one another, organize to meet their needs and generally cope as members of society. The term also includes cultural impacts involving changes to the norms, values, and beliefs that guide and rationalize their cognition of themselves and their society."[50]

Socioeconomic variables and values primarily define and measure social impact. These variables include per capita income, housing availability, and employment opportunity. Social impact also considers, to a lesser extent, the potential effect to cultural resources. Defining and measuring potential impact to all cultural resources that are important to Native peoples are inadequate. Traditional indigenous values defining environmental and cultural sustainability fall in between the socioeconomic environment described under the NEPA and the cultural environment defined under the NHPA.[51] The effects of a proposed action over sacred places, like highway construction or surface mining, are usually limited to a discussion about material, or archaeological, remains and their intrinsic scientific or educational values. Social impact analysis of effect resulting from an action on sacred natural places does not routinely include discussions of ceremonies, stories, songs, dance, language, technology, or art forms linking land and cultural identity.

The process outlined in NEPA guidelines for defining impact to cultural properties generally includes defining concrete boundaries for places of cultural or spiritual interest. Assigning rigid physical boundaries to places of spirituality and power is an incommensurable practice to Native peoples. For example, the sacred mountains defining the Diné Bikeyah are imbued with such deep personal spiritual meaning transcending the physical and the metaphysical, that the notion of demarking a physical boundary around discrete locations of "sacredness" is an incommensurable concept. "There are no boundaries. Boundaries don't make sense. All ceremonies go to the four sacred mountains. Ceremonies and mountains are inside us. The land is within us and we take it with us. You can't put a boundary around that."[52] Legal and administrative boundaries ultimately supplant cultural boundaries for sacred lands definition and protection. To illustrate, the Dinétah is a Navajo sacred landscape spanning several hundred square miles in northwestern New Mexico. According to origin stories, the modern Navajo people, Nihookáá Diné, emerged into the modern world within the Dinétah. This region is also the birthplace of some of the most important spiritual beings in Navajo creation. Gobernador Knob, or Ch'ool'íí, a prominent dome-shaped rock outcrop, is the birthplace of Changing Woman. She created the four pairs of Diné who became the originators of the four original clans.[53] The fundamental values for Navajo identity, culture, and "charter of life" are based on Changing Woman's life.[54] Dził Ná oodiłii, commonly known as Huerfano Mesa, is the first terrestrial hogan marking the center of the Navajo world around which the people were to travel.[55] Gobernador Knob and Huerfano Mesa are situated within the Dinétah and are two of the six most sacred and revered mountains in the Navajo physical and metaphysical universe.

Today, the Dinétah is not managed as a whole or culturally defined sacred or heritage landscape. Most of this region is divided among multiple federal, state, and private landowners, as well as the Navajo Nation. The physical and spiritual integrity of the Dinétah as a holy land is deteriorating from large-scale energy, commercial, and recreational development. The Dinétah is located in the San Juan Basin, one of the largest natural gas fields in the United States. Oil and gas production in this region has been ongoing for more than fifty years.[56] In 2003, the US Bureau of Land Management (BLM) approved additional large-scale oil and gas resources development.[57] The proposed wells, pipeline, and road network expand over one hundred thousand acres of northwest New Mexico, including the sacred lands of the Dinétah. The Navajo Nation rejected BLM approval of this proposal, expressing concerns over the adverse effects to Ch'ool'íí and Dził Ná oodiłii and inadequate compliance with federal environmental and cultural protection statutes.[58]

Ch'ool'íí and Dził Ná oodiłii, along with several other important cultural properties within the Dinétah, are individually managed as a discretely defined Area of Critical Environmental Concern (ACEC).[59] An ACEC is a special management designation applied to protect and prevent irreparable damage to important historical, cultural, and scenic values; fish or wildlife resources; or other natural systems or processes, or to protect human life and safety from natural hazards.[60] What is problematic about the ACEC concept relative to sacred landscapes is that an ACEC is a narrowly defined management unit encompassing a natural or human-built physical feature. Consequently, the larger cultural or spiritual landscape is arbitrarily fragmented into noncontiguous "islands of preservation." Additionally, the cultural landscape of the Dinétah is fragmented into multiple federal, tribal, and state management jurisdictions, missions, and management priorities, none of which are organized around the traditional cultural concept of the Dinétah or the traditional philosophy of *hozho*.

Finally, preservation of resources in the ACEC is limited to visible surface features and does not normally include the air space or the substrate. Although surface gas wells, pumping stations, roads, and pipelines are not permitted inside the ACEC, the sacred properties inside this protective unit are still vulnerable to desecration or destruction as consequences of directional drilling from locations outside of the ACEC boundary or from hydraulic fracturing. Directional drilling is the process of drilling a curved or angled well in order to reach a target that is not directly beneath the drill site, and where a vertical hole may not be optimal, such as when trying to reach a gas reservoir located beneath a body of water.[61] Hydraulic fracturing, or fracking, involves high-pressure injection of fluids into the bedrock to break up formations surrounding the oil and gas, allowing it to flow more freely. According to the Environmental Protection Agency, fracturing fluids can include a long list of hazardous materials and carcinogens, such as diesel fuel and formaldehyde. Fracking can result in physical damage to surface features, and any injected fluids that remain trapped underground are sufficiently toxic to contaminate groundwater.[62]

Another incommensurable NEPA and NHPA concept relative to the treatment of sacred places is the idea of "mitigating" adverse effects to sacred lands. Common mitigation measures implemented by project proponents include avoiding the impact altogether, minimizing impacts by limiting the degree or magnitude of the action, rectifying the impact by repairing or restoring the affected environment, reducing or eliminating the impact over time by preservation and maintenance operations, or compensating for the impact by replacing or providing substitute resources or environments.[63] Indigenous sacred lands can be places of spiritual power and can have physical and metaphysical elements or metaphysical or intangible characteristics. Places of power can be esoteric and even dangerous; therefore, the standard alternatives provided under

NEPA regulations, or standard archaeological practice, cannot apply to sacred lands or traditional cultural properties (TCPs). Tribes argue that mitigating adverse effects to the metaphysical or spiritual components of sacred lands is not always possible.[64] The only option for mitigating impact to sacred lands is no action at all.[65]

Navajo elders echoed these opinions in reaction to the treatment of Dook'o'oosłííd (San Francisco Peaks), the westernmost of the four Diné sacred mountains, located in northeastern Arizona.[66] Dook'o'oosłííd is a living being created and brought from the underworld by the Holy People. It is the residence of the Holy People who guide and support the Diné. This mountain range is a significant source of food, water, and medicine, and it is an essential place of worship.[67] Navajo elders living near Dook'o'oosłííd first argue that desecration of sacred lands cannot be mitigated. Second, they suggest that if mitigation or "repair" of sacred lands is a possibility, mitigation is not limited to measures applied by non-Navajos like a federal agency or project proponents. Navajo people, specifically medicine people, need to aid the mountain.

> Stop talking about the mountain. Only climb the mountain with song and prayer . . . and the snow will come back. We need to teach this to everyone and our future generations.[68]

> Effect to the physical properties or significance of traditional cultural properties cannot be mitigated by any measure other than avoidance. If TCPs are adversely affected their power can be diminished or lost. This loss can be measured by success in healing.[69]

Today, the US Forest Service manages Dook'o'oosłííd. Although there are numerous commercial and recreational uses of forest resources on the mountain, the citizens of the Navajo Nation consider a facilities improvement project at the seven-hundred-acre Snowbowl Ski Area as one of the most egregious threats of desecration to this sacred landscape. More specifically, variable levels of natural snowfall affect ski area operations, and in drought years, snow levels are not sufficient for the Snowbowl to remain open long enough each year to make the business profitable. To augment natural snow levels, Snowbowl management has proposed using reclaimed wastewater from the city of Flagstaff to make artificial snow and then spread it throughout the ski area. Navajo Nation President, Joe Shirley Jr., stated, "To Navajos, the use of effluent on one of its four sacred mountains surrounding the Navajo Nation is an outrageous desecration of a holy site. The proposed development of the sacred *Dook'o'oosłííd* would be like having a child witness the brutal violation of its mother, leaving it emotionally and psychologically scarred forever."[70]

The Navajo Nation along with twelve other tribes sued the Forest Service for its 2005 decision permitting the Snowbowl Ski Area to upgrade its existing facilities and utilize treated sewage effluent for snowmaking.[71] *Navajo Nation et al. v. U.S. Forest Service et al.* (January 2006) is the most recent case testing the Religious Freedom and Restoration Act (RFRA).[72] The 1993 RFRA affirms the language and intent of the American Indian Religious Freedom Act to recognize the inherent right of Native peoples as a group to believe, express, and exercise their religious beliefs and declares it the policy of the United States to protect that right.[73] The RFRA further mandates that the federal government shall not "substantially burden" a person's exercise of religion unless that burden is in the "compelling interest" of the government.

For tribal governments, the legal fight to save Dook'o'oosłííd from desecration evolved into an argument over the definition of *substantial burden*. Tribal attorneys argued that the purity of the water and the soil on the peaks would be compromised by the use of recycled sewage and would, therefore, put a substantial burden on the ability of tribal members to practice their traditional faith.[74] The US District Court judge rejected arguments from the tribes that upgrading existing facilities and dispersing snow made with reclaimed water within the Snowbowl Ski Area present a substantial burden to thirteen Native nations considering the mountains sacred. After a three-member panel of the Ninth Circuit Court of Appeals reversed the lower court's decision and sided with the tribes, the court later reheard the case and, in an eight to three vote, finally rejected the tribal RFRA claim.[75] The court concluded that the Forest Service decision to permit the use of treated effluent does not require Native peoples to act contrary to their religious beliefs.[76]

The Navajo Nation petitioned the US Supreme Court to review the Ninth Circuit ruling. In June 2009, the Supreme Court officially declined to hear the case.[77] This decision leaves the Ninth Circuit's interpretation of substantial burden in place and marks the end of the intertribal, four-year struggle to protect the mountain with a religious freedom argument. This standing judicial interpretation of substantial burden also serves as another example of incommensurability and interest convergence in US law. A dominant Western institution interpreted the concept of substantial burden in a manner that privileges economic and property values. Consequently, this decision impedes the fundamental human right of Native peoples to worship at a reverent natural place that is free of desecration. Snowbowl management remains focused on implementing planned improvements at the resort.[78] Additionally, in October 2009, the Navajo Nation Council voted to consider legislation that would allow the tribe to try to buy the Snowbowl.[79]

Preservation and protection of this nation's most important historic and cultural resources is at the core of the NHPA.[80] The NHPA "represents the cornerstone of federal historic and cultural preservation policy, and it is the most widely litigated federal statute in the area of cultural property law."[81] The National Register of Historic Places (NRHP), authorized by the NHPA, gives recognition to places meeting "historical significance" criteria in American history, architecture, archaeology, engineering, and culture. Places significant to indigenous peoples were not adequately recognized until 1992 when amendments to the act provided explicit recognition of traditional religious and cultural values and places important to American Indians, Alaska Natives, or Native Hawaiian organizations and stated that these may be eligible for National Register listing. For the first time, an indigenous TCP could be defined and evaluated for National Register eligibility against criteria that are inclusive of traditional cultural perspectives and priorities.[82] An important advantage of listing sacred sites on the National Register is that it honors the property and its significance as an indigenous spiritual place and signals the property's worthiness of protection for traditional cultural reasons.

Managers and scholars have raised questions about the effectiveness of listing an indigenous sacred place on the NRHP, designating it as a National Historic Landmark, or naming it to the Endangered Historic Places List, or other similar historic or heritage designation.[83] To illustrate, Mount Graham, or Dzil Nchaa Si An, is a sacred mountain to the Western Apache and is "eligible" for listing on the National Register. This mountain, home to sacred beings, is central to Apache religion and life.[84] Designating this TCP as eligible to the National Register is a positive administrative step toward recognizing the nature, extent, and importance of the mountain as a sacred place, but designation of a property does not guarantee its protection according to the expectations of Native people.

Although Mount Graham is eligible for listing on the National Register, the current land steward, the Forest Service, is considering permit renewal for continued operations of three existing telescopes within the University of Arizona's Mount Graham International Observatory (MGIO). As many as seven telescopes have been approved for construction within the MGIO.[85] According to the Western Apache, construction of the MGIO, and associated infrastructure, has profoundly desecrated Dzil Nchaa Si An and has elicited significant controversy among Apache traditional practitioners, the Forest Service, project proponents, and the local communities over Apache demands for telescope removal.[86] In the end, a National Register listing, or a positive eligibility determination for a sacred mountain like Dzil Nchaa Si An, does not, by itself, define a special protocol for sacred lands management, nor does it necessarily achieve the desired protection of the physical or spiritual integrity of the property. Site protection is a public-interest decision that is made at the discretion of the property manager. Finally, determining the significance of indigenous sacred lands within a Western process is incommensurate with Native values. Listing properties on the National Register follows a rigid bureaucratic process in which disclosure of sensitive traditional cultural information occurs to convince the US government, and the general public, of its significance and that a sacred place is sacred and worthy of preservation.

## RESOLVING INCOMPATIBLE IDEOLOGIES AND LANGUAGES

### *Traditional Navajo Values and Knowledge*

Meeting the legal requirement and moral imperative to protect the physical and spiritual integrity of sacred lands depends on traditional indigenous philosophies and bodies of knowledge. For the Navajo Nation, a sacred lands management policy, applied on and off the reservation, should be based on a combination of the principles of *hozho*, natural law, tribal law, and federal environmental and cultural resources protection law. *Hozho* is an abstract, complex, highly spiritual doctrine of Navajo philosophy and spiritual practice described as "perfection so far as it is attainable by man, the end toward which not only man but also supernaturals and time and motion, institutions, and behavior strive. Perhaps it is the utmost achievement of order."[87] This Navajo philosophy of harmony and natural beauty is intrinsic to how Navajo people treasure their land and is, therefore, intrinsic to sacred lands preservation. It is also the incentive and direction for all Navajos to work together. "Religious leaders need to be involved in creating a Navajo Nation sacred lands management policy. Sacred lands need to be foremost managed as sacred. They constitute a part of Navajo identity which is defined by language, land base and culture. This is the guiding philosophy for sacred lands treatment."[88]

A sacred lands management policy based on the doctrine of *hozho* may have important spiritual and practical benefits. Such a plan could be applied to all Navajo traditional territory, the Diné Bikeyah, which is inclusive of all sacred places located on reservation and nonreservation lands. A sacred lands policy based on the doctrine of *hozho* may resolve some of the incommensurable ideologies and languages embedded throughout federal environmental and cultural protection laws. With a central plan guiding local decision making across the Diné Bikeyah, sacred lands will be treated competently and consistently according to a vision based on tradition and to what constitutes compliance with all Navajo Nation and federal environmental and cultural protection laws. A sacred lands policy grounded in *hozho* may be an important means to assure that all Navajo people representing a wide spectrum of interests have the opportunity to express concerns and take part in decisions.

> A uniform policy would eliminate the influence of single individuals. The person with authority for decision-making at the time has tremendous influence over policy and individual site protection. This applies to tribal positions as well as federal positions. Individual people, philosophy, and policy all work together to influence sacred lands management.
>
> A uniform policy would also address the need to decide what is the role of economic development on sacred lands both on reservation and off. An internal disagreement among Navajo Nation citizens exists regarding alteration of a sacred place from a proposed action related to economic development. Some feel that sacred lands should never be altered for economic development regardless of who benefits (including Navajo communities).[89]

Some Navajo citizens expressed concerns over the absence of a commitment to the traditional philosophy of *hozho* in the treatment of sacred lands. Navajo people collectively need to decide what their commitment to sacred lands protection and tradition is going to be in relationship to decisions about proposing or permitting projects like communications towers, energy production, or tourism development. One Navajo citizen stated, "Sacred lands should be treated as sacred lands," because the consequences of not protecting sacred lands and conducting ceremonies extend far beyond noncompliance with tribal or federal environmental and cultural laws.[90]

The wisdom shared by Navajo elders is that complying with the law is not what the Navajo or anyone else should be worried about. Our collective concern should be about the health and survival of local communities practicing traditional subsistence off the land. Without proper understanding of, and respect for, the profound effects of landscape loss to traditional cultures and ways of life, federal management practices remain agents of adverse change in indigenous cultures. One Native scholar describes the most severe of these consequences as "environmental genocide."[91] The elders clarified that beyond the well-being of the Navajo people, the larger issues are caring for the environment in order to ensure the survival of all humanity.

A sacred lands policy based on the doctrine of *hozho* may raise as many complex issues as it resolves because this would be an attempt to blend traditional sacred doctrine with secular US law. For example, because the doctrine of *hozho* can be characterized as an abstract, complex, highly spiritual, unconscious operation, then it is largely unavailable for precise explanation or codification.[92] It may be a challenge for Navajo Nation lawmakers to introduce concepts of true *hozho* into a secular policy that also incorporates Western concepts of property law and science. Additionally, lawmakers may be challenged to blend *hozho* with the doctrines and sacred beliefs of other cultures, including other Native cultures. For example, the Hopi tribe would vigorously seek to have their doctrines and beliefs considered in the management of their traditional cultural places that are under Navajo or federal jurisdiction. Finally, the doctrine of *hozho* is a spiritual paradigm in which to manage cultural property that, for some communities, may be a source of economic development and heritage tourism. Native communities and individuals may have to debate the compatibility of spiritual and economic paradigms for sacred lands management.

## INNOVATIVE STRATEGIES FOR SACRED LANDS MANAGEMENT

Traditional indigenous philosophies and bodies of knowledge are essential to meet the legal requirement and moral imperative to protect the physical and spiritual integrity of sacred lands. A culture's vitality is dependent on individuals living in community with the natural world. The land's features, and the sense of place and kinship they create, are central to the identity of a Native individual and a people. Sacred lands' loss, desecration, or neglect can result in spiritual, practical, cultural, and political risk to Native peoples.[93] Eroded sacred lands diminish the spiritual practices that are central to religious belief systems, personal and cultural identity, and human survival. One Navajo elder pointed to contamination of ground water and plant communities on Dook'o'oosłíid as a practical example of potential adverse effect to the health and survival of local communities living directly off the land. Environmental and human rights are at risk for all Native nations because the Forest Service and the Ninth Circuit Court of Appeals have forced the Navajo Nation into a compelling, but very risky, decision to argue their position on the Snowbowl Ski Area expansion proposal to an, historically, unsympathetic Supreme Court. Now the Navajo Nation is forced to contemplate using limited economic resources to attempt to purchase the ski area in order to protect not only the mountain but also their faith, culture, and sovereignty.

In the United States, a complex environmental and cultural legislative and regulatory framework governs indigenous sacred places that are in federal stewardship. Unfortunately, this legal architecture, intended to protect sacred lands, ultimately conflicts with traditional indigenous values relative to land and religious practice, privileges the values of the dominant society, erodes tribal identity and sovereignty, and leaves sacred lands vulnerable to desecration or destruction. An examination of the ideologies and languages in US environmental and cultural protection laws demonstrates sacred lands management is another arena of tribal rights and environmental justice in which the critical theory concepts of incommensurability and interest convergence are operative. Effective strategies for sacred lands protection and access are those that identify and reflect on incompatible and hegemonic ideologies and languages in the law and in practice and then take action to transform them. The examples of terms and concepts I discuss in this article, codifying a definition of *sacred land*, defining and measuring *social impact* and *mitigation*, delineating discrete boundaries for sacred landscapes, determining historical significance, and defining *substantial burden* on the free exercise of religion, do not form an exhaustive list. They comprise a small sample of unambiguous demonstrations of how the law privileges Western values of science and property rights over indigenous spiritual values in the treatment of sacred lands and fails to balance the inequity by imposing procedures largely giving the appearance of equality rather than actual equality.

For Native peoples, just complying with existing environmental and cultural laws does not alone result in meaningful and effective sacred lands protection and access. Meeting the legal requirement and moral imperative to protect the physical and spiritual integrity of sacred lands depends on a commitment to traditional indigenous philosophies and bodies of knowledge. Resolving the problem of incompatible ideologies and languages in sacred lands protection law and practice may include integrating traditional indigenous worldviews directly into federal and tribal law. For the Navajo Nation, a uniform sacred lands management policy could be based on a combination of the principles of *hozho*, natural law, tribal law, and federal environmental and cultural resources protection law.[94]

Discussions about the Navajo Nation revealed that directly integrating the sacred ideologies and languages of Native tradition into secular law may result in important spiritual and practical benefits, as well as present its own unique suite of complex issues.[95] It may be a challenge for Navajo Nation lawmakers to introduce concepts of true *hozho* into a secular policy that also incorporates Western concepts of property law and science. Additionally, lawmakers may be challenged to blend *hozho* with the doctrines and sacred beliefs of other cultures, including other Native cultures. Finally, the doctrine of *hozho* is a spiritual paradigm in which to manage cultural property that, for some communities, may be a source of economic development and heritage tourism.

Regardless of these issues, directly integrating traditional ideology into sacred lands protection laws is a significant step in developing innovative strategies for sacred lands management. Also important, effective sacred lands protection depends on cultivating a willingness among federal lawmakers, land managers, project proponents, and stakeholders to commit to honoring traditional values and working with Native governments and traditional practitioners in order to identify and change incommensurate and hegemonic ideologies and languages prior to drafting new legislation or implementing negotiations or environmental evaluations mandated in existing US law.[96] Although not impossible, this will be a formidable challenge because the larger social and political context involves convincing those with the power to share it.

## NOTES

Reprinted with permission from Sharon Milholland, *American Indian Culture and Research Journal* 34:2 (2010): 103–124.

1. Derek C. Haskew, "Federal Consultation with Indian Tribes: The Foundation of Enlightened Policy Decisions, or Another Badge of Shame?" *American Indian Law Review* 24, no. 1 (1999–2000): 21–74; Jack Trope and Dean Suagee, "Consultation Protocols for Protecting Native American Sacred Places, Preliminary Draft, 10/28/03." Paper presented at the Summit on Consultation Protocols for Protecting Native American Sacred Places, 2003 November 14–16, Santa Fe, NM; Kyme McGaw and Rob Roy Smith, "Rethinking Sacred Sites Consultation: Achieving Meaningful Tribal/Federal Relations." Paper presented at the Summit on Consultation Protocols for Protecting Native American Sacred Places, 2003 November 14–16, Santa Fe, NM; Richmond Clowe and Imre Sutton, "Prologue," in *Trusteeship in Change: Toward Tribal Autonomy in Resource Management*, ed. Richmond L. Clowe and Imre Sutton (Boulder: University Press of Colorado, 2001), xxi; Shirley Powell and Sharon Hatch, "The Falls Creek Archaeological Area and Contemporary Native Americans: Background, Consultations, and Recommendations." Special report prepared for the US Department of Agriculture Forest Service (hereinafter referred to as USDA FS), San Juan National Forest, Durango, CO, September 1999.

2. National Congress of American Indians (hereinafter referred to as NCAI), "Essential Elements of Public Policy to Protect Native Sacred Places," Resolution #SD-02-027. Adopted at the Annual Session of the NCAI, San Diego, CA, 2002.

3. Christopher Vecsey, ed., *Handbook of American Indian Religious Freedom* (Chestnut Ridge, NY: Crossroad Publishing, 1991); Erica-Irene Daes, *Protection of the Heritage of Indigenous People* (New York: United Nations, 1997); Frank Occhipinti, "The Enola Hill Controversy: Deconstructing an American Indian Sacred Site" (PhD diss., University of Colorado, 2000); Imre Sutton, "Indian Cultural, Historical, and Sacred Resources: How Tribes, Trustees, and the Citizenry Have Invoked Conservation," in Clowe and Sutton, eds., *Trusteeship in Change*, 165; Jill Oakes et al., ed. *Sacred Lands: Aboriginal World Views, Claims, and Conflicts* (Edmonton, AB: Canadian Circumpolar Institute Press, 1998); Vine Deloria Jr., *God Is Red* (Golden, CO: Fulcrum Publishing, 1994), 271.

4. Christopher Quinn, "Mounds of Controversy: Is Sacred Tribal Land in the Path of Progress?" *Atlanta Journal-Constitution*, 14 April 2002; Heather S. Duncan, "Sites of Ancient Culture in Macon Ga., Could Be Destroyed in Firm's Expansion," *Macon Telegraph*, 5 November 2003; US Department of the Interior, National Park Service (hereinafter referred to as DOI NPS), "Ocmulgee National Monument" (US National Park Service), http://www.nps.gov/ocmu/historyculture/index.html (accessed 20 May 2009).

5. Brian Hansen, "Nuclear Waste," *CQ Researcher* 11 (June 2001): 489–504; U.S. Department of Energy, Office of Civilian Radioactive Waste Management, *Recommendation by the Secretary of Energy Regarding the Suitability of the Yucca Mountain Site for a Repository Under the Nuclear Waste Policy Act of 1982* (February 2002), 6, http://www .ocrwm.doe.gov (accessed 12 June 2009); Geoffrey Fattah and Suzanne Struglinski, "Pressure Used to Stop Nuclear Dump, Lawsuit Says," *Deseret Morning News*, 19 July 2007.

6. Courtney Ann Coyle, "Coyle: Defending Quechan Indian Pass—Again," *Indian Country Today*, 10 September 2008, http://www.indiancountry.com (accessed 27 January 2010); Larry Hogue, "Victory for Indian Pass," DesertBlog: News and Views from the Desert Protective Council, comment posted 10 June 2009, http://www .dpcinc.org/blog (accessed 27 January 2010).

7. Office of Mauna Kea Management, "Mauna Kea Comprehensive Management Plan: Fact Sheet," 2 May 2008, http://www.MaunaKeaCMP.com (accessed 14 March 2009).

8. Erica Bolstad, "Committee Votes Against Directional Drilling in ANWR," *Anchorage Daily News*, 29 June 2009; Sarah James, "We Are the Caribou People," *Earth Island Journal* 17, no. 2 (Summer 2002): 48; Zachary Coile, "The Last Refuge: Caribou Migration, Drilling Plan Symbolic of Battle between Oil and Environment," *San Francisco Chronicle*, 28 August 2005.

9. Robert A. Hershey, e-mail message to author, 27 March 2009.

10. David Suzuki and Peter Knudtson, *Wisdom of the Elders: Sacred Native Stories of Nature* (New York: Bantam Books, 1992), 156; Wilson Aronilth Jr., *Diné Bi Bee Óhoo'aah Bá Silá: An Introduction to Navajo Philosophy* (Tsaile, AZ: Navajo Community College, 1994). Aronilth applies the more comprehensive term Sa'ah Naagháí Bik'eh Hozhóón, 14.

11. Deloria, *God Is Red*, 279.

12. Gregory Cajete, *Native Science, Natural Laws of Interdependence* (Santa Fe, NM: Clear Light Publishers, 2000), 94.

13. Steven Field and Keith H. Basso, eds., *Senses of Place* (Santa Fe, NM: School of American Research Press, 1996).

14. Robert S. McPherson, *Sacred Land, Sacred View: Navajo Perceptions of the Four Corners Region* (Salt Lake City, UT: Brigham Young University, 1992), 11.

15. Cajete, *Native Science*, 211.

16. Klara Bonsack Kelley and Harris Francis, *Navajo Sacred Places* (Bloomington: Indiana University Press, 1994), 38–40.

17. Peggy V. Beck et al., *The Sacred: Ways of Knowledge, Sources of Life* (Tsaile, AZ: Dine College Press, 2001), 70.

18. Kelley and Francis, *Navajo Sacred Places*, 40.

19. McPherson, *Sacred Land, Sacred View*, 17.

20. James Riding In, "Spiritual Genocide: The Snowbowl Case." Paper presented at the Seventh Annual Conference of the American Indian Studies Consortium, Arizona State University, Phoenix, 15 February 2006; "The Snowbowl Effect, When Recreation and Culture Collide," DVD, directed by Klee Benally (Flagstaff, AZ: Indigenous Action Media, 2005).

21. Kelley and Francis, *Navajo Sacred Places*, 170.

22. Wilson Aronilth Jr., *Foundation of Navajo Culture* (Tsaile, AZ: Navajo Community College, 1991), 31.

23. *American Antiquities Act*, Public Law 59–209, June 1906 (34 Stat. 225, 16 U.S.C. 431–433); *National Historic Preservation Act*, Public Law 89-665, 15 October 1966 (16 U.S.C. 470 et seq.); *Archaeological Resources Protection Act*, Public Law 96-95, 31 October 1979 (16 U.S.C. 470aa–mm).

24. Jack F. Trope and Walter R. Echo-Hawk, "The Native American Graves Protection and Repatriation Act Background and Legislative History," in *Repatriation Reader: Who Owns American Indian Remains*, ed. Devon Mihesuah (Lincoln: University of Nebraska Press, 2000), 129.

25. Angela Riley, "Indian Remains, Human Rights: Reconsidering Entitlement under the Native American Graves Protection and Repatriation Act," *Columbia Human Rights Law Review* 34 (2002): 49–94; John W. Ragsdale Jr., "Some Philosophical, Political and Legal Implications of American Archaeological and Anthropological Theory," *University of Missouri at Kansas City Law Review* 70 (2001): 1.

26. Bill Ashcroft et al., *Key Concepts in Post Colonial Studies* (London: Routledge, 1998); Colin Perrin, "Approaching Anxiety: The Insistence of the Postcolonial in the Declaration on the Rights of Indigenous Peoples," in *Laws of the Postcolonial*, ed. Eve Darian-Smith and Peter Fitzpatrick (Ann Arbor: University of Michigan Press, 1999), 19–37; Edward Said, *Orientalism* (New York: Vintage, 1978); Frantz Fanon, *The Wretched of the Earth* (New York: Grove, 1968); John McLeod, *Beginning Post-Colonialism* (Manchester, UK: Manchester University Press, 2000); Patrick Williams and Laura Chrisman, *Colonial Discourse and Post-Colonial Theory: A Reader* (New York: Columbia University

Press, 1994). Derrick A. Bell Jr., *Faces at the Bottom of the Well: The Permanence of Racism* (New York: Basic Books, 1992); Kimberle Crenshaw et al., *Critical Race Theory: The Key Writings That Formed the Movement* (New York: The New Press, 1995); Richard Delgado and Jean Stefancic, *Critical Race Theory: The Cutting Edge* (Philadelphia: Temple University Press, 2000); Richard Delgado and Jean Stefancic, *Critical Race Theory: An Introduction* (New York: New York University Press, 2001); Robert A. Williams Jr., "Vampires Anonymous and Critical Race Practice," *Michigan Law Review* 95 (1997): 741.

27. Said, *Orientalism*; Fanon, *The Wretched of the Earth*.

28. Ania Loomba, *Colonialism/Postcolonialism: The New Critical Idiom* (New York: Routledge, 1998).

29. Peter Fitzpatrick, "Passions Out of Place: Law, Incommensurability and Resistance," in Darian-Smith and Fitzpatrick, eds., *Laws of the Post-Colonial*, 39–55.

30. Bryan A. Garner and Henry Campbell Black, *Black's Law Dictionary* (St. Paul, MN: West Group, 1999).

31. Crenshaw et al., *Critical Race Theory*, 103–22; Delgado and Stefancic, *Critical Race Theory*, 21–23.

32. John F. Dovidio and Samuel L. Gaertner, "Aversive Racism and Selection Decisions: 1989 and 1999," *Psychological Science* 11, no. 4 (July 2000): 315–19.

33. Ian F. Haney Lopez, "The Social Construction of Race," in Delgado and Stefancic, eds., *Critical Race Theory*, 168.

34. Delgado and Stefancic, *Critical Race Theory*, 9.

35. Ibid., 7.

36. Derrick A. Bell Jr., "*Brown v. Board of Education* and the Interest-Convergence Dilemma," *Harvard Law Review* 93 (1980): 518.

37. *Brown v. Board of Education*, 347 U.S. 483 (1954).

38. Andrew Gulliford, *Sacred Objects and Sacred Places* (Boulder: University of Colorado Press, 2000); Joseph Bruchac and Thomas Locker, *Between Earth and Sky: Legends of Native American Sacred Places* (San Diego, CA: Harcourt Brace Jovanovich, 1996); Keith H. Basso, *Wisdom Sits in Places* (Albuquerque: University of New Mexico Press, 1996).

39. Executive Order no. 13007: Indian Sacred Sites, sec. 1 (b) (iii), "Accommodation of Sacred Sites" (24 May 1996).

40. *Native American Sacred Lands Act of 2003*, HR 2419, 108th Cong., 1st sess. (11 June 2003).

41. Ibid., sec. 6, "Transfer of Land."

42. Ibid., sec. 7, "Cooperative Agreements."

43. Ibid., sec. 1, "Short Title; Definitions."

44. Suzan Shown Harjo, "American Indian Religious Freedom Act at 25," *Indian Country Today*, 1 August 2003, http://www.indiancountry.com (accessed 28 March 2008).

45. Deloria, *God Is Red*, 275–85.

46. Basso, *Wisdom Sits in Places*; Kelley and Francis, *Navajo Sacred Places*.

47. Cajete, *Native Science*; Beck et al., *The Sacred*; Deloria, *God Is Red*; Vine Deloria Jr., *The World We Used to Live In: Remembering the Powers of the Medicine Men* (Golden, CO: Fulcrum Publishing, 2006).

48. Beck et al., *The Sacred*, 6.

49. *National Environmental Policy Act of 1969*, Public Law 91-190, 42 *U.S. Code* 4321 and 4331-4335.

50. Interorganizational Committee on Guidelines and Principles for Social Impact Assessment, "Guidelines and Principles for Social Impact Assessment," *Environmental Impact Assessment Review* 15, no. 1 (1993): 11.

51. *National Historic Preservation Act*, Public Law 89-665, 15 October 1966 (16 *U.S. Code* 470 et seq.).

52. Interview by author with anonymous Navajo elder, 6 November 2007.

53. Raymond D. Austin, personal communication, 29 March 2008. Dr. Austin is adjunct assistant professor at James E. Rogers College of Law. He served on the Navajo Nation Supreme Court from 1985 to 2001.

54. Maureen Trudelle Schwartz, *Navajo Lifeways: Contemporary Issues, Ancient Knowledge* (Norman: University of Oklahoma Press, 2001); Beck et al., *The Sacred*, 76.

55. Aronilth Jr., *Diné Bi Bee Óhoo'aah Bá Silá*.

56. US Department of the Interior, Bureau of Land Management (hereinafter referred to as DOI BLM), *Record of Decision: Farmington Proposed Resource Management Plan and Final Environmental Impact Statement* (Farmington, NM: Farmington Field Office, 2003), 1.

57. Ibid., 9.

58. Meeting with anonymous Navajo Nation government staff, 11 October 2006.

59. DOI BLM, *Record of Decision.*

60. Ibid., 133.

61. "Directional Drilling," http://www.NaturalGas.org (accessed 27 January 2010).

62. US Environmental Protection Agency, *DRAFT Evaluation of Impacts to Underground Sources of Drinking Water by Hydraulic Fracturing of Coalbed Methane Reservoirs*, EPA 816-D-02-006 (August 2002).

63. US Council on Environmental Quality, *Code of Federal Regulations*, Title 40 sec. 1508.20, "Mitigation" (1 July 1998).

64. Suzan Shown-Harjo, "Gathering to Protect Native Sacred Places: Consensus Position on Essential Elements of Public Policy to Protect Native Sacred Places (Essential Elements and Objectionable Elements)," San Diego, CA, 8–9 November 2002. Report presented to the NCAI Subcommittee on Human, Religious, and Cultural Concerns, 12 November 2002, and to the NCAI Convention Session on Sacred Lands: Protecting Our Most Precious Resources, 13 November 2002; Tom King, *Places That Count: Traditional Cultural Properties in Cultural Resources Management* (Walnut Creek, CA: AltaMira Press, 2003), 193.

65. Interview with anonymous Navajo Nation government staff, 24 August 2007.

66. Sharon Milholland, "Native Voices and Native Values in Sacred Landscapes Management: Bridging the Indigenous Values Gap on Public Lands through Co-Management Policy" (PhD diss., University of Arizona, 2008), 178.

67. James Riding In, "Spiritual Genocide"; Benally, "The Snowbowl Effect."

68. Interview by author with anonymous Navajo elder, 6 November 2007.

69. Interview with anonymous Navajo Nation government staff, 24 August 2007.

70. Navajo Nation, Office of the President and Vice President, "Navajo Nation President Joe Shirley, Jr., Calls Proposed Arizona Snowbowl Development Violation of Navajos' Mother," news release, 3 November 2005.

71. USDA FS, *Record of Decision: Arizona Snowbowl Facilities Improvements Final EIS and Forest Plan Amendment #21* (Coconino County, AZ: Peaks Ranger District, Coconino National Forest, February 2005).

72. *Navajo Nation et al. v. U.S. Forest Service et al.*, WL 62565 (D. Ariz. 2006); *Religious Freedom Restoration Act*, Public Law 103-141, 42 *U.S. Code* 21 (1993).

73. *American Indian Religious Freedom Act*, Public Law 95-341, 95th Cong., 2d sess. (11 August 1978) and amendments, HR 4230, 103rd Cong., 2d sess. (8 August 1994).

74. Howard Fischer, "Snowmaking Wins Legal OK," Capitol Media Services, 9 June 2009, http://www.savethepeaks.org (accessed 27 October 2009).

75. *Navajo Nation et al. v. U.S. Forest Service et al.*, No. 06-15371, No. 01-15436, No. 06-15455 (9th Cir., 12 March 2007).

76. Fischer, "Snowmaking Wins Legal OK."

77. US Supreme Court Docket, Case No. 08-846 (8 June 2009).

78. Cindy Yurth, "High Court Refuses to Hear Dook'o'oosłííd Case," *Navajo Times*, 11 June 2009, http://www.navajotimes.com (accessed 27 October 2009).

79. Jason Begay and Noel Lyn Smith, "Navajo Nation Considers Purchasing Arizona Snowbowl," *Navajo Times*, 23 October 2009, http://www.navajotimes.com (accessed 27 October 2009).

80. *National Historic Preservation Act*; Public Law 89-665, 15 October 1966 (16 *U.S. Code* 470 et seq.).

81. Sherry Hutt et al., *Cultural Property Law: A Practitioner's Guide to the Management, Protection, and Preservation of Heritage Resources* (New York: John Wiley and Sons, 1999), 5.

82. DOI NPS, National Register, *Guidelines for Evaluating and Documenting Traditional Cultural Properties*, Bulletin 38 (Washington, DC: National Park Service, 1990).

83. Frank Occhipinti, "The Enola Hill Controversy: Deconstructing an American Indian Sacred Site" (PhD diss., University of Colorado, 2000); King, *Places That Count*, 213.

84. Resolution of the White Mountain Apache Tribe of the Fort Apache Indian Reservation, Resolution No. 07-99-153, adopted 15 July 1999.

85. *Arizona-Idaho Conservation Act*, Public Law No. 100-696, 102 Stat. 4571, 4597 (1988); USDA FS, *Term Special Use Permit (Draft)* granted to the Board of Regents, University of Arizona (Steward Observatory), Tucson (1988).

86. Resolution of the White Mountain Apache Tribe of the Fort Apache Indian Reservation, Resolution No. 12-2003-296, adopted 17 December 2003. Elizabeth A. Brandt, "The Fight for Dzil Nchaa Si An, Mt. Graham: Apaches and Astrophysical Development in Arizona," *Cultural Survival Quarterly* 19, no. 4 (1996): 50–57; John Welch, "White Eyes Lies and the Battle for Dzil Nchaa Si An," *American Indian Quarterly* 21, no. 1 (1997): 75–109; Robert A. Williams Jr., "Large Binocular Telescopes, Red Squirrel Piñatas, and Apache Sacred Mountains: Decolonizing Environmental Law in a Multicultural World," *West Virginia Law Review* 96 (1994): 1133.

87. Gladys Reichard, *Navajo Religion: A Study of Symbolism* (1950; repr., Princeton, NJ: Princeton University Press, 1977), 45.

88. Interview with Navajo Nation government staff, 24 August 2007.

89. Ibid.

90. Ibid.

91. Manny Pino, "Assaulting Mother Earth: Natural Resource Development and Sacred Site Protection." Paper presented at the Seventh Annual Conference of the American Indian Studies Consortium, Arizona State University, Phoenix, 15 February 2006.

92. Raymond D. Austin, "Navajo Courts and Navajo Common Law" (PhD diss., University of Arizona, 2007), 81–84.

93. Deloria, *God Is Red*, 284.

94. Milholland, "Native Voices and Native Values in Sacred Landscapes Management," 192.

95. Austin, "Navajo Courts and Navajo Common Law," 81–84.

96. Hershey e-mail.

# III.

# GENDER AND SEXUALITY

# TOWARD A MARIPOSA CONSCIOUSNESS

## Reimagining Queer Chicano and Latino Identities

DANIEL ENRIQUE PÉREZ

Butterfly iconography is ubiquitous in cultural production and serves many purposes. In this essay I explore how it has been appropriated by some artists and writers to reimagine queer Chicano and Latino identities in innovative ways. I begin by laying the foundation for what I call *mariposa theory*, a theoretical framework drawing on postcolonial theory, queer theory, an examination of butterfly imagery in ancient and contemporary cultural texts, and the reappropriation and resignification of the term *mariposa*. Several artists and writers have used butterfly imagery to represent Chicana/o and Latina/o identities in cultural production. Their works have provided a means for the mariposa subject to develop a *mariposa consciousness*—a decolonial site that is grounded in an awareness of the social location, social relations, and history of the mariposa subject.

Gloria Anzaldúa (1987) theorized mestiza consciousness from a multidisciplinary and mixed-genre approach, and by taking a similar approach to this essay I hope to fuse the various perspectives into an overarching argument. I intentionally employ the first-person point of view at key junctures because I identify as a mariposa, and approaching the topic from a mariposa standpoint is integral to the nature of this essay as a *marifesto* (mariposa manifesto).[1] The essay builds on a body of work that emerged from my collaboration with other mariposas. A number of poems that were inspired by and written for this research project appear at the end of various sections; they are my own.

Daniel Enrique Pérez is a fierce mariposa warrior and a Jotería studies scholar. His books include: *Rethinking Chicana/o and Latina/o Popular Culture* (2009), an edited collection of plays titled *Latina/o Heritage on Stage: Dramatizing Heroes and Legends* (2015), and a collection of poems titled *Things You See in the Dark* (2018). He was born in Texas to a migrant farmworking family and raised in the onion fields outside of Phoenix, Arizona. He obtained his PhD from Arizona State University. He is the director of the Core Humanities program and professor of Chicanx and Latinx studies at the University of Nevada, Reno.

## MARIPOSAS IN THE BORDERLANDS

Links between human beings and animals have been forged throughout history and across cultures. The relationship between the two is represented in a wide array of cultural texts, from ancient pictorial narratives to contemporary written or visual texts, and animals have often served as metaphors for human beings and human behavior. Animals are also frequently employed as semiotic devices to signify human sexuality or genitalia, as well as to delineate gender variances. In "Queer Ducks, Puerto Rican Patos, and Jewish-American *Feygelekh*: Birds and the Cultural Representation of Homosexuality," Lawrence La Fountain-Stokes focuses on bird metaphors associated with queer gender and sexuality in Puerto Rican and other cultures: *pato/a*, *pájaro/a*, and *feygele*. He argues that these terms have historically been used in pejorative contexts to describe effeminate and homosexual males; he also demonstrates how they are often reappropriated and transformed by the subjects they were intended to marginalize (2007, 194). With respect to *pato/a*, *pájaro/a*, *mariposa*, and *mariquita*—all terms historically used as epithets to describe queer males in several Hispanic cultures—he identifies an important link with similar terms in other languages and cultures: "all of these animal words refer to insects or birds that have wings and fly, associating their use to terms in other languages such as *fairy* in English and *feygele* in Yiddish" (200).

Here, I will focus on the term *mariposa*, which is commonly used to describe Hispanic males who engage in non-heteronormative gender and sexual behavior, with an emphasis on attributes typically associated with femininity. I am especially interested in examining the way butterfly imagery is employed and reappropriated as a metaphor for non-heteronormative gender and sexuality. Such uses contest the traditional use of the term *mariposa* as an epithet and help construct alternative modes of seeing gender and sexuality. In "The Latin Phallus," Ilan Stavans includes *mariposa* in a lengthy list of terms that have historically been used to stigmatize gay men in the Hispanic world and points out that gay men were typically considered "oversensitive, vulnerable, unproved in the art of daily survival" (1996, 155). Moreover, early depictions of gay Chicanos in literature were largely negative or peripheral. According to Karl J. Reinhardt, such representations can be placed into one of three categories: (a) incidental gay characters not pertinent to the plot who are presented derogatorily and who are virtually asexual, (b) gay characters somehow pertinent to the plot who commit unacceptable acts and suffer retribution, and (c) gay Chicano characters who do not participate in a Chicano space (1981, 47).

The use of the term *mariposa* to refer to men who have sex with men can be traced all the way back to sixteenth-century Spain. A Jesuit priest by the name of Pedro de León (1545–1632), who listened to the final confessions of men who were serving time in la Cárcel de Sevilla for committing acts of sodomy, associated these men with moths or butterflies because like the insect, they had an inexplicable attraction to fire. León claimed that the men who had sex with men repeatedly played with fire even though they knew they could be executed for doing so. In the following account recorded in 1592, he relates the story of a man who is executed for committing sodomy, as countless men have been in other cultures and eras:

The story of this constable—named Quesada—is that he had a guest house where he received young, good-looking men, and he managed to grope and caress some of their hands and faces, and others he managed to induce to commit the sins of the flesh. . . . He ended up in the fire, and as I typically say (and the day they executed him, I said it), those who don't straighten up and who run around committing sins are like moths [*mariposillas*] that are fluttering near the fire: and in one brush with the fire a little wing is burned, and in another encounter another piece, and in yet another encounter they are left burnt. That is why those who engage in these types of exchanges are left with their honor tinged and scorched, and, finally, they end up in the fire.[2] (León 1981, 480, my translation)

León's use of the term *mariposilla* is consonant with the other Spanish terms that have been used to describe men who commit same-sex acts or those deemed effeminate: *mariposa*, *marica*, and *maricón*. Besides their pejorative uses, what these terms have in common is their derivation, from María or La Virgen María. According to Federico Garza Carvajal, these terms were used as early as the fifteenth century to describe men who exhibit effeminate traits (2003, 68). *Marica* and *maricón* are defined as "hombre afeminado" in the *Diccionario crítico etimológico castellano e hispánico* (Corominas and Pascual 1980, 3: 852). The same etymological dictionary suggests that *mariposa* is derived from "la Santa María posa" (the Virgin Mary rests) or "María, pósate," which was most likely a line in a children's song (852). Besides meaning to sit still or rest, *posar* can mean to pose or lie down, and the familiar command form, *pósate*, is still used in some Spanish-speaking communities as a directive to lie in a position suitable for sexual intercourse. Thus the use of the term *mariposa* can be seen as an invitation to engage in an erotic act.

Matthew Rabuzzi (1997) suggests that the association between the term *mariposa* and "la Santa María posa" or "the Virgin Mary rests" is a reference to the deification of the soul and the Psyche legend. In ancient Greek, *psyche* meant butterfly, and also mind, breath, and soul. As Greek legend maintains, Psyche was a female mortal and was considered the most attractive person in Sicily. She remained a mortal until she married Cupid (aka Eros) and Zeus transformed her into a goddess. Thus, besides symbolizing an ultimate form of beauty, Psyche and butterflies came to represent transformation and the deification of the human soul.

Rabuzzi points out that the modern Greek word for butterfly is *petalouda*, which is related to the words for petal, leaf, wing, and spreading out. The Latin term, *papilio*, and the French, *papillon*, are the origins of the terms *pavilion* in English and *pabellón* in Spanish, historically used to describe a large tent with a decorative top that often resembled a butterfly. Today, *pavilion* and *pabellón* are still associated with beauty but describe a large, sheltered cultural space. One might imagine a pavilion as a large, beautiful butterfly providing shelter and a space in which to celebrate some of the most coveted traditions of many cultures.

Moths and butterflies have been used in many cultures throughout recorded history to represent a range of concepts: nature, beauty, balance, the human soul, deities, love, rebirth, and transformation. Although they may occasionally symbolize something negative—an omen, the souls of witches, or death, for example—they are overwhelmingly used in more positive contexts. In general, the butterfly symbolizes the beauty of nature and is typically associated with the feminine (Gagliardi 1997).

Chicana and Latina writers and artists have employed moth and butterfly imagery as powerful symbols of transformation, life, death, resilience, migration, and the soul. In Helena María Viramontes's "The Moths" (1985), the insects are a spiritual element of the story used to solidify the bond between the young protagonist and her dying Abuelita. When the grandmother passes away, the moths become a symbol of her soul and facilitate her journey to the other side. In Julia Alvarez's *In the Time of the Butterflies* (1994), Mariposa #1, Mariposa #2, and Mariposa #3 are the code names given to the Mirabal sisters when they join the 14th of June Movement in the Dominican Republic—a resistance movement dedicated to freeing the country from the Trujillo dictatorship. In Alma López's 2008 screen print, *El vals de las mariposas*, viceroy butterflies engage in the traditional quinceañera waltz along with La Sirena and her dance partner; besides emphasizing the quinceañera as a transformative period in a young lady's life, this underscores migratory and other traits associated with the viceroy butterfly.[3] The works of these and several other Chicana and Latina artists and writers are fruitful sites for exploring mariposa consciousness. However, in this essay I am interested in examining the way in which queer Chicano and Latino identities are reconfigured in cultural production using butterflies as metaphors, as well as the resignification and reappropriation of the term *mariposa* from a pejorative term associated with the nonnormative gender and sexual behavior of Hispanic males to a term of empowerment.

Butterfly imagery is also prevalent in Chicano and Latino cultural expression, especially among queer writers and artists. Such imagery is evoked repeatedly in the works of Rigoberto González, which I examine below, and in important queer Chicano and Latino collections like *Mariposas: A Modern Anthology of Queer Latino Poetry* (Xavier 2008); *Gay Latino Studies: A Critical Reader* (Hames-García and Martínez 2011); *From Macho to Mariposa: New Gay Latino Fiction* (Rice-González and Vázquez 2011); and *Queer in Aztlán: Chicano Male Recollections of Consciousness and Coming Out* (Güido and Del Castillo 2013). Artist Julio Salgado often incorporates butterfly iconography into his images of undocumented immigrants and undocuqueer individuals. In artist Héctor Silva's *José* (2009), the use of butterflies softens an otherwise rough-edged and hypermasculine homeboy. Artists Virgo Paraíso and Tino Rodríguez often incorporate them in their innovative works, which I also examine below.

I argue that the manner in which some artists and writers employ butterfly imagery in cultural production can create decolonial sites for the formation of a mariposa consciousness, which may vary according to gender, social location, sexuality, or other elements integral to subjectivity. Mariposa consciousness is not limited to any particular gender or sexual identity; various individuals can and do identify as mariposas. Instead, I see mariposa theory as a tool that can be appropriated to raise awareness of the social location, social relations, and history of the mariposa subject, which in turn can facilitate a mariposa consciousness. In other words, mariposa theory can provide the mariposa subject the epistemological and ontological tools to affirm an identity that is shaped by a unique heritage and positionality.

My focus on artists and writers who use butterfly imagery to affirm queer Chicano and Latino identities underscores the way queer Chicanos and Latinos are being reimagined in social locations that stand in direct opposition to the negative stereotypes that have historically maintained them at the margins of society. Although one will still find stereotypical and negative depictions in Hispanic cultural production today, the writers and artists I examine reconfigure queer Chicano and Latino identities by creating characters that do not fall into any of Reinhardt's three categories or possess the traits Stavans underscores. Instead, these writers and artists portray more complex, empowered, and positive queer Chicano and Latino identities by using the butterfly as a liberatory semiotic device. The mariposas they create are strong, fierce, and resilient while also embodying some of the traditional elements associated with butterflies: beauty and femininity, for example.

The act of reclaiming and resignifying a term that has historically been used to denigrate a group of people can function as a liberatory device in a variety of contexts, especially when appropriated by the subject the term was originally intended to marginalize. According to Gloria Anzaldúa, this process is directly related to the consciousness of the borderlands. For her, calling yourself mestiza/o or Chicana/o is a way to affirm your identity, become aware of a reality, and acquire a name and language that reflects that reality (1987, 63). Besides shaping a mestiza consciousness, Anzaldúa and other Chicana lesbian feminists have been instrumental in shaping Jotería consciousness, an awareness of the social locations, social relations, and histories of Jotería subjects, especially Chicana lesbians. Anzaldúa insisted that embracing all aspects of identity and developing a tolerance for contradictions and ambiguity was how the subject-object duality could be transcended (79). Cherríe Moraga envisioned a "queer Aztlán" (1993, 164), and Emma Pérez (1999) and Chela Sandoval (2000) theorized decolonial imaginaries and practices—and they are just some of the Chicana lesbians who have helped shape a Jotería consciousness.

Several Chicano and Latino writers and scholars have engaged in decolonizing projects that have also shaped Jotería consciousness, especially as it relates to gay Chicanos or Jotos. John Rechy's sexual outlaw trope and Michael Nava's renegade gay Chicano lawyer from his Henry Ríos mystery series have been instrumental in helping gay Chicano males overcome various forms of oppression—especially homophobia—while creating important links to their unique heritage. José Esteban Muñoz and Lawrence La Fountain-Stokes have also been influential in theorizing decolonial sites and practices. Muñoz suggests that disidentificatory processes can function as a means of making the disembodied whole (1999, 161). La Fountain-Stokes examines how some queer Latinos reappropriate the term *pato* as a term of empowerment and lays a foundation for *teoría pata*, which he suggests aligns with a "global project of liberation" (2007, 218).

By reimagining the way Jotería are represented in cultural texts, these and several other writers, scholars, and artists provide Jotería with an opportunity to learn about themselves and their unique heritage. I believe such works are instrumental in contributing to a Jotería consciousness in general while also addressing the needs and concerns of specific groups of Jotería: Chicana lesbians, gay Chicanos, and others. Similarly, I see mariposa consciousness as part of an ongoing decolonial project in which several writers, artists, and scholars have engaged to facilitate an awareness of the social locations, social relations, and history of the mariposa subject, with several parallels and links to mestiza consciousness and Jotería consciousness.

With respect to mestiza/o consciousness, Anzaldúa suggests that mestiza/os must know their history and embrace all aspects of their identities, as disparate as they may seem (1987, 62). Similarly, developing a mariposa consciousness requires that we know our history and embrace all elements of our identity, down to the core of our true selves. We must never allow ourselves to feel ashamed of who we are or of what we do naturally. We cannot deny what we are. We cannot reject or undervalue a single part of ourselves or one another. Because most people have been colonized by patriarchy, most have privileged masculinity and undervalued femininity; besides contributing to the oppression of women, this has led to the persecution of males who exhibit feminine traits, sometimes regardless of their age or sexual orientation. As a result, from a young age most mariposas are taught that certain behaviors are unacceptable and a deep-seated culture of shame, denial, and rejection is implanted. Homophobia and internalized homophobia have led to the destruction of countless mariposas, many of whom continue to take their own lives or have their lives taken from them in violent ways.

Like the black-white dichotomy, the masculine-feminine dichotomy is an ideological construct; these are terms that can be dismantled and redefined. Like racism and the privileging of whiteness, the invention and privileging of masculinity has real and dire consequences. Therefore, one must resist any acts—verbal, physical, or mental—that devalue the feminine or any acts of love and desire in which a person may engage. Love is valuable and legitimate in all its forms. Masculinity and femininity are not mutually exclusive; instead, they can be considered mutually constitutive. As several civilizations throughout recorded history have recognized, to maintain equilibrium all elements of nature must coexist: the yin and the yang, or the sun and the moon, for example. Having a mariposa consciousness is about recognizing your outer and inner beauty and strength; it is about being yourself, in your true nature, in your own words, in all your *mariposada*—the full splendor of your beauty, strength, gender expression, and sexuality. It is about knowing your history and yourself fully, and embracing all aspects of your identity. It is about maintaining a physical and mental equilibrium so that you can soar in all your glory.

Toward a Mariposa Consciousness

Being a Mariposa means you're beautiful
and resilient that you soar
as you migrate
you have the strength
to survive
harsh conditions and the skills
to thrive with conditions just right

Being a Mariposa means you hold your head high
spread your wings and fly wherever
the winds
may take you
and when you
return home you are at home
naked and glorious in all your mariposada

## CONSTRUCTING FIERCE MARIPOSA WARRIORS: BUILDING A MARIPOSA NATION IN THE WORKS OF RIGOBERTO GONZÁLEZ

One of the most ubiquitous symbols in Rigoberto González's writing is the butterfly, and I contend that it functions to position queer Chicanos and Latinos in unique and innovative social locations that allow for the materialization of a mariposa consciousness. Besides serving as a metaphor for queer Chicano and Latino males, butterfly imagery is used to construct characters that share common traits: they suffer acts of retribution for being visibly queer, they remain resilient in harsh, foreign, and homophobic environments, they are beautiful in their own nature, and they undergo significant transformations.

González's memoir *Butterfly Boy: Memories of a Chicano Mariposa* (2006) begins with "butterfly kisses"—hickeys given to a young and sometimes naïve González by his lover, a man more than twice his age who has learned how to control him through emotional and physical abuse. The lover has managed to convince González that love is supposed to be painful, and the "butterfly kisses" are one way of making his point clear. However, butterflies also remind González of his childhood in Michoacán, Mexico, the final destination of the monarch butterfly as it migrates in search of a more hospitable climate.

The monarch (*Danaus plexippus*) is one of the largest and most recognized butterflies of North America. Monarchs feed on milkweed, which makes them poisonous to their predators. The bright orange on their wings warns predators of their toxicity.[4] The Aztecs believed that monarchs were the incarnation of fallen warriors and that the colors on their wings were emblematic of the battles the warriors had fought.[5] Many consider the monarch to be the most beautiful of butterflies; besides its beauty, it is known for its resilience and lengthy migrations.

Like the monarch, González bears the emotional and psychological scars of the many battles he has managed to survive: extreme poverty, difficult migrations, abandonment by his father, the death of his mother when he was only twelve, the teasing he suffered for being an effeminate and overweight child, the physical abuse he has experienced throughout his life, and the many dysfunctional relationships he has. All these traumas mark him as a warrior about to embark on a migration that takes him to a past he is unable to escape. He flees one battlefield only to find himself in another, where he must relive painful memories and interact with people who cannot show affection for him in the way he desires.

Nevertheless, one of the salient aspects of González's memoir is his ability not only to survive but to overcome the oppression he experiences from multiple sources, especially poverty, patriarchy, and homophobia. As painful as his experiences are, he remains resilient and constantly ventures into unfamiliar territory. I posit that many of his characters, like González himself in his memoir, share traits that closely align them with butterflies. Their feminine features are often lauded and deemed beautiful; although the threat of death may loom, they are resilient and survive harsh conditions; they migrate in patterns similar to that of the monarch butterfly; and they typically undergo a personal transformation that allows them to transform their own families and communities in positive ways—often tackling patriarchy and homophobia. Moreover, his use of butterfly imagery resonates with the myriad uses of such imagery in ancient Mexican cultural texts. It also contests the negative uses of the term *mariposa* to signify queer Chicano and Latino males as passive, vulnerable, oversensitive, and tragic figures.

Like the serpent, the butterfly appears on many ancient Mexican cultural artifacts. The insects were studied carefully by indigenous people in ancient Mexican civilizations and were important components of indigenous poetry, music, art, and religion. As anthropologist Carlos R. Beutelspacher reveals in his excellent study *Las mariposas entre los antiguos mexicanos,* for ancient Mexicans butterflies represented fire, souls, travelers, warriors, and death (1988, 12).[6] Many people still believe that they hold valuable answers to philosophical questions about life and death, and they remain integral to the cultural expression and spiritual beliefs of several cultures today.

As Beutelspacher points out, if one looks closely at the Aztec calendar, butterflies appear on the outer ring as the flaming tongues of fire serpents (1988, 75). Also included on the Aztec calendar is Cozcacuauhtli, a vulture used to represent day-sign number 16. Cozcacuauhtli is associated with wisdom, longevity, and mental equilibrium. The day itself was believed to be a good day to confront the challenges one suffers in life. This particular day is protected by the warrior goddess Itzpapálotl, who is also known as the obsidian butterfly or the clawed butterfly. Among her many attributes, Itzpapálotl was a great hunter, warrior, and traveler; she was also a representation of Venus and had the ability to transform herself into a beautiful woman in order to seduce men. Her name derives from the combination of *itz* and *papálotl*; *itz* is the Náhuatl prefix for "go toward" or "come" (Launey 2011, 281) and *papálotl* means "butterfly" (Bierhorst 1985, 260). Therefore, her name means to "go toward" or "come to the butterfly." Today, *papalote* is used in Mexico and other Spanish-speaking cultures to signify a kite; it is derived from the Náhuatl for butterfly.

In the Codex Magliabechiano (c. 1528–53) one will find a pictorial glossary of the cosmological and religious symbols venerated by the Aztecs; among them is the "manta de may posa" (Nuttall 1903, 10). Art historian Elizabeth Hill Boone identifies this figure as the "mantle [or cloak] of the butterfly" (1983, 174). The codex contains illustrations and short annotations of forty-five ritual cloaks that were worn in religious ceremonies. Other butterfly-like symbols include the "manta de agua de araña," which appears to be four interlocking insects resembling butterflies (Nuttall 1903, 5).[7] The *manta de agua de araña* is today more commonly referred to as the *hunab ku,* or the galactic butterfly.[8]

I posit that González's use of butterfly imagery resonates with several of the etymological and epistemological traits associated with the term *mariposa*. Consider the image on the cover of *Butterfly Boy*, which is a photograph by Luis González Palma titled *La coraza* (1993). The image of a young mestizo male dressed in armor with wings attached to his back is emblematic of the way González reconfigures the mariposa subject as strong and resilient; it also resonates with the epistemology of the term *mariposa* as the boy assumes a Virgin Mary–like pose. In his memoir, González claims the term *mariposa* as an integral part of his identity and as his favorite term among those used to refer to queer males: "In México the homosexual has many names: joto, puto, marica, maricón, margarita, and my favorite, *mariposa*, butterfly, an allusion to the feminine fluttering of eyelashes" (2006, 184). González proudly identifies himself as a mariposa, and the "fluttering of eyelashes" he describes can be seen as a visible marker of mariposa identity, a way to highlight feminine features in men as beautiful and also as an act of resistance. The use of the mariposa as a metaphor for the beauty and strength of heroic queer Chicano males is a common thread in González's work.

González's mariposas are often Chicano males who have been persecuted for being effeminate, but they are also fierce warriors who do not fear the varied social locations they inhabit; they are deemed beautiful in their own skin, and they remain resilient. His collection of stories, *Men without Bliss* (2008), is a good example. The figure on the cover of this book is emblematic of the queer males one will find in the collection. The image, *¿Qué culpa tengo de ser tan guapo?* (2006) by artist Artemio Rodríguez, is a queer Chicano male adorned with feminine attributes. His eyelashes are pronounced and evoke the "fluttering of eyelashes" in González's memoir; he is associated with beauty and nature; he embodies both the sun and the moon; and he is in a Virgin Mary pose, which portrays mariposas as saintly in and of themselves. The aura around his head is emphasized, indicating *sabiduría* (wisdom) and consciousness, the knowledge and awareness of his self-worth and social location.

Although the characters in *Men without Bliss* live gloomy lives, there is typically a ray of hope that they too will survive despite living in conditions that are unfavorable to queer males. Abi, in the story "Plums," is a good example: he is a young man who manages to create a space in a cheap motel to be himself in all his *mariposada*. Because he has no privacy at home, he rents a room at the local Palm Tree Motel in Caliente Valley, California. Besides pampering himself and tending to his personal needs, he attempts to meet a lover, Gilberto, a married man who can offer Abi little more than a brief erotic encounter. However, Gilberto does not show up and Abi is left alone, burning with desire. Abi would be considered a tragic figure were it not for Tony-Raúl, the front desk clerk who works the night shift at the hotel and is interested in Abi. Tony-Raúl, it turns out, sabotaged Abi's rendezvous with Gilberto because he wanted Abi for himself. Although their relationship starts off haphazardly, the last few lines of the story give us a remnant of hope that Abi will find more than just empty sex to comfort him in this unforgiving town: "When the music starts playing, Abi rests his head against the tattooed cushion of Tony-R's shoulder, and breathes in the musk of a cologne that probably didn't cost very much, but for Abi, it's quite valuable and deliciously real" (González 2008, 57).

I consider González's *The Mariposa Club* (2009) to be a sort of how-to manual for young queer Chicanos. Using an engaging narrative, González teaches young queer Chicano males how to organize to overcome poverty, patriarchy, and homophobia. These themes can also be found in *The Mariposa Gown* (2011) and will surely play a role in what is slated to be the last novel in the series, *Mariposa U* (2014). These three young-adult novels make up the first series targeting this specific group. González is undoubtedly invested in empowering young queer Chicano males. He clearly does not want others to experience the painful childhood he had. Like the monarch butterfly, he is in essence returning to his home, the Coachella Valley, in order to transform it after he himself has undergone significant transformations: first, through his educational achievements and, now, through his professional development and writing (he is currently a professor of creative writing at Rutgers University in Newark, New Jersey). Notice that the majority of his works, like *The Mariposa Club*, are set in "Caliente Valley"—a variation on Coachella Valley, where González was raised. There are several other similarities between the characters in *The Mariposa Club* and the author himself. For example, like González, Maui/Mauricio, the narrator, loses his mother when he is only twelve, and Lib/Liberace shares many of the physical features and effeminate mannerisms González describes in his memoir. All four members of the "Fierce Foursome" are smart and have lots of potential. They take advanced courses like calculus, and although each faces individual challenges, they all have what it takes to graduate from high school and succeed in college. They are strong and "fierce"—the word González employs throughout the novel to describe these young mariposas.

The mission of the Mariposa Club, which the four youths organize, is to build alliances in order to combat homophobia and to create a space where other LGBTQ people can feel free and safe to be themselves. In the first novel, the antagonist, Tony Sánchez, is one of the greatest obstacles standing in their way. As a closeted queer Chicano, Tony suffers from internalized homophobia, which leads him to engage in an act of gay bashing after Trini tries to get him to join the club. It also eventually leads to his demise. The group recognizes Tony as one of their own, but he ultimately commits suicide by shooting himself after threatening to kill Lib and others for publicly recruiting members at the Holiday Village Arts & Crafts Fair. Tony's character demonstrates how dangerous and destructive homophobia can be to individuals and communities. After his death, Trini, Maui, and Lib hold a ceremony to posthumously induct Tony into the club—"the first official function of the Mariposa Club" (González 2009, 215). They claim Tony as one of their own fallen warriors and his death becomes a symbol of the birth of the club itself.

At the end of the novel, each member makes the official sign of the club, crossing his hands and placing them over his breasts with thumbs locked in place, fluttering his fingers wildly. Maui's closing words inform the reader that these mariposas are going to do just fine in life, transforming all the communities they may touch with their splendid wings: "We're butterflies alright, except we're still strengthening our wings inside the cocoon we call Caliente, the small mostly-Mexican town that still needs to grow up as well. But, like Papi says, it's *our* town. And after all that's happened, I'm more determined than ever to do some good here before I fly away" (216).

The way in which González highlights traits traditionally considered feminine in his characters and forges alliances between mariposas so that they can survive and thrive can be considered a nation-building, decolonial project, where the fluttering of eyelashes, the painting of nails, the lisps, and other effeminate traits are acts of resistance in the never-ending battle between mariposas and the homophobic patriarchal communities where they may reside. By juxtaposing seemingly disparate elements—"fierce" and "mariposa"—González links the mariposa subject to past and present struggles as a way of facilitating a mariposa consciousness and building a Mariposa Nation.

Those of us who have the privilege of living as visibly queer Chicanos and Latinos can do so thanks to our ancestral warriors, many of whom lost their lives in battle. They assisted in the construction of a Mariposa Nation where others could live freely and safely. Although we still face severe acts of condemnation and persecution, several of us proudly display our colorful wings and are bold enough to venture into inhospitable terrain because we know the value of our presence. With each flutter of our wings, we honor those who no longer fly among us.

Ode to Lorca

You are one                                        of millions of
Mariposa warriors
killed
so that I can live   and write freely

Verde          Verde
que te
quiero
Verde      Verde

Quiero verte                            en tu cuero
quiero                                  probar
el dulce infierno
me muero          me muero
por verte          Verde te quiero

## PORTRAITS OF FIERCE MARIPOSA WARRIORS: VISUALIZING A MARIPOSA NATION IN THE WORKS OF TINO RODRÍGUEZ

The work of visual artist Tino Rodríguez has captivated many. He often creates portraits that tell a unique story and that are simultaneously aesthetically pleasing and disturbing. Much as González juxtaposes love with pain and suffering, for Rodríguez beauty does not exist without pain and suffering. He also juxtaposes seemingly disparate elements to portray the true complexity of lived and imagined experiences, where all elements are synthesized. As he explains, "My work is my search for a spiritual philosophy that transcends simple duality . . . I want to continue creating a syncretic universe in which all is integrated, whether it be good or evil" (Rodríguez 2002, 234). Because Rodríguez's cosmology aligns with that of other queer Chicano and Latino artists and scholars, his portraits have been selected as cover art for several works. *Gay Latino Studies: A Critical Reader* (Hames-García and Martínez 2011) has Rodríguez's *La voz del poeta* (2005) on the cover; Francisco Alarcón's *From the Other Side of Night/Del otro lado de la noche* (2002) has *El amante* (1998); and Rigoberto González's *Autobiography of My Hungers* (2013) has *When You Hurt Me (I Won't Let It Show)* (1999). Moreover, Rodríguez occasionally collaborates with his partner Virgo Paraíso, an artist who also incorporates butterfly iconography in his works. In a 2012 San Francisco exhibition titled *Pagan Poetry: Tino Rodríguez and Virgo Paraíso*, the two debuted *Pagan Poetry* (2012), a piece they created together that is replete with bird and butterfly iconography. Although Paraíso's work is a rich site for conducting a similar analysis, for the purposes of this essay I will focus on Rodríguez.

The masterful way in which Rodríguez synthesizes what are typically viewed as disparate elements gives his portraits a synergy that evokes a visceral response. The

**Figure 1.** Tino Rodríguez, *Beauty Is Harsh*, 1996. Oil on wooden panel, 5 x 7 inches. © 1996 by Tino Rodríguez; reproduced by permission of the artist.

observer is often drawn to a work by the beauty of the subject or the array of flowers and winged creatures present in several of his scenes. However, a closer look will typically reveal wounds or dark images that disrupt a utopian narrative (fig. 1). The subject, often portrayed as a beautiful, mystical, and ambiguous being (fairylike, sometimes with both male and female genitalia, and often adorned with wings of some sort), may have a severed limb or wound gushing blood or may be decapitated. Flowers and winged

**Figure 2.** Tino Rodríguez, *Xochipilli's Ecstatic Universe*, 2004. Oil on wooden panel, 12 x 18 inches. © 2004 by Tino Rodríguez; reproduced by permission of the artist.

creatures emerge from the macabre scene. Despite the darkness in some of his works, beauty radiates from each portrait, overpowering evil and the repulsive. Icons evoking spring often emanate from the mouths of the subjects, suggesting inner beauty as the ultimate form of beauty; when it is made visible, it can triumph in the never-ending battle between good and evil. This technique also positions the subject as the giver of life and signifies transformation. The use of flowers and winged creatures evokes beauty, spring, and life; they offer the observer a sense of hope in an otherwise bleak scenario. Wings signify freedom and the ability to transcend a social location; they are integral to the courting rituals of several species; they also frequently serve as camouflage or as a means to escape predators. Wings may also be given to human-like subjects to mark them as divine messengers with special gifts that allow them to move between different worlds (Nagel 2009, 45). Moreover, as La Fountain-Stokes suggests, winged creatures—birds, butterflies, and fairies—have commonly been used to symbolize males who engage in nonnormative gender and sexual behavior (2007, 200).

Rodríguez uses flowers and winged creatures to assist him in telling unique stories. In one published interview, the artist underscores his desire to tell stories through his work: "I would like [observers] to have a conversation with the piece and get something good out of it. To be able to get a story that they have never heard before. Maybe they will get an image that they could never imagine could happen before" (Rodríguez 2005, 11). Rodríguez's pictorial narratives are sometimes a mixture of cultural and religious imagery. A good example is *Xochipilli's Ecstatic Universe* (2004) (fig. 2). As a tribute to "the prince of flowers" and patron god of beauty, art, music, and poetry, the scene is replete with flowers and winged creatures that are larger than some of the other iconic figures: the sculptures of Aztec deities, the Hindu temples and goddesses, the sphinx, and the ballet-dancing *calavera*. At the center is the artist himself as a sentient being fully aware of his history while giving birth to new life forms. These are depicted by the large bird emanating from his mouth and a cornucopia of elements related to spring; the artist himself springs from and is grounded in the earth as his head protrudes from the foliage in a flower-like fashion. By combining these elements, Rodríguez positions the subject at the center of a cosmic universe, fully conscious and seemingly omniscient. When asked about the inspiration for his pictorial narratives, he explains, "Basically I intertwine all those stories [I read] and a lot of [my] stuff comes from dreams . . . I would present the dream in a pictorial way to where it's not a dream anymore but a conscious perception of what the dream was about" (Rodríguez 2005, 11).

By imagining himself as Xochipilli, Rodríguez makes important links between the contemporary queer Chicano/Latino subject (Rodríguez is openly gay) and a lengthy history reaching back to ancient Mexican civilizations. Xochipilli is the patron god of dances, games, art, beauty, fertility, summer, and love; he is also associated and commonly depicted with flowers and butterflies. He is known as the "flower prince" or the "ghost warrior prince."[9] Xochipilli is also associated with erotic desire, sins of the flesh, licentiousness, and debauchery (Beutelspacher 1988, 32). Sociologist David F. Greenberg claims that Xochipilli was "the patron of male homosexuality and male prostitution" and was idolized by those who identified with him—especially trans individuals who were sex workers (1988, 165). He surmises that the Aztecs appropriated this god from Toltec civilization, which "had a reputation for sodomy" (165).

In the Codex Borgia (c. AD 1500), Xochipilli is often depicted with a white butterfly painted around his mouth or on his chin.[10] As a sun god, he is also often depicted in yellow and is considered a manifestation of Tonatiuh, the supreme sun god of Mesoamerica. According to anthropologist Susan Milbrath, "Xochipilli is specifically linked with flowers and butterflies, perhaps indicating that he is an aspect of the sun associated with the rainy season" (2013, 50). Moreover, he is considered the twin of Xochiquétzal, the Aztec goddess who was believed to have been a butterfly in her original form and who corresponds to the *Papilio multicaudata* species (the two-tailed swallowtail), which can still be found today from the western part of North America all the way to Central America. The large butterfly in the lower left-hand corner of Rodríguez's image closely resembles this species (see fig. 2). Xochiquétzal is the goddess of love and flowers (Bierhorst 1985, 395). According to Beutelspacher (1988, 41), she is also the goddess of the earth and vegetation, making her responsible for yielding food; he contends that she symbolizes fire as well as the souls of those who have died. Her name is a derivation of *xóchitl* and *quetza* or *quetzalli*, signifying something precious as well as a "ghost warrior" (Bierhorst 1985, 283).[11] Therefore, she can be considered the precious ghost warrior who stands or rests on flowers (283).[12] *Xóchitl's* connotation of "warrior" or "ghost warrior" and the links to butterflies mentioned above permit both Xochipilli and Xochiquétzal to be located in the realm of mariposa warriors. Furthermore, the term *xóchitl* was often used in ancient Mexican poetry to symbolize the warrior's heart, the heart given in sacrifice, or the body given in battle.[13]

A closer look at *Xochipilli's Ecstatic Universe* reveals three additional butterflies surrounding the central figure's head. While it is not easy to decipher the three, the dark one at the top resembles the black witch moth, also known as "la mariposa de la muerte" in Mexico (*Ascalapha odorata*); the middle one resembles the queen butterfly (from the same genus as the monarch, *Danaus*); and the smallest one near the sphinx resembles the eyes of Tláloc, which I explain below. The presence of Xochiquétzal as a butterfly along with additional butterflies in *Xochipilli's Ecstatic Universe* creates a unified front of mariposas that are integral to the subject's understanding of his social location, social relations, and heritage. The butterflies create links to an ancestral past while completing an aura of *sabiduría* around the central figure's head, which is shaped by various winged creatures: the small swan below the chin, the large yellow bird emanating from his mouth, the black birds near the Aztec sculptures, the hummingbird, the three butterflies, and the bird prominently displayed on his forehead. The use of flower petals resembling wings adds to the aura, and if one considers the Greek origin of the word *petal*, and *petalouda* as the modern Greek word for butterfly, the flowers themselves become extensions of the butterfly wings.[14] Wings are essential components of Rodríguez's oeuvre; however, he often does not clearly distinguish between wings of different species. The wings of a bird resemble the wings of a dragonfly or those of a butterfly, while the petals of a flower or the leaves of a plant also often appear as wings. In this way, his association of wings with human-like subjects makes important links to a natural history while also mapping his characters with multiple traits that one can associate with wings: freedom, the ability to transcend a social location, divine messengers, beauty, eroticism, protection, and resilience.

In *Tlaloc's Paradise* (2002), Rodríguez pays tribute to an ancestral past and the famous mural itself (*The Paradise of Tláloc*, c. AD 600) but privileges the unique (hi)story of the present-day subject: a young, attractive individual adorned with tattoos, with a large butterfly in place of the mouth (fig. 3). In light of Rodríguez's other work, we can assume that the subject gave birth to the butterfly through the mouth, so that the butterfly represents the subject's soul; the butterfly might also be the subject's familiar or an incarnation of Tláloc. Regardless, there is an obvious link between the

**Figure 3.** Tino Rodríguez, *Tlaloc's Paradise*, 2002. Oil on wooden panel, 12 x 12 inches. © 2002 by Tino Rodríguez; reproduced by permission of the artist.

Aztec butterflies on Tláloc's wall and the butterfly as the subject's mouth. The butterfly gives voice to the subject and tells a unique story while positioning the subject in a safe, stable, and comfortable social location. This corresponds to what Rodríguez refers to as "the impossible voice": "I have found a lot of beauty in pain and transformed it into something I call *la voz imposible*" (Rodríguez 2002, 234). Therefore, the butterfly permits the articulation of a narrative that would otherwise be impossible or taboo; it is an integral link to the past and enhances the subject's *sabiduría* in the present.

In this way, Rodríguez's mariposa subjects can also be considered fierce mariposa warriors who speak truths and the forbidden. This social location is useful as a means of survival and key to prospering in the present. In other words, beauty and strength materialize in the present because of the subject's knowledge of the past. Although Rodríguez's work suggests an interest in recognizing how the past shapes the individual, he is primarily invested in the present and embraces it with all its joys, beauty, and hardships, which is why the central figures are often contemporary subjects associated with mythical figures and Aztec or Greek deities. In this way, although they sometimes suffer horrific deaths, the beauty and strength they exude function as both a celebration of queerness and a critique of the spaces they inhabit, which remain terrorized by homophobia, patriarchy, and racism. The artist's personal philosophy clearly drives his focus on the present. As he explains, "Because of the way I live on a daily basis I don't like to think about the future or the past that much. I like to embrace the present as much as I can and live as fully as I can every day" (Rodríguez 2005, 11).

As one of the most important Toltec and, later, Aztec deities, the butterfly was one of the symbolic representations of Tláloc, the god of rain and lightening. The term *tláloc* derives from the Náhuatl for earth, *tlālli* (Bierhorst 1985, 337). According to anthropologist and historian Nigel Davies, Tláloc was originally more important than Quetzalcoatl (1987, 57). Davies also contends that representations of a "bird-butterfly god" are more prevalent in the murals of Teotihuacán than representations of a "plumed serpent" (59). Besides being worshipped for his ability to provide water, Tláloc was feared for his ability to bring about thunder, lightening, and floods. Therefore, Tláloc is often depicted with water in the shape of flames. Beutelspacher suggests the butterfly as a link between fire and water in ancient Mexico, especially as it pertains to the deity Tláloc. According to him and other social scientists, the eyes of the butterflies commonly depicted in cultural artifacts of ancient Mexicans are intended to evoke the sun, and the insect itself is a symbol of flames, representing Tláloc's ability to deliver rains of fire (Beutelspacher 1988, 29). Beutelspacher highlights the murals and other artifacts found in Teotihuacán, where butterflies were used to evoke the deity; *The Paradise of Tláloc* contains several large butterflies bearing Tláloc's eyes and flying among human figures (images of the mural are available online).[15] The association between butterflies and fire is essential to the construction of a fierce mariposa warrior identity, as I explain below.

Butterflies figure prominently on the heads and faces of several of Rodríguez's subjects in works such as *Serenity* (2008), *Afterglow* (2008), *The Small Girl Who Knew Dreams* (2006), *Sonnet* (2002), and *Oberon (King of Faeries)* (2000)—just to name a few.[16] The butterflies are the incarnation of the subject, the soul transformed into something material, an inner beauty made visible, while also marking the subject as a warrior with the ability to survive and transcend a social location. A butterfly may mask the eyes or mouth of the subject or serve as a veil covering the subject's face; sometimes a butterfly will perch on the subject's head or some other part of the upper body. By adorning his subjects with butterfly wings, Rodríguez highlights their beauty, strength, and resilience while transforming them into messengers that facilitate dialogues between past and present struggles. The presence of the butterfly is integral to maintaining the subject fully awake and in equilibrium, in all her/his *mariposada*. Rodríguez's work thus exemplifies the process by which a mariposa consciousness can come to fruition.

The use of butterfly iconography in the works of González and Rodríguez also resonates with the way large butterflies were used by the Toltecs as emblems for their elite warriors. These can still be seen today prominently displayed on the chests of the Toltec Atlantean Warriors (c. AD 900) in Tula, the ancient capital of the Toltecs. Besides representing the souls of fallen warriors, these butterflies personified deities and were regarded as symbols of strength and courage. In this way, the ancient mariposa warriors can be considered an integral part of a lengthy history of fierce mariposa warriors struggling to build a Mariposa Nation.

Fierce Mariposa Warriors

Fierce Mariposa warriors fly boldly into the future
We cannot sit still or leave the world unchanged
Many will fall Many will soar
Mariposas will land
on unchartered territory create space
where other mariposas spread their wings
and fly, we will spread our wings and fly

## LA LENGUA DE LA MARIPOSA

Rigoberto González and Tino Rodríguez develop a unique aesthetic and voice in their works. González's fierce mariposa warriors speak out about injustices and affirm their identities on various occasions, and Rodríguez's fierce mariposa warriors express *la voz imposible* in an array of contexts. Similar to the way Anzaldúa conceptualized the serpent's tongue, these artists use a mariposa standpoint to affirm a queer sexual and gender identity that stands in direct opposition to the way queer Chicanos and Latinos have historically been depicted as the abject. They also unearth a lost history and unleash the unspeakable. As Anzaldúa asserts, having your own voice and letting it be heard is a way to overcome oppression and break silences: "I will no longer be made to feel ashamed of existing. I will have my voice: Indian, Spanish, white. I will have my serpent's tongue—my woman's voice, my sexual voice, my poet's voice. I will overcome the tradition of silence" (1987, 59).

"La lengua de la mariposa," like that of the serpent, remains coiled until it is ready to strike. The tongue is lengthy and strong. The butterfly relies on its tongue to nourish itself by feeding on the nectar or pollen of flowers. The tongue is hollow, like a straw (technically, a proboscis), which allows the insect to slurp nectar or water. Although it varies by species, some butterflies have tongues that are longer than their bodies.

In the Spanish film *La lengua de las mariposas* (1999), that butterflies have tongues is one of many lessons a young child named Moncho (played by Manuel Lozano) learns from his beloved teacher, Don Gregorio (Fernando Fernán Gómez). As he comes of age, Moncho learns valuable lessons about nature and sexuality, among other things. The teacher and Moncho's father, Ramón (Gonzalo Uriarte), are Republicans—which, in this context, means liberals—during the 1930s, when Spain is about to fall into the grip of the Catholic Church, ultraconservatism, and fascism. The teacher tries to explain the physical and biological functions of the butterfly tongue to his students: "La lengua de las mariposas es una trompa como la de los elefantes" (the butterfly's tongue is a trunk like that of an elephant). However, he is unable to show them an actual butterfly tongue because the school does not yet have a microscope. The use of the butterfly tongue in the film is multifaceted. It represents sexuality, rebelliousness, and loss of innocence, as Moncho's lessons on the butterfly are intertwined with the life lessons he learns about sexual intercourse between adults; it serves as a metaphor for the penis while the flower is a metaphor for the vagina; and it serves as a medium by which the forbidden is spoken out loud.

Don Gregorio becomes the target of the fascist regime due to his willingness to speak about liberty and other anticonservative views; he is eventually arrested and silenced.[17] On the day he is taken away along with other individuals who are marked as subversives, he is paraded past the townspeople, including Moncho and his family. In order to save her family from a similar fate, Moncho's mother, Rosa (Uxía Blanco), prods her son and Ramón to publicly shout epithets at their beloved teacher: "¡Asesino! ¡Anarquista! ¡Cabrón! ¡Hijo de puta! ¡Ateo! ¡Rojo! ¡Rojo! ¡Rojo!" Reluctant and dismayed, they participate in denigrating Don Gregorio, who is dressed in the tailored suit Ramón made for him and gave him as a gift. Once the truck leaves with the prisoners mounted on the back, Moncho joins the other children running behind it and throwing stones at the men. As he hurls stones, his epithets become coded specifically for Don Gregorio: "*¡Tilonorrinco! ¡Proboscis!*" (the scientific name for the bower bird, known for engaging in elaborate courting rituals, and the tongue of the butterfly, respectively). In this way, Moncho cleverly takes advantage of this heart-wrenching moment to thank his teacher for the lessons he has learned and to assure him that they were not in vain. Therefore, "la lengua de la mariposa" speaks taboos and in codes; some will use it to nourish their souls, and others will use it to engage in a revolution.

Don Gregorio is one of several examples of how "la lengua de la mariposa" can be used to facilitate transformations. By being true to himself and speaking out, he was able to inspire others and participate in a resistance movement while cultivating a new generation of freedom fighters, like the fierce mariposa warriors in the works of González and Rodríguez. Similar dynamics can be witnessed in other films that center on queer *latinidades*, especially documentaries where testimonios made by queer subjects are documented: *Blossoms of Fire* (2001), *De colores* (2009), and *Mariposas en el andamio* (1995). In these documentaries, one will bear witness to gay men, lesbians, and trans individuals revealing their true identities and sharing their stories. They actively engage in transforming their lives, their families, and their communities in constructive ways. All the films also contain "coming-out" stories. Some of the individuals have tumultuous coming-out experiences, while others have more positive ones. In the Cuban documentary on trans individuals who transform an entire community through their varied performances, *Mariposas en el andamio*, Yosvany López Trujillo (aka Pimpinela) describes the day he told his mother he was gay. During an interview with his mother sitting at his side and his partner, Henry, behind them, he recounts how when he told her, she slapped him and then dared him to repeat it: "Repítemelo," she exclaimed. He reiterated, "Mami, que soy homosexual." She slapped him again and dared him to repeat it again. According to Yosvany, that's when they both began to cry. Although this was a painful process, as the interview proceeds it is clear that she has managed to accept Yosvany, albeit with some concerns, as he and his partner are almost fully integrated into the family.

Compare this scene with a scene in *Blossoms of Fire*, where Armando López (aka Mandy) describes what happened when his father caught him curling his eyelashes. Initially, his father didn't say a word, but later he grabbed the eyelash curler and, with the mother also present in the room, asked Armando, "¿Por qué usas esto?" Armando hesitated a bit but felt compelled to reply, "Pues, porque soy homosexual. ¿No te has dado cuenta? Soy homosexual." Instead of slapping him, his father extended his hand to Armando and told him, "Qué bueno que tuviste el valor de decírmelo."[18]

De esto, sí se habla
La lengua de la mariposa es su weapon
Which it must learn to use to survive
It often speaks those words others fear
It is often targeted by those who fear it
La lengua de la mariposa es su weapon
It is filled with courage and strength
When it speaks the truth, sacred words
It unleashes a beauty that has no limits
La lengua de la mariposa
Es su weapon

## FANNING THE FLAMES, BURNING WITH DESIRE, AND THE ACT OF BEING BURNED

Although the moths and butterflies that venture too near fire and are burned are sometimes assumed to have some type of malfunction, the relationship between these insects and fire is a natural one. As lepidopterists explain, some insects are biologically phototactic, or attracted to light. Moths and butterflies depend on natural light, mainly the moon and the sun, for navigational purposes. Artificial light and fire disorient them in ways that sometimes lead to their demise (Cowan and Gries 2009).

The link between butterflies and fire that is found in the cultural expression of ancient Mexicans is often evoked today. As described earlier, butterflies were used by the Aztecs to represent the tongue of fire serpents or Tláloc's rain of fire; they were also used in Spain as early as the sixteenth century as metaphors for men accused of sodomy who figuratively played with fire and were literally burned to death. The images of fierce mariposa warriors that González and Rodríguez create can be considered in a similar vein. González uses Caliente Valley as a setting for his flaming fierce mariposas in *The Mariposa Club* and *The Mariposa Gown*, while Rodríguez depicts queer subjects associated with Tláloc, Xochipilli, and other ancient deities that are also associated with butterflies and warriors; these are just a few examples of the way these artists portray mariposas as both wielding fire and being consumed by it. Both artists depict queer Chicanos and Latinos as beautiful beings burning with and for desire.

Today, besides the term *faggot,* effeminate males in the United States are often referred to as "flamers" or men who are "flaming," as in "flaming queens"; they may also be described as "flamboyant." In Spanish, to be *soflamero* means to be melodramatic. Someone who is acting melodramatically or fanning the flames may be told to tone things down using the Spanglish vernacular: "No seas flamer." Moreover, in Spanish the expression "Te quemaste" (you burned yourself) is used to signify that you ruined your reputation because you engaged in some form of illicit behavior: got caught in a lie, had unsanctioned sex, or committed some other socially unacceptable act. Related expressions include "Estás tostado" and "Estás en el horno" (you are toast or you are in hot water). According to one dictionary, *quemar*, to burn, can also mean to discredit someone, for example by revealing a damaging secret ("hacer quedar mal a alguien, por ejemplo revelando algún secreto que le perjudica"), or, alternatively, to be consumed by passion.[19]

In *The Construction of Homosexuality*, David Greenberg (1988) examines the history and politics of homosexuality, sodomy, and transvestism among several indigenous groups in the Americas. Greenberg highlights how homosexual and trans individuals were treated, which he claims varied greatly among indigenous groups; perceptions also depended on the time period and often became negative after colonization. Greenberg points out that even though there is plenty of evidence of homosexual relations and gender transgressions, both were punishable by law in some societies. He cites the Inca laws, which called for death by burning for those who engaged in homosexual acts, and the Aztec death penalty laws for homosexuality and transvestism, although he finds that the enforcement of Aztec and Inca laws was sporadic and varied by region (166). Greenberg suggests that these laws were devised to encourage reproduction in order to strengthen the military and thus fortify the capacity to conquer others: "Anything that might weaken the military strength of the empire by encouraging licentiousness was to be suppressed." Because of this, he concludes, "Male effeminacy became intolerable" (167). As evident in an account documented in the seventeenth century by Fernando de Alva Ixtlilxochitl (c. 1568–1648), a descendant of the kings of Texcoco, gender transgression among the Chichimeca was often seen as a greater offense than homosexuality; although both were punishable by death by burning, those who engaged in some form of gender transgression often suffered harsher penalties than those who committed same-sex acts:

> To the one acting as a female, they removed his entrails from the bottom, he was tied down to a log and the boys from the town covered him with ash, until he was buried; and then they put a lot of wood and burnt him. The one acting as a male was covered with ash, tied down to a log until he died. (Greenberg 1988, 165)[20]

According to Federico Garza Carvajal's *Butterflies Will Burn: Prosecuting Sodomites in Early Modern Spain and Mexico*, the prosecution of men who did not exhibit appropriate masculine behavior increased considerably by the middle of the seventeenth century in Spain and Mexico City. This often led to the execution of those accused of sodomy: "Notions of effeminacy in association with a man's proper dress and perceptions of sodomy would gradually gain notoriety in the peninsula and reach a high-pitched level of hysteria in mid-seventeenth-century Mexico City" (Garza Carvajal 2003, 68). As an example, Garza Carvajal cites the execution of Domingo Palacios, a cook who, tragically and ironically, was burned at the stake in Sevilla in 1593; he was ousted by an innkeeper from his quarters because he looked like a *maricón* or a *marica* (68).

Flaming, burning with desire, and being burned have been metaphors and realities for queer males for centuries. In "La mariposa, el amor y el fuego: De Petrarca y

Lope a Dostoievski y Argullol," José Manuel Pedrosa (2003) examines the association between mariposas and fire as represented in literary texts from medieval Spain to the twentieth century. He suggests that the butterfly in literary texts during this period was primarily used to represent the poet engulfed by passion: "No es exagerado afirmar, para empezar, que decenas, o quizás centenares de poemas españoles de los siglos XVI y XVII desarrollaron el motivo de la mariposa abrasada en las llamas del amor" (650).[21] He also claims that Federico García Lorca repeatedly used the butterfly to represent tragic love. As examples, he references Lorca's *El maleficio de la mariposa* and suggests that Lorca's use of the tragic love theme is often associated with fire and being consumed by the flames of passion, as in his celebrated play *Bodas de sangre* (Lorca 1963). The image of the artist engulfed in flames due to a burning desire persists today. Besides the prevalence of this image in the work of González and Rodríguez, one will find it in the work of Francisco X. Alarcón, especially his collection of poems *Body in Flames/Cuerpo en llamas* (1990).

Yes, queer Chicano and Latino males have a long history of playing and living with fire. It is a reality of our daily lives, and it is a product of our own desires. As mariposas, we are attracted to the flames. We do not fear them because fire is a natural element, and it too requires oxygen to exist.

La Mariposa y el Fuego

la mariposa no teme
el fuego
sino abraza las llamas

porque prefiere
el calor
de un amor ardiente

que el frío de una cama vacía.

## CONCLUSION

Queer Chicanos and Latinos have often been told that we are not real men y que no valemos nada. We are often viewed as traitors to our people por no portarnos como los hombres se deberían portar—como un hombre "verdadero."[22] We have historically been silenced, abused emotionally and physically, made to feel ashamed of what we are, and punished, executed, or murdered for who we are. We are the targets of homophobic epithets in both English and Spanish: *maricón*, *faggot*, *puto*, *sissy*, *joto*, *cocksucker*, and *chupa verga*. As I have demonstrated, queer Chicanos and Latinos also have a rich and lengthy history with ancient roots in the Americas and Europe. In order to shine today, we must know our ancestral past. Our ancestors are deities, warriors, those who have been executed for speaking out or committing unacceptable acts, and those who have soared in their full glory. We are still the ones who speak taboos, commit rebellious acts of love, and play with fire. We are the *chupa vergas*, the *sinvergüenzas*, the *maricones*, and, above all, the *Mariposas* of a Mariposa Nation.

Mariposas en el cielo, Mariposa en la tierra

Mariposas are abused and killed daily around the world
we have been for centuries but we will not stop flying
we must soar above it all we must continue to fly
to our destinies wherever the winds
may take us and when we land
Mariposas
wherever we land we will be *there*
present, fluttering, and grounded in our full splendor
in all our glory in all our mariposada


## *Acknowledgements*

I would like to thank the fierce mariposa warriors who provided valuable feedback for this research project at various stages of its development: Michael Hames-García, Ernesto Martínez, Guillermo Reyes, Trino Sandoval, Eddy Alvarez, and Gibrán Güido. I am also grateful for the generosity, enthusiasm, and valuable input provided by the two fierce mariposa warriors whose work inspired this project: Rigoberto González and Tino Rodríguez. I must also thank the anonymous reviewers and the editorial staff of *Aztlán*; their generous and insightful feedback helped shape and strengthen this piece considerably. I am grateful for the assistance and valuable insight provided by my former graduate student, Gabriel Uriel Chávez. I would like to dedicate this piece to all the fierce mariposa warriors out there, especially those who are on the verge of discovering themselves in all their *mariposada*.


## NOTES

Reprinted with permission from Daniel Enrique Pérez, *Aztlán: A Journal of Chicano Studies* 39:2 (2014):

1. The term *marifesto* was coined by Gibrán Güido. See *Queer in Aztlán: Chicano Male Recollections of Consciousness and Coming Out* (Güido and Del Castillo 2013, xxix). My essay in the collection, "Out in the Field: Mariposas and Chican@ Studies," uses the mariposa as a metaphor for the way queer Chicanos travel through and survive in academia.

2. "La historia de este alguacil—un tal Quesada—es que él tenía casa de juego y acogía allí algunos mocitos de los pintadillos y galancitos, y a unos procuraba palparlos y tocarles las manos y caras, y a otros procuraba inducir al pecado consumado. . . . Al fin vino a parar en el fuego y como suelo decir (y aquel día que lo mataron lo dije), que los que no se enmiendan y se andan en las ocasiones de pecar son como las mariposillas, que andan revoloteando por junto a la lumbre: que de un encuentro se le quema un alilla, y de otro un pedacillo, y de otro se quedan quemadas; así los que tratan de esta mercaduría una vez quedan tiznados en sus honras y otra vez chamuscados y, al fin, vienen a parar en el fuego."

3. The viceroy butterfly is commonly mistaken for the monarch butterfly. The former is typically smaller and possesses a postmedian black line that runs across the veins of its hindwing. The viceroy mimics the monarch and queen butterflies as a means of protection from predators.

4. For more information on the monarch, see "Butterflies and Moths of North America," http://www.butterfliesandmoths.org/species/Danaus-plexippus.

5. See Beutelspacher (1988) and Allard (2013) for more information linking butterflies with ancient myths.

6. Beutelspacher provides examples of butterfly imagery in ancient Mexican poetry (24–26). Several additional examples are found in Miguel León-Portilla's *Cantares mexicanos* (2011).

7. Boone (1983) surmises that "agua de araña" was merely a mistaken rendition of "water spider." Therefore, the image may show not interlocking butterflies but other insects, although Beutelspacher (1988, 86) believes them to be butterflies.

8. There is much debate regarding the true meaning of the symbol. Whereas the Toltecs and Aztecs worshipped many deities and important elements of nature, in popular culture and among New Age enthusiasts, the *hunab ku* has come to represent a supreme creator or the sum of all consciousness in the universe. The symbol gained widespread attention when José Argüelles altered the image slightly and associated it with galactic convergences in *The Mayan Factor* (1987).

9. In Náhuatl, *xóchitl* means "rose" or "flower," and, figuratively speaking, "ghost warrior" (Bierhorst 1985, 395). *Pilli* means "child" or "prince" (266).

10. For an analysis of the pictorial representation of Xochipilli in the Codex Borgia, see Milbrath (2013, 49–52).

11. *Quetza* means "to stand up," and *quetzalli* means "long green plume" or "tail feather of the quetzal," which signifies something precious (Bierhorst 1985, 281, 283).

12. She is also sometimes referred to as Xochiquetzalpapálotl.

13. See Edward Kissam and Michael Schmidt's introduction to their translation of Aztec poems in *Poems of the Aztec Peoples* (1983, 16).

14. As Beutelspacher (1988), Bierhorst (1985), and Milbrath (2013) suggest, the distinctions between flowers, birds, butterflies, and other iconic images found in ancient Mexican cultural texts are often blurred.

15. According to Beutelspacher and other scholars, the renowned Templo de las Mariposas in Teotihuacán is actually misnamed. When the tattered ruins were discovered, the segmented wings were thought to represent those of the butterfly, so the site was christened Templo de las Mariposas. Once the artifacts were cleaned and assembled, however, the wings turned out to be those of the quétzal. Nevertheless, the name persists (Beutelspacher 1988, 97).

16. To view these and other works by Tino Rodríguez, visit his website: http://tinorodriguez.com.

17. I also suggest that Don Gregorio is very queer; he has no heterosexual markings and reminds me of El Californio in the film *Mi Familia* (1995). See Daniel Enrique Pérez (2009, 97–111).

18. "Why are you using this?" "Well, because I'm homosexual. Haven't you realized? I'm homosexual." "That's good you had the courage to tell me."

19. *Diccionario de María Moliner*, s.v. "quemar," DicLib.com, http://www.diclib.com/cgi-bin/d1.cgi?l=en&base=moliner&page=showid&id=64709.

20. Fernando de Alva Ixtlilxochitl's chronicles are published in Spanish in *Historia de la nación chichimeca* (1985).

21. "It is no exaggeration to assert, to begin with, that dozens or maybe hundreds of Spanish poems from the sixteenth and seventeenth centuries described the butterfly engulfed in flames of passion" (my translation).

22. We have often been told that we are not real men and that we are worthless. We are often viewed as traitors to our people for not behaving as men are supposed to behave—like "real" men.

## WORKS CITED

Alarcón, Francisco X. 1990. *Body in Flames/Cuerpo en llamas.* Translated by Francisco Aragón. San Francisco: Chronicle Books.

———. 2002. *From the Other Side of Night/Del otro lado de la noche*. Translated by Francisco Aragón. Tucson: University of Arizona Press.

Allard, Simone Hébert. 2013. *Manitoba Butterflies: A Field Guide*. Winnipeg: Turnstone Press.

Alva Ixtlilxochitl, Fernando de. 1985. *Historia de la nación chichimeca*. Madrid: Historia 16.

Alvarez, Julia. 1994. *In the Time of the Butterflies*. Chapel Hill, NC: Algonquin Books.

Anzaldúa, Gloria. 1987. *Borderlands/La Frontera: The New Mestiza*. San Francisco: Aunt Lute.

Argüelles, José. 1987. *The Mayan Factor: Path beyond Technology*. Rochester, VT: Bear and Company.

Beutelspacher, Carlos R. 1988. *Las mariposas entre los antiguos mexicanos*. Mexico City: Fondo de Cultura Económica.

Bierhorst, John. 1985. *A Nahuatl-English Dictionary and Concordance to the* Cantares Mexicanos. Stanford, CA: Stanford University Press.

Boone, Elizabeth Hill. 1983. *The Codex Magliabechiano and the Lost Prototype of the Magliabechiano Group*. Berkeley: University of California Press.

Corominas, Joan, and José A. Pascual. 1980. *Diccionario crítico etimológico castellano e hispánico*, vol. 3. Madrid: Editorial Gredos.

Cowan, Thomas, and Gerhard Gries. 2009. "Ultraviolet and Violet Light: Attractive Orientation Cues for the Indian Meal Moth, *Plodia interpunctella*." *Entomologia Experimentalis et Applicata* 131, no. 2: 148–58.

Davies, Nigel. 1987. *The Toltecs: Until the Fall of Tula*. Norman: University of Oklahoma Press.

Gagliardi, Ronald A. 1997. "The Butterfly and Moth as Symbols in Western Art." *Cultural Entomology Digest* 4. http://www.insects.org/ced4/butterfly_symbols.html.

Garza Carvajal, Federico. 2003. *Butterflies Will Burn: Prosecuting Sodomites in Early Modern Spain and Mexico*. Austin: University of Texas Press.

González, Rigoberto. 2006. *Butterfly Boy: Memories of a Chicano Mariposa*. Madison: University of Wisconsin Press.

———. 2008. *Men without Bliss*. Norman: University of Oklahoma Press.

———. 2009. *The Mariposa Club*. New York: Alyson Books.

———. 2011. *The Mariposa Gown*. Maple Shade, NJ: Tincture.

———. 2013. *Autobiography of My Hungers*. Madison: University of Wisconsin Press.

———. 2014. *Mariposa U*. Maple Shade, NJ: Tincture.

Greenberg, David F. 1988. *The Construction of Homosexuality*. Chicago: University of Chicago Press.

Güido, Gibrán, and Adelaida R. Del Castillo, eds. 2013. *Queer in Aztlán: Chicano Male Recollections of Consciousness and Coming Out*. San Diego: Cognella Academic.

Hames-García, Michael, and Ernesto Javier Martínez, eds. 2011. *Gay Latino Studies: A Critical Reader*. Durham, NC: Duke University Press.

Kissam, Edward, and Michael Schmidt, trans. 1983. *Poems of the Aztec Peoples*. Ypsilanti, MI: Bilingual Press/Editorial Bilingüe.

La Fountain-Stokes, Lawrence. 2007. "Queer Ducks, Puerto Rican Patos, and Jewish-American *Feygelekh*: Birds and the Cultural Representation of Homosexuality." *CENTRO Journal* (Center for Puerto Rican Studies, Hunter College) 19, no. 1: 192–229.

Launey, Michel. 2011. *An Introduction to Classical Nahuatl*. Translated by Christopher Mackay. New York: Cambridge University Press.

León, Pedro de. 1981. *Grandeza y miseria en Andalucía: Testimonio de una encrucijada histórica, 1578–1616*. Granada, Spain: Facultad de Teología de Granada.

León-Portilla, Miguel. 2011. *Cantares mexicanos*. 3 vols. Mexico City: Universidad Nacional Autónoma de México.

Lorca, Federico García. 1963. *Federico García Lorca: Obras completas*. Edited by Arturo del Hoyo. Madrid: Aguilar.

Milbrath, Susan. 2013. *Heaven and Earth in Ancient Mexico: Astronomy and the Seasonal Cycles in the Codex Borgia*. Austin: University of Texas Press.

Moraga, Cherríe. 1993. *The Last Generation*. Boston: South End Press.

Muñoz, José Esteban. 1999. *Disidentifications: Queers of Color and the Performance of Politics*. Minneapolis: University of Minnesota Press.

Nagel, Alexandra. 2009. "From the Symbolism of Wings to the Symbolism of Tarot Cards." *Playing-Card: Journal of the International Playing-Card Society* 38, no. 1: 40–55.

Nuttall, Zelia. 1903. *The Book of the Life of the Ancient Mexicans*. Berkeley: University of California.

Pedrosa, José Manuel. 2003. "La mariposa, el amor y el fuego: De Petrarca y Lope a Dostoievski y Argullol." *Criticón* 87–89: 649–60.

Pérez, Daniel Enrique. 2009. *Rethinking Chicana*/o *and Latina*/o *Popular Culture*. New York: Palgrave Macmillan.

Pérez, Emma. 1999. *The Decolonial Imaginary: Writing Chicanas into History*. Bloomington: Indiana University Press.

Rabuzzi, Matthew. 1997. "Butterfly Etymology." *Cultural Entomology Digest* 4. http://www.insects.org/ced4/etymology.html.

Reinhardt, Karl J. 1981. "The Image of Gays in Chicano Prose Fiction." *Explorations in Ethnic Studies* 4, no. 2: 41–55.

Rice-González, Charles, and Charlie Vázquez, eds. 2011. *From Macho to Mariposa: New Gay Latino Fiction*. Maple Shade, NJ: Tincture.

Rodríguez, Tino. 2002. Artist's statement. In *Contemporary Chicana and Chicano Art: Artists, Works, Culture, and Education*, vol. 2, by Gary D. Keller, Joaquín Alvarado, Kaytie Johnson, and Mary Erickson, 234–35. Tempe, AZ: Bilingual Press/Editorial Bilingüe.

———. 2005. "Tino Rodriguez: Art." Interview by Veronica Chanel. *Kitten Magazine* 2, no. 3: 10–11.

Sandoval, Chela. 2000. *Methodology of the Oppressed*. Minneapolis: University of Minnesota Press.

Stavans, Ilan. 1996. "The Latin Phallus." In *Muy Macho: Latino Men Confront Their Manhood*, edited by Ray González, 143–64. New York: Anchor Books.

Viramontes, Helena María. 1985. *The Moths and Other Stories*. Houston: Arte Público.

Xavier, Emanuel. 2008. *Mariposas: A Modern Anthology of Queer Latino Poetry*. Mountain View, CA: Floricanto Press.

## FILMOGRAPHY

*Blossoms of Fire*. 2001. Directed by Maureen Gosling and Ellen Osborne. Written by Maureen Gosling and Toni Hanna. New Yorker Films.

*De Colores*. 2009. Directed by Peter Barbosa and Garrett Lanoir. Iron Rod Motion Pictures.

*La lengua de las mariposas*. 1999. Directed by José Luis Cuerda. Written by Rafael Azcona, José Luis Cuerda, and Manuel Rivas. SOGETEL and Las Producciones del Escorpión.

*Mariposas en el andamio*. 1995. Directed by Luis Felipe Bernaza and Margaret Gilpin. Kangaroo Productions.

# THE FUTURE OF THE LGBTQ ASIAN AMERICAN AND PACIFIC ISLANDER COMMUNITY IN 2040

GLENN D. MAGPANTAY

## INTRODUCTION

As Paul Ong and his team have uncovered, the Asian American and Pacific Islander (AAPI) populations will grow significantly in the next twenty-five years (Ong, Ong, and Ong 2016). According to the US Census Bureau, the number of AAPIs will increase 74 percent, from 20.5 million in 2015 to 35.7 million in 2040, making AAPIs the fastest-growing racial population in the nation. In addition, those identifying as lesbian, gay, bisexual, transgender, and queer (LGBTQ) are higher among AAPIs compared to the general population (Gates and Newport 2012). This demographic trajectory will have profound social, cultural, political, and economic implications as AAPIs become nearly a tenth of the total US population.

This article provides some insights into the implications of the AAPI population growth of the LGBTQ AAPI community as well as the exponential growth of multiracial Asians over the next twenty-five years. Before reviewing the impact on public policies, advocacy, and community infrastructure, I will present a short discussion of the census data and the history of the LGBTQ rights movement. I anticipate tremendous advancement in substantive rights and protections, a sea change in AAPI attitudes toward LGBTQ people, and significant growth among LGBTQ AAPI community organizations.

Glenn D. Magpantay, esq. is the executive director of the National Queer Asian Pacific Islander Alliance, a federation of LGBT Asian American, South Asian, Southeast Asian, and Pacific Islander organizations that seeks to build the organizational capacity of local LGBT AAPI groups, develops leadership, promotes visibility, educates our community, enhances grassroots organizing, and challenges homophobia and racism. Magpantay is also an adjunct assistant professor of Asian American studies, Hunter College, CUNY and adjunct assistant professor of law, Brooklyn Law School. He received his BA from the State University of New York at Stony Brook and JD cum laude from New England School of Law, Boston, MA.

## INITIAL CONSIDERATIONS ON THE DATA AND LGBTQ MOVEMENT

### *Limitations of the Data*

Although the US Census reports on the AAPI population and ethnic subgroups, future censuses must count LGBTQ people, which is not currently done.[1] Currently, the US Census recognizes both "married couples" and "unmarried partners" who may be of the same sex. However, being in a same-sex partnership is a limited identifier of the LGBTQ community. Advocates are exploring asking the "LGB" question and reforming the gender question. Knowing an approximate population size of the LGBTQ community is necessary to explore the need for and impact of an array of public policies, social services, and substantive rights and protections.

The Williams Institute at UCLA has researched how to collect data about the LGBTQ community (Gates 2011). One challenge in measuring sexual orientation is that lesbian, gay, and bisexual individuals may be identified strictly based on their self-identity or based on their sexual behavior or sexual attraction. Identifying the transgender population can also be challenging because the transgender experience includes aspects of both gender identities and varying forms of gender expression or nonconformity. Moreover, sexual orientation and gender identity, like race, are ever-changing concepts. Today, there are more than fifty gender options on Facebook. The Census Bureau has already started to analyze this trend (Harris 2015).

It is also important to recognize that LGBTQ people may be reluctant to honestly answer such questions for fear of stigma and discrimination. In a study by the National Center for Transgender Equality and the National Gay and Lesbian Task Force, 71 percent of transgender people said they do not typically disclose their gender identity or gender transition in order to avoid discrimination (Grant et al. 2011). Many people feel that these are private questions, inappropriate for a governmental survey. Nevertheless, there are some commonly used survey questions to gather data on sexual orientation and gender identity.

The census relationship question may need to change as well. LGBTQ people are beginning to develop more dynamic relationships. They are more complex than just monogamous partnerships. There is a growing movement for polyamory (Easton and Liszt 1997; James 2010), which is a relationship that has multiple partners. Some of these relationships are triads or have even more people involved. Human relationships are complex, and I could foresee a census policy movement developing to recognize these multiparty partnerships.

The next twenty-five years will also see an exponential growth in the population of multiracial Asians. Complex racial identities go hand in hand with complex sexual and gender identities in terms of recognition. Racial, sexual, ethnic, and gender identification are powerful unifiers but also imperfect categories. As we look to 2040, the census will need to look at new ways to document the demographic diversity of America.

### *History of the LGBTQ Movement in the United States*

The early LGBTQ rights agenda was focused on being left alone, to live free, but not necessarily openly, as lesbian, gay, and transgendered people (Egan and Sherrill 2005).

In the 1970s and 1980s, antigay and anti-trans harassment, violence, and hate crimes were commonplace. Gay bars were frequently raided by the police, no one was LGBTQ in high school, college-aged young people were being harassed in dormitories, and gay men were contracting HIV and dying from AIDS.

Today, so much has changed. LGBTQ people no longer simply seek tolerance, but affirmative acceptance, if not celebration, of who we are, whom we love, how we love, and our gender presentation. LGBTQ people can now legally marry. LGBTQ acceptance has changed considerably where, today, a majority of Americans are supportive of LGBTQ rights (Baunach 2012). It is common for someone to know an out LGBTQ person.

And yet more work still needs to be done. LGBTQ people can get married but we still need to ask, "Who will come to the wedding?" Marriage is an important legal right, but also a familial recognition of our partners. Parental acceptance of their LGBTQ children and their partners is still needed. LGBTQ people can get married, but they can also get fired from a job in many states or beaten up because of whom they chose to marry. People of transgender experience, especially trans-women of color, are facing horrific rates of violence. While the LGBTQ community has secured many rights in the United States, the world can still be a dangerous place for LGBTQ people to live. So much work is ahead of us.

## *Rights for LGBTQ People*

Before delving into the issues of the LGBTQ community and movement over the next twenty-five years, we must consider how rights are developed. The agenda for LGBTQ AAPI rights and equality is often a function of being LGBTQ or being a racial minority. LGBTQ AAPIs live at the intersection of race, gender, and sexuality. When LGBTQ people win the right to marry or are protected from discrimination in housing, employment, and public accommodations, LGBTQ AAPIs win those rights as well. When race-based affirmative actions are preserved, undocumented immigrants given legal status, and limited English proficient Asians can vote in their native languages, American society and democracy becomes more inclusive of LGBTQ AAPIs. So forecasting an LGBTQ AAPI rights agenda must lie at this unique intersection.

The victories of today can be lost tomorrow. The 1970s feminist movement fed into a sexual liberation movement. The National March on Washington for Gay and Lesbian Rights in 1979 saw the beginnings of a more politicized gay community. And then there was AIDS. Lesbian and gay organizations and communities were decimated. Gay men and trans people were dying. Discriminatory policies were written into federal immigration and state adoption laws. Agendas shifted from rights based on sexual orientation to health care access. In 1986, the US Supreme Court upheld state sodomy laws in *Bowers v. Hardwick*. The opinion's legal reasoning surprisingly cited William Blackstone from the eighteenth century (*Bowers v. Hardwick* 1986). A second national march on Washington in 1987 demonstrated the communities' resilience. But it was not until much later that the LGBTQ community began to make some headway in public policies.

The 1990s saw a different rhetoric and much more access to the White House and top public policy officials under the presidency of Bill Clinton. Yet, LGBTQ leaders wondered whether winning access was the same as winning policy changes. The obvious setbacks were the passage of the Defense of Marriage Act (DOMA) and the military's Don't Ask Don't Tell policy. The George W. Bush years saw an LGBTQ regrouping and refocusing on state and local initiatives, especially state DOMAs that prohibited same-sex marriage. This laid the foundations for what would become a powerful political machine. Under the presidency of Barack Obama, the LGBTQ community won a string of federal as well as state and local victories (Human Rights Campaign 2015; On the Issues 2015; Ring 2015).

Policies affirmatively discriminating against people with AIDS and LGBTQ people were overturned. Obama signed the federal Matthew Shepard and James Byrd Jr. Hate Crimes Prevention Act into law. Military discrimination ended with the overturning of Don't Ask Don't Tell. The Supreme Court recognized a federal right to marriage for same-sex couples. These substantive rights are incredible. But they are yet to be fully implemented to truly alter the everyday lives of LGBTQ people. At the same time, for LGBTQ AAPIs, many of us are immigrants and deportations reached an all-time high under Obama. Transgender people still faced ongoing violence.

The civil rights movement provides ample evidence for continued struggle. The US Supreme Court's decision outlawing segregation in *Brown v. Board of Education* was in 1954 but Dr. Martin Luther King Jr.'s "Letter from a Birmingham Jail" underscoring the need for action against segregation and injustice was written in 1963, nearly ten years after Brown was decided. Rights must be institutionalized. And cultural shifts are necessary prerequisites to institutionalization.

## DEMOGRAPHIC IMPLICATIONS ON PUBLIC POLICIES

Three substantive public policy areas that can be directly implicated with the increase of the AAPI community over the next twenty-five years are immigration, nondiscrimination, and family-building policies.

AAPIs will comprise 10 percent of the US population by 2040 due to large waves of immigration. This rise in immigration will shift the AAPI population from being predominantly US-born to a mainly immigrant constituency. The Williams Institute found that AAPIs comprised a larger share of LGBTQ immigrant populations, with 15 percent of undocumented LGBTQ adults and 35 percent of documented LGBTQ adults identifying as AAPI (Gates 2013). Immigration issues are vitally important to the LGBTQ AAPI community. By 2040, I hope that advocates will have developed the ability to win a legalization program that allows undocumented immigrants to gain status and US citizenship.

Today several states and municipalities outlaw employment discrimination on the basis of sexual orientation and some on gender identity. I hope that in the next twenty-five years we will not just see the passage of the federal Employment Non-Discrimination Act but also a more comprehensive measure, like the Equality Act, modeled after the Civil Rights Act of 1965, that prevents discrimination in employment, housing, and public accommodations on the basis of sexual orientation and gender identity.

The new law will have to cover both intentional discrimination and discrimination in effect (Rutherglen 1987). Current laws prevent racial discrimination when it is done openly and is easy to prove. Today, racial discrimination in employment and housing tends to be more nuanced or race-neutral (Kang and Lane 2010). For instance, offending parties may claim that they are not discriminating against African American people per se, but against those who are "unqualified" or have criminal prolixities if not actual convictions. There is then a disproportionate impact, or "effect," on African Americans.

Similarly, firing a LGBTQ person may be motivated on the basis of sexuality or gender identity, but an oral record to illustrate that animus was the reason is far more difficult to prove. Jerry Kang's work on implicit bias has also uncovered discrimination without any intent or even awareness. Over the next twenty-five years, my hope is that advocates will develop a legal standard to outlaw discrimination in effect that will more competently address discrimination against both LGBTQ people and racial and ethnic minorities (US Equal Employment Opportunity Commission 2015). The latter includes remedying discrimination against multiracial people who will grow in population.

Today there is a baby boom among LGBTQ people. There is already a growth of AAPIs who have come out and openly identify as LGBTQ. More and more LGBTQ people, including LGBTQ AAPIs, are raising children, either through adoption or artificial insemination (Badgett et al. 2007; Goldberg, Gartrell, and Gates 2014). AAPI parents of LGBTQ kids have sometimes said that coming to terms with their children being LGBTQ has meant coming to terms with no longer becoming a grandparent. For AAPIs, having children and grandchildren is especially powerful. It is about legacy and long-term security and gives status and meaning to one's life.

The children of LGBTQ parents are often from a different racial background than their LGBTQ parents, or they are of mixed race. In domestic adoption, there are simply more black and Latino children to adopt than white and AAPIs. Lesbians often secure sperm from a donor of a different race. Many Asians still harbor old prejudices against adoption and artificial insemination, but the desire to have a family is powerful. I anticipate that these prejudices will subside as more and more LGBTQ AAPIs demand recognition, resources, and support for family building.

Today, we already know that a large number of AAPI same-sex unmarried parents are raising children, oftentimes children of a different race or of mixed race (Kastanis and Gates 2013). The projected 104 percent increase in the multiracial AAPI population between 2015 and 2040 is attributable to the large number of interracial marriages. I believe that AAPI LGBTQ families will contribute to the growth of the AAPI multiracial population over the next twenty-five years.

## DEMOGRAPHIC IMPLICATIONS ON LGBTQ ACCEPTANCE

There will be a sea change in the acceptance of LGBTQ people among AAPIs. This will largely be driven by the growth of the US native-born AAPI population and as the AAPI young people of today grow up, more inclined toward acceptance. Young people will be more inclined to accept LGBTQ people. Such changes in attitudes, coupled with increased voter eligibility and voter registration of AAPIs, will result in a new landscape of LGBTQ people advocating for public policy changes.

### *Public Opinion*

Today, a majority of Americans support the right of same-sex couples to legally marry (Clement and Barnes 2015). Yet, AAPIs have been less accepting, if not opposed. In 2012, the Asian American Legal Defense and Education Fund (AALDEF) polled 9,096 Asian American voters during the elections in fourteen states in twelve Asian languages. It was the largest multilingual exit poll of its kind and it was the first time that AAPI support for LGBTQ issues had been polled on such a national and representative scale (Tran, Magpantay, and Fung 2013). AALDEF found that only a third (37 percent) of Asian American voters supported the right of same-sex couples to legally marry. Almost half (48 percent) were opposed.

The greatest opposition came from Asian Americans who were foreign-born, limited English proficient, and older. This cut makes up the largest portion of the Asian American electorate today. Only a fifth (21 percent) of Asian American voters polled were born in the United States and 79 percent were foreign-born citizens who naturalized. Majority support did not break by gender, college education, or Democratic Party affiliation.

The greatest support for same-sex marriage came from Asian American voters who were native-born, younger, highly educated, and fully English proficient. In fact, 75 percent of Asian Americans born in the United States and 65 percent between the ages of eighteen to twenty-nine supported same-sex marriage.

AALDEF conducted another exit poll in 2014 of 4,102 Asian American voters in thirty-eight cities across eleven states. That year, Asian Americans showed support for laws that protect LGBTQ people from discrimination in employment, housing, and public accommodations, with an overall result of 56 percent indicating their support and 24 percent expressing opposition. The greatest support again came from native-born and younger voters, at 89 percent of native-born voters and 82 percent for those between the ages of eighteen and twenty-nine.

In 2040, the increase in the US-born AAPI population, coupled with a larger share being younger, could push forth AAPI support for same-sex marriage and legal protections for LGBTQ people.

### *Advocacy*

Electoral and attitudinal changes will also fuel changes in public policy advocacy. By 2040, one in fifteen registered voters will be AAPI. The increase will make AAPIs one of the fastest-growing electorates in America. Ong and other commentators (2016) predict that politicians will reach out more deliberately to the AAPI community.

Likewise, I anticipate that mainstream national LGBTQ advocacy organizations will not only reach out to, but also substantively address the needs of, AAPIs. This would occur not only to keep their base of donors and members satisfied, but also for political advantage through coalitions. National LGBTQ organizations may need to press for immigrants' rights because so many LGBTQs will be immigrants. Indeed, AAPI registered voters who are foreign-born are predicted to continue to be in the majority. Demographic changes could thereby promote more racial inclusion in the LGBTQ rights agenda.

### *Family Acceptance*

As public opinion changes, the acceptance of LGBTQ people by their families will surely change as well. Today, the parents who are visible and who have publicly proclaimed that they love their LGBTQ kids are almost all white or only say so in English. Few AAPI parents have stepped forward to say the same (Aizumi 2015). Traditional cultural attitudes sometimes dissuade such outness. To address this conundrum, the National Queer Asian Pacific Islander Alliance (NQAPIA) spearheaded an effort to present parents who love their LGBTQ children through public service announcements and multilingual leaflets (National Queer Asian Pacific Islander Alliance 2015a, 2015c).

AAPI parents are often stuck in a "time warp" when it comes to awareness about LGBTQ people. Parents tell their children that "there are no gays back home" or share their perception of LGBTQs as being all "transsexual prostitutes." That is what they remember from when they immigrated to the United States in the 1960s, 1970s, and 1980s. Today the LGBTQ community has flourished abroad. There are sizable LGBTQ pride celebrations and public parades in Manila, Mumbai, Beijing, Taipei, Hanoi, Seoul, and the Pacific Islands (Mediator News Group 2015; Pawar 2014; Senzee 2014). But AAPI parents who are in the United States today never saw those parades so they understand being LGBTQ as a "Western influence," something that would never happen back home.

The trajectory of the AAPI community in 2040 will see a tremendous rise in US-born Asians and Asian immigration. These individuals will come to the United States with an increased awareness of the existence of the LGBTQ community, which may enable them to contribute to the movement for increased understanding and ultimately the acceptance of LGBTQ people.

## DEMOGRAPHIC IMPLICATIONS ON LGBTQ AAPI COMMUNITY INFRASTRUCTURE

The rapid growth of the AAPI population by 2040 will have a tremendous impact on LGBTQ AAPI community infrastructure. Between 2015 and 2040, AAPIs will grow 74 percent, from 20.5 million to 35.7 million (Ong, Ong, and Ong 2016). By 2040, nearly one in ten Americans will be AAPI. These numbers are not so far off from the size of the black population today, and one can anticipate that the level of the black community's infrastructure today will be what is to come for AAPIs in the next twenty-five years. Today, the LGBTQ AAPI community is primarily served by two models of institutions: HIV/AIDS agencies and volunteer community-based organizations. These are enduring independent groups, but it is important to note that there are also professional associations, employee networks, and queer Asian student groups that form from time to time within larger institutions. With the rapid rise of the LGBTQ AAPI community, these institutions will be transformed.

## *Transformation AAPI-Serving Institutions from HIV/AIDS to Health*

Today we already see that HIV/AIDS institutions are transforming themselves. Just a few years ago, in 2010, there were five HIV/AIDS organizations primarily serving AAPIs.[2] These institutions were founded because mainstream AIDS service organizations were incapable, or unwilling, to provide HIV services, outreach, and education with sufficient cultural competency to AAPIs.

In 2015, these agencies have changed considerably. API Wellness Center in San Francisco and APICHA in New York are becoming full-fledged community health centers that provide a host of health and wellness services far beyond HIV/AIDS. Asian Pacific AIDS Intervention Team in Los Angeles also tried to become a community health center but found the process too arduous and too political. The smaller agencies in Philadelphia and Boston have since folded.

As the population of AAPIs dramatically grows over the next twenty-five years, demands for cultural competent health services in the fields of HIV and transgender health will assuredly increase. Current and/or new agencies will step up and respond to changing demographics. Some cities may follow current models in Chicago, Washington, DC, and Seattle, where mainstream AAPI health agencies or minority AIDS service agencies address the needs of AAPIs. The undeniable demographic changes will encourage, if not require, changes in HIV/AIDS services.

## *Community-Based Organizations*

The second model of community infrastructure has been community-based organizations (National Queer Asian Pacific Islander Alliance 2009). About thirty-five local LGBTQ AAPI community organizations across the nation currently exist. Most are all-volunteer groups, and only a handful has full-time staff.

In 2005, NQAPIA was founded as a federation of LGBTQ AAPI organizations to build their organizational capacity, develop leadership, invigorate organizing, and challenge homophobia and racism. NQAPIA conducted a survey of these organizations in 2009 and again in 2015 (National Queer Asian Pacific Islander Alliance 2015b). NQAPIA found that they all have limited capacity. Only a quarter of them are incorporated as tax-exempt nonprofits. Half have budgets under $10,000 and only a quarter (those with staff) have budgets of more than $50,000.

LGBTQ AAPI organizations engage in social, support, educational, outreach, and political activities. They provide essential social networking spaces where they can connect with people of common heritage and experiences. They provide an alternative space to gay bars and clubs, which is and will continue to be especially important for young people given that the AAPI population in 2040 will be younger on the whole.

Educational activities include workshops, guest speakers, or discussion groups on a variety of topics. Peer support provides help for those coming out of the closet, or who experience other forms of marginalization due to their identities as women, people of transgender experience, or young people.

All LGBTQ AAPI groups engaged in some form of political advocacy or activism. They have written letters to editors, launched campaigns, and participated in rallies, protests, and lobby days. They challenge racism in the LGBTQ community and homophobia in AAPI communities. Some groups engaged electorally, through their companion 501(c)(4) Political Action Committee (PAC) to endorse candidates or to host nonpartisan public forums on the elections. But there are internal tensions in this work.

Some organizations' members pushed back regarding political work. One faction focused on social activities and had a distaste for political activism. Another faction believed that it had a duty to be politically engaged and speak up for LGBTQ AAPIs. These dynamics have been seen with many local grassroots LGBTQ AAPI organizations, such as Asian Queers and Allies (AQUA), Durham, NC; Queer & Asian, Houston, TX; Shades of Yellow (SOY), Minneapolis, MN; Invisible-to-Invincible (i2i): Asian Pacific Islander Pride of Chicago; Trikone-Chicago; Asian Pacific Islander Queer Sisters (APIQS), Washington, DC; Khush-DC, Washington, DC; Gay Asian & Pacific Islander Men of New York (GAPIMNY); Q-WAVE; SALGA; Massachusetts Area South Asian Lambda Association (MASALA), Boston, MA; Queer Asian Pacific- Islander Alliance (QAPA), Boston, MA; Asian Pacific Islander Pride of Portland, OR; Trikone-Northwest, Seattle, WA; Pride Asia, Seattle, WA; Gay Asian Pacific Alliance (GAPA), San Francisco, CA; South Bay Queer and Asian, San Jose; Trikone, San Francisco, CA; Barangay–LA; Satrang; Gay Asian Pacific Support Network (GAPSN); and Viet Rainbow Orange County (VietROC).

Digging deeper, NQAPIA found that the struggle emanated from membership demographics. The more socially oriented leaders and members tended to be immigrants. The more politically oriented were US-born. This is understandable. Many AAPIs come from countries where homosexuality is still frowned upon, that have palpable histories of government repression, or where speaking out has direct consequences for them and their families. With the tremendous rise of native-born AAPIs in 2040, I hope this pushback will subside and more of the groups will more affirmatively seek the same rights and dignities as all Americans.

I suspect that in the next twenty-five years, there will be a proliferation of these community-based organizations, in new cities and states with large AAPI growth. For current organizations, I see their programs expanding considerably in the future. Many groups want to provide specific support on immigration matters or professional counseling services, for example, but they lack the capacity to do so. But the demands may continue as the population increases. In order to accommodate more expansive programs and regular services, these organizations will need a higher level of infrastructure. These organizations will incorporate, acquire tax-exempt status, attract more institutional funding, and hire staff. Today, they have been reluctant to take on such infrastructure, but as they grow, they will find themselves needing to do so.

In some places, like Los Angeles, San Francisco, and New York, the local LGBTQ AAPI organization may have the requisite infrastructure and local AAPI population may be sufficiently large enough in 2040 where they will be able to develop full-fledged community centers. These may be needed because mainstream LGBTQ community centers lack the diversity and cultural competency to service all sectors of the LGBTQ community.

## CONCLUSION

The dramatic increase of the AAPI population and electorate has many implications on the LGBTQ rights agenda and manner in which the movement is organized. Greater acceptance of LGBTQs by AAPIs will not only be fueled by ongoing education but because the demographic who are the greatest supporters of LGBTQ rights today will be become the AAPI electorate of the future. Likewise, community needs will increase as the population increases, and so the infrastructure of the LGBTQ AAPI community will mature and formalize. I believe that multiculturalism within existing legislation, programs, and agencies will normalize, and civil rights protections will more sufficiently address discrimination in a more dynamic and diverse American society. The noted author, activist, and thinker Urvashi Vaid (1993) once said, "The gay rights movement is an integral part of the American promise of freedom." I hope we will achieve that freedom in the next twenty-five years.

## ACKNOWLEDGMENTS

The author acknowledges scholars Mari Matsuda, Kevin Nadel, Gary Gates, and Stephanie Hsu, and research assistant Kristy Medina for their help on this article.

## NOTES

Reprinted with permission from Glenn D. Magpantay, *AAPI Nexus* 14:2 (2016): 33–48.

1. It is notable that many other federal, state, and local data collection efforts include sexual orientation and gender identity. Sexual orientation identity is now measured on the National Health Interview Survey, and sexual orientation and gender identity measurement is currently being tested for inclusion on the National Crime and Victimization Survey. The National Survey of Family Growth includes measures of sexual orientation, behavior, and attraction. The California Health Interview Survey has just added measurement of gender identity for adults and gender expression for adolescents and has expanded sexual orientation identity measurement to all adults.

2. The groups are API Wellness Center in San Francisco, APICHA in New York, and Asian Pacific AIDS Intervention Team in Los Angeles, as well as smaller agencies such as AIDS Services in Asian Communities in Philadelphia and MAP for Health in Boston (see Wong et al., 2011).

## REFERENCES

Aizumi, Marsha. 2015. "Op-ed: Embracing the Role of Asian Mother to a Trans Son." Advocate, 27 May. Accessed February 29, 2016. http://www.advocate.com/commentary/2015/05/27/op-ed-embracing-role-asian-mother-trans-son

Badgett, M. V. Lee, Kate Chambers, Gary J. Gates, and Jennifer Ehrle Macomber. 2007. "Adoption and Foster Care by Gay and Lesbian Parents in the United States." Los Angeles: The Williams Institute, UCLA School of Law and the Urban Institute.

Baunach, Dawn Michelle. 2012. "Changing Same-Sex Marriage Attitudes in America from 1988 through 2010." *Public Opinion Quarterly* 76(2): 364–78.

Bowers v. Hardwick, 478 U.S. 186 (1986).

Clement, Scott, and Robert Barnes. 2015. "Poll: Gay-Marriage Support at Record High." *Washington Post*, 23 April.

Easton, Dossie, and Catherine A. Liszt. 1997. *The Ethical Slut: A Guide to Infinite Sexual Possibilities.* San Francisco: Greenery.

Egan, Patrick J., and Kenneth Sherrill. 2005. "Marriage and the Shifting Priorities of a New Generation of Lesbians and Gays." *PS: Political Science and Politics* 2: 229–32.

Gates, Gary. 2011. "How Many People Are Lesbian, Gay, Bisexual, and Transgender?" The Williams Institute, UCLA School of Law. April. Accessed February 29, 2016. http://williamsinstitute.law.ucla.edu/wp-content/uploads/Gates-How-Many-People-LGBT- Apr-2011.pdf

———.2013. "LGBTQ Adult Immigrants in the United States." Los Angeles: The Williams Institute, UCLA School of Law.

Gates, Gary J., and Frank Newport. 2012."Special Report: 3.4% of U.S. Adult Population Identify as LGBTQ?" Gallup, 18 October. Accessed February 29, 2016. http://www.gallup.com/poll/158066/special-report-adults-identify-LGBTQ.aspx

Gifts of Speech - Urvashi Vaid. (April 25, 1993). From http://gos.sbc.edu/w/vaid.html

Goldberg, Abbie E., Gartrell, Nanette K., and Gary Gates. 2014. "Research Report on LGB-Parent Families." Los Angeles: The Williams Institute, UCLA School of Law.

Grant, Jaime M., Mottet, Lisa A., Tanis, Justin, Harrison, Jack, Herman, Jody L., and Mara Keisling. 2011. *Injustice at Every Turn: A Report of the National Transgender Discrimination Survey.* Washington, DC: National Center for Transgender Equality and National Gay and Lesbian Task Force.

Harris, Benjamin Cerf. 2015. "Likely Transgender Individuals in U.S. Federal Administrative Records and the 2010 Census." CARRA Working Paper Series, Working Paper #2015-03, May 4. Washington, DC: US Census Bureau.

Human Rights Campaign. 2015."Summary of President Obama's Commitment to LGBTQ Equality." Summary Report. Accessed February 29, 2016. amazonaws.com//files/assets/resources/Obama_Administration_Accom- plishments_Document.pdf

James, Scott. 2010. "Many Successful Gay Marriages Share an Open Secret." *The New York Times*, 28 January. Accessed August 17, 2015. http://www.nytimes.com/2010/01/29/us/29sfmetro.html?_r=0

Kang, Jerry, and Kristin Lane. 2010. "Seeing through Colorblindness: Implicit Bias and the Law." *UCLA Law Review* 58: 465–520.

Kastanis, Angeliki, and Gary J. Gates. 2013. "LGBTQ Asian and Pacific Islander Individuals and Same-Sex Couples." Los Angeles: The Williams Institute, UCLA School of Law.

Mediator News Group. 2015. "Thousands March in Seoul for S Korea's Gay Pride Parade." Channel NewsAsia, 28 June.

National Queer Asian Pacific Islander Alliance. 2015a. "Japanese Parents Who Love Their LGBTQ Kids." NQAPIA, 22 May. Accessed February 29, 2016. http://www.nqapia.org/ wpp/japanese-parents-who-love-their-LGBTQ-kids-psas

———. 2015b. "LGBTQ AAPI Member Profile." Chicago: National Queer Asian Pacific Islander Alliance.

———. 2015c. "South Asian Parents Who Love Their LGBTQ Kids." NQA- PIA, 22 May. Accessed February 29, 2016. http://www.nqapia.org/wpp/south-asian-parents-who-love- their-LGBTQ-kids-psa/

———. 2009. "Queer Asian Compass: A Descriptive Directory of Lesbian, Gay, Bisexual, and Transgender (LGBTQ) Asian American, South Asian, and Pacific Islander (AAPI) Organizations." New York: National Queer Asian Pacific Islander Alliance.

On the Issues. 2015. "Bill Clinton on Civil Rights." On the Issues, 30 April. Accessed February 29, 2016. http:// www.ontheissues.org/Celeb/Bill_Clinton_Civil_Rights.htm

Ong, Jonathan, Paul Ong, and Elena Ong. 2016. "The Future of Asian America in 2040." *AAPI Nexus Journal* 14(1): 14–29.

Pawar, Yogesh. 2014."Seventh Edition of Mumbai Gay Pride Gets Bigger and Bolder, Attracts People from across the World." *DNA India*. 2 February.

Ring, Trudy. 2015. "The 11 Most Significant Presidents for LGBTQ Americans." *Advocate*, 16 February. Accessed February 29, 2016. http://www.advocate.com/politics/politicians/2015/02/16/11-most-significant-presidents-lgbt-americans

Rutherglen, George. 1987. "Disparate Impact under Title VII: An Objective Theory of Discrimination." *Virginia Law Review* 73, no. 7: 1297–345.

Senzee, Thom. 2014. "PHOTOS: Taiwan Pride 2014 Is All About Marriage Equality." *Advocate*, 27 October. Accessed February 29, 2016. http://www.advocate.com/pride/2014/10/27/photos-taiwan-pride-2014-all-about-marriage-equality

Tran, Chi-Ser, Glenn D. Magpantay, and Margaret Fung. 2013. "The Asian American Vote 2012." New York: The Asian American Legal Defense and Education Fund. Accessed February 29, 2016. http://aaldef.org/Asian%20American%20Vote%202012. pdf

U.S. Equal Employment Opportunity Commission. 2015. "Addressing Sexual Orientation and Gender Identity Discrimination in Federal Civilian Employment: A Guide to Employment Rights, Protections, and Responsibilities." June. Washington, DC: Equal Employment Opportunity Commission.

Wong, Frank Y., Vincent A. Crisotomo, Daniel Bao, Brian D. Smith, Darwin Young, Z. Jennifer Huang, Michelle E. Buchhloz, and Stephanie N. Frangos. 2011. "Development and Implementation of a Collaborative, Multistakeholder Research and Practice Model on HIV Prevention Targeting Asian/Pacific Islander Men in the United States Who Have Sex with Men." *American Journal of Public Health* 101(4): 623–31.

# NEGOTIATING AMERICAN INDIAN INCLUSION:
## Sovereignty, Same-Sex Marriage, and Sexual Minorities in Indian Country

VALERIE LAMBERT

On April 17, 2013, two intertwined, symbolic actions occurred in the New Zealand Parliament. In a vote of 77 to 44, this nation became the thirteenth country in the world to legalize same-sex marriage.[1] When it became clear that the bill had passed, lawmakers and spectators broke into song, specifically a Maori song, "Pokarekare Ana," sung in the Maori language.[2] As an American and an enrolled member of the Choctaw Nation, I felt a mix of emotions at the time, including happiness for New Zealand and sorrow for Americans and American Indians. In the United States, a comparable victory for what some activists have termed "marriage equality" was not achieved until June 26, 2015, more than two years after New Zealand's passage of the bill and more than fourteen years after the Netherlands became the first country to legalize same-sex marriage. Moreover, as far as I am aware, no American Indian even speculated that a Native-authored song would be sung in a Native language in court when the decision was announced. And indeed, no such song was heard issuing from the US Supreme Court building on that historic day.

The legalization of same-sex marriage in New Zealand, celebrated with a Maori song, was one of several events that prompted me to help document how American Indians—a population that Russ Hepler rightly describes as "one of the American groups overlooked in the debate"—participated in the same-sex marriage movement in the United States.[3] That American Indians have been excluded and marginalized from the historiography of this major US social movement is puzzling, and especially so given that the movement has, at least in some arenas, attempted to foreground the queer subject in the larger social context of a settler-colonial investment in "constructing Native peoples as hypersexual and nonheteronormative."[4] In 2011, queer Native scholar Chris Finley explains this and other holes in the scholarship by asserting that queer

Valerie Lambert is an enrolled member of the Choctaw Nation. She is an associate professor of anthropology and an affiliate of American Indian and Indigenous Studies at the University of North Carolina at Chapel Hill. She is president-elect of the Association of Indigenous Anthropologists.

studies "only rarely addresses Native peoples and Native issues" and that neither queer studies nor Native studies "has shown much interest in critically engaging the other," a condition that fortunately has been changing.[5] She adds that American Indian sexualities in general have been overlooked, partly because a Native "silencing of sexuality" exists in Indian Country—one that "especially applies to queer sexuality."[6]

Adopting Vasu Reddy's conceptualization of *queer* as that which "signals an active force challenging compulsory heterosexuality," this article explores American Indian efforts to both queer marriage and to impede and halt that queering.[7] I focus on the ten-year period when same-sex marriage received the most national attention, the decade prior to the 2015 Supreme Court decision that affirmed the right to marry as a right under the US constitution.[8] Amy Brandzel has pointed out that during this period, gay and lesbian rights activists who supported advocating for same-sex marriage were divided from queer theorists who were critical of that objective on the grounds that marriage reifies identity categories and is "assimilationist in tone and/or outcome."[9] My research has found abundant evidence of American Indian challenges to homophobia and heteropatriarchy—challenges which help queer marriage and thus resonate with queer-theorist goals. Nonetheless, as will be seen, like many non-Native LGBTQ activists in the United States during this period, many Indians embraced the goal of legalizing same-sex marriage, engaging in complex processes of resistance, evasion, and even annexation of institutional power.[10]

The descriptions and analysis in this article have benefited greatly from and build upon queer theorists' explorations of the forms and consequences of institutional power used to discipline and align Native queer subjects. Mark Rifkin, for example, systematically deconstructs and denaturalizes institutions, among them marriage, and identifies the ways institutions and institutional power work to erase and marginalize the experiences of Natives and Native writers.[11] Scott Lauria Morgensen insightfully discusses both non-Native and Native queer modernities, productively framing the latter as creative assertions of resistance to settler-colonial narratives and institutions.[12] Together with the stellar ethnographic work on Native sexual minorities by both Brian Gilley and Jenny Davis (Chickasaw Nation), this scholarship attests to the value of attending to the subjectivities of queer Natives living in exile from reservation homelands, a number of whom claim a Native identity but cannot meet the membership requirements of any tribe.[13]

Following the work of Jennifer Nez Denetdale (Navajo Nation) and Chris Finley (Colville Confederated Tribes), my study continues the work of extending these explorations more fully into early-twenty-first-century tribal homelands and addressing them as part of contemporary internal tribal domestic affairs.[14] For example, this article provides comprehensive coverage of the state of tribal same-sex marriage law during the second decade of the twenty-first century. My discussion centers on negotiations among Indians of Indian-authored tribal marriage laws, and the immediate context for most of my materials are tribal governments, tribal courts, and other institutions controlled almost exclusively by Indians. Additionally, I hope to supplement the growing literature on queer Natives and issues by deploying a different lens and angle than those generally used in queer studies, as well as by addressing often-bypassed spaces. This article pools and helps make sense of diverse Indian perspectives and seeks to bring issues of same-sex marriage in Indian Country beyond legal specialists to wider scholarly audiences. A central goal of the second half of the discussion is to present a range of Indian voices, in Indians' own words, that emanate from these spaces. At the same time, my goal is to illuminate aspects of the social and political contexts in which these voices are expressed and these actions take place.

As this journal's readership and others familiar with Indian Country are aware, the legal status of "tribal member" is a prerequisite to participation in tribal legal and political affairs and is the bedrock upon which other tribal rights are layered. Tribal members thus have different sets of rights in their tribes; most have a partial set, while some have a full set of tribal rights. As will be seen, queer tribal members—a category that almost always has only a partial set—have been working to expand their set of rights, challenging homophobia and heteropatriarchy and queering marriage in tribal nations by legalizing same-sex marriage. To be sure, in many homelands homophobia is a part of modern Native nation-building, as Denetdale has noted, and may help explain a queer, largely non-Native "suspicion of Native nationalisms," as Melanie Yazzie has described.[15] This suspicion is sometimes dismissive and disrespectful of tribes and tribal sovereignty, and it is hoped that my findings will lessen some of this disrespect.

My exploration of tribal lawmaking around same-sex marriage began partly in response to the pressing need for a scholar to assemble, synthesize, and provide a framework for understanding the growing primary materials on same-sex marriage in Indian Country and Indian voices. The sketch I provide here is best conceptualized as mapping; that is, it is intended to provide a bird's-eye view of institutional shifts in marriage in Indian Country, rather than an up-close, comprehensive examination of same-sex marriage debates in a single tribal nation, for example. It finds inspiration in Finley's excellent question, "How does the queering of Native bodies affect sovereignty struggles?" but can take only a small step toward addressing that question.[16] My materials implicitly address another fruitful question, herein adapted to the reservation context: "How exactly [do] we want LGBT people and queer others to align themselves with [tribal] citizenship[?]"[17]

I begin by discussing at some length the demographic, political, and legal contexts that profoundly shape some of the key ways in which Indians in tribal homelands participate in debates over same-sex marriage. I then focus attention on the lack of uniformity in the early-twenty-first-century tribal laws that govern same-sex marriage in Indian Country. Tribal marriage laws, of course, emerge from particular social and cultural contexts. Drawing upon interview evidence with queer Natives, I describe and discuss the reality that some tribal homelands are welcoming to this sexual minority, others are hostile, and the overwhelming majority are uneven and thus are not dissimilar to most US communities. In the course of tracing some of the contours of queer Native experience in tribal homelands, I identify and analyze some of the arguments Indians have been using to debate the issue of same-sex marriage. Like the sovereignty that Indians exercise over marriage and marriage laws, these arguments help define the distinctiveness of Indian participation in the US movement to legalize same-sex marriage. In this, my descriptions and analyses have benefited greatly from the work of legal scholars Matthew L. M. Fletcher (Grand Traverse Band) and Ann Tweedy in tribal law and federal law regarding same-sex marriage. Their penetrating insights have inspired me to use anthropological approaches and perspectives to further investigate and analyze these issues.[18]

Several different research methods were used. The vast majority of my research mined "narrative spaces," to use Morgensen's phrase, examining newspapers, web-based publications, books, and archives.[19] As an American Indian sociocultural anthropologist with training in legal anthropology and American Indian studies, I also drew from participant-observation field research data and interviews that I have conducted in Indian Country over the course of two decades. I received permission for all interviews and field research I conducted, which included visits to the homelands of a number of the tribes discussed. Lastly, I drew upon my prior professional experience working in the Bureau of Indian Affairs in Washington, DC. My sixteen months working in the Division of Tribal Government Services helped me to forge a broader and more complex understanding of Indian tribes, especially of their marked diversity.

Although I occasionally use "Native" and "Native nation," most often I use the words "American Indian" and "Indian tribes," both because these terms denote legal categories and because Indians themselves use them widely in Indian Country. In accordance with federal and tribal legal conventions, I capitalize the word "tribe" when referring to a specific tribe, but not when referring to a non-specific tribe or group of tribes. Several times I use "LGBTQ" (lesbian, gay, bisexual, transgender, queer) to refer to sexual minorities, an acronym (and its variations) that is in widespread use among queer Natives. Despite this, Jenny Davis has made the critical point that the meanings and boundaries of these terms are not always "synonymous with dominant understandings" when used by Indians.[20] For example, she explains that some Indians understand sexual and gender binaries as "potentially overlapping states" rather than "mutually exclusive opposing poles." Likewise, she cautions that Indians may frequently and "simultaneously" "align and diverge from mainstream discourses regarding sexuality."[21] Throughout this article, Davis's important insights should be kept in mind.

## AMERICAN INDIANS AND MARRIAGE LAWMAKING

The societal context for American Indian participation in debates over same-sex marriage helps illuminate the ways in which Indians engage with this issue. The apparent lack of visibility of Indians in public debates about marriage equality is most striking, especially from 2005 to 2015, when such debates were at their height. Demographics provide a partial explanation: Indians comprise less than one percent of the US population. In addition, Indians are underrepresented in the legislative branches of the US state and national governments, some of the most visible sites for these public debates. From 2005 to 2015, for example, in seven out of the ten years only one member of the US Congress was Indian out of the total of 535 members.[22]

Yet American Indians in the United States do exercise leadership on issues that include the topic of same-sex marriage. It is simply that this leadership tends to be limited to the islands of authority that are our tribal homelands; Indian agency would be significantly more apparent if our primary domestic political actions took place within mainstream US politics. A constellation of legal facts helps shape this context. Indian tribes are recognized as possessing "a significant sovereignty"[23] that US and tribal law often characterize as "preconstitutional," because this sovereignty predates the formation of the United States, and also "extraconstitutional," because this sovereignty exists outside the US Constitution. As preconstitutional and extraconstitutional sovereigns who did not participate in or consent to the provisions of the US Constitution and were never incorporated into the federal union, Indian tribes are not subject to the US Constitution and Bill of Rights. Consequently, the 2015 Supreme Court decision which found that the equal protection and due process clauses of the Fourteenth Amendment include a "fundamental right to marry," *Obergefell v. Hodges*, does not apply to the homelands of Indian tribes.[24] Prior to this landmark decision, the state laws and amendments to state constitutions that banned same-sex marriage in many states also did not apply to tribes, as "states have no authority to regulate on-reservation domestic relations."[25] Interestingly, the Defense of Marriage Act passed by Congress in 1996, which was ruled unconstitutional in 2015, specifically included Indian tribes.[26]

Despite the fact that federal agents and missionaries spent much time and effort attempting to regulate Native sexuality and "exercised a heteronormative influence,"[27] Indian sovereignty over marriage and related domestic law is legally well established, "quite pronounced," and represents some of the most secure rights exercised by Indian tribes in the United States.[28] Tribes have "undisturbed inherent authority to decide matters of domestic and family law within Indian Country," Matthew Fletcher (Grand Traverse Band) explains in his foundational article about same-sex marriage in Indian Country.[29] "The hard inner core of tribal sovereignty," he continues, is "the *Williams v. Lee* formulation that Indians have the right to make their own laws and be governed by them. At the center of this core are domestic relations and family law."[30] As justices of the Navajo Nation Supreme Court have explained, exclusive control over marriage law is critical to "enhance Navajo sovereignty, preserve the Navajo marriage tradition, and protect those who adhere to the Navajo tradition."[31] Such assertions are common in Indian Country.

Fletcher explains that the assemblage of US case law that supports the "plenary and exclusive inherent authority" of Indian tribes over marriage begins with cases from the late-nineteenth century.[32] The earliest such case appears to be *Kobogum v. Jackson Iron Co.* In 1889, the Michigan Supreme Court justice declared,

> We had no more right to control [tribal] domestic usages than those of Turkey or India . . . [A]mong these Indians [Chippewa] polygamous marriages have always been recognized as valid. . . . We must either hold that there can be no valid Indian marriage, or we must hold that all marriages are valid which by Indian usages are so regarded. There is no middle ground which can be taken, so long as our own laws are not binding on the tribes.[33]

In the 1906 Cherokee intermarriage cases and *U.S. v. Quiver* in 1916, the courts reiterated that "domestic relations issues within tribes should be regulated by tribes themselves according to their own laws and customs," and added that US courts should not and "would not get involved in these issues."[34] In *Ortley v. Ross* (1907) the court declared, "It has always been the policy of the general government to permit the Indian tribes as such to regulate their own domestic affairs, and to control the intercourse between the sexes by their own customs and usages."[35] A final example of a foundational case in early case law that affirmed tribes' sovereign rights over marriage is *Hallowell v. Commons* (1914). The court pointed out that the Omaha tribe had a "right" to practice polygamy in accordance with their "customs" and that this right "must be respected."[36] More than one hundred years later, in the aftermath of the *Obergefell v. Hodges* decision, in 2015 BIA public affairs director and my former co-worker Nedra Darling (Prairie Band Potawatomi Nation) referred to this weighty legal foundation, explaining that "because the tribes have the ability to regulate domestic relationships" the federal government would not "interfere" in the marriage laws of tribes.[37] This legal foundation is an important resource for tribes exercising their sovereign right to regulate domestic relations, especially given the extensive history of efforts by federal agents, missionaries and others to interfere in Indian marriage and other tribal domestic affairs.[38]

## TRIBAL LAWMAKING ON SAME-SEX MARRIAGE

An overview of Indian tribal law on same-sex marriage shows that Indian tribes have been engaged with lawmaking on same-sex marriage longer than many world nations, with lack of uniformity across tribes being this lawmaking's defining feature. Ann Tweedy has analyzed the content of many of these tribal laws and the processes by which they were enacted, building upon Fletcher's brilliant overview of their legal foundations. She rightly points out that such laws "have been under-researched and under-theorized" and argues for more scholarship in this area.[39] As is well-known in Indian Country, the first tribe to explicitly legalize same-sex marriage is the Coquille Indian Tribe. From the passage of the Coquille law in 2008 until the 2015 *Obergefell v. Hodges* decision, a period when many US states banned same-sex marriage and the period when Tweedy published her important survey, more than a dozen additional Indian tribes either legalized same-sex marriage or performed marriages of same-sex couples under existing tribal, sex-neutral marriage laws. While lengthy, to list these tribes by name may help dissipate the stereotype that tribes are highly homophobic, a belief that is common in some circles. During the period from 2005 to 2015, tribes with laws allowing same-sex marriage included the Suquamish Indian Tribe, Little Traverse Bay Bands of Odawa Indians, Mashantucket Pequot Tribal Nation, Pokagon Band of Potowatomi Indians, Iipay Nation of Santa Ysabel, Confederated Tribes of the Colville Reservation, Cheyenne and Arapaho Tribes, Eastern Shoshone and Northern Arapaho Tribes, Leech Lake Band of Ojibwe, Minnesota Chippewa Tribe–Leech Lake Band, Puyallup Tribe, Tlingit and Haida Indian Tribes, Oneida Nation (Wisconsin), and Keweenaw Bay Indian Community.[40] Since 2015, other tribes have also legalized same-sex marriage, most notably the Cherokee Nation and the Osage Nation. Most often, tribal councils or other tribal lawmaking bodies vote to change or uphold tribal marriage laws; alternatively, tribes may hold national referenda on same-sex marriage.[41]

Referring to these tribes' legalization of same-sex marriage prior to the *Obergefell* decision, Tweedy makes the critical point that "tribal sovereignty is very important to tribes. They don't want to just adopt what the U.S. does."[42] Indeed, in at least three states that banned same-sex marriage between 2009 and 2013 (Oregon, Michigan, and Oklahoma), the first same-sex couples to be legally married were married by Indian tribes under tribal law. As journalist Gyasi Ross (Blackfeet Nation) has commented, "there were many Tribes who were ahead of the game and said, 'No, we can't treat humans like that. We have to treat them all equally.'"[43] To be married under tribal law, however, many tribes require at least one of the parties to be a tribal member.[44] An individual who is not enrolled in their spouse's tribe may or may not receive benefits from that tribe. When the Coquille Tribe married two women in 2009, for example, non-member spouse Jeni Branting acquired health insurance fully funded by the Tribe and the right to participate in tribal events,[45] but some tribes (such as my own) do not provide direct tribal benefits to non-member spouses. (My husband, who is enrolled in the Eastern Band of Cherokee Indians, receives no direct benefits from the tribe in which I am enrolled, the Choctaw Nation.)

A number of Indian tribes ban same-sex marriage, a fact that is well-known in Indian Country.[46] In 2005, when same-sex marriage was legal in the nearby states of Arizona, New Mexico, and Utah, the legislature of the largest Indian tribe, the Navajo Nation, passed the Diné Marriage Act outlawing same-sex marriage.[47] In 2004, the second-largest tribe, the Cherokee Nation, banned same-sex marriage, but importantly, twelve years later the Cherokee law was overturned. By July 2017, among the tribes that outlawed same-sex marriage were the Chickasaw Nation, Choctaw Nation, Seminole Nation, Muscogee (Creek) Nation, Kickapoo Tribe, Navajo Nation, Kalispel Indian Community, Sac and Fox Tribe of the Mississippi in Iowa, and the Ak-Chin Indian Community (Arizona).[48]

If nearly "1,000 federal benefits hinge on marital status,"[49] the benefits of tribal recognition of a marriage can also be significant. For example, Navajo law banning same-sex marriage denies same-sex couples the right to participate in medical decisions that pertain to their partner, the right to share in a home on a lease site, and other rights enjoyed by married heterosexual couples who live on the reservation.[50] Not only is same-sex marriage against tribal law in the Ak-Chin Indian Community, but so is the cohabitation of couples who are unmarried or whose marriage is not recognized by the Tribe.[51] In the 2010s, Cleo Pablo, a lesbian with a home on the Ak-Chin Indian reservation who married a woman under Arizona state law, gave up that home rather than risk arrest by tribal police simply for living with her family. She and her spouse and their children relocated to Phoenix fifty miles north.[52] Thus, as Native journalist Julian Brave NoiseCat has pointed out, same-sex couples living on the reservations of tribes that ban same-sex marriage "are denied the same rights and benefits afforded to heterosexual couples . . . in areas like housing, property rights and custody of children."[53] Explaining her decision to take legal action against her Tribe, Pablo said, "As Native people in the community, we're taught to stand in the background, not create waves . . . [before,] I wouldn't rock the boat, [but recently] I've done the opposite. . . . It gets to the point if you don't say anything, nothing is going to change."[54]

Not all tribal marriage laws explicitly approve or prohibit same-sex marriage, a fact that contributes to the lack of uniformity in tribal marriage laws. For example, in the marriage law of the Cheyenne and Arapaho Tribes, the gender of participants is unspecified.[55] Tribal law states that at least one spouse must be a tribal member, at least one must live within tribal jurisdiction, and both must have Indian ancestry.[56] At least three same-sex couples have married under this sex-neutral tribal marriage law. Yankton Sioux tribal marriage law uses the terms "husband" and "wife." It does not, however, specify that a husband must be male and a wife be female, thereby providing room for same-sex couples to marry under Yankton Sioux marriage law. A third example is the marriage law of the Eastern Band of Cherokee Indians (EBCI). In 2014 the tribal council amended their marriage law that was based on North Carolina marriage law, declaring, "the licensing and solemnizing of same-sex marriages are not allowed within this jurisdiction."[57] At the same time, however, the tribe's acting attorney general affirmed that the EBCI recognizes as legal the marriages of same-sex couples married elsewhere and that same-sex couples can "live on [EBCI] tribal land with no penalty."[58] Lastly, there are perhaps a dozen tribes, including the Sault Ste. Marie Tribe of Chippewa Indians, that define the marriage law of their tribe as the marriage law of the US state where their tribe's homeland is located.[59] As a result, when the 2015 *Obergefell* decision determined that US state marriage laws banning same-sex marriage were unconstitutional, same-sex marriage became legal for these tribes as well.

Emerging as they do from particular social and cultural contexts—as this article will later explore in greater detail—tribal laws governing same-sex marriage have been made and carried out with varying levels of dissent among tribal lawmakers and citizenries. Some tribes have reached near-consensus on same-sex marriage. Both the 2011 vote of the Suquamish Tribe's legislature and the 2015 vote of the business committee of the Oneida Nation (Wisconsin) were unanimous in legalizing same-sex marriage.[60] In regard to the Cheyenne and Arapaho Tribes, Lieutenant Governor Amber Bighorse asserted that the marriage of same-sex couples has been unremarkable because same-sex marriage "has never been controversial."[61] About her Tribe's decision to legalize same-sex marriage, Chief Justice Debra O'Gara of the Tlingit and Haida Indian Tribes remarked, "There was very little controversy over the same gender aspect because everybody believed it [marriage] should be open. Whoever our citizens are should have the same rights as everyone else."[62] She added that there was a lot more discussion of whether members of the same clan should marry.[63] By contrast, in some tribes there has been near-agreement not to approve, but to limit or even ban tribal recognition of same-sex marriage. For example, the 2014 EBCI law that did recognize same-sex marriages performed elsewhere but banned marriage ceremonies for same-sex couples on tribal land was passed with only one dissenting vote.[64]

Historian Gregory Smithers has correctly pointed out that many Indian "communities are divided—sometimes bitterly so—over the issue."[65] In the early 2010s this was the case for the Little Traverse Bay Bands of Odawa Indians. In 2012 the tribal legislature voted down a bill to legalize same-sex marriage by five to four; the following year the bill passed, but by another highly divided vote of five to four.[66] John Keshick III, a Little Traverse representative, remarked, "It was a close vote, and I [simply] voted the way I was brought up," which was against same-sex marriage.[67] In 2005 the Navajo legislature voted to ban same-sex marriage by a significant margin, by a vote of sixty-two to fourteen.[68] Though these results may suggest the presence of only a small amount of dissent, by all accounts great "bitterness and divisions" resulted from what Navajo lawmaker Otto Tso described as the "heated debate" over this law (termed the Diné Marriage Act), a debate that occurred both in the tribal legislature and throughout the Tribe's more than 27,000-square-mile homeland.[69] Following the vote, Navajo Nation President Joe Shirley, Jr. then vetoed the act, citing its "discriminatory nature," "violation of a basic human right," and alleged "low priority for Navajo citizens."[70] Navajo lawmaker Larry Anderson launched a counterattack and eventually obtained the necessary votes to override the veto and make the act into law.[71] Both then and now, Navajos have engaged in vocal protests of the Diné Marriage Act and have mobilized extensively to expand the set of tribal rights accorded LGBTQ Navajos.[72]

## THE CLIMATE FOR QUEER INDIANS ON OR NEAR TRIBAL HOMELANDS

The marriage laws of Indian tribes, as we have seen, range broadly from laws that accord same-sex couples and heterosexual couples the same rights, to laws that discriminate against same-sex couples and individuals who do not conform to hegemonies of sexuality and gender. The foregoing overview speaks to existence of a range of spaces in tribal homelands, some of which harbor hostile or mixed attitudes towards sexual minorities, and others which welcome and include these populations. The remaining discussion provides richer descriptions of these spaces and the perspectives and experiences of queer Indians. After first tracing some of the contours of these experiences and perspectives, I then turn to some of the arguments Indians have been using in debating same-sex marriage. Like the previous survey of the sovereignty that Indians exercise over marriage laws and the lack of uniformity of these laws across tribes, these arguments help define the distinctiveness of Indian participation in the US marriage-equality movement. In addition, such distinctiveness stems from the particular individuals who have exercised leadership in the movement and have helped to bring about social change. The influence of some of these figures deserves greater scholarly and popular attention.

A good number of scholars and activists have worked during the past few decades to document what Brian Gilley characterizes as the "ubiquitous homophobia that alienates" queer Indians.[73] By all accounts both Indians and non-Indians are perpetrators of the bullying, discrimination, and hateful treatment that many queer Indians experience. Alarmingly high rates of victimization plague the American Indian and Alaska Native LGBTQ population, a report of the National Gay and Lesbian Task Force found, with the violent beating death of Fred Martinez, Jr. in 2011 serving as a powerful symbol of the widespread mistreatment of LGBTQ Indians in general, and transgender Indians in particular.[74] Martinez, Jr., a sixteen-year-old transgender Navajo woman, was brutally murdered near the reservation border town of Cortez, Colorado by non-Indian Sean Murphy, who later told others that he had "bug-smashed a fag."[75] The grassroots organization Native OUT has focused needed attention on the story of Martinez and other queer Indians who have been murdered, with Navajos comprising a disturbing two-thirds of the murder victims listed on the group's website.[76]

Heather Purser, a Suquamish Indian and a lesbian, reported that she was attacked and beaten by fellow Indian students at Haskell Indian Nations University "for being different" when she attended the BIA-run, Indian-only school in the early 2000s.[77] She was victimized again, she added, when the university first thwarted an investigation into the crime, then prematurely terminated it. Purser shared that after these types of incidents "You hide yourself so well that you forget who you are. I know I did for such a long time."[78] Darren Black Bear, a citizen of the Cheyenne and Arapaho Tribes, said that while traveling in about 2007, he and his then-boyfriend Jason Pickel (now his spouse), "were denied entrance to a hotel because we were gay."[79]

The findings of scholars and activists who are helping to document this discrimination suggest that such incidents are not uncommon. A substantial number of the dozens of queer Native consultants whom Gilley interviewed between 1998 and 2010 reported experiences of discrimination, ostracism, and rejection by both members of the larger, non-Indian society and citizens of their own tribes. Gilley conducted field research in Colorado and Oklahoma on the experiences of queer, mostly male Indian members of two different "two spirit" organizations.[80] His book, *Becoming Two-Spirit: Gay Identity and Social Acceptance in Indian Country*, provides much insight into the psychological and emotional pain his consultants experience, their strategies of resistance, and the climates for queer Indians on or near their tribal homelands (many of Gilley's consultants are affiliated with tribes located in the US Southwest and Southern Midwest). Gilley's work after *Becoming Two-Spirit* explored the ways that some of these men pursued "personal empowerment" in ceremonial contexts by means of an orientation grounded in "docility to cultural authority" that did not "disrupt."[81]

Despite the great diversity of tribal affiliations that Gilley's consultants likely represent, their accounts exhibit striking similarities. Gilley reports, for example, "Most believed the common Native idea that they were (and still are) harming their families by being gay."[82] In addition, he found that many of his consultants' families and fellow tribal members associated "same-sex relations and gay culture-related behaviors . . . with "whiteness" and white-dominated geographic space, such as the major cities."[83] Gilley found a related belief to be common in this part of Indian Country: "If an Indian man is recognized as gay, it is thought that he learned this behavior from white people."[84] Finally, Gilley documents resemblances among his consultants' coming-out stories. "We tried to come out to the elders a couple years ago," said one, "and the elders were very much against it, and were very mean-spirited."[85] Another reported, "There's homophobia alive and well on many Native reservation communities. The families, the friends, they say you are no longer welcome here: 'If you wanna engage in that kind of activity, there are places . . . the big cities. That's where you go to do it. Here, we do not condone that type of activity. We will not tolerate that kind of activity."[86]

The writings of Zachary Pullin (Chippewa Cree Tribe) lend much-needed insight into the feelings of alienation and exclusion experienced by queer Indians in the northern Great Plains and Pacific Northwest. Of his childhood experiences on Rocky Boy's reservation in Montana and later in Spokane, Washington, Pullin writes "I had grown up with the idea in my own mind that I was less of a man" and "[t]here was a deep sense that I couldn't present my whole self in that space."[87] Nearly all Gilley's consultants describe themselves as having found healing and belonging in two-spirit spaces created mostly outside tribal homelands; likewise, Pullin continues, "It wasn't until I attended a two-spirit gathering—a cultural event that draws together two-spirit individuals for traditional dancing, storytelling and other customs—that I entered a dance arena and felt authentic about who I was in my place in the circle [and did not have to hide my identity as both Native and gay]."[88]

The Navajo Nation and the Cherokee Nation have received public attention for the antagonism that some of their citizens have shown to their queer fellow tribal members; they are the first- and second-largest tribes in the United States, respectively. By many accounts, it is common for queer Navajos to feel unwelcome on their reservation. As an older female Navajo told Gilley, "Indian gay men . . . went into the white community, 'cause our tribes didn't want 'em."[89] Gay activist and Navajo Alray Nelson hints at an indirect shunning or near-banishment of queer Navajos by some on the reservation. "We still have leaders today," he said, "that say, 'It is fine to get a marriage license off the reservation and to live in a city like San Francisco or in a border town like Farmington or Gallup, but don't get married here at home because we're not going to recognize it.'"[90] In an attempt to educate the broader public about Indian issues in 2014, Pullin asserted, "There are complicated debates about the rights of LGBTQ Native men and women on reservations, like the one taking place on the Navajo Nation, where LGBTQ rights advocates have received support from some and resistance from others in their attempt to undo the 2005 Diné Marriage Act."[91] About the Navajo debate, tribal member Amber Crotty remarked, "Hopefully it attracts Navajos who are living in urban settings to come back home and have this discussion."[92]

Reactions to a tribal same-sex marriage in the early 2000s helped some of the citizens of the Cherokee Nation to earn a reputation for being unwelcoming to queer tribal members. In May 2004, two female citizens of the Cherokee Nation, Kathy Reynolds and Dawn McKinley, were granted a marriage license under the tribe's marriage law, then sex-neutral. The Tribe's attorney general, followed by a group of Cherokee Nation lawmakers, then filed petitions seeking to invalidate the same-sex marriage. These were dismissed by the Cherokee Nation Judicial Appeals Tribunal because petitioners failed to show that they had been harmed by the marriage.[93] Cherokee tribal council representative Lina O'Leary declared, "We don't want gay marriage in the Cherokee Nation. It's that simple."[94] About such reactions to her marriage, Reynolds remarked, "Dawn and I are private people, and we simply wish to live our lives in peace and quiet, just as other married couples are permitted to do."[95] By the end of 2004, the Cherokee Nation legislative branch had banned same-sex marriage pursuant to the Cherokee Nation Marriage and Family Protection Act. Twelve years later, in December 2016 the Cherokee Nation Supreme Court ruled this law unconstitutional, and same-sex couples can now marry under Cherokee Nation law.

Although a number of queer Natives, as we have seen, report discrimination, prejudice, and hate in Indian Country, others state that they have experienced love, acceptance, and affirmation of their difference on reservations and in other Native spaces. Heather Purser, a lesbian who faced hate from fellow Indian students at Haskell Indian Nations University, said that her Tribe, the Suquamish, has embraced her for who she is both on and off the reservation, which is about twenty miles from Seattle in central Puget Sound. "Indian people, especially in my community, are way more understanding [about discrimination] because they've been through it," she explains.[96] "The elders know what it's like to go to school and have their hair cut off and be called a filthy, sick person just because of who they are."[97] Further reflecting upon her Tribe, Purser adds, "Suquamish are very live-and-let-live. Very progressive. Here, we were all family. Suquamish has always been my safe place."[98] The Squaxin Island Tribe is also widely described as accepting of queer tribal members. For example, Ron Whitener, executive director of the University of Washington's Native American Law Center and a tribal member, has an openly gay brother who was elected to the Squaxin Island tribal council. Whitener reports that his brother's sexuality "was [simply] not an issue" in the election that brought him into office; his explanation is that Squaxin Island tribal members "have a much more fluid spirituality."[99]

Legalizing same-sex marriage has been a way for some tribes to show acceptance and support of their queer tribal members. As Ken Tanner, chief of the first tribe to legalize same-sex marriage, explained the Tribe's decision: "Our directive is to provide recognition and respect to all . . . Native Americans, more than anyone, know about discrimination."[100] When the Iipay Nation of Santa Ysabel passed a resolution in support of same-sex marriage in 2013, California was a state that outlawed same-sex marriage. Tribal Chairman Virgil Perez "aggressively defended marriage equality" in his public announcement to the tribe's citizenry, as well as to non-Indians where the Tribe's reservation is located in south-central California. Our Tribe "won't ever forget the sting of prejudice," he cried, "or stand passively by when others suffer discrimination or denial of basic human rights!"[101] Also that year, the tribal council of the Confederated Tribes of the Colville Reservation in Washington voted unanimously to legalize same-sex marriage. Gays "have a special place in . . . [our] society," tribal leader Michael Finley explained; "they've always been accepted."[102] Finley's words were echoed that year by Dexter McNamara, the tribal chairman of the Little Traverse Bay Bands of Odawa Indians, whose headquarters is in Michigan, a state that banned same-sex marriage at the time. "This is about people being happy," McNamara explained.[103] "I've always felt that either you believe in equal rights or you are prejudiced. We [Odawa Indians] don't have a dividing line . . . Everyone deserves to live the lives of their choice."[104]

Tribal chairman McNamara himself married two men under tribal law: Tim LaCroix, an enrolled tribal member, and his boyfriend of thirty years, Gene Barfield, a non-Native. Barfield, deeply moved by the actions of McNamara and the Tribe, stood humbly in the tribal building after the ceremony and said: "This is their turf. They have their own government, they have their own police force, they have their own rules and regulations. They're very big on respect, and for them to say to us, 'We respect your relationship and your prerogative to define it as you choose,' is really special." Nearly speechless after the ceremony, newlywed LaCroix said, "I'm so proud of my tribe for doing this. I just can't say enough." Tribal communications coordinator Annette VanDeCar explained to the public, "We as Indians are taught to respect people as individuals, and as individuals people have the right to decide what is best for them."[105] Indeed, more than one hundred tribal citizens organized a wedding reception for the gay couple.[106] A similar experience followed the 2013 wedding of another gay couple under Cheyenne and Arapaho tribal law. These tribes are located in the state of Oklahoma, which banned same-sex marriage until 2014, when the Supreme Court ruled such laws violated the US Constitution. Private donors paid for the major expenses of the couple's reception, including the catering, the cake, and the use of the reception hall. The couple reported the "vast majority" of tribal members to be "very supportive."[107]

## DEBATES OVER SAME-SEX MARRIAGE

Although American Indians, like other populations, deploy a wide range of arguments in promoting and defending their positions either for or against same-sex marriage, two distinct categories of arguments pervade Indian Country regarding Natives' participation in the marriage equality movement: arguments that appeal to "tradition" and arguments that invoke Christianity and its teachings. In Indian Country, these two arguments tend to be used to support opposed positions on same-sex marriage, but this is not always the case, as will be seen.

However, before analyzing this rhetoric and discussing the insights into Indian participation in these debates that it provides, a critical point should be made about how "culture" and "tradition" operate in American Indian contexts. It can be challenging and even dicey for actors in any society to claim and legitimize a practice or belief as "traditional" or as part of a group's "culture," but for American Indians the process is further complicated by problematic and offensive stereotypes produced by non-Natives. An Indian tribe's culture, for example, is often simply presumed to be singular, while its traditions, or what are recognized as such, are often constructed by outsiders as cloudless, uncomplicated, and immobile, treated like a time capsule from an implicitly static, simple past. For these stereotypes to be replaced by more accurate and productive conceptualizations of Indian traditions and cultures, each tribe's culture should be treated as a collection of diverse practices and ideas, as collective creative assemblages. These products should be understood as complex, open-ended, and shifting, and it should be expected that, as is the case for all societies, parts of such assemblages are piecemeal and contradictory. Finally, it should always be kept in mind that these collective creative assemblages are products of history and thus have multiple authors and origins.

Such a reconceptualization of Indian traditions and culture is important for many reasons. For one, it fosters greater appreciation for the enormity and complexity of Native legal projects, including tribes' efforts to exercise their legal right to interpret the Indian Civil Rights Act of 1968 "in terms of their own cultures and traditions" and to incorporate tribally specific traditions into tribal laws and judicial proceedings.[108] Lopez asks how Navajo tribal judges "determine relevant Navajo culture" and, hinting at the many challenges this question presents, identifies one of a myriad of questions these judges face: "Do they look to the culture of pre-European contact . . . [or to] the contemporary [Navajo] community?"[109] Related questions include who gets to decide what is "traditional," and what role these constructs should have in tribal lawmaking, adjudication, and enforcement. In Navajo debates concerning the tribal law banning same-sex marriage, each side has argued that Navajo traditions and culture support their position. Tradition is actually at "the heart of the [marriage equality] issue" in this Tribe, as NoiseCat points out.[110]

Indeed, some Navajos contend that embracing multiple gender identities and extending marriage to non-heterosexual partners is following ancient Navajo cultural prescriptions. LBGTQ Navajos and their supporters cite the *nádleeh*—a gender identity that is neither male nor female and that sanctions non-heterosexual sex—as proof that, in ancient times "third, and possibly fourth, genders were accepted and celebrated,"[111] and that same-sex couples "were recognized" and "had every right to be productive members of our community."[112] Denetdale adds that in the Navajo creation narratives "the *nádleehí* played a crucial role in bringing about harmony between men and women after a period of conflict and unrest between the two sexes."[113]

A coalition headed by some past and present Navajo lawmakers has opposed this position, among them Kenneth Maryboy and Larry Anderson. Maryboy has argued that "in the traditional Navajo way, gay marriage is a big no-no ... It boils down to the circle of life ... We are put on the earth to produce off-spring."[114] Anderson, who has argued that the ban on same-sex marriage is necessary "to strengthen family values,"[115] has explained, "[t]raditionally, Navajos have always respected the woman and man union. Family values are important. The Navajo elders said we should respect both men and women."[116] Denetdale contends that such claims are best understood as a "conflation of Navajo traditional values with mainstream American values" including "monogamy, the nuclear family, and heterosexuality."[117] Indeed many non-Indians, including the leaders of the National Organization for Marriage, define heterosexual marriage as "traditional" American marriage.[118]

Similar debates have transpired elsewhere in Indian Country. Both supporters and opponents of the 2004 Cherokee Nation law banning same-sex marriage, which was overturned in 2016, claimed to have "tradition on their sides."[119] Additionally, in Colorado and Oklahoma many members of a two-spirit movement construct and deploy "tradition" toward the goals of acceptance, empowerment, and inclusion, while some other American Indians in these parts of Indian Country circulate their opposing views that "[h]omosexuality is not a traditional value" and "gay is not a part of our [tribe's] traditions."[120] Moreover, some "traditionals" see themselves as "preserving tribal social values" in condemning homosexuality and multiple gender identities.[121] Tweedy argues that these traditionals' claims are "contemporary prejudice" being made "to masquerade as tribal tradition."[122] To prevent such exclusions from being institutionalized in the name of tradition, she argues, tribal judges should require "solid evidence" that the exclusions are indeed tribal traditions.[123] While such a directive is likely to raise many more questions than it answers, it hints at how messy it can be when the tribal processes that regulate domestic relations involve the evaluation of proposed rules or actions in terms of culture and tradition.

It is also common in Indian Country to appeal to Christianity when opposing same-sex marriage.[124] In a debate over legalizing same-sex marriage during a tribal council meeting of the Little Traverse Bay Bands of Odawa Indians, for example, tribal elder Doug Emery cited "Romans 22 of the Old Testament" about "man not being with man."[125] He explained, "[G]ay marriage is against the Bible. If two men can't reproduce with each other, we become extinct."[126] "God created woman for man," he continued, "and when you try to rewrite creation you can expect judgment to fall on your people."[127] Likewise, Cherokee Nation lawmakers "referred to Christianity" when they banned same-sex marriage."[128] Finally, according to Navajo priest Dale Jamison the Navajos who attend the "influential churches" on the reservation tend to see same-sex marriage not only as against their Christian religion, but also as "a foreign imposition creeping into Navajo life from cities like Albuquerque and San Francisco."[129]

Although Christianity is a commonly cited reason for opposing same-sex marriage in the United States, it should be pointed out that a number of Christian religious bodies officially approve of same-sex marriage, including the Quaker, Unitarian Universalist, Episcopal, Evangelical Lutheran, and Presbyterian churches.[130] Officially opposed are the American Baptist, Mormon, Roman Catholic, and Southern Baptist Convention churches, among others.[131] Providing additional evidence that US Christians' opinions are divided over same-sex marriage, one poll found that 66 percent of US Christians reported "no conflict between homosexuality and their religious belief."[132]

## NEGOTIATING INCLUSION

This article has gathered, supplemented, synthesized, and framed materials from tribal homelands in the United States in order to shed light on American Indian participation and involvement in debates over same-sex marriage. During the decade from 2005 to 2015 on which this article has focused, and even beyond, both popular and scholarly attention to Indian engagement in these debates has been disappointingly sparse. An unfortunate impression may have developed that Indians are indifferent to, or uninterested in, the inclusion or exclusion of sexual minorities and the queering of marriage. To be sure, Indian voices have been almost entirely absent from the spaces in the United States where these debates have been given the most public attention and where lawmaking and legal decisions about marriage equality and queer rights have taken place: namely, the legislatures of the state and national governments and the Supreme Court. Even so, Indian engagement, decision-making, and leadership on these issues have been extensive.

This article's ethnographic descriptions and analyses support my contention that, in and around our tribal homelands and outside of the public view of most Americans, Indians have been deeply ensconced in conversations about marriage, sexuality, gender, and belonging. In many parts of Indian Country, questions are pressing about whether and how to queer marriage, to extend fuller rights to tribal members who are also sexual minorities, and to effectively combat heterosexism and heteronormativity. Whether they are working toward disrupting existing arrangements in tribal homelands or trying to stem those efforts, Indians have been making substantial use of tribally controlled political and legal institutions, including tribal legislatures, courts, and political processes. As this article has discussed, since 2008 tribal marriage laws have been extensively revisited and revised.

Another central finding and argument of this article is that Indians in the United States have taken a range of positions on same-sex marriage, both as Native nations and as individuals. On the one hand, my materials show that Indians cannot be construed as paragons of tolerance and compassion—the way they have been rendered by some queer non-Natives who seek their "primordial" counterparts, as Jenny Davis aptly puts this impulse.[133] On the other hand, this study's materials demonstrate that Indians also cannot be characterized as wholly contemptuous, dismissive, and rejecting of individuals of nonconforming sexualities and gender identities. Delving into the content and character of the debates over marriage, sexuality, gender, and citizenship that have unfolded in tribal homelands reveals not only Indian individuals who creatively appeal to "tradition," "culture," and Christianity (among other symbols, institutions, and ideas), but also those who work to discredit these appeals. In order to better understand these and other debates in Indian Country, the most promising approaches treat tribal "traditions" and "culture" as variegated, contradictory, contested, and piecemeal. American Indians, like other human beings, have at their disposal a strikingly wide range of ideas and practices that can be (and are) reassembled, reinterpreted, divided, combined, and in other ways reworked. We are all, both Native and non-Native, still quite far from a thorough, or even an adequate, understanding of the complex processes by which these creative assemblages are legitimized, and exactly how they are used to transform tribal institutions, including the institution of marriage.

## *Acknowledgments*

I would like to thank my consultants, my co-workers at the Bureau of Indian Affairs, and my friends and colleagues Mike Lambert and Jean Dennison. I would also like to thank my undergraduate student Lindsey Terrell, who conducted valuable research on this topic that prompted me to think about the issues in new ways. Finally, I would like to thank the anonymous reviewers of this manuscript and *AICRJ* acting editor Pamela Grieman. The help that each of them provided was invaluable.

## NOTES

Reprinted with permission from Valerie Lambert, *American Indian Culture and Research* 41:2 (2017): 1–21.

1. Abby Ohlheiser, "New Zealand Lawmakers Burst Into Song as They Legalize Gay Marriage," *The Slatist*, April 17, 2013, www.slate.com/blogs/the-slatest/2013/04/17/new-zealand-gay-marriage-law-passes-supporters-sing-maori-love-song-in-parliament.html.

2. Ibid.

3. Russ Hepler, "Native Americans Say 'No' to Gay Marriage," *The Federalist Papers Project*, n.d., www.thefederalistpapers.org/us/native-americans-say-no-to-gay-marriage.

4. Chris Finley, "Decolonizing the Queer Native Body (and Recovering the Native Bull-Dyke): Bringing 'Sexy Back' and Out of the Native Studies' Closet," in *Queer Indigenous Studies: Critical Interventions in Theory, Politics, and Literature*, ed. Qwo-Li Driscoll, Chris Finley, Brian Joseph Gilley, and Scott Lauria Morgensen (Tucson: University of Arizona Press, 2011), 40.

5. Ibid., 33.

6. Ibid., 32.

7. Vasu Reddy, "Queer Marriage: Sexualising Citizenship and the Development of Freedoms in South Africa," in *The Prize and the Price: Shaping Sexualities in South Africa,* ed. Melissa Steyn and Mikki Van Zyl (Cape Town: Human Sciences Research Council, 2009), 345.

8. Obergefell v. Hodges, 576 U.S. 15-556 (2015).

9. Amy Brandzel, "Queering Citizenship? Same-Sex Marriage and the State," *GLQ: A Journal of Lesbian and Gay Studies* 11, no. 2 (2005): 187, https://doi.org/10.1215/10642684-11-2-171.

10. In this connection, an important next step would be to extend the approach and analysis of this article into the homelands of the First Nations. Canada legalized same-sex marriage in 2005, ten years prior to the United States; comparative work on the actions taken by Native peoples in that country would be fruitful.

11. Mark Rifkin, *When Did Indians Become Straight? Kinship, The History of Sexuality, and Native Sovereignty* (New York: Oxford University Press, 2011), and *The Erotics of Sovereignty: Queer Native Writing in the Era of Self-Determination* (Minneapolis: University of Minnesota Press, 2012).

12. Scott Lauria Morgensen, *Spaces Between Us: Queer Settler Colonialism and Indigenous Decolonization* (Minneapolis: University of Minnesota Press, 2010).

13. Brian Joseph Gilley, *Becoming Two-Spirit: Gay Identity and Social Acceptance in Indian Country* (Lincoln: University of Nebraska Press, 2006); Jenny Davis, "More Than Just 'Gay' Indians,' Intersecting Articulations of Two-Spirit Gender, Sexuality, and Indigenousness," in *Queer Excursions: Retheorizing Binaries in Language, Gender, and Sexuality*, ed. Lal Zimmerman, Jenny Davis, and Joshua Reclaw (Oxford: Oxford University Press, 2014), 63–81.

14. Jennifer Denetdale, "Carving Navajo National Boundaries: Patriotism, Tradition, and the Diné Marriage Act of 2005," *American Quarterly* 60, no. 2 (2008), https://doi.org/10.1353/aq.0.0007; Finley, "Decolonizing the Queer Native Body."

15. Denetdale, "Carving Navajo National Boundaries"; Melanie Yazzie, "Rifkin, Mark, The Erotics of Sovereignty: Queer Native Writing in the Era of Self-Determination," *Studies in American Indian Literatures* 26, no. 2 (2014): 106.

16. Finley, "Decolonizing the Queer Native Body," 32.

17. Brandzel, "Queering Citizenship?", 172.

18. See especially Fletcher, "Same-Sex Marriage," and Ann Tweedy, "Tribal Laws and Same-Sex Marriage: Theory, Process and Content," *Columbia Human Rights Law Review* 46 (2015): 104–65.

19. Morgensen, *Spaces Between Us.*

20. Davis, "More Than Just 'Gay' Indians," 62.

21. Ibid., 62, 65.

22. In 2005, there were three Indians in the US Congress: Ben Nighthorse Campbell (Northern Cheyenne), Brad Carson (Cherokee Nation), and Tom Cole (Chickasaw Nation). From 2006 to 2012, Tom Cole (Chickasaw Nation) was the only American Indian in the US Congress. From 2013 to 2015, Tom Cole was joined by Markwayne Mullin (Cherokee Nation).

23. Fletcher, "Same-Sex Marriage," 66.

24. Obergefell v. Hodges, 576 U.S. 15-556 (2015).

25. Fletcher, "Same-Sex Marriage," 81.

26. Pub.L. 104–99, 110 Stat. 2419 (1996), 1 U.S.C. 7 and 28 U.S.C. 1738C; Jeffrey S. Jacobi, "Two Spirits, Two Eras, Same Sex: For a Traditionalist Perspective on Native American Tribal Same-Sex Marriage Policy," *University of Michigan Journal of Law Reform* 39, no. 4 (2006), 823–50, http://www.heinonline.org/HOL/Page?handle=hein.journals/umijlr39&id=833.

27. Jacobi, "Two Spirits," 845; Rifkin, *When Did Indians Become Straight*; Morgensen, *Spaces Between Us.*

28. Antoinette Sedillo Lopez, "Evolving Indigenous Law: Navajo Marriage-Cultural Traditions and Modern Challenges," *Arizona Journal of International and Comparative Law* 17, no. 2 (2000): 305, http://www.heinonline.org/HOL/Page?handle=hein.journals/ajicl17&collection=journals&id=297.

29. Fletcher, "Same-Sex Marriage," 59.

30. Ibid., 79.

31. *In re: Validation of Marriage of Francisco*, 16 Indian L. Rep 6113 (Navajo Nation S. Ct. 1989), quoted in Lopez, "Evolving Indigenous Law," 298.

32. Fletcher, "Same-Sex Marriage," 54.

33. 76 Mich 498, 43 N.W. 602 (1889), quoted in Fletcher, "Same-Sex Marriage," 53–54.

34. Paula Burkes, "Same-Sex Marriage May Not Extend to Indian Country Land," *The Oklahoman*, August 13, 2015, http://www.newsok.com/article/5439817.

35. 78 Neb. 339, 110 N.W. 983 (1907), quoted in Lopez, "Evolving Indigenous Law," 305.

36. 201 F. 793 (8th Cir. 1914), quoted in Lopez, "Evolving Indigenous Law," 305. About these early cases, some of which affirm the right of tribes to practice polygamy, the point should be made that on the ground, federal officials often discouraged and even imposed criminal penalties on Indians practicing polygamy; see Tweedy, "Tribal Laws and Same-Sex Marriage, 157n284, and Lopez, "Evolving Indigenous Law."

37. Sarah Netter, "Brides Look Forward to Marrying under Tribal Same-Sex Marriage Law," ABCNewsgo.com, August 27, 2008, http://abcnews.go.com/TheLaw/story?id=5659821.

38. Rifkin, *When Did Indians Become Straight*; Morgensen, *Spaces Between Us*.

39. Tweedy, "Tribal Laws and Same-Sex Marriage," 162.

40. Freedom to Marry, "Why Marriage Matters to Native Americans," Freedomtomarry.org, http://www.freedomtomarry.org/communities/entry/c/native-americans; see also Tweedy, "Tribal Laws and Same-Sex Marriage."

41. In 2015 the Keweenaw Bay Indian Community approved same-sex marriage by tribal referendum and Navajo president Russell Begaye said that, if elected, he would put same-sex marriage to a "reservation-wide vote"; see Jonathan Drew and Felicia Fonseca, "Handful of Holdout Tribes Dig In Against Gay Marriage," CNS News, April 6, 2015, http://www.yahoo.com/news/ap-handful-holdout-tribes-dig-in-against-gay-marriage-153352266.html?ref=gs.

42. Felicia Fonseca, "Gay Marriage Is Legal but Not on Tribal Lands," ABCNewsgo.com, November 27, 2015, http://abcnews.go.com/US/wireStory/gay-marriage-legal-tribal-lands-35448512.

43. Gyasi Ross, "Smear the Queer, the Supreme Court, and Same Sex Marriage: Love For the Win (Finally)," Indian Country Today Media Network.com, June 25, 2015, http://www.indiancountrytodaymedianetwork.com/2015/06/26/smear-queer-supreme-court-and-same-sex-marriage-love-win-finally-160872; emphasis in the original.

44. Most Indians today marry under US state law and concomitantly receive tribal recognition of most of these marriages.

45. Netter, "Brides Look Forward to Marrying."

46. Jacobi, "Two Spirits," 823.

47. Fletcher, "Same-Sex Marriage," 70.

48. This is as of July 10, 2015; see Matthew Tharrett, "Some Native American Tribes Are Still Banning Same-Sex Marriage," NewNowNext.com, July 7, 2015, http://www.newnownext.com/some-native-american-tries-are-still-banning-same-sex-marriage/07/2015/.

49. Jacobi, "Two Spirits," 832.

50. Drew and Fonseca, "Handful of Holdout Tribes Dig In."

51. Fonseca, "Gay Marriage Is Legal."

52. Ibid.

53. Julian Brave NoiseCat, "Fight for Marriage Equality Not Over on Navajo Nation," *Huffington Post*, July 2, 2015, http://www.huffingtonpost.com/2015/07/02/navajo-marriage-equality_n_7709016.html.

54. Fonseca, "Gay Marriage Is Legal," 3.

55. Henrietta Mann, interview with author, Chapel Hill, North Carolina, April 12, 2016.

56. Elizabeth Dias, "A Gay Marriage Loophole for Native Americans," Nationtime.com, November 1, 2013, http://nation.time.com/2013/11/01/a-gay-marriage-loophole-for-native-americans/.

57. Gregory Smithers, "Will Gay Marriage Split Indian Country?" Indian Country Today Media Network.com, May 30, 2015, http://www.indiancountrytodaymedianetwork.com/2015/05/30/will-gay-marriage-split-indian-country.

58. Drew and Fonseca, "Handful of Holdout Tribes Dig In."

59. Other tribes with such marriage laws include the Blackfeet Nation and the Fort McDowell Yavapai Nation; see Tweedy, "Tribal Laws and Same-Sex Marriage," 139.

60. The Circle Staff, "Oneida Nation Approves Gay Marriage," *The Circle*, June 1, 2015, http://thecirclenews.org/index.php?option=com_content&task=view&id=1174&Itemid=76; Samantha Mesa Miles, "A Foot in Two Worlds: The Battle for Gay Marriage on Tribal Lands," Indian Country Today Media Network.com, April 28, 2015, http://indiancountrytodaymedianetwork.com/2015/04/28/foot-two-worlds-battle-gay-marriage-tribal-lands-160178.

61. Dias, "A Gay Marriage Loophole."

62. Fonseca, "Gay Marriage Is Legal."

63. Ibid.

64. Drew and Fonseca, "Handful of Holdout Tribes Dig In."

65. Smithers, "Will Gay Marriage Split Indian Country?"

66. Rob Hotakainen, "Among Indian Tribes, A Division Over Gay Marriage," *Washington Post*, May 12, 2013, http://www.washingtonpost.com/politics/among-indian-tribes-a-division-over-gay-marriage/2013/05/12/4c77bf3e-bb3a-11e2-9b09-1638acc3942e_story.html; see also John Carlisle, "Tribe Hosts Mich.'s First Legal Same-Sex Marriage," USA Today.com, March 15, 2013, http://www.usatoday.com/story/news/nation/2013/03/15/tribe-hosts-first-legal-gay-marriage/1991781/.

67. Hotakainen, "Among Indian Tribes, A Division."

68. Denetdale, "Carving Navajo National Boundaries," 293.

69. Ibid., 294; Fonseca, "Gay Marriage Is Legal"; Tweedy, "Tribal Laws and Same-Sex Marriage," 135.

70. Denetdale, "Carving Navajo National Boundaries," 293.

71. Ibid.

72. NoiseCat, "Fight for Marriage Equality Not Over"; Freedom to Marry, "Why Marriage Matters to Native Americans."

73. Brian Joseph Gilley, "Native Sexual Inequalities: American Indian Cultural Conservative Homophobia and the Problem of Tradition," *Sexualities* 13, no. 1 (2010): 47, https://doi.org/10.1177/1363460709346114.

74. Zachary Pullin, "Two Spirit: The Story of a Movement Unfolds," Native Peoples.com, May–June, 2014, http://www.nativepeoples.com/Native-Peoples/May-June-2014/Two-Spirit-The-Story-of-a-Movement-Unfolds.

75. NoiseCat, "Fight for Marriage Equality Not Over."

76. Nativeout.com.

77. Kevin Taylor, "Diver Heather Purser Pioneers Same-Sex Marriage for Suquamish," Indian Country Today Media Network.com, January 18, 2012, http://indiancountrytodaymedianetwork.com/2012/01/18/diver-heather-purser-pioneers-same-sex-marriage-suquamish-72993.

78. Ibid.

79. Lisa DeBode, "Native American Tribes Challenge Oklahoma Gay Marriage Ban," AlJeezera America, October 22, 2013, http://america.aljazeera.com/articles/2013/10/22/native-american-tribeschallengeoklahomagaymarriageban.html.

80. Gilley, "Native Sexual Inequalities," and *Becoming Two-Spirit: Gay Identity and Social Acceptance in Indian Country* (Lincoln: University of Nebraska Press, 2006). "Two spirit," as Jenny Davis has explained, is a term that aims "to encompass all the localized realizations of indigenous gender and sexual variation." See Davis, "More Than Just 'Gay' Indians," 65. It has been in use since at least the early 1990s, and though it has been rejected by some queer youth activists and others, many prefer the term "two spirit" to the alternatives. See, for example, Sue-Ellen Jacobs, Wesley Thomas, and Sabine Lang, *Two-Spirit People: Native American Gender Identity, Sexuality, and Spirituality* (Urbana and Chicago: University of Illinois Press, 1997).

81. Brian Gilley, "Joyous Discipline: Native Autonomy and Culturally Conservative Two-Spirit People," *American Indian Culture and Research Journal* 38, no. 2 (2014): 30–31, https://doi.org/10.17953/aicr.38.2.l874w4216151vp23.

82. Gilley, "Native Sexual Inequalities," 53.

83. Ibid., 55.

84. Ibid.

85. Ibid., 57.

86. Ibid., 59.

87. Pullin, "Two Spirit."

88. Ibid.

89. Gilley, "Native Sexual Inequalities," 55.

90. NoiseCat, "Fight for Marriage Equality Not Over."

91. Pullin, "Two Spirit."

92. NoiseCat, "Fight for Marriage Equality Not Over."

93. Fletcher, "Same-Sex Marriage," 70; National Center for Lesbian Rights, "Cherokee High Court Rules in Favor of NCLR and Same-Sex Couple," press release, January 4, 2006, http://www.nclrights.org/press-release/cherokee-high-court-rules-in-favor-of-nclr-and-same-sex-couple/; Tweedy, "Tribal Laws and Same-Sex Marriage," 136.

94. Quoted in Jacobi, "Two Spirits," 828.

95. National Center for Lesbian Rights, "Cherokee High Court Rules in Favor of NCLR."

96. Taylor, "Diver Heather Purser Pioneers Same-Sex Marriage."

97. Ibid.

98. Ibid.

99. Hotakainen, "Among Indian Tribes, A Division."

100. Netter, "Brides Look Forward to Marrying."

101. Steve Russell, "The Headlines Are Wrong! Same-Sex Marriage Not Banned Across Indian Country," Indian Country Today Media Network.com, April 23, 2015, https://indiancountrymedianetwork.com/news/native-news/the-headlines-are-wrong-same-sex-marriage-not-banned-across-indian-country/.

102. Tweedy, "Tribal Laws and Same-Sex Marriage," 121.

103. Ibid., 120.

104. Carlisle, "Tribe Hosts Mich.'s First Legal Same-Sex Marriage," 2.

105. Ibid.

106. Miles, "A Foot in Two Worlds."

107. Tweedy, "Tribal Laws and Same-Sex Marriage," 123.

108. 25 U.S.C. 1301–1304 (1968), quoted in Tweedy, "Tribal Laws and Same-Sex Marriage," 149.

109. Lopez, "Evolving Indigenous Law," 301.

110. NoiseCat, "Fight for Marriage Equality Not Over," 3.

111. Denetdale, "Carving Navajo National Boundaries," 294.

112. Well-known Navajo activist Alray Nelson, quoted in Tharrett, "Some Native American Tribes Are Still Banning Same-Sex Marriage," 2.

113. Denetdale, "Carving Navajo National Boundaries," 293.

114. Anna Macias Aguayo, "Navajo Nation Council Overrides President's Veto of Same-Sex Marriage Ban," *Arizona Daily Sun*, June 3, 2005, http://azdailysun.com/navajo-nation-council-overrides-president-s-veto-of-same-sex/article_75f82c28-2da0-5c56-a70a-0db6024ddec4.html.

115. Russell, "The Headlines Are Wrong," 2.

116. Quoted in Denetdale, "Carving Navajo National Boundaries," 293.

117. Ibid., 289, 293.

118. Mark Walsh, "A 'View' From the Courtroom: A Marriage Celebration," Scotusblog.com, http://www.scotusblog.com/2015/06/a-view-from-the-courtroom-a-marriage-celebration.

119. Tweedy, "Tribal Laws and Same-Sex Marriage," 154.

120. Gilley, "Native Sexual Inequalities," 55.

121. Ibid., 54.

122. Tweedy, "Tribal Laws and Same-Sex Marriage," 154.

123. Ibid.

124. Jacobi, "Two Spirits," 829, 849.

125. Quoted in Miles, "A Foot in Two Worlds," 3.

126. Ibid.

127. Quoted in Hotakainen, "Among Indian Tribes, A Division."

128. Russell, "The Headlines Are Wrong," 2.

129. NoiseCat, "Fight for Marriage Equality Not Over," 4.

130. David Masci and Michael Lipka, "Where Christian Churches, Other Religions Stand on Gay Marriage," Pew Research.org, July 2, 2015, www.pewresearch.org/fact-tank/2015/07/02/where-christian-churches-stand-on-gay-marriage.

131. Ibid.

132. Ibid.

133. Davis, "'More Than Just 'Gay' Indians,'" 64.

# IV.

# ARTS AND CULTURAL PRODUCTION

# POETRY WITHIN EARSHOT

## Notes on an Asian American Generation 1968–1978[1]

RUSSELL C. LEONG

"In the process of finding out what one has learned, one learns once more."
—Bertolt Brecht[2]

Poetry is practical, so I have learned.

Because I wanted to relearn—and relive—the stirrings of an Asian American generation, I sought out its poetry.[3] For poetry, like a hammer, can nail down the times.

Contrary to what is taught, poetry has its practical side. Poems are portable. They are easily held, to a paper or between the brows. They do not need leather bindings, do not require a light projector, a picture frame, a wind or percussion instrument to carry their images or produce their sounds. Poetry is the form which, given the unity of speaker and listener, can quicken our emotions and color our perceptions. "It is the literary form that depends most directly on pure verbal resources—the sound and evocative power of words, meter, alliteration, rhyme, and other rhythmic devices, associated images, repetitions, archaisms, and grammatical twists."[4] Poems may be understood better by listening, though some poems read faster by the eye.

For our generation, poetry was the most broadly-based of crafts. Asian Americans from different walks of life wrote, some for the first—and last—time.

Some wrote from behind prison bars.[5] Others, between raising daughters and sons, or between jobs. Before or after work. For, or against, a political idea. Because of love or beauty or revolt, or due to their lack. Each person had reasons—what matters is that each made the choice to write.

Here, then, are notes on a generation of Asian American poets and what they wrote. The poets were mainly Japanese, Chinese, and Filipino Americans—and a few Korean and Vietnamese—who wrote, and who were published between 1968 and 1978. We were a post-World War II generation mostly in our twenties and thirties; in or out of local schools and colleges. A few had been incarcerated, in desolate

---

Russell Leong is an acclaimed writer and poet. He served as the long time editor of *Amerasia Journal*, retiring in 2010.

American-style concentration camps at the tail end of World War II.[6] The writers gravitated toward cities—San Francisco, Los Angeles, New York—where movements for ethnic studies and inner city blocks of Asian communities coincided. Others—in Seattle, Honolulu, Chicago, etc.—also wrote. But their writings were less inclined toward third world movements.

Of those whom I had known or worked with in the San Francisco Bay Area in the late 1960s and 1970s, many were part of Third World Communications, a multicultural arts group, or of the Asian American Writers' Workshop, located in the basement of the International Hotel.[7]

We read as we wrote—not in isolation—but in the company of our neighbors in Manilatown pool halls, barrio parks, Chinatown basements. And though some of us had books published in our own names, most of our writings were collected in anthologies, newspapers, and journals, published on the West and East Coasts.[8]

Borne of adversity and spun of diversity, we poets formed a loosely aligned "tribe." In the West, the term "tribal" has been used to define the "other"—non-western, primitive, Indian, African—or to those who live in Africa, the Near and Middle East, and parts of Asia.[9] But we must drive the term back to its roots—to affiliation based upon blood and generational lines, upon folk and cultural ties. Tribal bespeaks of the consciousness of the third world—of attempts to rescue memory and culture from total colonization, or to reclaim and transform that which is left from annihilation. "Tribal" is based upon shared experience—even the shared experience of subjugation—and on an integration of self with community. Rather than accepting the divisive ideologies and splintering imagery of the Eurocentric West, we can use tribalism to unlock the original keys to memory, and to provide a base for unity.[10]

Above all, we poets were a tribe of storytellers. Throughout place and time, storytellers have shared certain traits.[11] Storytellers live in communities where they write for family and friends. The relationship between the teller and listener is neighborly, because the teller of stories must also listen.[12] Storytellers, in their work, utilize the beliefs, feelings, and common dialects of those around them.

"The storyteller takes what he tells from experience—his own or that reported by others. And he in turn makes it the experience of those who are listening to his tale."[13] Thus, their stories are opposed to the detached, official versions of history and experience. The storyteller is a keeper of "popular memory," as opposed to the recorder of diluted, sanitized, and expurgated versions of history.[14]

Some Asian American poems encapsulize stories, though lacking the full-blown development of character, dialogue, and action. For even a single line can tell a story. A noun places an event, a verb promotes action, an adjective sets the tone. Hear these lines written by a first-generation Japanese American:

All my living days
Gripped tightly and pressed into
That old hoe handle![15]

At least, the poems must possess "organic form, something that springs from a single detail and embraces past, present, and future."[16]

For our generation, the Vietnam War hit home. We Americans of Asian blood were engaged in the dogged killing of Asian peoples across the sea. The conflagration of the war moved us to write. As one Asian American poet put it:

> . . .
> There is no way to keep their
> blood from sticking in my skin and
> no single music to measure
> the circumference of their wound. . . .[17]

We saw the war as part of an unfinished revolution against Western colonialism in Algeria, Dien Bien Phu, China, South Africa. We took lessons, as did Malcolm X, from those Asian and African compatriots who spoke out against their countries' subjugation at the Bandung Conference in 1955.[18] Closer yet, we looked toward the first and second generations for cues. We dug out World War II camp journals squirreled away in boxes, fingered graffiti carved on Angel Island immigration station's walls, untied Manila letters in brown suitcases.[19] Search even upon the sand, a poet observed, that was sprinkled with "birthmarks."[20]

By looking at poetry only, I am ignoring other forms: novels, plays, short stories, essays. Yet the writings—seen as a whole—form a larger generational response to the times. So narrative works, wherever they illuminate approaches to seeing the world, will be touched upon.[21]

Jeffery Chan, founder of the first classes on Asian American literature and writing at San Francisco State College after the Third World Strike, says the writers in his classes—then, as now—were "compelled, confused, or repelled, by family, race, and sex."[22] These preoccupations revealed themselves in attempts to

- Restore historical lineage, and recover a "cultural bloodline," through tracing the first- and second-generation experiences.
- View our experiences as grounded in the triangle of America, Asia, and the Third World.
- Define an Asian American women's persona and poetic voice.
- Exhibit multi-lingualism-usage of non-English words and phrases in lyrics.

Besides looking at the poets' thoughts on family, race, and sex, we must touch upon the language, idiom, and the strategies by which we forged meaning from words. What strategies did we invent, borrow, or beg to clothe our politics, prejudices, and passions? These poetic strategies included:

1. Frames of reference—singular or multiple—as in America and Asia
2. Unity of the speaker—listener
3. Elements of the oral tradition such as naming, chanting, repetition, polemic, and direct address
4. Reversal and transformation of stereotypes—through ironic and satirical images and metaphors
5. Compilative, archival approaches to language and speech

## DEPOSITS OF EXPERIENCE

N. V. M. Gonzalez describes the Filipino writer as one who mines the "inherited 'deposits' of experience," and delves into the "banked" answers to life's riddles, motifs of initiations and discoveries.[23]

What were the "deposits" and "motifs" of Asian American poets of the 1960s and 1970s? Due partially to patterns of immigration, and to the development of full-bodied second and third generations, the main communities of writers who wrote in English were Chinese, Japanese, and Filipino. Key experiences, roughly sketched below, served as motifs.

| **CHINESE** | **JAPANESE** | **FILIPINO** |
|---|---|---|
| **journey to US settlement:** | **journey to US** | **journey to US** |
| Chinatowns | Little Tokyos | Manilatowns |
| C-town society | Issei society | manong society |
| family/culture | family/culture | family/culture |
| women's roles | women's roles | women's roles |
| Sino/US relations | internment/WWII | WWII |
| Mao Zedong | Hiroshima/Nagasaki | US naval bases |
| Vietnam war | Vietnam war | Vietnam war |
| civil rights | civil rights | civil rights |
| black power | black power | black power |
| ethnic studies | ethnic studies | ethnic studies |

For groups, these key experiences differed. Yet, the paths of individuals crossed as they stepped upon American shores.[24] Our lives were rooted in work in the fields and factories. And our settlement in towns and cities meant enclaves of "bachelor" Chinatowns, "Little Tokyos," and Manilatowns clustered on the West Coast.[25]

World War II and its aftermath—the internment and resettlement of Japanese Americans; the bombing of Hiroshima and Nagasaki; the establishment of the communist government in China; the continued US occupation of the Philippines; the division of Korea into north and south; also served as ready material for us. The decolonization of Asian and African countries and the emerging role of women there provoked us to write.[26]

The 1960s' and 1970s' charting of Chinese immigrant society led to our rereading of poetry and prose depicting the Cantonese bachelor society, and new translations of the Angel Island poetry. Writers Frank Chin, Jeffery Chan, Maxine Hong Kingston, and Shawn Wong in their plays, novels, and short stories—and Alan Chong Lau and Wing Tek Lum, in their poetry—attempted to revise conceptions of life within and without Chinatown.[27]

In contrast, those Japanese American writers who were the Sansei, or third generation, tended to see their history—and literature—tied to the World War II internment experience of their parents. The reprinting and reading of works by writers such as

Toshio Mori, Hisaye Yamamoto, Wakako Yamauchi, and John Okada broadened the view of Japanese Americans before the war. The editors of *Aiiieeeee!* anthologized these second-generation authors, enfolding new readers.[28]

## LIFE UNFOLDING LIKE A CORAL SEA

As we strove to trace a poetic bloodline through those who had written before us, we envisaged our writing as part of "life unfolding like a coral sea"—to paraphrase the words of Carlos Bulosan. This Filipino novelist, poet, and labor organizer was key to the bloodline.

Filipino American writers, heeding their rediscovery of the first-generation manongs and Manilatown culture, recognized a history dyed and warped with the threads of Spanish and US colonialism. This knowledge imbued Filipino writers with a heightened sensitivity to the promise, contradiction, and lie of the American dream, as exemplified by the rediscovery of the writings of Carlos Bulosan in the 1960s.

Bulosan is best known for his novel, *America Is in the Heart.* His essays, short stories, and poetry have received less attention. Dolores S. Feria, and E. San Juan Jr., however, have edited and written extensively about his works.

E. San Juan states that the rediscovery of Bulosan's writings in the 1960s "announces and seals the fact of Bulosan's advent as a revolutionary force in the battlefield of Western culture."[29]

San Juan provides the most cogent analysis to date of Bulosan's works. On Bulosan's poem, "Biography," San Juan says: "When the child is born in winter, the past and future interlock to determine his fate":[30]

> . . .
> Delicately the film
> Of his life unfolded like a coral sea,
> Where stone is a hard substance of wind
> And water leaking into memory like pain. . . .[31]

On Bulosan's imagery, San Juan points out

> The mineral hardness of nature is translated into sensory impressions that form the imaginative faculty, the faculty of desire and need. . . . What Bulosan communicates here is the sense of growth, of self development as a creative use of the past, the determinisms of nature and social life, in an unrelenting process of confrontation and analysis.

Following is another poem in its entirety, "When I Woke upon My Twenty-First Year":

> When I woke up in my twenty-first year the journey
> ended. Life was the one word cursed by the soldiers
> when they died. America commenced with a desolate range
> of weathered porches. The long shadow of the swastika
> loomed. It crucified my thoughts and meditation. . .
> I rushed from the jailhouse screaming and sat on the
> cold snow, cursing like a dying soldier.[32]

Compressed within seven lines, a strong narrative premise reveals the paradox—of waking up, of being twenty-one, and of ending the journey. As E. San Juan has found, the poems of Bulosan are "constructed with firm dramatic scaffolding, with carefully delineated scenes that objectify the moods and concretize the feelings of the speaker."[33]

Bulosan, merging motive and form, intensifies our perceptions of everyday life.

## AT THE TIP OF THE PAST

> Our living is an extension of our remembrances
> We are at the tip of the past,
> Balancing,
> As dancers do.
> —Bayani Mariano[34]

January twenty-ninth, nineteen hundred and seventy-two: San Francisco, congealed in fog. A friend and I drove across the Bay Bridge to Berkeley at UC's Zellerbach playhouse. Tonight was the first gathering of Filipino, Chinese, and Japanese American poets in a reading called Poetry of the New Asian Nation.

The reading was divided into the Chinese, Filipino, and Japanese "nations"—with Al Robles representing the "Asian American nation."

Those who read: Nanying Stella Wong, Curtis Choy, Kitty Tsui, Russell Leong, George Leong, Bayani Mariano, Serafin Syquia, Samuel Tagatac, Russell Robles, Alfred Robles, Emily Cachapero, Lawson Fusao Inada, Janice Mirikitani. Filipino Igorot dance, Chinese music, and Japanese mask dance were performed.

The poetry, dance, and music not only signified the cultural forms of a "New Asian Nation." It reflected the political thrusts of the times, including the movement by some blacks toward establishing a "Black Nation," and the call for a "United Front of Asians in America" by community activists.[35]

As well, the program represented sources of spiritual unity: musical and dance renditions and poetic traditions, a celebration of Asian cultural nationalism one evening in America.[36]

In the printed program, each poet had penned a brief, revealing statement. Serafin Syquia for instance, recalled the first poem that he wrote in grammar school—and where he ended up—"back to Bulosan, Rizal, Mirikitani, Cleaver."

Russell Robles, brother of Alfred, spoke on growing up in the Fillmore, an Afro-Asian neighborhood, in these passages:

> I was born in the womb of yellow pissgutters & brown
> brown sweet potato pie, hamhocks, neck bones, adobo, pig head,
> and tons of rice. . . .
> I was born in a bowl of STEAMED FISH COVERED WITH PATIS
> I was born when a monkey looked at me and said I was not white but
> pinoy.[37]

Here, Robles as the "Filipino everyman," connects his history to a multiple framework of Filipino and soul foods, to the American continent and the islands, and to a natural order where—a monkey—not a Catholic priest—gives him back his name.

Robles, like other community poets, was "balancing" life in the present, yet seeking "the tip of the past" to give fuller vein to his ideas.

Nanying Stella Wong, in a poem, "The Return," intertwines the fates of Saigon and San Francisco in her vision of two cities:

> . . .
> the islands huddled like renounced camels,
> the parasol of sky closing
> here is San Francisco
> there is Saigon
> their locks of mouths
> damming the Pacific![38]

Wong provided yet another angle on the "New Asian Nation," due to her earlier work on Chinatown folklore sources. In the 1950s, she went back to China and became interested in village bridal songs. Upon her return to San Francisco, she visited sewing factories, where she recorded and translated some of the folk songs that the older Chinese workers sang.

Delving into folk materials is essential to restoring the tribe and the cultural lineage.[39]

The peasant, the tiller of the soil; the traveler, the seaman, and the hunter all combine the lore of the past with the lore of faraway places, to conserve and deposit into popular memory what has transpired in life and in every day social existence.[40]

## MEMORY AND MUSIC

Memory and music join forces in Lawson Fusao Inada's book, *Before the War* (1971). As the dust jacket notes, "he lived through the War with his family in 'evacuation camps'," resettling afterward in the black and Latin section of Fresno, California. Within this vortex of ethnicity, Inada developed a phrasing with jazz at its heart, intoned to Asian American life. His poems are dedicated to jazz musicians and singers who influenced him—among them, Clifford Brown, John Coltrane, Miles Davis, Billie Holiday, Milt Jackson, Charlie Parker. Inada's phrasing is lean and his textures rich: ironic, humorous, tender. The following poem is a polemic which differs from his other verse, but reveals linkages—and differences—between Asian and other groups. Entitled "Projected Scenario of a Performance to Be Given before the U.N.," it begins:

> I am a mad mother-
> fucker, or in other
> words, a very irate
> citizen—that's what
> you call the black
> and white of it all.

(general applause)
But that's an over-
simplification—how
about other colors?
(scattered applause)
And I'm supposed to
be yellow as butter
or expensive spread?
Call me a very irate
fatherhugger, that's
what we Asians have
to be, making these
various variations. . . .[41]

The speech continues, driving polemic to its sardonic edge—from Confucius to fortune cookies, to "Madame Butterfly Rag." It ends with a "Bong." Inada reverses the epithet—tossing and turning it on its head. Then, as now, Inada's poetry strikes back.

## AN IFUGAO NOSE-FLUTE TELLS NO LIES

Al Robles has changed the way that Filipino American poets see, think, and write about their neighborhoods. Since 1969, after the strike at San Francisco State, Robles began going to Kearny Street, the center of Manilatown and the site of the International Hotel until its demolition.

> I went to Kearny Street because the manongs told me a thousand stories of my father. So the best way to know my family better is to talk with the manongs. And, I found the answers in a poolhall, in the sounds of cueballs. Suddenly, they were all here—all the dreams, myths, celebrations of people—tending the last waterbuffalo, walking in this room, in the delta, in Agbayani Village.[42]
>
> Robles has recorded hundreds of conversations with the manongs, or old-timers, and funnels their experiences into his writings.

But Robles' poems do not try to "reproduce social reality." They leapfrog time and place between the islands and the continent. His poems delight in the reclamation of the tribal—body, blood, and tongue. Through naming, Robles traces lineages between urban Filipino manongs and rural Ifugao tribes.

"In a thousand pilipino songs: pilipino ako" Robles recasts origins in such lines as:[43]

. . .
i am the slated pink salmon from alaska
barreled in thick seasoned wood-floating round like
orange-persimmon buttocks fermenting in a bursting semen-sky. . . .

The poem is dedicated to Filipinos "in the jungles, in the cities, in the ghettos." The frame of reference is both the United States and the Philippines—in one breath—possible only in a poem. The method is archival—gathering, sorting, and sifting out of the collective patterns of speech, chant, song, English and Pilipino words. This poem harkens to the oral tradition. The speaker is "the blood-earth patis flowing through the mountain soil—veins of my people." Robles restores the spirit, that sense of undivided lineage. His response is tribal, defying the imperative of western address.

Robles says:

> There were 20,000 spirits of trees, mountains, animals, on the islands—before the Christians came. So 'primitive' to me is a kind of unfinishedness, and says that we live out natural everyday life in a very natural way. But once the colonizers set up the church—we discovered we were brown. The children of God. And we had to repent. What was more powerful than to kiss the padre's hand? The Spanish divided us with guilt, confession, and conscience. They made us walk around with a confessional box. Our spirit was divided.[44]

Yet, his poetry is not a false escape into the past, a romanticization of history. Aware of that danger, Robles counsels in "Tagatac on Ifugao Mountain":

> . . .
> A Filipino fisherman once said
> that looking for your roots
> will get you all tangled up
> with the dead past. . . .
> The reason, the fisherman continues, is that
> . . .
> If the mind bothers with the roots
> It'll forget
> all about the weeds
> the weeds and roots. . . .[45]

The seeker does not ever find Tagatac, instead ending up on Seventh Street, or in Manilatown on Kearny Street. "But how does the manong survive?" asks Robles:

> . . .
> Does he spread his mind
> far back into the past?
> or does he forget everything
> like a Zen monk
> and live from day to day
> in his old rags
> without attachment?

Perhaps as Robles did, as a Zen monk in Japan.

Robles ends the poem:

> . . .
> There is only one sound
> that comes from ifugao mountain

Tagatac says that it tells you
all you need to know
An ifugao mountain nose-flute sound
tells no lies.

Robles reframes history and experience, producing a poetics in which the present reorders the past.[46]

Aside from poems which are litany, Robles can shift to narrative stanzas. "Carlos Bulosan: Pilipino Poet," reveals another side of an immigrant generation.[47] Robles describes manongs holding Bulosan's thin body to an old cot, leaving him naked for "the first and last embrace of a naked pilipino man and chicana woman." The poem ends with nothing but Bulosan remembering the words of the woman, "do you like it? do you like it?"

The poem not only refers to Bulosan as an individual, but to the Filipino worker: men without wives. It follows the fields where Filipinos and Mexicans worked shoulder to shoulder. At the same time, the sexual encounter is deromanticized: Bulosan's body is wracked by tuberculosis, so that he could not even unbuckle his pants. His friends, without a second thought, help him out, then retreat to their music and card playing. Yet the tryst does not lead to a longer relationship: it was "a zero in a pocket of erections."

## THE *LIWANAG* WRITERS

The poems and stories of Al Robles, together with those of over forty other writers, were anthologized in 1975. *Liwanag* is the name bestowed upon this first collection of Filipino American expression by its editors—Emily Cachapero, Bayani Mariano, and Luis Syquia. To clarify, illuminate, and understand is the meaning of *liwanag* in the Pilipino and Tagalog dialects.

The poem/preface describes the writers as "tribal storytellers keeping the legends alive—making up new stories to delight the young and entertain the old with tales of wonder & long ago monsoon thunder. . . ." The *Liwanag* writers thus link surnames in a tribal litany—Albert, Amelia, Begonia, Belale, Cabanero, Cachapero, Cerenio, Dacanay, Badajos, Fajunio, Feria, Gomez, Gonzales, Hagedorn, Ignacio, Jundis, Kikuchi-Yngojo, Lanosa, Larosa, Legaspi, Likong, Macabasco, Magsino, Mariano, Mateo, Nino, Penaranda, Prisco, Ramos, Remington, Reyes, Robles, Salvador, Santos, Syquia, Tagatac, Talaugon, Tamayo-Lott, Ticke, Valledor, Vila, Zarco.

Of these writers, Oscar Penaranda, and Samuel Tagatac, both born in the Philippines, imbue their works with a sense of the Filipino's land and livelihood.[48] Each writer requires attention: Oscar Penaranda for his subtle renderings of family, friendship, and generation in his short stories that span California to Alaska.

Then, there is Samuel Tagatac. A filmmaker, he visualizes his images to the frame, his poems to the syllable. He experiments with dual languages, line-breaks, montages of English and Pilipino dialects. He coins new expressions such as "chinkujapfilerpino," a composite epithet of the three Asian groups—coming out of the mouth of a white man in "I Came to Tell You Something."[49]

In "The Husking" he speaks to the loss of an ancestral Philippine rice culture to the West:

Clarke's Field deep in
Asia Luzon
Spread the gentle datu
Sea of Ancestral

Birth
Lay

Burning
The palay

Plains for the U.S. wheat dream
That final
Year of infection. . . .[50]

Tagatac recalls the sources of his experience:

> When I was a little boy there were all these legends and tales about trees and the spirits which abound in them. Now that I think about it, the spirits my father and mother spoke of are really the ancestral heritage, unconscious coming to life through legend and myth, except that they are very real. We felt and saw them. Then when we came to America something happened. The smooth flow of life was suddenly snipped, I mean like the jump cut in a film when you know it isn't right. I think the legends and myths ceased then when I was about eight. Why, I had heroes like Randolph Scott, John Wayne, George Montgomery, and favorite names like Jane, Mary, sweetheart, honey, and one day found myself standing under a doorway where I measured out a mark on the frame and decided then that I was going to be six feet tall.[51]

For Tagatac, the "jump cut" is the journey to America: the sharp break with the past and hurtling into a present not of your own making.

Poets such as Tagatac suggest ways to survive the "breaks" of history and the "flows" of life.[52]

## WOMEN WHO KNOW THE MAP BY HEART

The profile of our generation has been redrawn by Asian American women. They trace new territories of mind, body, and earth in their poetry. They see and render the Asian woman as creator, transformer, and lover—and as an exploited object of western imperialism.

Emily Cachapero evokes a disturbing image of beauty and subjugation in her satire of the Miss Universe contest and the candidate from the Philippine islands. The poem begins

miss PI at the miss universe contest
has highways across

her body
everyone at the show
has a map
and those men
un-fresh from nam
know the map by heart. . . .[53]

Cachapero uses the body as a metaphoric map not only for women, but for the Philippines and Southeast Asia, surrendering to war. The poem continues:

. . .
across her body
and mindanao
muslim land
moro land
is under the fold in her belly
it's a secret
kept between the thighs. . . .

It is the territory of insurrection, of land that cannot be quelled. Cachapero concludes that in this contest "the winner is the loser."

To counter the physical, erotic, and political subjugation of the Third World by the West, a coalition of black, Raza, Asian American, Indian, and Native Island peoples founded Third World Communications in San Francisco in 1970. They published *Third World Women* in 1972, followed by *Time to Greeze: Incantations from the Third World* in 1975.[54]

The extension of the personal body, and its rebirth in that of a larger historical body, girds consciousness. Thus Geraldine Kudaka in her poem, "i was born. . ." places her birth in multiple contexts—of the personal—"i was born from the seed of a ford motor co. lineman nakedly given with love to my mother; of the community—"i died and was born again in the streets of chinatown / in the rising sun The East Is Red;" between Dien Bien Phu and the Vietnam War—"i was born seven hundred and twenty four days before the/thundering fall of b-52s. . . ."[55]

In the poem, the east is her "fetal cord," yet she dies many times, in the "schizophrenia of the west."

In another mode, but touching again upon subjugation and liberation, is an unsigned essay in *Third World Women* entitled "Pomegranate Breasts." It is the story of a young Asian woman who has been through the job mill, selling encyclopedias for $1.65 an hour, applying for jobs as a cashier, who finally ends up as a topless dancer.[56] "I, a daughter of third world, was brought up to believe that topless dancers were the same as prostitutes."

The experience changes the dancer's perspective: on the white women with whom she worked, on the customers, mainly white and Asian, or the ex-Vietnam servicemen who either loved or hated Asian women. Rather than condemning the servicemen, she says: "A lot of times I just wanted to tell some racists to 'fuck off,' but my patience sprang from seeing the servicemen so dehumanized."

The writer concludes that within the women who worked at the bar, "we shared a sisterhood, an unspoken oath that we can cheat those who come in to fulfill their perverted fantasies, but not each other."

This essay reveals how individuals can develop their "own brand of humanity," not just through correct study, or involvement in certain "political" or social activities, but even through an alienated form of work.

Moreover, the writer sees that the relationship which is based on male power, though more blatant at the topless bar, can be found in other workplaces. Rather than passive acceptance of her body and her work as viewed/subjugated by the male voyeur—the author has used the experience to develop a psychological bond to other women.

In *A Dying Colonialism,* Frantz Fanon explores the relationship of Algerian women to the veil and to their body, in the context of developing a revolutionary society. Some women had to take off their veils in order to infiltrate European society. At times they would be misunderstood by those in traditional Algerian society. Fanon points out that "The Algerian woman who walks stark naked into the European city relearns her body, reestablishes it in a totally revolutionary fashion."[57]

For Asian American women, their development as writers meant imagining and fashioning poetics which reflected the new ways in which they viewed Asia and the Third World, men, and themselves. Tomi Tanaka's "from a lotus blossom cunt" probes the difficulties that Asian men have in forging relationships with women based on equality:[58]

> . . .
> my eyes have the ol' epicanthic fold
> my skin is the ideologically correct color
> a legit lay for the revolutionary
> well, let me tell you, brother
> revolution must be total. . . .

The message is clear: the bite comes from her use of political rhetoric pitted against sexual rhetoric. The juxtaposition sets up a contradiction between what is stated—and what is acted in relation to women and men. The point here is who is defining the relationship; in this case, it is Tanaka.

Women define and desire themselves, as Kitty Tsui does. She writes for, and about, other women: grandmothers, mothers, aunts, cousins, friends, and lovers. In "Para Todas Crazywomen, Este Poema," Tsui ventures outside of traditional family boundaries.[59] The ode, in eighteen stanzas, is for a woman

> . . .
> who drinks red wine
> and passes out to avoid the night.
>
> este poema is for the crazywoman
> who lets me wear her favorite blue shirt
> and takes my tongue into her mouth
> and massages it.

este poema is for the crazywoman
whose husband burned her
full of holes
and tried to take her son. . . .

Tsui says she continues to write poems to "link arms with women, with men to fight the diseases of a patriarchal past."

Others, like Jessica Hagedorn, incorporate black, Latino, Filipino, and Puerto Rican cadences and charms into their poems and plays, as in the one-act play "Chiquita Banana." The parody takes place in Don Juan's bar with a gaggle of caricatures—Carmen Miranda, Cesar Romero, Miss Harlow—and Koumiko, the lady bartender.[60]

There is conflict among various women—some who want to go with the white male patrons, those who refuse to go with "the pigs." By the end, Carmen points the gun at the audience and shoots, stating: "And you . . . my father . . . it doesn't really matter . . . because you had forsaken us long ago . . . at our expense. This is for you—the real pimp." The play ends with

The militant banana
said fuck you in the grocery stand
peeled his chiquita sticker
and split saying:
I'm no chiquita freak banana—
I gits browner and better
sweeter and cheaper for de people.

In this comedy of Hollywood grotesques, the audience is not lulled into realism or naturalism: Hagedorn utilizes entertainment—music, dance, street, and popular and movie vernacular to ask questions about women in relation to: a single mother raising children, to other women, to the expectations of men, to money and violence. Bottom line, Hagedorn raises the question of the male as pimp.

Hagedorn shares with Cachapero, Robles, Tagatac, and others, the pain of the journey—the cutting off, and reclaiming, of their past. In a poem, "Songs for My Father," a daughter returns from America to the Philippines, finding "i have not understood my obsession to return. . . ." The poem ends with these lines:

. . .
i am trapped
by priests and nuns
whispering my names
in confession boxes
i am trapped
by antiques and the music
of the future

and leaving you
again and again

for america
the loneliest of countries

my words change. . .
sometimes
i even forget english.[61]

It is a narrative of return, of relearning about "dope dealers" and "corrupted senators," that "and decay is forever/even in the rage of humorless revolutionaries." There is familiarity—and futility—with life in the home country, but loneliness in America. The distance from both countries produces self-knowledge—beyond language, alienation, or assimilation.

Hagedorn teases, cajoles, provokes—especially about politics and sex in relation to her Filipino American identity. She visualizes herself in other women, and does not separate the body from ideology. She thus joins other women in "a politics of the body."

Teshome Gabriel suggests that third world artists—be they poets, writers, or filmmakers—are eyewitnesses to both tradition and change. As artisans, they may retain the traditional religious or folkloric forms or vessels, but instill them with new ideologies and purposes.[62]

Anti-Marcos activist, teacher, and writer Dolores S. Feria provides us with an example of the wedding of traditional form and radical content in her poem "Underground Christmas, Circa 1973."[63] Here, she utilizes traditional images of Herod from biblical sources. But through choices of diction and image, she subverts, demystifies, and deromanticizes the Christmas story. She begins:

At midnight
They came, the outcast and the madman
Evading the policemen of Herod
To that stable so pungent with
Newly cut straw and small dunghills
The night I was born
underground. . .

The story advances:

. . .
Verily I say unto you:
Arise now and take the gold, frankincense
And mirth from the vaults of the overfed.
Strip the palaces and the gilded
Cathedrals of all the booty
Snatched from the hungry mouths
of the trampled multitudes.

For the meek will at last inherit the earth:
I say verily, lay down your plowshares and
Melt them back into swords and bullets

At the midnight mass of fire and infinite
Anger, as the herald angels inundate
The mountains and the seas with their
Marching songs
Underground.

The piece attacks the Marcos regime. The poem plays traditional forms against political content in order to reveal the contradictions of Philippine society under siege. Feria's technique—drawing from the form and material of popular lore and altering them toward a different ideological effect, offers a method to follow.

## BY HER OWN INNER EAR

Janice Mirikitani's writings reveal an Asian American persona as poet, activist, and woman of the third world. With others, she founded and edited for Asian and third world publications of the 1960s, 1970s, and 1980s: *Aion, Third World Women, Time to Greeze,* and *Ayumi*. Of her own voice, there are two books.[64]

In the first issue of *Aion,* Mirikitani's "Poem to the Alien Native" gathers images of the seasons, of woman and child.[65] The ode begins:

All seasons were one
The child wore trees in her limbs
and wove leaves to drape her breasts.
I held that child in me
as we walked through seasons together. . . .

Here, no signposts point to Asia or Asian Americans. Other references prevail: to stone, roots, worms, moths, silken graves, and memories of birthing and dying. Her choices reflect an ability to internalize the externals of women's experience. Whether it is marriage or war, Mirikitani is able to cross it. Mirikitani's lyrics speak to her concerns: the incarceration of Japanese and other third world peoples, birthing, war and violence, unity and rift between women and men.

In "Sing with Your Body," about her daughter, she again hears "the beat of a child/dangled by her own inner ear," and directs her daughter "to go quickly/to who you are/before your mother swallows/what she has lost."[66]

The process of creating and retaining, of claiming and letting go, are the constants in her poetry. With hand and knife "preparing fish" or sharpening metaphor, Mirikitani confronts herself and the world.

In "Loving from Vietnam to Zimbabwe,'" Mirikitani pitches the intensity of love-making against the violence of war, in alternating stanzas.[67] She contrasts crimson and silk with boots and delta mud; a massage freely given with the capturing and stripping of a soldier. She ends with

. . .
call me strange Names
hanoi

bachmai
haipong
loving in this world
is the sliver splinter edge
is the dare
in the teeth of the tiger
the pain of jungle rot
the horror of flesh unsealed
the danger of surviving.

Like other Asian American women poets, Mirikitani identifies herself with other women—in this case, the Vietnamese who dared to love, work, and raise children—stepping "through the minefields" of war.[68]

Mirikitani forges dual worlds of "inside and outside," letting her own skin act as the cloth upon which the desires, beliefs, and actions of women "before me, beyond me," are inscribed. As she states: "In my writing I am a lot of women—young girls with the pain, the desires, the dreams, that I have experienced in a lot of women."[69]

Mirikitani does not lack levity. See her parody "A Lecherous Poem to Toshiro Mifune." In this poem she sets up tradition as a ploy: the flute or *shakuhachi, obi,* and the squared-off image of a samurai/rebel squared in the snow. To these clichéd images she directs a series of disarming questions:

. . .
Toshiro, don't you ever get down
with your women
why don't you. . . .[70]

She positions the coy, kimono-clad woman, watching her "hero" stalk away in the twilight. Suddenly, she reverses the subject/subjugated relationship in direct address:

. . .
Turn around Mifune.
stop cleaning your blade. . . .

The statement parodies traditional images of Asian women and men, where the woman usually is the one addressed by the "man of action." Mirikitani pulls it off by her quick imperative, thereby reversing the traditional male and female stances.

Janice Mirikitani sums up her writing "as a whole reaction against what a 'good poem' is: what is iambic or free verse? And besides, all the models were white in those days. So for myself, I rebelled against who I was not."[71]

As her generation responded, rebelled, and created new forms, the next generation recasts their stories—thereby tying a knot to the future. How Asian American poets, the storytellers of each generation—have heard, written, and spoken is part of the unfolding of the tribe.

Their voices are still within earshot. We choose, whether or not, to listen.

## TWENTY-FOUR HOURS FROM NOW

The poets of each generation harbor a future which they can see, hear, and smell, but still cannot touch.

I see the future moving: across the formalities between poetry and prose; across the boundaries between history and passion. Poems which are stories; stories which act as poems. In Theresa Hak Kyung Cha's *Dictee,* for instance.[72] The chronicle of her mother. A refugee, a fighter, for Korean Independence. Maps, Korean and Chinese ideograms, constellations of images, paragraph bulk. English, French, and Korean syllables colliding, conversing. Sure-footed modes: history, lyric, chorus, and epic.

I hear a return to song: how Jeff Tagami illuminates Filipino American history:[73]

. . .
Remember me?
I'm Fermin, the young one,
forever twenty-two
whose name is forming
like a dead son, even now,
on the pursed lips
of my brothers whispering,
'Tobera, Tobera, Tobera'

(Fermin Tobera, a Filipino laborer, was shot and killed as he lay sleeping in a labor camp during the 1930 Watsonville race riots.) The past, forever alive in the future.

I can smell what the new immigrant smells—in Vietnamese writer Nhat-Tien's short story, "The Night Janitor," as yet unpublished in English. The janitor, Mr. Thai, is a refugee who works in an American factory. Every night, he smells the "obnoxious and peculiar odor coming from the office section." The odor is compounded of bookshelves, file cabinets, and computers in rank air. The dankness of the Pacific Ocean, of his recent journey, seeps through the walls, floods his membranes. The journey leads to the interior—of memory, history, and experience. There is no dialogue: only the territory of "trash cans, pictures of sons and daughters next to photos of dogs and cats" in an alien society. As each strange object jolts his senses, each homeland memory is a poem recalled in silence.

I imagine other journeys taken. Writers—Cambodian, Indian, Chinese, Burmese, Samoan, Korean, Hawaiian, Filipino—hauling languages, images, and rhythms from hemisphere to hemisphere. Or poets who have abandoned paper altogether and now write twenty-four frames per second on film.

Departures and arrivals. Our poems, our graffiti. In hardcore English syllables. Spoken in twenty-four Pacific languages in twenty-four-hour noodle houses. Renewed, in twenty-four-year-old Asian Pacific faces.

Twenty-four hours from now, the future will arrive.

A woman's voice will announce: "Deplane."

## NOTES

Reprinted with permission from Russell Leong, *Amerasia Journal* 15:1 (1989): 165–193.

1. Those interviewed for this article provided the impetus: Jeffery Chan, Janice Mirikitani, Geraldine Kudaka, Amy Uyematsu, Alfred Robles, Russell Robles. Over the years, the members of the Kearny Street Asian American Writers' Workshop, and N.V M. Gonzalez, Marlon Hom, Glenn Omatsu, Frank Chin, Emma Gee, Teshome Gabriel, Sam Solberg, have shared their insights on literature with me, for which I am indebted.

2. Bertolt Brecht, "Where I have learned," in *Bertolt Brecht, Poems 1913–1956,* edited by John Willet and Ralph Manheim (New York, 1976): 472–477. See also, Betty Nance Weber and Hubert Heiner, *Bertolt Brecht: Political Theory and Literary Practice* (Athens, Georgia, 1980).

3. On the relationship between literature and society, see, George Plekhanov, "The social mentality of an age is conditioned by that age's social relations. This is nowhere quite as evident as in the history of art and literature," quoted in Terry Eagleton, *Marxism and Literary Criticism* (Berkeley, 1974): 6. For a discussion of Marxism, literature, and ideology, see Raymond Williams, *Marxism and Literature* (London, 1977), especially chapter 3, "Literature," 45–54, on the way the concept developed; and chapter 4, "Ideology," 55–71, on the way ideology is conceptualized in Marxist thought, as 1. a system of beliefs characteristic of a particular class or group, 2. a system of illusory beliefs, or "false consciousness," and 3. the general process of the production of meaning and ideas. Also, see Lu Hsun, "Literature and Revolution'" in *Writing for the Revolution* (San Francisco, 1976): 29–32, where he discusses literature as a tool of revolution.

4. Susanne K. Langer, *Feeling and Form: A Theory of Art* (New York, 1953), especially chapter 15 on "Virtual Memory," 259; Etheridge Knight, "On the Oral Nature of Poetry," *The Black Scholar* 19:4 and 19:5 (1988): 92–95.

5. Henry Miyaji, "Poems from Soledad," in *Gidra,* October 1973, 7.

6. See, the biographies of Japanese American writers who were incarcerated in World War II concentration camps in, Janice Mirikitani, *et al.*, eds., *Ayumi, A Japanese American Anthology* (San Francisco, 1980).

7. The Asian American Writers' Workshop, based in the Chinatown/Manilatown communities, attempted to utilize its writings toward social ends. For example, *We Won't Move/Kearny Street Workshop* (San Francisco, 1976). The purpose of this collection was to raise monies for, and also to raise awareness about the International Hotel struggle. Also, George Leong, *A lone bamboo doesn't come from Jackson St.* (San Francisco, 1977).

8. For a summary of 1970s periodicals which "have in common an honesty, conviction and freshness of creation not found in the so-called 'establishment' Asian ethnic press," see Rockwell Chin, "Getting Beyond Vol. 1, No. 1: Asian American Periodicals," in *Bridge* 1:2 (1971): 29–32. Chin states that these publications were instrumental in helping Asian Americans "create a new culture." Newspapers included: *Gidra*, an English monthly out of Los Angeles; *Rodan*, serving the northern California community; *Chinese Awareness*, a Southland publication connected with the Chinatown Youth Council; *Getting Together,* the official publication of the I Wor Kuen organization in New York; the English section of the *New York Nichibei; Third World News,* covering the UC Davis campus; *Kalayaan International: Philippine international Community News Service* (anti-Marcos, based in San Francisco); *Hawaii Pono Journal,* which analyzes the Pacific area; *Huli!* (Hawaiian for overthrow, published by the Hawaiian community); and *New Dawn.*

Other community journals: *Aion* (1970–71); *Amerasia Journal* (1971–); *Bridge Magazine* (1971–1985); *Bulletin of Concerned Asian Scholars* (esp. issue 4:3 1972); *Echoes from Gold Mountain* (1977); *Yardbird Reader* (1974); *Bamboo Ridge* (1988–). Anthologies included: Emma Gee, et al., eds., *Asian Women* (Berkeley, 1971), *Counterpoint: Perspectives on Asian America* (Los Angeles, 1976); Amy

Tachiki, ed., *Roots: An Asian American Reader* (Los Angeles, 1971); Kaiyu Hsu and Helen Palubinkas, *Asian American Authors* (Boston, 1971); Frank Chin, et al., eds., *Aiiieeeee! An Anthology of Asian American Writers* (Washington, DC, 1974); Joseph Bruchac, ed., *The Next World, Poems by Third World Americans*, (Trumansburg, New York, 1978); Garrett Kaoru Hongo, Alan Chong Lau, Lawson Fusao Inada, *Buddha Bandits down Highway 99* (Mountain View, California, 1978); Janice Mirikitani, *et al.*, eds., *Time to Greez! Incantations from the Third World* (San Francisco, 1975); Brenda Paik Sunoo, *Korean American Writings* (New York, 1975); David Wand, *Asian American Heritage* (New York, 1974); Nick Harvey, ed., *Ting: Chinese Art and Identity in San Francisco* (San Francisco, 1970); Basement Workshop, *Yellow Pearl* (New York, 1972); Asian American Student Alliance, *Rising Waters* (Santa Cruz, 1975–76); Emily Cachapero, et al., eds., *Liwanag: Literary and Graphic Expression by Filipinos in America* (San Francisco, 1975); Jovinna Navarro, ed., *Lahing Pilipino: A Pilipino American Anthology* (Davis, 1977); Mayumi Tsutakawa and Alan Chong Lau, *Turning Shadows into Light* (Seattle, 1982); Ishmael Reed, *Calafia: The California Poetry* (Berkeley, 1979); Shawn Wong, *et. al.*, eds., *Yardbird Reader* 3 (Berkeley, 1974).

For an extended listing of individual works, King-Kok Cheung and Stan Yogi, *Asian American Literature: An Annotated Bibliography* (New York, 1988). Bruce Iwasaki, "Introduction" to the literature section of *Counterpoint: Perspectives on Asian America*, for a listing of poets and writers of the 1968–1978 period, 452–463.

9. Edward Said, *Orientalism* (New York, 1978) especially on cultural hegemony of the West, Introduction, 1–28.

10. Teshome Gabriel, "Third Cinema as Guardian of Popular Memory: Towards a Third Aesthetics," manuscript, forthcoming in Paul Willeman and Jim Pies, eds. *Third Cinema: Theory and Practice* (London, 1989). Also, Kazue Matsuda, *Poetic Reflections of the Tule Lake Internment Camp 1944* (California, 1987), and Wakako Yamauchi, "The Poetry of the Issei on the American Relocation Experience," in *Calafia*, lxxi–lxxviii.

11. Deben Bhattacharya, translator, *Songs of the Bards of Bengal* (New York, 1969), especially the introduction, 23–38. Also, Jan Vansina, Oral *Tradition as History* (Madison, Wisconsin, 1985) especially 13–25, on the dynamic processes of oral history, and on performance and tradition, 39–54.

12. Gabriel, "Third Cinema."

13. Walter Benjamin, "The Storyteller, Reflections on the Work of Nikolai Leskov," in *Illuminations,* edited by Hannah Arendt (New York, 1978): 83–109.

14. Gabriel, "Third Cinema." "Popular memory . . . considers the past as a political issue. It orders the past not only as a reference point but also as a theme of struggle. . . . Popular memory, then, is neither a retreat to some great tradition, nor a flight to some imagined 'ivory tower,' neither a self-indulgent escapism, nor a desire for the actual 'experience' or 'content' of the past for its own sake. Rather, it is a 'look back to the future,' necessarily dissident and partisan, wedded to constant change."

15. Horai, quoted by Stephen Sumida in "Hawaii, the Northwest and Asia: Localism and Local Literary Development in Creation of an Asian Immigrants' Sensibility," in *The Seattle Review* 11:l (1988): 14.

16. Frank O'Connor, *The Lonely Voice: A Study of the Short Story* (New York, 1985): 13–45.

17. Alex Kuo, "Green Tanks and Other Hidden Vehicles of Destruction," in *The Next World,* 106–107.

18. Carlos Romulo, *The Meaning* of *Bundung* (Chapel Hill, 1956) for full text of final communiqué. In 1955, twenty-nine nations excluding those of Europe and America, and the Soviet Union, met in Bandung, Indonesia on April 18–24. Also, Malcolm X, "A Message to the Grass Roots," in *Malcolm X Speaks,* edited by George Breitman (New York, 1966): 3–17. "Once you study what

happened at the Bandung Conference, and the results of the Bandung conference, it actually serves as a model for the same procedure you and I can use to get our problems solved."

19. For a discussion of early immigrant Asian literature, Shawn H. Wong "Longtime Californ'," in *Calafia,* lv–lxx; on Angel Island, see Him Mark Lai, Genny Li, Judy Yung, eds., *Island: Poetry and History of Chinese Immigrants on Angel Island 1910–2940* (San Francisco, 1980); on the first wave of Filipino immigrants, including their expressive writings, Jesse Quinsaat, ed., *Letters in Exile: An Introductory Reader on the History* of *Pilipinos in America (Los* Angeles, 1976).

20. Alan Lau, "Origins," in *Songs for Jadina* (Greenfield Center, New York, 1980).

21. For a broader discussion of third world arts in this period, see *Other Sources, An American Essay* (San Francisco, 1976), a catalog of the San Francisco Art Institute 17 October–7 November 1976, on artists, videos, poetry. The poetry readings were coordinated by the Asian American Writers workshop. Especially see Paul Kagawa, "Third World Art as a State of Mind," 8–16, and Rupert Garcia, "Sources," 23–29 which speaks about Amilcar Cabral and the "seeds of opposition in culture," and also about murals by third world artists, including "International Hotel Fight for Low Income Housing," by Jim Dong and Nancy Hom.

Later publications which evolved from this period include Crystal Huie, Zand Gee, and Jim Dong, eds., *Texas Long Grain*, photos by the Kearny Street Workshop (San Francisco, 1982). Also, Mayumi Tsutakawa and Alan Chong Lau, eds., *Turning Shadows into Light, Art and Culture of the Northwest's Early Asian/Pacific Community* (Seattle, 1982).

22. Chan to Leong, November 14, 1988 interview. Some of the writers in his beginning classes included: Cliff Yoza, Chris Fujimoto, Ed Illumin, Bayani Mariano, Laureen Chew, Juanita Tamayo, George Leong, Connie Chan, Curtis Choy, Russell Leong, Russell Robles, Samuel Tagatac, Luis Syquia, Serafin Syquia, Nathan Lee, Kitty Tsui, Paul Chi, Alan Lau.

23. N.V.M. Gonzalez, "In the Workshop of Time and Tide," in *Mindoro and Beyond: Twenty-One Stories (*Quezon City, Philippines, 1979): 231–256.

24. General historical works include: Norris Hundley, Jr., ed., *The Asian American: The Historical Perspective* (Santa Barbara, 1976); Him Mark Lai and Philip P. Choy, *Outline History of the Chinese in America* (San Francisco, 1971); Victor G. and Brett de Bary Nee, *"Longtime Californ'": A Documentary Study of an American Chinatown* (Boston, 1974); Kazuo Ito, *lssei: A History of Japanese Immigrants in North America* (Japan, 1973); Yuji Ichioka, *The lssei: The World of the First Generation Japanese lmmigrants 1885–1924* (New York, 1988); Lawrence H. Fuchs, *Hawaii Pono: A Local History* (New York, 1961); Michi Weglyn, *Years of Infamy: The Untold Story of America's Concentration Camps* (New York, 1976); Ronald Takaki, ed., *From Different Shores: Perspectives on Race and Ethnicity* (New York, 1987); Sucheng Chan, *This Bittersweet Soil: The Chinese in California Agriculture, 1860–1910* (Berkeley, 1987).

On Filipinos: see Jesse Quinsaat, ed., *Letters in Exile, An Introductory Reader on the History of Pilipinos in America* (Los Angeles, 1976); Carlos Bulosan, *America Is in the Heart* (Seattle, 1973); and "Filipinos in American Life," *Amerasia Journal* 13:1 (1986–87).

On Koreans: Illsoo Kim, *New Urban Immigrants: The Korean Community in New York* (Princeton, 1981); Wayne K. Patterson, *The Korean Frontier in America: Immigration to Hawaii, 1896–1910* (Honolulu, 1988); and Kingsley K. Lyu, "Korean Nationalist Activities in Hawaii and the Continental United States, 1900–1945," *Amerasia Journal* 4:l and 4:2 (1977); and Warren Won Yong Kim, *Koreans in America* (Seoul, 1971).

For updates on these and other groups, see the annual *Amerasia Journal* selected bibliography.

25. Jack K. Masson and Donald K. Guimary, "Pilipinos and Unionization of the Alaskan Canned Salmon Industry," *Amerasia Journal* 8:2 (1981): 130; Carey McWilliams, *Factories in the Field: The Story* of *Migratory Farm Labor in California* (United States, 1969); and Bienvenido Santos, "Pilipino Old Timers: Fact and Fiction," *Amerasia Journal* 9:2 (1982): 89–98.

26. Emma Gee, ed., *Asian Women* (Berkeley and Los Angeles, 1971,1975), especially the section on "Third World Woman," and the report on the "Indochinese Women's Conference: Asian Delegates from Berkeley," 77–80.

27. Frank Chin, "Confessions of a Chinatown Cowboy," *Bulletin* of *Concerned Asian Scholars* 4:3 (1972): 58–70; Robert Murray Davis, "Frank Chin: An Interview with Robert Murray Davis," *Amerasia Journal* 14:2 (1988): 81–95; Maxine Hong Kingston, *The Woman Warrior: Memoirs of a Girlhood among Ghosts* (New York, 1976); Shawn Wong, *Homebase* (Berkeley, 1979); Alan Chong Lau, *Songs for Jadina* (Greenfield Center, 1980); and Wing Tek Lum, *Expounding the Doubtful Points* (Honolulu, 1987).

28. The Combined Asian American Resources Project, taped interviews with Asian American writers and artists, the Bancroft Library, University of California, Berkeley. Also see Louis Chu, *Eat A Bowl of Tea* (New York, 1961), John Okada, *No No Boy* (Rutland, Vermont, 1957), Toshio Mori, *Yokohama California* (Caldwell, Idaho, 1949), *The Chauvinist and Other Stories* (Los Angeles, 1979), and the literature section of *Counterpoint: Perspectives on Asian America,* which includes works by Hisaye Yamamoto and Wakako Yamauchi. Also, Hisaye Yamamoto, *Seventeen Syllables and Other Stories* (Lathan, New York, 1988), and; *Nikkei Review: Japanese American Literary and Cultural Newsletter* 1:l (1989), for news on second generation Nisei writers and artists.

29. *Amerasia Journal* 6:1 (1979), Introduction, 3–29.

30. E. San Juan, Jr., "The Poetics of Anti-Individualism," in *Carlos Bulosan and the Imagination of the Class Struggle* (Quezon City, 1972): 65, and *Only By Struggle, Literature and Revolution in the Philippines* (Mansfield Depot, Connecticut, 1980) for a discussion of contemporary art and politics.

31. *Ibid.,* 65, also *Amerasia Journal* 6:1 (1979): 103.

32. S.E. Solberg, "Carlos Bulosan: A Selected Bibliography," *Amerasia Journal* 6:l (1979): 167-172.

33. *Imagination of the Class Struggle,* 79.

34. *Poetry of the New Asian Nation* (Berkeley, 1972), printed program.

35. Alex Hing, "The Need for a United Asian Front," *Aion* 1:l (1970): 9-11. Interview with Alex Hing, Minister of Information of the Red Guard Party, by Neil Gotanda, 32–42, where he discusses parallels between the black and Chinatown communities.

36. Hisaye Yamomoto sums up the major literary conferences of the period in her introduction to Toshio Mori's *The Chauvinist and Other Stories* (Los Angeles, 1979): 3: "Out of this growing ethnic consciousness emerged the first Asian American Writers' Conference, sponsored at Oakland Museum, by the Combined Asian American Resources Project (March 1975); the second similar event, the Pacific Northwest Asian American Writers' Conference, sponsored at the University of Washington in Seattle (June 1976); the Talk Story Ethnic Writers' Conference at Mid-Pacific Institute in Honolulu (June 1978)."

37. Russell Robles, New Asian Nation program note.

38. Nanyang Stella Wong, "The Return," in *Third World Women,* 43, and "Nuptial Songs of a Chinese Village," in *NUMBER* 1:2 (1950): 3–17. Also, Marlon K. Hom, *Songs* of *Gold Mountain, Cantonese Rhymes from* San *Francisco Chinatown* (Berkeley, 1987).

39. "Where I have learned," Bertolt Brecht, in *Poems*, 472–476. He discusses sources and influences on his writing—overheard in factories—folksongs sung and improvised, and the ditties of childhood.

Ralph Ellison, in an essay, "Hidden Name and Complex Fate," in *The Writer's Experience* (Washington, D.C., 1964): 1–15, talks about a writer's sources: "The places where a rich oral literature was truly functional were in the churches, the schoolyards, the barbershops, the cotton-picking camps; places where folklore and gossip thrived."

Stephen Sumida, in "Hawaii, the Northwest and Asia" refers to the *hole hole bushi* work songs created in the sugar plantation fields to break the monotony of labor (see note 14): "Like American spirituals and grassroots work songs, *hole hole bushi* are authentic American folk songs, their form and content inspired directly by the particular circumstances which the issei discover themselves."

In the same essay, Milton Murayama states that his characters would speak any of four basic tongues, standard English, pidgin English, pidgin Japanese, or standard Japanese. Also see Eric Chock, et al., eds., *Talk Story: An Anthology of Hawaii's Local Writers* (Honolulu, 1978) on the discussion of pidgin.

40. Gabriel, "Third Cinema."

41. Lawson Fusao Inada, *Before the War, Poems as They Happened* (New York, 1971): 110–113.

42. Robles to Leong, 14 November 1988.

43. In "a thousand pilipino songs: pilipino ako," *Liwanag,* 149.

44. Robles to Leong.

45. "Tagatac on Ifugao Mountain," *Liwanag,* 152–153.

46. Jean Chesneux, *Pasts and Futures or What Is History For?* (London, 1978). "Reversing the Past–Present Relationship," chapter 5, 37–44: "The primacy of the present over the past is based on the fact that it is the present alone that forces us to change."

47. "Carlos Bulosan: Pilipino poet," *Liwanag,* 146.

48. Oscar Penaranda's works in *Liwanag,* 103-130, in *Aiiieeeee!,* 14–149, in *Asian American Authors,* 151–153.

49. Tagatac: "I came to tell you something," in *Liwanag,* 197–198, in *Aiiieeeee!,* "The New Anak," 150-168, Poetry of the New Asian Nation program note.

50. Tagatac, "The Husking," in *Liwanag,* 190.

51. Editor's Note: This citation is missing from the original.

52. Other *Liwanag* poets include Luis Syquia, Jr., 163–171, and Serafin Syquia, 172–187.

53. Cachapero, *Liwanag,* 32.

54. Third World Communications, *Third World Women* (San Francisco, 1972); Janice Mirikitani, Luis Syquia Jr., Buriel Clay II, Alejandro Murguia, Roberto Vargas, Jim Dong, Janet Campbell Hale, eds., *Time to Greeze! Incantations from the Third World* (San Francisco, 1975).

55. Kudaka, *Time to Greeze,* 35. Also, *Numerous Avalanches at the Point of Intersection* (Greenfield Center, New York, 1978).

56. "Pomegranate Breasts," in *Third World Women,* 30.

57. Frantz Fanon, "Algeria Unveiled," in *A Dying Colonialism,* discusses the new Algerian women (New York, 1982): 35–67.

58. Tomi Tanaka, in *Roots* (reprinted from *Gidra),* 109.

59. Kitty Tsui, *The Words of a Woman Who Breathes Fire* (San Francisco, 1983): 23–25.

60. Jessica Tarahata Hagedorn, "Chiquita Banana," in *Third World Women,* 118–122.

61. "Songs for My Father," *Dangerous Music* (San Francisco, 1975).

62. Gabriel, "Third Cinema."

63. Dolores Feria, "Underground Christmas, 1973," in *Time to Greeze,* 72. Also see Feria, *Sound of Falling Light: Letters in Exile* (Quezon City, Philippines, 1960).

64. Janice Mirikitani, *Awake in the River, Poetry and Prose* (San Francisco, 1978); *Shedding Silence* (Berkeley, 1987).

65. "Poem to the Alien Native," *Aion,* 28–29.

66. "Sing with your body," in *Awake in the River.*

67. Ibid., "Loving from Vietnam to Zimbabwe."

68. Quoted from the title of a reading, "Through the Minefields," by the Pacific Asian American Women Writers—West, 26 September 1987, Asian American Journalists Association First National Conference. Adapted and produced by Emma Gee.

69. Mirikitani, in "Why is Preparing Fish a Political Act?," documentary videotape, produced by Russell Leong, forthcoming.

70. In *Awake in the River.*

71. Theresa Hak Kyung Cha, *Dictee* (New York, 1982).

72. Jeff Tagami, *October Light: Poems* (San Francisco, 1987).

73. Nhat-Tien, "The Night Janitor," from *Mot Thoi Dang Qua* [*The Passing of an Era*], translated by Anh Tran. For contemporary Vietnamese literary and cultural expression, see *The Vietnam Forum*, a periodical published by the Yale Council on Southeast Asian Studies. On the demographics of new Asian immigration, see James Fawcett and Benjamin Carino, *Pacific Bridges: The New immigration from Asia and the Pacific Islands* (Staten Island, New York, 1987).

# INTRODUCTION TO *RESISTANCE, DIGNITY, AND PRIDE: AFRICAN AMERICAN ARTISTS IN LOS ANGELES*

PAUL VON BLUM

African Americans and other representatives of diverse communities are prominent among the thousands of talented visual artists who live and work in Los Angeles today. These artists have produced exemplary works in every medium, including painting, sculpture, printmaking, photography, and others. Their efforts have helped to make Los Angeles an important center among artists, critics, and scholars.

African American artists may be drawn to Los Angeles by its substantial black population. The 2000 US Census showed that more than 930,000 African Americans reside in Los Angeles County alone. This includes the city of Los Angeles along with substantial black populations in such independent municipalities as Inglewood, Compton, Long Beach, and Pomona. Thus, a familiar and supportive environment exists to encourage African American visual production.

Los Angeles has also served as a center for oppositional political activity and supports a resistance culture. In addition, despite its complex and continuing social and economic problems, the Los Angeles area has historically been a fertile ground for artists who work outside the framework of the white-dominated mainstream. As a result, the area now enjoys an impressive black cultural infrastructure encouraging visual expression and exhibition. Such institutions as the California African American Museum, the Museum of African American Art, the Watts Tower Arts Center, and the William Grant Still Community Arts Center offer major venues for the works of local and national African

Paul Von Blum is a senior lecturer in African American studies and communication at UCLA where he has taught since 1980. Previously, he taught at UC Berkeley for eleven years, where he participated vigorously as a young faculty member in the Third World Liberation Front struggle that helped to create ethnic studies programs at the University of California. He has received numerous teaching awards and is the author of ten books and numerous articles on art, law, education, history, and politics. His most recent book is *Creative Souls: African American Artists in Greater Los Angeles*. The introduction and subsequent discussions of four artists are taken from Von Blum's *Resistance, Dignity, and Pride: African American Artists in Los Angeles* (Los Angeles: Ralphe J. Bunche Center for African American Studies, 2005).

American artists. The Golden State Mutual Life Insurance Company's African American art collection, including the famous 1949 murals on *The Negro in California History* by Charles Alston and Hale Woodruff, also provides a rich and supportive cultural context.

At present, no one has written a comprehensive history of African American art in California, much less Los Angeles specifically. This endeavor remains a compelling challenge for scholarly investigation; detailed documentation of this visual tradition would enable scholars and the general public alike to understand the roots of contemporary African American art in Los Angeles. While moving in this direction, the present work has a less extensive reach.

*Resistance, Dignity, and Pride: African American Artists in Los Angeles* introduces readers to the lives and works of sixteen African Americans prominent in the Los Angeles art world of the late twentieth century. While the artists discussed here include many of the brightest stars of the African American art community, their selection was not intended to reflect any critical judgment in the sense of a top ten list. Serendipitously, the author became acquainted with each of these artists during the course of his work as a professor of African American Studies at UCLA. Therefore, it should be added that this book is not intended to provide a comprehensive critical appreciation of these artists in the context of the American art scene, though again it moves in that direction. While various works and artistic genres and styles are described and discussed, the author is unequivocally and unapologetically a fan of the artists reviewed here.

The sixteen African American artists featured in *Resistance, Dignity, and Pride* have made powerful and enduring contributions to the local and national art world, engaging and challenging thousands of people, especially African Americans, to reflect critically about major historical and social themes. They have built a vibrant and powerful creative community in the Los Angeles area. In particular, the focus here is on the period of the 1960s and 1970s, when this art community in many ways came into being.

To fully understand the work of these artists, one must not only recognize its sources in American history and the art world but also acknowledge the barriers many of the artists have overcome to achieve a professional reputation and economic stability. Thus, their efforts must be viewed in the context of slavery, racism, and their more subtle sequelae, the changing dynamics of race relations in contemporary America. This book will show how their experience as African Americans interacted with their artistic abilities in producing an impressive body of work.

The introduction is intended to provide a context for the individual profiles. First, it will briefly sketch the political and social events and trends that characterized the times these artists lived in and helped to record. Then, it will look at the African American art community in Los Angeles. Finally, it will provide an overview of the sixteen artist profiles to follow.

## A HISTORY OF STRUGGLE

As African Americans born in the twentieth century, the sixteen artists this book features have emerged from a distinctive and too often negative experience. Like others of their ethnicity and generation, they responded to their times with resistance, dignity, and pride.

African Americans are descended from people who were seized against their will, carried out of their homelands and across an ocean under the most appalling conditions, and sold into slavery in a strange land, often without their families. Although this history lies more than a century in the past, its impact remains.

Moreover, some of the artists profiled in this book were born when segregation was still the law of the land. They have personal memories of water fountains and restrooms labeled white or colored. Growing up in the 1930s and 1940s, they knew the indignity of racial slurs; they knew the dangers they faced in encounters with white police—or any white men. Some were children in places where lynchings were common: White men, in Klan regalia or not, dragged black men off in the night and hanged them for imagined crimes or no crimes at all.

The bias was both pernicious and pragmatic. A North Carolina museum docent informed the young Ernie Barnes that African Americans did not express themselves in the visual arts. Roland Charles was repeatedly turned away from mainstream galleries that cavalierly rejected his photographic images of ordinary black people. And a college art teacher rudely objected to Lavialle Campbell's explanation of the historical implications of her racially focused work.

With the 1950s and 1960s, the Civil Rights Movement combined organized social protest with legal action to put America onto a path toward true freedom for all. We have made some progress on that road, but the destination is still over the horizon. Despite affirmative action and less formal forms of outreach to African Americans, their representation among the middle class, among college graduates, and in several professions remains small in proportion to their presence in the population. Racial profiling and police assaults against African Americans continue to occur. Twice in the last half of the twentieth century—during the Watts riots of 1965 and the rebellion sparked by the acquittal of Rodney King's police assailants in 1992—the Los Angeles community experienced widespread race-related violence.

Provocative scholars Derrick Bell and Andrew Hacker have repeatedly argued that millions of whites still believe Americans of African origin are fundamentally inferior, both morally and intellectually. The accomplished men and women featured in this book know well the power of institutional resistance to blacks and other ethnic minorities. They recognize that their work must proceed in an atmosphere of continuing, if more subtle, racial discrimination.

This atmosphere influences their work in several ways. Besides shaping their sensibilities and lives, the social history of their people has become the subject of these artists' works, just as improving the situation of African Americans has become a frequent motivation. These larger issues of social justice are mentioned in this book only as they affect the artists and their work. The racial climate of the nation has had a profound effect on the art world and those African Americans who try to find a place for themselves within it. This merits further attention.

African American art has historically received scant recognition from academic institutions. A few prominent black artists, such as Henry O. Tanner, Jacob Lawrence, Romare Bearden, Charles White, and perhaps a few others, may appear in standard art history texts and university courses. Even then, African American works may be treated as ethnic curiosities, a reflect ion of "primitivism" better consigned to anthropological inquiry. University art schools compound the problem by admitting relatively few African American students to MFA programs; even fewer African American artists have permanent faculty positions in such schools.

Until quite recently, historically black colleges were the only institutions where students could learn about the intellectual and cultural contributions of African Americans. In the past thirty years, modest attempts to broaden the curriculum at other colleges and universities have met vigorous resistance from those who misrepresent these efforts as "political correctness" and issue hypocritical calls for restoring "excellence" and "quality" to the curriculum. This structural denigration means that many of the artists discussed here grew up in ignorance about their predecessors and had to find means outside the mainstream to learn about their legacy.

The media have not helped. Reviewers for newspapers and some art journals may dismiss work by artists of color and ignore art exhibitions in alternative African American (and Latino and Asian American) cultural institutions and venues. In addition, they rarely write about murals, which constitute a major expression of alternative ethnic consciousness.

This exclusionary pattern persists in the institutions that make up the art world itself. Major American art museums primarily collect and exhibit the work of established white male artists. Art galleries are capitalist enterprises created to make profits. Many gallery officials believe, with some justification, that their affluent white audiences have little interest in purchasing artworks addressing black themes, especially those criticizing society's attitudes, policies, and institutions.

It is reasonable to ask why the growing black middle class is unable to support African American artists. Increasingly, educated African Americans have realized that the visual arts can provide a durable legacy of their culture for future generations. This process, however, is slow and the market small. The underlying reason lies in the differences between wealth and income. In *Black Wealth, White Wealth*, Melvin Oliver and Thomas Shapiro show how historic patterns of American racial inequality are reflected in continuing imbalances in black and white wealth. Whereas affluent whites often own houses and other wealth-producing property and inherit substantial estates, upwardly mobile blacks may have good incomes alone. Their lack of a supporting base of real estate and other liquid assets inhibits their financial ability to purchase artworks.

Against these negative forces, some positive developments have occurred, particularly in the past thirty or forty years. The central catalyst was the civil rights and black power ferment of the 1960s and 1970s, which influenced American cultural and intellectual life. At colleges and universities, the creation of black and other ethnic studies programs inspired scholars to document and validate the long-ignored cultural products of African Americans, Latinos, American Indians, Asian Americans, and women. Many of their works involved effective critiques of white cultural hegemony.

A tradition of scholarly literature on African American art has existed for decades. Pioneering books by Howard University scholars James Porter and Alain Locke defined and legitimized the field in the early 1940s. In the 1960s and 1970s, new books described the lives and works of artists from non-white communities, detailing how they functioned in adverse social and economic circumstances. Other books or catalogs dealt with individual minority artists, movements, or art forms. These more recent works responded aggressively to the exclusionary patterns of traditional white research and scholarship.

Perhaps most significantly, scholars have recently argued that the time has come to reexamine traditional standards of artistic quality. As Thomas McEvilley persuasively maintains in *Art and Otherness*, the Plato- and Kant-inspired vision that quality can be judged by universal and unchanging criteria has dominated modern art criticism. This perspective suggests that artistic judgments are purely objective; those with sufficient training and experience can capably apply these universal standards to any works of art they may examine. McEvilley contends that these artistic judgments are hardly objective. Rather, they are a neo-conservative political expression that devalues contemporary multicultural and politically radical visions to protect established interests. A more authentic critical approach should involve greater sensitivity to the value standards of groups historically excluded from political power and cultural influence, he suggests.

The implications for African American art are obvious. The black experience in America has differed dramatically from that of other racial and ethnic populations. An understanding of this history must inform an expanded and ultimately more comprehensive set of critical standards. Moreover, viewers should be empowered to make their own determinations about artistic quality and effectiveness, drawing constantly on their experiences as well as on so-called objective standards. For example, if, after seeing Elliot Pinkney's mural *Ceremony for Smokers*, an African American teenager decides to quit smoking, that public artwork succeeds effectively in the terms in which it was created and presented. If a viewer happens on Ramsess' poster portraits of Jomo Kenyatta and Paul Robeson and vows to learn more about African and African American history as a result, those works also succeed on their own terms. If a person attending an exhibition showing Alison Saar's *Terra Firma* is stimulated to work politically to address homelessness, that sculpture is effective. Scores of comparable examples fill this book.

## A HISTORY OF ACCOMPLISHMENT

Besides their impact on individuals, the historic struggles for justice and racial equality helped to galvanize a strong African American arts community in Los Angeles. Those struggles also promoted specific anti-racist political agitation that eventually brought African American art closer to the exposure and recognition it justly deserves.

Ever since they arrived unwillingly on these shores, African Americans have produced a remarkable and prolific body of paintings, prints, sculpture, photography, murals, and other forms of art. From its slave craft beginnings, African American art has come to embrace the contributions of thousands of gifted black men and women, not only in big cities but also in the rural South and elsewhere.

African American art also has impressive roots in Southern California. Although early representatives of this tradition, like black artists everywhere, received inadequate attention from both the art world arid the larger society, their efforts nevertheless had a profound effect on their audiences and on the artists featured in this book.

The artists of *Resistance, Dignity, and Pride* especially acknowledge the relentless efforts of Claude Booker and Cecil Fergerson in promoting local African American artists. Booker, a shipping clerk at the Los Angeles County Museum of Art, developed a passionate interest in African American art. As Fergerson indicates, Booker felt that he had a mission to bring black artists to public attention. Self-educated in the field, he was instrumental in pressuring museum officials to end the pattern of racial exclusion in the visual arts. He relentlessly insisted that black artists be given proper representation. His pressure catalyzed the first major exhibition entitled *Two Centuries of Black American Art*, which David Driskell organized at the Los Angeles County Museum of Art in 1976, several years after Booker's premature death of a heart attack at thirty-six.

As employees of the Los Angeles County Art Museum, Booker and Fergerson had daily acquaintance with the irrelevance of that major institution to the lives and interests of millions of black citizens. Their formation of the Black Art Council in 1968 (with Booker as president), along with subsequent efforts, played a major role in generating a more cohesive African American artistic community. Thus, they are properly recognized as seminal figures in the twentieth century history of African American art in Los Angeles. As artist John Outterbridge has explained, this organization functioned as the art world's equivalent of the NAACP, serving as a watchdog entity to check racist excesses and to promote reforms that served African American artists.

Fergerson, who started as a janitor and tenaciously worked himself into a professional position, organized the art exhibition at the Watts Summer Festival for many years. He retired from his curatorial assistant position at the Los Angeles County Museum of Art in 1985 and has continued to be a major advocate, organizing exhibitions and demanding recognition and support for African American visual art.

Another milestone in the development of the Los Angeles African American art community occurred in 1967: Artists Alonzo and Dale Davis founded the Brockman Art Gallery, providing a major exhibition venue for African American artists. Visually accomplished themselves, the brothers contributed significantly to local institution building. The gallery in Leimert Park, an exhibition space and think tank, fostered solidarity and networking among black artists and stimulated a deeper intellectual consciousness about their work.

Perhaps the dominant figure of the 1960s and 1970s was Charles White, who had already established a national reputation that was rare among black artists in America. As many of the men and women in this book attest, White was a role model, inspiring them to incorporate the historic challenges and joys of African American history and life in their creative work.

Charles White's story is well known. Born in 1918, he struggled as a young man to build an artistic career in Chicago, where racist institutions and incidents caused regular frustration. In 1956, he moved to the Los Angeles area, where he quickly established himself as a major artistic presence.

Beginning around 1960, White's association with the Heritage Gallery brought him to national prominence. Owner Benjamin Horowitz promoted White's art vigorously, providing him several exhibitions, encouraging sales of his works, and, in 1967, producing a pictorial book about his art entitled, *Images of Dignity: The Drawings of Charles White*. By the early 1960s, White had secured a teaching position at the Otis

Art Institute, where he worked closely with younger artists, many of whom went on to make their own significant contributions to African American art history.

Before his death in 1979, White had created many striking murals, drawings, and prints that captured the essential dignity and strength of his people. White's portraits of historic figures in African American political, cultural, and intellectual life remain classics. His influence on other generations of African American artists has been enormous, extending well beyond Southern California.

Another key figure of White's era was Ruth Waddy. Born in 1909, Waddy founded Art West Associated, an organization that encouraged African Americans to pursue their artistic interests. Several of the younger artists featured in subsequent chapters have spoken passionately of her personal support and encouragement.

Waddy's work as a self-taught painter and printmaker was widely recognized during her productive artistic years. Along with Samella Lewis, who is profiled in this book, Waddy helped to chronicle the contributions of black artists throughout America. Her cumulative efforts in mentoring other black artists and her own visual efforts led to her selection in 1995 as one of the "legends" honored at the annual Artist's Salute to Black History Month in Los Angeles.

Also honored as a legend in 1995 was Noah Purifoy, a powerful artistic figure from the 1960s and 1970s. Born in 1917, Purifoy founded the Watts Tower Arts Center and cofounded the Watts Summer Festival. His remarkable institution building was combined with intellectual vigor and pioneering personal efforts in assemblage work. Accomplished senior artists such as Betye Saar and John Outterbridge, both profiled in this book, have repeatedly acknowledged their creative debts to Purifoy.

Trained as a social worker, Purifoy turned to visual art later in life. His distinctive personal style involved the collection of discarded materials that he fashioned together into creative wholes. He was a major participant in the historic *66 Signs of Neon* exhibition, based on artworks assembled from the debris of the 1965 Watts rebellion. This traveling show had a profound effect on black artists all over America. Artistically active throughout his eighties, Noah Purifoy died in his desert home in Joshua Tree, California in 2004.

Purifoy's engaging philosophical interests generated deep respect among his African American artistic peers. He encouraged the use of art as a tool for social change, a goal that has long pervaded African American art history. His influential presence in the developing community of Los Angeles-based black artists in the late 1960s and early 1970s helped establish the tone for African American artwork of the next quarter century and beyond.

Like White, Waddy, and Purifoy, John Riddle also played a prominent role in the multiple creative developments of the 1960s and 1970s. President of the Black Arts Council, Riddle also exhibited his work at the Brockman Gallery. A teacher in the public schools, he had a deep understanding of black history, and that passion led him to share his knowledge through art.

Born in 1933, Riddle was a sculptor who, during the late 1960s, collected discarded objects to serve as his basic artistic source material. He regularly accompanied his friend and colleague, John Outterbridge, on early morning field trips around Los Angeles to salvage materials. His welding ability also contributed to his works' quality and impact.

Riddle left Los Angeles in 1976, eventually moving to Atlanta, where he continued to produce compelling works of visual art chronicling the black experience. In 1999, he returned to Los Angeles to head the Visual Arts division of the California African American Museum. His untimely death in 2002 ended his brilliant career as an artist and educator. Virtually every major black artist in Los Angeles attended his memorial service at the Watts Towers Art Center on April 7, 2002.

Like Riddle, several artists left Southern California after contributing to the cultural ferment of the 1960s and 1970s that eventually gave rise to the present regional community of African American artists. Canadian-born Artis Lane is a good example. She trained at the Ontario College of Art and at UCLA, forging a distinguished career in both painting and sculpture. Her three-dimensional works in particular have focused on black identity as well as broader spiritual themes.

Lane's sculptural series entitled *Emerging into Spirit* pioneered a technique that leaves part of the ceramic casting material on the finished product. These striking figurative works suggest that emergence from racial oppression and spiritual darkness is a continuing process. Lane spent most of her productive life working in a Santa Monica studio and influencing a younger generation of local African American artists. After living in New Mexico for several years, Lane returned to Los Angeles in 1998 following her husband's death. She continues in her seventies to produce powerful figurative works as a senior member of this vital artistic community.

David Hammons, born in 1943, is one of the most celebrated visual artists from the civil rights/ black power era in Los Angeles. A student of Charles White at the Otis Art Institute, he emulated his time in Los Angeles, Hammons pioneered the technique of body prints, using his own body as the printing plate. In the mid-1970s, Hammons moved to New York, where his remarkable sculptures, instillations, performance works, and other artistic efforts have brought him international honor and recognition, including a prestigious MacArthur Foundation grant.

*Resistance, Dignity, and Pride* celebrates some of the major contemporaries and descendants of this accomplished and energetic African American community of Los Angeles based artists. Many were personally engaged in the inseparable intellectual, cultural, and political activities of the 1960s and 1970s. All have profited from their participation in the artistic community that developed then. By documenting their lives and works, the book reveals the historical continuity of that tradition.

## RESISTANCE, DIGNITY, AND PRIDE

The artists featured in the following chapters are at various stages of their careers. Some are just starting, others are in mid-career, while still others, now in their sixties and seventies, continue many decades of outstanding artistic production. For the most part, these artists know each other personally and professionally and often provide generous assistance for each other's artistic endeavors. The men and women of this coherent, loose-knit artistic community regularly attend each other's openings and include each other in group exhibitions whenever possible. Their common African identity and experience fosters higher levels of cooperation, support, and mutual respect than might be typical in the art world.

Most of these artists are well trained in the traditional fine arts. Many have completed formal university degrees in studio art, some with terminal degrees in their field. Others have undergone rigorous apprenticeship training; their extensive artistic experience transcends the background and training they could find in contemporary BFA or MFA programs.

As the following chapters reveal, these artists work in a striking variety of visual media. Some use traditional drawing, printmaking, and photography to communicate their visions of the African American experience, while others have developed sculptural and assemblage techniques for this purpose. Many have pioneered or adopted new ways to attract nontraditional audiences, especially African Americans, to their artistic commentary. Images of their murals, installations, and other art forms appear throughout these pages.

Rather than organized around genre or medium, age or gender, this book groups these artists by the themes delineated in the title—resistance, dignity, and pride. While the artists have been placed according to the emphasis in their careers, most could have appeared in more than one section.

Sympathetic to the historic "others" exploited by the dominant race, class, and gender, the artists in this book regularly use art to criticize the existing social and political order and to call attention to the dramatic racial injustices that have marred so much of American history. Part 1, "Resistance," includes artists who have created a range of politically provocative works on subjects ranging from slavery and police brutality to economic inequity and media bias.

African American artists routinely offer positive visual perspectives that empower people of color to find the dignity often denied them in mainstream media and popular attitudes. Part 2, "Dignity," includes artists whose primary protest has taken the form of presenting positive images of black people: political leaders, artistic and athletic icons, and ordinary mothers and fathers, aunts, musicians, even insurance men.

Moreover, some of the African American artists profiled here have participated in building alternative institutions where their colleagues can be exhibited with pride appropriate to their achievements. In Part 3, "Pride," the book examines the personal art works of four people who have made a significant contribution in this way.

A common thread among these sixteen artists is that their works continue one of the traditions of African American artists rooted in the nineteenth century and aggressively extending into the twentieth century: using art to tell stories. As distinguished artist and scholar David Driskell has noted, in numerous interviews with the author, most African American artists have had little patience with the ideology of art for art's sake, preferring instead to communicate messages about the urgent realities of their lives as black people in a white society.

The artists in *Resistance, Dignity, and Pride* provide alternative visions to those that have dominated American cultural life for more than two centuries. Their superbly executed efforts have affected and informed audiences of all ages and backgrounds. Their fundamental objective, passionately felt and unshakably persistent, is to invite viewers to reflect seriously about history, society, politics, and personal creativity. Only the future can reveal the final success and impact of their work.

# ERNIE BARNES

In 1995, Ernie Barnes published his autobiography, *From Pads to Palette*, an engaging account of his dual careers as a professional football player and a visual artist. Therein he chronicles his unique path in endeavors that most people might reflexively perceive as entirely unrelated. Against stereotype, Ernie Barnes has made the move from successful offensive lineman to highly accomplished figurative painter. In addition, his depictions of athletic events and scenes from daily life add immense luster to the long tradition of American genre painting. Barnes's specific portrayals of African American themes have made him one of the most renowned African American artists of the late twentieth century. Contributing powerfully to the vibrant tradition from which he emerges, his works underscore the vitality of Los Angeles as a center of exceptional African American visual art.

Barnes's personal odyssey began in Durham, North Carolina. Born in 1938, Barnes was an overweight, shy, and reserved child whose extraordinary sensitivity would eventually inform his mature artistic production. Throughout his early life, he had the good fortune of having a loving family and of receiving the positive support of most of his neighbors. Decades later, he recalls fondly how the "village raised the child," offering hope and encouraging his dreams, despite overt racial discrimination. He found repeated encouragement to read, take music lessons, converse, and appreciate the black experience, especially the rich and dynamic tradition of African American music.

Barnes also recalls vividly the barriers and affronts that he and others encountered each day in the Jim Crow South of that era. He remembers the indignity of segregated water fountains, distant seating in movie theaters, and many other institutional means of promoting subordination among the black population, all of which left him feeling emotionally strangled. In one incident, when he was nine or ten years old, a clerk at the Kress five and dime store threw a bag of popcorn at him, exhibiting the pervasive disrespect for black customers that virtually all shoppers experienced in southern states.

He reflects even now about how both law and culture enforced racist attitudes and practices. Above all, he has come to understand how hatred is ingrained in people and how profoundly destructive that emotion can be for them individually and for society generally. To his regret, moreover, he realizes that despite the surface changes fostered by the Civil Rights Movement, the deeper manifestations of racism remain in the South and throughout the United States. This consciousness has affected his artistic focus for the past thirty years and explains his passionate desire to use his art to showcase the essential dignity and humanity of people of all races and ethnic backgrounds.

While in junior high school, Barnes discovered his natural athletic prowess. At first, he went out for football in order to acquire popularity he desperately hoped would offset his insecurity. He coveted athletes' applause and other accolades, imagining those as the solution to his low self-esteem.

As he progressed through high school, however, it became apparent to everyone that he had extraordinary athletic talent. He strengthened himself through a rigorous bodybuilding program and grew bigger, heavier, faster, more muscular, and more self-confident. He also refined his specific skills under the careful tutelage of his high school coach. By his senior year, he had captured the football team, become state champion in the shot put, and garnered twenty-six college and university scholarship offers.

Significantly, Barnes continued to pursue the sketches and drawings that he had done since early childhood. This was for him a natural expressive outlet that his teachers encouraged. In fact, school authorities once asked him to paint a mural in the school cafeteria. This effort focused on the foods of various cultures, including dishes from China, Hawai'i, the US mainland, and elsewhere. As Barnes eventually discovered, he was at heart an artist, an identity that never faltered even during his grueling five seasons in professional football.

As he tellingly reveals in his autobiography, no scholarship offers came from such noted institutions near his hometown as Duke or the University of North Carolina. The racist ambiance of the times precluded a black football player from participation at that level of Southern collegiate athletics. Barnes decided to accept a football and track offer at North Carolina College (now North Carolina Central University), an all-black institution only one block away from his neighborhood high school.

His undergraduate years there proved to be valuable preparation for both of his subsequent careers. Off the football field, the most significant feature of his college life involved his efforts as a studio art major and the influence of his various instructors. Two teachers, in particular, helped him establish an enduring basis for his future role as a figurative artist.

One was Ed Wilson, one of the chairs of the Art Department, who had studied as an apprentice with noted Jewish American sculptor William Zorach. The other was Wilson's co-chair, Winston B. Fletcher. These two men helped train the many gifted but unprepared students who often came from poorly equipped and poorly funded primarily-black high schools. Barnes himself had enjoyed decent artistic facilities in high school but mediocre training. Most of his fellow classmates, coming from rural largely-African American schools, had lacked both adequate facilities and instruction.

From Wilson and Fletcher, Barnes learned about proper artistic form and the fundamentals of drawing and painting; human anatomy; perspective; light and shade; design; and basic art history. During college, Barnes developed competence and confidence in such media as charcoal, pencil, pen and ink, and oil. This foundational work has served him well for more than forty years.

Wilson's and Fletcher's influence, which stemmed in part from the art education writings of renowned Hampton Institute teacher Viktor Lowenfeld, went far beyond artistic technique alone. In particular, they encouraged their students to develop individual styles, pushing Barnes and others to trunk critically and to have an informed vision of their lives and their world. They inspired students to look closely at their experiences and to use them as the foundation for their artistic expression. Barnes has incorporated this advice in all his subsequent artistic efforts. A former college football player himself, Wilson also showed Barnes the close connection between sports and the visual arts, a perspective he has retained and implemented throughout his artistic career.

These teachers' most valuable gift, however, was the knowledge and appreciation of the neglected tradition of African American art that they imparted to their students. As Barnes poignantly relates in *From Pads to Palette*, he and his fellow art students once visited the recently desegregated North Carolina Museum of Art. When he asked the docent there to talk about paintings by Negro artists, she replied, "I'm afraid that your people don't express themselves that way." When they returned to North Carolina College, Ed Wilson told the young art students that they now could see what they were up against. Then he proceeded to show slides of the works of such African American masters as Robert Duncanson, Henry O. Tanner, Edmonia Lewis, Archibald Motley, Hale Woodruff, Sargent Johnson, and Palmer Hayden.

Meanwhile, on the athletic field, Barnes's undergraduate years propelled him to high visibility and excellence in football. From his freshman through his senior years, he played center, developing extraordinary skills in blocking. Because few players from black colleges were seriously considered as professional prospects, however, he gave little thought to a football career. Instead, he prepared himself to work as an artist. To his surprise, though, he began to receive inquiries during his senior year and was drafted by the Baltimore Colts in 1959.

For the next five years, Ernie Barnes spent his life as a professional football player, playing with the Baltimore Colts, the San Diego Chargers, and the Denver Broncos. He is the first to admit that be had a journeyman's career, with solid accomplishments short of Hall of Fame status. His experiences, both positive and negative, have profoundly affected both his life and artistic work since be retired in 1965. *From Pads to Palate* provides a detailed account of his five pro seasons.

Barnes was one of the first blacks drafted into professional football. Not surprisingly, be continued to encounter racism during his football career. He discovered, for example, that a quota limited the number of black players, another barrier to full racial dignity and equality in America. In addition, African American players were frequently forced to eat and sleep in separate facilities, a legacy of the Jim Crow environment of his youth. More insidiously, Barnes was, in effect, compelled to play while injured, a practice that reflected the dominant attitude among the white ownership and coaching staff that black bodies somehow endured pain better than white bodies. Barnes recalls even now the pervasiveness of this stereotype during the 1960s. Interestingly, all of this occurred against the background of the emerging Civil Rights Movement, catalyzed by the courageous actions of African American students throughout the South.

Barnes also recalls the more beneficial consequences of his five professional seasons. For the first time in his life, he was living and working closely with whites, providing him with more subtle knowledge of the multicultural reality of modern America. In particular, he experienced an intense camaraderie emerging among people who worked together with almost military discipline and precision. As a result, teamwork and the spirit of common endeavor among people of different races and backgrounds have informed his subsequent efforts as a painter. In addition, be experienced and observed human physical movement in depth. More than anything else, this intimate engagement with movement provided the foundation for the dynamic energy that characterizes his artistic work.

Barnes continued his artistic production throughout his playing days. Like most artists, he drew in his sketchbook, frequently using his football experiences as subject matter. He also created various paintings during his football career, including his first work with a football theme, entitled *The Bench*, which he still owns more than thirty-five years later. He developed a solid reputation among teammates and other football personnel (some of whom have become collectors of his work) for his artistic skill and sensitivity. Common athletic objectives and general camaraderie encouraged a genuine interest in teammates' private lives and other activities, including Barnes's passion for drawing and painting.

During his football years, Barnes also learned more about his artistic roots. In 1964, while browsing in a Harlem bookstore, he discovered a portfolio of Charles White's artwork. He recalls this experience as almost indescribably intense. Years later, Barnes reflects on how the encounter with White's work—dignified portraits of African Americans—went to his core. He realized intuitively that this discovery was much bigger than football. As he put it in a conversation in 1996, it "kicked my ass!" Later, as a Los Angeles resident, he had the good fortune to develop a relationship with Charles White. Through a mutual friend, Ivan Dickson, Barnes met and visited the legendary artist at his Altadena home. Barnes and White continued their relationship until White's death in 1979, meeting often at gallery exhibitions and other occasions. Their conversations helped Barnes reflect more precisely about his aspirations as a visual artist. White also provided a powerful model for success in a difficult and socially marginalized activity.

In 1965, Ernie Barnes retired from the Broncos. Playing in an era before the vast escalation of salaries for professional athletes in the 1980s and 1990s, he left football with no basis of financial security. His child and spousal support obligations exacerbated his uncertainty about what he should do next. Returning to San Diego, where he had served in the off-seasons as a YMCA youth director, he sought out his former contacts hoping to find a patron. Instead, a wealthy board member at the YMCA discouraged his artistic aspirations and provided a referral that led to a job as a construction worker.

Unhappy in that role, Barnes yearned to paint. At one point, financial pressures sent Barnes to Canada, hoping to resume his football career, but a foot injury put a permanent end to that phase of his life. Drifting again, he found his way to Los Angeles, seeking to fulfill his lifelong aspiration to be a professional artist. His first weeks in the city were disconcerting at best because he had little money and few contacts. He used his meager funds to buy a sketchpad, pencil, and paints, in lieu of nutritious food and decent lodging.

Then, he saw an opportunity to use his pro football contacts to advance his new career. He contacted Barron Hilton, whom he had known while playing for the San Diego Chargers, at the Hilton Corporation headquarters in Beverly Hills with an audacious suggestion: He should become the official artist of the American Football League. Hilton, who was chief executive officer of the hotel corporation and president of the Chargers, responded warmly. Hilton advanced him $1,000 to produce a painting of

Chargers' end Lance Alworth and also arranged for Barnes to make a presentation at an upcoming owners' meeting, where good fortune struck again.

At that gathering, Sonny Werblin, the wealthy, well-connected owner of the New York Jets, took an interest in Barnes, his ideas, and his artistic prospects. He invited the struggling artist to come to New York and arranged meetings with important people in the art world there. He also put Barnes under contract, with an exceedingly livable salary, to produce thirty paintings during the next six months. Ernie Barnes had found a patron, a circumstance he candidly recognizes as both extremely lucky and extremely rare. In due course, Werblin arranged a major exhibition for Barnes in New York City at the Grand Central Art Galleries, a major institution that encouraged artists working in the traditional figurative manner. Others who had shown there included the distinguished artists George Bellows, John Sloan, Robert Henri, as well as African American luminary Henry O. Tanner.

Barnes was twenty-six and at a transitional point in life when he got this first exposure to a cosmopolitan audience. It was highly successful. Most of the art he showed at the gallery had football as its subject matter. Several sports and business notables, including Werblin, the late sportscaster Howard Cosell, and various players on the New York Jets, purchased paintings. Having penetrated the art world's major leagues, Barnes returned to Los Angeles, intent on deepening his skills and implementing the vision that had pervaded his consciousness since his North Carolina childhood.

Finding a place to live in the predominantly Jewish Fairfax section, Barnes undertook to solidify his growing artistic reputation. Initially, he encountered little enthusiasm among mainstream Los Angeles galleries. He walked up and down La Cienega Boulevard, the city's gallery center in the late 1960s, attempting to find someone who would show his paintings. Finally, he connected with the Mackenzie Gallery, where he presented a major exhibition of sports-oriented work in 1968.

In 1970, Benjamin Horowitz of the Heritage Gallery began to represent him. This gallery also handled Charles White, Barnes's major inspiration in the African American visual tradition. Compared to other gallery owners Horowitz was far more enthusiastic about black artists and had worked prodigiously to build White's national reputation. In Barnes, Horowitz saw an artist of growing stature and enormous potential whose thematic focus could not only incorporate but transcend his athletic experiences. Barnes responded by producing and showing numerous paintings, culminating in 1971 in his landmark exhibition, "The Beauty of the Ghetto," which drew on a wide variety of personal experiences painted in Barnes's increasingly imaginative style. This exhibition marked one of the few times in American art history that a major artist had showcased the joys of African American pool halls, barbershops, musical and dance clubs, and churches—some of the key gathering places within the black community. The collected paintings in that show brought a comprehensive vision of African American cultural vibrancy to audiences of all backgrounds.

Throughout his life in Southern California, Ernie Barnes has enjoyed high public visibility, an unusual achievement for an African American artist. During the 1970s, he exhibited widely throughout the United States. His paintings were also featured on the CBS television program *Good Times*, a popular show about a working-class black family. Then, in 1984, he was the official artist of the twenty-third Olympic Games, which were held in Los Angeles. He won this position by convincing Los Angeles Olympic Organizing President Peter Ueberroth and the board that his artworks would both capture the Olympic spirit and be accessible to most spectators at the events. Over the years, Barnes's collectors have come to include prominent figures in sports, government, and the professions, and he has received numerous awards and honors.

This recognition is somewhat unusual because he is a traditional painter who has deliberately avoided the dazzling array of modern and postmodern styles that generally preoccupy art circles. His work is properly characterized as neo-mannerist, based on the style popular in Italian painting and sculpture between the Renaissance and Baroque periods. Like the efforts of Tintoretto and Michelangelo, Barnes's paintings and drawings emphasize elongated figures and carefully conceived distortions of color and perspective. Above all, his efforts highlight a dramatic sense of movement, emerging from his lifelong athletic involvement. He refers to his style as "the tension generated by conflict and paradox."

Barnes also recognizes the influence of many modern artists on his development. Beyond the seminal inspiration of Charles White, he has found the efforts of the entire American "ashcan" school useful and attractive. And, through their paintings, George Bellows, Thom as Hart Benton, and Andrew Wyeth have also served as his artistic mentors.

Some of Barnes's works pay explicit tribute to his predecessors and strengthen the idea of a continuing black visual tradition. For example, *Homage to Charles*, an acrylic on canvas, reinforces Charles White's depictions of the liberating effect of education on African American youth. Loosely based on White's Los Angeles mural *Mary McLeod Bethune*, the painting similarly emphasizes a young black person reading. With his arms extended, the teenager seems to envelop the book, absorbing both its contents and its durable significance for his future. Two other young people grasp the youth, drawing the same intellectual sustenance from him that he has drawn from the act and habit of reading. Together, these three figures suggest the collective commitment of many young African Americans to seek education for both personal growth and social advancement. The alphabet in the background, following Charles White's own compositional strategy in several works, fortifies the focus on learning. Barnes repeats this theme in several paintings, including *Mother Hale*, *The Story Teller*, *Commencement*, and *Study Break*, among others.

Barnes's athletic paintings similarly reveal the fundamental humanism of his artistic vision. His football works enable viewers to understand the intensity of gridiron combat. *Half Time* illustrates the huge physical and emotional toll on team members each week. Battered and exhausted, the players struggle to find the strength to compete with equal vigor in the second half. By focusing on the halftime locker room interlude, Barnes conveys the spirit of brotherhood uniting the team and sustaining their common endeavor. Significantly, black and white players share the common emotional territory of anxiety and hope. Thanks to their commitment to the singular goal of victory, racial divisions and animosities fade into irrelevance.

As the Official Olympic Artist in 1984, Barnes made a series of paintings that deal with numerous athletic events, feature people of all races and nationalities, and promote the ideals of tolerance and cooperation. Over the years, Barnes has deliberately created favorable images of white people. He explains that he has lived and worked with extensively in white settings and is comfortable in extending his artistic scope beyond his own African American culture and heritage. Cumulatively, these depictions suggest that the visual arts might have a role in resisting racial misunderstanding and promoting multiculturalism.

One vibrant painting from the Olympic series deals with young people who live in the vicinity of the Los Angeles Coliseum, the main site of the 1984 games. *The Neighborhood Games* combines Barnes's signature neo-mannerist style with substantial thematic detail. As residents recall, the 1984 Olympics generated considerable community spirit throughout Southern California. The work captures this exuberance in depicting several young men and women playing volleyball and basketball as part of the *Olympic Neighbor Games*. The group is conspicuously multiracial, and the message of community solidarity is reinforced with background textual references to supportive activities such as cooking, dancing, and bake-off event. At the top of the piece, colored balloons soar, signifying, perhaps, Barnes's hope that this community spirit will endure.

In another acrylic from the Olympic series, Barnes focused on a marginalized population. In *Special Olympics*, he affectionately depicts five young, physically and mentally handicapped participants in a racing event. Struggling despite the constraints of wheelchairs, crutches, and other barriers, these youngsters show the Olympics and in professional sports leagues. The competitive intensity suggests their deeper commitment to thrive against all odds. At the top of the painting, Barnes employs the cloud-like imagery if the Coliseum and of the Olympians in motion to show how these special athletes share the same hopes and aspirations as everyone else. He may indeed, be drawing on his own disadvantaged background, particularly his encounters with racism during his youth and football career, to provide a sensitive account of others who struggle against irrational fear and institutional discrimination. Like his mentor Charles White, Barnes is determined to provide images of dignity for all people.

A major thrust of Barnes's artistic work is a celebration of the positive elements of African American life and expressive culture. A typical example is *The Sugar Shack*, a genre painting reminiscent of Archibald Motley's black club life scenes set in Chicago in the 1930s and 1940s. Like those African American visual classics, his work is a model of energy. The fusion of music and dance underscores the dynamism of the entire hall. The frenetic activity suggests a highly sexualized ambiance by Marvin Gate and of other events indicate that this is a well-established place to escape the pressures of daily life. In the midst of this exuberance, Barnes depicts a seated figure, at the bottom, right of the composition, who appears to be headed toward an alcohol-assisted despair. Not even the loud music and joyful dancing alleviate his pain. The artist invites viewers to speculate on the deeper causes of his malaise.

African American jazz and its performers have profoundly affected Ernie Barnes. Several of his paintings reflect the deep impact of music, as its rhythms and emotions inform his art. An outstanding example is *Quintet*, from his exhibition "The Beauty of the Ghetto." Like his other genre works chronicling African American daily life, this painting portrays the beauty of the black experience. The faces of these five musicians, their skills predicated on years of practice, reveal the same determination and exhaustion that Barnes's football players and other athletes reveal in his sports-related artwork. Above all, the musicians show the consummate seriousness of their craft.

In *The Tunesmith*, Barnes deepens this perspective by adding an educational theme to his celebration of the black musical heritage. The young musician displays a typical Barnesian intensity of purpose: dedicated to his craft, he meticulously plots out his compositional strategy. The young man's hand is poised to make whatever changes and corrections are necessary, determined to achieve perfection. Barnes's neo-mannerist style is useful in conveying the painting's underlying message. Thoughtful viewers understand that creative expression requires protracted, often frustrating work, represented by the stretch and strain of the figure's body language.

When Barnes organized his "Beauty of the Ghetto" show, he understood that the term ghetto has historical origins beyond the segregated residential arrangements of African Americans. Specifically, it refers to the historic Jewish quarters in European cities, where millions of Jews lived and developed their impressive heritage of learning and culture. Barnes speaks with passion of the five years he lived in the Los Angeles Jewish community, where he learned of Jews' enduring spiritual sense and their determination to overcome hardships and persecution. In *Sam and Sidney*, Barnes pays artistic tribute to the Jewish ghetto's resilience and vigor.

The painting features two Jewish men engrossed in conversation. The men appear to be arguing, with the man in the foreground making his point in animated fashion, while his friend seemingly resists with equal intensity. More important than their theological or political dispute, however, is the closeness of their relationship, signified by their linked arms. This gesture suggests the unity of the Jewish people, fortified by their historic capacity to argue and debate with both vigor and mutual respect. *Sam and Sidney* reflects Barnes' broader sympathy with people of all cultural and ethnic backgrounds at the same time that it pointedly rejects the destructive media-inspired myth of black anti-Semitism.

For three decades now, Ernie Barnes has lived his childhood dream of being a successful visual artist. Unlike many artists, especially African Americans, he has made a good living and has achieved the high recognition and visibility his work deserves. Fully realizing his good fortune, he continues to be extremely active. Recently, he completed a large commissioned painting with a football theme for the National Football League's Carolina Panthers. His 1996 painting, *The Advocate*, honors courageous black lawyers like the late Supreme Court Justice Thurgood Marshall and others who fought (and continue to fight) to implement American constitutional ideals. In 200l, Barnes created a powerful painting, *In Remembrance*, in response to the horrific terrorist attack on September 11.

Barnes has ambitious artistic plans for the future, including a portrait of Paul Robeson, probably the greatest athlete-artist of all time. Painting most deeply for himself, Barnes also has a powerful desire to communicate his visions and ideas to ordinary people. His special commitment is to use his art to influence young people, extending to a new generation the benefits of mentorship that served him so well. Barnes's unique ability to depict the central themes of daily life ensures the success of this worthy objective.

# VARNETTE HONEYWOOD

Los Angeles artist Varnette Honeywood is an exceptional descendant in the long line of African Americans who use their art to provide a more positive image of their people. A highly versatile artist currently in mid-career, she has produced scores of vibrant and colorful artworks that reveal the exuberance and creativity of black life. Her paintings, collages, and prints use visual language to continue the long story-telling tradition of her people. Like many of her African American predecessors and contemporaries, she eschews the notion of "art for art's sake," instead opting to produce work that communicates deeply felt thoughts and ideas to her audiences.

A lifelong resident of Los Angeles except for her college years in Atlanta, Honeywood's artistic sensibility has been shaped by the effects of racism on her family as well as her own encounters with it. Her mother and father, who migrated from Mississippi and Louisiana respectively, often discussed their memories of the Jim Crow environment of the early twentieth century. They were also subjected to white racial harassment in Los Angeles when they moved into a mixed neighborhood. Her parents recall numerous telephone calls filled with racial slurs. Their complaints to the authorities were ignored, leaving them vulnerable and without protection.

The artist's maternal grandparents were victimized by a Klan cross burning. This ugly act towards their family reinforced Honeywood's grandfather's determination to gain his human and constitutional right to dignity and respect. A church deacon and appliance salesman in Mississippi, he had extensive contact with other African Americans. For the Ku Klux Klan in Mississippi, that marked him as a trouble maker and civil rights advocate. Refusing to be morally intimidated, however, Honeywood's grandfather retained his dignity in the face of the Klan's racist affront.

Among Honeywood's own experiences, she recalls that, in high school in the late 1960s, she and her fellow African American students were prohibited from wearing Afros, then a visible symbol of black power and resistance. Even more importantly, she observed the insidious policy of discouraging minority students from proceeding to higher education and channeling them instead into low-paying, menial jobs that lacked future prospects.

On the positive side, high school enabled Honeywood to learn about the history of her own people. As a teenager, she took one of the first courses in African American history, a curricular development that emerged directly from the civil rights ferment of the l 960s. Through that class, she achieved a fuller understanding of the tragedy of the forced migration of her ancestors from the African continent. She also came to know the many accomplishments of African Americans in all fields of human endeavor. This led her, in turn, to realize that African American history and culture are inextricably part of to the wider American history and culture.

Honeywood's consciousness about black history gave birth to a strong desire to become a history teacher herself, a role that would allow her to make major contributions to her community. Although she subsequently spent a few years teaching, her work as a visual artist has provided her primary identity and livelihood, and her artworks have constituted her most enduring legacy to African American cultural pride and dignity.

Unlike many accomplished artists, Honeywood had no strong youthful inclination to pursue a professional artistic career, even though she had demonstrated impressive artistic talent in her youth. Nevertheless, she benefited from her parents' encouragement to pursue the arts. Her mother, for example, enrolled her in an art program at the highly regarded Chouinard Institute in Los Angeles. Honeywood participated as a teenager in the Watts "chalk- in" in 1967, a community venue for young blacks to showcase their artistic talent. She was also involved in an art club while a student at Los Angeles High School.

However, her systematic development of this gift came only during her collegiate years. Enrolled at Spelman College in Atlanta, a historically black college for women, Honeywood took a drawing course, where she soon received serious recognition and encouragement. She recalls vividly how her African American instructor Joseph Ross fostered her confidence, which led her to declare art as her undergraduate major. Later, Floyd Coleman added his strong visual expertise to her efforts. He had a dramatic impact on her thinking and on her art making. He also assisted her technical development, propelling her to the road of lifelong creativity. Another major influence at Spelman was the renowned African American artist Kofi Bailey, who served as artist-in-residence during Honeywood's undergraduate studies. The pan-African perspective that infused Bailey's socially conscious figurative art deeply affected Honeywood. To this day, its influence is apparent throughout her works. Spelman College art instructors exposed students to working black artists, ensuring that they would never work in an historical vacuum. By emphasizing the efforts of such luminaries as Romare Bearden, Elizabeth Catlett, Benny Andrews, Howardina Pindell, Barrington Watson, and others, the instructors encouraged Honeywood and her fellow students to aspire to their own artistic greatness.

Like many young people during that era, Honeywood also attended civil rights rallies and protest demonstrations. She discovered that visual art played a powerful role in the broader struggles for equality and human dignity. This recognition merged with her formal studies in art.

Following her graduation from Spelman, Honeywood returned to Los Angeles, where she obtained her master's degree in education from the University of Southern California. For five years, she worked at the Joint Educational Project (JEP), developing visual arts programs that helped USC students to design various multicultural arts and crafts programs and mural projects for mostly minority students in local public schools. Honeywood's work, with this program was far-reaching, since her students, from several academic fields, had a unique opportunity to interact with minority communities. While at JEP, she also joined and became an active member of the National Conference of Artists, an organization that fostered African American history and art in the United States, Brazil, and Nigeria.

Previously, Honeywood taught art at the Central Juvenile Hall, an experience she remembers as extremely difficult. This work emerged from Teacher Corps-Urban Corrections and provided a creative and controversial educational alternative to the tradition custodial focus of the juvenile justice system, but dealing with those warring value systems was frustrating for Honeywood. This background furthered her commitment to young people, however, fortifying her desire to provide positive visual images for black children, one of the central premises of her artistic career.

Honeywood's visit to Nigeria in 1977 had a similarly profound effect upon her artistic work. Her African travels solidified her emotional connection to her ancestors and reinforced her view that African Americans must look to Africa as a source of identity, pride, and creativity. During her stay, Honeywood was welcomed by Nigerian families and observed African dance, music, and visual art, leaving with strongly positive impressions that would inform her own efforts in painting, printmaking, and other visual forms. Above all, she had a strong impression from her travels that art infused all aspects of Nigerian life.

From 1978 to the present, she has collaborated with her sister, Stephanie Honeywood, in creating and sustaining an art business based on her own work, including both original works and reproductions. Together, they produce and distribute note cards, posters, and similar products to the public, thereby ensuring a substantial audience for Honeywood's artwork. These efforts provide all people with the opportunity to acquire copies of her vibrant and colorful images of African American life and give her a source of income in a society that still devalues the efforts of visual and other artists. It enables viewers of all income levels to enjoy high quality visual art. With sales of her artwork at exhibitions, her work as an illustrator for books with African American themes, and her and her sister's reproduction business, Honeywood has successfully forged an artistic career. Her inclusion in the Cosbys' renowned collection of African American art has also fostered her career, a recognition that has increased her stature and visibility throughout the United States.

Major figures in the African American art community in Los Angeles have helped this gifted and emerging artist. Like many prominent African American artists in that community, Honeywood owes the most immense gratitude to Cecil Fergerson, curator and community activist, whose assistance to and encouragement of black artists has been instrumental both in their personal careers and in the wider recognition of their artistic tradition and legacy. Fergerson has regularly selected Honeywood's works for inclusion in local exhibitions.

She also received extremely valuable help from older well-established African American female artists Ruth Waddy and Samella Lewia. Waddy became a lifelong friend and mentor and talked to Honeywood's parents about recognizing the need to support young artists. Lewis in particular has always been a powerful role model and community artistic leader. Their encouragement and active support facilitated her artistic efforts, in process forging the same type of powerful cross-generational bond that pervades the entire community of African American visual artists in Southern California and elsewhere in the United States.

Honeywood has also drawn on the vast tradition of African American art as a major source of inspiration for her own work. Jacob Lawrence's migration series, for example, reflected the experiences of Honeywood's parents, stimulating her commitment to memorialize the lives of African American people in Los Angeles and elsewhere. From Archibald Motley, she learned how artists can use visual forms to capture the essence of daily life. From William H. Johnson, she discovered the power of color to communicate her personal vision of African American life and experience. From Romare Bearden, she discovered the effectiveness of the collage form in accomplishing the same objective. Honeywood has also emulated the underlying political consciousness evident in the works of Elizabeth Catlett and Charles White a perspective she specifically and proudly acknowledges. Finally, the influence of the contemporary Afri-Cobra artists reinforced Honeywood's commitment to her artistic endeavors.

From these many sources of inspiration, Honeywood has developed a coherent artistic philosophy. Above all, she seeks to provide a personal and positive vision of black life to her audiences. Her primary commitment as an artist is to convey her sense of history and struggles of her people. She views her works as visual documents that create a historical record of African American suffering and triumphs. For her, this objective reflects her identification of the spirit of social consciousness and protest of the 1960s.

A collage from 1973 effectively exemplifies this perspective. *Slavery* vividly depicts the tragic origins of African American history in the New World. Emerging from his forced labor in a Southern cotton field, a black male at the top right of the composition expresses his intense agony at being driven from his ancestral homeland and brutalized into submission. Few viewers can remain indifferent to the pathos of this work. Like other socially conscious artists, Honeywood uses individual portraits to communicate deeper historical realities. By highlighting one sorrowful human being, the artist reveals the true human consequences of massive social injustice.

A recurring theme in Honeywood's work is the vibrancy of black culture despite the barriers of racial oppression. Her 1981 watercolor *entitled Club Alabam: Down at the Dunbar* combines strong composition, striking color, and historical content. The scene of the painting dates from the 1940s and is based on her parents' vivid memories of the black lifestyle of that period. The effort highlights Central Avenue in Los Angeles, then the center of a thriving African American community. For Honeywood's parents and thousands of others, Central Avenue was the place to congregate: the West Coast counterpart to New York's Harlem. As the work reveals, people strolled the avenue, savoring the multiple delights of food, music, dance, and general conviviality.

The locus of both commerce and culture, Central Avenue attracted major black luminaries in all fields. In the background, the artist depicts the Dunbar Hotel, the legendary stop for black musicians, artists, and others who were excluded from the major white hotels in the Jim Crow environment of Los Angeles in the early twentieth century. Engaging in its artistry, Honeywood's work promotes an awareness and appreciation of the exuberant street culture of African American life. In the spirit of Archibald Motley's depictions of Chicago and William Pajaud's of Los Angeles, the work stands as a thoughtful corrective to negative portrayals of blacks in the popular media.

Throughout her career, Honeywood has also used her art to express solidarity with black women throughout the world. *Virtuous Woman*, a serigraph from 1988, reflects the impact of her trip to Africa. Around the central image of a strikingly attractive black woman, the artist has placed the twisting African symbol of toughness and adaptability, Nkyimkyim. Drawing on her impressive capacity as a colorist, Honeywood presents the woman as ready and fully able to handle any adversity. Most importantly, the image speaks eloquently to young African American women, for whom the dual barriers of racism and sexism present daily challenges.

The special strengths and contributions of African American women have been a recurring subject of Honeywood's art. In *Taking Care of Business*, she identifies and celebrates the political role of black women in America. From the abolitionist movement to the civil rights struggles of the recent past and present, women have provided both leadership and organizational skill in the fight for political and social justice. In this collage, Honeywood depicts three women working hard to get out the vote to ensure that African Americans are adequately represented in the electoral contests of the day. The artist also places pictures of her own family members in the background of the work, which underscores its deeply personal meaning.

Created in 1983, the work was made in the context of the strong support African American communities gave to Jesse Jackson's candidacy for the Democratic nomination for president. The artist's own grandfather, his family having been victimized by a Klan cross burning, for example, felt great excitement and gratification in finally being able to vote for a black candidate for the nation's highest office. *Taking Care of Business* documents a major historical reality and encourages other blacks (especially women) to extend the legacy of the politically active sisters depicted in it.

Honeywood has also made it part of her artistic mission to focus on the underrecognized creative activities of black people. *Kuumba* appropriates (and incorporates into the work itself at the left side of the image) the Swahili word for creativity as it draws on one of the seven Kwanzaa principles to provide a strongly positive image of the multiple talents of people of African descent. In this mixed media effort, Honeywood portrays several archetypal figures of impressive creative accomplishments in various fields, including architecture; historical research and communication; photography; printmaking; sculpture; and painting. Significantly, she highlights people of varying skin colors, a celebration of the diversity of black people in America and throughout the world.

Like many African American artists since the early part of the twentieth century, Honeywood pointedly identifies Africa as a key source of blacks' creative energy. In *Kuumba*, she provides a detailed and colorful background of West African fabric and symbols. This visual recognition of Africa's influence provides an alternative perspective to the Eurocentricity still dominant in American education. Her art deliberately emphasizes African themes and imagery, encouraging young black viewers in particular to discover their heritage. Fulfilling her deepest communicative objectives, her artworks promote recognition of the African genesis of black creativity, an insight of immense value to people of all ethnic backgrounds.

Honeywood has worked with this specific theme for many years, hoping that its repetition will inspire her audiences, especially young African Americans, to build socially productive and personally satisfying lives. In a silkscreen created for the National Black Arts Festival in Atlanta in 1990, she focuses on the unique and multifaceted contributions of black people to American arts. *Generations of Creative Genius* portrays, from left to right, a dancer, a writer, a painter, and a musician. Each of these artistic enterprises has deep roots in African American history. Once again, she emphasizes the African sources of these domains of accomplishment. Each figure is attired in African dress, with symbols from the motherland present to remind viewers of the inextricable links between Africa and its sons and daughters in the Diaspora. Well aware that the many contributions of blacks to the nation's cultural legacy remain largely unknown, Honeywood employs her artworks as a valuable antidote.

Throughout the 1990s, Honeywood intensified her effort to use her art to communicate messages of social relevance. As a resident of Los Angeles, she is keenly aware of the multiple dangers facing young people of color in that community, dangers originating in part from harmful generalizations about their attitudes and behavior. In a provocative acrylic painting from 1990, she critiques attitudes among white Americans (and even some black Americans) about African American family dysfunction and irresponsibility. *Don't B-Live the Hype* counters these stereotypes by depicting a young black family man warmly embracing his three children. Fully committed to authentic family values, the man exemplifies the loving relationships that people of all ethnic backgrounds cherish and attempt to establish. Honeywood's central point is deliberately unambiguous: African Americans—no less than anyone else—care deeply about their children.

In addition, the very title of the painting conveys a particular message to young African Americans, especially males. The artist implores them neither to "B" nor to "Live" the hype of media-promoted visions of black irresponsibility. Moreover, in a work specifically directed to the younger black community, she reinforces her affection for her subjects through various details in the work. In particular, she calls attention to their creative capabilities by highlighting the colorful spray-can art in the background. This highly imaginative art form, once disparaged as mere vandalism, repeats the central theme of the artwork. Also, the young man at the lower left of the painting wears an African medallion, underscoring the artist's identification of Africa as the source of all black accomplishments.

In 1991 Varnette Honeywood produced a painting that simultaneously acknowledged the value of her own college education and the continuing vitality of historically black colleges generally. *The Groundbreaking* commemorates that occasion for the new Camille Cosby Academic Center at Spelman College, a generous gift from the Cosbys, which houses the art museum, the Women's Center, and the library. Used as the cover for the *Spelman Alumni News Magazine*, the work depicts, from left to right, Camille Cosby, Spelman President Johnnetta Cole, the project architect, the chair of the board of trustees, a Spelman student, and Bill Cosby. Each participant in the ceremony is justifiably proud of the broader accomplishments of the college in providing education and opportunity for generations of African American students. That message has intimate personal significance for Honeywood, whose own experiences at Spelman nurtured the well-deserved professional recognition she presently enjoys.

Varnette Honeywood has accepted responsibility for extending the tradition of visual social commentary about the black experience. Her dedication to the rituals, traditions, hopes, and frustrations of her people assures her reputation as an artist of remarkable distinction and visibility. In addition, from 1997 to the present, she has done illustrations for the series of children's books for young readers called *Little Bill Books* and for the accompanying cartoon. With this work, Honeywood joins a distinguished tradition of African American children's book illustrators, including such luminaries as Faith Ringgold, Jerry Pinkney, Jacob Lawrence, and others. In her early fifties, she has decades of creative work to come.

# SAMELLA LEWIS

Few people have been as successful in promoting African American art as Samella Lewis, who has devoted her long career to bringing recognition and respect to this powerful tradition of visual creativity. Her outstanding efforts have made her one of the most internationally acclaimed art historians of the late twentieth century. Her teaching, writings, curatorial efforts, film productions, and institution building reflect her tireless commitment to black artists. Contemporary scholars and other working to discover, interpret, and validate the efforts of these talented men and women in the United States owe her a colossal debt of gratitude.

Because Lewis is widely acknowledged as one of the leading figures in African American art history, her stature as a visual artist is occasionally overlooked. For more than half a century, she has created a substantial body of paintings, drawings, prints, and sculptures that reflect her empathy with humanity in general and African Americans in particular. An artist of first-rank quality, she emerges from the same tradition of African American visual art that she has so effectively documented in her scholarly work. Her artworks frequently reflect the figurative, narrative, and socially conscious focus of that tradition. Like such masters as Jacob Lawrence, Romare Bearden, Charles White, and her early teacher Elizabeth Catlett, she has combined solid artistic training and highly developed techniques, with compassionate and critical subject matter. Her efforts simultaneously engage and educate her viewers, encouraging them to confront the compelling themes pervading her work.

Widely exhibited over the years, Lewis is also represented in the permanent collections of major art institutions across the United States, including the Atlanta University Gallery of Contemporary Art, the Baltimore Museum of Fine Arts, Hampton Institute Museum, the Oakland Museum, the Virginia Museum of Fine Art, Howard University Museum, the High Museum of Atlanta, and the Golden State Mutual Life Insurance Collection in Los

Angeles. She has also garnered a vast array of honors for her academic and artistic accomplishments: for example, the UNICEF Award for the Visual Arts, the Charles White Lifetime Achievements Award, the Honor Award for Outstanding Achievements in Visual Arts from the Women's Caucus for the Arts, and the Vesta Award from the Los Angeles Women's Building.

Like many prominent African American artists of her generation, Samella Lewis grew up in the South. Born in New Orleans, she was introduced as a child to black art, culture, and history, a background that would forever more inform her academic and artistic activities. She recalls the racism pervading Southern life at the time and remembers the impact of Jim Crow on her experience. As a young art student, for example, she was unable to visit the Delgado Museum because it was located in the municipal park that was reserved exclusively for whites. Despite this ban, her renowned teacher Elizabeth Catlett managed to organize a trip for her African American students to see a Picasso exhibition in that museum. Cleverly, she secured a bus and had everyone move directly from the bus onto the museum steps, thus technically avoiding the racial restrictions of the park itself. Decades later, Lewis sees this incident as one of the many ludicrous expressions of a racist policy that kept human beings from one another and inhibited mutual understanding.

Equally important, she recalls that black people were not as brutalized in New Orleans as they were elsewhere in the South and that they often fought back against racist practices and affronts. This spirit also influenced Lewis's work. Both her scholarship and her visual artworks advance the resistance perspective informing African American expressive culture.

Lewis began her formal studies in art at Dillard University in New Orleans, an experience that had an enormous impact on her life and career. As an undergraduate, she studied with Catlett, who became her mentor and lifelong friend as well as a major contemporary artist. Catlett was then a young art instructor who encouraged Lewis to transfer to Hampton Institute in Virginia to complete her artistic training.

Lewis's residence at Hampton, one of the oldest historically black colleges in America, inspired and solidified her commitment to an African American vision in her artistic work. Hampton in the early 1940s was an exciting environment for the visual arts. Viktor Lowenfeld, a refugee from Nazi Germany, played a key role in making its art department one of the main incubators of African American visual creativity during that era. His art classes were designed to stimulate students, including Lewis, to understand, appreciate, and express their identity through their work.

Lewis credits Lowenfeld's teaching with helping her to develop a deep self-knowledge that encompassed issues of race, gender, and social class. Lowenfeld also encouraged students to learn about and incorporate into their own artworks the African heritage and current social status of black people in the United States. This approach to art education instilled and reinforced a profound sense of racial identity, a focus with immense and progressive implications for the future of African American art generally.

This exhilarating ambiance attracted an unprecedented wealth of African American visual art talent to Hampton. One of Lewis's fellow Hampton students was John Biggers, who worked closely with Charles White and Lowenfeld and who later emerged as a leading figure in African American art.

Following her graduation in 1945, Lewis pursued advanced training at Ohio State University. After finishing her MA in fine arts there, she switched to art history and, in 1951, received her PhD, emphasizing Asian and African arts and culture. Her reluctance to follow the Eurocentric artistic emphasis demanded of graduate students in fine arts at the time precipitated her move to art history. As she explains it, she had no interest in becoming Pablo Picasso or Georges Braque; instead, she wanted to become herself, pursuing the African American artistic vision she had developed during her studies at Hampton.

After completing her doctoral work and doing advanced study in Taiwan, Lewis embarked on an extensive teaching career. She has served on the faculty of several colleges and universities, including various historically black institutions such as Morgan State University and Florida A&M University. During her work in Florida from 1953 through 1958, she encountered the anti-communist hysteria of the early Cold War era. Like many progressive educators, she declined to sign the required loyalty oath and was branded as a subversive, a not uncommon response of political and university officials during this time.

After her brief faculty service at State University of New York at Plattsburg, Lewis relocated to the Los Angeles area, where she has resided since 1964. She taught for a few years at various campuses of the California State University system, but then in 1969, she joined the faculty at Scripps College in Claremont, remaining there until her retirement. At Scripps, Lewis taught Chinese art history, while also teaching African American art through the Intercollegiate Black Studies Program of the Claremont College Consortium.

During her residence in California, Lewis produced major publications documenting the history of African American art. Her books have contributed profoundly to an understanding of this tradition among academics as well as the public. For example, her two-volume work, *Black Artists on Art*, coedited with fellow artist Ruth Waddy, highlights the efforts of numerous contemporary black artists working in various visual media. *African American Art and Artists*, authored exclusively by Lewis, has become one of the standard texts in the field since its original publication in 1978. And her monograph entitled *The Art of Elizabeth Catlett* is one of the finest works ever written about Lewis's teacher and friend. Then, in 1991, *African American Art for Young People* extended Lewis's commitment to documenting this tradition to include an audience especially in need of knowledge about black history and culture.

Lewis has gone far beyond publications in her drive to displace the hegemony of Eurocentric art in American educational and cultural institutions. Since 1976, for example, she has served as editor and editor emerita of *The International Review of African American Art*, a scholarly forum for disseminating knowledge about black artistic accomplishments. She has also curated numerous exhibitions throughout the hemisphere and produced several films about African American artists.

1n 1977 she founded the Museum of African American Art in Los Angeles, an important institution that regularly exhibits the artworks of historical and contemporary African

Americans. Frequently featuring local African American visual artists, this institution also sponsors symposia and other programs and encourages visits from schools throughout the region. Its dedication to the interpretation, promotion, and preservation of art by and about people of African descent has made it a powerful contributor to the vitality of black culture throughout Southern California.

Samella Lewis's creative works add further luster to her status in the world of African American visual art. She has been painting since she was five years old, pursuing her unique vision wherever it led her. Over the years, she has developed a complex theoretical foundation for her versatile efforts. Above all, her works contribute to the strongest current in the African American artistic tradition: the use of visual language to communicate reactions to black history, culture, and social life. Lewis expressed her artistic vision eloquently in Volume 1 of *Black Artists on Art* (Los Angeles: Contemporary Crafts, Inc.) in 1969: "Art offers avenues for exploring ideas and human experience. It is important to Black people because it adds to the enrichment and understanding of our ancient past and provides a significant source for documenting our contemporary present" (121).

Lewis also acknowledges the artistic influences that inform her work. Elizabeth Catlett's social vision and technical brilliance have clearly played a powerful role in Lewis's own development, and the renowned Mexican artist José Clemente Orozco has been a key influence as well. Indeed, his haunting murals, paintings, and prints in the early part of the century have inspired hundreds of socially conscious artists, including many African Americans. Finally, Lewis's extensive knowledge of Asian art has enabled her to make imaginative formal advances and adaptations in her paintings and prints for many decades.

An examination of one of Samella Lewis's paintings made during her Hampton years yields cogent insights about her socially conscious, African American artistic vision. A painting originally commissioned for the black chapel at Camp Lee in Virginia in 1944 was intended to be viewed by the black servicemen on the base during World WarII. This 4-by-8 foot work on plywood features a strong male worker as the Christ-like, central figure. The other figures reveal traits of character and determination, a striking contrast to the racist caricatures of blacks that were prominent in that era.

After Lewis presented her painting, the base commander refused to hang it, expressing "concern" that such bold images would offend white viewers. Rather than informing Lewis directly of his apprehensions, he sent the black chaplain to deliver the message. Her reply, that the effort was painted for black audiences, fell on deaf ears. The painting was returned to the Hampton Institute Museum, where it remained in storage for forty years before being exhibited as a regular feature of the institution's public programming. Like other works in the permanent collection, the painting has occasionally been displayed at the museum.

Several of Lewis's works extend the humanist strain of Western art that can be traced to such figures as Francisco Goya, Honoré Daumier, Georges Rouault, Kathe Kollwitz, José Clemente Orozco, and Ben Shahn as well as key representatives of African American art history. Her moving 1962 linocut entitled *Migrants*, for example, emerges from her experiences in Florida, where the artist frequently observed migrant bean pickers moving from field to field, earning minimal wages under unhealthy conditions. The anxious expressions of all seven figures dominate the composition, inviting viewers to understand and empathize with their plight. An ominous black cloud hovers over them, signifying the disturbing economic and social context of their lives and suggesting a deeper critique of American capitalism generally. Still, despite their collective despair, the figures remain strong, resolved to endure whatever hardships they encounter. *Migrants* is an image of dignity, an expression of faith in the capacity of downtrodden people not only to survive but to provide a legacy for their children.

Throughout her life, Lewis has regularly portrayed the quiet heroism of black people struggling to overcome institutional barriers. *Garbageman*, a 1969 oil painting, highlights an African American man collecting the discarded goods of his community's wealthier residents. What is garbage to them is sustenance to him. His defiant expression reflects his determination to make a living as a scavenger if necessary. Lewis employs this solitary figure to convey a broader social point. Like the thousands of destitute men and women who gathered recyclable newspapers, cans, and bottles from Los Angeles streets in the 1990s, he intends to do whatever he must to secure the economic necessities of life. As the painting clearly suggests, his actions deserve respect and admiration, not contempt and persecution.

*Royal Sacrifice*, another 1969 oil painting, calls attention to the strengths of black women in America. The specter of death dominates the background in this portrait of mother and son, symbolically revealing the multiple problems that African American children often face: inadequate education, massive unemployment, daily violence, insufficient health care, and pervasive hopelessness. The painting encourages viewers to pay homage to the millions of unrecognized black mothers who successfully nurture their sons and daughters in this environment.

In 1993, Lewis added a new dimension to this theme in a powerful colored pencil drawing. Reflecting the influence of the Mexican muralists, *Barrier* depicts a young African American boy pitted against a formidable steel barrier in human form. This creature, cloaked in armor, represents the unyielding and inhospitable character of social, economic, and political life in the United States for the African American population. The drawing suggests that the barriers to African American progress and justice are structural in nature. Despite its human form, the steel figure signifies that racism is embedded in the very fabric of America. Even so, since institutional racism is a human construction, it can be changed. The boy's expression of resistance encourages optimism.

Samella Lewis bas frequently used her art to expose some of the historical forces militating against progress. Over the centuries, for instance, police and private citizens have used unjustified violence against African Americans. American history includes accounts of lynchings in the South; white-inspired race riots following extensive black migration; terror against returning black veterans after World War I, World War II, and the Korean War; and numerous other incidents, culminating most recently in the 1991 beating by police of Rodney King.

Lewis's untitled graphite drawing from 1975 highlights this historical reality. Reminiscent of a painting from Jacob Lawrence's migration series, the work constitutes a powerful indictment of racist brutality. The perpetrator, dressed tellingly in a pure white shirt, assaults his victims with savage impunity. The central message is unambiguous: Racial violence in America has consistently reflected the unequal power relations among blacks and whites.

During her artistic career, Lewis has also expressed her affection and respect for the durable institutions enabling most black people to overcome the barriers of racism, poverty, and injustice. *Family*, a graphite drawing from 1969, communicates a genuine appreciation of family integrity. Celebrating the different physical types among blacks, the effort reveals the strong and loving bonds of the family, fortifying its individual members. Sharing a meal, the family portrayed here expresses the solidarity and mutual caring common to families of all ethnic and racial backgrounds.

In 1995, the artist created a compelling painting about the powerful role of the black church throughout African American history. *The Word* depicts a charismatic preacher with his enthusiastic and vocal congregation. Both the painting's title and its imagery convey justifiable pride in the brilliant orations that have inspired millions of African Americans and others who appreciate the power of public speech.

From the time of slavery to the present, the black church has provided its congregants with solace for and refuge from their burdens. Equally important, the church has regularly been at the center of social action, galvanizing African Americans and their allies in the struggle for civil rights. Such militant leaders as Adam Clayton Powell, Martin Luther King, and Jesse Jackson emerged from the pulpit. *The Word* simultaneously honors the legacy of the black church and reminds audiences of its continuing vitality in addressing the social ills of contemporary America.

During her distinguished career as both an art historian and a practicing artist, Samella Lewis has fostered recognition and respect for African American visual art. She has also eloquently promoted her vision of the responsibilities of African American artists. In her *African American Art and Artists* (Berkeley: University of California Press, 1990), she argues that artists should establish direct relationships with their communities by learning about and expressing their cultural heritage as people of African origin. She also urges black artists to interpret the "deepest, most meaningful aspirations of their people," including their most fundamental fears, hopes, resentments, and ambitions. Above all, she calls for artists to be major community resources, creating artworks that make sense first and foremost to African American audiences. No statement could better summarize the enduring and exemplary legacy of Lewis's own artwork.

# WILLIAM PAJAUD

In an article on African American artists in the *Los Angeles Times Magazine* in the summer of 1995, Wanda Coleman asked Santa Monica art dealer Eric Hanks for a list of emerging artists worth watching. Hanks mentioned several names, including William Pajaud, and then swiftly added that Pajaud was not exactly a new artist. Indeed, having turned seventy years old on August 3, 1995, Pajaud has had a long and distinguished career as a visual artist, even if the mainstream art establishment has been slow to recognize his contributions (along with those of other African Americans).

William Pajaud's artistic emergence dates from the 1950s. For several decades, he has produced hundreds of engaging paintings and prints that highlight the triumphs and chronicle the problems of his fellow African Americans. In addition, during his employment as an art director at Golden State Mutual Life Insurance Company, Pajaud made a lasting contribution to African American culture by developing one of the most striking collections of African American art in the nation. Operating within a minuscule budget, Pajaud used his knowledge of the tightly knit community of black artists to purchase works of world-class stature. A powerful presence among the ranks of Los Angeles African American artists, Pajaud has played a seminal role in the history of their visual tradition.

Born in New Orleans, Pajaud says that memories of his childhood in the South have informed his attitudes and artwork throughout his life. The rich and colorful experiences of African Americans in New Orleans, especially their world-renowned musical accomplishments, find vivid expression in his watercolors and other efforts. His more personal experiences with the overt racism of the era have also colored his artistic expression.

As a boy, Pajaud encountered the type of savagery that too often culminated in lynchings and false imprisonments of African Americans from the end of Reconstruction through the 1950s. In Chattanooga, Tennessee, for example, he was badly beaten when he was twelve or thirteen years old because he waved at a car with white passengers. Later, in Texas, he was hit with a rope for a similar "affront" to white supremacy. Like most African Americans of his generation, he has vivid memories of being called "nigger" and of experiencing other indignities in the Jim Crow South.

Despite these and other barriers, he was determined to accomplish his educational goals. His artistic inclinations dated back to his early childhood; at age seven, for example, he meticulously copied windmills from "Old Dutch Cleanser" containers. He also replicated pictures of the little Dutch boy and girl on the label. Following a family tradition, he enrolled at Xavier University in New Orleans. There, he majored in fine arts and received his degree. He spent two years in Chicago and then moved to Los Angeles, where he has lived and worked since 1948.

Postwar Los Angeles was hardly a hospitable environment for a young black artist. With rare exceptions, museums and galleries did not exhibit works by artists of color, and a racist atmosphere pervaded the city, even though it was usually (but not always) more subtle than the overt Jim Crow arrangements in the South. More than a half century later, Pajaud recalls that black people were discouraged from entering parts of Altadena and Pasadena, for example. He also remembers how he and his sons were told, sometimes quite directly, that they were not welcome at various Los Angeles-area department stores and supermarkets.

Almost invariably, African American artists had to find alternative employment in order to support themselves and their families. William Pajaud held in a variety of jobs on his arrival in Los Angeles, including work a wrapper in a department store, a janitor in a hotel, a sewing machine repairman, and a postal worker.

In the early 1950s, while working full-time at night in the US Post Office, he also enrolled at the Chouinard Art Institute, where he studied commercial art and took painting classes. The first African American day student, Pajaud was viewed with some trepidation throughout the school. In fact, an official explicitly warned him not to look up white girls' dresses as they climbed the steps of the main building ahead of him. Despite his relative isolation at Chouinard, he finished his studies with distinction, obtaining the formal training that would inform his work for the next 40 years. In 1957, Pajaud found employment at the Golden State Mutual Life Insurance Company, one of the largest black owned insurance companies in the United States. Hired as the art director in public relations, he spent approximately 30 years as a successful businessman, working a traditional eight-hour day.

The idea for the Golden State Collection originated with Pajaud, but it reflects the company's commitment to promoting a more accurate vision of African Americans' contributions. The collection encourages viewers of all ethnicities to augment their knowledge of black history, and it inspires African Americans to take pride in black artists and their accomplishments. Thanks to Pajaud's curatorial efforts, the collection contains works by Henry O. Tanner, Charles Alston, Richmond Barthé, Hale Woodruff, John Biggers, Jacob Lawrence, Romare Bearden, Charles White, Elizabeth Catlett, Betye Saar, Samella Lewis, John Riddle, Richard Wyatt, Varnette Honeywood, Noni Olabisi, William Pajaud himself, and many others. These artists' origina1 works decorate the lobby and virtually every private office in the striking building designed by famed African American architect Paul Williams.

Despite its importance, the Golden State Collection is but one facet of Pajaud's artistic career. While employed by Golden State, he continued producing art at home on his own time. Often, he would complete a full day in the office and then work another eight hours on his painting. Throughout his business career, he exhibited his artworks around Los Angeles in black churches, in community halls, at the Wilshire Presbyterian Church, and at the Westside Jewish Community Center. He also exhibited at the Heritage Gallery, which was the major exception to the exclusionary practices of mainstream art institutions in the region.

During these decades of extraordinary effort, Pajaud created hundreds of pieces depicting blacks' contributions to American history and civilization. His artistic philosophy emerges from his rich life experiences, including his close relationships with artists Charles White and John Biggers. In particular, Pajaud's deep friendship with Biggers, spanning more than thirty years, supplied him with an extensive knowledge of black history and of the African roots of African American life and culture. Indeed, Biggers emerged as a chief moral, spiritual, and professional influence on Pajaud.

An accomplished painter and muralist in his own right, Biggers also had a productive career as an art teacher and educator, inspiring generations of young African Americans who studied and worked with him at Texas Southern University in Houston. His exemplary attention to visual detail combined with his African and African American themes earned him status as a giant of twentieth-century African American art history. Biggers's death in 2001 ended a remarkable and influential career.

Following his mentor, Pajaud expresses strong views about his central objectives. He paints and draws in response to white society's continuing propensity to tell African Americans that they have little or no worth. For him, this disparagement is the most egregious sin of racism—worse than racial slurs, worse than discriminatory treatment in employment and education, worse even than beatings and lynchings. In response, Pajaud revels in his blackness, using his art to tell a different, more positive story.

Specifically eschewing the overt social protest of many African American artists, William Pajaud prefers a less obvious but no less effective form of communication. He routinely uses his works to provide an affectionate glimpse into the lives of African Americans. *Friday Night*, for example, depicts a typical street scene derived from the artist's recollections of Los Angeles more than fifty years ago. The image is neither startling nor provocative. It promotes no political agenda, raises no fists, promotes no slogans, and identifies no racist events or practices. Instead, it portrays ordinary people engaged in the everyday activity of shopping, in this case at a South Central Los Angeles fish market. The merchant and his customers show respect for one another as they conduct their transactions. Though commonplace, the content of this work reveals a deeper social truth: African Americans, like most people in the United States, conduct their affairs with diligence and honesty. As a visual corrective to harmful stereotypes, *Friday Night* constitutes a powerful resistance artwork.

African American music is a major theme of Pajaud's work. An especially gifted watercolorist, he uses this medium to call attention to the enduring influence and vitality of African American spirituals in *Wade in the Water*. Forged during slavery to express political resistance and the yearning for freedom, this venerable musical tradition has been a continuing inspiration to generations of civil rights and social activists. Strikingly aesthetic, *Wade in the Water* focuses on a choir singing a spiritual. The painting informs viewers of the seminal role of the black church and its music in African Americans' historical struggle to achieve freedom and dignity.

The artist's profound commitment to musical themes is no coincidence. His father was a renowned musician in New Orleans, playing with the Eureka Brass Band, and Pajaud has vivid childhood memories of the band playing at funerals and other functions. These recollections form the basis for his numerous artworks that treat musical themes and validate the accomplishments of African Americans. Some of these works were showcased in Pajaud's 1999–2000 retrospective entitled "The Sights and Sounds of My New Orleans" at the California African American Museum.

Included in that exhibition was *The Jazz Singer*, a colorful 1992 watercolor that reflects the extensive musical motif employed by such masters as Archibald Motley, Romare Bearden, William H. Johnson, and Charles White. Like Bearden, in particular, Pajaud celebrates jazz musicians as the embodiment of African American culture. More fundamentally, in this and many similar works, he draws attention to the exuberance of life in the jazz clubs of New Orleans and elsewhere, a sign of blacks' vigor in an often hostile society.

Throughout his career, Pajaud has also used his work to honor African American women for their strength and perseverance. For example, *Mother Love*, featuring a nude mother and her child, expresses a historical reality about black women that is widely understood in their own communities but remains largely unrecognized by whites. In discussing this painting, Pajaud notes that for generations, in their role as domestic workers, black women have spent their days with white children, providing them with excellent cate and even deep affection. Only after getting off work could these women attend t the needs of their own offspring.

In the painting, the mother literally envelops her child, her hands and hips serving as protection from any dangers that the child might encounter. For Pajaud, that protection reflects an abundance of motherly love. Rather than using female nudity for sexual titillation, he strips away the stereotypical image of black women as callous and insensitive, unconcerned about their children.

Pajaud's sympathetic treatment of women subjects transcends his own ethnic community. Over the years, he has spent considerable time in Mexico, observing its dynamic culture and developing affection for its people. Like several other African American artists, he has transformed this affection into striking works of visual art. *Mujer con Gallo*, for example, is an insightful portrait of an Indian woman in Mexico. Once again, the artist provides an alternative vision to stereotypical presentations in American culture.

Despite his discomfort with trenchant social protest art, Pajaud has created some works that call explicit attention to social problems in the United States. For instance, *Main Street Mission*, a lithograph from 1970, depicts an emaciated man eating a bowl of soup from a Skid Row mission in downtown Los Angeles. Like Picasso's famous 1904 etching, *The Frugal Repast*, this work evokes enormous sympathy for the subject's plight. Its focus on a solitary figure highlights the human impact of poverty and homelessness, transcending the abstractions of journalistic and scholarly accounts.

In *Someday I'll Be a Woman*, a lithograph from the same period, Pajaud depicts a young African American girl whose role model for success is a prostitute. Like *Main Street Mission*, this work expresses immense feeling for the victim while provoking reflection upon the underlying reasons for her situation. Viewers are invited to ponder the destructive cycle that will perpetuate itself if the girl is provided no reasonable alternative role models. Indeed, the artist offers little hope. A close view of the girl's expression reveals almost total hopelessness; her eyes in particular look nearly dead.

Pajaud's visual critique extends to the long history of white men's use of black women as sexual playthings. Behind the bathing nude woman in *View of the Kitchen* lurks a young white male, leering at her body. For him, the woman is a mere vehicle for personal pleasure, an unwitting stimulus for whatever erotic fantasy (or reality) he desires. Pajaud deliberately employs a double entendre in the painting's title. The word kitchen is widely used among African Americans to denote a woman's buttocks. In imagery and title, *View of the Kitchen* is a devastating treatment of attitudes rooted in American racism.

The impact of William Pajaud 's work as curator and artist is obvious. His paintings and prints, documenting and celebrating the experiences and accomplishments of his people, add depth and excellence to a visual tradition originating in the Harlem Renaissance. A pioneer in the growing community of black artists in Los Angeles, Pajaud passed away in 2015.

## NOTE

Reprinted and excerpted with permission from Paul von Blum, *Resistance, Dignity, and Pride: African American Artists in Los Angeles* (Los Angeles: Ralph J. Bunche Center for African American Studies at UCLA, 2005), ix–xvi, 39–45, 46–51, 85–89, 97–100.

# BLOOD MEMORY AND THE ARTS: INDIGENOUS GENEALOGIES AND IMAGINED TRUTHS

NANCY MARIE MITHLO

*Literary theory may provide the discourse to compare and construe the apparent evolution of literature, but the traces, tricky turns and visionary reach of Native narratives forever haunt interpreters and translators.*

—Gerald Vizenor, "American Indian Art and Literature Today"

For generations (and as some might argue, since contact), American Indian artists have grappled with the varied responses of a consumerist Western audience unversed in the interior logic of indigenous aesthetic impulses.[1] The public exchange of Native arts as goods for cash, trade, or opportunity has resulted in a largely object-based academic inquiry in the service of ethnography, voyeurism, and consumer class aspirations. The marked history of these objects and their circulation has to date effectively stood in for serious arts scholarship, obscuring and at times obstructing a more accurate reading of aesthetic expressions informed by the rich legacies of oral history, traditional exchange processes, religious uses, and even metaphysical interventions with the divine that are enacted in the private and often-interior settings of indigenous lifeways. Like Native literary theory, Native arts scholarship is "haunted" by the visionary complexity of indigenous arts practices. The inherent intellectualism of indigenous visual arts, design, performance, and media exceeds the means by which we have to describe them, even in our own contexts of Native arts teaching, learning, and enacting in national and global settings.

The translation of indigenous aesthetic worlds to a broader audience—tribal communities as well as numerous variations of consumers (those labeled tourists, collectors, and academics)—is fraught with constraints. The legacy of colonialism, still enacted in fine arts and ethnographic settings; the pressures of economically distressed tribal communities dependent upon income from arts commerce; and the

Nancy Marie Mithlo is a professor of gender studies and American Indian studies at the University of California, Los Angeles.

lack of requisite infrastructure, including American Indian art publications, professional training programs, and representative collections, inhibit the transference of knowledge among disciplines, institutions, constituents, and practitioners.[2] Indigenous source communities lack adequate motivation to enter the precarious dialogues that may illuminate the wealth of knowledge encoded in artistic practice with unversed consumers, given the many forms of exploitation that have and still may occur, including devaluation, appropriation, theft of culturally sensitive knowledge, and exile from fine-arts settings.[3] Similarly, the constituents who encounter Native arts through museums, galleries, film festivals, and popular culture are often content with the exterior visual trappings of indigenous arts alone—the skin of the goods. Commodities or even performances marked by Native registers are surface renditions of the deeper logic at play, the intellectual underpinnings of indigenous worldviews.

Given these mutually reinforcing tendencies, indigenous arts operate in something of a vacuum. Contemporary Native arts are rarely included in global arts settings that highlight any number of other disenfranchised artists seeking to gain recognition and a voice in the form of critical exhibition practice or scholarship.[4] This article argues that Native artists can benefit from an increased participation in these broader arts networks, given the resources and opportunities associated with institutions and organizations that give life and reason to the curation and reception of fine arts. Although I recognize the technical and logistical inhibitions for a rapprochement between indigenous arts and the places of its circulation (that is, books, exhibits, collections, and the Internet), in this article I focus my attention on the philosophical and emotional dimensions of audience reception and its impact on the Native arts world, implicating the gaze and problematizing key qualitative values that have largely remained unexplored in our field. Importantly, these values include emotional and imaginative saliences that may simultaneously attract and hold at bay the mutual exchanges implicated in the gaze.

My analysis highlights lens-based artistic practice, the power of biography, and the curatorial strategies of embodiment, including the senses, possession, and emotional connections. The iconic placeholder of "the blood" as an organizing principle is identified as a productive means of articulating the interior renderings of an indigenous aesthetic and recognizing the essential saliences of communal place-based logics and current political realities. Examples of work featuring Chippewa filmmaker Marcella Ernest and Ho-Chunk photographer Tom Jones will be mobilized in an effort to illuminate these varied theoretical directions.

## BEYOND IDENTITY TO BLOOD

Identity debates—meaning the delineation of self-identity in the highly charged political contexts of postmodernism—have largely defined the work of contemporary Native artists in the United States and Canada for more than two decades (the situation for indigenous artists in Australia and Aotearoa New Zealand are centrally related but will not be directly addressed here).[5] Although some critics have charged that a continued interest with identity arts is outdated and unnecessary, notions of self and biography continue to concern indigenous artists.

Art historian Sylvester Okwunodu Ogbechie correctly delineates the major problem inherent in the use of identity as a theoretical paradigm by referencing the multiple meanings of the term. Rather than referencing only a call for inclusion (concurrent with a romanticized depiction of authentic cultures in opposition to the West), Ogbechie demonstrates how identity debates can effectively present "a comprehensive demand for the radical overhaul of contemporary structures of power and privilege, rather than a call for tokenist inclusion of 'non-Western.'"[6] This spirit of a politically mobilized radical restructuring of the field accurately reflects the work discussed here and is more exemplary of the current practices of contemporary Native arts production and reception than the concessionary implications of inclusion alone. The fact that both strategies—simple acceptance into a mainstream institution and the absolute rejection of the same structural mode of knowledge circulation—may be described under the same term of *identity debates* renders the descriptive of identity inherently unstable and insufficient as a means of describing the variables at play.

Identity as a category of arts analysis is too broad to offer any productive implications for theory building and, consequently, for the advancement of Native art criticism. This problematic appraisal does not mean that all interest with identity is mistaken but rather that our thinking regarding identity requires nuance. A consideration of the physical nature of people, their bodies, and their familial linkages to their ancestors through blood and their land—when taken as a totality—provides the means to craft meaningful appraisals of indigenous arts. This work is something that a purely cognitive consideration of identity alone cannot accomplish.[7]

The articulation and advancement of a qualitative (and some might charge imaginative) approach to contemporary Native arts criticism—characterized by its attention to the body, the experience of belonging, and the implications of these attributes for collective memory and place by way of blood reckoning—has merit due to its centrality in the scope of indigenous collective thought and political realities. Writing in the journal *Cultural Anthropology*, scholars Pauline Turner Strong and Barrik Van Winkle assert that, although scholarship on identity as debated in tribal recognition cases and museum collections is well documented, "the need to objectify identity in the idiom of blood courses through Native American life."[8] Similarly, literary theorist and scholar Sean Teuton, citing Kiowa author N. Scott Momaday, declares, "The very pulse of Native literature seems to rely on blood. On this 'blood memory,' Momaday writes: 'The land, *this* land, is secure in the Native American's racial memory.'"[9]

The concept of blood memory is ageless, but the term gained currency with its use by Momaday in his Pulitzer Prize–winning first novel, *House Made of Dawn* (1968).[10] Developed further in his subsequent works and hotly debated by academics, primarily literary critics, blood memory has developed into a controversial premise for the most central issues in American Indian, First Nations, and Aboriginal studies. From the use of federal recognition regulations by blood quantum to consideration of the ultimate audience and purpose for indigenous arts (internal needs or external communication), the concept of blood has proven to be a central theme for exploring Native identity, but to date, the powerful concept of blood has not been significantly explored in contemporary indigenous artistic or curatorial practice.

The trope "blood memory," Chadwick Allen states, "blurs distinctions between racial identity and narrative."[11] I argue that the concept has the potential not only to "blur" but also to clarify key categories of indigenous wisdoms as expressed in the verbal and visual arts. Tribal museums, tribal colleges, and language-preservation offices are sites where indigenous peoples are encouraged to draw from their ancestral memories.[12] These spaces of remembrance are commonly characterized by efforts to heal the multigenerational impacts of genocide and historic trauma.

Blood relationships reference not only the common understanding of what is considered biological heritage or race but also, in an expanded sense, the internalized memories of communal history, knowledge, and wisdom. Blood memories are powerful political tropes mobilized to call attention to the legacies of colonialism in contexts as diverse as battlefields, boarding schools, and sacred sites. This common tribal value of multigenerational remembrance runs directly counter to prevailing Western traits of individual achievement, lack of transgenerational memory, and transcendence of one's genealogical fate and place of origin.

Theorizing race in the academy has proven to be even more demanding than advocating for the recognition of oppression in the political scene. In an age in which hybridity is celebrated, any sense of biological determinism is automatically charged as essentialist, regressive rhetoric. Heritage thus becomes either solely decorative or dangerously close to racially determined logic. Calls to blood relationships, either in a corporeal or abstracted sense, are negated in contemporary academic discourse, thus prohibiting the exploration and legitimization of indigenous knowledge systems.[13] If we cut loose the reactive exclusion of calls to blood memory, then the imaginative and affective qualities of indigenous arts practice today may be productively wrought in new and meaningful ways.

## THE CORPOREAL AS AN INDIGENOUS AESTHETIC

My interest in embodied knowledge is influenced by the work of documentary filmmaker and theorist David MacDougall, and in particular his text *The Corporeal Image: Film, Ethnography and the Senses*. In this work, MacDougall helpfully identifies three variables of experiencing film: the bodies of the spectator, filmmaker, and film.[14] This complicated layering of moving image, sound, space, and time is deeply personal, highly charged, and intensely challenging to conceptualize, even to document in written form. These physical saliencies overwhelm, overtax, and have historically prohibited viewers of Native arts from fully appreciating the absolute power of the work and the maker's intent. Consequently, I believe that the audience withdraws, for few viewers wish to engage in this embodied space, this intimate arena. However, it is exactly this physical closeness that artists often produce and that audiences, particularly audiences of Native arts, those who are satisfied with what I termed earlier in this essay as "the skin of the goods," seem unable to meet. My proposition in evoking the body as an inhibitor of a mutual engagement in the gaze is that this body knowledge exceeds the abilities of the audience.

In his classic "Outline of a Sociological Theory of Art Perception," theorist Pierre Bourdieu classifies the ability or inability to engage in fine-arts appreciation as a matter of understanding key codes of artistic expression and interpretation. These codes are viewed as ultimately exclusionary, marking his project as one of class-consciousness. Bourdieu's platform asserts, "The disorientation and cultural blindness of the less-educated beholders are an objective reminder of the objective truth that art perception is a mediate deciphering operation. Since the information presented by the works exhibited exceeds the deciphering capabilities of the beholder, he perceives them as devoid of signification—or, to be more precise, of structuration and organization—because he cannot 'decode' them, i.e. reduce them to an intelligible form."[15] This structural and cognitive theorizing seeks to make art appreciation a matter of legibility, a set of terms and concepts that may be articulated, learned, and enacted. In contrast, the "decoding" of the unique visual worlds of indigenous arts requires an engagement with the body, communal ideologies, the land, and motion. These qualifiers are necessary precursors to a deeper engagement in indigenous arts practice and a central point of engagement when one considers the importance of the viewer to the production of the work. Do indigenous artists, for example, make art in reaction to the limitations of the non-Native audience? Are concessions made in which communal and land/body-oriented concerns are ignored for the sake of translation, exhibition, and commodification?

MacDougall describes film as containing "traces of experience" that can sometimes overwhelm the filmmaker in "an intense engagement with the world that sometimes borders on the painful":

> In sharing the worlds of others so intimately, it is possible to lose sight of your own boundaries. It is not uncommon to discover yourself inhabited by your subjects. Long after making a film, you sometimes feel in yourself a gesture or hear in your mind an intonation of [a] voice that is not your own. Filmmakers and filmviewers have this in common, that things seen and heard are capable of reaching out and possessing us. This possession is not so much a matter of spirit as of material being.[16]

The intriguing suggestion here in reference to the gaze is that the relationship between the artist and his or her subject is as fraught as the relationship between the artist and the audience.[17] The introduction of the subject, especially in lens-based arts, complicates the standard theorization of the gaze, enhancing the discussions of spectatorship and objects in potentially productive and meaningful ways. The absence of Bourdieu's cognitive categories and competencies is evident in MacDougall's summarizing: "This is corporeal knowledge, only lightly mediated by thought."[18] I suggest that an engagement in this reciprocity among the audience, subject, and maker in Native arts analysis is required in order to craft an effective interpretative paradigm. But to be successful in this telling—in what MacDougall calls a type of "possession"—the work needs to be accessible on the level of experience; it must contain the depth of generations of relationships and engage the senses of memory.[19]

## THE WORK

To apply these variables directly to the work of Bad River Chippewa filmmaker Marcella Ernest, for example, we need to consider the individuals, often family members, who populate her films with evidence of Ernest's artistic choices as a filmmaker—the visual and the audio—and the impact of these variables on the audience: their histories, memories, and physical responses. Ernest's four-minute experimental film *Blood Memory* (2010) evidences corporeal attributes in a subtle and highly personal telling. Ernest opens her dream-like sequence with a shot of young men on motorbikes, joyfully riding across a rural landscape. The emphasis on raw movement, on youth, seems to parallel the essence of a young America—male, unbridled, like a Western, but without cowboys and horses—more of an *Easy Rider*. The subsequent image of a young woman in a white dress, shot modestly from behind, could not contrast more. Obvious connotations of purity, serenity, and innocence are associated with this image—a constellation of traditionally Western attributes of femininity. She lacks motion, she is caught in one place, and her only movement is an odd stamping of one foot as if a rope tethers her and she waits to be released. As viewers, we are even allowed to play with this female figure, much like we might play with a Barbie doll, turning her sideways, upside down, and over as the camera explores her from a variety of perspectives. This experimental camera technique reeks of a 1970s counternorm, a type of Andy Warhol manipulation of found objects.

So far, this piece may be interpreted as fairly formulaic with its obvious juxtapositions of female/male and motion/stationary. But then Ernest introduces us to the extended family, and this is where her experiential memory narrative begins (see fig. 1). Of her grandfathers, Ernest comments in a 2010 interview with the author,

> My dad's dad is the first grandparent you see in the beginning. He punches the camera. He's awesome! The SWEETEST man alive. I think he's mid-80s now. Anyway, he was abandoned at the age of 4 and grew up in and out of foster homes and orphanages. He's real dark but we don't know what he is. He found out that his mother was in the circus!!! And left him with his father, Oscar, and then Oscar went for milk and never came back. The circus??!! So we have [been] told that he might be Gypsy given that he has dark skin and his mom was in the damn circus. But we don't know. And my last name, Ernest, which comes from him is not even his last name. I think when he joined the war he had to get a last name so he picked the first name of his favorite foster parent.[20]

**FIGURE 1.** *Film still from* Blood Memory *by Marcella Ernest (US, 2010, 4 min.). Image courtesy of Marcella Ernest.*

The estrangement from home, the longing that often accompanies an indigenous search for identity is supplanted with the fascination of the unexpected. Ernest's biography is complicated by loss, but her visual narrative is not restrained by this lack; it is informed by the presence of her ancestors and their dynamic and unpredictable lives. The playful, self-deprecating, and open-ended exploration of the older men's bodies brings us, the viewer, back into Ernest's vivid imagination. These men even appear more powerful than the young dudes on dirt bikes. They laugh, impose themselves into the camera's lens, punch us, and then ride their bicycle backward without a shirt and sporting tattoos. In these sequences, Ernest seems to say "Ha! And you thought you were tough!" She obviously adores these older men; the camera toys with their features, lingers on their absurdity. We become a child, placed beside Ernest as a child, left in their wonder and their power. Significantly, these powerful and comedic men are from her non-Native father's side of the family. Ernest states,

> I have found, and read, and listened to people of mixed race talk about who they are or where they come from. And many times we tend to emphasize heavily more upon the side "of color." For instance, if they are black and white, it would be more of a black identity.
>
> I try in this piece to include both my Ojibwe mother and my white father. My blood is through my mother, and thus I repeat that my mother is Ojibwe more than my father is white. Grandparents, and great grandparents, on both sides however are included in the piece as well. My great grandfather on my father's side is riding the bike backwards. And both maternal and paternal grandpa and grandma are included in the film, as are my mom's sister, and other relatives. Predominately though, we see my mom and my dad and my grandparents.[21]

This extended visual foray into the family archives places us among the family members lingering over a photo album on the living room couch, but this is a film and there are other means of crafting the quality of "possession." The sound of a heartbeat opens the film segment with a lulling cantor, something like a drum or even the hum of a motorcycle engine. Then we hear Ernest's voice almost mumbling as if she is shy or withholding, "Yes, yes, no, no." She is not celebratory, but pained, obviously pinned to the wall with some unseen interviewer questioning her. Of this encounter Ernest states,

> I always tend to be asked the same questions by people. Mostly non-Native people. I have always had this, "what are you question" from Native and non. And then when it comes to talking about being Native American they are always so very curious. And comment on my eyes. Sometimes rudely. HAHA! So I keep having to repeat Ojibwe to non-Native people all the time too because we are not one of those tribes that everyone knows. So they are like, "Who? Say that again? How do you say it? Where are THEY from? Who? Tell me one more time? Hmmmm, no I never heard of them and I know Native Americans!" And then I say Chippewa and most people are like, "Ohhhh Okay I have heard of that." And then people always feel so comfortable asking me all about shit that is none of their business in terms of Native Americans. So I find myself doing a lot of "Yes, yes, yes, yes, no, no, no, no, maybe, I don't think so."[22]

This interrogation leads us to Ernest's recounting of her parents' divorce, which she corresponds visually to a series of hopelessly romantic wedding-film sequences. Her mother, absolutely layered in white—is stunning in her Native beauty and her presence.

The father has shades of his grandparents—proud and a bit nonconformist. Shots of Ernest as a baby follow. She is dressed in white tights and layers of calico, bald, innocent, drooling, sassing at a birthday party, being held, and obviously loved.

These are very personal images that as viewers we are drawn to because of their rawness. The technology alone is evocative; we are transported to a time we think of as innocent, but we are not allowed to stay because the pain of the memory is too real, too raw. Although all the video segments are historic and "found" as a part of the artist's family archive, the audio is completely new. The juxtaposition of the heartbeat with the sound of Chippewa ceremonial singing was recorded by Ernest on an iPhone and downloaded onto the film tracks. The combination of historic images and recent audio adds a surreal quality to the piece, as if we are traveling the distance between time and place on the platform of new digital technologies.[23]

In terms of spectatorship and the gaze, Ernest is highly involved in mining her family's archives—these are vintage family VHS tapes that she has strategically repurposed to her own demands. She stops the film, rewinds it at places, and talks over it. It is as if she, as an adult and no longer the child of the film, takes pleasure in being the one in control now. Yet her premise for the piece is not entirely self-referential. It is the persistence of the audience—those who question her authenticity—that she works to subdue in this piece. Her "yes, yes" and "no, no" are in answer to the prying questions posed to her by primarily non-Natives who question her being—how she looks, the color of her eyes, her place of belonging. As an urban Native who has lived in several parts of the country, this definitive answer of self-identity must be empowering, perhaps freeing even as it is enacted in a reactive fashion at heart. For Native viewers who experience the same questioning (this author included), it is reassuring that one's individual experience is the experience of many.

Whereas Ernest's film talks back to impositions of identity by evoking personal narrative, Ho-Chunk photographer Jones mobilizes a traditional social norm of self-effacement. Both artists choose to work in the media of lens-based craft, what I argue to be a largely personalized and highly autobiographical format. The camera, unlike the brush, the welder's torch, or the mediums of performance and installation, is a familial tool, one that today is an inherent part of cell phone technology and ubiquitous surveillance cameras. Jones gravitates to the documentary impulses of the audience in order to capture personal and familial memories; however, his craft is deeply infused with the intimate details of his tribe's orientation as original peoples of the Great Lakes area. Born into the Ho-Chunk community, Tom Jones has worked closely with his tribe in order to portray it from the inside out. By showing some of the tribe's adaptations to the "white" culture of mainstream America, he hopes to give "a name and face to the individuals and their way of life in our own time" instead of simply depicting the "beads and feathers."[24]

In his newest work, Jones addresses the idea of phenotype in which enrolled tribal members present as white and unenrolled members appear as stereotypically Native. These physical attributes are utilized as a means of questioning federal recognition policies based on the genealogies of blood, not culture. Many of the photographs in his portrait series could appropriately be termed self-portraiture for their completeness as an example of Ho-Chunk visual sensibilities. This formalistic aesthetic is defined by an admonishment not to talk of oneself; it is a modesty and privacy that is palpable in his complete engagement with line, form, and composition.

Jones's emphasis on the intricacies of how the world inside his camera lens appears in final form could be interpreted as an overriding concern with Western aesthetics rather than indigenous norms. He is fond of crediting abstract expressionists, for example, as influences for his stark, abstract landscape compositions; however, the patterns he replicates could easily be delineated as essential geometric grids for traditional Ho-Chunk basketry and ribbon work. This perceived tension is regularly explored in the scholarship on Native arts. For example, is modernism an appropriation of indigenous expression or vice versa? Jones is explicit about his Western influences—Mondrian and Rothko are primary muses. Yet Jones's aesthetic choices have everything to do with his community's norms, in this instance the norm of refusal. As he states, "Even though there's a lot of baggage, I'm only showing you what I want you to see. I want our people to have pride about themselves."[25] Form becomes a way to shield the viewer and the subject from exposing information that is too personal. Abstraction serves indigeneity.[26]

To understand how these attributes of experiential, blood relationships function in Jones's work, I will consider two images to discuss from his formal portrait series titled *Honoring the Ho-Chunk Warrior*. Jones's choice of documenting tribal members who are active in the US military may signal to an unversed viewer an anomaly, given the fraught history of US imperialism and expansion on American soil, yet this preconception is a false one. The legacy of American Indians active in the military is aptly documented and forms a major component of any accurate rendering of America. However, like many aspects of American Indian history, its salience is frequently overlooked or misunderstood. Jones's engagement with the veterans consequently signals a counternarrative to the unversed viewer who may react with surprise or even humor upon encountering these "unexpected" images.

Margaret Garvin (see fig. 2), a self-possessed veteran in a brilliant blue Indian shirt, cradles her newborn child. Garvin is positioned against a distressed tin building that echoes the blue of her shirt, making her appear larger and more powerful than her physical presence alone. The baby, also wrapped in blue, is held securely by her mother's flexed hand. Garvin's protective stance, her squinted eye, challenges the viewer to dare and threaten this precious child. A jagged tear in the blue tin backdrop exaggerates this powerful stance, as if she herself was responsible for mutilating it. She is proud, just as Jones has intended, but she is also to be feared. In terms of a visceral experience, the viewer

**FIGURE 2.** *Margaret Garvin from* Honoring the Ho-Chunk Warrior, *2001. Digital archival print courtesy of Tom Jones.*

feels her strength. The pale color of her skin and hair subvert the expectedness of the Native warrior icon, inserting a counternarrative of Native resiliency and strength grounded in the matriarchal values of leadership and power.

**FIGURE 3.** *Sergeant Jessika Greendeer and Corporal Kristen Greendeer from* Honoring the Ho-Chunk Warrior, *2006. Digital archival print courtesy of Tom Jones.*

The second image from the same series shows two sisters (Sergeant Jessika Greendeer and Corporal Kristen Greendeer) in army uniforms, fully decorated (see fig. 3). The women are so physically similar that they appear as one. They are turned toward each other in a fashion that suggests one body. Again, their presence is enlarged just as Garvin's was by the staging of a similarly colored background. The Greendeer photo is set in a wooded area, forming a backdrop that almost implicates the two sisters as creatures of the natural environment. They present as deer, their heads turned in union to meet the viewer. It is as if we had accidently come across these two women in the forest, but instead of startling and running, they turn and face us, fully present in the moment. Their eyes engaging ours creates a bond; they implicate us in their recognition that we stand in their territory, we have interrupted their moment—we are the interloper on Ho-Chunk land. Jones's intent—to convey self-possession—is accomplished.

These somewhat contemplative images reflect Jones's desire to examine issues that affect American Indian communities, in particular his Ho-Chunk community. His concern with how traditional standards of family and blood are changing was heightened by tribal legislation that required all new members to have DNA testing in order to prove their Ho-Chunk ancestry.[27] Jones dubs this new policy "identity genocide," describing the implications of this legislation as self-imposed tribal eradication:

> Traditionally, the Ho-Chunk have adopted non-Ho-Chunks (whether they were Native or white) into the tribe. Before contact with whites, there was constant intermarriage among the tribes. This did not change who you were culturally, if you were raised within that specific community.
>
> Today, we have children whose parents [may be] a one-quarter Chippewa, one-quarter Potawatomi, one-quarter Mesquakie, and one-quarter Ho-Chunk. All of these children are full-blooded Indians, but according to new tribal enrollment policies, the children will no longer be considered a member of any federally recognized tribe, because they are only one-eighth of each individual tribe.
>
> Through DNA testing, the tribe is terminating or self-colonizing its people with federally-imposed ideas of what an American Indian is. This new form of eradication did not arise from wanting biological purity, but instead from the desire to keep

people from jumping ship from one tribe to another, in order to receive per capita checks from casino revenues.[28]

For this new series, *Identity Genocide*, Jones plans to photograph enrolled Ho-Chunk tribal members who are one-quarter Ho-Chunk and are not distinguishably "Indian looking" alongside non-enrolled individuals of Ho-Chunk descent who are distinguishably "Indian looking."[29] This contested history regarding the complexities of regulating race is a potent analysis of the ways in which blood unites as well as divides. Jones's approach finds congruence with scholars such as Kimberly TallBear who assert that "tribal ideas of kinship and community belonging are not synonymous with biology. If tribal political practice is not meaningfully informed by cultural practice and philosophy, it seems that tribes are abdicating self-determination."[30] This fraught territory of tribal recognition using genealogy is not imaginary and is not informed by postmodern aesthetic theory or identity politics, but is a matter of tribal legislation. Jones's concern with these issues cannot be synonymous with the misnomer "identity politics," for his realities are informed by self-segregations, federal legislations, and the sovereign relationship of Native nations. The content is a grounded political reality as salient as US aggressions abroad, the trauma of AIDS, or the crisis of feminist representations, which are typical fodder for consideration as serious fine-arts endeavors, but somehow dismissed when the art is cast as Native and labeled "identity art."

## IMAGINARY TRUTHS

Jones and Ernest utilize genealogical mapping to define their statements on identity and belonging, making varied uses of the concept of addressing blood memories. Although non-Native artists may be concerned with family or community, this engagement lacks the extreme relationality that exists within indigenous contexts and an embracement of the metaphysical. Sean Teuton summarizes this divide by stating "to Western eyes, tribal forms of experience such as dreams, visions, and ceremonial, athletic—and certainly narcotic revelations—can't possibly produce reliable knowledge. And yet these have been fundamental to Indigenous lives."[31] The defining quality of indigenous life and identities as a continued engagement with the colonial experience and as a means of defining sovereignty—who belongs and how we belong—is central to the interpretation of indigenous arts. It is the power of blood, linkage to the land, and memory of painful histories of genocide that form the absolute space of what MacDougall terms "possession."

I began this article with MacDougall's call for a holistic syncretism between filmmaker, subject, and spectator as a means of understanding imagery as a corporeal experience. Although audience reception may present as a reactive form of scholarship, I forward the premise that the audience may be, and frequently is, the artist's originating source community. Clearly this is the case for both artists featured in this article, given Jones's documentary impulse with Ho-Chunk veterans and Ernest's less obvious off-screen mentorship of Native youth in a variety of settings.[32] The field's collective understanding of spectatorship and the gaze must then allow for the challenge of multiple interpretations between and within communities.

MacDougall states that the spectator typically experiences a convergence with the objects and faces on film: "Films exceed normal observation and yet throw up huge barriers to it. They give us the privileged view point of the close-up of the enclosing frame . . . yet at the same time they confine us to limited frames, give us limited time to inspect them and in other ways deprive us of our will. This becomes a gap on a larger scale, of a different order."[33] I suggest that this "gap" is more than the distance between the concerns of indigenous communities—including land, survivance, and identities as embodied in genealogy and blood—and non-Native communities. These concerns are multivalent, enduring, ever-present, and essential to crafting a theoretical approach to indigenous aesthetic expressions.

Vizenor states that "Native literary artists create the tropes of oral stories in the silence of narratives, and in the imagist scenes of eternal motion, totemic transmutation, pronoun waves, gender inversion, the presence of creatures, visionary voice and in a sense of survivance."[34] The active imaginations of Native artists embodied in multiple exchanges with their subjects and audiences allow for a more nuanced and telling delineation of indigenous aesthetics than identity and counternorms alone.

## NOTES

Reprinted with permission from Nancy Marie Mithlo, *American Indian Culture and Research Journal* 35:4 (2011): 103–118.

This article was first presented at the Native American Indigenous Studies Association Meeting, May 20, 2010, as part of the session titled "ART SPEAKS: Translating and Interpreting Indigenous Art through Curatorial Practice, Exhibition and Theory," which was organized by Ryan Rice, chief curator, Museum of Contemporary Native Arts, a center of the Institute of American Indian Arts, Santa Fe, New Mexico. The author is grateful for the financial support to travel provided by the University of Wisconsin's Vilas Fellowship. The associated exhibition—tentatively titled "Blood Memory: Indigenous Genealogies and Imagined Truths," featuring the work of Greg Staats (Canada), Anna Tsouhlarakis (US), Tom Jones (US), and Brenda Croft (Australia)—will open in January 2013 at the Museum of Contemporary Native Arts.

1. Gerald Vizenor, "American Indian Art and Literature Today: Survivance and Tragic Wisdom," *Museum International* 62, no. 3 (2010): 50.

2. An assessment of these infrastructure challenges was completed at the 2008 American Indian Curatorial Practice: State of the Field conference hosted at the University of Wisconsin–Madison and funded by the Ford Foundation. A PDF catalogue of the proceedings may be found at http://www.nancymariemithlo.com/aicp_menu.htm (accessed July 21, 2011).

3. Peter Kulchyski, "From Appropriation to Subversion: Aboriginal Cultural Production in the Age of Postmodernism," *American Indian Quarterly* 21, no. 4 (Autumn 1997): 605–20.

4. Smithsonian National Museum of the American Indian, *Vision, Space, Desire: Global Perspectives and Cultural Hybridity* (Washington, DC: National Museum of the American Indian, 2006).

5. For a helpful overview of the field see Mario Caro, "Owning the Image: Indigenous Arts since 1990," in *Manifestations: New Native Art Criticism*, ed. Nancy Marie Mithlo (Santa Fe: Museum of Contemporary Native Arts, 2011), 56–71.

6. Although I recognize the exciting development of "the senses" in the literature (e.g., Constance Classen and David Howes, "The Sensescape of the Museum: Western Sensibilities and Indigenous Artifacts," in *Sensible Objects: Colonialism, Museums and Material Culture*, ed. Elizabeth

Edwards, Chris Gosden, and Ruth Phillips [Oxford: Berg Publishers, 2006], 199–222), I choose to focus my energies in this article on the affective qualities of audience and gaze.

7. Pauline Turner Strong and Barrik Van Winkle, "'Indian Blood': Reflections on the Reckoning and Refiguring of Native North American Identity," *Cultural Anthropology* 11, no. 4 (November 1996): 552.

8. Sean Kicummah Teuton, "Native Literature, Native Art, and How There Might Be 'Memory in the Blood.'" Paper presented at the Smithsonian National Museum of the American Indian Essentially Indigenous? Symposium, New York, May 6, 2011 (Smithsonian Press, forthcoming).

9. N. Scott Momaday, *House Made of Dawn* (1968; repr., New York: Perennial Library, 1989).

10. Chadwick Allen, "Blood (and) Memory," *American Literature* 71, no. 1 (March 1999): 93–94.

11. The Saginaw Chippewa Indian Tribe's Ziibiwing Center offers a powerful demonstration of the concept of blood memory in an interpretative exhibit. See http://www.sagchip.org/ziibiwing/ (accessed July 21, 2011). See an informative review of the exhibits by scholar Amy Lonetree, "'Diba Jimooyung: Telling Our Story,' Ziibiwing Center of Anishinaabe Culture and Lifeways, Mount Pleasant, MI," *The Journal of American History* 95, no. 1 (June 2008): 158–63.

12. See Future of Minority Studies for proactive means of addressing these ills: http://www.fmsproject.cornell.edu/ (accessed July 21, 2011).

13. David MacDougall, *The Corporeal Image: Film, Ethnography, and the Senses* (Princeton, NJ: Princeton University Press, 2006).

14. Pierre Bordieu, *The Field of Cultural Production: Essays on Art and Literature* (New York: Columbia University Press, 1984), 4.

15. MacDougall, *The Corporeal Image*, 137.

16. For more on multiple gazes, see James Elkins, *The Object Stares Back: On the Nature of Seeing* (New York: Simon and Schuster, 1996).

17. MacDougall, *The Corporeal Image*, 137.

18. Sam Pack, "Reversing the Gaze: 'The Whiteman' as Other," *International Journal of Business and Social Science* 1, no. 3 (December 2010): 295.

19. Marcella Ernest, e-mail communications with author, April 27–28, 2010.

20. Ibid.

21. Ibid.

22. Ibid. Ernest adds, "The most interesting thing to me about this film, in terms of the process of making it is that all of the footage—all of the visuals are from old S-8 film captured by my dad from about 1960–1981. I simply digitized the old footage and added the sound. I only added one transition! Which is rare in any film, especially experimental! I usually do the opposite and add multiple layers of video with a simple soundtrack. Interestingly again, is that ALL of the audio added was recorded from my iPhone. All of it, even the Ojibwe song and prayer which is playing in the background. And my own voice was also recorded by iPhone as well. The juxtaposition of the two (archival family films from my dad without computer manipulation and the audio of a very modern tool such as the iPhone). I don't know, I find that interesting and it adds something to it."

23. Tom Jones, artist's statement, Museum of Contemporary Photography, http://www.mocp.org/collections/mpp/jones_tom.php (accessed July 21, 2011).

24. Tom Jones, presentation to the University of Wisconsin–Madison Tribal Libraries and Museums course, March 29, 2009.

25. Nancy Marie Mithlo, "'On the Other Side of this Ocean': The Limits of Knowledge as an Aesthetic Framework." Paper presented at the 2011 College Art Association panel "Toward an Indigenous Artistic Sovereignty: Theory, Criticism, and Native Art," Michigan State University.

26. Nancy Marie Mithlo, "'On the Other Side of this Ocean': The Limits of Knowledge as an Aesthetic Framework." Paper presented at the College Art Association panel "Toward an Indigenous Artistic Sovereignty: Theory, Criticism, and Native Art," New York, February 9–12, 2011.

27. Ho-Chunk Nation Code, Title 2, Government Code Section 7, Tribal Enrollment and Membership Code Enacted by Legislature, October 16, 2007.

28. Tom Jones, *Identity Genocide* exhibition statement, 2009.

29. At press time, Jones stated that his intent in the new series may change: "I am currently photographing people who are no longer seen as Ho-Chunk by the tribe." Personal communication with author, May 19, 2011.

30. Kimberly TallBear, "DNA, Blood, and Racializing the Tribe," *Wicazo Sa Review* 18, no. 1 (Spring 2003): 84.

31. Teuton, "Native Literature, Native Art, and How There Might Be 'Memory in the Blood.'"

32. For more on Ernest's impact with Native youth see http://www.nativenetworks.si.edu/nafvf/filmmakers_ernest.aspx (accessed July 21, 2011).

33. MacDougall, *The Corporeal Image*, 26.

34. Vizenor, "American Indian Art and Literature Today," 48–49.

# THE OPPOSITIONAL CONSCIOUSNESS OF YOLANDA M. LÓPEZ

KAREN MARY DAVALOS

In the 1970s, when Yolanda M. López began to investigate media representations of Chicanas, she was shocked to notice that "not even Dolores Huerta" was present in the public images of the Chicano civil rights movement. Huerta's role as cofounder of the United Farm Workers could not surmount the ideology of patriarchy that erased Chicana activists and leaders. When López began her analysis of the function of images, representations of Chicana activists, labor organizers, and student leaders were not prevalent, and the Catholic and Mexican icon of the Virgin of Guadalupe was the most popular female figure within Chicano public and private space. Guadalupe appeared on banners, placards, murals, and calendars, and in home altars and store windows, although it was difficult for López to find the icon at Catholic religious stores or parish shrines in her hometown of San Diego, California. For ten years, López explored the function of the sixteenth-century painting of Guadalupe, and as a result she produced one of the most widely circulated images in Chicana/o art history: *Portrait of the Artist as the Virgin of Guadalupe* (1978, fig. 1). Consistently reproduced in the 1980s and 1990s to represent major traveling exhibitions as well as regional group shows of Chicana and Chicano art, the oil pastel self-portrait drawing is probably the most recognizable work of art associated with the Chicano art renaissance.[1]

Drawing on an extended life history interview, this essay examines the work of López and argues that it articulates the multivocal, or polyvalent, identity consciousness developed by US Third World feminists, thereby enacting oppositional consciousness—the method, epistemology, and praxis described by Chela Sandoval (2000).[2] As it traces the oppositional consciousness within the art of López, the essay documents her earliest political activism and the subsequent aesthetic strategies that emerged from social

Karen Mary Davalos is professor of Chicano and Latino studies at the University of Minnesota, Twin Cities. Her research and teaching interests include Chicana feminist scholarship, spirituality, art, exhibition practices, and oral history, and she has published widely on Chicana/o art, spirituality, and museums. Among her publications are *Yolanda M. López* (UCLA Chicano Studies Research Center Press, 2008), recipient of two book awards, and her latest book, *Chicana/o Remix: Art and Errata since the Sixties* (NYU Press, 2017).

**Figure 1.** Yolanda M. López, *Portrait of the Artist as the Virgin of Guadalupe*, from the Guadalupe series, 1978. Oil pastel on rag paper, 22 × 30 inches. Reproduced with the permission of the artist.

protest. The larger study that gave rise to this essay investigates the artist's biography, documenting her family as a source of her artistic expression, her activism as a source of her conceptual approach, and her formal arts training as the place where she develops a language for her deconstructivist and semiotic aesthetic project (Davalos 2008b). It also places López's art within American art history. An underlying goal of the essay is to draw out the conceptual, deconstructivist, and semiotic approach that is usually overshadowed by the figurative composition, a misinterpretation that has led critics and scholars to misclassify her work as representational, figurative, or Catholic romanticism.

Since much of the work discussed here was created in the 1970s, I argue that it anticipates the 1980s feminist scholarship on intersectionality. I do not wish to imply that López was the first to visually render the matrix of gender, race, class, ethnicity, and, to some extent, sexuality. Rather, my intention is to balance the uneven scholarship on literature, performance, and visual arts. As Laura Pérez notes, scholars have not paid the same amount of intellectual attention to the visual arts as they have to literature and performance (2007, 13). We are familiar with the creative writing of and critical scholarship on Sandra Cisneros, Denise Chávez, Lorna Dee Cervantes, Helena María Viramontes, Cherríe Moraga, and Gloria Anzaldúa—to name a few. The Chicana/o studies canon is rich with Chicana feminist literary voices that braid race and class with gender consciousness. In addition, scholarship on these and other writers has brought sexuality, citizenship, migration, and language into the *trenza* of intersectionality.

Yet as Rita González (2003) points out, scholarship on Latina and Latino visual artists is lacking. Using the primary search engines of art history, such as Art Abstracts, Art Index Retrospective, and the Getty Research Institute's Union List of Artist Names, as well as six major teaching texts for twentieth-century American art history, González searched for citations on a sample of ninety-three Latina and Latino artists, focusing on established artists in midcareer. She found that "few artists on [the sample] list had more than one article published about their work; and more often than not the few articles published consisted of brief exhibition reviews. In comparison, searching for one hundred of the most exhibited non-Hispanic White artists would yield thousands of entries" (2). Chicana artists faired especially poorly. For example, the survey revealed thirteen works on Amalia Mesa-Bains, eleven works on Carmen Lomas Garza, seven on Diane Gamboa, six on Judith Baca, five on Barbara Carrasco, one on Yolanda López, and none on Santa Barraza or Yreina D. Cervántez. In contrast, the indexes record thirty works on Luis Jiménez, twenty-two on Anthony Hernandez, eighteen on Carlos Almaraz, fourteen on Gronk, twelve on Rupert García, and eleven on John Valadez.[3] The picture is very bleak. Therefore, I wish to intervene, and similar to the way Pérez positions her book-length study on Chicana art since the 1980s, I offer this essay as homage to López's work and her participation in the most important advance in ethnic and feminist studies: recognition of the intersecting and multiple subjectivities of women of color.[4]

Recent scholarship on López does not consistently or systematically account for the complexity of her consciousness.[5] More critically, scholars rarely address within the scope of a single analytic piece López's shifting oppositional consciousness. Some authors emphasize her Mexican heritage, and others focus on her Latino and Third World orientation (Cordova 2005; Ferreira 2003). The majority of visual arts and social analyses describe her antisexism and her Chicana consciousness (Chabram-Dernersesian 1994; Goldman 1990; Keale 2000; Mazurana 1999). López was frequently associated with the visual arts and religious movement that redeemed feminine spiritual authority (Gadon 1989; Orenstein 1996; Stott 1995). For example, Gloria Feman Orenstein used López's Guadalupe triptych as an example of the California-based goddess art movement of the 1970s. This interpretation amused López because she was not concerned with the divine or with the sacred powers of women. Claire Joysmith (1995) did not analyze the Guadalupe triptych, but it was the central illustration for an argument about reclaiming female figures that empower mothers, grandmothers, and women's traditions. In contrast, López was interested in the power of working-class women rather than in feminine mystical power. As I argue below, López was not concerned with recuperating Guadalupe.

Within Chicana scholarship, Alicia Gaspar de Alba and Angie Chabram-Dernersesian offer solid efforts to account for López's antiracist, antisexist, and anticlassist orientation. Gaspar de Alba briefly describes López as "upholding Marxist ideologies of el Movimiento that focused on class and worker solidarity" (1998, 125). While this analysis suggests some of the multiple subject positions that compose López's oppositional consciousness, it elides the role her family played in developing López's criticism of capitalism. Chabram-Dernersesian acknowledges "linkages between sexism, racism, patriarchy, homophobia, and economic exploitation" (2006, 179) and argues that the Guadalupe triptych "echoes the resolution of many Chicana activists who clarified, once and for all," that liberation is not negotiable. In her short examination, Chabram-Dernersesian correctly connects López's triptych to the work of other Chicana feminists, including artist Ester Hernandez, who also explored female iconography. However, the brilliantly argued article by Chabram-Dernersesian is an example of the imbalance in Chicana literary criticism, performance, and art history, since the bulk of the analysis is devoted to textual works; the visual arts are addressed only briefly. This essay contributes to scholarship on López by considering her childhood and youth, analyzing a range of her artistic productions, including work produced within the Guadalupe series as well as work produced after it, and exploring the complex and multiple subject positions rendered in her visual project.

## CHARTING DIFFERENTIAL CONSCIOUSNESS OF US THIRD WORLD FEMINISTS

Chela Sandoval argues that the differential consciousness of US Third World feminists of color is mobile rather than permanently aligned with a singular ideology or form of resistance to US social hierarchy. This mobility allows for a new subjectivity and mode of perception that accounts for the social conditions of racialization, sex and gender heteronormativity, and material inequality. The new mode, known as the differential mode or mestiza consciousness, combines four other political modes of resistance: equal-rights, revolutionary, supremacist, and separatist. It is the ability to merge existing political positions that makes the work of US Third World feminists of color historic, particularly during the period of activism, scholarship, and creative expression that lasted from the late 1960s through the 1980s (C. Sandoval 2000, 44). A shifting consciousness that bridges multiple modes makes clear that the social conditions of racism, sexism, homophobia/heteronormativity, and classism are complementary and competing forms of social control. In the visual arts of Yolanda López, an oppositional consciousness makes visible the previously invisible and unimaginable Chicana feminist working-class subject position. A shifting consciousness launches a new Chicana subjectivity, and it is rendered in López's image bank. One example is the Guadalupe series, in which López joins formerly separate political projects of feminism, cultural nationalism, and anticapitalism into a proposal for Chicana womanhood that empowers. In short, Sandoval posits that differential consciousness is the necessary position, tactic, and epistemology for authentic liberation.

Indeed, the bulk of Sandoval's project in *Methodology of the Oppressed* is devoted to a critique of the ways in which social theorists of postmodern, poststructural, postcolonial, feminist, and ethnic studies rely upon separatist disciplinary methods and practices that limit the possibility of social transformation. Ruby Tapia makes this observation in a review of the book, noting that Sandoval asserts that social theorists in these fields "have not spoken to each other or read each other's work," even though they share a vision for liberation (Tapia 2001, 734). Unfortunately, as a result of this intellectual seclusion, the contributions of US Third World feminists of color are ignored or appropriated. The theoretical genealogies that Sandoval reconstructs through the advancements made by US Third World feminists enable resistance and emancipation and plot a path for authentic liberation previously unimagined by the legitimated citizen-subject.

The shifting and braided consciousness of US Third World feminists of color creates tools and methods for survival under global capitalism and its imperatives of racism, sexism, and imperialism. It travels between and mixes equal-rights, revolutionary, supremacist, and separatist tactics, creating a new modality in the process. Unlike the "formerly centered and legitimated bourgeois citizen-subject of the first world" that was "once anchored in a secure haven of self" but is now "set adrift under the imperatives of late-capitalist cultural conditions," the "historically decentered citizen-subject" has precisely the tools needed for survival (C. Sandoval 2000, 27). "The colonized, the outsider, the queer, the subaltern, the marginalized" (27) developed an oppositional consciousness "in response to such fragmentation" under colonialism, imperialism, material and political inequity, and other systems of oppression (33). Gloria Anzaldúa names this response "*la facultad*," by which she means a knowledge that emerges from fragmentation (1987, 38). López uses her knowledge of subordination and daily inequalities to create a visual world filled with dignified Chicanas and Mexican women. I turn now to her life and education to trace the foundations of her differential consciousness.

## FAMILY AND POLITICAL PRACTICES

Born in 1942, Yolanda M. López grew up in San Diego at a time when the town was developing a military-industrial complex to support US involvement in World War II (Villa 2000). The household of her childhood comprised her grandparents, Senobio and Victoria Franco, who had migrated from Mexico in 1918; her mother, Margaret; and several uncles, including Uncle Mikey, who became her surrogate father after Senobio passed away when López was eleven years old (López 2007). Senobio's tailoring skills permitted him a remunerative profession in a town that otherwise locked Mexicans, Southern white migrants, and African Americans into unskilled and semiskilled jobs. His employer vouched for him during the 1940s and he was able to avoid deportation, but unfortunately his wife, Victoria, was not so lucky, and she was deported to Mexico in 1941. This incident outraged the family. López recalls, "Even though my grandmother had two or three sons in the [US] military, they deported her. She spent about a year in Tijuana before she could migrate" back to the United States (2007). López credits the family's survival to Victoria's ingenuity and self-taught knowledge: her grandmother kept her adult children and sometimes their spouses as well as López and her younger sisters fed and clothed. No one went hungry. The multigenerational household allowed López to become close to her grandparents, who took her on frequent short trips to Tijuana and on a few extended vacations to Acapulco and Mexico City. According to López, her grandparents offered her unconditional love, protection, and comfort, and before her younger sisters were born they even considered raising her as their own child (2007).

The extended family household also offered her several models for womanhood, since Margaret worked outside the home for most of López's childhood and teenage years. Working first at the Grant Hotel and later at the Naval Training Center, Margaret was employed as a seamstress and presser. For a brief period during her second marriage she labored exclusively inside the home, but she returned to paid labor when her husband lost his job and could not maintain the myth of patriarchal economic authority. The artist recalls that her mother, like Senobio and his sons, enjoyed sewing well-made clothes, although she rejected other forms of domesticity such as cooking. When López was a teenager, Margaret created for her children fashionable outfits using inexpensive fabrics, a strategy that the artist would employ during her graduate training in order to challenge highbrow art. For Margaret, finding the time to sew must have been a challenge, since she left for work before the sun rose and returned after it had set. With family time limited to the long bus rides to and from day care, López found she enjoyed the otherwise monotonous trips on public transportation because it allowed for intimate conversation between her and her mother. It was during these bus trips that Margaret taught her daughter to respect labor, to support unions, and to "never cross a picket line" (López 2007).

Victoria was also a model of female autonomy. She was the head of the household, even before Senobio died around 1953. With only a third-grade education, Victoria taught herself to read and managed a household by growing food and raising goats and chickens (and later, pigeons). Senobio respected her ingenuity and treated her with dignity, although her sons did not always grant her the same consideration. These two models of patriarchy—one polite and respectful of women, the other insisting that women perform the dirty work, pick up after men, and serve men first—taught López to question gender expectations. Nevertheless, the household largely supported women's autonomy. López did not recall anyone chastising Margaret for staying out late on Saturday nights, divorcing two men, or eventually living on her own with her daughters (López 2007).

While growing up in San Diego, López did not think of herself as a Mexican American girl. Her first language was Spanish, her family ate Mexican food and frequently traveled to the border, and Victoria's dark skin, hair, and eyes clearly marked her as indigenous Mexican; nonetheless, López's schooling shaped her identity. She was taught to recognize George Washington as a forefather. At a young age, López associated Mexican culture with tourist art and *arte popular*, and these markers were not part of her family's experience or aesthetic (López 2007). While in college, however, she learned from other students of color to recognize that assimilation was the goal of her childhood education, and she no longer wished to deny the historical presence of Mexicans in California, her heritage, or the role women played in shaping Chicano communities.

The education in public schools was largely subtractive of her home language and culture, but within the family and elsewhere, López and her sisters were encouraged to develop their creative expression. Her uncles taught her to appreciate working with one's hands, and she delighted in watching them make furniture and rebuild bicycles and car engines. The entire household enjoyed music and theater, read popular magazines, and created toys and playthings for Margaret's girls. Victoria cared for a garden and arranged family photographs and *recuerdos* near a crucifix, although the family was not religious.[6] She allowed López to create hats from pie tins and flowers. Aesthetic expression was also reinforced at the Bayside Settlement House, where López and her sisters attended day care: the program took them on trips to museums and the zoo, taught them how to create dolls and games, and provided them with a library of books and magazines. Margaret also shared with her oldest daughter her hobby of arranging images in scrapbooks, a leisure activity that developed among women during World War II. While this feminine craft supported consumerism, domesticity, and Eurocentric and middle-class images of beauty, it was for Margaret and López a chance to reformulate mainstream images into their own visual and gender narrative. López and her mom cut pictures from glamour magazines, initiating López's first explorations into the collage and photomontage techniques, and they imagined lives outside of gender expectations.

Her sensibility to push against gender norms is seen in her childhood dream of becoming a set or costume designer. During her teenage years, after working in the costume department at the Globe Theatre, López hoped to study for a career in animation. She set her sights on attending the Chouinard Art Institute, which was known as a major force in training and employing West Coast artists. But these adolescent dreams were born of the notion that her artistic talent was not useful and that she would therefore need a career in set or costume design. She enjoyed Disney full-length animation movies, but she did not have a deep desire or aspiration to emulate the Disney animators or costume designers that had trained at Chouinard. She simply did not know how or why an artist could make a living; more important, she saw no immediate necessity for her art, although her uncles, grandparents, and mother were constantly creating clothes, furniture, and other useful household items. It was not until she became involved in student activism at San Francisco State College and later in the Mission District, where she met Emory Douglas of Oakland's Black Panther Party, that she began to focus on the power of images to create social change (López 2007).

## DECONSTRUCTION OF IMAGES

López grew up in a generation that was critical of the liberal state. Living in the San Francisco Bay Area, she found her political voice on the picket lines of the Third World Liberation Front (TWLF) at San Francisco State College. There she developed the ability to organize on behalf of workers, women, and people of color while at the same time referring to herself as a Chicana. When twenty-four-year-old López transferred to San Francisco State College, she was already participating in the cultural revolution in Northern California. She had ventured into the counterculture scene through fashion, style, books, and music. In March 1968 the TWLF, a multiracial and multiethnic student coalition at State College, began mobilizing to demand ethnic studies, a voice in faculty hiring, and admissions and financial aid policies that would create a student body more reflective of the demographic profile of the city. Underlying their activism was a determination to "overturn the pejorative meaning" of the term "Third World" and to create solidarity across lines of race, ethnicity, national heritage, color, and immigration status in their struggle to win these demands (Cordova 2005, 8).[7] After the administration failed to deliver on its promises, the group of African American, Latina/o, Native American, and Asian American students led a five-month strike, using radical tactics that included building occupations, chanting, trash can fires, amplified speeches, picket lines, and sit-ins.

Several factors influenced López's decision to join the strike rather than attend classes. First of all, her mother had raised her to respect worker solidarity, a political strategy she continues to practice. She would not have crossed a picket line under any circumstances. Second, her household was filled with people who were self-taught. For López, learning was never confined to the classroom. Another major factor in her decision to join the TWLF was the participatory democracy she learned at home, which was reinforced in multiple ways. López remembers excitement in the family as they watched several Democratic conventions. She recalls that her mother took all three sisters to "stuff envelopes for Jack Kennedy's [presidential] campaign" in 1960 (Cordova 2005, 15). In addition, her mother's union membership signaled the importance of collective action, and the collective action of the students proved invaluable for the TWLF when the president of the university attempted to split the coalition by making promises to the Black Student Union. This sense of shared interests and goals was the high point of López's education at State College. Throughout the five-month student strike, López learned to see herself as a person of color whose history and experience was connected to that of African Americans, Asian Americans, Native Americans, and other Latinos. She also began to identify as a Chicana, shedding the constraints of a childhood in which the curriculum of Americanization and denial had taught her to see herself as a descendant of Mayflower Pilgrims (López 2007).

The Third World Liberation Front taught López that inclusive political action and self-determination could coexist. A shifting consciousness allowed her to understand the structural inequalities common to people of color while affirming the need for Chicanas and Chicanos to become the producers of their own history, creative imagination, visual library, and futures. López began to question the production and function of images, and this was more than an epistemological exercise. She noted how some images and image makers were valued over others and understood that the valuation was a matter of unearned power due to race, class, or gender privilege. In fact, as she continued her activism she formulated an artistic goal to deconstruct images and to propose new representations of Chicanas and Chicanos.

After the strike came to a successful end, López and some friends focused their organizing skills on the Mission District. There they founded a youth empowerment group that changed into Los Siete de la Raza, a defense committee for seven young Latino men accused of killing a police officer. As the organization grew, it offered services as well as advocacy to the largely immigrant Latino community. The direct political engagement of Los Siete de la Raza helped López strengthen her identity as an artist.

It was through Los Siete that she met Douglas, minister of culture for the Black Panther Party. He taught her inexpensive methods for laying out the Los Siete newspaper, *¡Basta Ya!* More important, his direct style and combination of text and image inspired her to identify as a political artist.

> One of the reasons I liked Emory Douglas . . . what I learned from Emory . . . is that he loves his people so much. He's done a lot of beautiful, haunting [images]. . . . He did a very poignant piece . . . the profile of a black man with a helmet—it was an Army man . . . and in his helmet were pictures of Vietnamese dead and murdered

> black people in the United States. And there was just a single tear going down the side [of his face]. And it was so beautiful. And one of the most, I felt, eloquent [antiwar] statements. . . . He was talking about their humanity; he was talking about their humanness. And that's what it was. So it wasn't like a stereotypic image of a black person. (López 2007)

Activism within Los Siete provided López with her "function as an artist" (López 2007). She created the artwork and graphic designs for the newspaper as well as the buttons, placards, and posters used at mass demonstrations to rally support for Los Siete. Because the media portrayed the Latino defendants as "hoodlums" and "militants" (López 2007), López was determined to examine the role and function of these images by offering new ones (figs. 2, 3). Indeed, just as Douglas crafted images of black leaders as strong, intelligent, and ready for military conflict in contrast to the happy sambo, the illiterate and lazy drug user, or the baffoon, López was determined to show that Latino youth were not gang members. For example, she provided illustrations and graphic designs for articles that told how two of the defendants were student organizers who assisted Latinos with college applications (Ferreira 2003, 296).

Influenced by Douglas, she realized that the audience for new images of Latinos was the Mission District community itself. The masthead of the newspaper and the photomontage and collage techniques are examples of López's effort to reimagine Chicanos and other Latinos. By overlapping a variety of images, López could document the diversity within the Latino community. In the masthead of the earliest editions, an open hand holding a broken chain visually represents new possibilities. The palm gestures up to the sky as if to signify the hope and future of Chicanos and Latinos. Unlike the closed fist raised to signify solidarity and black power, the open hand and powerful forearm presents an empowerment already achieved; the struggle is over and it was a success. The chains of institutionalized racism, capitalist exploitation, and exclusion are literally broken. Using this and other images in *¡Basta Ya!*, López offered radically new representations of Chicanos and Latinos, and she avoided romantic images of noble native people or overly idealized themes and motifs. That is, she did not indulge in an exotic or sentimental view of Mexicans and their ancestors.

## ENACTING DIFFERENTIAL CONSCIOUSNESS: ITS SHADE, FORM, AND COLOR

In 1970 López decided to return to school to complete her bachelor's degree in painting and drawing, and she enrolled at California State University, San Diego. While studying there, she created several portraits of her grandmother in order to "show her at different ages: young, middle-aged, and older" (López 2007, figs. 4–6). Working from photographs and using the techniques of photomontage and collage, the series of portraits is her first homage to "ordinary women," a phrase she uses to describe the commonplace fashion, comportment, and simple appearance of Mexican-origin, working-class women. The phrase "ordinary women" is meant to counter the objectifying visual vocabulary of the media; it was not meant to position women as lowly or intellectually inferior. Instead it asserts the everyday and nonenticing corporeal presence of women.

**Figure 2.** Cover of *¡Basta Ya!* no. 5 (October 1969). Reproduced with the permission of the artist.

**Figure 3.** Yolanda M. López, *Libertad para Los Siete: Bring the Brothers Back Home to the Mission!* Printed in *¡Basta Ya!* no. 8 (March 1970). Reproduced with the permission of the artist.

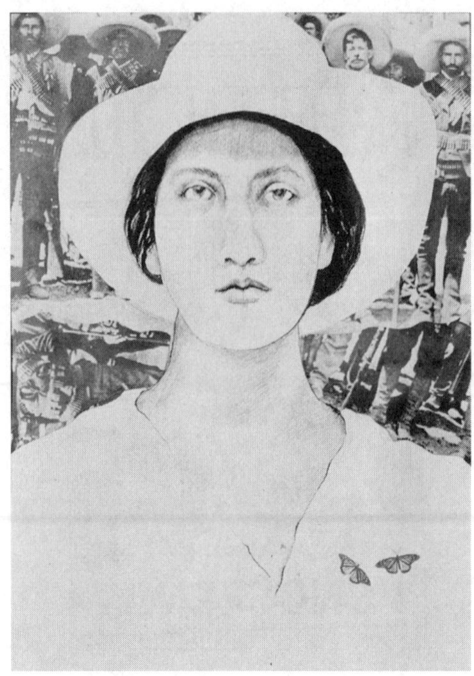

**Figure 4.** Yolanda M. López, Victoria F. Franco series (1 of 4), 1974. Mixed-media collage, 18 × 15 inches. Reproduced with the permission of the artist.

**Figure 5.** Yolanda M. López, Victoria F. Franco series (3 of 4), 1974. Mixed-media collage, 18 × 15 inches. Reproduced with the permission of the artist.

**Figure 6.** Yolanda M. López, Victoria F. Franco series (4 of 4), 1974. Mixed-media collage, 18 × 15 inches. Reproduced with the permission of the artist.

López's eye began to focus on the nonglamorous or nonsexualized woman, and the work visually legitimated elderly skin, eyes, arms, and breasts that sag or droop from age and labor. Moreover, Victoria was in her late eighties when López created the portraits, and the goal was to render an elderly woman as fully active, which López signified through coloration: "I did it in color, because I wanted to express she's alive—in color" (López 2007). The early series is also an example of her experimentation with multiple images of Mexican-origin women. López did not assert a single portrait but crafted at least four portraits, each showing a distinct aspect of Victoria's beauty and experiences.

Funding from the Ford Foundation allowed López to immediately enter the master of fine arts (MFA) program at the University of California, San Diego in 1975.[8] During this time López enhanced the artistic vision she had been developing while living in San Francisco. Her graduate training with artist-scholars Allan Sekula and Martha Rosler provided a language for her feminist deconstructivist and semiotic approach that had initially emerged on the front lines of the Third World Liberation Front strike and with Los Siete in the Mission District. She explores concepts, signs, and meanings; unlike her contemporaries, she is little interested in figuration and pigmentation, internal self-expression, or abstraction. Her monumental compositions, notably the series Tres Mujeres/Three Generations, are explorations in the large format; the formal approach draws on feminist analysis of images and the gaze (figs. 7–9). In this series produced for her MFA exhibition, López successfully joins the feminist critique of the patriarchal gaze and rejects racist objectification of Mexican women and Chicanas. This dialogue of critique and rejection serves as the conceptual backdrop of the series. The refusal of the

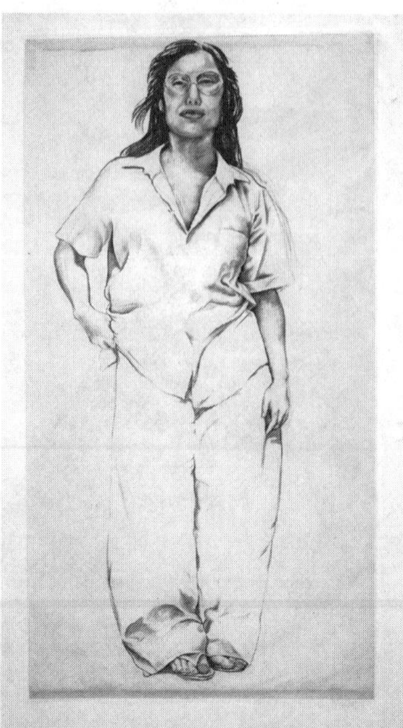

**Figure 7.** Yolanda M. López, *Self-Portrait,* from Tres Mujeres/Three Generations series, 1975–76. Charcoal on paper, 8 × 4 feet.

**Figure 8.** Yolanda M. López, *Mother*, from Tres Mujeres/Three Generations series, 1975–76. Charcoal on paper, 8 × 4 feet. Reproduced with the permission of the artist.

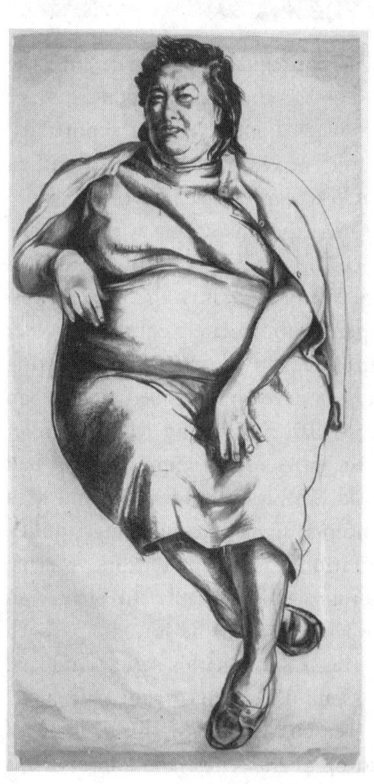

**Figure 9.** Yolanda M. López, *Grandmother,* from Tres Mujeres/Three Generations series, 1975–76. Charcoal on paper, 8 × 4 feet. Reproduced with the permission of the artist.

patriarchal male gaze visually renders the work of film critic Laura Mulvey (1975), who in the same decade argued that Hollywood film depends upon the fetish, the spectacle, and the sex object in its representation of women. López advances the argument in two ways. First, by noting that Mexican women and Chicanas are objectified differently than white women, the portraits remind us that looking is also racial. Second, by presenting women in plain and unadorned ways, the portraits reject a heteronormative stare. The portraits offer new images of Chicanas and Mexicans, bringing into view representations of brown-skinned Latinas that are not possible under sexism, racism, and economic exploitation and middle-class bias.

As implied by the monumental presence of the women in Tres Mujeres/Three Generations, who engage the viewer with their gaze, a major part of the MFA exhibition was its dialogic premise. López forged a collaboration between the art department and El Centro Cultural de la Raza, a community arts organization in San Diego's Balboa Park. She joined with El Centro in order to bring residents from her hometown to the university gallery. Operating in the cultural nationalist mode of pride in heritage, but also registering rights politics and the acknowledgment of women's presence, the exhibition invited Chicanos and Mexicans to bear witness and to claim ownership in the university. As López wrote about the series in her artist's statement,

> Tres Mujeres represents one of the first systematic efforts on my part to explore the presentation of Raza women as we see ourselves. It is a subject that has long interested me as an artist. And it is in general the subject matter of this exhibition. (1978)

This statement indicates her deliberate attempt to dialog with Raza, or people of Latin American heritage; she was interested in Raza-gazing, exploring how "we see ourselves." She produced this type of looking by providing transportation across town from the southeastern neighborhoods of San Diego to the university in La Jolla. Yet the exhibition also shifts its political register to women, those not yet present as citizen-subjects in the nation-state or within Chicano cultural nationalism. This feminist mode avoids the romanticism she saw inside and outside of Chicano communities.

> My intention was to consciously work against traditional commercial stereotypes. . . . A common Chicano/Latino experience in contemporary American culture is the lack of positive visual representations of Latin Americans as normal, intelligent human beings. This omission and the continued use of such stereotypes as the Latin bombshell and the passive long suffering wife/mother negate the humanity of Raza women. (1978)

Through Tres Mujeres/Three Generations and also the Guadalupe triptych, López proposed new signs in the semiotic landscape by representing three generations of women. Both series visually render a mestiza or indigenous Mexican woman (Victoria), a Mexican American woman (Margaret), and a Chicana (the artist). In the statement, López weaves in a gender analysis and expands the discussion of Chicano cultural nationalism and its privileging of patriarchy. López aimed to challenge the racist and sexist portrayals of Latinas. The charcoal-on-paper portraits of Tres Mujeres, a set of nine in total, accomplish this complex oppositional consciousness though the "simple device of scale" and by having the model "confront the viewer directly" (1978). The gaze of patriarchal heterosexism and racism is cut off by the larger-than-life direct gaze and frontal posturing of the women. It is an invitation to view ordinary women as heroes, but their valor is accomplished through proportion rather than through flattery or sexual appeal.

Tres Mujeres/Three Generations, more than the Guadalupe series, is a semiotic exposition of the female human form. López accomplishes this in two ways. First, the line drawings offer minimal but realist interpretations of the female form. A woman stands, sits, or leans. She wears an apron, baggy pants, or a housedress. The portraits are uncluttered and feature expanses of blank space; in fact, they isolate each woman in space. Each female figure has no landscape or surroundings, and she exists in a blank and, thus, illusory space. She stands and leans without a wall or sits without a chair; each woman exists nowhere and everywhere. López uses only the title to anchor the viewer, a point to which I will return. But their isolation in space is not intended to heighten or reinforce objectification of the female body. The portraits are not for "pleasurable looking" (Mulvey 1975, 17); rather, they are mirrors for Chicanas. But the scale transforms the portraits into affirmations of Chicanas and Mexican women that are otherwise obscured. As both semiotic investigation and feminist psychoanalysis argue, this mirror is the articulation of subjectivity, but again López advances the discourse of recognition through multiplicity and size. And this is her second method of accomplishing a semiotic analysis.

She creates not just one portrait but three of each woman, and the different generations and body types are important. The ages, experiences, and physicality of the women are vital to López's semiotic presentation. Moreover, each sitter is asked to duplicate the pose of the other two, an experiment in body language and mimicry to suggest new signs and subjects. The following titles reveal who is mimicking whom and the original pose:

*Grandmother: Victoria F. Franco* [also known as *Grandmother*]
*Mother: Margaret F. Stewart* [also known as *Mother*]
*Daughter: Portrait of the Artist* [also known as *Self-Portrait*]
*Grandmother Sitting as Mother*
*Artist Sitting as Mother*
*Grandmother Standing as Mother*
*Artist Standing as Mother*
*Grandmother Standing as Artist*
*Mother Standing as Artist* (1978)[9]

Each title reinforces the act of imitation and repetition, a process that Judith Butler argues is essential to gender formation—and, Jonathan Inda adds, to racialization (Butler 1993; Inda 2000). The nine monumental drawings express Chicana and *mexicana* similarity (imitation) *and* difference. The series is a collective articulation of multiple subjectivities and the recognition of the self in relation to others. However, a shift occurs when López names herself "the artist" rather than the daughter or granddaughter: it is a maneuver that pushes against the law of the father and asserts a self that does not depend upon the patriarch. This identity outside of patriarchy evokes the separatist or insurgent mode.

## BRAIDING POLITICAL MODES

Mapping an equal rights project within the work of López is not difficult to do, since much of her activism and her artistic product aimed to rectify the inability of the nation-state to secure liberty, equality, and justice for its residents. Her aesthetic choices clearly point to insurgent rather than reformist strategies. A celebrated poster that presumes the ideology of equal rights is *Who's the Illegal Alien, Pilgrim?* The messenger formulates the radical mode or consciousness with an angry snarl and jabbing finger. This revolutionary political gesture questions the nation's early settlers of European heritage, pointing out their immigrant status; by implication it demands the same open border, economic and political opportunities, and legal protections for recent immigrants as the colonial settlers enjoyed (Lipsitz 2001, 77). But the poster is also a vision of settlers' fear: the indigenous inhabitants will take back their land and territory and deport everyone else. The text—European settlers are illegal aliens—and the image of a man dressed in an Aztec headdress propose a time and place where the European conquest has not happened, or at least has not succeeded. Insurgent and separatist modes are used ironically and with humor, a strategy that demonstrates the creative and tempered shifts of a differential consciousness.

This mobility allows López to align experiences across time and space. Two posters in the series Women's Work Is Never Done illustrate how she bridges past and present social conditions to express a different future. *Your Vote Has Power* was López's invention to frighten then governor Pete Wilson and other proponents of California's anti-immigrant Proposition 187 (fig. 10). To render this nightmare, López selects a fertile Latina who votes to confront the xenophobic misperception of Latinas as welfare mothers who burden society. In this new social imaginary, the Latina—taken from a journalist's photograph of an Ecuadorian woman—supports democracy and self-empowerment as indicated by the repeated X, a sign of her past voting record. The image of a dark-brown-skinned woman who casts her ballot while also caring for a child requires new mental calculations: Latinas are politically informed, active, and at the same time caretakers; they repeatedly engage in democracy, and they do so to maintain their liberties and ensure their children's future liberties.

The poster is a unique articulation of Latina autonomy and intellect coupled with motherhood and leadership. The series title, Women's Work Is Never Done, an old adage, calls attention to the economic exploitation of women and particularly women of color, but an ironic twist of meaning changes it into a description of women's leadership. Latina leadership is never done because the Latina's knowledge is needed to ensure society's future survival and democracy. Latinas must protect the world from those unwilling or unable to participate in a democratic society and childrearing. Is López pointing her finger at Wilson and his xenophobia? At deadbeat fathers? At cynics who forego democratic participation? I suggest that López's multivalent consciousness allows for a critique of each: it is an antiracist, antisexist, anti-imperialist, and pro-participatory democracy message.

**Figure 10.** Yolanda M. López, *Your Vote Has Power*, from Women's Work Is Never Done series, 1997. Silkscreen, 24 × 20 inches. Reproduced with the permission of the artist.

Another poster from this series also joins activism and labor of women across time and space. *Homenaje a Dolores Huerta* is a silkscreen print that commemorates three decades of women's labor in the fields, women's leadership, and the continued struggle for workers' rights and dignity (fig. 11). Repairing the damage of patriarchal authority, López pairs Huerta, as the symbol of historic UFW activism, with California broccoli workers, who represent the contemporary fight for safe labor conditions and economic justice. Four Latinas, wearing hats, scarves, and gloves to protect themselves from pesticides and the sun, dominate the center and right side of the print. They gaze away as if to suggest apprehension, up as if to imply hope, and down as if to document their exhaustion. These women are not present to pay respect to Huerta. Their labor is a testimony—women's work in the fields, on the picket lines, and in the union halls is never done. The poster is a bitter reminder of the ongoing battle and endless labor of women; for this reason, López venerates the history and presence of Latina activists and fieldworkers.

Perhaps the most compelling composition of antisexism, antiracism, and anticapitalist exploitation is the installation *The Nanny* (fig. 12). The installation is set into a corner and makes use of the perpendicular walls. A grey uniform hangs on a white screen. On either side of the screen are two advertisements, one for the wool industry and the other for travel to Mexico on Eastern Airlines; both degrade dark-skinned indigenous Mexican women by contrasting them to light-skinned white, beautiful, and smiling women (Pérez 2007). The installation challenges viewers to consider the

**Figure 11.** Yolanda M. López, *Homenaje a Dolores Huerta*, from Women's Work Is Never Done series, 1995. Silkscreen, 20 × 20 inches. Reproduced with the permission of the artist.

**Figure 12.** Yolanda M. López, *The Nanny*, from Women's Work Is Never Done series, 1994. Mixed-media installation. Reproduced with the permission of the artist.

so-called hidden labor of Latina domestic workers and the matrix of racism and sexism that undergirds the low wages paid to these workers.

An analysis of the uniform, however, suggests that López is articulating the nanny's potential political consciousness. The uniform has several images silkscreened or drawn on the fabric: Guadalupe covers a pocket on the chest; a naked infant, taken from a portrait of the artist's son, is placed in the lower register, near the womb; a plumed serpent emerges from the hip pocket; and the necklace of Coatlicue is drawn around the bodice. A necklace of human hearts and hands symbolically indicates female power over life and death. A cultural nationalist reading would presume that the nanny is, therefore, an Aztec female goddess.

But López does not allow the viewer to romanticize the nanny and turn her into the all-powerful preconquest goddess. The romantic or sentimental interpretation is blocked by the arrangement on the floor. A large white laundry basket contains dirty clothes, toys, and objects to remind the viewer that the nanny works in two households. This double labor provides some economic support for her own family, but because of her low wages and physically demanding work, it also ensures a distance between the nanny and her own children. Coming home late at night, she is simply too tired to enjoy leisure time or play with her children. If her power to create life is doubled, so is her labor. The basket also illustrates the harsh realities of domestic work. The nanny washes the clothes and dishes, cleans the house, and cares for the employer's children. She is asked to perform other duties, but usually for no extra remuneration.

The romantic impression of the nanny is further dissolved by a color reproduction of the airline ad, placed on the floor near the basket of dirty clothes and thus within the space of the nanny's world. López places a cutout of the light-skinned smiling woman near a cutout of the dark-skinned woman (fig. 13). Between them is a magazine on Mexican cuisine, and the smiling white woman's hand gestures toward the magazine as if to offer it to the indigenous woman. The extended hand and the magazine signify the double consciousness of the nanny. She is aware of the way she is viewed by her middle-class white female employer. She cannot escape the patronizing gaze or degraded position. While the nanny is paid to labor in the home of white middle-class families, her knowledge of her own heritage, symbolically represented by the magazine on Mexican cuisine, is insufficient or lacking. The white woman is the authority or expert who knows best and must teach the nanny how to do her job. This double consciousness surfaces through daily exchanges—the small and large gestures of racial superiority—in which middle-class employers instruct their nannies in cooking, cleaning, and caring for children. The presumed ignorance that necessitates these instructions serves to justify the low wages the nanny is paid. From this experience of overlapping sexism, racism, and economic inequality, the nanny develops a critical consciousness of her condition.

**Figure 13.** Yolanda M. López, *The Nanny* (detail), from Women's Work Is Never Done series, 1994. Mixed-media installation. Reproduced with the permission of the artist.

## "ORDINARY WOMEN" AS THE PROPOSAL

López's investigation of images is part of a larger Chicana feminist movement to locate and create alternative identities for Mexican-origin women. It is an aesthetic method that emerges from her upbringing, her activism in the social movements of the 1960s and 1970s, and her training in graduate school. Her formal education honed an existing antisexist and antiracist orientation, but it also provided her with a language for the ways in which she would look at, analyze, and deconstruct images. That is, her aesthetic productions are evidence of shifting strategies against containment, submission, erasure, and absence. The work defies the nationalist presumption of a singular or homogeneous citizen and the fantasy of the neoliberal nation-state's promise to guarantee liberty and equality. In formulating a critique of the potent figure of the Virgin of Guadalupe and offering alternatives for women, López paralleled in some sense the work of other Chicana feminists engaged in recuperating historical figures known as "monstrous women," such as La Malinche (Malintzin Tenepal, the so-called mistress and translator for Hernán Cortés) and La Llorona (the weeping woman who cries for her dead children).[10] Yet unlike recuperations of La Malinche and La Llorona, which uncover valuable skills, honor survival strategies, or simply acknowledge the ways in which patriarchy or colonialism have injured, erased, or elided these historical women, López's renderings of Guadalupe did not point to *la virgencita*'s endearing qualities. On the contrary, she highlighted the ways that Guadalupe functioned to support the subordination of Latinas within the home, church, and society.

This divergence is significant. While Chicana and Chicano artists such as Yreina D. Cervántez, Rupert García, Celia Herrera Rodríguez, Santa Barraza, René Yáñez, and Amalia Mesa-Bains created tributes to Frida Kahlo, La Malinche, La Llorona, Emiliano Zapata, Dolores del Rio, and other Mexican figures in order to recuperate a historical and cultural legacy, López invoked Guadalupe to question her meaning for contemporary Latinas.[11] She was not interested in recovering the previously lost qualities of Guadalupe that may have been subordinated by racism or sexism. According to López, Guadalupan iconography functions to support these ideologies.[12] López raises the questions: What does Guadalupe permit for Chicanas and Mexican women? Does the long gown represent control? What is the meaning of her posture? Does it signify her passivity? Does her virginity idealize motherhood within Chicano and Mexican communities?

Through an investigation of Guadalupan iconography, López recovered "ordinary women" and expanded popular representations of Chicanas and Mexican women by depicting them at work, engaged in activity without a man, or aging and near death. They are distinctly unglamorous. She did not wish to portray the predictable and romantic image of the folkloric Chicana with braids, peasant blouse, and *juaraches*, an image that reinforces the Spanish fantasy heritage made popular by European and Eureopan American settlers in the Southwest. Nor did she invoke the urban aesthetics of Chicano nationalism by showing the loyal woman in the arms of her cholo or pachuco. In both cases, Chicana autonomy and diversity is invisible, hidden, or denied. Therefore López created women of marked plainness and banality, and her intentional compositions avoid the heterosexist male gaze and draw out the power, beauty, and wisdom of women.

López depicted women of various ages, sizes, occupations, skin colors, cultural identities, and connections (or not) to men. Her proposal for Chicana womanhood emphasizes multiplicity and complexity and challenges the singular gendered subject of Chicano nationalism, La Chicana. Now acknowledged as a problematic ideology, Chicano nationalism structured solidarity and unity through the heterosexual family, and like other feminists, López did not support this ideology. Several factors influenced her ability to question the romantic image of the Chicano family and community. As a child, she witnessed two women, Margaret and Victoria, take responsibility for and control of their households. While organizing in the Mission District, she saw firsthand the gender inequality within the movement as well as the material differences throughout the Chicano community. Her objective, therefore, was to portray the diversity of Chicana womanhood. The multiple subject positions conveyed in her work depict survival under the forces of sexism, racism, and political and economic injustice. Her consistent compositions of women without men implicitly resist heteronormative constructions of women. By expanding the space for challenges against heteronormativity, López also opens up the possibility for discursive and aesthetic interventions against homophobia and affirmations of lesbian desire.

Making use of various tactics and ideological positions, her work belongs within, and in some regions predates, the artistic and cultural projects that express oppositional consciousness. It is a mobile and contingent art strategically critical of the images and institutions that have provided her with a material and aesthetic foundation. It is the oppositional mode that allows for disidentification and countermemory; without it López could not construct a proposal for female subjectivities, racial equity, transnational solidarity, class consciousness, or self-determination. As Chela Sandoval argues, oppositional consciousness emerges from everyday strategies of survival, and López began to articulate these strategies in the early 1970s through quotidian images of working women: the voter, the seamstress, the nursing mother, and the runner, to name a few (1991, 3).

The rejection of an image and its message relies upon oppositional consciousness, especially when the deconstruction of the master narrative builds toward new meanings. When López takes apart or analyzes an image, she turns to the oppositional mode to aesthetically express a multitude of displacements. The artist sees the previously unseen, looks beyond the icon, and pulls out new forms and symbols. Similar to the work of Emory Douglas, López's conceptual projects make the unreal real; she takes the previously unimaginable social bodies of Chicanas and Mexican women and figuratively expresses a new reality. By moving into the realm of what is unthinkable—or at least unimaginable to heteronormative patriarchy, racism, classism, imperialism, and other institutions of oppression—López calls up countermemory, that is, histories and pasts not yet told by or not acknowledged within these institutions and systems. The open hand holding a broken chain on the cover of *¡Basta Ya!* was an example of this countermemory, as the battle against social and political freedom had not yet been won. Such is also the case in *Your Vote Has Power*, since white privilege and supremacy cannot imagine an intelligent, fertile Latina who regularly participates in democracy. Nor can patriarchy envision a Chicana who controls her own body with ease, as in *Portrait of the Artist as the Virgin of Guadalupe*. American myths of Manifest Destiny and immigrant assimilation cannot admit to the realities of annexation and extermination of indigenous populations, but López presents this countermemory in *Illegal Alien*.

Moreover, the aesthetic political project of deconstruction consistently acknowledges the viewer, the author, the message, and the channel or medium by which the message is conveyed. This semiotic venture is one that supports López's avoidance of romanticism or sentimentalism. Each work pulls the viewer back to the construction of the object, forcing her or him to reconcile and ultimately abandon the celebratory relationship to the image or a sentimental reading of the artist. López's grandmother or the reference to *las abuelitas* may tug at our heartstrings, but the portrait of Victoria from the Guadalupe triptych as well as other portraits of López's grandmother are ruthlessly honest in their references to death, its inevitability or its nearness. Likewise, *The Nanny* requires us to accord dignity to domestic workers but it does not romanticize their labor conditions. The installation, with its laundry basket of dirty clothes and bottles of cleaning solution, suggests that the nanny is hired to care for children but is required to perform other domestic chores as well. The tableau prompts a mental consideration of what it is like to clean other people's dirty laundry or care for other people's children while your own are left alone. Similarly, in *Homenaje a Dolores Huerta*, the women farmworkers are our contemporary warriors in the battle for better wages and working conditions, but it is difficult to become celebratory about their position since the scarves covering the women's faces and the rubber gloves protecting their hands convey the dangers of pesticides. López has no tolerance for the social detachment that can emerge from sentimentality and romanticism.

The power of her work also stems from its complexity, as López uses these aesthetic articulations to challenge overlapping systems of subordination and control. Oppositional consciousness allows for a tactical maneuver against these interlocking systems of dispossession. Within one aesthetic project, López can voice cultural nationalism and simultaneously outline its limitations for women. Or she measures racism as it functions to support imperialism in Latin America but does not flatten the differences among Latino populations. She turns away from heterosexist patriarchal assumptions that only value women in their relationships to men, as mothers, daughters, or wives, but she never disowns the mother. Her work is never about a singular social position or form of injustice; it inhabits the matrix of domination and privilege, acknowledging that her own Chicana identity carries more political value than her grandmother's undocumented status. Within Chicano communities, López recognizes the authority carried by images of *las abuelitas*, and her compositions aim to undermine the romanticization of the ancestors or the appropriation of indigenousness.

In short, she proposes new subjectivities but encourages Chicanas to invent themselves again and again as she questions the image, its context, and what it accomplishes for them. The project is never static. Underscoring López's art is a pedagogy of liberation, and the method of deconstruction is a tool that can be applied to multiple representations, those created by Mexican-origin people and those created by non-Mexicans.

Finally, because the site of recuperation is the Chicana and Chicano body, her political project need not depend on the neoliberal nation-state or other sites or sources of regulation. The subjects of López's work wait for no one, and yet the artist would be the first to question the utopia imagined by the active or self-possessed female figure. After all, her mother's body behind the industrial sewing machine is not in perfect health, and the nanny she brings to public attention must still divide her time between her own children and those whom she is paid to tend. López is uncomfortable with sentimental projections onto her mother and grandmother, even onto herself, and she consistently argues for the valuation of "ordinary women," not the female superheroes who manage work and kids, fight for workers' rights, and still have time for themselves. The viewer may find joy and hope in the images, but the celebration of new forms of Chicana subjectivity need not arise from idealization. This is her "proposal" (López 2007).

## *Acknowledgements*

The wisdom and experience that Yolanda M. López shared with me is so precious; I continue to seek outlets that allow me to share it. I am deeply grateful to her. Colin Gunckel's editorial wand made magic; it is possible to repeat Wendy Belcher's spell and I am thankful. Anonymous reviewers at *Aztlán* made the work stronger. Finally, I acknowledge Tiffany Ana López for tutoring me in the fine art of effective argumentation. All errors are mine.

## NOTES

Reprinted with permission from Karen Mary Davalos, *Aztlán: A Journal of Chicano Studies* 34:2 (Fall 2009): 35–66.

1. *Portrait of the Artist as the Virgin of Guadalupe* was used to illustrate reviews, press announcements, and critical analysis of major traveling exhibitions, such as *Chicano Art: Resistance and Affirmation, 1965–1985* and *The Once and Future Goddess*, as well as regional group shows of Chicana visual arts, such as *Chicana Voices and Visions* at SPARC. Furthermore, it is typically reproduced and made to represent all of Chicana and Chicano art in major art history textbooks. Some works by López have been published with various titles; in this essay, I use the titles that López herself preferred.

2. The author's two-day interview with López was conducted in Los Angeles in 2007, and the transcript is housed at the UCLA Chicano Studies Research Center Library and Archive.

3. The survey was published in 2003, four years before the first scholarly book on Gronk was published. See Benavides (2007).

4. Although I do not have the space to address the significance of intersectionality as the major paradigm to advance the fields of ethnic and feminist studies since the 1980s, the insertion of race, class, gender, and sexuality challenges the assumed sameness among mainstream feminists, cultural nationalists, and imperialists. Moreover, the acknowledgment of multiple subjectivities interrogates disciplinary conventions in the humanities and social sciences. See also Davalos (2008a).

5. Betty LaDuke (1986) produced the first major scholarly analysis of Yolanda M. López's work, including two series of the MFA exhibition in 1978, that have rarely been exhibited or critically examined since then. See also LaDuke (1994).

6. Yolanda and her sisters were allowed to attend a Catholic church on their own, but her connection to Catholicism ended when a priest refused to bless one sister who died at age twenty-two in a car accident (López 2007).

7. This section benefits from rigorous original research by Cordova (2005), Ferreira (2003), and T. F. Sandoval (2002).

8. López (2007) acknowledges that Arturo Madrid helped her directly to secure the highly coveted Ford Foundation scholarship.

9. The titles are written here as they appear in López's 1978 MFA exhibition brochure. In some other publications on the artist, the shorter titles in brackets are used for figures 7–9.

10. On La Malinche, see Romero and Harris (2005) and Del Castillo (1977). On La Llorona, see Cano Alcalá (2001), Alarcón (1990, 1998), and Anzaldúa (1998). For the quoted phrase, see Chavoya (2006, 93).

11. Carla Trujillo (1998) offers to recuperate Guadalupe for lesbian Chicana feminists, but she does so by questioning the meaning of the Virgin for contemporary women, much as does López.

12. Although López is not interested in recuperating Guadalupe, she uses works such as *Nuestra Madre* (1981–88) to uncover "the thin veil of Christianity" by "superimposing an image of an actual Aztec statue from the state of Coxcatlán, Puebla over the Virgin's radiant mandorla." Most scholars identify the statue as a depiction of Tonantzin or Coatlicue, Nahuatl goddesses known for their powers to create and extinguish life. The first quote comes from López (2007) and the second from Villaseñor Black (forthcoming).

## WORKS CITED


Alarcón, Norma. 1990. "The Theoretical Subject(s) of *This Bridge Called My Back* and Anglo-American Feminism." In *Making Face, Making Soul/Haciendo Caras: Creative and Critical Perspectives by Feminists of Color,* edited by Gloria Anzaldúa, 356–69. San Francisco: Aunt Lute.

———. 1998. "Chicana Feminism: In the Tracks of 'The' Native Woman." In *Living Chicana Theory*, edited by Carla Trujillo, 371–82. Berkeley, CA: Third Woman Press.

Anzaldúa, Gloria. 1987. *Borderlands/La Frontera: The New Mestiza.* San Francisco: Aunt Lute.

———. 1998. "Chicana Artists: Exploring *Nepantla, el Lugar de la Frontera.*" In *The Latino Studies Reader: Culture, Economy, and Society*, edited by Antonia Darder and Rodolfo D. Torres, 163–69. Malden, MA: Blackwell.

Benavidez, Max. 2007. *Gronk.* A Ver: Revisioning Art History, vol. 1. Los Angeles: UCLA Chicano Studies Research Center Press. Distributed by University of Minnesota Press.

Butler, Judith. 1993. *Bodies That Matter: On the Discursive Limits of "Sex."* New York: Routledge.

Cano Alcalá, Rita. 2001. "From Chingada to Chingona: La Malinche Redefined, or a Long Line of Hermanas." *Aztlán: A Journal of Chicano Studies* 26, no. 3: 33–62.

Chabram-Dernersesian, Angie. 1994. "And, Yes . . . The Earth Did Part: On the Splitting of Chicana/o Subjectivity." In *Building with Our Hands: New Directions in Chicana Studies*, edited by Adela de la Torre and Beatríz M. Pesquera, 34–56. Berkeley: University of California Press.

———. 2006. "I Throw Punches for My Race, but I Don't Want to Be a Man: Writing Us—Chica-nos (Girl, Us) / Chicanas—into the Movement Script." In *The Chicana/o Cultural Studies Reader*, edited by Angie Chabram-Dernersesian, 165–82. New York: Routledge.

Chavoya, C. Ondine. 2006. "Malcriada: Delilah Montoya, Photographer." In *Women Boxers: The New Warriors*, 90–93. Photographs by Delilah Montoya and essays by María Teresa Márquez and C. Ondine Chavoya. Houston: Arte Público.

Cordova, Cary. 2005. "The Heart of the Mission: Latino Art and Identity in San Francisco." PhD diss., University of Texas, Austin.

Davalos, Karen Mary. 2008a. "Sin Vergüenza: Chicana Feminist Theorizing." In "Chicana Feminism," special issue, *Feminist Studies* 32, no. 1-2: 151–71.

———. 2008b. *Yolanda M. López.* A Ver: Revisioning Art History, vol. 2. Los Angeles: UCLA Chicano Studies Research Center Press. Distributed by University of Minnesota Press.

Del Castillo, Adelaida R. 1997. "Malintzin Tenépal: A Preliminary Look into a New Perspective." In *Essays on La Mujer*, edited by Rosaura Sánchez and Rosa Martinez, 124–49. Los Angeles: Chicano Studies Center Publications.

Ferreira, Jason Michael. 2003. "All Power to the People: A Comparative History of Third World Radicalism in San Francisco, 1968–1974." PhD diss., University of California, Berkley.

Gadon, Elinor W. 1989. *The Once and Future Goddess: A Symbol for Our Time.* San Francisco: Harper and Row.

Gaspar de Alba, Alicia. 1998. *Chicano Art Inside/Outside the Master's House: Cultural Politics and the CARA Exhibition*. Austin: University of Texas Press.

Goldman, Shifra M. 1990. "The Iconography of Chicano Self-Determination: Race, Ethnicity, and Class." *Art Journal* 49, no. 2: 167–73.

González, Rita. 2003. *An Undocumented History: A Survey of Index Citations for Latino and Latina Artists*. CSRC Research Report 2. Los Angeles: UCLA Chicano Studies Research Center Press.

Inda, Jonathan Xavier. 2000. "Performativity, Materiality, and the Racial Body." *Latino Studies Journal* 11, no. 3: 74–99.

Joysmith, Claire. 1995. "Chicana Writers: Recovering a Female Mexican Legacy." *Voices of México: Mexican Perspectives on Contemporary Issues* 32 (July–September): 39–44.

Keale, Susan Britt. 2000. "Issues of Female Mobility in Yolanda López's *Artist as the Virgin of Guadalupe*." Master's thesis, California State University, Chico.

LaDuke, Betty. 1986. "Trivial Lives: Artists Yolanda López and Patricia Rodríguez." *Trivia: A Journal of Ideas*, no. 8 (Winter): 74–84.

———. 1994. "Yolanda Lopez: Breaking Chicana Stereotypes." *Feminist Studies* 20, no. 1: 117–30.

Lipsitz, George. 2001. "Not Just Another Social Movement: Poster Art and the Movimiento Chicano." In *Just Another Poster? Chicano Graphic Arts in California / ¿Solo un cartel mas? Artes gráficas chicanas en California*, edited by Chon Noriega, 71–90. Santa Barbara: University Art Museum, University of California.

López, Yolanda M. 1978. *Yolanda M. López: Works 1975–1978*. MFA exhibition brochure. La Jolla, CA: Mandeville Center for the Arts.

———. 2007. Interview by author, Los Angeles, March 22–23.

Mazurana, Dyan Ellen. 1999. "Uprising of Las Mujeres: A Feminist and Semiotic Analysis of Mexicana and Chicana Art." PhD diss., Clark University, Worcester, MA.

Mulvey, Laura. 1975. "Visual Pleasure and Narrative Cinema." *Screen* 16, no. 3: 6–18.

Orenstein, Gloria Feman. 1996. "Recovering Her Story: Feminist Artists Reclaim the Great Goddess." In *The Power of Feminist Art: The American Movement of the 1970s, History and Impact*, edited by Norma Broude, Mary D. Garrard, and Judith K. Brodsky, 174–89. New York: H. N. Abrams.

Pérez, Laura Elisa. 2007. *Chicana Art: The Politics of Spiritual and Aesthetic Altarities*. Durham, NC: Duke University Press.

Romero, Rolando, and Amanda Nolacea Harris, eds. 2005. *Feminism, Nation and Myth: La Malinche*. Houston: Arte Público.

Sandoval, Chela. 1991. "U.S. Third World Feminism: The Theory and Method of Oppositional Consciousness in the Postmodern World." *Genders* 10 (Spring): 1–24.

———. 2000. *Methodology of the Oppressed*. Minneapolis: University of Minnesota Press.

Sandoval, Tomás Francisco, Jr. 2002. "Mission Stories, Latino Lives: The Making of San Francisco's Latino Identity, 1945–1970." PhD diss., University of California, Berkeley.

Stott, Annette. 1995. "Transformative Triptychs in Multicultural America." *Art Journal* 57, no. 1: 55–63.

Tapia, Ruby C. 2001. "What's Love Got to Do with It? Consciousness, Politics and Knowledge Production in Chela Sandoval's *Methodology of the Oppressed*." *American Quarterly* 53, no. 4: 733–43.

Trujillo, Carla. 1998. "La Virgen de Guadalupe and Her Reconstruction in Chicana Lesbian Desire." In *Living Chicana Theory*, edited by Carla Trujillo, 214–31. Berkeley, CA: Third Woman Press.

Villa, Raúl Homero. 2000. *Barrio-Logos: Space and Place in Urban Chicano Literature and Culture*. Austin: University of Texas Press.

Villaseñor Black, Charlene. Forthcoming. "Inquisitorial Practices Past and Present: Artistic Censorship, the Virgin Mary, and St. Anne." In *Art, Piety and Destruction in the Christian West, 1500–1700*, edited by Virginia C. Raguin. Burlington, VT: Ashgate.

# V.

# SOCIAL MOVEMENTS, JUSTICE, AND POLITICS

# NEGOTIATING CÉSAR

## César Chávez in the Chicano Movement

JORGE MARISCAL

> We want radical change. Nothing short of radical change is going to have any impact on our lives or our problems. We want sufficient power to control our own destinies. This is our struggle.
>
> —César Estrada Chávez

An aggressive militancy, symbolized by the ubiquitous image of Ernesto Che Guevara, pervaded the discourse and activities of the Chicano movement in the late 1960s in the Southwest. This militancy is visible in the fiery rhetoric of Reies López Tijerina, the charismatic leadership of Rodolfo Corky Gonzales, and the paramilitary formations of the Brown and Black Berets. In this context, the figure of César Chávez and his philosophy of nonviolence strike us as incongruous.[1] Armando Navarro writes: "The militant actions of Tijerina and Gonzales, coupled with the nonviolent direct action of Chavez, provided role models for both students and barrio youth" (1995, 23).[2] Navarro is surely correct, yet in retrospect we are struck by the incompatibility of the different leadership styles practiced by *los jefes*. F. Arturo Rosales notes as much when he points out: "Interestingly, the leader of the farmworkers, César Chávez, contrasted sharply with other Chicano leaders. The former farmworker . . . did not possess an imposing figure; he did not swagger or project a tough persona as did many militant activists of the era. Chávez's short stature and soft-spoken, quiet demeanor was often mistaken for the stereotypical look of passivity rather than forceful leadership" (1997, 130–31).

For some contemporary observers of the Movimiento, Chávez was the necessary complement to the more traditional "warrior" styles of Corky Gonzales and López Tijerina. Three weeks before he was assassinated by law enforcement agents on August 29, 1970, *Los Angeles Times* reporter Ruben Salazar offered this analysis of the Chicano movement: "César is our only real leader . . . [Gonzales and Tijerina] rant and rave and threaten to burn the establishment down. That's good because most people won't

JORGE MARISCAL is professor emeritus at the University of California, San Diego. Among his publications are *Aztlán and Viet Nam: Chicano Experiences of the War* (University of California Press, 1999) and *Brown-Eyed Children of the Sun: Lessons from the Chicano Movement, 1965–1975* (University of New Mexico Press, 2005). He is editor of the forthcoming *To Serve the People: The Long Pilgrimage of LeRoy Chatfield.*

listen unless you rant and rave. But this provides the community with little more than emotional uplift; nothing palpable" (Gómez 1982, 501). In retrospect, Salazar's assertion that Gonzales and Tijerina produced no concrete gains for their communities and functioned merely as a rhetorical sideshow is open to debate. Ironically, even as moderates like Salazar designated Chávez as the only authentic Chicano leader, young activists criticized him for being too narrowly focused on one issue and too conciliatory toward traditional liberal organizations such as the Democratic Party.

In this essay I will trace the complex and often contradictory relationship between César Chávez and the various sectors of the Chicano movement during the crucial period of the American war in Southeast Asia.[3] To do so, I will draw upon the entire field of discursive practices that contributed to the construction of multiple images of Chávez and the ways in which these images were put to political use. Chávez's own self-fashioning, his public statements and actions, will make up one area of inquiry, but this will be complemented by journalistic, artistic, and literary representations of the leader as well as critiques from both the political right and the political left. By mapping the broader cultural field in order to understand what the figure of César Chávez signified for various groups, I do not adhere to the naive empiricist notion that so-called historical sources (archival documents, testimonials, and so forth) are somehow more authoritative (that is, "real") than cultural materials. A passage in a novel or a poem dedicated to La Causa, for example, may have had as much to do with the construction of Chávez as a powerful sign for the Movimiento as did the actualized practices of the fast and the march, themselves to a great extent political and artistic interventions rooted in Mexican cultural traditions. Rather than seeking access to "what really happened" during the movement period construed as a totalized and objective historical whole, I am interested in charting the ideological systems that generated a diverse array of organizational styles, political languages, and leaders.

The reinsertion of the public figure of César Chávez into the rich discursive archive that was the Vietnam War period will help us to understand the interplay among various sectors of the politicized Chicana/o community and the ways in which these sectors negotiated with Chávez as both leader and symbol. The contrast to which I alluded above between Chávez's public figure and those of other movement leaders, for example, produces on one level "points of incompatibility" (following Michel Foucault's archaeological method). However, what seem to be incompatible historical agents are in fact all consequences of the same general set of social relations or discursive constellation that I will call the "critique of liberalism." That diverse movement figures and organizations assumed different forms in their realization of that critique does not signify a "weakness" in the movement. According to Foucault's concept of discursive formations, the relationships among cultural and political objects or statements that appear to be in conflict are not gaps or flaws: "Instead of constituting a mere defect of coherence, they form an alternative . . . [and] are characterized as link points of systematization. . . . One describes it rather as a unity of distribution that opens a field of possible options, and enables various mutually exclusive architectures to appear side by side or in turn" (1972, 65–66). At issue, therefore, are not historical figures as metaphors or images created by subjective "perceptions" but rather the manner in which discursive objects participate in political projects and thereby exercise a direct impact on material conditions, in this instance as part of a major social movement created by ethnic Mexicans in the United States.[4]

By the time of the Delano grape strike in late 1965, the political, cultural, and economic project that was the National Farm Workers Association (NFWA), and later the United Farm Workers Organizing Committee (UFWOC) and the United Farm Workers (UFW), had already established the groundwork for the multiple forms of Chicana/o activism that emerged in the final years of the decade. Years before the full-blown Movimiento burst onto the historical stage, the NFWA had become a classic version of what Raymond Williams (1989) called a "militant particularism"—in which a group of workers in a specific geographical locale, faced with intolerable conditions, organize to change those conditions for the better. But the particularities of the farmworkers' struggle spoke to a wide range of related issues that affected virtually every Mexican American community in the United States during the Vietnam War period. As other militant particularisms developed across the Southwest, the UFW functioned as an affective link and practical training ground for movement organizations with diverse agendas. In a dialectical and often contradictory process, the union's project fed into an emergent cultural nationalism and provided it with a repertoire of symbols and tropes even as it worked against the construction of a sectarian ethnicity-based identity by insisting on multiethnic coalition building and international solidarity with workers around the world.[5]

By both underwriting and destabilizing a "resistance identity" designed to create a collective subject based on shared cultural traits ("our essentially different life style" invoked in the Plan de Santa Barbara [Muñoz 1989, 191]), the UFW indirectly assisted in the formulation of a more radical Chicana/o "project identity" that critiqued the entire structure of US capitalism at home and abroad (Castells 1997, 8). I will argue, therefore, that just as the Movimiento is inconceivable without the UFW, the most dramatic successes of the UFW are inconceivable without the Movimiento in its emergent stages within the broader radicalized condition of US society, especially among youth. For many non-Latino activists, the efforts of the UFW embodied a utopian project composed of diverse ethnic groups and classes. As one observer put it:

> Something remarkable has happened in the town of Delano, something that a scant few months ago no one foresaw. A pattern for a New America has emerged out of the chaos of a bitter labor dispute, the pattern of people of all races and backgrounds working and living together in perfect and unprecedented harmony. Idealistic people in other parts of America talk about this ideal; in Delano today it is working. When the strike began last September "Huelga" meant only that: "Strike." But something has happened along the way; "Huelga" has come to mean something more than "Strike"; it has come to mean cooperation, brotherhood, Love. (Nelson 1966, 122)

The distance between this statement, written in 1965, and the subsequent Summer of Love in 1967, the youth counter-culture, and the antiwar and Third World people's movements is not terribly great. The connection between César Chávez and the revolutionary period of the 1960s was perhaps best captured in the title of Peter Matthiessen's classic book first published in 1969: *Sal Si Puedes (Escape If You Can): Cesar Chavez and the New American Revolution.* According to Matthiessen's ambivalent characterization, this new "American Revolution" was an "American renaissance" led by young radicals whose "philosophical poverty and abrasive attitudes should not obscure the fact that these people are forming the front line in a *necessary* revolution" (2000, 113; emphasis in original).[6]

But how exactly did César Chávez fit into the panorama of 1960s radicalism? As we shall see, Chávez's unconventional leadership, drawing on religious and pacifist traditions, placed some Chicanos in the movement in the uncomfortable position of balancing the admiration they held for him with a preference many of them also held for warrior models of manhood. One of the more militant Chicano writers unfavorably compared Chávez to Che Guevara. Nephtalí de León's play, *¡Chicanos! The Living and the Dead!*, places Che in direct confrontation with Chávez's philosophy (represented by the character Manuel) and argues that nonviolence is of no use to Chicanos:

> Manuel: Yet there are many of us who had and still have faith. Cesar Chavez has faith and look how far he has advanced.
>
> Che (somewhat exasperated): And how far is that hermano? Don't our people still do stoop labor? Only it's by contract now. Now they are really true slaves, for they have told the yankee farmers: "We will sell our bodies and our souls to you, but only if you promise us you'll buy them!" He should have asked not for contracts to pick grapes or lettuce, but for contracts for an education and a preparation to cope with the technical-industrial age that now governs the world—an age that still enslaves him and his people. How different are California's farm laborers from the Chinese peasants who sweat their lives away stuck in their rice paddies? No, Manuel, my heart has bled for Cesar, a giant of a man, stuck by his children into that earth that enslaves him and his people. While America basks in plenty, our dear brown Saint starves with his brothers and sweats his life out for a contract that has chained them. (de León 1972a, 61–62)

The criticism voiced by el Che, one of the more powerful symbols of the Movimiento, is harsh but captures some of the tensions that existed in left-leaning activist circles with regard to the objectives of the UFW. Elsewhere in his writings, however, de León praises Chávez (without sarcasm) as a "modern prince of peace," "a very human man," and "one of those rare happenings that occur every time a people are oppressed and every time the universe and man join hands to yield us such a being" (1972b, 43). The contradiction in de León's writing underscores the dilemma Chávez presented to movement militants. What many of them did not understand well were the origins of Chávez's spiritual praxis and its function in a time of revolutionary rhetoric, police brutality in the barrios, and massive military aggression in Southeast Asia.

In a curious column that appeared in an issue of the UFW newspaper *El Malcriado* (52: 22), it was announced that the paper's official logo would be Don Quixote (fig. 1). Wearing a UFW button on his lapel and with the union eagle on his shield, this farmworker version of Cervantes's *caballero andante* would be "a Quixote who represents accurately the spirit of our struggle, always in good humor in spite of the risk." According to the unnamed author:

**Figure 1.** Andy Zermeño, drawing of Don Quixote with the UFW Eagle. Published in *El Malcriado*, no. 52, December 29, 1966. Used by permission of the artist.

> Quixote symbolizes the spirit of man which always believes in human strength; in defense of the weak; in protection of women and children; in sacrifice for one's fellow-men; in the struggle against evil; in the fight against the powerful in favor of the disinherited; he represents these and many similar things, in the spirit of battle even when there are not enough resources for it, in the great causes in which man has involved himself.

What is interesting about this attempt to link the traditional image of Don Quixote to the farmworker movement is that it invokes both idealism and militancy at the same time.[7] Although Cervantes's character never killed anyone, his actions were at times quite violent, and at one point in the 1605 novel he is denounced by another character whose leg he has broken. The column in *El Malcriado* develops the theme of militancy by devoting some space to Cervantes himself. It specifically emphasizes his career as a soldier and participant in the battle of Lepanto, the 1571 naval conflict in which Catholic forces defeated the Muslim Ottoman Turks. According to the UFW author, Lepanto was "the first act in the establishment of what we now call 'Western Civilization.'"

Cervantes and Don Quixote, then, represented both the defense of traditional Catholic/Western values and the idealistic struggle to defend the disenfranchised. Whatever the traces of Eurocentrism that informed this interpretation of Don Quixote, the emphasis for the UFW writer fell primarily upon the call to service and social activism. The key ideological link, therefore, was to be found in the idea of "militancy," a concept Chávez himself had written about in reference to Dr. Martin Luther King Jr.: "His nonviolence was that of action—not that of one contemplating action" (1968a, 5). Chávez's distinction is between the "philosopher of nonviolence" and the active practitioner of nonviolence in the pursuit of justice. It was this latter idea that would inform Chávez's entire career.

## HYBRID AND HYPER-MASCULINITIES

> We must respect all human life, in the cities and in the fields and in Vietnam. Nonviolence is the only weapon that is compassionate and recognizes each man's value.
>
> —César Estrada Chávez

In terms of his political persona, Chávez presented urban Chicanas and Chicanos with a form of masculinity virtually unknown outside the Catholicism of their *abuelitas*.[8] At its very core was the principle of "militant nonviolence." Seemingly an oxymoron, the phrase retains a commitment to social change but disassociates that commitment from aggression against other individuals or groups by incorporating a strong Christian-based empathy for the oppressor. Nonviolent change, therefore, is to be sought not only on the level of institutions but in the very attitudes of the antagonist. In their practical effects, Chávez's actions constructed a hybrid form of masculinity that combined "passive" elements most often linked by Western patriarchal structures to "feminine" subjectivities with a fearless determination that traditional gendered representations have reserved exclusively for "masculine" practices.

At the core of this hybrid agency is the belief that by resorting to physical violence the political activist is actually admitting his or her own weakness. A nonviolent approach requires a deeper and more sustained engagement. According to Chávez, "In some instances nonviolence requires more militancy than violence. Nonviolence forces you to abandon the shortcut in trying to make a change in the social order" (1969, 27). This is essentially what Martin Luther King Jr. advocated consistently throughout his career. Shortly before his death, Dr. King told an interviewer: "To be militant merely means to be demanding and to be persistent, and in this sense I think the nonviolent movement has demonstrated great militancy. It is possible to be militantly nonviolent" (Washington 1986, 661). In one of his most succinct definitions of nonviolence as he practiced it, Chávez articulated a similar view: "Our conviction is that human life and limb are a very special possession given by God to man and that no one has the right to take that away, in any cause, however just. . . . Also we are convinced that nonviolence is more powerful than violence. . . . We operate on the theory that men who are involved and truly concerned about people are not by nature violent. If they were violent they couldn't have that love and that concern for people" (1970, 1). As he would many times during his public life, Chávez argued that those who resort to violence do so because of their inability to organize their constituencies in an effective way.

Although neither Chávez's nor King's concept of nonviolence was as deeply wed to an elaborate religious and philosophical framework as was Mahatma Gandhi's method of *satyagraha* ("holding to truth"), in which the spiritual soul-force of existence triumphs over material reality, both men drew freely from Gandhi's practical methods.[9] Chávez's use of the fast, for example, combined Catholic practices with Gandhian ideas about self-purification. According to Gandhi's reading of the *Gita* and *Upanisads*, fasting ought not be used to produce direct political effects but rather to cleanse the sensory perceptions and strengthen the moral resolve of the subject and potentially facilitate a spiritual change of heart in the adversary.

In the Gandhian view, fasting as coercion designed to force specific political concessions was itself a form, albeit a lesser form, of violence, and ultimately could only produce a violent reaction (Borman 1986, 107).[10] Upon ending one of his more famous fasts on March 10, 1968, Chávez explained his use of the fast: "Some of you still wonder about its meaning and importance. It was not intended as a pressure against any growers. For that reason we have suspended negotiations and arbitration proceedings and relaxed the militant picketing and boycotting of the strike during this period. I undertook the fast because my heart was filled with grief and pain for the sufferings of farmworkers. The fast was first for me and then for all of us in this Union. It was a fast for nonviolence and a call to sacrifice" (1968c).[11] Three years later in an informal talk in which he elaborated on the negative consequences produced by the combination of large financial contributions and unions, he argued that the fast was an organizing tool of greater value than traditional fundraising. The fast modeled the sacrifice demanded of all supporters: "When you sacrifice, you force others to sacrifice. It's an extremely powerful weapon. When somebody stops eating for a week or ten days, people come and want to be part of that experience. Someone goes to jail and people want to help him. You don't buy that with money. That doesn't have any price in terms of dollars" (1971).

While Chávez modeled a Mexican American variation on Christian asceticism and studied the works of Gandhi, Aquinas, and St. Paul, young Chicano militants were reading Fanon and Che Guevara (Yinger 1975, 25).[12] Nonetheless, Chávez's rhetoric at times intersected with that of leaders elsewhere in the movement. In what seems an unlikely pairing, two photographs that shared the wall of Chávez's office at UFW headquarters were those of the pacifist Gandhi and of the armed revolutionary Emiliano Zapata. The word "revolution" had appeared in UFW documents as early as 1966, in Chávez's letter written before the march to Sacramento. With the Mexican Revolution as its primary inspiration, the letter portrayed Mexican Americans as the heirs to a tradition of insurgency, and invoked the historical fact that the Southwest was a conquered land whose original inhabitants had been colonized by foreigners: "Delano is [the farmworker's] 'cause,' his great demand for justice, freedom, and respect from a predominantly foreign cultural community in a land where he was first. The revolutions of Mexico were primarily uprisings of the poor, fighting for bread and for dignity. The Mexican American is also a child of the revolution. Pilgrimage, penance, and revolution. The pilgrimage from Delano to Sacramento has strong religio-cultural overtones. But it is also the pilgrimage of a cultural minority who have suffered from a hostile environment, and a minority who means business" (Yinger 1975, 106).[13] Chávez would claim that the religious underpinnings of his beliefs did not diminish the radical nature of his political objectives. The phrase "means business" invokes a more traditional form of masculinity premised upon the threat of physical action, but links it to religious practices associated with saintliness. The hybrid nature of Chávez's masculinity maintained these tensions in a precarious balance throughout the various stages of his public life.[14]

To "mean business" nonviolently was precisely what Dr. King had proposed in his use of the term "nonviolent gadflies" to describe militant activists. Taking the "gadfly" image associated with Socrates, King argued that to mean business, at least in the initial stages of a social movement, was to demand the attention of the powerful in order to shine light on the problems of the disempowered. According to the 1963 "Letter from the Birmingham Jail," nonviolent militancy, far from being a passive stance, was designed to create a crisis of consciousness within the ranks of the ruling majority: "Nonviolent direct action seeks to create such a crisis and establish such creative tension that a community that has constantly refused to negotiate is forced to confront the issue. It seeks so to dramatize the issue that it can no longer be ignored" (Washington 1986, 291). Less than two years later, he elaborated on the pedagogical goals of mass mobilization: "Our nonviolent direct action program has as its objective not the creation of tensions, but the surfacing of tensions already present. We set out to precipitate a crisis situation that must open the door to negotiation. I am not afraid of the words 'crisis' and 'tension.' I deeply oppose violence, but constructive crisis and tension are necessary for growth. . . . To cure injustices, you must expose them before the light of human conscience and the bar of public opinion, regardless of whatever tensions that exposure generates" (350).

César Chávez understood that the strategy of nonviolent militancy would expose to the light of day not only the plight of the invisible farm worker but the conditions of the vast majority of ethnic Mexicans in the United States. In the 1969 "Good Friday Letter" addressed to a California grower who had accused the UFW of using violent tactics, Chávez presented a brilliant analysis not only of the farmworkers' situation but also of the demands and aspirations of Chicanos and Chicanas in urban centers across the Southwest. Three sections in particular suggest the ways in which Chávez's analysis participated in the discursive field I have called the "critique of liberalism." In light of these correspondences, Chávez's occasional reluctance to refer to himself as a Chicano movement leader can be seen as unfortunate; they reveal his profound understanding of what the Movimiento, in all of its diverse sectors, took to be its principal issues and political objectives:

> The color of our skins, the languages of our cultural and native origins, the lack of formal education, the exclusion from the democratic process, the numbers of our slain in recent wars—all these burdens generation after generation have sought to demoralize us, to break our human spirit. But God knows that we are not beasts of burden, we are not agricultural implements or rented slaves, we are men. . . .
>
> While we do not belittle or underestimate our adversaries, for they are the rich and the powerful and possess the land, we are not afraid nor do we cringe from the confrontation. We welcome it! We have planned for it. We know that our cause is just, that history is a story of social revolutions, and that the poor shall inherit the land. . . .
>
> We advocate militant nonviolence as our means for social revolution and to achieve justice for our people, but we are not blind or deaf to the desperate and moody winds of human frustration, impatience and rage that blow among us. Gandhi himself admitted that if his only choices were cowardice or violence, he would choose violence. Men are not angels and the time and tides wait for no man. Precisely because of these powerful human emotions, we have tried to involve masses

of people in their own struggle. Participation and self-determination remain the best experience of freedom; and free men instinctively prefer democratic change and even protect the rights guaranteed to seek it. Only the enslaved in despair have need of violent overthrow. (quoted in Yinger 1975, 112)

If Che Guevara had dreamed of a society in which "new men and women" would fundamentally transform the nature of capitalist social relations, Chávez saw the union as a means to decolonize the farmworkers' subjectivity and sufficiently transform surrounding conditions, albeit without addressing the farmworkers' place in the relations of production. Chávez argued that farmworkers, with their "natural dignity" restored, would no longer be at the mercy of the corporate bosses: "Workers whom they previously had treated as dumb members of a forgotten minority suddenly are blooming as capable, intelligent persons using initiative and showing leadership" (1968b, 9). But the newfound agency of the farmworker would not necessarily be shaped by the dominant ethic of capitalist individualism, which led necessarily to self-interest and personal rivalries, but rather by the idea of community solidarity and service. Speaking on the occasion of the historic contract signings in the summer of 1970, Chávez said of his union members: "They found that only through dedication to serving mankind—and in this case to serving the poor and those who are struggling for justice—only in that way could they find themselves" (Yinger 1975, 87).

The religious underpinnings of Chávez's message resonated with the tenets of liberation theology as they had been formulated in the 1960s in Latin America and elsewhere. Pope John XXIII and Vatican Council II had attempted to shift the role of the Church toward service of the poor, and liberation theologians drew upon thinkers in both the Christian and Marxist traditions in order to formulate a powerful concept of religious activism or "orthopraxis" as opposed to abstract orthodoxy (G. Gutiérrez 1971). In fundamental ways, both the Vatican II reforms and Chávez's project embodied the earliest forms of Mexican Catholicism in which the role of the indigenous poor took precedence over institutionalized religion. One of the earliest treatises on la Virgen de Guadalupe, for example, depicts a scene in which Juan Diego, the indigenous man who had seen the Virgin on the hill at Tepeyac, complains that because he is a commoner (*macehual*) he is ill suited to carry the Virgin's message to the bishop. The Virgin replies: "Do listen, my youngest child. Be assured that my servants and messengers to whom I entrust it to carry my message and realize my wishes are not high-ranking people. Rather it is highly necessary that you yourself be involved and take care of it. It is very much by your hand that my will and wish are to be carried out and accomplished" (Sousa, Poole, and Lockhart 1998, 71). The idea that it is the poor who carry out God's work was at the core of Chávez's public style and it resonated with the foundational working-class membership and principles of the vast majority of Chicana/o movement organizations.

Because of his conscious decision to draw upon Mexican Catholic iconography and rituals, Chávez would soon find himself in a position he had not anticipated and certainly did not seek. For some of his followers, Chávez became less a Don Quixote than a Christ figure who incarnated the saintly virtues of humility and service to the poor in a corrupt and immoral world. The beatification of Chávez coincided with

**Figure 2.** George Ballis, *César Chávez Ends Fast,* 1968. César Chávez and Robert Kennedy talk after Chávez ends his hunger strike on March 11. Copyright 1976 by George Ballis/Take Stock/The Image Works; image courtesy of The Image Works.

the elevation of the murdered Kennedy brothers as figures in the Mexican American imaginary. Chávez's association with Robert Kennedy, martyred in June 1968, served to increase each man's stature, and indeed Bobby Kennedy's role in the development of Chávez's national reputation cannot be underestimated. His ties to the UFW leader were captured perhaps most dramatically in the widely circulated account and photographs of Kennedy feeding Chávez a piece of bread and conversing with him as he ended his fast on March 10, 1968 (fig. 2).[15] Although Chávez met Kennedy for the first time in 1960, the two men actually spent very little time together over the ensuing years. Once Robert Kennedy was assassinated, however, the symbolism linking the two leaders took on an enhanced power.

## THE ELABORATION OF THE LEADER

Instrumental in the earliest representations of Chávez as the leader for whom La Raza had been waiting was playwright and Teatro Campesino founder Luis Valdez. In 1970 he told the Berkeley, California, newspaper *La Voz del Pueblo*: "Pero allí teníamos al líder esperando y no nos dábamos cuenta. Era César Chávez, y estaba allí consumiéndose a fuego lento, pobre como nosotros y hablándonos, sugiriéndonos lo que debíamos hacer—nunca ordenando—y poco a poco nos fuimos reuniendo en torno suyo . . . un hombre, en fin, que había sufrido en carne propia las vicisitudes de toda la Raza en los Estados Unidos" (*La Voz del Pueblo* 1970, 5). By this time, as the Delano grape strike was coming to a successful conclusion, the identification of Chavez with earlier holy figures was so great that California poet Ricardo C. Pérez (1970) could compose the following:

Con un libro de Gandhi en la mano
Cual héroe en un mundo putrefacto
Buscando la justicia en un pacto
Anda con alta frente el chicano.

Sufre como un hereje el desprecio
Sufre como un Cristo el martirio
Sufre por sufrir que es el precio
Del que ama la llama de amor, el lirio.

Pero grande en su humilde aspecto es
Y por todo lo que sinceramente cree
Porque es suya la única vía que

Es tocada por la redentora fe
Que hará todo humilde a la vez
Tan grande en heroísmo cual los Andes!

At once a Chicano "Everyman" and Christ himself, Pérez's Chávez is linked in the final stanza to all of Latin America and by implication to the struggles of Spanish-speaking communities throughout the hemisphere. The religious language of the poem ("la llama de amor, el lirio") taken from the Catholic mystic tradition, together with the reference to Gandhi, produce a tone of holiness, and establish Chávez as less a union organizer than a twentieth-century saint.

Other movement writers contributed to the canonization process. San Francisco poet Elías Hruska-Cortés (1973), for example, wrote:

Delano the strategy and César
César and Cristo and Victory
César and filipino hall and victory
Delano and Solidarity and People
Delano the boycott and victory
Delano the strike and César
                    the strike and victory
                                        huel-ga huel-ga huel-ga

Shortly after he ended his career as a movement attorney, candidate for sheriff of Los Angeles County, and all-around *vato loco*, Oscar Zeta Acosta solidified for the Chicana/o imaginary the image of Chávez the saint. Early in the 1973 novel *Revolt of the Cockroach People*, Acosta's literary alter ego makes a pilgrimage to Delano. As the character of the Brown Buffalo approaches the room in which Chávez has been fasting for twenty-five days, an air of other-worldliness permeates the scene: "I enter and close the door behind me. It is very dark. There is a tiny candle burning over a bed, illuminating dimly a wooden cross and a figure of La Virgen on the wall. My ears are buzzing. There is a heavy smell of incense and kerosene. I don't move. I hear nothing. I no longer have any idea of why I have come or what I will say. 'Is that you, Buffalo?' The voice is soft, barely audible" (Acosta 1989, 44). Seeking spiritual and political guidance, Buffalo is surprised to learn that Chávez is aware of his activities in Los Angeles: "In the darkness, I think again of his words. The Father of Chicanos, César Chávez, has heard of me" (45). For Acosta, then, the figure of Chávez functions as a powerful touchstone against which all other agendas and practices will be measured. Not only a saint, Chávez in Acosta's hands becomes the moral and ethical core of the Movimiento in stark contrast to the depravities of the Brown Buffalo and his associates. By giving his blessing to Acosta and "the Militants" in LA, César Chávez assumes his role at the symbolic center of movement history.[16]

In a concluding section of the novel the figure of Chávez reappears as a character witness for Corky Gonzales, who had been detained after the Chicano Moratorium, the antiwar demonstration that took place on August 29, 1970. Chávez's stature is intact, according to the narrator, who tells us: "They [Chávez and Gonzales] are number one and two in the Nation of Aztlán" (Acosta 1989, 249). But the Brown Buffalo himself has moved away from the ideal of nonviolence: "I have not seen Cesar since I first began in LA. He is still my leader, but I no longer worship him. I am pushing for Corky because when things go political, I will push for the more militant of the two. Corky laughs at me. He tells me that Cesar's work is more important than both of us combined. Speak for yourself, I tell him" (250). Given Acosta's real-life role as a movement participant, we must read this statement as more than a mere declaration made by a fictionalized character. The passage captures well the tension between Chávez's militant nonviolence and alternative Movimiento practices that viewed insurgency as necessarily linked to hypermasculine acts of physical aggression.

Even as militant nationalist and leftist groups in the movement mounted critiques of the strategies preferred by the UFW, right-wing attacks on Chávez proliferated as the union continued to achieve moderate success. Ironically, what bothered conservatives more than anything else was Chávez's public image as a Gandhi-like pacifist. In a vitriolic book aimed at discrediting Chávez, conservative writer Ralph de Toledano wrote: "A small man with an oversize messianic complex has put his mark on Delano. He has been able to do so by mobilizing in this small town the raw power of organized labor, the hysteria and psychosis of the New Left, and the pressure apparatus of the clergy" (1971, 16–17). Toledano, the son of Spanish immigrants to the United States, had made a career in Republican Party circles by writing laudatory biographies of J. Edgar Hoover and Richard Nixon. As an early incarnation of a "Hispanic intellectual" in the service of corporate and law enforcement interests, Toledano made it his business to represent the growers as the victims of the UFW's evil intentions.[17]

Other writers inclined to follow Toledano's lead sought to portray Chávez as just another corrupt union boss: "Chávez has been depicted as an almost Gandhiesque character, loving his fellow man, eschewing violence, calling for peaceful resolution of human problems. His detractors view him as a conniving labor czar who deliberately defrauded the grape pickers in order to aggrandize his labor union. Generally, this latter view seems more accurate and to the point, for it dwells on the ability of one man to manipulate others and to use what can best be described as shady tactics to achieve his ends" (Machado 1978, 99).[18] Such attempts to cast Chávez as a thug were doomed to fail despite backing from a well-funded public relations campaign sponsored by the growers. The right-wing and anti-Mexican John Birch Society ran a small cottage industry throughout the Vietnam War period whose sole objective was to produce attacks against Chávez and the UFW in books such as *Little Cesar and His Phony Strike* (Huck 1974) and *The Grapes: Communist Wrath in Delano* (Allen 1966).[19] One of the more hysterical efforts to link the UFW to a communist conspiracy was produced by Orange County, California, reporter John Steinbacher: "The young who follow a Chavez are not unlike the Narodniks, those bearded beatnik young of the Czarist regime, who helped to bring on the blood bath that led to the Red takeover of Russia. . . . The young follow a Hitler or a Stalin or a Kennedy—or a Chavez—in a mad lust for power through the darkling bye-ways of America" (1970, 128–29). Rhetorical flourishes such as this, the product of an almost irrational hatred of liberalism, remained on the margins of public discourse in the 1970s.[20] Even conservatives could only view the implication that Chávez was somehow equivalent to Hitler and Stalin as extreme.

But not only conservative Birchers, Republicans, and their hired "Hispanic" writers criticized Chávez. As I have demonstrated, activists within the various sectors of the Movimiento itself were at times at odds with Chávez's political stances. In the early years of the movement, the most contentious point had to do with the UFW's public statements regarding undocumented labor. Advocating strict immigration controls and a closed-border policy, Chávez, Dolores Huerta, and other union leaders hoped to deprive growers of a vast pool of potential strikebreakers. In his 1969 testimony before the congressional subcommittee on labor, Chávez referred to "illegals" and "green carders" as "natural economic rivals of those who become American citizens or who otherwise decide to stake out their future in this country" (Jensen and Hammerback 2002, 43). From the union's perspective, the logic of this position made sense but many movement activists viewed it as misguided and complicit with reactionary and anti-immigrant rhetoric and legislation. By the early 1970s the critique of the UFW on this issue reached a breaking point, primarily on account of threats by the Department of Justice to begin deporting undocumented workers. Chávez, sensing the growing discontent among many of his supporters, published a defense of "illegal aliens" in a 1974 letter to the *San Francisco Examiner*. But tensions on the issue continued unresolved, and Chávez himself angrily told an interviewer in *El Malcriado* that "most of the left attacking us has no experience in labor matters. They don't know what a strike is. . . . And they don't know because really they haven't talked to the workers" (quoted in D. Gutiérrez 1995, 199).[21] Beyond the specific issue of immigration, however, other differences of opinion emerged from within a movement that increasingly encompassed diverse ideologies and agendas.

As early as 1965, members of Tijerina's Alianza Federal de Mercedes had declared the philosophy of nonviolence to be less desirable than the actions taken by the black community in Los Angeles during the Watts riots. Alianza member Felix Martinez had visited both Watts and Delano in 1965, and upon his return to New Mexico he reported: "revolution speeds up evolution" (Navarro 1995, 24). In this view, Chávez's reformist agenda lacked the necessary urgency that drove alternative Chicano political programs. In his 1970 poem titled "Los caudillos," therefore, Tejano poet raúlrsalinas (1971, 74) could write:

In rich Delano vineyards
Chavez does his pacifist thing
"lift that crate
and pick them grapes"
stoop labor's awright—with God on your side.

Small wonder David Sanchez
impatient and enraged in L.A., dons a beret . . .

Tijerina, Indo-Hispano
you're our man.

From a more strictly leftist position, activist Froben Lozada complained: "And the pacifists want us to preach morality to them who have none!" (1968, 6). One labor and antiwar activist took a more pragmatic position with regard to Chávez's perceived pacifism: "They [UFW] have been able to win broad public support by demonstrating that it is their enemies who are violent. But in elevating nonviolence to an absolute principle, the union's leadership has unfortunately given up the right of the union to physically defend itself in any circumstances" (J. Pérez 1973, 13). For many Chicanos, self-determination would never be realized without the right to self-defense, given the high degree of racialized violence and economic exploitation that characterized institutional practices in the United States.

Other sectors of the movement found themselves in disagreement with UFW strategies. Chicano organizers struggling to create a third political party were particularly critical of Chávez for his unwavering allegiance to the Democratic Party. The union newspaper *El Malcriado* had stated repeatedly that John F. Kennedy would "always be our president," and as we have seen Robert Kennedy had given the union his support in public statements and appearances. For some of the founders of La Raza Unida Party (LRUP), therefore, Chávez's efforts to keep Chicanos in the Democrat camp were counterproductive if not outright "treason":

> [Chávez] would be doing a disservice to people about the crying need to break with the Democratic Party. He would be miseducating people, and it's a lot harder to educate people after they've been miseducated about what is necessary. . . . It would make it harder for us to talk about a Chicano party if Chavez was at the same time campaigning and registering people in the Democratic Party. And the truth of the matter is that this has already been tried again and again and nothing has come from it. Malcolm X made a very strong statement on this. He said, "Anyone who supports the Democratic Party after its record of oppression, and what it has done to our people, is not only a fool, but a traitor to his race." (Camejo 1970, 346)

The exaggerated rhetoric of the attack was certainly divisive and the use of Malcolm X's remark misleading and out of context. In practical terms, the tensions between LRUP and Chávez produced serious signs of disunity. Filmmaker Jesús Treviño reports that

Chávez turned down an invitation to attend the LRUP convention in 1972 because both José Ángel Gutiérrez and Corky Gonzales had made clear to him that they were displeased with the union's endorsement of Democratic candidate George McGovern (2001, 281). According to one account, several LRUP officials in the Texas delegation saw the break with Chávez as a necessary step in the eventual displacement of older organizers considered to be too accepting of the status quo and their replacement by younger, more radical leaders (Castro 1974, 96–111).

The criticisms of Chávez by some members of LRUP precluded potential alliances that could have furthered the movement's agenda. Historian Juan Gómez-Quiñones has summarized these unfortunate developments:

> For all his visibility and connections, La Raza Unida viewed Chavez negatively; absurdly, they felt he was negligent in pursuing broader Chicano issues or in demanding political concessions for Chicanos. To LRUP, Chavez was simply an arm of the Anglo political establishment; and allegedly he represented the traditional negotiating posture in politics, one that clashed with La Raza Unida's rhetorical emphasis on Chicano "self-determination." LRUP, however, overlooked UFW strength in California and the fact that they were seeking electoral office in the system for themselves. La Raza Unida was weakened by the inability to incorporate support from a prominent Chicano organization. (1990, 138)[22]

The question of whether or not the UFW was a "Chicano organization," however, depended on how the latter term was defined. On various occasions Chávez himself had declared that he was a union leader, not a leader in the Chicano movement. Some activists noted early on that Chávez was conspicuously absent from important movement events such as the Poor People's Campaign in 1968 or the 1970 Chicano Moratorium antiwar demonstration in Los Angeles.[23] Had they been readers of the *New Yorker*, young Chicano and Chicana activists would have been surprised by Chávez's comments in Peter Matthiessen's 1969 essays. Stressing the need to avoid narrow race-based nationalism, Chávez seemed to attack some of the basic principles of emergent Chicana/o identities:

> "I hear more and more Mexicans talking about la raza—to build up their pride, you know," Chavez told me. "Some people don't look at it as racism, but when you say 'la raza,' you are saying an anti-gringo thing, and it won't stop there. Today it's anti-gringo, tomorrow it will be anti-Negro, and the day after it will be anti-Filipino, anti-Puerto Rican. And then it will be anti-poor-Mexican, and anti-darker-skinned Mexican. . . . La raza is a very dangerous concept. I speak very strongly against it among the chicanos. At this point in the struggle, they respect me enough so that they don't emphasize la raza, but as soon as this is over they'll be against me, because I make fun of it, and I knock down machismo, too." (Matthiessen 1969b, 66; 2000, 178–79)[24]

Matthiessen's conversation with long-time UFW organizer LeRoy Chatfield about Chávez's attitude toward the movement might have added fuel to the fire. Chatfield remarked: "Everyone should be proud of what he is, of course, but race is only skin-deep. It's phony, and it comes out of frustration—the *la raza* people are not secure. They want to use Cesar as a symbol of their nationalism. But he doesn't want any part of it. He said to me just the other day, 'Can't they understand that that's just the way Hitler started?' A few months ago, a big foundation gave some money to a *la raza* group—they liked the outfit's sense of pride, or something—and Cesar really told them off" (Matthiessen 1969b, 69; 2000, 179).

It was moments like these that had the potential to strain the otherwise strong links between Chávez and younger Chicana/o radicals. Reflecting more than just a "generation gap" or even ideological differences, tensions arose around issues of leadership style and organizational structures. Veteran organizer Bert Corona, for example, recalled an argument between student militants at the University of California, Santa Barbara, and Chávez, in which the students complained about a lack of consultation despite the fact that they had provided the manpower for recent union pickets (1994, 261). When asked whether or not the organizing strategies of the Crusade for Justice were in conflict with those of the UFW, in particular with regard to coalition building, Corky Gonzales replied that there was no disagreement between the two but insisted that Chicanos ought not to enter into alliances as "junior partners." He said: "There's a difference between that [Chávez's] and my philosophy. He feels that maybe it's the only way he could do it, that is, to get this outside help and make this outside alliance in order to remain autonomous. That's quite a contradiction, but it's an irony that's true. In order to have autonomy he had to have financial support. We work differently. We feel that no matter how long it takes, we have to develop our own leadership. We don't want those alliances. We'll take their support, but they can't make any decisions for us. They can't influence us" (1971, 4). Differences of opinion continued to separate the organizing strategies of major movement leaders, despite their joint appearances and public pronouncements as to shared objectives.[25]

In the end, however, the most astute commentators of the period understood that the activities of the UFW and Chávez himself served as crucial points of reference for the Movimiento as a whole. At its core the movement was a working-class project and who, after all, was more exploited than the farmworker? As the poet Abelardo Delgado put it: "Many movement people charge that Chavez may be one hell of an organizer, but not a leader in the Chicano movement in that he fails to embrace many other areas of concern affecting millions of other deprived Chicanos. Whether the charge is a valid one or not, the fact remains that we can rally behind our national leaders, and whether movement Chicanos claim Chavez owes them something or whether Chavez himself acknowledges the movement, the fact remains that he is a Chicano whose immense contribution cannot be ignored or belittled" (1971, 17).[26] Delgado's sentiments were widely shared by movement activists. At the same time, some activists argued that the UFW's successes themselves were inconceivable without the mass mobilizations organized by various movement organizations. In a period in which the trade union movement was not particularly strong and the number of farmworkers relatively small, Chávez's efforts, they believed, depended on the popular base created by the Movimiento.[27] Even *chavistas* like author Peter Matthiessen—who in his book had constructed a subtle division between Chávez and what he called "la raza Mexicans," that is, movement activists—understood the strong ties that bound the various groups together. For Matthiessen, however, the source of "Brown Power" identities could be traced directly to the founder of the UFW: "The new-born pride in being chicano, in the opinion of most people, is due largely to Chavez himself" (2000, 109).

By the 1970s, with the exception of revolutionary groups like the August 29th Movement, which accused Chávez of reformism and class collaborationism, the artificial division between "movement people" and Chávez to a large extent had been repaired. After the arrest of Corky Gonzales on a fabricated concealed-weapons charge at the Chicano Moratorium, Chávez agreed to serve as a character witness for Gonzales at the Los Angeles trial. In response to questions from attorney Oscar Zeta Acosta, Chávez testified that Gonzales's "general reputation for truth, honesty, and integrity is excellent" (Villaseñor 1970, 3). Even Chicano socialists were rethinking the role of the UFW within the overall Movimiento. Writer and activist José G. Pérez, for example, who had covered Chávez for the *Young Socialist* newspaper, argued in 1973: "Because the UFW is part of both the Chicano Movement and the labor movement, both must rally to its defense—otherwise both will be weakened and the way will be cleared for further assaults by the employers and their racist government" (1973, 14).[28] As the American war in Southeast Asia came to an end, UFW publications became less critical of the concepts of "Aztlán" and "La Raza," although they always subordinated them to the discourses of trade unionism.

## EL LEGADO DE CÉSAR

Attempts to organize farmworkers in California had met with failure in every decade of the first half of the twentieth century. The relative success of the UFW was the product of a historical conjuncture in which grassroots mobilizations around a variety of issues affecting Mexican Americans, the ascendancy of the liberal wing of the Democratic Party, Pope John XXIII's shifting of the Catholic Church's agenda toward the poor, the elimination of the Bracero Program in 1964, the general politicization of US society caused by the Vietnam war, and an emerging Chicana/o consciousness created a context in which it was possible to extract long-sought concessions from political and economic elites. At the end of this extraordinary historical moment, capital continued to treat labor as a commodity, but at least working conditions had improved and the discourse of the worker's inherent dignity had achieved a temporary prominence. The Chicana/o critique of liberalism had forced capitalist democracy in the United States to deliver on some but not all of its promises.

At once a union movement and an ethnic Mexican movement, La Causa was thus a result of the more generalized social transformation known as the 1960s. As one astute student of farmworkers' movements wrote: "The United Farm Workers story is significant for three reasons. In general terms, the UFW exemplified the basic goals and strategies of the social movements of the stormy 1960s. The major social movements of the period were insurgencies, that is, organized attempts to bring the interests of previously unorganized and excluded groups into the centers of economic and political power. By organizing farmworkers, the UFW took up the interests of one of the more disorganized and marginal segments of American society" (Jenkins 1985, x). As I have argued in the present essay, a unique characteristic of the UFW was the fact that its most recognizable leader deployed a nontraditional form of leadership that was often at odds with other forms typical of the period.[29]

By the mid-1980s, the conservative counterattack against progressive social movements was winning on many fronts. In California, Governor George Deukmejian, backed by affluent corporate growers, brought the "Reagan Revolution" to the farmworkers by gutting the Agricultural Labor Relations Act that had been passed in 1975. Chávez reacted to these rollbacks with anger: "There is a shadow falling over the land, brothers and sisters, and the dark forces of reaction threaten us now as never before. The enemies of the poor and the working classes hold power in the White House and the governor's office. . . . They have created a whole new class of millionaires while forcing millions of ordinary people into poverty" (1984a). At this moment perhaps more than previous ones, Chávez understood that the early activities of the UFW had been inextricably linked to a broader movement having to do with the construction of new and contestatory ethnic identities that challenged the racial and economic status quo. In a speech to the Commonwealth Club of California, he said: "Our union will forever exist as an empowering force among Chicanos in the Southwest. And that means our power and our influence will grow and not diminish. . . . The consciousness and pride that were raised by our union are alive and thriving inside millions of young Hispanics who will never work on a farm" (1984b). Whereas Chávez had criticized the "Brown Power" agenda in his 1969 *New Yorker* interviews, his recognition that the UFW had been an integral part of el Movimiento now tempered his concerns.[30]

As the decade of the 1990s began, Chávez reflected upon the legacy of Dr. King. In a speech delivered in January 1990, his critical analysis of the current state of affairs wove together the language of the movement with fundamental messages about coalition building and nonviolence:

> My friends, as we enter a new decade, it should be clear to all of us that there is an unfinished agenda, that we have miles to go before we reach the promised land. The men who rule this country today never learned the lessons of Dr. King, they never learned that nonviolence is the only way to peace and justice. Our nation continues to wage war upon its neighbors, and upon itself. The powers-that-be rule over a racist society, filled with hatred and ignorance. Our nation continues to be segregated along racial and economic lines. The powers-that-be make themselves richer by exploiting the poor. Our nation continues to allow children to go hungry, and will not even house its own people. The time is now for people, of all races and backgrounds, to sound the trumpets of change. As Dr. King proclaimed, "There comes a time when people get tired of being trampled over by the iron feet of oppression." (1990, 2)

Throughout the years of the Bush Sr. and Clinton administrations, the conservative reaction Chávez had warned about during Reagan's presidency gained momentum. This was particularly so in California, where ballot initiatives attempted to destroy the social safety net for undocumented workers, eliminated affirmative action, and gutted bilingual education programs. Although the UFW grew in membership in the 1990s and carried out large organizing campaigns such as the one in the California strawberry industry, victories were few and far between. On the more than four hundred farms where the union had won elections since 1975, less than half the growers agreed to sign contracts. The problem of unsafe transportation for farmworkers, an issue captured in Tomás Rivera's classic novel set in the 1950s, *Y no se lo tragó la tierra*, had been responsible for numerous deaths over the previous thirty years. Despite Chávez's personal efforts to win reforms on this issue, it was not until 2002 that the California state legislature finally passed a law mandating that growers provide safe vehicles (Chávez 1974; Ingram 2002). Also in 2002, after a well-publicized march on Sacramento to force the hand of Governor Gray Davis, the union won the right to have outside mediators and the Agricultural Labor Relations Board decide disputes between workers and growers (Maxwell 2002). Not unlike his disembodied voice that speaks from beyond to all those who visit the UFW's official website, the image of Chávez hovers over these victories and all contemporary acts of Chicana/o activism.

Today, Chávez enjoys widespread admiration throughout Mexican American and Latino communities and even within Hispanic corporate culture. For progressive Chicanas and Chicanos, of course, he continues to be the major historical icon, and it would be difficult to imagine a contemporary Chicana/o rejection of Chávez's legacy like the backlash Michael Dyson records in his book on Martin Luther King Jr. Dyson reconstructs a conversation in which a thirty-something African American scholar vehemently denounces King for being upper middle class, accommodationist, and an Uncle Tom (and implicitly not "man enough") (2000, 101).[31] Unlike earlier critiques of Chávez from within some movement sectors that raised doubts about his political alliances and tactics, contemporary Chicana/o intellectual projects have refrained from such a harsh reinterpretation, perhaps because many ethnic Mexican professionals have rejected outright the more contestatory aspects of the Movimiento. In the context of a generalized dispersion and fragmentation of progressive forces in the United States, the image of Chávez has become one of the safer ones associated with a revolutionary period, a period that still frightens many in both the corporate art world and the corporate university.

The death of César Chávez in 1993 solidified his position as a historic Mexican American leader, and by 2001 the state of California had instituted an official holiday in his honor. Although neoconservatives in their attempts to block the holiday continued to represent Chávez as a union mafioso, for the majority of Americans Chávez had become a somewhat romanticized and non-threatening figure that was less associated with unions and social movements than with nonviolence or religion or dot-com "creativity." The commodification of Chávez's image proceeded along the lines of that of King. Featured in Apple's "Think Different" series, Chávez joined his ally Robert Kennedy as one more pitchman for corporate gain. Even as the depoliticization of Chávez moved forward, the general public's understanding of the plight of contemporary farmworkers in the United States improved only slightly, if at all, from what it had been in 1962 when Chávez, Dolores Huerta, Larry Itliong, and others created the UFW (fig. 3). At the turn of the century, conditions in the fields were still deplorable, with Mexican farmworkers reporting significantly higher rates of cancer than other Latinos in California and a higher risk of contracting HIV/AIDS; 63 percent had only six years of school or fewer and 75 percent lacked health insurance.[32]

**Figure 3.** Lalo Alcaraz, *Farmworkers*, 2002. Copyright 2002 by Lalo Alcaraz; used by permission of Lalo Alcaraz and Andrews McMeel Syndication.

In contemporary Chicana/o culture, Chávez continues to fulfill a number of functions, not the least of which is that of a spiritual force at one with the powers of nature. Recently, novelist Rodolfo Anaya (2000, 26) has written:

> Our César has not died!
> He is the light of the new day.
> He is the rain that renews parched fields.
> He is the hope that builds the House of Justice.
> He is with us! Here! Today!
> Listen to his voice in the wind.
> He is the spirit of Hope,
> A Movement building to sweep away oppression!
> His spirit guides us in the struggle
> Let us join his spirit to ours!

In a process not unlike the one that transformed Che Guevara into a revolutionary saint, the mythologizing of Chávez removes him from the historical reality in which he lived and worked, and effaces his militant critique of economic inequality in order to construct a figure for the ages. In its weakest form, then, the image of Chávez becomes one more petrified icon deployed to demonstrate the virtues of American pluralism and liberal democracy—an aestheticized sign on a postage stamp. Poet César Cruz (2002) brilliantly captured the contradiction between this assimilated figure and the radical pursuit of social justice to which Chávez devoted his life:

I am wearing a
César Chávez t-shirt
driving a car with
César Chávez stickers
on César Chávez Boulevard
passing by
César Chávez school
on César Chávez Day
hearing
César Chávez commercials
on the local radio
and seeing
César Chávez billboards
announcing a
César Chávez march
sponsored by multinational
corporations
wondering
if
we praise you
or curse you
when farmworkers are still underpaid
under-appreciated
when immigrants
are scapegoated
when nothing you stood for
is respected. . . .

And yet even as the historical reality of Chávez recedes into the distant pantheon of "American" heroes, there can be no doubt that his name may still be deployed as a catalyst for ongoing struggles to end exploitation and win full political rights for working-class people. In 2001, recently organized janitors and service workers made up overwhelmingly of Latina/o immigrants marched through the streets of San Diego, California, chanting "Sí se puede" as they locked arms behind the image of César Estrada Chávez.

## NOTES

Reprinted with permission from Jorge Mariscal, *Aztlán: A Journal of Chicano Studies* 29:1 (2004): 21–56.

1. Based on Chávez's own comments in which he insisted that he was a labor leader and not a Chicano movement leader, several historians have argued that his connection to the Movimiento was tentative. Carlos Muñoz Jr., for example, writes: "Chavez was a union organizer and lent his increasing prestige and astute leadership abilities only to farmworkers" (1989, 60). It is my contention that on account of the immeasurable impact that Chávez and the United Farm Workers (UFW) had on Chicana/o activism throughout the movement period, as well as his direct or indirect support of movement sectors such as the anti–Vietnam War National Chicano Moratorium Committee, it would be misleading to isolate his efforts—regardless of his own declarations. Historian Ignacio García argues similarly that both Tijerina's Alianza Federal de Mercedes and the UFW were essential to the broader Movimiento: "Some scholars argue that César Chávez's farmworkers' union and the Alianza were not part of the Movement because they never emphasized their *chicanismo*. I counter by saying that these two organizations were fundamental to the development of the militancy of the period" (1998, 14). Manuel G. Gonzales artificially separates the Movimiento into "radical and moderate wings" and situates the UFW in the latter (2000, 196).

2. Tijerina's rhetoric in particular was dependent upon traditional forms of masculinity and on homophobia. Referring to government agents who had threatened him and his family, he said: "Most of them are homosexuals now and very few men are found among them" (1969, 4). Tijerina's use of homosexuality as a "charge" with which to dismiss his political enemies is reminiscent of the novels of Oscar Zeta Acosta.

3. I take for granted that scholars of the Chicano movement agree that far from being a "monolithic" social movement (has there ever been such a creature?), the Movimiento was made up of diverse organizations with regional and ideological differences. In my opinion, attempts to totalize the movement under any one political language are reductive and therefore distort what was a complex tapestry of agendas and rhetorical strategies. I take up many of these issues in my forthcoming *Brown-Eyed Children of the Sun: Lessons from the Chicano Movement.*

4. A reviewer for *Aztlán* charged me with "mythologizing Chavez once again." Let me say at the outset that by recontextualizng both Chávez and cultural representations of Chávez, my intention is not to demythologize his legacy but to clarify its origins so that current and future generations of students and activists can comprehend its complexity and thus refashion it for use in their own struggles for social justice.

5. In 1971 Carlos Blanco astutely pointed out that few if any of the farmworkers (approximately half of them Mexican nationals in the early 1970s) felt compelled to "construct" a new ethnic identity, since they understood themselves to be Mexicana/os *and* workers: "They know exactly where they stand in terms of their Mexicanidad and of their working-class condition and, therefore, of their relationship to the ever-present and clearly definable bosses. . . . The Chicano aspect of the struggle, the Mexican 'identity' of the 'causa' did not even have to be alluded to for the simple reason that the talk [by César Chávez] was given in Spanish" (1971, 2). Indeed, in the earliest days of the UFW, Chávez often appealed not only to the workers' *mexicanidad* but also to each one's specific regional identity within the Mexican context. One participant in a rally during the grape strike in 1965 reported: "Speaker follows speaker as the enthusiasm of the crowd grows. 'Who is here from Jalisco?' Cesar Chavez asks. 'Who is here from Michoacan?' A man from Tanguancícuaro rises: 'What have we to lose by going on strike?' . . . Men from state after Mexican state rise to pledge the aid of those from their part of the homeland, followed by cries of 'Viva Chihuahua! Viva Nuevo Leon! Viva Tamaulipas!'" (Nelson 1966, 27).

6. A new edition of Matthiessen's book was published in 2000, containing versions of some but not all of the materials in Matthiessen's original *New Yorker* articles. I have chosen to quote from the original articles because of their more properly *testimonio* style but I have included page references to both sources in those instances where material was either revised or reprinted.

7. Early in his activist career, Reies López Tijerina was referred to as "Don Quixote." After the June 5, 1967 courthouse raid on Tierra Amarilla, however, one media outlet declared: "Don Quixote has become El Cid" (Tijerina 2000, 102). On Chicano literary appropriations of the Don Quixote figure, see Childers (2002).

8. That Chávez's masculinity signified an implicit critique of traditional forms of leadership was noted early on by perceptive observers. In their book on farmworker organizing in California, Henry Anderson and Joan London (daughter of Jack London) wrote: "He is challenging the long-standing, deeply embedded folkways which equate aggressiveness with manliness in the cultures of Mexico, the Philippines, the United States—and in the culture of labor organizing itself. It is a breathtaking challenge" (1970, 184).

9. Chávez told Peter Matthiessen in 1969: "I didn't know much about Gandhi, so I read everything I could get my hands on about him, and I read some of the things that he had read, and I read Thoreau, which I liked very much. But I couldn't really understand Gandhi until I was actually in the fast. Then the books became much more clear" (Matthiessen 1969a, 64; 2000, 187). Central to Chávez's understanding of the activist Catholic tradition were the figures of Father Thomas McCullough and Father Donald McDonnell who founded a migrant ministry in the 1950s associated with the Spanish Mission Band and later the Missionary Apostolate. Father McDonnell exerted a direct influence over Chávez during his time in east San Jose. See London and Anderson (1970).

10. Chávez himself seemed to have practiced the fast according to this strict Gandhian interpretation, although many subsequent Chicana/o political actions have misunderstood the function of the fast and employed it as coercion. In their recent cartoon history, Lalo Alcaraz and Ilan Stavans perpetuate this misunderstanding by depicting Chávez on a fast saying: "I will not eat again until the grape growers concede" (2000, 121). During the Movimiento period, not all youth activists were convinced that the fast was an important strategy. In 1970 Ysidro Macias advised: "hunger strikes may be effective because of their sentimental value" (1969, 47). According to Peter Matthiessen, some UFW members left the union specifically because of Chávez's use of the fast: "One dismissed the entire fast as a 'cheap publicity stunt.' The other, who had once been a priest, accused Chávez of having a Messiah complex. Both soon quit the United Farm Workers for good" (1969b, 56).

11. Many years later, upon ending a fast in August 1988, Chávez explained: "The fast was first and foremost a personal act. It was something I felt compelled to do—to purify my own body, mind, and soul. The fast was also an act of penance for those in positions of moral authority and for all men and women who know what is right and just. It is for those who know that they could or should do more" (Jensen and Hammerback 2002, 169).

12. In his autobiography, African American leader Andrew Young recalls Chávez as "a small man with a soothing, spiritual presence" and "eyes that expressed the kind of loving determination with which the apostle Paul spread the Gospel" (1996, 445).

13. This quotation is from the so-called Sacramento March Letter. In documents such as these it is difficult to determine authorship since Chávez, Luis Valdez, Eliezer Risco, and others may have written the text collectively. On the practice of multiple authorship in the UFW and El Teatro Campesino, see Broyles González (1994).

14. Questions have been raised about the ways in which Chávez's hybrid masculinity, in a sense "feminized" by its indebtedness to religious traditions, might have worked to "hail" or attract women activists during the movement period. This is an important issue that, in my opinion, deserves

separate and multiple studies. Espinoza (2001) offers a possible model for such research. Equally needed are studies of the real-life ways in which farmworker women experience gender relations.

15. According to Peter Matthiessen's eyewitness account, a photographer staged the now famous 1968 tableau with RFK feeding Chávez (1969a, 68; 2000, 195). In his biography of Kennedy, Evan Thomas claims that meeting with Chávez initially did not appeal to Kennedy: "His involvement followed a familiar pattern: at first, he grumbled, he didn't want to fly to California to meet with some striking Mexicans. . . . But reluctantly, as a favor to his liberal activist friends in the United Auto Workers, he flew out to Delano, California, in mid-March" (2000, 320). Once he met Chávez, however, Kennedy became a staunch supporter.

16. Acosta's scene captured the tone of actual events in which movement leaders made the journey to Delano to consult with Chávez. In my personal conversations with Rosalío Muñoz, one of the founders of the National Chicano Moratorium Committee, he described a similar visit he made before deciding to refuse induction into military service.

17. Toledano's writings bear many of the marks of COINTELPRO disinformation and so there is some reason to believe they were subsidized by government agencies. The FBI had begun to construct a file on Chávez as early as 1965 on the premise that "communists" had infiltrated the UFW. In October 1969, the Nixon White House requested a "name check" on Chávez. J. Edgar Hoover relayed the Bureau's information to Nixon aide John Ehrlichman. Some of Chávez's FBI files are available online at http://foia.fbi.gov/chavez.htm.

18. Machado's attacks on Chávez's character would be repeated twenty years later by opponents of a César Chávez state holiday in California. Despite a well-funded opposition, the holiday was officially established in 2000 and celebrated for the first time in 2001.

19. Another example is *Cesar Chavez* by W. E. Dunham (1970).

20. Steinbacher was a reporter for the local *Anaheim* (California) *Bulletin*. His writings predated by a decade the reactionary "family values" project of the Reagan–Bush Sr. era. The hero of Steinbacher's book on the UFW is a certain Alfred Ramirez, founder of a group called "Mothers Against Chavez" and California chairman of the Spanish Surname Citizens for Wallace (George Wallace, the former Alabama segregationist governor, ran for president as a third-party candidate in 1968). By the 1990s an even more virulent strain of anti-liberalism was common currency. Right-wing hatred for centrist President Bill Clinton, for example, produced in Southern California bumper stickers that read "Clinton = Socialism" or juxtaposed "Clinton" with a hammer and sickle.

21. Although he disagreed with the UFW on the undocumented worker issue, Bert Corona later recalled: "Despite our differences with the United Farm Workers, we never had a major confrontation, even though on our side some people on the extreme left tried to provoke it (Corona and Garcia 1994, 249).

22. Elsewhere, Gómez-Quiñones further criticizes LRUP's position: "La mesquina exclusión de César Chávez y de su sindicato fue espuria y ejemplo de la falta de visión de largo plazo. Se dejó fuera a una organización de estructura nacional, con una base de más de 70 mil trabajadores, con equipos organizados, considerable apoyo público y una fuerza que podía ser reconocida en elecciones tanto estatales como nacionales. Viniendo de donde venían, los cargos en contra de Chávez eran hipócritas: trabajar con el Partido Demócrata y aceptar el apoyo de grupos no mexicanos" (1996, 247). The troubled relations between the UFW leadership and leftists within the union itself have yet to be chronicled. See remarks by union co-founder Philip Vera Cruz in Scharlin and Villanueva (2000, 120).

23. In a speech at a Los Angeles antiwar rally in May 1971, Chávez said: "It is hard for me because we in the farmworkers' movement have been so absorbed in our own struggle that we have not participated actively in the battle against the war" (Jensen and Hammerback 2002, 63). When asked why he did not attend the 1968 Poor People's Campaign, Chávez answered that he could not abandon his responsibilities in California in order to travel to Washington, D.C. (Matthiessen 2000, 242).

24. Many movement activists, for whom indigenous histories and traditions had become a central part of their new identity, would have been disappointed by Chávez's favorable remarks in the same interview about the California mission system (Matthiessen 1969b, 65–66; 2000, 300).

25. To the degree that radical organizations adopted an increasingly strident rhetoric threatening the use of violence, the mainstream media cast Chávez as a safe alternative and someone who could be reasoned with. In the April 1, 1969, issue of *Look* magazine, for example, readers were told: "At a time when many American radicals are saying that nonviolence—as an instrument for social change—died with Martin Luther King, Jr., it is reassuring to meet a man of faith who preaches compassion rather than bloody confrontation, practices what he preaches, and gets results" (52). Throughout the interview, Chávez's religiosity is emphasized. He praises Bobby Kennedy for his "hechos de amor, deeds of love" and eloquently states: "It may be a long time before the growers see us as human beings. . . . But we will win, we are winning, because ours is a revolution of mind and heart, not only of economics" (57). What one writer called Chávez's "tenacious idealism" sat in uneasy juxtaposition to traditional images of the union leader (Daniel 1995, 401).

26. According to Ernesto Vigil, Corky Gonzales "admired Chavez and praised his dedication to the farmworkers, but he—like Chavez himself—saw the latter mainly as a labor leader" (1999, 10). Bert Corona, on the other hand, convincingly argued that the UFW deployed a form of Mexicano nationalism that "complemented the stress on ethnic nationalism and ethnic revival in the sixties. . . . It was ethnic nationalism but it was interpreted through Cesar's earlier experience and conscious- ness which reflected a broader and more class-based approach" (1994, 248).

27. "It was the Chicano community that saw the struggle of the farm workers as its own struggle and formed the backbone of the [farmworkers'] movement" (Pendás 1976, 7).

28. Pérez argued further: "The UFW is the closest thing today to the militant, socially conscious unionism of the CIO in the late thirties. It supported the movement against the Vietnam War when few labor leaders would go near it. The struggle of these oppressed workers and their attempts to link up with broader concerns of the working masses point in the direction of a new labor radicalism" (8–9).

29. Chávez's spiritualized masculinity contradicts recent historiography and cultural criticism that casts the entire Chicano movement as a hyper-masculinist orgy, as if Oscar Zeta Acosta and not César Chávez were its primary inspiration. While there can be no doubt that the feminist critiques of the movement carried out in the 1980s were necessary correctives to the sexist practices that characterized all organizations, arguments about the "origins" of the Movimiento that posit "emasculation" as its primary cause are misleading. A sense of emasculation among working-class men (of any ethnicity), the product of racializing capitalist formations, may produce a variety of pathologies ranging from alcoholism to domestic violence. In and of itself, however, emasculation cannot generate social movements. To argue that it can is to return to an older "pathological tradition" of social movement theory, a tradition for the most part rejected by contemporary scholars (Gamson 1992). For a rather hastily constructed analysis of the Chicano movement along these "pathological" lines, see R. Gutiérrez (1993).

30. As early as 1968, Chávez had spoken about the unavoidable links between labor organizing and other struggles in the Southwest: "People raise the question: Is this a strike or is it a civil-rights fight? In California, in Texas, or in the South, any time you strike, it becomes a civil-rights movement. It becomes a civil-rights fight" (Jensen and Hammerback 2002, 33).

31. Dyson's colleague who denounces King begins boldly enough: "Fuck Martin Luther King. The nigga was the worst thing to happen to black people in the twentieth century" (101).

32. On the situation for farmworkers in the 1980s and 1990s, see Acuña (2000) and Hanson (2002). In his groundbreaking study of farm labor in the late twentieth century, Daniel Rothenberg writes: "The basic statistics regarding agricultural labor reveal an ethical challenge that raises questions about our professed belief that honest labor should be justly rewarded" (1998, xiii).

## WORKS CITED


Acosta, Oscar Zeta. 1989. *Revolt of the Cockroach People.* New York: Vintage.

Acuña, Rodolfo. 2000. *Occupied America: A History of Chicanos.* 4th ed. New York: Longman.

Alcaraz, Lalo, and Ilan Stavans. 2000. *Latino USA: A Cartoon History.* New York: Basic Books.

Allen, Gary. 1966. *The Grapes: Communist Wrath in Delano.* Belmont, MA: Review of the News.

Anaya, Rodolfo. 2000. *Elegy on the Death of César Chávez.* El Paso: Cinco Puntos Press.

Blanco Aguinaga, Carlos. 1971. "Unidad del trabajo y la vida—Cinco de mayo, 1971." *Aztlán* 3, no. 1: 1–5.

Borman, William. 1986. *Gandhi and Non-violence.* Albany: State University of New York Press.

Broyles González, Yolanda. 1994. E*l Teatro Campesino: Theater in the Chicano Movement.* Austin: University of Texas Press.

Camejo, Antonio. 1970. "A New Ideology for the Chicano Party." In *La Causa Política: A Chicano Politics Reader*, edited by F. Chris Garcia, 343–46. Notre Dame, IL: University of Notre Dame Press.

Castells, Manuel. 1997. *The Power of Identity.* Vol. 2 of *The Information Age: Economy, Society and Culture.* Oxford: Blackwell.

Castro, Tony. 1974. *Chicano Power: The Emergence of Mexican America.* New York: Saturday Review Press.

Chávez, César E. 1968a. Telegram to Mrs. Martin Luther King, Jr. Reprinted in *El Malcriado*, April 15.

———. 1968b. "National Council Policy Statement." *Tempo* (summer–fall): 9–10.

———. 1968c. Speech ending fast, March 10. http://chavez.scientech.com:8080/research (site discontinued).

———. 1984a. Address to UFW's Seventh Constitutional Convention, September. http://chavez. scientech. com:8080/research (site discontinued).

———. 1984b. Address to the Commonwealth Club of California, San Francisco, November 9. http://www.chavezfoundation.org/_cms.php?mode=view&b_code=001008000000000&b_no=16&page=1&field=&key=&n=8.

———. 1970. "Cesar Chavez: Apostle of Non-Violence." Interview. *Observer*, May.

———. 1971. "On Money and Organizing." Speech delivered in Keene, California, October 4. https://libraries.ucsd.edu/farmworkermovement/essays/essays/MillerArchive/041%20On%20Money%20and%20Organizing.pdf.

———. 1974. "Chavez Blames Fatal Bus Accidents on Greed: 'Inhuman Treatment of Farmworkers Must End.'" *National Chicano Health Organization (NCHO) Newsletter* 3 (April): 7.

———. 1990. "Lessons of Dr. Martin Luther King, Jr." http://www.chavezfoundation.org/_cms.php?mode=view&b_code=001008000000000&b_no=11&page=1&field=&key=&n=3.

Childers, William. 2002. "Chicanoizing Don Quixote: For Luis Andres Murillo." *Aztlán* 27, no. 2: 87–117.

Corona, Bert, and Mario T. García. 1994. *Memories of Chicano History: The Life and Narrative of Bert Corona.* Berkeley and Los Angeles: University of California Press.

Cruz, César A. (Teolol). 2002. "Turning in Your Grave." Unpublished manuscript.

Daniel, Cletus E. 1995. "Cesar Chavez and the Unionization of California Farmworkers." In *Working People of California*, edited by Daniel Cornford, 371–404. Berkeley and Los Angeles: University of California Press.

de León, Nephtalí. 1972a. *Five Plays.* Denver: Totinem Publications.

———. 1972b. *Chicanos: Our Background and Our Pride.* Lubbock, TX: Trucha Publications.

Delgado, Abelardo. 1971. *The Chicano Movement: Some Not Too Objective Observations.* Denver: Totinem Publications.

Dunham, W. E. 1970. *Cesar Chavez*. Belmont, MA: Review of the News.

Dyson, Michael Eric. 2000. *I May Not Get There With You: The True Martin Luther King, Jr.* New York: Touchstone Press.

Espinoza, Dionne. 2001. "'Revolutionary Sisters': Women's Solidarity and Collective Identification among Chicana Brown Berets in East Los Angeles, 1967–1970." *Aztlán* 26, no. 2: 17–58.

Foucault, Michel. 1972. *The Archaeology of Knowledge and the Discourse on Language*. New York: Harper & Row.

Gamson, William A. 1992. "The Social Psychology of Collective Action." In *Frontiers in Social Movement Theory*, edited by Aldon D. Morris and Carol McClurg Mueller, 53–76. New Haven, CT: Yale University Press.

García, Ignacio M. 1998. *Chicanismo: The Forging of a Militant Ethos among Mexican Americans*. Tucson: University of Arizona Press.

Gómez, David. 1982. "The Story of Ruben Salazar." In *Introduction to Chicano Studies*, edited by Livie Isauro Durán and H. Russell Bernard, 499–505. New York: Macmillan.

Gómez-Quiñones, Juan. 1990. *Chicano Politics: Reality and Promise 1940–1990*. Albuquerque: University of New Mexico Press.

———. 1996. "La era de los setenta." In *El México olvidado: La historia del pueblo chicano*, edited by David R. Maciel, 239–61. Colección Sin Fronteras, vol. 2. Ciudad Juárez, Mexico: Universidad Autónoma de Ciudad Juárez; El Paso: University of Texas at El Paso.

Gonzales, Manuel G. 2000. *Mexicanos: A History of Mexicans in the United States*. Bloomington: Indiana University Press.

Gonzales, Rodolfo Corky. 1971. Interview in *La Voz del Pueblo*, June.

Gutiérrez, David G. 1995. *Walls and Mirrors: Mexican Americans, Mexican Immigrants, and the Politics of Ethnicity*. Berkeley and Los Angeles: University of California Press.

Gutiérrez, Gustavo. 1971. *Teología de la liberación: Perspectivas*. Lima: CEP.

Gutiérrez, Ramón A. 1993. "Community, Patriarchy and Individualism: The Politics of Chicano History and the Dream of Equality." *American Quarterly* 45, no. 1: 44–72.

Hanson, Pat. 2002. "Migrant Farmers Suffering in Silence: California Groups Look at Problems and Solutions." *Hispanic Outlook in Higher Education*, June 3, 28–32.

Hruska-Cortés, Elías. 1973. "Recuerdos." *La calavera chicana* (University of California, Berkeley), September, 15.

Huck, Susan. 1974. *Little Cesar and His Phony Strike*. Belmont, MA: Review of the News.

Ingram, Carl. 2002. "Farm Workers Celebrate Safety Law, Chavez Holiday." *Los Angeles Times*, April 2.

Jenkins, J. Craig. 1985. *The Politics of Insurgency: The Farm Worker Movement in the 1960s*. New York: Columbia University Press.

Jensen, Richard J., and John C. Hammerback. 2002. *The Words of César Chávez*. College Station: Texas A&M University Press.

*La Voz del Pueblo*. 1970. "El poder Chicano." December, 4–5.

London, Joan, and Henry Anderson. 1970. *So Shall Ye Reap: The Story of Cesar Chavez and the Farm Workers' Movement*. New York: Thomas Y. Crowell.

*Look*. 1969. "Nonviolence Still Works." April 1, 52–57.

Lozada, Froben. 1968. Speech delivered at California State University, Hayward, November 1. Typescript in author's possession.

Machado, Manuel A., Jr. 1978. *Listen Chicano!: An Informal History of the Mexican-American*. Chicago: Nelson Hall.

Macias, Ysidro Ramón. 1969. "Plan de Political Action for Chicano Campus Groups." Document produced at a political action workshop at the University of California, Santa Barbara, April. Reprinted in *El Pocho Che*, April 1970.

Matthiessen, Peter. 1969a. "Profile: Organizer-1." *New Yorker*, June 21, 42–85.

———. 1969b. "Profile: Organizer II." *New Yorker*, June 28, 43–76.

———. 2000. *Sal Si Puedes (Escape If You Can): Cesar Chavez and the New American Revolution.* Berkeley and Los Angeles: University of California Press.

Maxwell, Lesli A. 2002. "Davis Gives UFW Major Victory." *Sacramento Bee*, October 1.

Muñoz, Carlos Jr. 1989. *Youth, Identity, Power: The Chicano Movement.* London and New York: Verso.

Navarro, Armando. 1995. *Mexican American Youth Organization: Avant-Garde of the Chicano Movement in Texas.* Austin: University of Texas Press.

Nelson, Eugene. 1966. *Huelga: The First Hundred Days of the Great Delano Grape Strike.* Delano: Farm Worker Press.

Pendás, Miguel. 1976. *Chicano Liberation and Socialism.* New York: Pathfinder Press.

Pérez, José G. 1973. *Viva la Huelga! The Struggle of the Farm Workers.* New York: Pathfinder Press.

Pérez, Ricardo C. 1970. "César." *El Chicano* (San Bernardino, California), January 12.

raúlrsalinas. 1971. "Los caudillos." *La Raza* 1 (January): 74.

Rosales, F. Arturo. 1997. *Chicano! The History of the Mexican American Civil Rights Movement.* Houston: Arte Público Press.

Rothenberg, Daniel. 1998. *With These Hands: The Hidden World of Migrant Farmworkers Today.* Berkeley and Los Angeles: University of California Press.

Scharlin, Craig, and Lilia V. Villanueva, eds. 2000. *Philip Vera Cruz: A Personal History of Filipino Immigrants and the Farmworkers Movement.* Seattle: University of Washington Press.

Sousa, Lisa, Stafford Poole, and James Lockhart, eds. 1998. *The Story of Guadalupe: Luis Laso de la Vega's "Huei tlamahuiçoltica" of 1649.* Palo Alto, CA: Stanford University Press; Los Angeles: UCLA Latin American Publications.

Steinbacher, John. 1970. *Bitter Harvest.* Whittier, CA: Orange Tree Press.

Thomas, Evan. 2000. *Robert Kennedy: His Life.* New York: Simon & Schuster.

Tijerina, Reies López. 1969. Interview in the *Indicator* (University of California, San Diego), January 29, 2.

———. 2000. *They Called Me "King Tiger": My Struggle for the Land and Our Rights.* Translated by José Ángel Gutiérrez. Houston: Arte Público Press.

Toledano, Ralph de. 1971. *Little Cesar.* Washington, DC: Anthem.

Treviño, Jesús Salvador. 2001. *Eyewitness: A Filmmaker's Memoir of the Chicano Movement.* Houston: Arte Público Press.

Vigil, Ernesto. 1999. *The Crusade for Justice: Chicano Militancy and the Government's War on Dissent.* Madison: University of Wisconsin Press.

Villaseñor, Rudy. 1970. "Chavez Gives Testimony for Gun Suspect." *Los Angeles Times*, November 26, II: 3.

Washington, James Melvin, ed. 1986. *A Testament of Hope: The Essential Writings and Speeches of Martin Luther King, Jr.* San Francisco: HarperSanFrancisco.

Williams, Raymond. 1989. *Resources of Hope.* London and New York: Verso.

Yinger, Winthrop. 1975. *Cesar Chavez: The Rhetoric of Nonviolence.* Hicksville, NY: Exposition Press.

Young, Andrew. 1996. *An Easy Burden: The Civil Rights Movement and the Transformation of America.* New York: HarperCollins.

# AWAKENING THE NEW "SLEEPING GIANT"?

## Asian American Political Engagement

PAUL M. ONG, MELANY DELA CRUZ-VIESCA, AND DON NAKANISHI

The 2008 Primary's "Super Tuesday" was a milestone in the emergence of Asian Americans as a factor in American politics. The national television news networks openly discussed and analyzed California's Asian American voters, who comprised an estimated 12 percent of the state's registered voters. Most mainstream analysis, however, had very little in-depth understanding of this population with some initial commentaries claiming that a large majority of California's Asian American voters went for Senator Clinton because of racial bias. This essay provides some insights into the absolute and relative size of the Asian American population, along with key demographic characteristics, their participation in electoral politics, some of the barriers they encounter, and future prospects. The brief is based on analyzing the most recently available data, the 2006 American Community Survey (ACS) and the 2006 November Current Population Survey (CPS). This analysis builds on a previous analytical brief which examined the emergence of Asian Americans as California politics' new "sleeping giant," a term that was applied to Hispanics in the 1980s and 1990s because of their rapid growing numbers.

## INTRODUCTION

Super Tuesday of the 2008 Primary (February 5, 2008) was a milestone in the emergence of Asian Americans as a factor in American politics. The national television

Paul M. Ong is a professor at the UCLA School of Public Affairs and Department of Asian American Studies. He also serves as the director of the UC AAPI Policy Multi-campus Research Program. Melany Dela Cruz-Viesca is the assistant director of the UCLA Asian American Studies Center. She is also the managing editor of the *AAPI Nexus Journal*, in addition to coordinator and researcher of the Center's highly acclaimed Census Information Center, a joint partnership with the National Coalition of Asian Pacific American Community Development (CAPACD) and the US Census Bureau. She serves on the Human Relations Commission of the City of Los Angeles. Don T. Nakanishi (1949–2016) was the director of the UCLA Asian American Studies Center. He was also a professor at the Department of Asian American Studies and Department of Social Sciences and Comparative Education Division, GSE&IS.

news networks openly discussed and analyzed California's Asian American voters, who comprised an estimated 12 percent of the state's registered voters.[1] A CNN exit poll indicated that Asian Americans in California voted for Senator Hillary Clinton by a 3-1 margin (71 percent), allowing her to win the popular vote by eight points through an Asian American and Latino voting bloc.[2] To a lesser extent, newscasters took note of the Asian Americans in other primary elections. The focus has been on the Democratic race because more Asian Americans are registered with that party than any other party. A report by the Asian American Legal Defense and Education Fund (AALDEF) on the 2004 Presidential Elections surveyed Asian Americans in twenty-three cities in eight states: New York, New Jersey, Massachusetts, Rhode Island, Michigan, Illinois, Pennsylvania, and Virginia. AALDEF affirmed that 57 percent of Asian Americans were registered Democrats, over a quarter were not enrolled in any political party, and 15 percent were registered Republicans.[3] Similarly, a study by the Asian Pacific American Legal Center (APALC) found 35 percent of Asian American Voters registered as Democrats in the Los Angeles County 2006 General Election and 28 percent registered as Republicans.[4]

Most mainstream analysis, however, had very little in-depth understanding of this population with some initial commentaries claiming that a large majority of California's Asian American voters went for Senator Clinton because of racial bias.[5] That proved to be too simplistic and inaccurate because a significant number of Asian Americans went for Senator Barack Obama in Hawai'i's primary election, which was held two weeks later. The lack of well-informed opinions on how this population voted, however, does not distract from the historical acknowledgement of Asian American voters by the national media, even if it has proven to be somewhat brief and fleeting.

This paper provides some insights into the absolute and relative size of the Asian American population, along with key demographic characteristics, their participation in electoral politics, some of the barriers they encounter, and future prospects. The brief is based on analyzing the most recently available data, the 2006 American Community Survey (ACS) and the 2006 November Current Population Survey (CPS). This analysis builds on a previous analytical brief which examined the emergence of Asian Americans as California politics' new "sleeping giant," a term that was applied to Hispanics in the 1980s and 1990s because of their rapid growing numbers.[6]

## CITIZENSHIP STATUS

As of 2006, Asian Americans comprise nearly 5 percent of the total US population, with 10 states having more than 5 percent of their population being Asian Americans.[7] What is more important in terms of potential political engagement is the Asian American percent of those eligible to register to vote. What is particularly noticeable is the fall off in the Asian American share when the analysis is limited to either those with citizenship or adult citizens (18 years and older), which is documented in Table 1.[8] Nationally, the share drops by 1 or more percentage points. In other words, while one in twenty Americans is Asian, between one in twenty-five and one in thirty adult citizens is Asian. These figures, however, vary tremendously among the states. Asians constitute a majority of adult citizens in Hawai'i, and they comprise one-eighth of the population

**Table 1:** 2006 Asian American Population Estimates

| Area | Total population | Asian Population | Percent Asian | Percent Asian, Citizens | Percent Asian, 18+ Citizens |
|---|---|---|---|---|---|
| United States | 299,398,485 | 14,656,608 | 4.9% | 3.9% | 3.6% |
| **STATES** | | | | | |
| California | 36,457,549 | 4,896,851 | 13.4% | 12.2 % | 12.3% |
| New York | 19,306,183 | 1,391,510 | 7.2% | 5.4% | 5.2% |
| Texas | 23,507,783 | 859,588 | 3.7% | 2.8% | 2.7% |
| Hawai'i | 1,285,498 | 725,436 | 56.4% | 55.3% | 54.0% |
| New Jersey | 8,724,560 | 685,013 | 7.9% | 5.9% | 5.4% |
| Illinois | 12,831,970 | 583,538 | 4.5% | 3.5% | 3.3% |
| Washington | 6,395,798 | 497,782 | 7.8% | 6.4% | 6.1% |
| Florida | 18,089,889 | 460,641 | 2.5% | 2.1% | 1.8% |
| Virginia | 7,642,884 | 409,035 | 5.4% | 4.0% | 3.7% |
| Massachusetts | 6,437,193 | 334,954 | 5.2% | 3.8% | 3.3% |

Source: US Census Bureau, 2006 ACS PUMS

in California. Four additional states listed in Table 1 have percentages higher than the national average (New York, New Jersey, Washington, and Virginia). The numbers show considerable regional differences in the potential of Asian Americans to be an important political force.

The primary reason for the difference in the Asian American share of the total population and the Asian American share of adult citizens is the fact that this is predominantly an immigrant population. In 2006, 61 percent of Asian Americans were immigrants, and 76 percent among Asian American adults.[9] The percent that is comprised of immigrants varies greatly among the ten states listed in Table 2. They comprise a small minority majority of those in Hawai'i, and three-quarters of those in California. The highest fraction is in New Jersey, where seven in eight are immigrants. This difference can influence the political issues that Asian Americans are most concerned about because immigrants and US-born have different concerns. Equally important is the naturalization rate among the immigrants. The good news is that nationally a majority has acquired citizenship, and the rate of naturalization appears to have increased.[10] Nonetheless, there is still a substantial minority who are not citizens, and the rates tend to be lower outside the West Coast.

## VOTER REGISTRATION AND VOTING PATTERNS

Even after achieving citizenship, there are two additional steps required to become fully politically engaged—registering to vote and turning out to vote. According to estimates from the Voter Supplement to the November 2006 Current Population Survey,[11] Asian

**Table 2:** Citizenship Status of Asian Americans

| State | Adults (x1,000) | Born Citizen | Naturalized | Not Citizen | Naturalization Rate |
|---|---|---|---|---|---|
| United States | 10,951 | 24.1 percent | 43.4 percent | 32.5 percent | 57.2 percent |
| **States** | | | | | |
| California | 3,722 | 25% | 47% | 28% | 63% |
| New York | 1,090 | 15% | 46% | 38% | 55% |
| Texas | 625 | 17% | 46% | 37% | 56% |
| Hawai'i | 551 | 70% | 19% | 11% | 63% |
| New Jersey | 515 | 12% | 49% | 39% | 56% |
| Illinois | 440 | 19% | 46% | 35% | 57% |
| Washington | 376 | 29% | 44% | 27% | 62% |
| Florida | 337 | 19% | 48% | 33% | 59% |
| Virginia | 303 | 18% | 48% | 34% | 58% |
| Massachusetts | 255 | 20% | 39% | 41% | 49% |

Source: US Census Bureau, 2006 ACS PUMS

American adult citizens exhibit lower registration rates, which can be seen in the top panel of Table 3. The national registration rate among Asian Americans is substantially lower than for their non-Asian counterparts, a difference of 19 percentage points. With the exception of Hawai'i, registration rates among Asian Americans by regions are lower than for their non-Asian counterparts. On the other hand, the rate for naturalized Asian Americans is only slightly lower than for naturalized non-Asians, which indicates that the typical immigrant regardless of race tend to have lower odds of registering. Thus, the observed lower registration rate among Asian American adult citizens is due in part to its population being dominated by naturalized immigrants. What is surprising is that the registration rate for native Asian Americans is lower than that for native non-Asians. This indicates that inter-generational acculturation does not necessarily translate into greater political engagement. In fact, there seems to be greater apathy among US-born Asian Americans, although it may be due in part to the fact that this group tends to be younger.

Table 3 also reports voting rates. Nationally, relatively fewer Asian American citizens turned out to vote in 2006, a difference of 15 percentage points compared with non-Asians. Asian American subgroups also lag behind their non-Asian counterparts, with the exception of those in Hawai'i. The gaps are not as great when examining the turnout rate among those registered to vote. Nonetheless, even with this more limited population base, there is room for improvement in terms of enhancing Asian American political engagement. One strategy is to use an alternative to going to the polls, that is, by mail voting. Interestingly, a higher percentage of Asian American voters used this method, 24 percent compared with 13 percent for non-Asian voters. The one exception

**Table 3:** Registration and Voting Rates, 2006

| | Registered | | Voted | |
|---|---|---|---|---|
| | **Asians** | **Non-Asians** | **Asians** | **Non-Asians** |
| Adults (18+) Citizens | | | | |
| United States | 49% | 68% | 33% | 48% |
| Citizen by Birth | 46% | 69% | 31% | 49% |
| U.S. Naturalized | 52% | 55% | 34% | 38% |
| California | 49% | 64% | 34% | 49% |
| Hawai'i | 56% | 53% | 47% | 39% |
| New York/New Jersey | 51% | 64% | 29% | 44% |
| All Other Regions | 48% | 69% | 30% | 49% |
| Registered Voters | | | | |
| United State | | | 66% | 71% |
| Citizen by Birth | | | 68% | 71% |
| U.S. Naturalized | | | 65% | 68% |
| California | | | 71% | 77% |
| Hawai'i | | | 83% | 72% |
| New York/New Jersey | | | 57% | 68% |
| All Other Regions | | | 62 % | 71% |

Source: US Census Bureau, 2006 CPS

to the low turn-out rate is, again, the Aloha state. The Asian Pacific American Legal Center reported approximately 37 percent of Asian Americans voting in the LA County 2006 General Election voted by absentee ballot. APALC also noted while 48 percent of all voters in Orange County's 2006 General Election voted by mail, approximately 61 percent of Asian Americans countywide did so.[12] The Hawaiian exception may be due to the fact that Asian Americans are highly influential in state politics, and this greater efficacy may provide incentives for greater participation.

The November 2006 CPS provides some additional explanations for the lower political engagement levels for Asian American citizens. As the above analysis indicates, the more important challenge among those eligible to vote is to increase their registration rate. Moreover, an analysis of the responses to the survey indicates that registered Asian Americans who did not turn out to vote had similar problems as non-Asians, such as the inability to get to the polls because of illness, being away from home, conflicts with other obligations, and transportation problems. There are, however, distinctive differences in the relative frequency of reasons for not registering. One positive finding is that Asian Americans are not more politically apathetic. While 42 percent of non-Asian citizens stated that they did not register because they were "Not interested in the election or not involved in politics," only 30 percent of Asian American citizens gave the same reason. On the other hand, 11 percent of the non-registered Asian American citizens stated that they "Did not know where or how to register" and another 7 percent stated that they had "Difficulty with English." The respective percentages for non-Asians were 5 percent and 1 percent. According to the Asian American Legal Defense and Education Fund, 41 percent of all respondents in their 2004 Multilingual Exit Poll were limited English proficient (LEP).[13] The 2004 exit poll covered jurisdictions that were either legally required to provide or voluntarily provided language assistance to the voter, under Section 203 of the Voting Rights Act. In the Manhattan-Brooklyn-Queens areas of New York, 56 percent of Chinese were limited English proficient and 37 percent required an interpreter; 67 percent of Koreans were LEP and 34 percent required an interpreter in Queens, NY; and 59 percent of Bangladeshi was LEP and 26 percent needed an interpreter in Hamtramck, MI.

These barriers to registration are not surprising given that most Asian American citizens are immigrants; consequently, they are more likely to encounter language and informational barriers.

## FUTURE TRAJECTORY

Rapid growth has been the driving force behind the emergence of Asian Americans as a potential new "sleeping giant" in politics. And that force will not abate anytime soon. The most recent Bureau of Census populations projects that Asian Americans alone, a more restrictive definition that does not include those who are part Asian, will increase to 5.4 percent of the population by 2020, up from 3.8 percent in 2000.[14] The more inclusive count of Asian Americans would put the 2020 figure at perhaps over 6 percent. If the percentage point increase in the Asian American share of the population is similar at the state level, then three to four states will join Hawai'i and California as having at least one-tenth of the population being Asian American.[15] Demographics, however, is not political destiny. Asian Americans still face a number of hurdles to translating their growing numbers into growing political strength. The above analysis highlights some of the challenges. Although the number of US-born Asian Americans will grow faster than the number Asian American immigrants, our projections indicate that immigrants will continue to constitute a large majority of Asian Americans twenty-years-old or older, over three quarters in 2020.[16] Over 3 million will be recent immigrants, that is, those in the country 10 years or less. As a consequence, there will continue to be the challenge of promoting naturalization in order to increase the number of Asian Americans eligible to register and vote. Even with citizenship, the current patterns indicate that much work is still needed to get naturalized Asians to register and go to the polls. While the growing number of US-born Asian Americans will automatically increase the number of Asian Americans eligible to vote, the analysis show that this group has low registration and turnout rates. The population trajectories clearly create the potential for an awakened sleeping giant in American politics within less than a generation, but that will only materialize through public policies that promote greater political engagement and the concerted efforts of a myriad of community-based organizations.

Note: The analysis in this analytical brief was partially supported with grants from the Russell Sage Foundation and Carnegie Foundation. Additional support was provided by the UCLA Asian American Studies Center, the UC AAPI Policy Multi-Campus Research Program, and LEAP (Leadership Education for Asian Pacifics). We are grateful to J.D. Hokoyama, our many colleagues within higher education, and the national, state, and local Asian American community leaders who provided their input. The authors alone are responsible for the content.

### *Co-Sponsoring Organizations:*

The UCLA Asian American Studies Center is the nation's leading research center in the field of Asian American Studies and houses a Census Information Center, which will continue to analyze data from the ACS as they become available.

The UC AAPI Policy MRP brings together University of California researchers, elected officials and their staff, and community organizations to conduct research focusing on the policy concerns of the AAPI community.

Leadership Education for Asian Pacifics, Inc. (LEAP) has been intent on "growing leaders" within the Asian American and Pacific Islander (AAPI) communities across the country. LEAP's mission is to achieve full participation and equality for Asian Americans and Pacific Islanders through leadership, empowerment, and policy.

## NOTES

Reprinted with permission from Paul Ong, Melany Dela Cruz-Viesca, and Don Nakanishi, *AAPI Nexus* 6:1 (2008): 1–10.

1. "Election08 Political Dashboard," <http://news.yahoo.com/election/2008/dashboard/?d=NC> as of February 5, 2008.

2. "Election Center 2008 Primaries and Caucuses," <http://www.cnn.com/ELECTION/2008/primaries/results/epolls/#CADEM> as of February 5, 2008.

3. Asian American Legal Defense and Education Fund (AALDEF). "*The Asian American Vote: A Report on the AALDEF Multilingual Exit Poll in the 2004 Presidential Election.*" <http://www.apiavote.org/documents/multimedia/04-20-05_exit_poll_report.pdf>

4. Asian Pacific American Legal Center (APALC). "*Asian Americans at the Ballot Box: The 2006 General Election in Los Angeles County.*" <http://apalc.org/demographics/wpcontent/uploads/2007/05/apalc_ballotbox2006_final.pdf>

5. National Election Pool Exit Poll 2008. "Demographic Profile of California Voters." *Los Angeles Times* Website: <http://www.latimes.com/news/politics/la-020708-me-calif-g,0,1300314.graphic> as of May 5, 2008.

6. Ong, et al., The New "Sleeping Giant" in California Politics: The Growth of Asian Americans," UCLA Asian American Studies Center, http://www.aasc.ucla.edu/archives/sleepgiants.htm, posted September 6, 2006. In 1990, Hispanics made up 14 percent of adult citizens in California, and in 2006, Asian Americans approached that level, with over 12 percent of California's adult citizens.

7. When possible, the counts include those who are Asian alone or Asian in combination with another race. The most recent estimates from the US Bureau of the Census places the Asian American population at 5 percent of the US population on July 1, 2007. The ten states with the highest Asian American percentages are Hawai'i, California, New Jersey, Washington, New York, Nevada, Alaska, Maryland, Virginia and Massachusetts.

8. The estimates in Table 1 on total population, Asian population, percent Asian, and Asians as a percent of citizens are based on information extracted from tabulations reported by the Bureau of Census on its American FactFinder web site. The estimated Asian share of adult population is based on Paul Ong's tabulation of the 2006 ACS Public-Use Micro Sample (PUMS).

9. Immigrants are defined as those who are not citizens by birth. The statistics on adult Asian Americans and the statistics in Table 2 are tabulated by Paul Ong from the 2006 ACS PUMS.

10. See for example, Paul Ong and Joanna Lee "Naturalization of S.F. Chinese Immigrants: The Surge In The 1990s," UCLA California Center for Population Research, January 2007.

11. The tabulations in Table 3 were done by Paul Ong. The Asian category includes those who are Asian alone and one of seven multiracial categories that include Asians. The weights for Asian Americans were slightly adjusted upward to account for those who are part Asian but not in one of the seven listed multi-racial categories. Subpopulations were created to ensure an adequate sample. The smallest sample is the number of Asians in the New York and New Jersey, which numbered 311. The next smallest sample is the number of Asians in Hawai'i, which numbered 708.

12. Asian Pacific American Legal Center (APALC). *"Asian Americans at the Ballot Box: The 2006 General Election in Orange County."* <http://demographics.apalc.org/wp-content/uploads/2008/04/oc-ballot-box-final-032708.pdf> *and "Asian Americans at the Ballot Box: The 2006 General Election in Los Angeles County."*< http://apalc.org/demographics/wp-content/uploads/2007/05/apalc_ballotbox2006_final.pdf>

13. Asian American Legal Defense and Education Fund (AALDEF). *"The Asian American Vote: A Report on the AALDEF Multilingual Exit Poll in the 2004 Presidential Election."* <http://www.apiavote.org/documents/multimedia/04-20-05_exit_poll_report.pdf>

14. US Census Bureau, 2004, "U.S. Interim Projections by Age, Sex, Race, and Hispanic Origin," http://www.census.gov/ipc/www/usinterimproj/, Internet Release Date: March 18, 2004. The number of Asian Americans is projected to increase by 67 percent over the two decades, from 10.7 million to 18 million. The more inclusive Asian American count for 2000 is 11.9 million.

15. The likely states are New Jersey, Washington, New York, and Nevada.

16. These projections by nativity were made by the author based on the Bureau of the Census' overall population projections. The modified projections starts with the distribution by nativity in 2000, assumes that the age-specific survival rates are the same for both US-born and foreign-born Asians, and uses the Bureau's assumptions about future immigration flows.

# SEARCHING FOR *HAKNIP ACHUKMA* (GOOD HEALTH):

## Challenges to Food Sovereignty Initiatives in Oklahoma

DEVON MIHESUAH

In the last three decades, tribes and grassroots organizations comprised of determined tribal members have initiated numerous food projects, including seed distribution, food summits, farmers' markets, cattle and bison ranches, and community and school gardens.[1] These enterprises are steps towards achieving what many food activists refer to as "food sovereignty," although there are various ideas about what food sovereignty is, or can be. Further, there is no universal solution to achieving food sovereignty. Tribal food self-sufficiency involves the coordination of complex social, political, religious, economic, and environmental concerns. Those efforts vary by tribe because tribes adapted to colonization differently and they do not have access to the same resources; therefore, their food sovereignty goals also differ, provided they even have any. Many do not. While British food activist Raj Patel writes about the idea of food sovereignty in general, his statement that "there are so many versions of the concept, it is hard to know exactly what it means" certainly applies to indigenous people in the United States.[2]

The title theme of this special issue of the *AICRJ* is "Indigenous Food Sovereignty," so as a point of departure I begin with the most complete vision of the concept as it is basically defined in the 2007 Declaration of Nyéléni: "The right of peoples to healthy and culturally appropriate food produced through ecologically sound and sustainable methods, and their right to define their own food and agricultural systems." The declaration also asserts that food sovereignty "ensures that the rights to use and manage lands, territories, waters, seeds, livestock and biodiversity are in the hands of those of us who produce food."[3]

---

Devon A. Mihesuah, an enrolled citizen of the Choctaw Nation of Oklahoma, is the Cora Lee Beers Price Professor in the Humanities Program at the University of Kansas. She is the author of numerous award-winning books on indigenous history and current issues, including *Ned Christie: The Creation of an Outlaw* and *Cherokee Hero*; *Choctaw Crime and Punishment: 1884–1907*; and *American Indigenous Women: Decolonization, Empowerment, Activism*. She is former editor of the *American Indian Quarterly* and oversees the American Indian Health and Diet Project at the University of Kansas.

To be a "food sovereign" tribe ideally would mean, then, that a tribe has the right to control its food production, food quality, and food distribution. It supports tribal farmers and ranchers by supplying machinery and technology needed to plant and harvest. The tribe is not answerable to state regulatory control, and follows its own edicts, regulations, and ways of governance. Its members have educational and job opportunities. The tribe collectively decides if it wants to purchase foods produced outside its boundaries and if it wants to trade with other groups. The tribe has renewable energy infrastructure, such as solar and wind power.[4] Elders are honored for their ability to teach language and for imparting traditional indigenous knowledge about planting, harvesting, seed saving, hunting, basket and tool making, as well as ceremonies associated with sustenance. They remind us about female deities who among many tribes originally brought them sustenance. Rather than viewing environmental resources as commodities for monetary gain, tribal members show reverence for the land that sustains them. They protect and respect the natural world because thriving relationships between healthy ecosystems and indigenous peoples underlie tribal political, social, and religious systems. For indigenous activists concerned with food injustice, that is the ideal scenario. But if food sovereignty is defined in this way, is it possible?

## OKLAHOMA

Oklahoma presents opportunities for discussion about food sovereignty because of its multifaceted history, environmental issues, and current politics, which include uneven food quality, poor indigenous health, intratribal factionalism, trenchant racism, and the glaring dichotomy between those tribal members who are affluent and those suffering from extreme poverty.

Oklahoma became a state in 1907. Prior to that time, it was Indian Territory. The Indian Removal Act of 1830, signed by President Andrew Jackson, was a cruel and devastating policy that forced thousands of Indians to Indian Territory in order to make way for white settlement in the Southeast and elsewhere.[5] Today there are thirty-eight tribal nations in Oklahoma; sixty-seven tribes have lived there.[6] For Oklahoma tribes wishing to follow their foodway traditions, there is no "one-size-fits-all" model. Some tribes have an agricultural legacy, but also depended on wild game and plants. Plains tribes that arrived in the 1870s hunted bison and other animals, but they expanded their resource base by gathering wild flora and trading with tribes and non-Indians. Some, such as Comanches ("Lords of the Plains"), had no agricultural tradition but had access to a variety of foods and were adept at taking what they wanted.

Among those Native peoples who, under great duress and loss of life, came to Indian Territory, were the "Five Tribes" (Cherokee, Chickasaws, Choctaws, Mvskoke-Creeks, and Seminoles). They found that much of their new lands resembled their Southeastern homelands. There was plentiful game in the forests and grasslands and fertile soils allowed them to farm. They had ample water and a variety of nut trees and wild fruits.[7] Yet despite the assortment of foods that many Natives grew, gathered, and hunted, by the time of the Civil War different foods were becoming available and many Natives began suffering the consequences of altering their diets of vegetables, fruits, and game meats to rely upon sugary, fatty, and starchy foods instead.[8]

The reasons for these health changes are complex. Boarding schools, missionaries, and intermarriage with whites contributed to the disassociation from tribal language, religion, and foodways. Particular population groups that were affected include tribal members who were affluent—a group that included full-blood Native persons, although most were racially and culturally mixed—and Native students at the boarding schools, who were fed white flour and sugar three times a day. These populations developed digestive disorders, with some becoming diabetic or pre-diabetic. In addition, as non-Native intruders surged into Indian Territory throughout the 1800s, the plants and animals Indians once used for sustenance and medicine diminished. The ecosystems were transformed by dams, mines, deforestation, invasive species, and ranching. Those Native people who could not afford to purchase store goods survived on what they could grow; some suffered from malnutrition. The bison herds diminished, drastically altering the lifeways of Plains tribes. After being placed in Indian Territory in the late 1800s, Comanches, Cheyennes, Kiowas, and other hunters were forced to depend on inadequate rations provided by the federal government.[9]

Today, at least 16 percent of Native people in the United States suffer from diabetes and 33 percent are obese.[10] Among the Oklahoma population, Indians have the highest rates of heart disease, "unintentional injury deaths," diabetes, and asthma. They eat fewer fruits than whites, blacks, and Hispanics. The Oklahoma Department of Health assigns Natives Americans a grade of "D" for low physical activity and incidences of obesity, and an "F" for "poor mental health" and "poor physical health" days.[11] Of the Cherokees who seek treatment at Cherokee clinics, 34 percent are overweight or obese.[12] The rate of diabetes on the Osage reservation is 20.7 percent, double that of the rate in the United States. The rate of heart disease among reservation Osages is double that of those off-reservation. Twenty-one percent of reservation Osages live in poverty compared to 10.3 percent of the US population.[13] Children spend less time playing outdoors and adults are increasingly isolated from the land, resulting in waning interest in the natural world. Smoking and depression exacerbate their health issues.

It is not only people in Indian country who feel effects from environmental degradation, climate change, food-borne illnesses, industrial chemicals, and soil erosion.[14] Water and air are polluted, seafood is overharvested, and the cost of animal feed has risen. All consumers now face prices that are 40 percent higher in recent years for bread, baked goods, canned vegetables, fruit, eggs, beef, pork and chicken.[15] The avian flu, porcine epidemic diarrhea virus, and excessively dry and wet seasons have resulted in sick animals and failed wheat, lettuce, and corn crops. Food sovereignty activists are situated in an economy in which four seed companies, Dow AgroSciences, DuPont/Pioneer, Monsanto, and Syngenta, control 80 percent of the corn market, 70 percent of the soybean market, and half of the world's seed supply.[16] Ten companies own almost every brand of food and beverage.[17] Environmental activist Wendell Berry sums up what we all want: "Food that is nutritionally whole and uncontaminated by pesticides and other toxic chemical residues."[18]

Many tribal members who do not qualify for government commodities find that stores are not conveniently located and the products are inadequate. For example, the 2,251 square miles of the Osage reservation in Osage County has only four grocery stores, making it a "super food desert." Most of the land is for livestock ranching, not for agriculture, and there is no public transportation.[19] Most stores on Indian land offer produce that comes from farms that use genetically modified seeds. These pest-resistant crops grow bigger and more quickly, but they are less nutritious and leave behind eroded and depleted soils.[20]

Among Oklahoma Indians, the lack of food, or lack of nutritious food, is the result of their having no money to purchase it; being dependent on the government; having no control over resources; and being unable to produce food. Many Indians have eaten their traditional foods, hunted, and gardened their entire lives. Most, however, have not. Natives who take advantage of the commodities offered under the USDA's Food Distribution Program have about one hundred food-buying choices, but often they opt for white flour, lard, cheese, and sugary and salty items. Notably, food distribution commodities are available to low-income tribal members who live within a tribal nation's boundaries.[21] Yet not all residents on tribal lands are members of that tribe and, given the differing food histories of each tribe, their food choices are both likely to be different and to affect the diets of those around them. For example, the majority of the 233,126 persons residing within the Choctaw Nation are not Choctaws.[22] In addition, in Oklahoma's program, as long as there is one member of a federally recognized tribe in the residence, non-Indians also in the home can receive commodities under the Food Distribution Program. Their food choices may not include items that are culturally connected or healthy and their preferences might influence others in the house.

## "TRADITIONAL" FOODS

Health and traditionalism intertwine. Tribal members can consume non-indigenous foods and be healthy, but food sovereignty activists are hopeful that a return to traditional foodways will provide something more: empowering links to their cultures and histories. Of course, it must be determined what those traditional foodways are and if everyone agrees on what is "traditional."[23] The Choctaw Nation's website and the 2017 calendar, for example, feature some reasons many tribal members are obese and diabetic: a "traditional" recipes section heavy on unhealthy food items, including sugar, white flour, cheese, and butter, used for making grape dumplings, cheddar and corn chowder, crisp salt pork, cobblers, fried corn, fry bread, Indian tacos, and creamed Indian corn (sugar, flour, milk, and pork). A sweet potato dish that would be flavorful without any seasoning calls for adding two cups of sugar and onte cup of flour.[24] The Chickasaw Nation does the same, with "Chickasaw" appearing in the names of some dishes even though the ingredients are not indigenous.[25] Similarly, Osage cooking classes teach young tribal members how to make "Indian food" such as wheat flour rolled out in the "Osage custom"—that is, fried in hot grease—as well as to how to cook chicken and dumplings, and meat with wheat gravy.[26]

Defining traditional food is tricky because some Oklahoma tribes adopted European and African foods and material goods centuries ago and some define traditional foods as what their grandparents ate. Those traditionalists who advocate for precontact foods may clash with tribal members who argue that fried bread, mutton, and grape dumplings made with wheat flour and sugar are traditional, as are dishes made with dairy, eggs, beef, pork, and chicken. Ancestors of tribespeople in Oklahoma started growing European-introduced crops on a large scale for profit by the 1840s. After the Civil War, Choctaws cultivated sixty thousand acres of corn and potatoes, but also non-indigenous wheat and oats. By this time, members of the Five Tribes used metal axes, plows, hoes, harrows, scrapers, shovels, spades, threshers, mowers, and reapers. Backyard gardens featured more European-introduced foods: lettuce, turnips, peas, and mustard. Many cultivated European-introduced apple, peach, and plum trees. Some of the farmers along the North Fork and Arkansas Rivers grew cotton and tobacco and ranchers raised non-indigenous horses, cattle, mules, sheep, goats, and hogs.[27]

If the goal is to eat only precontact foods, then the list might include alligator, elk, waterfowl, deer, antelope, wild turkeys, and bison. Those animals have to be hunted or raised, and both options require financial planning. Tribes historically gathered flora such as mulberries, wild plums, grapes, onions, and nuts (such as pecan, hickory, walnuts, and acorns), but today those foods may only grow on private property. Traditional foods are not always available, so some food projects and families might use only a few indigenous foods as symbols of culture. For example, the Delawares were originally hunters and coastal people and were removed several times before settling in Indian Territory in 1867. They no longer have access to marine life so they stock their ponds with fish, hold annual fishing tournaments, and teach their children to hunt.[28]

Some tribes have vested economic interests in food production such as cattle, wheat, hogs, and sorghum, none of which is indigenous. However, supplying traditional foods to their members may not be their goal. Hunting tribes followed bison herds for hundreds of miles each year and obviously, they cannot do that today. The Quapaw Tribe of Indians moved to Indian Territory in 1834 and settled on 96,000 acres in what is now Quapaw County.[29] Traditionally, Quapaws hunted, gathered, and farmed, but like other tribes, they were not ranchers.[30] In June 2016, the Quapaw Tribe opened the Quapaw Cattle Company distribution center, The Quapaw Mercantile. The store sells beef and bison ribeye steaks, beef bacon, and bratwursts from the tribe's herds in Miami and Quapaw. They provide meat to the tribe's elder center, daycare centers, and the Quapaw and Downstream casino restaurants. The tribe is in the process of designing its own meat-processing plant and has plans to grow feed for the animals.[31] The Iowa, Modoc, Cheyenne and Arapaho Tribes, and Cherokee Nation raise bison. Some ranchers breed bison with cattle to create "beefalo."

### *Poverty*

"Food security" has been defined as members of households having, at all times, "physical and economic access to sufficient, safe and nutritious food that meets their dietary needs and food preferences for an active and healthy life."[32] Eric Holt-Giménez writes, "Where one stands on hunger depends on where one sits."[33] Some Natives in Oklahoma are quite affluent and can buy whatever they want; others are poverty-stricken and have little opportunity for advancement.

The Choctaw Nation of Oklahoma lands consist of 10,613 square miles of rural area in 10.5 counties in southern Oklahoma. In 2016 the Choctaw Nation had 9,000 workers on a payroll of $300 million. The tribe operates seven casinos, thirteen travel plazas, twelve smoke shops, two Chili franchises, a resort in Durant, and document-archiving companies; along with manufacturing, it manages seven Black Angus cattle ranches and provides other management services. In 2016 the Nation generated $658 million, with $148 million of that from state and federal funds.[34] The previous year, moreover, a 2015 tribal trust court settlement awarded the Choctaw and Chickasaw Nations $139.5 million and $46.5 million, respectively, for the federal government's failure to protect tribes' interests when it sold over one million acres of timberlands in the decades between 1908 and 1940.[35]

My tribe should not be an impoverished one, yet despite the millions of dollars produced each year, some of the poorest counties in the country are within the Choctaw Nation. Atoka, Coal, Haskell, Latimer, LeFlore, McCurtain, Pittsburg, and Pushmataha counties all have high-risk factors such as smoking, obesity, physical inactivity, and low consumption of fruit and vegetables. One census tract has a poverty rate of more than 52.8 percent, with leading causes of death being heart disease and cancer.[36] Those who do find work receive low wages. Recognizing the dire situation, in 2014 then-president Barack Obama named the Choctaw Nation one of five "Promise Zones." The award entails tax incentives for businesses that invest in the community and promises them "competitive advantage" when applying for federal grants.[37]

After the Promise Zone award, the chief business and economic development officer enlisted several Choctaws with expertise about traditional foods, medicine, and gardening to brainstorm strategies for the Farm-to-Table Agriculture initiative. The focus was to be on nutrition and natural medicines, in addition to myriad other issues such as Native foods, backyard gardens, agri-art, and farmers' markets. The new tribal chief elected that year, however, dismissed the business development officer, thereby severing ties with those of us who had contributed a plethora of ideas to the Promise Zone initiative. The initiative's leadership then created the Choctaw Small Business Development Services (CSBDS), which currently offers advice, planning, and counseling for tribal entrepreneurs, but not financial support.[38]

One of its stated goals is that "natural, historic, and cultural resources" serve as the foundation for initiatives, including "technology-enhanced traditional farming and ranching," large greenhouses, and training for women-owned businesses.[39] Choctaws did not traditionally ranch, so it is not clear what is meant by "traditional farming and ranching." Indeed, backyard gardens had been among the suggestions initially submitted to the Choctaw Promise Zone initiative. Families desirous of cultivating gardens would have been given seeds, basic tools, soil, and water. The tribe would finance the plowing of land, and would provide lessons on basic gardening. That idea apparently has been discarded. The monthly tribal newspaper, the *BISKINIK*, includes columns about traditional foods, but there are no indigenous gardens or classes to teach tribal members how to grow or gather them.[40]

Part of the Choctaw Nation's plan is to create an educated workforce that can succeed in the business world. This is a crucial initiative considering that Oklahoma is ranked forty-ninth in the nation in educational services and performance.[41] If that workforce education strategy also includes implementing "traditional" farming methods, that workforce must know how to cultivate traditional foods and how to save seeds. The plan calls for partnerships with Oklahoma State University, Eastern Oklahoma State

College, and the Kiamichi Technology Center.[42] However, none of those schools offers courses dealing with Choctaw history and culture.

For low-income seniors residing in the Choctaw Nation's 10.5-county area, the Choctaw Nation has instituted the Senior Farmers' Market Nutrition Program. Qualified seniors receive $50 and an additional 3,800 participants receive $30 to purchase locally produced foods. Funded by both the USDA and the Choctaw Nation, the program is "designed to encourage participants to make better food choices and raise awareness of farmers and farmers markets." Only about half of the ninety-five farmers who sell their produce to the market are tribal members, which might defeat the purpose of supporting tribal farmers. Non-Natives over 60 years of age living in a household that includes one enrolled Choctaw are eligible for checks.[43]

An additional concern is lack of data regarding what consumers do with the produce. The Choctaw Nation has a number of health initiatives, but there is little research revealing their successes beyond the number of people using the vouchers. The tribal newspaper includes articles about diabetes, obesity, and exercise, and the Diabetes Multi-Resource Task Force travels across the Choctaw Nation to educate tribal members about healthy lifestyles. However, as seen on the calendars, the Choctaw Nation's website, and at tribal celebrations, the tribe also provides and promotes unhealthy food.

## IMPACT OF DIMINISHED HEALTH CARE FUNDING

As of March 2018, the Trump administration has weakened the Affordable Care Act and continues to seek its repeal. Through the Indian Healthcare Improvement Act (IHCIA) that is part of the ACA, Indian health centers can bill third-party insurers, Medicare, and Medicaid. Almost 2.2 million people who use the IHS will be impacted negatively if the ACA is repealed.[44] The IHS could potentially lose over $800 million in funding from Medicaid programs.[45] The Choctaw Nation recently completed a 143,000 square-foot regional medical clinic, the first tribal clinic in the United States with an outpatient ambulatory surgery center. The ambitious project features dental services, podiatry, endoscopy, pediatrics, respiratory therapy, cardiology, diabetic and pulmonology care, in addition to behavioral health services and an on-site laboratory.[46] The tribe pays for the construction of the facility, and the Indian Health Service works with Congress to provide funding for staff. Considering that President Trump has called for a 16.2 percent cut in funding for the Department of Health and Human Services, this is cause for alarm.[47] Everyone needs medical and dental care. Nonetheless, to improve physical and mental health and avoid hospital visits to treat maladies caused by poor diet and inactivity, we know that it is key to adopt an exercise regime and a diet of unprocessed and fresh foods, and to quit smoking.

## TREATIES AND ACCESS TO TRADITIONAL FOODS: HUNTING, FISHING, AND GATHERING RIGHTS

Treaties between tribes and the federal government are legally binding contracts that contain assurances of self-determination, healthcare and educational services, religious freedom, and rights to hunt and fish. The federal government has a responsibility to protect tribal treaty rights, tribal lands, and resources. Those who were forcibly sent to Indian Territory were understandably suspicious about the government, as are their descendants. Removal treaties guaranteed tribes that they would retain their lands, but Oklahoma has a long history of racism and dispossessing tribes of their property—27 million acres during the allotment period. Portraits of men such as Governor Haskell, who stole land from tribes during the allotment period, hang in the statehouse.[48] The discovery in 1897 of oil under Osage lands not only resulted in the murders of dozens of tribal citizens at the hands of unscrupulous whites intent on taking their resources, but also caused socioeconomic rifts within the tribe.[49] University of Oklahoma students are nicknamed "Boomer Sooners," after the intrepid pioneers who illegally jumped the gun on the Appropriations Act of 1889 in order to claim land belonging to tribal peoples.

Tribes must know how to negotiate the various challenges from outside forces (e.g., racism, climate change, pollution) as they relate to the powers of their tribe, the states, and federal government, as well as abrogation of treaty agreements that guarantee water, hunting, fishing, and gathering rights. Several treaties in the 1830s guaranteed to Cherokees "free and unmolested use" of lands not within the bounds of Cherokee Nation.[50] It was not until 2015 that the Cherokee Nation became the first tribe to sign a compact giving their members hunting and fishing rights in all seventy-seven counties in Oklahoma. Cherokees over the age of sixteen can receive one "dual license" (Cherokee Nation and Oklahoma) and one free turkey and deer tag per year. Beginning in January 2017, Choctaw Nation citizens in Oklahoma did not have to pay for licenses either; the tribes pay a fee for each tag received and Oklahoma in turn receives federal monies for wildlife conservation.[51]

These are indeed important compacts, but one cannot (or should not) just pick up a gun and go hunting. Procuring a deer or turkey requires skill, patience, and knowledge of hunting safety and protocol. Proper equipment and clothing is expensive. Moreover, physical fitness is essential for those who stalk birds all day or who must drag a heavy animal back to camp. Then it must be dressed and butchered. Although some Natives are adept at using traditional blowguns, rabbit sticks, and bows to hunt small animals, it should be pointed out that not everyone has the wherewithal to hunt game.

## TRADITIONAL FOODS AND ECOSYSTEM CHANGES

A return to traditional ways of eating requires access to healthy ecosystems and its resources. After the 1830s removal to Indian Territory, human actions brought about serious environmental changes and resource depletion, including building fences, dams, and railroads, harvesting timber, mining, and digging lakes, as well as drought and overgrazing. For example, in the 1830s much of the Choctaw Nation's fertile lands were crossed by streams of clear water and lush with edible plant foods. After removal, my family settled in Atoka County, then moved to the Kully Chaha ("high spring") township in the shadow of Nvnih Chufvk (Sugar Loaf mountain), once deemed both by Choctaws and newspaper reporters as an "oasis" of springs, bountiful game, nuts, and berries.[52] Despite its relative isolation, the nearby cattle ranching, diversion of waterways, and deforestation caused the disappearance of many wild fruit plants, turkeys, deer, and pollinators. Many Natives stated that they were careful not to overhunt, and throughout the Choctaw Nation the complaints were the same: when white intruders arrived onto their lands the herds and flocks declined—some said to the point of "extinction"—mainly because whites engaged in unchecked sport hunting.[53] In response, in 1895, the Oklahoma Territorial Legislature created the first game laws to address severe wildlife depletion.[54] Fish, game, and environmental problems remain, however.

## BLUNDERING INTRUDERS AND ENVIRONMENTAL DAMAGE

Turner, et al. use the term "blundering intruders" to describe policies and external projects that impede indigenous peoples' efforts to protect their cultures, resources, and independence.[55] A major blunderer is Oklahoma's fracking industry, which opens fissures into the earth in order to extract oil and gas with high-pressure forcing of sand, liquid, and sometimes chemicals. Fracking's waste liquid often flows into underground aquifers and pollutes water and soil.[56] The rocks fracture because of the force of the injection. Disposal wells with millions of gallons of liquid cause faults to slip, resulting in earthquakes; the state of Oklahoma has the highest number of induced earthquakes in the country. There were 889 earthquakes in 2015 and 1,055 from March 2017 to March 2018.[57] The September 2016 earthquake damaged the Pawnee Nation's administrative buildings and tribal members' homes. The Nation responded by filing suit against the Bureau of Indian Affairs (BIA) and Bureau of Land Management (BLM) in an effort to rid their nation of drilling permits and oil and gas leases on their land, which the agencies approved without consulting the tribe or adhering to natural-resource protection laws.[58]

Fracking is not the only problem. In June 2017, the Oklahoma Department of Environmental Quality warned that fish in fifty-four Oklahoma lakes have high levels of mercury and that consumers should limit their intake.[59] The Poncas, who were removed to Indian Territory from Nebraska in the 1870s, find that fish in the nearby Arkansas River are polluted from raw sewage and a ConocoPhillips refinery and other factories in Ponca City. They also battle air pollution from carbon-black emissions. The Poncas suffer from what Mekasi Horinek, the coordinator of Bold Oklahoma, calls a "tirade of cancer" because of "environmental racism."[60] The problems are so severe that the Ponca Nation will be the first tribal nation to add a statute to enact the "Rights of Nature."[61] Osage oil still causes serious environmental problems because the BIA will not enforce oil and gas drilling regulations.[62] The Cherokee Nation established the Inter-Tribal Environmental Council (ITEC) in 1992 for protecting tribal national resources and their environments. The consortia consists of thirty-nine tribes in Oklahoma, Texas, and New Mexico. Recently, the Cherokee Nation filed a restraining order against Sequoyah Fields Fuels Corporation to prevent it from dumping radioactive waste into the Arkansas and Illinois rivers.[63]

Conservationists will continue to resist those who emphasize economic development over a healthy environment. In February 2017, President Trump appointed Oklahoma Attorney General Scott Pruitt to head the Environmental Protection Agency (EPA). Pruitt's office previously sued the EPA at least a dozen times in efforts to curb environmental protection regulations, including pollution policies.[64] A few months later,

Oklahoma Governor Mary Fallin signed into law House Bill 1123, which makes it illegal for anyone to trespass on property containing a "critical infrastructure facility," and that includes pipeline interconnections for oil, gas, and chemicals. Trespassers could receive a $1,000 fine, six months in jail, or both. Those who damage or destroy property might face a $100,000 fine and/or ten years in prison.[65] The Diamond Pipeline will cross 491 waterways and is set to transport almost 200,000 barrels of crude oil each day from Cushing, Oklahoma, to Memphis, Tennessee. Peaceful protesters have camped at the Oklahoma Coalition to Defeat the Diamond Pipeline's Oka Lawa Camp (Choctaw for "many waters") since March 2017. The camp is located on private, allotted land east of McCurtain, Oklahoma, and from that safe spot protesters can educate the country about the pipeline without being harassed.[66]

## POACHING, INVASIVE SPECIES, AND LOSS OF POLLINATORS

Poachers illegally take many deer, elk, fish and other animals every year in Oklahoma and trespass onto private land. For example, the Mihesuah family allotment on Little Beaver Creek in southern Oklahoma is 180 acres of forest and grassland that the family has hunted and fished since 1902. Multiple times a year my husband hunts for deer, turkeys, and quail, and every time he removes illegally placed deer stands and cameras and contends with poachers, who invariably argue that they were "lost." There also is the problem of runoff from the multitude of cows that graze on ranchland surrounding the allotment. Cows destroy vegetation, contaminate ground water, and emit nitrogen into the atmosphere. Cattle need pastureland and ranchers often cut trees. In fall 2016, one neighboring white rancher clear-cut an entire swath of cottonwoods to make way for more pasture, thus causing more contaminated drainage. The bass, carp, catfish, crappie, perch, and turtles that used to inhabit Little Beaver Creek are almost gone now.

Non-indigenous flora and fauna such as Poison hemlock (*Conium maculatium*), Dutch elm disease (a fungus), Eastern Red Cedar (out of control because of fire suppression), salt cedar, tamarisk, Chinese bush clover, musk thistle, and Bradford pear have spread throughout Oklahoma.[67] *Sericea lespedeza*, a perennial legume, was introduced in Kansas in 1900 to control erosion, but now it has spread far beyond that area and is considered a hard-to-eradicate noxious weed. It has, for example, overgrown the bison-grazing area in the Seneca-Cayuga Nation and the animals will not eat it.[68] Many of the more than two hundred lakes in Oklahoma (all but sixty-two of which were created by dams) now contain non-indigenous Zebra mussel, bighead carp, golden algae, and hydrilla, among others. Wild boar (also known as wild pigs and wild hogs) can weigh hundreds of pounds. The aggressive and intelligent animals now inhabit all seventy-seven Oklahoma counties. They reproduce quickly and destroy agriculture, livestock, and ecosystems. Rush Springs, also known as the "Watermelon Capital of the World," is my family's favorite place to acquire watermelons, but feral hogs now destroy multiple acres when the fruits are ripe.[69]

Pollinators—butterflies, moths, flies, beetles, wasps, and hummingbirds—collect nectar from flowering plants and in the process spread pollen. Their activity is crucial to the survival of fruit, vegetable, and nut plants. Residents of Indian Territory and Oklahoma observed healthy populations of pollinators until habitat loss and pesticides reduced their numbers.[70] In recent years, Oklahoma has lost more bees than any other state to drought, pesticides, undernutrition, and varroa mites.[71] Natives stated that during the late 1800s they had access to plenty of bee trees and hives in caves and under cliffs, and many men and women kept aviaries. One man recalled finding a hive so big that he collected a "washtub" of honey.[72] In an effort to increase the pollinator population, the Monarch Watch Program at the University of Kansas and the Euchee Butterfly Farm in Bixby were awarded a $250,000 grant from the National Fish and Wildlife Foundation dedicated to planting milkweed and other plants for monarchs and pollinators. TEAM (Tribal Environmental Action for Monarchs) consists of Chickasaw, Citizen Band Potawatomi, Miami, Muskogee-Creek, Osage, Seminole Nations, and Eastern Shawnee tribes that have pledged to plant 35,000 milkweed plants and 28,000 native wildflowers in the next two years.[73]

## THE FAMILY AND COMMUNITY GARDENING MODEL

A challenge facing those tribes desiring to provide food for all their members is how to produce it on a large scale in a safe and sustainable manner. Tribes historically did raise crops in just that way, but it was a community effort. Today, larger farms invest in machinery and other technologies that make production easier, maximize profits, and minimize costs.[74] Many of those large-scale agricultural endeavors, however, use technological innovations such as fertilizers and pesticides that result in depletion of groundwater.[75]

Anthony "Chako" Ciocco, National Program Coordinator of the Ancestral Lands Program on the Navajo Nation and former communications coordinator for the Mvskoke Food Sovereignty Initiative in Okmulgee, believes that "Our agricultural practices are a major part of who we are. If we were really sovereign we'd be living in the Mvskoke way."[76] Prior to the removal of the Mvskoke-Creeks in the 1830s, each town worked a large garden divided into family parcels. Everyone worked them: women cared for the small family gardens and in summer, when men did not hunt, men helped women tend the larger community gardens. Other times, women did the bulk of the labor with the assistance of older men who could no longer hunt.[77] One man blew a conch shell to call the men to work. They arrived at the garden with their hoes and axes while the women arrived with food for the day. William Bartram, who observed them farming in the eighteenth century, described them as "marching in order to the field as if they were going to battle." Those who did not work were fined. The farmers sang as they worked, usually through early afternoon, when they sometimes broke to play games. Children sat in small shelters that were interspersed in the fields in order to scare away pests such as birds and raccoons. Men patrolled the fields at night to deter deer. When it was time to harvest, each family gathered plants from their parcel and donated a portion of their corn crop to the "king's crib," a cache of corn for use in hard times, for guests, and for war parties.[78]

Their main foods were corn, sweet potatoes, rice, squashes, and pumpkins, as well as the non-indigenous watermelons. Creeks pounded, boiled, and then strained hickory nuts to extract the oily, sweet liquid to use in corn dishes. In addition to produce, they consumed waterfowl, rabbits, turkey, venison, alligator, bear, deer, trout, catfish, sunfish, bream, and soft-shelled tortoise, as well as the European-introduced beef, goat, and pork.[79] Creeks had festivals every month and almost all were dedicated to hunting or agriculture, most notably their principal festival that takes place when their corn crops mature in August, called the "feast of first fruits."[80]

Choctaws also used a plethora of flora and fauna, including acorns, alligators, blackberries, chestnuts, chinquapin, several varieties of corn (dent, flint, flour, and pop), deer, fish, geese, wild grapes, hickory nuts and oil, mulberries, mushrooms, pecans, persimmons, wild plums, potatoes, pumpkins, strawberries, sunflowers, squirrels, sweet potatoes, turkey, walnuts, and wild onions.[81] Each Choctaw family was responsible for their own sustenance and families cultivated backyard gardens. Men and women procured game. Families often lived far from each other, but feasts and religious ceremonies necessarily brought families and clans together.[82]

After removal to Indian Territory, many families continued with their small gardens around their houses, what nineteenth-century residents of Indian Territory referred to as "patches" and "roasting-ear patches."[83] Some family gardens were larger. One Atoka family that moved to Indian Territory from Mississippi in 1889 maintained an ambitious garden of corn, potatoes, pumpkins, beans, peas, and peanuts, together with an orchard of apple, peach, plum, pear, and cherry trees, as well as berry bushes and grapevines. They managed cattle, hogs, and horses, along with chickens, turkeys, and bees. Another resident cultivated five acres of corn, peas, beans, and pumpkins. When planting corn he dropped a minnow into the hole along with a corn kernel.[84] The variety of cultivated plants allowed farmers to recycle nutrients and organic matter. Choctaw seed-savers took great pride in saving the best kernels and stringing cobs in a dry place.[85] If people lost kernels or seeds or had a poor growing season, they could trade something of equal value with a neighbor for more seeds.

I recount the importance of family gardens as a lifeline to cultural, emotional, and physical survival through multiple generations in my first novel, *Roads of My Relations* (2000). My ancestors were removed from the Southeast in the 1830s, and like many other Choctaws and Chickasaws, they cultivated backyard gardens that supplied a good portion of their diet. Understanding the seasons and knowing when to plant and harvest were crucial to survival. My parents had a variety of plant foods growing around their home, but I have duplicated the large garden my grandparents cultivated in Muskogee, which was a copy of what came before them.[86] As I write this in July 2017, there remains in one of our freezers frozen peppers, okra, dried tomatoes, and squash soup from plants grown last summer, as well as approximately one-quarter of a white-tailed deer, a wild turkey, two pheasants, numerous quail, and catfish from our pond. Our modest greenhouse and inexpensive cold frames allow me to start planting in early spring and to keep foods going into the cool fall and cold winter. Since spring we have harvested potatoes, herbs, carrots, beets, spinach, bok choy, kale, broccoli, raspberries, mulberries, and strawberries. Corn, peppers, green beans, okra, squashes, and another round of potatoes are yet to come. We save seeds, make compost, use rain barrels, and created four large pollinator gardens around the property. Not all the foods are indigenous and the gardens do not supply us with everything we need. Still, this kind of gardening provides quite a bounty and is realistic for families willing to spend time outside and to exert themselves. If tribal members are physically unable to garden, the tribe should provide a workforce to do it for them.

### *Comanches and the Need for Food Initiatives*

Not every tribe now in Oklahoma farmed historically and therefore they do not have an agricultural tradition to revive. It can be a dilemma for those Kiowas, Cheyennes, Arapahos, Plains Apaches, and Comanches who are looking for cultural connections to traditional foods. Comanches, for example, once roamed over "Comancheria," a vast area of various ecosystems with myriad resources.[87] They historically ate mainly game meats, but they also relied on a variety of wild fruits and trade items (as well as food they stole, notably corn, squashes, and sheep).[88] The Comanche Nation has a diabetes awareness program and an environmental program that monitors hazardous materials in eight Oklahoma counties, but as of November 2017 it has no food sustainability plan. The monthly publication, *Comanche Nation News*,[89] includes recipes for untraditional and unhealthy foods: patty melts with one stick of butter and eight slices of cheese; cabbage casserole with butter, Cheez Whiz, and grated cheese; pecan pie with butter, sugar, and dark Karo syrup; cottage pudding with flour, sugar, milk, and shortening; and a host of other recipes that include overabundances of fat, lard, sugar, and salt. Cultural disconnection and the lack of both resources and food initiative planning are among the reasons why Comanches suffer from high rates of diabetes and obesity.

## SUSTAINING ENTHUSIASM AND INSTITUTING BIOSAFETY

Producing food in the backyard sounds enticing, but the reality of the work involved deters many. To illustrate, in 2006 the then-provost of the University of Kansas allotted me an acre of land on campus to establish an indigenous demonstration garden that would operate out of the Indigenous Studies Department. Funding provided fencing, equipment, soil, a water line, benches, birdbaths and feeders, gloves, plant labels, a kiosk, composting, water barrels, and an information center. Colleagues with similar weather from around the country promised to donate heirloom seeds. The idea was to give students a hands-on experience in cultivating plants their tribes used. Planning was to be done by students so they could research their tribes' agricultural techniques, ceremonies associated with food, the names of foods and animals in their tribes' language, and how to save the foods for cold months. They would take that knowledge home to their families and tribes. Indigenous students expressed excitement at the idea of a garden featuring foods of their ancestors, but what ultimately killed the initiative was that only one student was willing to get his hands dirty.

Maybe that attitude is changing. Individuals often feel they have no say in their tribes' decisions. However, many understand that their collective actions can go a long way towards creating tribal cohesion and supplying food for their households and communities. In 2014, the Cherokee Nation distributed heirloom corn, beans, squash, and gourd seeds to more than 1,500 Cherokees.[90] In 2013, the Cherokee Nation began its "Learn to Grow" project, teaching children how to plant, cultivate and harvest. The next year, over 3,500 children cultivated a variety of garden produce.[91] In

August 2010, AmeriCorps awarded the Osage Nation a $1.1 million grant to create a twelve-acre Wah-Zha-Zhi "ecological park" and develop the Bird Creek Farm located near Pawhuska to include walking trails, gardens, and a farmers' market. Plans include classes on cooking and "traditional Osage dishes."[92] Vann Bighorse, who directs the Wah-Zha-Zhi Cultural Center, is attempting to collect heirloom seeds, grow crops, and then distribute seeds to tribal members.[93]

It will be interesting to learn the fate of tribal heirloom seeds. Do any individuals who receive seeds sell theirs to non-Indians? Do any of them work for biotech companies? Many tribes have instituted strict research guidelines in order to protect their intellectual and cultural property, but enforcing a ban on nontribal use of heirloom seeds will be challenging, especially when those seeds leave the tribal nation.[94] In addition, blunders include allowing GMO plants to cross-pollinate with fields of heirloom plants. Without biosafety policies, tribal plants will become endangered.

## SOVEREIGNTY AND FOODWAYS SYSTEMS: NOW WHAT?

A common goal among activists is to achieve tribal autonomy and the ability to supply nutritious and affordable foods to tribal members.[95] At the very least, there must be clean air, uncontaminated water, fertile soil, regular weather patterns, adequate pollinators, clean energy, farm equipment, and a recycling and composting system. There also must be laws to protect the environment and resources.[96] A solid healthcare system must be in place. Indeed, significant hurdles must be overcome in order to return to traditional ways of eating (or to have nutritious food), to maintain a healthy environment, and to inspire tribal pride through recovering cultural knowledge.

Webster's defines a "sovereign state" as autonomous, free from external control.[97] The federal government declares that tribes are sovereign entities with the right to govern themselves, but the United States also deems them "domestic dependent nations" and ultimately holds power over every tribe. As Corntassel and Bryce wrote in 2012, "the indigenous rights discourse has limits and can only take struggles for land reclamation and justice so far."[98] Tribes can attempt revitalization of traditional foodways and will succeed in many endeavors, but until they have control over their lands and resources and are independent from neoliberal food policies, they will not achieve food sovereignty. Kanien'kehaka activist Taiaiake Alfred reminds us that "sovereignty" is a European concept and does not adequately describe indigenous peoples' traditional philosophies.[99] Indeed, if the goal is to revert to traditionalism, then the quest for food sovereignty is further complicated because not only are many tribal governments patterned after the US government, many tribal members have vested interests in keeping them that way.

Highly motivated individuals instigate food initiatives and the entire tribe does not always support them. Not every Indian has an emotional investment in eating tribes' traditional foods and not everyone is concerned about the environment. Many avoid political activism because it can be emotionally exhausting. There are vast socioeconomic differences among members of some tribes and the internal politics among some are volatile. Some community-based food autonomy and health endeavors are hampered by inadequate management, shortage of finances, lack of nutritional knowledge, absence of long-range planning, and intratribal factionalism. As Hope Radford discovered after an investigation of food sovereignty efforts among seven tribes in Montana, "Tribes are making progress, but many people are still hungry, many people are still unhealthy, and many people are still left without a voice in deciding what their community eats and where it comes from."[100] Anyone familiar with tribal politics knows that one tribal council might approve a project requiring tribal funds, but future councils can deny that venture. That includes food initiatives.

Tribes cannot overhaul their foodways system without assistance from outside entities and without adhering to governmental laws and regulations. Many business owners need loans and food project organizers seek aid from indigenous and non-indigenous foundations. Institutes such as the Intertribal Agriculture Council,[101] Native Food Systems Resource Center,[102] Seeds of Native Health,[103] and the Indigenous Food and Agriculture Initiative at the University of Arkansas School of Law[104] have assisted tribes with heirloom seed distribution, community and school gardens, business and cattle ranching initiatives. However, these organizations are in turn funded by, or partnered with, foundations such as W. K. Kellogg Foundation, American Association of Retired Persons, and Walmart Foundation, among other non-indigenous entities. The grants and advice offered by these institutes are crucial in helping certain projects flourish, but it takes much more than a few projects to make tribes truly food sovereign.

In order for food initiatives to prosper (that is, to be sustaining), plans must be long range, taking into account available finances and resources and identifying people committed to the goals. Tribal and community discussions are crucial in order to determine what is already being attempted, identify the most critical concerns, pinpoint policies that have negative impact, ascertain what resources are needed and which endeavors are successful, and decide how best to proceed. The decision-making entity should be comprised of tribal members with knowledge about traditional plants, seed saving, cultivating, harvesting, and animal processing, as well as those with political, economic, and scientific expertise. These knowledgeable and culturally connected tribal members (not just friends and political cronies of the current leadership) should have major roles in food education and Native-owned farms.

There are numerous indigenous food success stories. Schoolchildren cultivate garden plots, more conference papers about traditional foodways are presented each year, indigenous haute cuisine is a new trend, and more grants are forthcoming. Many Native people are just now discovering their traditional foods, and any news story about an indigenous chef or a successful garden harvest is felt to be unique and an exciting step towards their vision of food sovereignty. It remains to be seen, however, if schoolchildren are inspired enough to continue gardening; if recently formed pan-Indian indigenous food organizations benefit communities; and if indigenous foodie gatherings and summits will serve only those who can afford to attend them. Moreover, research is needed to determine if the tribal food initiatives that have emerged across the United States improve health. Indeed, gatherings, chefs' cooking demonstrations, food tastings, and philosophizing are easy compared to the work of confronting the political, economic, and social realities of building food sovereignty. That is why the indigenous food sovereignty movement might stay in a state of "sovereignization"—that is, continual planning and constructing, including negotiation, protest, and debate—until these questions are answered.[105]

In January 2017, Michael Wise wrote a blog entry, "Native Foods and the Colonial Gaze," asserting that "if there are important lessons to be learned by the food movement that are buried in the Native American past, they aren't embodied by ancient vegetables or archaic fishing techniques, but by stories of Indigenous resistance and accommodation to forces of colonialism and capitalism that have refashioned the lives, livelihoods, and dinner plates of us all over the last few centuries."[106] Wise is partially correct. A common way for the Five Tribes to catch fish, for example, was to daze them by dragging the mashed perennial herb white snakeroot (*Ageratina altissima*) through the water, then netting or shooting the paralyzed fish with arrows.[107] This "Devil's Shoestring" is toxic and today the practice is illegal in Oklahoma.[108] Some, however, still catch fish in an "archaic" way by spearing or shooting them with a bow (my son catches catfish in our pond in this manner). Yet Wise overlooks key facts: those "ancient vegetables" in large measure accounted for the good health of Native peoples and the foundation of their cultures is their relationship to the Earth that produced those plants. Many of us will continue what Wise refers to as our "quixotic quests for authenticity." We know that past diets, activities, and reverence for the natural world can help us avoid many modern health problems.

Regardless of the challenges, we will endeavor to accomplish what is realistic for our tribes and communities.


## *Acknowledgments*

Thank you to Peggy Carlton, Anthony "Chako" Ciocco, Jeff Corntassel, Pat Gwin, Nicky Michael, and Chip Taylor.


## NOTES

Reprinted with permission from Devon Mihesuah, *American Indian Culture and Research* 41:3 (2017): 9–30.

1. Indigenous Food and Agriculture Initiative, *A National Intertribal Survey and Report: Intertribal Food Systems* (Fayetteville: Indigenous Food and Agriculture Initiative, 2015) (funded by W. K. Kellogg Foundation).

2. For a discussion of the history of the term "food sovereignty," see Raj Patel, "What Does Food Sovereignty Look Like?" *The Journal of Peasant Studies* 36, no. 3 (July 2009): 663, https://doi.org/10.1080/03066150903143079.

3. "Declaration of Nyéléni: Declaration of the Forum for Food Sovereignty," February 27, 2007, https://nyeleni.org/spip.php?article290.

4. See, for example, "Winning the Future: Navajo-Hopi land Commission Leverages DOE Grant to Advance Solar Ranch Project," October 22, 2015, https://energy.gov/indianenergy/articles/winning-future-navajo-hopi-land-commission-leverages-doe-grant-advance-solar; Katherine Saltzstein, "Hopi Woman Brings Power of the Sun to the People," *Native Sun News*, October 9, 2014.

5. Act of June 30, 1834, Pub. L. No. 23–161, § 12, 4 Stat. 729, 730 (codified as amended at 25 U.S.C. § 177 (2006).

6. See Blue Clark, *Indian Tribes of Oklahoma: A Guide* (Norman: University of Oklahoma Press, 2009).

7. See Devon Mihesuah, "Sustenance and Health among the Five Tribes in Indian Territory, Post-Removal to Statehood," *Ethnohistory* 62, no. 2 (April 2015): 263–84.

8. See Devon Mihesuah, "Historical Research and Diabetes in Indian Territory: Revisiting Kelly M. West's Theory of 1940," *American Indian Culture and Research Journal* 40, no. 4 (2016): 1–21, https://doi.org/10.17953/aicrj.40.4.mihesuah.

9. See Devon A. Mihesuah, "Comanche Traditional Foodways and the Decline of Health," *Great Plains Journal* 50 (forthcoming).

10. Anne Gordon and Vanessa Oddo, "Addressing Child Hunger and Obesity in Indian Country: Report to Congress" (Princeton, NJ: Mathematica Policy Research, January 12, 2012), 5–7.

11. Oklahoma State Department of Health, *2014 State of the State's Health,* 13, 15, 24, 26, 28, 30, 35, 36, https://ok.gov/health2/documents/SOSH 2014.pdf.

12. Sarah McColl, "With Heirloom Seeds, Cherokee Nurture Cultural History and Future Health," *takepart,* January 29, 2016, http://www.takepart.com/article/2016/01/29/cherokee-seeds/.

13. Benny Polacca, "Health Survey: Reservation Osages Report 'Poorer Health' Than Osages Living Elsewhere," *Osage News,* August 30, 2010.

14. "Oklahoma Academy of Science Statement on Global Climate Change," November 8, 2013, http://www.oklahomaacademyofscience.org/uploads/4/6/0/5/46053599/oas_statement_of_global_climate_change__2013_.pdf.

15. Alexander Kent, "20 Grocery Items That Are Driving Up Your Food Bill," *USA Today,* February 22, 2016.

16. Ken Roseboro, "The GMO Seed Monopoly: Fewer Choices, Higher Prices," *Food Democracy Now,* October 4, 2013.

17. Kate Taylor, "These Ten Companies Control Everything You Buy," *Business Insider,* September 28, 2016.

18. Wendell Berry, *The Unsettling of America: Culture and Agriculture* (San Francisco: Sierra Club Books, 1977), 218.

19. See http://www.nationalservice.gov/blogs/2014-03-07/gardening-osage.

20. See Mark Shepard, *Restoration Agriculture* (Austin, Texas: Acres USA Inc., 2013); Akihiko Michimi and Michael C. Winmerly, "Associations of Supermarket Availability with Obesity and Fruit and Vegetable Consumption in the Conterminous United States," *International Journal of Health Geographics* 9, no. 1 (October 8, 2010): 49, https://doi.org/10.1186/1476-072X-9-49.

21. Food Distribution Program on Indian Reservations (FDPIR), https://www.fns.usda.gov/fdpir/eligibility-how-apply.

22. Choctaw Nation, "When Catastrophe Strikes: Responses to Natural Disaster in Indian Country," https://www.choctawnation.com/news-events/press-media/when-catastrophe-strikes-responses-natural-disasters-indian-country.

23. This is discussed in detail in Devon Mihesuah, "Indigenous Health Initiatives, Frybread, and the Marketing of Non-Traditional "Traditional" American Indian Foods," *Native American and Indigenous Studies* 3, no. 2 (Fall 2016): 45–69, https://muse.jhu.edu/article/641379.

24. Choctaw Nation, "Food," https://www.choctawnation.com/history-culture/choctaw-traditions/food.

25. Chickasaw Nation, "Foods," https://www.chickasaw.net/our-nation/culture/foods.aspx. Chickasaws did not grow corn, squash and beans together in the manner of the "Three Sisters."

26. Shannon Shaw Duty, "Osage Cooking Classes Begin with Young Crop of Students," *Osage News* (Pawhuska, OK), August 20, 2010.

27. Muriel H. Wright, "A Report to the General Council of the Indian Territory Meeting at Okmulgee in 1873," *Chronicles of Oklahoma* 34, no. 1 (1956): 9–10.

28. Delaware tribal council member Nicky Michael, personal communication. See also C. A. Weslager, *The Delaware Indians: A History* (New Brunswick: Rutgers University Press, 1990).

29. Barbara Harper, "Quapaw Traditional Lifeways Scenario," Superfund Research, Oregon State (2008), http://superfund.oregonstate.edu/sites/superfund.oregonstate.edu/files/harper_2008_quapaw_scenario_final.pdf.

30. W. David Baird, *The Quapaw Indians: A History of the Downstream People* (University of Oklahoma Press, Norman, 1980).

31. Kimberly Barker, "Quapaw Tribe Opens New Meat Distribution Center," June 7, 2016, *Miami News-Record*; "Bumpers College, School of Law Help Quapaw Tribe With Processing Plant," December 7, 2016, University of Arkansas News, http://news.uark.edu/articles/37330/bumpers-college-school-of-law-help-quapaw-tribe-with-processing-plant. Pima and Maricopa tribal members in Arizona also are attempting to revitalize their food traditions by cultivating as many of those traditional foods as they can. They face resistance from federal food safety laws that restrict their food production and processing, so now they are writing their own laws. These regulations will ensure that foods will be properly refrigerated, and free of contaminants such as salmonella and E-coli. The challenge is that bison is considered "exotic," each animal must be inspected (for a fee), and the animals have to be processed in facilities approved by the FDA. Tristan Ahtone, "Tribes Create Their Own Food Laws to Stop USDA from Killing Native Food Economies," *Yes!* Magazine, May 24, 2016, http://www.yesmagazine.org/people-power/tribes-create-their-own-food-laws-to-stop-usda-from-killing-native-food-economies-20160524.

32. Food and Agriculture Organization of the United Nations (FAO), World Food Summit, "Rome Declaration on World Food Security," November 13–17, 1996, http://www.fao.org/docrep/003/w3613e/w3613e00.HTM.

33. Eric Holt-Gimenez, "Food Security, Food Justice, or Food Sovereignty?" in Alison Hope Alkon and Julian Agyeman, eds., *Cultivating Food Justice: Race, Class, and Sustainability* (Cambridge: MIT Press, 2011), 319.

34. *The 2016 State of the [Choctaw] Nation*, 4, https://www.choctawnation.com/sites/default/files/[/2016 State of Nation.pdf.

35. "U.S. Government, Chickasaw, Choctaw Tribes Announce Historic Settlement Worth Millions," *Times Record* (Fort Smith, AK), October 7, 2015.

36. Oklahoma State Department of Health, "2014 State of the State's Health."

37. Amy Pereira and Trymaine Lee, "Hope on the Horizon for Choctaw Nation," March 19, 2014, MSNBC, http://www.msnbc.com/msnbc/choctaw-nation-hope-on-horizon - slide1.

38. Choctaw Nation Small Business Development Services, https://www.choctawnation.com/business/division-commerce/small-business-development-services.

39. The White House, "Fact Sheet: President Obama's Promise Zones Initiative," January 9, 2014, https://www.choctawnation.com/sites/default/files/pzwhitehousefact_original.pdf.

40. See https://www.choctawnation.com/biskinik-newspaper-archive.

41. Jessica McBride, "The Cost of Education," MvskokeMedia.com, June 13, 2017.

42. The White House, "Fact Sheet," 3.

43. Peggy Carlton, director of the program, personal communication; "The 2016 State of the [Choctaw] Nation," 17.

44. Dana Hertneky, "Oklahoma Native Americans Concerned About Future of Indian Healthcare," January 31, 2017, *Newson6.com*: http://www.newson6.com/story/34394277/oklahoma-native-americans-concerned-about-future-of-indian-healthcare.

45. Amanda Michelle Gomez, "Native Americans and Alaska Natives Will Disproportionally Suffer Under the GOP Health Care Plan," *ThinkProgress*, June 7, 2017.

46. Ronni Pierce, "A Healthy Outlook: New Regional Clinic to Open its Doors," *BISKINIK* (Talihina, Oklahoma), February 2017.

47. Mark Trahant, "How Bad Could It Be? Don't Get Sick if Senate (or House) Bill Becomes Law," June 23, 2017, TrahantReports.com: https://trahantreports.com/.

48. See in particular, Angie Debo, *And Still the Waters Run: The Betrayal of the Five Civilized Tribes* (Princeton: Princeton University Press, 1940).

49. Terry Wilson, *The Underground Reservation: Osage Oil* (Norman: University of Oklahoma Press, 1985); David Grann, *Killers of the Flower Moon: The Osage Murders and the Birth of the FBI* (New York: Doubleday, 2017).

50. Ralph Keen II, "Tribal Hunting and Fishing Regulatory Authority within Oklahoma," *Oklahoma Bar Journal* v 86 #24 (September 12, 2015): http://www.okbar.org/members/BarJournal/archive2015/SeptArchive15/OBJ8624Keen.aspx.

51. *Choctaw State of the Nation 2016*, 21.

52. Muriel H. Wright, "Notes and Documents: Sugar Loaf Mountain Resort," *Chronicles of Oklahoma* 36 (1960), pp. 202–3. South McAlester Capital, July 12, 1894; Interview with Elijah Conger, Indian and Pioneer Papers (hereafter IPP) vol. 2: 196–7, at the Western History Collections, University of Oklahoma, Norman.

53. Limon Pusley interview, December 28, 1937, IPP 73: 346; J.T. Poston, September 16, 1937, IPP 72: 286; Elijah W. Culberson, November 4, 1937, IPP 72: 215–16; Sarah Noah and Robert Noah, April 12 1937, IPP 67:254 Jim Spaniard, June 25, 1937, IPP 86: 7.

54. Oklahoma Department of Wildlife Conservation, *Fishing in the Schools Manual* (Oklahoma Department of Wildlife Conservation: Oklahoma City, 2014), 4.

55. Nancy J. Turner, Fikret Berkes, Janet Stephenson, Jonathan Dick, "Blundering Intruders: Extraneous Impacts on Two Indigenous Food Systems," *Human Ecology* 41, no. 4 (August 2013): 563–74, https://doi.org/10.1007/s10745-013-9591-y.

56. Darryl Fears, "This Mystery Was Solved: Scientists Say Chemicals from Fracking Wastewater Can Taint Freshwater Nearby," *Washington Post*, May 11, 2016; Jim Kelly, "On Oklahoma, Earthquakes and Contaminated Water: The Fracking Connection," *A New Domain*, December 8, 2015, http://anewdomain.net/oklahoma-earthquakes-contaminated-water-fracking-connection/.

57. See "Recent Earthquakes Near Oklahoma," *Earthquake Track*, http://earthquaketrack.com/p/united-states/oklahoma/recent; Katie M. Keranen, Matthew Weingarten, Geoffrey A. Abers, Barbara A. Bekins, and Shemin Ge, "Sharp Increase in Central Oklahoma Seismicity since 2008 Induced by Massive Wastewater Injection," *Science* 345, no. 6195 (July 25, 2014): 448–51. See also "Oklahoma and Fracking," http://www.sourcewatch.org/index.php/Oklahoma_and_fracking; and Jessica Fitzpatrick, "Induced Earthquakes Raise Chances of Damaging Shaking in 2016," March 28, 2016, *USGS Science Features*, https://www2.usgs.gov/blogs/features/usgs_top_story/induced-earthquakes-raise-chances-of-damaging-shaking-in-2016/.

58. Matthew L. M. Fletcher, "Pawnee Nation and Walter Echo-Hawk Sue over Fracking," *Turtle Talk*, November 21, 2016, https://turtletalk.wordpress.com/2016/11/21/pawnee-nation-walter-echo-hawk-sue-over-fracking/. See also Liz Blood, "Fracking in Bad Faith," *The Tulsa Voice* January-B, 2017, http://www.thetulsavoice.com/January-B-2017/Fracking-in-bad-faith/.

59. "14 More Oklahoma Lakes Have Elevated Mercury Levels in Fish," *NewsChannel 4*, June 22, 2017, http://kfor.com/2017/06/22/14-more-oklahoma-lakes-have-elevated-mercury-levels-in-fish/.

60. "Battling Pollution on Our Lands: Mekasi Horinek," *Cultural Survival Quarterly Magazine*, September 2016, https://www.culturalsurvival.org/publications/cultural-survival-quarterly/battling-pollution-our-lands-mekasi-horinek.

61. Movement Rights, "Ponca Nation of Oklahoma to Recognize the Rights of Nature to Stop Fracking," *Intercontinental Cry*, October 31, 2017, https://intercontinentalcry.org/ponca-nation-oklahoma-recognize-rights-nature-stop-fracking/.

62. Chalene Toehay-Tartsah, "Osage County Landowners Speak Out against Bad Drilling Practices," *Osage News*, August 18, 2014.

63. Inter-Tribal Council, http://itec.cherokee.org/; "Cherokee Nation Files, is Granted Emergency Restraining Order," *Anadisgoi*, February 9, 2017, http://www.anadisgoi.com/archive/1519-cherokee-nation-files-is-granted-emergency-restraining-order-halting-disposal-of-radioactive-waste-near-the-arkansas-and-illinois-rivers.

64. Kristin Hugo, "Native Americans Brace for Impact as EPA Undergoes Changes," *PBS Newshour*: The Rundown, February 17, 2017, http://www.pbs.org/newshour/rundown/native-americans-brace-impact-epa-undergoes-changes/.

65. See House Bill No. 1123, House of Representatives-Floor Version, State of Oklahoma, 1st Session of the 56th Legislature (2017), http://webserver1.lsb.state.ok.us/cf_pdf/2017-18%20FLR/HFLR/HB1123%20HFLR.PDF; Alleen Brown, "Oklahoma Governor Signs Anti-Protest Law Imposing huge Fines on 'Conspirator' Organizations," *The Intercept*, May 6, 2017, https://theintercept.com/2017/05/06/oklahoma-governor-signs-anti-protest-law-imposing-huge-fines-on-conspirator-organizations/.

66. Casey Smith, "The Diamond Pipeline," *Tulsa World*, February 3, 2017; Mark Hefflinger, "Fight Against Diamond Pipeline Spans Three States," *Bold Oklahoma*, January 30, 2017; Oka Lawa Camp, https://www.facebook.com/OkaLawaCamp/.

67. Oklahoma Invasive Plant Council: https://okipc.wordpress.com/the-dirty-dozen/; Brianna Bailey, "The Bradford Pear: Oklahoma's Worst Tree or Just Misunderstood?" *NewsOK*, March 5, 2017.

68. Chip Taylor, personal communication.

69. Oklahoma Department of Wildlife Conservation, "Feral Hogs in Oklahoma," https://www.wildlifedepartment.com/feral-hogs-in-oklahoma; "There Was Nothing I Could Do," *Oklahoma News 4*, September 5, 2017, http://kfor.com/2017/09/05/there-was-nothing-i-could-do-feral-hogs-wreaking-havoc-on-oklahoma-watermelon-farmers/.

70. For an overview of pollinators in Oklahoma in 1917, see Sister M. Agnes, "Biological Field Work," *Oklahoma Academy of Science* 1 (1917): 35–38, http://digital.library.okstate.edu/OAS/oas_pdf/v01/p35_38.pdf.

71. Logan Layden, "Why Oklahoma Had the Nation's Highest Percentage of Bee Deaths Last Year," *National Public Radio*: StateImpact-Oklahoma, June 25, 2015, https://stateimpact.npr.org/oklahoma/2015/06/25/why-oklahoma-had-the-nations-highest-percentage-of-bee-deaths-last-year/.

72. Edmund Flint interview, April 23, 1937, IPP 3, 527; Ben Cartarby, June 29, 1937, IPP 19, 203; Josephine Usray Lattimer, September 23, 1937 IPP 33, 84; T. P. Wilson, n.d., IPP 11, 498; Elijah W. Culberson, Nov. 4, 1937, IPP 22, 216; W. C. Mead interview, January 17, 1938, IPP 62, 17; Johnnie Gipson interview, April 21, 1927, IPP 34, 175.

73. Chip Taylor, personal communication. See also *Tribal Environmental Action for Monarchs*: http://www.nativebutterflies.org/saving-the-monarch; "Native American Tribes Pledge to Save the Monarch," *Trilateral Committee for Wildlife and Ecosystem Conservation and Management*: http://www.trilat.org/index.php?option=com_content&view=article&id=1197:native-american-tribes-pledge-to-save-the-monarch&catid=17&Itemid=256.

74. Tamar Haspel, "Small vs. Large: Which Size Farm is Better for the Planet?" *Washington Post*, September 2, 2014.

75. Bhat, "Food Sustainability Challenges," 2, 4.

76. National Family Farm Coalition and Grassroots International, *Food Sovereignty* (Washington, DC: Grassroots International, 2010), 11.

77. William Bartram, "The Creek and Cherokee Indians," *Transactions of the American Ethnological Society* 111 (1789): 39–40. See also the series of "Mvskoke Country" articles authored by James Treat, https://mvskokecountry.wordpress.com/category/mvskoke-country/.

78. William Bartram, *Bartram: Travels and Other Writings* (NY: Literary Classics of the United States, 1996), 506–7. See also James Adair, *History of the American Indians* (London: Edward and Charles Dilly, 1775), 405–10.

79. Bartram, *Travels*, 56, 319, 557–60.

80. Ibid., 404–5.

81. T. N. Campbell, "Choctaw Subsistence: Ethnographic Notes from the Lincecum Manuscript," *Florida Anthropologists* 12 #1 (1959): 9–24; H. B. Cushman, *History of the Choctaw, Chickasaw, and Natchez Indians* (Greenville, TX: Headlight, 1899), 74, 168, 231–32, 250, 272.

82. Campbell, "Choctaw Subsistence," 10–11; John R. Swanton, "Aboriginal Culture of the Southeast," in *Forty-Second Annual Report of the Bureau of American Ethnology* (Washington, DC: US Government Printing Office, 1924–1925), 695. There is no evidence that Choctaws planted corn, squash, and beans in the manner of the "Three Sisters."

83. See Mihesuah, "Sustenance and Health among the Five Tribes in Indian Territory."

84. J. C. Moncrief interview, November 1, 1933, IPP 64: 57.

85. Meton Ludlow interview, April 26, 1934, IPP 56: 182.

86. I expound on this in "The Garden Meal," in Linda Murray Berzok, ed., *Storied Dishes: What Our Family Recipes Tell Us about Who We Are and Where We've Been* (Santa Barbara: ABC–CLIO, 2010), 57–60.

87. For general works on the Comanches, see John Frances Bannon, *The Spanish Borderlands Frontier, 1513–1821* (Holt, Rinehart and Winston, 1970); Pekka Hämäläinen, *The Comanche Empire* (New Haven: Yale University Press, 2009); Ernest Wallace and E. Adamson Hoebel, *The Comanches: Lords of the South Plains* (/Norman: University of Oklahoma Press, 1952); Elizabeth A. H. John, *Storms Brewed in Other Men's Worlds: The Confrontation of Indians, Spanish, and French in The Southwest, 1540–1795* (Texas A&M University Press, 1975); Thomas W. Kavanagh, *The Comanches: A History, 1706–1875* (Lincoln: University of Nebraska Press, 1999); Stanley Noyes, *Los Comanches: The Horse People, 1751–1845* (Albuquerque: University of New Mexico Press, 1993); W. W. Newcomb, Jr., "Comanches: Terror of the Southern Plains," in *The Indians of Texas: From Prehistoric to Modern Times* (Austin: University of Texas Press, 1961), 155–91.

88. Gustav G. Carlson and Volney H. Jones, "Some Notes on Uses of Plants by the Comanche Indians," *Papers of the Michigan Academy of Science* 25 (1940): 517–42. See also Mihesuah, "Comanche Traditional Foodways and the Decline of Health," *Great Plains Journal* 50 (forthcoming).

89. *Comanche Nation News*, http://www.comanchenation.com/index.php?option=com_k2&view=itemlist&layout=category&task=category&id=109&Itemid=171.

90. Rick Wells, "Cherokee Seed Bank Program Provides Connection to Past," February 3, 2017, *NewsOn6.com*.

91. Sheila Stogsdill, "Cherokee Nation Garden Project Seeks to Teach Nutrition in Oklahoma," *The Oklahoman*, June 15, 2014.

92. Lenzy Krehbiel-Burton, "Osage Nation Awarded AmeriCorps Grant for Park, Gardens to Address Diabetes, Obesity," *Tulsa World*, August 20, 2015.

93. Tara Madden, "Community Gardens Being Grown by Osage Nation TA–WA AmeriCorps," *Osage News*, August, 14, 2014.

94. Pat Gwin, personal communication.

95. Kyle Powys Whyte, "Indigenous Food Sovereignty, Renewal, and US Settler Colonialism," in Mary Rawlinson and Caleb Ward., eds, *The Routledge Handbook of Food Ethics* (London: Routledge, 2016), 354–65.

96. Rajeev Bhat, "Food Sustainability Challenges in the Developing World," in *Sustainability Challenges in the Agrofood Sector* (New Jersey: John Wiley and Sons, 2017), 3–4.

97. "Sovereignty," Merriam-Webster, https://www.merriam-webster.com/dictionary/sovereignty.

98. Jeff Corntassel and Cheryl Bryce, "Practicing Sustainable Self-Determination: Indigenous Approaches to Cultural Restoration and Revitalization," *Brown Journal of World Affairs* 18, no. 2 (Spring/Summer 2012): 152.

99. For discussion about the implications of using the term "sovereignty," see Taiaiake Alfred, "Sovereignty," in Philip J. Deloria and Neal Salisbury, *A Companion to American Indian History* (Malden, MA: Blackwell Publishing, 2004), 460–74.

100. Hope Radford, "Native American Food Sovereignty in Montana," August 2016, 6, http://aeromt.org/wp-content/uploads/2016/10/Native-American-Food-Sovereignty-in-Montana-2016-1-1.pdf.

101. Intertribal Agriculture Council, http://www.indianaglink.com/our-programs/technical-assistance-program/.

102. Native Food Systems Resource Center, http://www.nativefoodsystems.org/about.

103. Seeds of Native Health, http://seedsofnativehealth.org/partners/; "Smokehouses, Farmers' Markets and More," *Indian Country Today*, June 20, 2017.

104. University of Arkansas School of Law Indigenous Food and Agriculture Initiative, http://indigenousfoodandag.com/about-us/. The initiative offers strategic planning and technical support for tribal governance infrastructure in the areas of business and economic development, financial markets and asset management, health and nutrition polities, and intellectual property rights. It also supports the increase of students into land grant universities, and creating academic programs in in food and agriculture.

105. Food sovereignty construction is discussed in Christina M. Schiavoni, "The Contested Terrain of Food Sovereignty Construction: Toward a Historical, Relational and Interactive Approach," *The Journal of Peasant Studies* 44, no. 1 (2017): 1–32.

106. Michael Wise, "Native Foods and the Colonial Gaze," *Process: a blog for American History*, January 10, 2017, http://www.processhistory.org/wise-native-foods/.

107. Elizabeth Ross, June 10, 1937, IPP 109, 190–92; Emiziah Bohanan, May 10, 1937, IPP 9, 139; T. J. Johnson, July 16, 1937, IPP 48, 402; Elizabeth Witcher, April 18, 1939, IPP 99, 390.

108. 29 OK Stat § 29-6-301a (2016), "Prohibited Means of Taking Game or Nongame Fish–Poison, Explosive, or Electrical Shock Devices," http://law.justia.com/codes/oklahoma/2016/title-29/section-29-6-301a/.

# THE PRICE FOR FREEDOM: BAIL IN THE CITY OF L.A.

## A MILLION DOLLAR HOODS REPORT

ISAAC BRYAN, TERRY ALLEN, KELLY LYTLE HERNANDEZ, AND CONSULTANT, MARGARET DOOLEY-SAMMULI, ACLU-CA

In California, all persons facing criminal charges are guaranteed the *right to freedom* before trial, except in a few cases. But there is a price for that freedom. Across the state, the money bail system requires many people to pay for pretrial release. When a person, or their representative, pays money bail up front and in full, the money is refunded so long as the person charged with a crime shows up for all of their court proceedings. But most people eligible for money bail cannot afford to pay the total sum up front.[1] Instead, most people eligible for money bail are left with one of two options. The first is to stay in jail until the conclusion of their court proceedings, which can take weeks, months, or even years. The second is to contract with a bail bond agent who provides

Isaac Bryan serves as the public policy adviser of the Ralph J. Bunche Center for African American Studies at UCLA. Working for Los Angeles Mayor Eric Garcetti, Bryan also co-authored the first City of Los Angeles comprehensive report on the reentry needs of community members. He is best known for his 2018 TEDxUCLA talk, which focused largely on the injustices found in the criminal justice system. Terry Allen is a doctoral candidate at UCLA's Graduate School of Education & Information Studies. He is also the director of Oral History and Ethnographic Research for the Million Dollar Hoods project, which maps how much is spent on incarceration per neighborhood in Los Angeles County. Allen received his master's degree in education policy from Columbia University and his bachelor's degree in rhetoric from UC Berkeley. Prior to his doctoral studies, Allen served President Barack Obama as an advance associate for the White House. Kelly Lytle Hernandez is a professor of history and African American studies at UCLA, and the interim director of the Ralph J. Bunche Center for African American Studies. A leading expert on race, immigration, and mass incarceration, she is the author of *Migra! A History of the U.S. Border Patrol* (University of California Press, 2010) and *City of Inmates: Conquest, Rebellion, and the Rise of Human Caging in Los Angeles* (University of North Carolina Press, 2017). Currently, Lytle Hernandez is the research lead for the Million Dollar Hoods project. Margaret Dooley-Sammuli is senior campaign strategist with the ACLU Campaign for Smart Justice, an unprecedented, multiyear effort to cut the nation's jail and prison population by 50 percent and combat racial disparities in the criminal justice system. Based in San Diego, she works with ACLU affiliates across the country to advance bail reform in order to dramatically reduce pretrial detention, fight racial bias in the justice system, and center the leadership of formerly incarcerated people. She has more than a decade of experience working on criminal justice and drug policy reform in California, including spearheading historic campaigns to reduce the state's drug possession penalties.

a surety bond to the court on their behalf. The surety bond operates like a promissory note: the bail bond company does not pay up front but, rather, promises to pay the full bail money amount if the accused fails to appear in court. For this service, a bail bond agent requires the arrested person, or their representative, to pay a nonrefundable deposit, typically amounting to 10 percent of the total bail amount. A bail bond agent will also charge a series of service fees and often requires some form of collateral, such as a home or car. In California, an estimated 97 percent of the people who pay money bail use a bail bond agent.[2]

In the City of Los Angeles, the money bail system is massive. According to new data provided to the Million Dollar Hoods research team, the Los Angeles Police Department (LAPD), using the Los Angeles County Superior Court's misdemeanor and felony bail schedules, levied $19,386,418,544 in money bail on persons arrested by the LAPD between 2012 and 2016. This $19.4 billion only reflects the amount of money bail set during LAPD booking proceedings. It does not reflect any changes later made by judges to bail assessments. It does not reflect arrests made by any other police departments in the Los Angeles area. And it does not reflect what was actually paid.

Of the $19.4 billion set between 2012 and 2016, 62,118 people bailed out of LAPD custody by paying cash or contracting with a bail bond agent. Collectively, they delivered $17,561,473 in cash to the court and paid an estimated $193,786,349 in nonrefundable bail bond deposits to bail bond agents. These payments do not include any additional service fees an arrested person or their representative might pay to a bail bond company after seeing a judge for the first time (at a hearing called "arraignment"). Nor do they include the value of any assets later seized by bail bond agents.

Of the $193.8 million paid to bail bond agents, Latinos paid $92.1 million, African Americans paid $40.7 million, and whites paid $37.9 million. But a recent study by the Ella Baker Center for Human Rights documents that it is women—the mothers, aunts, grandmothers, friends, and wives of the accused—who are most likely to contract with a bail bond agent on behalf of those in custody.[3] If so, the estimated $193.8 paid in nonrefundable bail bond deposits were disproportionately paid by women, namely black women and Latinas. Moreover, each community likely paid much more when accounting for post-arraignment payments, the service fees charged by bail bond companies, and, in some cases, asset seizures.

But most money bail was never paid. Of the $19.3 billion in money bail set, $13,508,414,069 was neither paid nor waived through an administrative procedure, such as release on "Own Recognizance." In fact, 70 percent of the amount levied was not paid during LAPD booking proceedings, which left 223,366 people in LAPD custody prior to arraignment between 2012 and 2016.

The reasons why people did not pay for release during the booking process are not recorded in LAPD records but poverty was likely a major factor. Mapping LAPD data shows that the greatest sums of money bail were levied in the City Council districts with the highest rates of unemployment. Moreover, nearly four billion dollars in money bail was levied on houseless persons.[4]

In sum, the money bail system is a multi-billion-dollar toll that demands tens of millions of dollars annually in cash and assets from some of LA's most economically vulnerable persons, families, and communities. For those who pay bail bond agents,

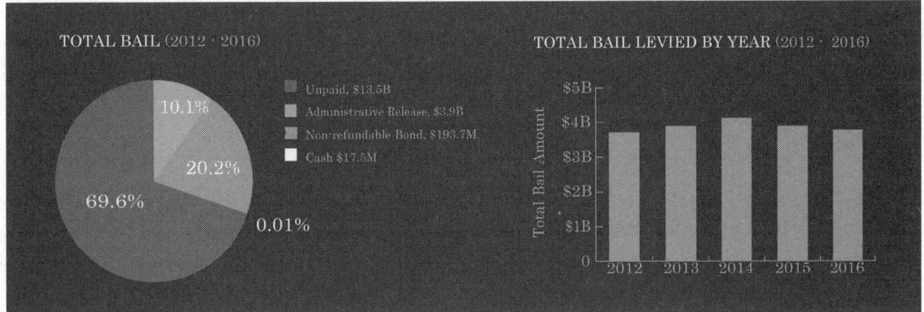


**Figure 1.** Total Bail (2012–2016).
**Figure 2.** Total Bail Levied by Year (2012–2016).

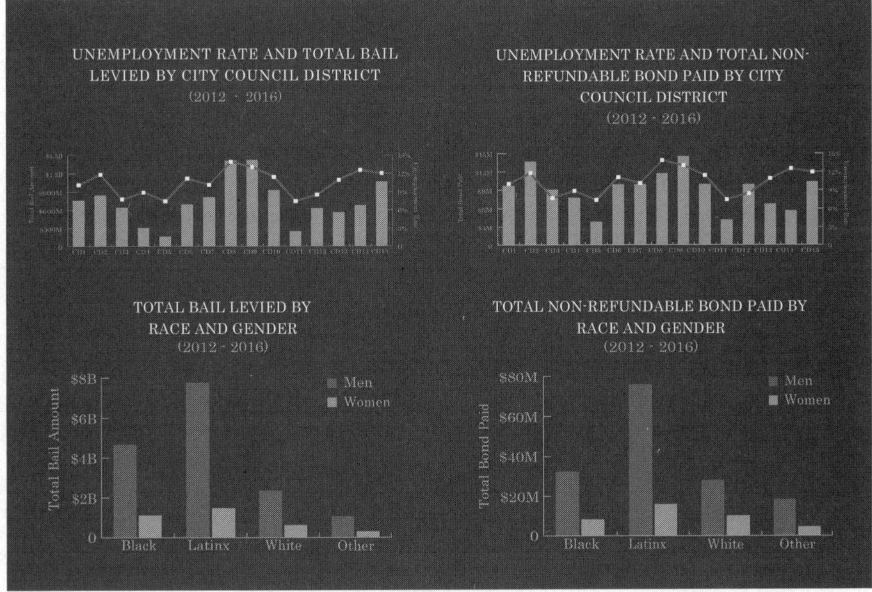


**Figure 3.** Unemployment Rate and Total Bail Levied by City Council District (2012–2016).
**Figure 4.** Unemployment Rate and Total Non-Refundable Bond Paid by City Council District (2012–2016).
**Figure 5.** Total Bail Levied by Race and Gender (2012–2016).
**Figure 6.** Total Non-Refundable Bond Paid by Race and Gender (2012–2016).

TOP 5 ZIP CODES BY TOTAL BAIL LEVIED AND NON-REFUNDABLE BOND PAID (2012 - 2016)

| | SOUTH CENTRAL | | | | ARLETA |
|---|---|---|---|---|---|
| Zip Code | 90044 | 90003 | 90037 | 90011 | 91331 |
| Total Bail | $506,280,304 | $475,136,066 | $415,821,902 | $411,301,117 | $294,164,928 |
| Non-Refundable Bond Paid | $3,769,368 | $4,225,251 | $4,013,070 | $4,870,101 | $3,106,637 |

**Figure 7.** Top 5 Zip Codes by Total Bail Levied and Non-Refundable Bond Paid (2012–2016).

that money is never returned and additional fees apply. But most people do not pay money bail. Among them, many individuals as well as their families and communities are simply too poor to pay the price for freedom.

## METHODOLOGY

On March 10, 2017, the LAPD fulfilled Public Records Act requests submitted by Professor Kelly Lytle Hernandez on March 8, 2016 and September 7, 2016. The data provided included more than twenty categories of information for all arrests and bookings made by the LAPD between January 1, 2012 and December 31, 2016. For this report, we utilized the following categories of information: Race, Sex (gender), Total Bail (the sum of all bail set), Rel_Reas (release disposition), and Home_Res (home address). Release dispositions include codes, such as "BOND," "CASH," "OR" (Own Recognizance), "CUST" (custody transfer), "IMP" (imperative release), and "49B1" (D.A. reject). To calculate total money bail set, we calculated the sum of all numeric values included in the "Total_Bail" category. To calculate how much was paid to bail bond agents, we estimated that for persons released on "BOND" 10 percent of their total money bail charge was paid to a bail bond agent. To determine how much money bail was unpaid we calculated "Total_Bail" for all entries without a release disposition. To determine total bail set and paid by neighborhood, we geo-coded and cross-referenced the home addresses provided in the "Home_Res" category with Los Angeles City Council District boundaries. Lastly, we used the most recently available US Census data to determine unemployment rates by City Council District.

## NOTES

Reprinted with permission from Isaac Bryan, Terry Allen, Kelly Lytle Hernandez, and Consultant Margaret Dooley-Sammuli (Los Angeles: Ralph J. Bunche Center on African American Studies at UCLA, 2017), https://bunchecenter.ucla.edu/wp-content/uploads/sites/82/2017/12/MDHHouselessReport-The-Price-for-Freedom-Bail-in-the-City-of-LA.pdf.

1. Bernadette Rabuy and Daniel Kopf, "How Money Bail Perpetuates an Endless Cycle of Poverty and Jail Time," Prison Policy Initiative, May 10, 2016, https://www.prisonpolicy.org/reports/incomejails.html.

2. Pretrial Detention Reform Workgroup, "Recommendations to the Chief Justice," October 2017, 31, https://newsroom.courts.ca.gov/internal_redirect/cms.ipressroom.com.s3.amazonaws.com/262/files/20179/PDRReport-FINAL%2010-23-17.pdf.

3. Saneta deVuono-powell, Chris Schweidler, Alicia Walters, and Azadeh Zohrabi, "Who Pays? The True Cost of Incarceration on Families" (Oakland, CA: Ella Baker Center, Forward Together, Research Action Design, 2015), 9, http://whopaysreport.org.

4. Houseless Persons are defined as those recorded as "transient" in LAPD data and those who, upon arrest, provide the address of a shelter as their home residence.

# INDEX

Pages followed by "n" indicate notes.